life

a complete operating manual

 *An Alliance of Angels Publishing Company*

Our Mission is to inspire and empower others to live life as a magical experience. By simplifying ageless wisdom, we will provide practical tools and techniques that improve the quality of life, alleviate unnecessary pain, and simultaneously re-create our world.

www.secrettolife.net

The Secret to Life is knowing how and why things happen. This book unveils that secret.

Twenty-three years before the thought of this book even entered my consciousness, I was forewarned of its forthcoming existence. While driving home late one evening, I inadvertently tuned in to a radio station featuring a psychic. Because I had never heard a psychic before, I was intrigued by the accuracy of this man's responses to the intimate questions people posed, so when I arrived home, I, too, placed a call. The psychic answered my question, and then added something that piqued my curiosity: I was going to do something "exciting" later in my life. Upon hearing that statement, the skeptical me wondered, "Okay, is this one of his 'pat' statements? One that could never be proved as having substance?" I implored him to define that "something" more specifically. His reply? "I would discover its meaning when I was 'supposed to.'" Hmmm…. The intrigue did not end there, however. This message was merely the first of many strikingly similar messages I would receive over the next thirteen years. That is, until I received another with far greater significance that explained that "something."

What precipitated these messages? At the core of my being I have always felt that there had to be more to life — that something was "wrong with this picture." As I observed the world around me, I saw so much pain, anguish, and suffering and always wondered why it occurred in the lives of some and not others. And this despair was not relegated to one socioeconomic class. Quite the contrary, it permeated all levels of society — the "haves" and the "have-nots." The answer eluded me. I continued to ask "why, why, why?"

You have probably heard the phrase "Seek and you will find." Well, my seeking began to produce curious findings. Late one evening a friend of mine called and asked if I would accompany her the following day to an appointment she and another friend had previously made with a psychic. Her scheduled friend had just canceled and she desperately wanted to see this man, but was afraid of going alone. Although I was a bit uncomfortable with the notion of having someone tell me "the future" once again, I conceded when her pleading became unrelenting. "What the heck," I thought, "Life's an adventure! After all, nothing "bad" happened after my first episode with a psychic, right?"

Well, this meeting was indeed an adventure, for in the midst of our session, this man abruptly stopped and announced that he was receiving an urgent message *for me* from a group of teachers. *Hello...?!?* I had no idea what he meant and felt that this experience was becoming a bit *too* weird for my taste. However, my uneasiness was soon dispelled when he implored me to write down what he was receiving before he lost it. The following was the message I received on that fateful day:

> *Things only happen when you make them happen. To let go and surrender is to let things happen to you. You have free will and must set things in motion. Planet Earth is on the verge of destructive power in the wrong hands. Things will only change when people change. To raise people's spiritual consciousness is the task at hand. It can only begin there and be demonstrated as such. There is much work to do. Begin by helping others become aware. You have the gift. Use it or it will be wasted. This is your Mission. DMA [Dimensional Mind Approach — a course I was then taking that dealt with the multi-dimensions of the mind] is your first step. Everyone's "universal truth" they espouse is holy unto them. Formulate your own truth, live by it, share it, and teach it. That is your Mission. To blend the psychological awareness of your past with the awareness of the reality of the future is the key. While men are building new and beautiful skyscrapers, energy should be channeled into consciousness into this world. They are blind — make them see. Various civilizations that were highly technical, fell. When there is technology without the awareness of God, it cannot work. God is before technology, and channeling the power properly will benefit and evolve mankind. It is time — the time is now for these events to happen. They happen only with individual people. That is the task at hand.*

I had no clue what this message meant — it was totally beyond my comprehension. However, I knew it meant *something* because of the haunting reference to the DMA course I was enrolled in, so I tucked that little piece of paper safely away. As the years passed, I continued to receive messages, all clues that led to the unraveling of this mystery, until one day I threw my hands up in surrender and uttered "All right, already. I'll do 'it'!" (I was afraid. I didn't know what "it" was, but I also never wanted to say "I coulda, woulda, shoulda.") The result? This book: my "Mission." Read it, and you may never look at life the same way again.

In sincerity,

Lauren

Do You Know Where You're Going To?

Do you know where you're going to?
Do you like the things that life is showing you?
Where are you going to?
Do you know?
Do you get what you're hoping for?
When you look behind you there's no open door.
What are you hoping for?
Do you know?
Once we were standing still in time.
Chasing the fantasies that filled our minds.
And you knew how I loved you,
but my spirit was free,
Laughing at the questions that you once asked of me.
Do you know where you're going to?
Do you like the things that life is showing you?
Where are you going to?
Do you know?
Now looking back at all we planned,
We let so many dreams just slip through our hands.
Why must we wait so long before we can see
how sad the answers to those questions can be?
Do you know where you're going to?
Do you like the things that life is showing you?
Where are you going to?
Do you know?[1]

Words by Gerry Goffin — Music by Mike Masser

Theme from the Valley of the Dolls

Gotta get off, gonna get, have to get off from this ride.
Gotta get hold, gonna get, need to get hold of my pride.
When did I get, where did I, how was I caught in this game?
When will I know, where will I, how will I think of my name?
When did I stop feeling sure, feeling safe,
and start wondering why, wondering why?
Is this a dream? Am I here? Where are you?
What's in back of the sky? Why do we cry?
Gotta get off, gonna get, out of this merry-go-round.
Gotta get on, gonna get, need to get on where I'm bound.
When did I get, where did I, why am I lost as a lamb?
When will I know, where will I, how will I learn who I am?
Is this a dream? Am I here? Where are you?
Tell me when will I know, how will I know,
when will I know why? [2]

Words by Dory Previn

Dedication

First, I would like to dedicate this book to the "Big Guy"
and to the Angels who have guided me along a path
to complete this work for the benefit of all.

Next, I dedicate this book to those who are searching,
for your search will lead you to the seeds of truth.
I honor you, for what you learn will help to
make this world a better place in which to live.

Last, I dedicate this book to those who feel helpless,
hopeless, and lost. You have not been abandoned.
Your journey may have been long and hard,
but that now can change.
You have nothing to lose. Here are the tools.
You deserve them, you have earned them,
and now the rest is up to you.

My love goes out to all.

Alfie

What's it all about, Alfie?
Is it just for the moment we live?
What's it all about, when you sort it out, Alfie?
Are we meant to take more than we give?
Or are we meant to be kind?
And if only fools are kind, Alfie,
then I guess it is wise to be cruel.
And if life belongs only to the strong, Alfie,
what will you lend on an old golden rule?
As sure as I believe there's a heaven above, Alfie.
I know there's something much more.
Something even nonbelievers can believe in.
I believe in love, Alfie.
Without true love you just exist, Alfie.
Until you find the love you've missed,
you're nothing, Alfie.
When you walk let your heart lead the way,
And you'll find love any day, Alfie.[3]

Words by Hal David — Music by Burt Bacharach

A Note of Thanks

I would like to express my gratitude to the many people who have unknowingly helped to create this book. First, to a myriad of fabulous authors who truly inspired me. I have quoted extensively from their work, for their wisdom, spiritual teachings, and words of enlightenment profoundly enrich the message I am seeking to convey. Second, I wish to thank another group of spiritual teachers who span the centuries and cultures of time, for through their wisdom and insightful prose, they too have contributed to the credibility and unfolding of this message. And last, I wish to express my gratitude to the songwriters whose beautiful lyrics are interspersed throughout these pages. Because songwriters are said to be the prophets of our time, you may discover an even deeper meaning to their lyrics as you read through these pages.

I consider each of these people to be a coauthor of this book and believe they are all messengers fulfilling their Missions to assist in the evolution of humankind. I greatly appreciate their contributions and hope they will be honored to once again share their important words with you through this book. I highly recommend their outstanding works to anyone searching for a deeper, more expansive understanding of life.

- Dr. Deepak Chopra for *The Seven Spiritual Laws of Success*

- Esther and Jerry Hicks, for *A New Beginning I & II, Sara,* and for the numerous audio tapes they have shared

- Shakti Gawain for *Creative Visualization* and *Living in the Light*

- Robert Fritz for *The Path of Least Resistance,* as well as the course, "DMA — Dimensional Mind Approach"

- Richard Bach for *Illusions: The Adventures of a Reluctant Messiah, Jonathan Livingston Seagull,* and *One*

- M. Scott Peck for *The Road Less Traveled*

～ James Redfield for *The Celestine Prophecy*

～ James Redfield and Carol Adrienne for *The Celestine Prophecy — An Experiential Guide*

～ Lee Carroll for *Kryon — The End Times, Don't Think Like a Human, The Alchemy of the Spirit*, and *The Journey Home: The Story of Michael and the Seven Angels*

～ Laurie Beth Jones, for *Jesus CEO*, and *The Path — Creating Your Mission Statement for Work and for Life*

～ Norman Cousins for *Anatomy of an Illness*

～ Ruth Montgomery for *Strangers Among Us*

～ Carolyn Myss for *Anatomy of a Spirit*

～ Julia Ingram and G. W. Hardin for *The Messengers*

～ The Foundation for Inner Peace for publishing *A Course in Miracles®*

～ Marianne Williamson for *A Return to Love* and *The Healing of America*

～ Jane Roberts for *The Nature of Personal Reality*

～ Neale Donald Walsch for *Conversations with God: An Uncommon Dialogue, Books 1, 2 and 3*

～ Dr. Wayne Dyer for *Manifest Your Destiny*

～ Peter McWilliams for *The Life 101 Quote Book*

～ James F. Twyman for *Emissary of Light*

～ Anne Morrow Lindbergh for *Gift from the Sea*

～ Florence Scovel Shinn for *The Game of Life and How to Play It, Your Word Is Your Wand, The Secret Door to Success*, and *The Power of the Spoken Word*

～ Joel Arthur Barker for *Paradigms: The Business of Discovering the Future*

～ Jon Peniel for *The Children of the Law of One and the Lost Teachings of Atlantis*

～ MSI for *First Thunder*

～ Dr. Herbert Benson for *Timeless Healing: The Power and Biology of Belief*

ᕃ   Glenda Green for *Love Without End: Jesus Speaks*

ᕃ   Gregg Braden for *Awakening to Zero Point, Walking Between The Worlds: The Science of Compassion*, and *The Isaiah Effect*

ᕃ   Dr. Brian Weiss for *Many Lives, Many Masters*

I would also like to thank other more earthly "Angels" who have been instrumental in my fulfilling this Mission. They are:

Mary Kay Krueger	*Jill Fawell*	*Irene Hughes*
Don Beck	*Verlene Gardner*	*Marsha Jones*
David Wright	*Robert Hilton*	*Diane Krueger*
Laura Medley	*Randy Nelson*	*Annemarie Osborne*

I especially wish to express my profound gratitude to my extraordinary husband, Ken, for without his help, this book would not be in your hands. Writing a book presents an ongoing challenge because of the need for time and space in which to work, and this project took more than four years to complete. During this period of time, I became so focused on this endeavor that I neglected many of my responsibilities (the garage and basement are bursting at the seams with accumulated stuff). Fortunately (serendipitously), I have been blessed with a wonderful, giving, and sacrificing man who filled in for me countless times as both mother and wife while simultaneously running his own company. By virtue of his support and love, oftentimes at his expense, Ken allowed me the freedom to accomplish this Mission. (Not that his halo doesn't fall off periodically when the tasks become overwhelming… just as mine does.) Ultimately, Ken is my greatest teacher, for through our continual interactions I have rather poignantly recognized my own unfinished business that seeks resolution. Underlying his occasionally brusque exterior — his protective crab shell — lies a beautiful, sensitive soul with an infinitely kind and generous heart as brilliant as gold.

I thank my ten-year-old son Zachary, another of my teachers, my primary student (guinea pig…), and a pure soul. His mere being has evoked a profound depth of love within me, and the fear that oftentimes accompanies it. I have a keen appreciation for the miracle of the day-to-day unfolding of his life and simultaneously, the underlying dread that it is all happening too fast. Zach understands this message at a very basic level and has applied the techniques presented with positive results (although he is embarrassed to admit it. At the age of ten, it's "uncool"). Although we have a difference of forty years in 'Earth time,' at a soul level we are the same. I am eager to know him at a mature stage of life and am trying to impart to him the *real* truth of life: He can *have* anything in life he wants, *be* anything he wants, and *do* anything he wants; that his life is an ever-evolving, exciting adventure born of his choices.

I thank my dad, a resident of Heaven since 1997, for always telling me I could do anything — because I *believed* him. Together we healed the trauma of my abusive childhood born of his alcoholism, and he went on to become the greatest supporter of whatever I pursued in life. My dad was the consummate philosopher and passed that propensity on to me.

I thank my mom, a resident of Heaven since 1988, for nurturing me, body and soul, and loving me as her 'baby' (along with my four siblings). Despite the traumas she endured in life, she found fun in almost everything and passed on that wonderful gift to me! She, too, was a great supporter of my various endeavors, but especially fond of my singing career. On occasion, however, she would take it to the extreme when she would 'crash' private parties that my band and I were hired for. My mom was a 'hoot' and loved by all who had the privilege to know her.

I thank my mother-in-law and father-in-law, Catherine and Frank Tratar, for always being there, intuitively responding to our family needs before we even knew we had them. Week after week they gifted us with home cooking so we could have a 'real' meal periodically. (I'm not too fond of cooking or cleaning the mess afterwards — it's so much easier to go out....) As they observed me pour my heart, soul, and every waking moment into this book, they went above and beyond the call of duty in a myriad of ways that I am extremely grateful for.

I thank my editors, Bonnie Kalar, Margaret Pinyan, and primarily Ro Sila, for having the patience to lovingly guide me along a path that reacquainted me with the English language and its proper use (or is that *usage?*). In complete honor, they addressed the issues that a first-time author would encounter and helped me to mold this book into a compre-
-hensive manual for you to use day after day, year after year. I wish to extend my deepest gratitude to them for their invaluable assistance.

And last, I thank myself. Writing this book has taken me on an incredible journey of introspection fraught with doubt, fear, and uncertainty. And each of those symptoms of "old-paradigm" thinking had to be processed, examined, and reassessed so I could remove the barriers they imposed and allow the energy of this work to flow. But at each juncture of despair, despondency, or inadequacy, I was always sent an Angel to offer me moral support and add fuel to my burning passion to help others. Lovingly, I was led to a multitude of books that all professed this profound knowledge in one way or another. And because humanity was still not living it, I knew, beyond a shadow of a doubt, that it was necessary to convey this message once again. Given such a profusion of overwhelming evidence, I was able to garner the courage of my convictions to publish this book and attempt to live on a daily basis what I believe to be truth. ☺

Contents

A NOTE TO THE READER

*I have devised two ways to read this book because I understand that you may be eager to discover the "secret to life." The first method is to read the book as it is written, providing you the most expansive, comprehensive perspective. The second is to opt for the shortcut, an overview of the "secret," by reading each chapter marked with an asterisk(*) I caution you **not** to skip around, for I have presented this information in a critical sequential order with step A providing the foundation for step B. Without gaining the knowledge in Step A, it will be difficult to fully comprehend the "secret." Whether you choose the "fast track," or choose to savor each and every word... enjoy!*

PART I

The Prelude

AN INTRODUCTION TO THE SECRET TO LIFE

PART II

The Puzzle

THE SECRET TO LIFE UNVEILED:
WHO YOU REALLY ARE AND HOW LIFE REALLY OPERATES

PART III

The Present

EXPLORING CURRENT REALITY:
PERSONALLY AND GLOBALLY

PART IV

The Past

DISSECTING YOUR PAST AND
UNCOVERING ITS HIDDEN TREASURES

PART V

The Pathway

REDEFINING YOUR PATH

PART VI

The Procedures

STAYING CENTERED ON YOUR PATH

PART VII

The Predicaments

GETTING BACK ON YOUR PATH
WHEN YOU HAVE LOST YOUR WAY

PART VIII

The Physical Body

ATTAINING PERFECT RADIANT HEALTH
AND A BODY YOU DESIRE

PART IX

The Postscript

LIVING HAPPILY EVER AFTER!

PART X

Appendices

PART I

The Prelude

AN INTRODUCTION TO THE SECRET TO LIFE

Part I

The Prelude

AN INTRODUCTION TO THE SECRET TO LIFE

$\mathcal{D}$iscovering a $\mathcal{G}$enie

Before you begin this book and become familiar with the "secret to life," please complete the following exercise that you will utilize later.

Imagine that you just discovered an old lamp with a genie inside. And your genie is *extra*-special, for he is able to grant you not just three, but *ten* wishes! What would you ask for?

1._____

_____

_____

_____

_____

_____

2._____

_____

_____

_____

_____

_____

3._____

_____

_____

_____

_____

_____

4._____

5._____

6._____

7._____

8._____

9._____

10._____

Beginnings

*Grasshopper, look beyond the game, as you look beneath
the surface of the pool to see its depths.* — MASTER PO
from the TV show "Kung Fu"

Have you ever heard the phrase "Your thoughts create your reality"? If so, your reaction may have been one of bafflement, "Excuse me, say that again?": one of wonder, "Hmmm, that's interesting; I'll ponder that for the next zillion years": or even one of fear, "That's far too overwhelming for me!" Whatever your reaction may have been, the concept of your thoughts creating your life experience is enormous and has far-reaching implications. But that concept is precisely what this book is all about, for it is the secret to life. However, because simply pondering those words can be both bewildering and intimidating, I have broken this concept down into simple steps, processes, and techniques that will allow you to harness the power of your thoughts to create a life that pleases you.

So, if you have ever wished there was an operating manual for life, a book that had answers — *real* answers — to help you resolve the various dilemmas you encounter day after day, this book is for you.

If you have ever longed for a bird's-eye view of life, a perspective that enabled you to comprehend what you observe and experience, this book is for you.

If you have ever felt a gnawing within that something was missing in life, this book is for you.

If you have ever desired to experience a life filled with passion, happiness, serenity, great relationships, radiant health, a job that lights your fire, prosperity, peace of mind, or a physical appearance that pleases you; if you have yearned to understand the *true* meaning of how life is meant to be lived, this book is for you. For the answers to those puzzles lie within these pages!

Buckle Up! You're Leaving Your Comfort Zone

There is a field beyond right or wrong. I will meet you there.
— RUMI
1207-1273

One doesn't discover new lands without consenting to lose sight of the shore for a very long time. — ANDRÉ GIDE
1869-1951

In order to truly find the Path, each of us must loosen our minds and begin from a point of wonder and openness — of being willing to not know.[1]
— LAURIE BETH JONES

Throughout my life I have always wondered *why*. Whenever I would ask a question, I was never content with a surface answer or trite explanation. I wanted to know *why*. Well, my incessant seeking and ceaseless questioning led to my "finding." The answers I found, though, may not be what you expect to hear. So the question I pose to you is: Are you willing to consider that the Truth as you know and understand it to be today ain't necessarily so?

Are you willing to embark on a journey that could change everything in your life for the better, a journey that offers you a bird's-eye view where life actually makes sense? Are you open, curious, and willing to take in the whole picture? Or are you filled with doubt, uncertainty, and skepticism when introduced to new ideas? Have you ever suffered from a condition known as "contempt *prior* to investigation"? Actually, that's a pretty normal reaction. Why? Whenever you meet with information that doesn't fit neatly inside your "comfort zone," your internal guidance system will alert you to a potential intruder. How did you acquire this comfort zone? Quite unconsciously. To understand just *how* your comfort zone was constructed, let's start at the very beginning: The day you arrived.

Your Indoctrination into Life

From the moment you arrived, your indoctrination into life began and with it, the construction of your comfort zone. As a child, your primary caretakers taught you 'the ropes.' "This is good, that is bad. This is right, and that is wrong. If you do what is good and right, you will be rewarded. Conversely, if you do what is bad or wrong, you will be punished." Once your indoctrination was complete within your family, the school system then took over with its set of rules along with its set of rewards and punishments. At the same time, society taught you its rules, regulations, rewards, and punishments, until pretty soon you were 'programmed' — your beliefs paralleled those of most folks around you. And though you didn't *consciously* choose to believe what you were taught, you adopted these prevailing beliefs. Consequently, whatever beliefs you adopted have created your comfort zone, and your life, along with it.

In order to undertake this journey, however, it will be necessary for you to leave your comfort zone — a task that will feel uncomfortable because your comfort zone houses your beliefs, and your beliefs form the foundation of your life. Therefore, it is beneficial to understand in advance that you're probably going to feel a degree of discomfort while reading this book. Even though your comfort zone may be imperfect and include a few cobweb-laden skeletons in a closet, a leaky faucet, a toilet that runs incessantly, or a roof fraught with holes, it has become 'home sweet home.' Nevertheless, this book is all about evolution, and in order to evolve, you must take a step *beyond* what is known — a step outside of your comfort zone. Furthermore, as you progress along this journey, you may become less and less attached to your current comfort zone, for not only was it built unconsciously, but its foundation actually contains fundamental flaws — flaws responsible for much of the pain and discomfort you have experienced in life.

How Heavily Guarded Is Your Comfort Zone?

The degree of discomfort you may experience along this journey will depend on the degree of discomfort you are currently experiencing in your life — either on a personal level or as you view the world globally. The more discomfort you're feeling in life, the less discomfort you will feel while reading this book. To determine your degree of discomfort, ask yourself a few questions: "Is the life I am now living bringing me more joy than sorrow, more laughter than tears, more love than indifference?" "Am I healing or hurting, growing or withering, expanding or contracting?"² "Am I content with our world situation, or do I feel sadness, despair, fear, or frustration when I observe the conditions that exist?" For the true gauge of your life is how you feel in the majority of your moments, because 'Now,' friends, is all that counts.

If you are now experiencing dissatisfaction or discomfort in your life, your comfort zone will more than likely sport a welcome mat at its front door. And though you may be cautious of someone who rings your doorbell, you will probably be willing to listen to the 'sales pitch' before responding. On the other hand, if you think that you already have all the answers, that life is just fine and dandy — regardless of how dysfunctional your life or the world may be, your comfort zone will more than likely sport a 'No Trespassing' sign. It may even resemble a thick-walled fortress, complete with trigger-happy armed soldiers stationed around its perimeter ready to shoot a 'trespasser' — one who rings your doorbell — if one dares to approach your front door.

Regardless of the type of comfort zone you have built, your challenge will be to restrain your knee-jerk response to pass premature judgment upon one who rings your doorbell. Why? In order to actualize your authentic power, it will be necessary for you to reevaluate your comfort zone.

The Missing Link in Life

Along this journey you will become acquainted with a critical missing link in life: your internal guidance system. Why is it critical? Because it guides you along your Path, alerting you if your thoughts are creating what you *want* or what you *don't* want — an essential aspect of living life the way it is meant to be lived. Many psychologists refer to this aspect of who you are as your superconscious self. Others have labeled it as your spirit, inner being, or the presence of God that resides within you. And one man, after seeing the movie *Austin Powers*, referred to it as 'mini me.' I have ascribed it yet another label, christening it as your "inner Angel." I hesitated to use the word 'spirit' because the definition of this word is so varied and conflicting that it evokes a plethora of reactions from person to person, and many folks reject a message in its entirety when they encounter words that 'ring their doorbells.' 'Spirit' is one of those words. Some mistakenly define it as an abstract, celestial aspect of life conjured by religions and thus dismiss it as nonsense. However, the context in which I speak of your internal guidance system refers to the powerful subtle force that resides within you as a human being, whether you are religious, spiritual without a religious affiliation, atheist, agnostic, or still gathering data from which to define yourself.

Although you may be unfamiliar with your guidance system, this aspect of Who You Are is as real as the head on your shoulders. Therefore, chapter by chapter, you will learn exactly how to utilize your spirit — to unify it with your body and mind, for when you do, you connect with the incredible untapped power that lies within you! In fact, failing to understand the mechanics of this interrelationship or how life operates at the most fundamental level, you and I — and most everyone else on this planet — are living life *backwards!* How do we reverse our direction? First, by understanding how life is *meant* to be lived.

Life Is Meant for Living, Loving, and Laughing!

Life is meant for living, loving, and laughing. To be lived with joy, freedom, love, peace, wisdom, power, abundance, blessings, acceptance, meaning, gratitude, and understanding — for *everyone.*

To live means more than to simply exist from day to day, more than to merely accomplish a "to-do" list. To live is to be eager to awake each morning, to look forward to the day ahead; to anticipate it with joy. To truly live means to be without fear, to be filled with love, to feel a connection with all things; to have a sense of inner peace, fulfillment, and a feeling of purpose.

To love means to appreciate the wonder of everything that surrounds you and feel joyful because of it. To love is to treasure every person for the unique being he or she is — even if you disagree with that person. To truly love is to look at the world in awe as a child does; to cherish everything for its intrinsic beauty; to be enveloped by a radiance of love to the core of your being.

To laugh means to enjoy the world around you, to have fun, and find humor in life. To laugh is to reconnect with the child within who is silly, funny, spontaneous, shouting with glee, and filled with a curiosity for the wonderful, magical world we live in.

How do you create this great life filled with love, laughter, and everything else that sounds too good to be true? By learning and applying the Four-Step Formula. The Formula is the step by step process that underlies *how* your thoughts create your reality. The Formula reveals how and why you are experiencing whatever you are experiencing in life. And because knowledge is power, you can utilize that knowledge to experience what you *want.*

Discovering the Secret

How did I stumble upon this Four-Step Formula? The story began to unfold in 1973 when a stream of rather unusual folks, under curious circumstances, told me that I was going to do something later in my life that was important, never disclosing or even knowing the actual 'something.' Well, I guess it must be 'later,' because one day in the summer of 1996, I connected with that something.

My search for greater truth led me to the enlightening books I mentioned in my note of thanks. As I read through these books, I dog-eared many pages, intending to outline the problem-solving, life-enhancing techniques they offered so I could get more of what I wanted out of life. But life was always moving too fast, I never had time, and I am one of those people who doesn't need to add yet another project to my list of 'things to do.'

On one fateful day, however, I experienced an epiphany — an *aha!* moment. Most of the books I had read conveyed a recurring message — a profound message. Underlying every experience in life — good, bad, or indifferent, there is a four-step process — a formula. This Formula is at the inception of every success or failure anyone has ever experienced. Additionally, it underlies any experience that a group of people has — a family, a corporation, a town, a country, our world, or any faction that comprises a collective entity — in the same manner! This Four-Step Formula is the genesis of every experience in life. And its *conscious* application has the potential to significantly impact many aspects of life. Tell me that is not profound! Once I recognized this truth, I experienced a 'knowing,' a 'click' in my mind that said: *"This is your Mission."*

I have never had the least inclination nor desire to be a writer, nor have I ever written a darn thing before in my life. (And my husband wondered if I had passed English upon scanning the first, second, third, hundredth, and every draft thereafter.) But I was meant to write this book. So, bear with me, for although I am a somewhat reluctant messenger, I have accepted this challenge and written this book from my heart. I now present to you the simple Formula incorporated within the context of a step-by-step workbook and guide that provides you the processes to attain whatever you want out of life *on a daily basis.* Actually, it is exactly what I always wanted, a "Cliffs Notes®" version of all the information I was inspired by. So, this book is really written for *me,* so that I can live the most wonderful life I have ever imagined! But not being selfish (well, maybe a little sometimes...), I thought I would share this secret with you so that you can live the most wonderful life you have ever imagined, too!

(Aren't I nice?) Think of this book as the *Rules for Life on Planet Earth* coming to you now rather than at birth. (Better late than never, right?)

The Four-Step Formula is the Foundation For Health, Prosperity, Love, and Joy!

As you learn the basis of the Formula, you will discover how to *be* everything you've always wanted to be, *do* everything you've always wanted to do, and *have* everything you've always wanted to have. And if you are not sure about what you want to be, do, or have, don't worry. This book will help you to uncover your desires. The steps to find your purpose in life; attain the job of your dreams; enjoy relationships that are loving and fulfilling; enjoy perfect radiant health; achieve a physical body that pleases you; have all the money you want; and find happiness, serenity, and a passion for life, are all included within these pages. Tall order? Indeed. But once you understand Who You *Really* Are and exactly how your thoughts create your reality, not too tall!

This "Secret" Has Been Around for a Long, Long Time

The information I share with you is not new. It is universal ageless wisdom, having neither religious affiliation nor bias. What lies at the core of this information is a principle of nature that has somehow escaped notice. In fact, as I researched this subject, I discovered book after book after book, dating as far back as 5000 B.C. to the secret mystery schools in ancient Egypt, *all* conveying the same information. And to tell you the truth, I am actually amazed that at the dawning of a new millennium, we, as humankind, still don't get it! Following in the footsteps of Dale Carnegie, I, too, have gathered my ideas from a multitude of visionaries:

> *The ideas I stand for are not mine. I borrowed them from Socrates. I swiped them from Chesterfield. I stole them from Jesus. And I put them in a book. If you don't like their rules, whose would you use?* — DALE CARNEGIE
> 1888-1955

I believe it is no coincidence that you are reading this book. I believe that you are ready to hear this message and whatever information you glean that will help to make your life more enjoyable, God bless. I am going to share a great deal with you, for life happens to be an all-encompassing subject. You may utilize some information right now, and other information you may 'put on the shelf' to ponder at a later date. Whatever you believe, it matters not; just try to *feel* with your heart rather than think with your head and know that you are in the right place at the right time. Trust yourself, try to keep an open mind, and don't be fooled by the greatest salesmen of all: Fear, Uncertainty, and Doubt. How do you recognize Truth? Truth resonates in your heart. Truth is that which empowers and unifies humanity.

> *Love breaks down the barriers and creates unity. That which creates barriers and creates separateness and differences is ignorance.*[3] — BRIAN L. WEISS, M.D.
> *a message received from a patient under hypnosis*

> *It is only with the heart that one can see rightly; what is essential is invisible to the eye.*
> — ANTOINE DE SAINT-EXUPÉRY
> 1900-1944

> *The heart knows truth as that which sets it free.*[4]
> — GLENDA GREEN
> *Love Without End: Jesus Speaks*

> *Only the heart knows how to find what is precious.*
> — FYODOR DOSTOEVSKY
> 1821-1885

I have divided the book into the following nine sections:

ᕀ Part I — *The Prelude* — introduces you to the secret to life and explores life on a hypothetical Earth living with the knowledge of the Four-Step Formula.

ᕀ Part II — *The Puzzle* — reveals the Four-Step Formula, its implications, and the far-reaching repercussions of *not* understanding it. Examining information from many diverse sources — medical, scientific, and metaphysical, you will connect the pieces of the puzzle of life and reconsider how it operates. You will become acquainted with your internal guidance system — your inner Angel — who continually guides you along your path of free will. Next, you will learn how you and Angel co-create what you desire in life.

ᕀ Part III — *The Present* — examines the state of being we exist in today, the evolution of humankind, and your current personal reality. You will begin to ponder new solutions to problems and issues, both global and personal, created as a result of being unaware of the Formula.

- Part IV — *The Past* — dissects your personal history and uncovers the hidden treasures that lie buried deep within it. By uncovering your beliefs and what you were taught as a child, you will learn how those beliefs have impacted your life experience.

- Part V — *The Pathway* — provides the tools to redefine your Path. By articulating the life you choose to live, you will define your Vision Statement — who you choose to be, and learn the steps to *consciously* create what you want in life. Next, you will discover both your personal Mission and the steps to actualize our collective global Mission: The recreation of our world.

- Part VI — *The Procedures* — provides the tools and techniques to stay on track. You will learn how joy, appreciation, compassion, and love are the key ingredients to living a life filled with happiness, health, and prosperity. By understanding the awesome nature of your authentic power, you will learn how to effectively help others, as well as the strategies to develop and sustain wonderful relationships.

- Part VII — *The Predicaments* — provides the processes that will guide you back to your Path when you lose your way. Step by step methods are articulated to help resolve the conflict that oftentimes arises between what you desire and what you believe.

- Part VIII — *The Physical Body* — explores the vast and enormous implications of the Four-Step Formula on your physical body. The steps to eradicate illness and attain a state of perfect radiant health are provided. Last, you will delve into the subject of food and diet and learn how to manifest a physical body that pleases you.

- Part IX — *The Postscript* — sums it all up and addresses how you add immeasurably to the joy in our world as you create the best possible life experience for yourself. To assist you in creating a magical life experience, I have included affirmations that you may choose to adopt. Afterward, I share my personal story — how I was 'called upon' to write this book, followed by my intention for you and your life.

Are you excited yet? I am!

> *I want to get you excited about who you are, what you are, what you have, and what can still be for you. I want to inspire you to see that you can go far beyond where you are right now.* — VIRGINIA SATIR

So, You Want Evidence?

While writing this manuscript, I encountered people who were experiencing painful issues in their lives. Having gained a knowledge that most people are unaware of, life now made complete sense to me. In fact, it was utterly *logical*. Therefore, I believed that in sharing my knowledge, these people might gain a clearer understanding of their problems and resolve them using a different approach. Thus, I gave each a copy of my manuscript. The results? Some were helped immensely. Some gained new insights that allowed them to change their lives. Some saved their marriages. Some became more prosperous. Some gained a new perspective on their illnesses. However, others (mostly members of my family who, incidentally, did not read the manuscript) felt otherwise. Their reactions? I was "full of it," "delusional," or "should start looking for a *real* job." (Ouch!) Rather than being open, curious, and willing to examine the potentiality of a new (old) truth, they found it easier to find things wrong with *me*, the messenger. After reeling from those less-than-supportive reactions, I took a step back and saw their *real* purpose: Those experiences were meant to teach me, for I then understood just how frightened people can be when presented with new information — regardless of its potential value. Although many people's lives are filled with blame, confusion, despair, and victimization, those nasty experiences are actually deemed safe because they are familiar and known.

As a result of my adverse experiences, I clearly understood that in order to reach people where they stand today — as perfectly normal, rational, analytical, logical, folks who have been 'programmed' to be skeptical of anything that 'pushed the envelope' beyond traditional thinking — it was essential that I present this information in a convincing manner. However, as I pondered that daunting task, I was overcome by feelings of inadequacy. I looked up and asked the 'powers that be' to send me help — quick. This 'Mission' was making my life miserable — destroying my credibility and integrity. I was in need of additional evidence, further validation of the profound truth I had discovered. The result? I was 'led' to supplementary material.

Initially, I chose the title of *Life 101 — Guess what? We're doing it backward, folks!* However, I soon discovered that another author, Peter McWilliams, had chosen *Life 101* as the title for a series of books he had written, so it was unavailable. Curious about his book's content, I ordered it over the Internet. What arrived, however, was *Life 101: The Quote Book*. My reaction? Frustration. I now had to go through the hassle of returning it. But when I opened this book, I became awestruck! This book contained a plethora of quotations from visionaries who represented a multitude of diverse cultures that spanned centuries — quotations that verified, validated, and confirmed exactly what I was writing! And these quotations were from familiar people — names you have heard before. People whose wisdom has stood the test of time. People who were not 'full of it' or 'delusional.' People, whose reputations would make this message far more difficult to dismiss. It was then that I experienced what I now refer to as the 'big wink' from above, or *"Get it, Lauren?"*

I also was 'led' to material from other sources, albeit non-earthly. For Christmas in 1997, I received the book *Conversations with God: Book 1* as a gift from my husband. My reaction? This was a rather unusual gift. How credible could this author be? After all, he purported to have had conversations with God — the Big Guy. How was I to know if what he conveyed was for real. As fate would have it, however, this book came to me at the perfect moment. I had just finished *The Nature of Personal Reality* by Jane Roberts, which I was also initially skeptical of, as its content was garnered from a highly evolved spiritual source who utilized Jane as a conduit. Incredibly, the information in *The Nature of Personal Reality* was consistent with the information conveyed in *Conversations with God*. Furthermore, the information from these two sources also was consistent with still other information I had been given. A few months prior to reading those books, I had serendipitously received audio tapes by authors/speakers Esther and Jerry Hicks, whose content was also garnered from a highly evolved spiritual source who utilizes Esther as a conduit. Although the wisdom conveyed through these sources differed in phraseology and grammar, the content was congruent and coherent. Therefore, I considered it far too coincidental to dismiss, and offer specific passages for your consideration. Even more interesting, though, the information conveyed by these sources sheds a whole new light on the wisdom imparted by the visionaries of our past.

To impart this message in a convincing comprehensive manner, I chose to present this information as an attorney would present a case to a jury — a jury having no previous knowledge of the case. I submit facts, ideas, witnesses, and evidence for your consideration in a logical sequential order to impart, in no uncertain terms, the validity of this truth in order to obtain a favorable verdict — one that will enable people to live their lives in a completely different way. To weave in the veracity of this truth, I have enlisted the credibility, integrity, and wisdom of my 'expert witnesses' (my new quote-book friends who heard my plea and came to my rescue): God, Plato, Socrates, Henry Ford, William Shakespeare, Mark Twain, Gautama Buddha, James Allen, Mother Teresa, Pope John Paul II, Jesus, Aristotle, Helen Keller, William James, Albert Einstein, Margaret Mead, Thomas Paine, Emily Dickinson, Ralph Waldo Emerson, Confucius, Chief Seattle, Mahatma Gandhi, Mohammed, George Bernard Shaw, Thomas Edison, Marie Curie, and many, many other notables.

Chapter by chapter I (we) present my (our) case: a synthesis of knowledge from a multitude of diverse sources, that when completed will hopefully present you with a clear, concise picture of how life really operates. And even though I am unknown, by the end of this book I hope that my friends and I will have succeeded in presenting a case that is so convincing that you render a verdict in our favor (which happens to be in your favor, too!).

I Believe...

My innermost wish is to inspire you to live the most magical life experience you can possibly imagine and to provide you with an insight that will enable you to ease any pain you may encounter along your journey.

> *If I can stop one heart from breaking, I shall not live in vain; if I can ease one life the aching, or cool one pain, or help one fainting robin into his nest again, I shall not live in vain.*
> — EMILY DICKINSON
> 1830-1886

As I share these pearls of wisdom with you, my intentions are pure, from my heart, and based in love. However, I also believe that you have a right to know what I believe. I am not asking you to believe what I believe, for I respect every person's spiritual values as I would appreciate their respecting mine. Actually, I believe this message broadens and expands on what you may already believe. I share my beliefs so you know where I am coming from, fully understanding that I am not intending to alienate, judge, or discriminate against anyone. I have a profound respect for each of you, *even if we embrace opposing viewpoints*, for you are my brother or sister and we're all in this thing called 'life' together. I have come to recognize that your unique perspective contributes to the essential diversity that makes our world a wonderful environment from which to experience life.

The following is a brief summary of my beliefs:

∿ First and foremost, I believe that a wonderful, loving, nonjudgmental Greater Power (God, to me) exists who has created this glorious world in which we live.

∿ I believe that life is eternal; hence, we have a lot of time on our hands. I believe that we incarnate in many lifetimes, donning the costumes of many different types of people. We may choose to experience life through the eyes of a man or woman, as a specific race, or as a person having an infirmity. Each life that we live provides us the opportunity to experience a unique perspective which results in our personal evolution.

∼ I believe that Earth provides us a rich environment endowed with a vast spectrum of people, beliefs, and experiences. And from this variety, we choose various experiences from which to evolve, define, and discover Who We Are.

∼ I believe that prior to our birth, each of us drafted an overall plan — a blueprint or Path — for the goals we wished to accomplish in this lifetime. Hence, the conditions, circumstances, challenges, or obstacles that we encounter in our lives are, in actuality, catalysts that allow us to accomplish our goals. I believe that our objective is to awaken to Who We Really Are and 'walk the talk,' but at every step we have a choice, or free will, in how we respond when presented with our opportunities.

∼ I believe that we are all sacred souls on a sacred journey of experience, all a part of God, and that there is essentially nothing — no race, religion, or physical difference — that separates us.

∼ I believe that we have been asleep for a long period of time, and as a result, adversity became the avenue most commonly used to reawaken us to Who We Really Are. Adversity offers opportunities for our evolution because it forces us to examine what is *truly* important in life. Adversity oftentimes manifests in loss: loss of employment, health, financial state, a family member or, on a global scale, worldly power. Loss presents the opportunity to grow by challenging our character, compelling us to define Who We Choose To Be in the midst of those experiences. In fact, those definitive moments provide our greatest opportunities for a turning point in life — one that compels us to reach beyond the pain we are experiencing and seek a better way.

∼ I believe that each moment we experience in life is an opportunity for growth, no matter how old or wise we are.

∼ I believe that life is meant for joyful living rather than simply existing; loving rather than hating; allowing rather than judging; appreciating rather than taking for granted; seeking to find points of harmony rather than those of disharmony; and laughing rather than suffering. I believe that life is meant to be a magical, creative experience.

Relax and Enjoy the Journey

Regardless of where you are on your Path right now, love yourself for who and what you are, for you are at the right place at the right time. Appreciate this moment for all its potential as it unfolds before you, for this moment is a gift. If you are not where you would like to be and have made mistakes that you regret, that's okay, for you will now be provided with the tools to learn from them, get past them, and understand their broader significance — that your mistakes have been essential elements of your experiential journey through life. And believe me, I'm struggling along my Path like everyone else — a work in progress. However, this message has allowed me to relax and enjoy the journey; for the journey is meant to be as much or more fun than arriving at the destination!

Graduation Day Is Approaching

I believe that we, as humankind, are on the threshold of a greater understanding of life; on the brink of a magnificent future and a new stage of evolution — *the Age of Spirit*. We are now on the verge of discovering the impenetrable triad of power: the connection between the three aspects of Who We Are — body, mind, *and* spirit — that allows us to accomplish anything! It is when we begin to apply this knowledge that we will graduate to a more expansive recognition of our true nature and the vast abilities we possess.

It has taken generations and generations of those who came before us to build the bridges and set the stage to create the potential for the rebirth of our world. There has never before been a more fertile time in history for this to occur. These are indeed the keys to the kingdom, my friend, for as each of us — you!☺ — becomes aware of our power and begins to create the life we wish to live, we will simultaneously create the world we wish to live in.

> *Come, my friends. 'Tis not too late to seek a newer world.*
> — ALFRED LORD TENNYSON
> 1809-1892

> *We have it in our power to begin the world again.*
> — THOMAS PAINE
> 1739-1809

In our time, what is at issue is the very nature of humankind, the image we have of our limits and possibilities. History is not yet done with its exploration of the limits of what it means to be human.
— C. WRIGHT MILLS
1914-1962

Prepare yourself for an exciting journey. My heart is with you as together we cross the bridge that leads to the best that life has to offer. I will accompany you on every step of your journey as your friend, your ally, and your cheerleader, interweaving my personal life experiences as well as the invaluable opportunities for insight they provided me. It is my hope that my experiences assist you in better understanding your own experiences, for in reality, it is not words that teach, but life experience. Now take a deep breath, relax, and let go of any anxiety or fear, because I will tell you in advance that this book has the happiest ending you could imagine, an ending that states: *You are powerful and you now have the tools to unleash that power!* So enjoy, enjoy, enjoy (as Angela, the most joyous server with a heart that sings at the Bakers Square® restaurant in Naperville, Illinois, would say)! Let's now forge ahead so you can begin to live your life as it is meant to be lived!

P.S. Throughout this book, you will be asked to write down your thoughts. Although you may have the urge to skip ahead with the good intention of filling in the blanks at a later date, please understand that this material will have a far greater meaning if you follow the steps in the order they have been written. Each step is a 'brick' that helps to build your foundation, ensuring its strength, and each 'brick' builds upon the previous. Therefore, following the book in the order it has been written (whether you choose the shortcut or read it from cover to cover) will allow you to fully understand and utilize the Four-Step Formula to create joy and abundance in your life. So control yourself and *do not "cheat"* (ha, ha, ☺)! (I have first-hand knowledge of this because my husband 'cheated.' He skimmed the book without filling in the blanks, and still doesn't quite 'get it.' He claims to know this material by osmosis after being subjected to my pontificating on countless occasions. However, to *know* this truth and to *live* it are two completely different experiences.)

I hear and I forget, I see and I remember, I do and I understand.
— CHINESE PROVERB

P.S. S. You will soon discover that I am repetitive and redundant, but bear with me, there is a method to my madness. Essentially you have been programmed backward to react and respond to life. However, the Four-Step Formula necessitates a proactive approach to life, so this is my attempt to help you begin to reprogram yourself. ☻

The Rose

Some say life is a river
that drowns the tender reed.
Some say life is a razor
that leaves your soul to bleed,
Some say life it is a hunger
an endless aching need.
I say life, it is a flower
and you its only seed.
It's the heart afraid of breaking
that never learns to dance.
It's the dream afraid of waking
that never takes a chance.
It's the one who won't be taken
who cannot seem to give.
And the soul afraid of dying
that never learns to live.
When the night has been too lonely
and the road has been too long,
And you think that life is only
for the lucky and the strong,
Just remember in the winter,
far beneath the winter snow,
Lies the seed
that with the sun's love,
In the Spring, becomes the rose.[5]

I have taken the liberty of substituting the word "life" for the word "love."

Words and music by Amanda McBroom

Your Life Holds Unlimited Potential

You have the ability
to attain whatever you seek.
Within you is every potential
you can imagine.
Always aim higher than
you believe you can reach.
So often, you'll discover
that when your talents
are set free
by your imagination,
you can attain any goal.
If people offer their
help or wisdom
as you go through life,
accept it gratefully.
You can learn much from those
who have gone before you.
But never be afraid or hesitant
to step off the accepted path
and head off in your own direction
if your heart tells you
that it's the right way for you.
Always believe that you will
ultimately succeed
at whatever you do,
and never forget the value
of persistence, discipline,
and determination.
You are meant to be
whatever you dream
of becoming.

Edmund O'Neill

Come in From the Rain

Well, hello again, good old friend of mine.
You've been reaching for yourself for such a long, long time.
There's so much to say, no need to explain,
just an open door to keep you from the rain.
It's a long, long road when you're all alone,
And a man like you will always choose the long way home.
There's no right or wrong, I'm not here to blame.
I just want to be the one to keep you from the rain.
And it looks like sunny skies, now that I know you're all right.
Time has left us older and wiser, I know I am.
And it's good to know my best friend has come home again.
'Cause I think of us like an old cliché.
But it doesn't matter 'cause I love you anyway,
Come in from the rain,
Come in from the rain,
Come in from the rain.[6]

Words and Music by
Melissa Manchester and Carole Bayer Sager

A Vision of our World
Living the Four-Step Formula

It is possible that our race may be an accident, in a meaningless universe, living its brief life uncared for, on this dark cooling star: but even so — and all the more — what marvelous creatures we are! What fairy story, what tale from the Arabian Nights of the Jinns, is a hundredth part as wonderful as this true fairy story of Simians! It is so much more heartening, too, than the tales we invent. A universe capable of giving birth to many such accidents is — blind or not — a good world to live in, a promising universe. We once thought we lived on God's footstool; it may be a throne.

— CLARENCE DAY
1874-1935

The evolution of humankind would have taken a far different path had we recognized the existence of the Four-Step Formula. A path void of hatred, war, destruction, frustration, anxiety, confusion, racism, stress, poverty, disease, crime, tension, discrimination, fear, and all the pain, anguish, and suffering that exists on Earth. Having taken this wrong turn, let's take a glimpse at life on Earth had we taken the right turn.

The Vision

For each one of us, there is a desire to travel. A star to discover. And a being within ourselves to bring to life.

—UNKNOWN

Life on Earth is a rich creative experience filled with love, laughter, or anything else that each of us chooses. Having free will, each of us selects a different perspective from which to experience life. Just as we might select a different movie each week — a thriller, sci-fi, romance, intrigue, drama, or comedy — we select different adventures to exper-ience on Earth. We understand that our lives provide us with the opportunity to expand our awareness — to experience the fullness of our being through our minds, bodies, and emotions.

We live in freedom and perfect radiant health, for those attributes are our birthrights. Our days are filled with the experiences we have chosen, and our lives with potential and excitement.

There is no one right or wrong way on Earth or one set of rules that applies to everyone. Each of us simply lives as we choose to and respects the uniqueness of others who have chosen a different path. Although there is great diversity among us, there is no conflict, for we fully understand that each of us is part of a great whole, dependent on one another. Those who think in similar ways simply gravitate to one another, not feeling threatened by those who think differently. We all realize that we have control over every aspect of our life experiences. In fact, we *appreciate* our differences, for we know that it is our differences that create the circumstances which allows us to choose the experiences we desire. If we were to do away with our differences, we would also do away with our choices.

We have a deep trust and awareness of our feelings and realize that each of us has different feelings. Our feelings act as our inner compasses that guide us along our paths of free will. When we encounter an aspect of life that doesn't please us, we simply utilize our displeasure as a stimulus to instead choose what we desire. We recognize that desire summons life energy, and whenever we block our desires with negative emotion, we restrict the flow of life energy to our physical bodies. The result? Our bodies age, decay, become riddled with disease, and eventually culminate in our physical demise.

Earth provides us with such an abundance of natural resources, that all of us enjoy prosperity. We respect and honor our planet for the exquisite environment she endows us. We have a reverence for Earth's breath-taking majesty and splendor — from her snow-capped mountains to her verdant prairies; from her thunderous and tranquil oceans to her awe-inspiring sunrises and sunsets. We share our home with all of Earth's elements, from her beautiful plant life to her creatures great and small. We understand the contribution that each living thing makes to the whole and our interdependence upon one another. As conscious beings inhabiting Earth, we care for her as the life-giving, life-sustaining being she really is.

Does This Glimpse Resemble Heaven?

Does this glimpse resemble what you might perceive as a Heaven on our Earth? For that is exactly what it is — a Heaven waiting to blossom. For eons we have longed for the knowledge that would allow us to manifest a new world. And though a myriad of authors and visionaries have provided us with the knowledge to recreate our world countless times before, each time we failed to embrace their words. Why? We weren't ready. We were so deeply entrenched in the reality of what we were living that we wore blinders when presented with the truth. The result? Fear triumphed and grew stronger. We became further separated from one another, further isolated, remote, and alone. The chasm between Who We Really Are and what we were living grew greater and greater.

To resolve this imbalance, adversity came knocking at our door. Adversity that appeared in the form of war, famine, poverty, hatred, racism, and disease. How could adversity help to resolve our imbalance? Adversity is a wake-up call. It challenges us to explore areas we may have heretofore denied. Adversity creates the contraction that impels expansion. Adversity produces degeneration that arouses regeneration. Adversity beckons us to look beyond what we now accept as truth, for the truth we are now living has not provided us with solutions to the myriad of problems we observe and experience daily.

We are now at a turning point where the questions before us are: Have we experienced enough anguish; enough suffering? Have we reached our threshold of pain? Have we recognized the futility of war? Have we experienced enough hatred, enough separation? Are we willing to reassess our comfort zones? Are we willing to reexamine the messages that others have passed down to us for centuries? Are we ready to admit that, although we are brilliant in many areas, we have failed to recognize the most fundamental aspect of life: how it *really* operates?

There are joys which long to be ours. God sends ten thousand truths, which come about us like birds seeking inlet; but we are shut up to them, and so they bring us nothing, but sit and sing awhile upon the roof, and then fly away.
— HENRY WARD BEECHER
1813-1887

Man will occasionally stumble upon the truth, but most
of the time he will pick himself up and continue on.
— WINSTON CHURCHILL
1874-1965

Many of us are indeed ready to take the next step. We somehow know that our world is not working as it should, and we feel this imbalance at an inner level. We yearn for a connection with something that has greater meaning. We ache for tangible solutions to the despair we feel. Marianne Williamson tells us in *The Healing of America*, [this yearning] "is penetrating the deepest levels of our psyche...and no amount of force can contain it...."[7]

Taking the next step in our evolution will include many challenges. Our greatest challenge? To overcome the hurdles in our minds — hurdles created by the powerful momentum of fear, uncertainty, doubt, and skepticism born of the domino-effect of our wrong turn. And each of us will encounter these hurdles as we make the transition from today to tomorrow, for in order to evolve, we must resolve them.

What We Are Taught from Birth

Beauty is all about us, but how many are blind to it? They take a look at the wonder of this earth — and seem to see nothing. Each second, we live in a new and unique moment of the universe, a moment that never was before and will never be again. And what do we teach our children in school? We teach them that two and two makes four, and that Paris is the capital of France. When will we also teach them what they are? We should say to each of them: Do you know what you are? You are a marvel! You are unique. In all of the world there is no other child exactly like you. In the millions of years that have passed there has never been another child like you. And look at your body — what a wonder it is! Your legs, your arms, your cunning fingers, the way you move! You may become a Shakespeare, a Michelangelo, a Beethoven. You have the capacity for anything. Yes, you are a marvel. And when you grow up, can you then harm another who is, like you, a marvel? You must cherish one another. You must work — we all must work — to make this world worthy of its children.
— PABLO CASALS
1876-1973

In my dream, the Angel shrugged and said "If we fail this time, it will be a failure of imagination." And then she placed the world gently in the palm of my hand.

— BRIAN ANDREAS

Let's now examine what we are taught from birth and subsequently take for granted, for the difference between the wrong turn and the right turn lies in what we assume. What are we taught that has precluded us from experiencing life the way it is meant to be lived?

From the time we are able to understand, we are programmed with the 'fact' that life is a struggle. We are programmed to fight for our fair share because there isn't enough. We are programmed to fear others, to keep our distance from anything dangerous. We are programmed to be cautious, suspicious, wary, skeptical, and to beware of the ulterior motives of others. We are programmed to blame others, to scream, shout, and lament about the miseries of life and the injustices we observe or experience.

We are *not* programmed to be human: to look for points of harmony, or to simply love one another. Why? Because we're afraid.

Unaware of how life operates at the most fundamental level, our lives are filled with fear because we cannot comprehend why 'bad' things happen. And this fear permeates all levels of our being. It debilitates and saps the strength out of life itself. In our fear and unawareness of how life really operates, we presume that we are helpless victims of forces beyond our control. We believe that we are tossed unmercifully by the twists and turns of fate. We accept that everything in life is an accident, luck, or circumstantial — outside of our control. Under these circumstances, it is really quite logical that we never learned to truly live, love, or laugh!

Now that you have a basic understanding of the underlying factors that spawned the state of being we exist in today, let's explore the 'secret to life' — the Four-Step Formula — how thought creates reality, so you can understand the basis of how life *really* operates.

Beginning with an evaluation of the 'haves' and 'have-nots,' let's see if you can uncover the four steps that underlie their vastly different realities. Are you ready to take your first step in living a life filled with love and laughter? ☯

Flashdance: What a Feeling!

First when there's nothing
but a slow glowing dream,
that your fear seems to hide deep inside your mind.
All alone I have cried silent tears full of pride.
In a world made of steel, made of stone.
When I hear the music, close my eyes,
feel the rhythm.
Wrap around take a hold of my heart.
What a feeling!
Being's believing!
I can have it all now I'm dancing for my life.
Take your passion and make it happen,
Pictures come alive you can dance right through your life.
Now I hear the music, close my eyes,
I am rhythm.
In a flash it takes hold of my heart.
What a feeling!
Being's believing!
I can have it all now I'm dancing for my life.[8]

Words by Keith Forsey and Irene Cara — Music by Giorgio Moroder

PART II

The Puzzle

THE SECRET TO LIFE:
WHO YOU REALLY ARE
AND HOW LIFE REALLY OPERATES

Part II

The Puzzle

THE SECRET TO LIFE UNVEILED:
WHO YOU REALLY ARE
AND HOW LIFE REALLY OPERATES

The Haves and the Have-Nots
Have a Lot in Common

Two men look through the same bars; one sees mud and one the stars.
— FREDERICK LANGBRIDGE
1849-1923

Man is not made by his circumstances, he is revealed by them.[1]
— JAMES ALLEN
1849-1925

Destiny is not a matter of chance, it is a matter of choice; it is not a thing to be waited for, it is a thing to be achieved.
— WILLIAM JENNINGS BRYAN
1860-1925

While one person hesitates because he feels inferior, the other is busy making mistakes and becoming superior.
— HENRY C. LINK

People are always blaming their circumstances for being what they are. I don't believe in circumstances. The people who get on in this world are the people who get up and look for the circumstances they want, and if they can't find them, make them.
— GEORGE BERNARD SHAW
1856-1950

Men are born to succeed, not to fail.
— HENRY DAVID THOREAU
1817-1862

Success is simply a matter of luck. Ask any failure.
— EARL WILSON

Success is ninety-nine percent failure.
— SOICHIRO HONDA
1906-1991
Founder of Honda Motor Corp

In order to see a rainbow you have to see through the rain.
— UNKNOWN

The Similarities Between the "Haves" and "Have-Nots"

Have you ever asked yourself *why* some people experience the wonderful aspects of life: lots of money, harmonious relationships, fantastic careers, fame, great bodies, good health, a centeredness in spirit, and why others are homeless, poor, sick, dying, unhappy, murdered, on drugs, or have a physical body that does not please them? "How could this be fair?" you might ask. Do you think that only a select few are meant to experience the wonderful aspects of life? I think not. So, what is responsible for impeding the wonderful aspects of life? Let's find out.

From where you stand today, you may define yourself as either a 'have' or 'have-not,' but, in reality, you are both. In certain areas of life you are gifted — a 'have;' and in other areas you may be lacking — a 'have-not.' Let's uncover what it takes to be a 'have' in most areas of life, by identifying the attributes that distinguish one from the other.

Although you may find the following examples to be simplistic, stereotypical, or even politically incorrect, they nonetheless impart what is most obvious and recognizable in our culture at a fundamental level. In fact, I purposely chose these examples to potentially push your buttons, for whenever you experience an adverse emotional reaction to *anything* in life, your reaction is actually a gift revealing something important to you — it is a catalyst for your growth. Therefore, whenever you experience an emotional reaction to anything in this book, be sure to note the page number so you can capitalize on the hidden treasure that lies within it.

The "Haves"

Many "haves" began their lives experiencing a scenario that resembles the following example, resulting in a seeming advantage for their life's journeys.

Jane grew up in a middle-class home where both her mother and father worked full-time so that their family could enjoy some of the extras in life. Jane was taught the value of working hard. If she went to school, achieved good grades, and then went on to a good college where she worked hard and achieved good grades, she would be successful in life. These 'facts of life' were conveyed to her from the time she was able to understand. She believed them to be true because validation was all around her. People, events, and circumstances — concrete evidence — proved these facts to be true.

What Most "Haves" Have in Common

○ Most "haves" feel that they have the ability to attain what they desire.

○ "Haves" somehow know they will find a way. If they just search and search, they will eventually discover it.

○ "Haves" utilize their failures as signposts that read, "This is the wrong way." These wrong-way signs intensify their determination and point them in other directions that eventually culminate in the right way.

○ "Haves" feel powerful, capable, and more than adequate in most areas of life.

Let's step into the shoes of a "have-not" and consider how he or she might perceive the life of a "have" living in prosperity.

Have you ever wondered why those who have an abundance of money seem to acquire more and more with such little effort? Were they born into it? Do you imagine that if *you* had their money, you would be wiser in how you spent it? Perhaps you would give your money to the poor or donate it to a research foundation that was dedicated to finding a cure for a fatal disease. Do you feel as though the rich squander their money? Do you believe that "it takes money to make money," so, if you didn't have any to begin with, how could you ever make it? Do you believe that the rich just get richer and the poor, poorer? Do you believe that the rich become richer because of our government? Do you believe that our legislators' create so many income tax loopholes for the upper-income earners that they're able to keep more of the money they earn (and consequently have the ability to contribute to the campaigns of the elected officials), whereas those who are just getting by ultimately pay the bulk of the taxes?

How do you think the "haves" became "haves"?

_____

_____

_____

_____

_____

_____

_____

_____

_____

_____

_____

_____

What were you taught to believe about the "haves," either verbally or by example?

_____

_____

_____

_____

_____

_____

_____

_____

_____

_____

_____

_____

The "Have-Nots"

Many "have-nots" began their lives experiencing a scenario that resembles the following example, resulting in a seeming disadvantage for their life's journeys.

David grew up in a poor family in the inner city. He was considered to be lucky because he had two parents living with him. He was taught, silently and subtly, that he would never have much of anything because no one around him ever did. David would have no recourse but to take from the government. In fact, they owed it to him because not only was he a member of a minority, but also a poor male — disadvantaged. David witnessed the world around him reward only those who were "haves." Or even worse, those who sold drugs, stole from others, or did whatever it took to beat the system. These facts of life were conveyed to him from the time he was able to understand. He believed them to be true because validation was everywhere. People, events, and circumstances — concrete evidence — proved these facts to be true.

What Most "Have-Nots" Have in Common

~ Most "have-nots" believe they do not have the ability to attain what they want. They have come to accept that what they desire is out of their reach, so eventually they stop dreaming and face what they believe to be reality.

~ The majority of "have-nots" grudgingly concede that they will live a life having less, that they will never find a way out, for that is what they have seen and experienced.

~ "Have-nots" utilize their failures as signposts that read: "I Told You So," or "Don't Try Again."

~ Most "have-nots" feel powerless, incompetent, unworthy, or inadequate in certain areas of life.

Let's step into the shoes of a "have" and consider how he or she might perceive the life of a "have-not" living in lack.

Have you ever wondered why the "have-nots" never seem to get ahead? Do you believe that if only they had the right education, lived in the right neighborhood, or had two parents supporting them spiritually and financially they could be a "have"? Do you believe that if they just stopped smoking, drinking, overeating, shopping, taking drugs, moaning, groaning, or whining and got a job, they would be just fine? Do you believe that our government gives them so much financial assistance that it creates a disincentive for them to find employment? Do you resent having to work forty to sixty hours a week only to have the government take 25 to 40 percent of your hard-earned money so the "have-nots" can stay at home and perhaps snicker at you — the working fool — thinking they have beat the system? Do you envision them watching television, eating food they have acquired from food stamps, and having more and more babies outside of marriage so they can qualify for more government funding to perpetuate their lives of freedom? Do you feel they just seem to lack focus and desire?

How do you think the "have-nots" became "haves-nots"?

_____
_____
_____
_____
_____
_____
_____
_____
_____
_____

What were you taught to believe about the "have-nots" either verbally or by example?

_____
_____
_____
_____
_____
_____
_____
_____
_____
_____

Were you able to recognize what the "haves" and "have-nots" have in common? Let's now explore the Four-Step Formula and see if you're right! ☺

Here's How You Get What You Get in Life: The Four-Step Formula

The real act of discovery consists not in finding new lands but in seeing with new eyes. — MARCEL PROUST
1871-1922

My function in life was to render clear what was already blindingly conspicuous. — QUENTIN CRISP

There are no new Truths, but only Truths that have not been recognized by those who have perceived them without noticing. — MARY MCCARTHY
1912-1989

I'm going to turn on the light, and we'll be two people in a room looking at each other and wondering why on Earth we were afraid of the dark. — GALE WILHELM

There is nothing so powerful as "Truth" — and often nothing so strange. — DANIEL WEBSTER
1782-1852

The secret to life, as well as the subject-matter of this book, is knowing *how* thought creates reality. Therefore, you probably recognized that the destinies of the "haves" and "have-nots" began with a thought — that was the common denominator they shared. However, there's more to this concept than just thought. Thought simply begins the process of creating life experience. So let's now dissect this concept.

As you recall, as Jane, our "have," and David, our "have-not," focused on what they were told was fact, they always observed people, events, or circumstances that corresponded with these facts. Logically, they concluded that these facts must be valid and as a result, believed them to be truth — a fact of life. Next, what they believed, whether it was conscious or unconscious, they expected to happen. And what they expected ultimately became their reality! Whatever they thought, believed, and expected, they got! *The Four-Step Formula.* This simple formula is the process underlying every experience in life, whether you're a "have," a "have-not," or a combination of the two. In general terms, the Formula reveals the process by which thought creates reality. Let's now take an even deeper look at the specifics that underlie each step.

STEP NUMBER ONE: *THINK*

All life experiences begin as a thought which is first conceived in your mind. This thought then produces a feeling in your heart — the center of your being. Your thoughts always precede your feelings, and your thoughts always return to you as a feeling. There is a dynamic point-to-point relationship between your thoughts and feelings. Think of an instance when you felt angry. What thoughts preceded your anger? Now think of a time when you felt happy. What thoughts preceded your happiness?

All feelings begin as thought. What was never fully understood was the tremendous *creative* power generated by thoughts and feelings. For each of your thoughts, after translating into a feeling, creates a *thoughtform* — a small parcel of concentrated magnetic energy (we will cover in depth in subsequent chapters). And each of your thoughtforms functions as an intense magnet attracting *other* thoughtforms that correspond with it. When enough similar thoughtforms join together, or coalesce, they manifest in people, events, or circumstances — evidence — that correspond with the feelings emanating from your heart. For example: Think of a time in your life that a male friend shared an experience with you. While he described the details of his experience, you automatically searched the 'database' of your mind for an experience in your life or the life of someone you knew that corresponded with his experience. If your experience concurred with his words, it validated, confirmed, and verified what he was saying to be 'truth.' And if it did not, think of how adamantly you may have opposed hearing it.

STEP NUMBER TWO: *BELIEVE*

∿   Unaware of the creative power of thought, once you have magnetized 'evidence' of your thoughts, you naturally conclude that your thoughts must be truth — an aspect of reality. In fact, how can you *not* believe in the face of 'evidence?' After all, in our culture, seeing *is* believing, right?

STEP NUMBER THREE: *EXPECT*

∿   Whatever you believe and hold in your heart as truth, you expect to happen. Consciously or unconsciously, you allow for it to occur.

STEP NUMBER FOUR: *GET*

∿   When you expect something to happen, guess what? It *does*, whether you want it or not! You always get what you think, believe, and expect, because your thoughts create your reality!

The Four-Step Formula

(1) think + (2) believe + (3) expect = (4) get

In the Bible it is written:

> As *you believe, so shall you receive.*

In the *Essene Gospel of Peace* it is written:

> There is no greater power in heaven and earth than the thought of the Son of Man. Though unseen by the eyes of the body, yet each thought has mighty strength, even such strength can shake the heavens.[2]

Take a moment to think about that. In short: *Your life experience is created by your beliefs, expectations, or whatever you focus your powerful thoughts on!* It's that basic. Whether your thoughts are positive or negative, the Four-Step Formula does not discriminate. It simply underlies all of life's experiences.

Evidence abounds that we have always possessed this ability, yet we have never fully understood the magnitude of its expansive, potent nature.

In Matthew 7:7,8 in the Bible it is written:

> *Ask, and it shall be given to you;*
> *Seek, and ye shall find;*
> *Knock, and it shall be opened unto you.*
> *For everyone that asketh, receiveth;*
> *And he that seeketh, findeth;*
> *And to him that knocketh, it shall be opened.*

Unfortunately, the Bible was a little vague in its explanation of *how* to specifically asketh, seeketh, and knocketh so we could receiveth! So, what does the Four-Step Formula imply? That

Whatever You Sow, You're Gonna Reap

ᕳ Have you ever noticed that people who talk about being a victim always seem to be victimized?

ᕳ Have you ever noticed that people who talk about being ill always seem to be ill?

ᕳ Have you ever noticed that people who talk about never having enough money never seem to have enough money?

ᕳ Have you ever noticed that people who talk about discrimination always seem to be discriminated against?

ᕳ Have you ever noticed that when someone's day starts out badly it always seems to get worse?

ᕳ Have you ever noticed that when someone is on a positive 'roll,' everything seems to fall in line for them?

What are all of these folks experiencing?
Exactly what they have focused their powerful thoughts on!

The Four-Step Formula ensures that they will experience whatever they focus their powerful thoughts on, whether they want it or not!

As you search for the Formula in your life or in the lives of others, you will discover the absolute association between thoughts, feelings, expectations, and life experience. And don't worry about seeing the evidence — it's always there. Ask prosperous folks what they believe. Ask folks who appear to have problem after problem what they believe. The evidence will always emerge. Perhaps not right on the surface, but if you dig deep enough, it will be unmistakable.

Although this information has always been under our noses, we failed to acknowledge it and thus apply it to our advantage. However, to live as life is meant to be lived, it is imperative that we now awaken to Who We Really Are and embrace our true power. Therefore, to ensure that this truth does not escape us once again, allow me to 'drive the point home' by presenting quotations from numerous visionaries who have previously conveyed this knowledge.

The ancestor of every action is a thought.
— RALPH WALDO EMERSON
1803-1882

Nothing occurs in your life — nothing — which is not first a thought. Thoughts are like magnets, drawing effects to you.[3]
— NEALE DONALD WALSCH
Conversations with God - Book 1

There is indeed a direct connection between what occurs in your conscious mind and what occurs in your life.[4]
— ROBERT FRITZ

Man sees first his failure or success, his joy or sorrow, before it swings into visibility from the scenes set in his own imagination.[5]
— FLORENCE SCOVEL SHINN
1871-1940

You attract the things you give a great deal of thought to. So if you give a great deal of thought to lack, you attract lack, if you give a great deal of thought to injustice, you attract more injustice.[6]
— FLORENCE SCOVEL SHINN
1871-1940

There is nothing either good or bad, but thinking makes it so...
— WILLIAM SHAKESPEARE
1564-1616

One receives only that which has been given. The game of life is a game of boomerangs. Our thoughts, deeds, and words return to us sooner or later, with astounding accuracy.[7]
— FLORENCE SCOVEL SHINN
1871-1940

The thing always happens that you really believe in; and the belief in a thing makes it happen.

— FRANK LLOYD WRIGHT
1867-1959

A thought or a word expressed and expressed and expressed becomes just that — expressed. It becomes your physical reality.[8]

— NEALE DONALD WALSCH
Conversations with God - Book 1

The world has a way of giving what is demanded of it. If you are frightened and look for failure and poverty, you will get them, no matter how hard you may try to succeed. Lack of faith in yourself, in what life will do for you, cuts you off from the good things of the world. Expect victory and you make victory.

— PRESTON BRADLEY

When the gods choose to punish us, they merely answer our prayers.

— OSCAR WILDE
1854-1900

What we steadily, consciously, habitually think we are, that we tend to become.

— ANN LANDERS

Be careful about what you wish for… you might just get it!

— UNKNOWN

Our life always expresses the result of our dominant thought.

— SOREN KIERKEGAARD
1813-1855

As a man thinketh in his heart, he is.

— JAMES ALLEN
1849-1925

To be is to do.

— JEAN PAUL SARTRE
1905-1980

To do is to be.

— JEAN JACQUES ROUSSEAU
1712-1778

Do, be, do, be, do.

— FRANK SINATRA
1915-1998
from the song "Strangers in the Night"☺

I think, therefore I am. — RENÉ DÉSCARTES
1596-1650

For as he thinketh in his heart, so is he.
— THE BIBLE
Proverbs 23:7

You create your life as you choose your thoughts.[9]
— ESTHER and JERRY HICKS

State of Mind

If you think you are beaten, you are;
if you think you dare not, you don't.
If you like to win, but think you can't,
it's almost a cinch you won't.
If you think you'll lose, you're lost;
for out in the world we find
success begins with a fellow's will;
it's all in the state of mind.
If you think you're outclassed, you are;
you've got to think high to rise,
you've got to be sure of yourself
before you can win the prize.
Life's battles don't always go
to the stronger or faster man;
but sooner or later the man who wins
is the man who thinks he can.

— UNKNOWN

Regardless of the nature of your beliefs, they are indeed
made flesh and material. The miracle of your being
cannot escape itself. Your thoughts blossom into events.
If you think the world is evil, you will meet with events
that seem evil. There are no accidents in cosmic terms,
or in terms of the world as you know it. Your beliefs
grow as surely in time and space as flowers do.[10]
— JANE ROBERTS
The Nature of Personal Reality - A Seth Book

Because of your likeness to your Creator, you are
creative. No child of God can lose this ability because it
is inherent in what he is, but he can use it inappropriately
by projecting.[11] — A COURSE IN MIRACLES®

You Cannot Escape the Miracle of Your Being

Every aspect of your life — your health, relationships, job, financial circumstances, physical body, happiness, peace of mind — has been created by your thoughts and beliefs. You are a creator. And because you're always thinking, you're always creating. Your every thought is an electromagnetic reality as real as this book in your hands, only invisible. But just as invisible microwaves or frequencies exist all around you, frequencies that transmit television shows, cellular phone calls, radio programs, conversations on walkie-talkies, etc., the same is true of your thoughts. Although you cannot see the energy projected by them, it exists. Therefore, you might as well learn how to use your thoughts to your *benefit*.

Are Your Buttons Being Pushed?

If you are now receiving 'red flags' — feelings of anxiety in the pit of your stomach as a result of this information, take a deep breath. I know this information may feel a bit unsettling. You've just left your comfort zone, so you may feel anxious. You might even feel overwhelmed because your thoughts are always 'on.' You're not really aware of them, they are as second nature to you as the beating of your heart. You may be thinking, "Now I have something *else* to worry about — my thoughts? Add *that* to my list of 'things to do'."

Consequently, you may experience a period of time where you feel uncentered. If you're like most, you have probably taken the way life operated for granted, believing it to be outside of your control. And now you're discovering that your assumption may be incorrect, which conjures a variety of implications. But accept your feelings — they are temporary. For once you get over the initial phase of incredulity and recognize that *you* have unknowingly created your life experience through your beliefs and thoughts, you will also discover that a belief is nothing more than a *habit* of thoughts, and you can *change* any habit if it no longer serves you.

Furthermore, consider the fact that if you are stuck in one place, however comfortable, you are not evolving. It is said that the comfort zone is equivalent to the 'dead zone.' Why? If you're not growing and expanding, you're withering and dying (not too pleasant a thought...).

The bottom line? You are getting exactly what you are getting in life because of the Four-Step Formula, whether you know it or not, whether you accept it or not, or whether you believe it or not. The good news is, however, knowledge is power: The power that gives you wings to soar! And now that you know the secret — how thought creates reality — you can utilize it to consciously create what you want in life. And don't worry about how to apply the Formula; I will guide you step by step through the process. So relax because the news is positive: it proclaims that YOU ARE POWERFUL.

There are really only two ways to approach life — as a victim or as a gallant fighter — and you must decide if you want to act or react, deal your own cards or play with a stacked deck. And if you don't decide which way to play with life, it always plays with you.
— MERLE SHAIN

The question is not, Why start off on a such a path? You have already started off. You did so with the first beat of your heart. The question is: Do I wish to walk this path consciously or unconsciously? With awareness or lack of awareness? As the cause of my experience or at the effect of it?[12]
— NEALE DONALD WALSCH
Conversations with God - Book I

Thought takes man out of servitude, into freedom.
— HENRY WADSWORTH LONGFELLOW
1807-1882

You are responsible for your own thoughts. You need to learn the power of thought and emotion, but this should fill you with the joy of creativity. Once you realize that your thoughts form reality, then you are no longer a slave to events.[13]
— ESTHER and JERRY HICKS

Jesus Christ said "And ye shall know the truth and the truth shall set you free." So we see freedom (from all unhappy conditions) comes through knowledge — a knowledge of Spiritual Law.[14] — FLORENCE SCOVEL SHINN
1871-1940

Jesus Christ claimed no miracles and told his followers that what he did they would also do and even greater things....What seemed miraculous was simply an understanding and operation of cosmic law.[15]
— RUTH MONTGOMERY

I have found power in the mysteries of thought.
— EURIPIDES
480-406 BC

Embrace the Process, and move through it with peace and wisdom and joy. Use the Process, and transform it from something you endure to something you engage as a tool in the creation of the most magnificent experience of All Time: the fulfillment of your Divine Self.[16]
—NEALE DONALD WALSCH
Conversations with God - Book 2

Fortunately, You Don't Need to Worry about Your 90,000 Daily Thoughts...

It is said that you have 90,000 thoughts a day,[16] the majority being negative. But don't worry about monitoring each of them. When you were born, you came prepackaged with an internal guidance system that knows *exactly* Who You Are and is fully aware of your Path — the blueprint you entered life with. Your guidance system is your spirit within — your superconscious self that I have christened as your inner Angel. Angel's assignment? To guide you along your Path and guard your comfort zone. How do you know when you're being guided? In any moment that you project a thought that contradicts a belief you hold, Angel will transmit a warning to you alerting you to the fact that whatever you are focused on is in conflict with what you believe. (We will explore this in greater depth as the book unfolds.) As you learn to utilize both the guidance of your Angel and the Four-Step Formula, you will experience just how exciting life can be.

Then What Is Truth?

The Four-Step Formula essentially states that each of us is equally powerful, therefore, 'truth' can sometimes be conflicting.

On the TV show "Nightline," two scientists debated the merits of salt and its correlation to health. One scientist had 'proof' that salt had a detrimental effect on our health, supported by empirical evidence. However, the other scientist also had 'proof' that salt had *no* detrimental effect on our health, supported by empirical evidence. Which 'truth' do you believe?

The Genesis of Truth

What does the Four-Step Formula imply? That what we assume to be true is subjective. For in reality, every truth began as a powerful magnetic thoughtform that attracted evidence and through logical deduction, culminated in belief. As person after person believed and magnetized more evidence of these truths, they became known as reality to us — the mass consciousness.

Programmed with beliefs that do not reflect an awareness of our real power — I refer to as 'old-paradigm thinking' — we have lived our lives oblivious to the potency of our thoughts. As a result, we sought to comprehend their seemingly random manifestations by attributing all sorts of reasons as to why they occurred. We labeled them, categorized them, and placed them in groups as statistics, and then lived our lives according to the conclusions we derived from these statistics. This, of course, led us further and further from ever recognizing the correlation between our thoughts, feelings, and life experience — further and further from the *real* truth and our authentic power!

> [Y]ou are locked into physical situations that are corroborated by the great evidence of sense data, and of course it is convincing because it reflects so beautifully, so creatively and so actively, your own ideas and beliefs, whether they are positive or negative.[18] — JANE ROBERTS
> The Nature of Personal Reality - A Seth Book

In our failure to recognize the existence of the Four-Step Formula, our thoughts have predominantly worked against us. The result? We've been living life backwards! We have grown fearful of many of life's facets, and in the process created much needless pain, suffering, and anguish. Therefore, we must now reconsider what we deem to be truth.

Go ahead and act on all that you know (now). But notice that you've been doing that since time began. And look at what shape the world is in. Clearly, you've missed something. Obviously, there is something you don't understand. That which you do understand may seem right to you, because "right" is a term you use to designate something with which you agree. What you've missed will, therefore, appear at first to be "wrong." The only way to move forward is to ask yourself, "What would actually happen if everything I thought was 'right' was actually 'wrong'?" Every great scientist knows about this. When what a scientist does is not working, a scientist sets aside all assumptions and starts over. All great discoveries have been made from a willingness, and ability, to not be right. And that's what's needed here.[19]

— NEALE DONALD WALSCH
Conversations with God - Book 1

The Power of Belief Is Surfacing Everywhere

First we have to **believe***, and then we believe.*
— G.C. LICHTENBERG

A groundswell of proof is mounting day after day that confirms the validity of the Four-Step Formula — that our thoughts do indeed create our realities. Oprah Winfrey, one of the Angels we have been blessed with, has taken the courageous step of using her television show to convey various aspects of this knowledge through her new format: "Change Your Life TV." Through her wisdom and insight, she has recognized that her Mission in life goes beyond offering entertainment to others (although we certainly need to laugh and have fun, too!). She has acknowledged her role as a teacher, one who inspires and uplifts others. Using both her personal influence and the power of the far-reaching medium of television, she is responsible for changing lives in spite of the criticism she has received. Her show is raising consciousness by presenting various people who specialize in key areas of personal growth to impart their wisdom and knowledge. These "Bringers of Light" (light = information; dark = lack of information), are helping to eradicate much of the needless pain and suffering that many of us have experienced as a result of not understanding how thought creates reality. It is no coincidence that Ms. Winfrey is in the position she is in at the dawning of our new millennium. We owe her a huge debt of gratitude because, fortunately for us, she is allowing her heart to guide her through this challenging transition.

It is not only Oprah who has recognized that our thoughts create our reality. Various other fields have recognized this truth as well, from the most mundane, affecting our lives in inconsequential ways, to the most formidable and respected, having the potential to completely alter our perceptions of the world. From golf instruction to corporate training; from medical science to scientific research; from religious study to sports psychology — all of these diverse fields are either employing facets of this knowledge or discovering its compelling impact on life. And because each of us has the power to *consciously* create our reality, some folks are already reaping in rewards! They are not waiting for science to catch up, for the medical field to 'see the light.' They are not asking for the Good Housekeeping™ seal of approval. They are moving into a new paradigm without even knowing exactly what 'it' is!

Various sectors of science are on the brink of recognizing the correlation between thought and its impact on reality. In December 1998, CBS-TV News aired a segment on "The Power of Prayer," a study conducted by Rice University in Houston, Texas. In this study, 30 patients were randomly selected from a group of 100 suffering from heart maladies. Researchers then dispensed these 30 names to different prayer groups representing different religious denominations all over the world, without informing the patients. The results? The 30 patients who received prayer experienced 50–100 percent better results than those who had not.[20]

In the medical field, Dr. Herbert Benson, founder of the Harvard Mind/ Body Medical Institute at the New England Deaconess Hospital in Boston, as well as chief of Behavioral Medicine, and on staff at the Harvard Medical School, explored aspects of healing that ventured beyond 'accepted' medical science. Through his experiences as a medical doctor, Dr. Benson found that a mysterious factor — belief, or the "placebo-effect" — appeared to contribute to a patient's recovery and/or the eradication of his illness. As a result of the remarkable findings he amassed, Dr. Benson authored *Timeless Healing: The Power and Biology of Belief,* concluding that contemporary medical science has completely disregarded the correlation between thoughts, emotion, belief, and healing. It is his belief that "medical science is now in the throes of a spiritual crisis, at a turning point regarding the neglected aspect of the power of belief and its impact on healing." Citing case after case, Dr. Benson presents overwhelming evidence, staggering proof that demonstrates the connection between belief and healing. In his opinion, "the power of belief can no longer be ignored or glossed over." "For far too long, most people believed that the only things that could help them were doctors and their treatments, when in reality the human body can utilize the power of belief to heal illness." He further states, "Belief is a powerful weapon against illness…. It can heal a multitude of conditions, including those previously thought of as incapable of being helped," that "no healing force is more impressive or accessible than the power to cure ourselves."

While conducting research, Dr. Benson found that three elements were necessary to produce healing in a patient: 1) a patient's *desire* for health, 2) his *belief* that a cure was possible, and 3) his ability to *remember* a state of calm and confidence associated with health and happiness. Labeling this process "remembered wellness," Dr. Benson has helped to bring relief to a majority of patients suffering from various illnesses.

One of the more dramatic examples Dr. Benson cites is the following:

> *In 1950, Dr. Stewart Wolf studied women who endured persistent nausea and vomiting during pregnancy. "These patients swallowed small, balloon-tipped tubes that, once positioned in their stomachs, allowed researchers to record the contractions associated with waves of nausea and vomiting. Then the women were given a drug they were told would cure the problem. In fact, they were given the opposite — syrup of ipecac — a substance that causes vomiting. Remarkably, the patients nausea and vomiting ceased entirely and their stomach contractions, as measured through the balloons, returned to normal. Because they believed they received antinausea medicine, the women reversed the proven action of a powerful drug….With belief alone, they cured themselves.*[21]   — DR. HERBERT BENSON

What did these ladies think, believe, expect, and get?

In November 1997, ABC-TV's *Good Morning America* ran a week-long segment on the topic of "Mind over Matter."[22] For the previous eighteen years, scientists at Princeton University had conducted studies on the power of the mind in relation to machinery. Upon completing these clinical trials, the scientists concluded that the operation of any form of machinery is influenced at various levels by the *mind* of its operator. By the way, this included any mishap or accident related to its operation! Michael Guillan, ABC-TV's science editor, stated that any time scientists delve into areas of life that are mysterious, they can either be completely frivolous or ushering in a new frontier of discovery.

"To Save a Life"

As I read through the wonderful heart-warming stories in *A Fourth Course of Chicken Soup for the Soul®* by authors Jack Canfield, Mark Victor Hansen, Hanoch McCarty, and Meladee McCarty, I discovered a story entitled "To Save a Life," by Hanoch McCarty, that vividly illustrated the far-reaching impact of the Four-Step Formula.

In those chaotic years of the late 1940s, just after World War II ended, an immigrant family in New York tried to contact their surviving relatives in Hungary. Communications were sporadic, the mails untrustworthy, records destroyed or inaccurate or lost. It could take many weeks or months for letters to travel to Europe and find their way to recipients and just as long for replies to return. Reliable information was hard, if not impossible, to get.

The immigrant family wondered if their relatives were still alive. Had they all survived the war? Where were they living? It was so hard to tell. Then, they received a letter, in Hungarian, from Uncle Lazlo in a small town near Budapest. Yes, some of the family had survived the war. The letter was tantalizingly incomplete in the news it offered. But it was clear that they were hungry and hurting. Food and other necessities were in very short supply. The black market was operating in full force, the currency was inflated and nearly valueless. It took all their energy and wit to survive each day.

The New Yorkers were appalled at the story of devastation and deprivation they could piece together by reading and rereading this crumpled letter, written on the tissue-thin paper of the airmail of that time. Grateful to be able to read again in Hungarian, the older members of the family translated for their America-born children. They argued about the translation of this phrase or that. But it was clear that they could be useful to their far-off family.

They determined to send survival supplies to their cousins, aunts, and uncles. They tried to imagine what would be needed and appreciated, but, not having directly experienced war themselves, it was not easy to come up with a list of things to send. They included canned meats and vegetables and chocolates. Necessities like toilet paper and bandages made the final list, too. In the end, the package grew to several cartons, stuffed to the brim with many items. Little spaces in each carton were filled with whatever odds and ends were at hand: candies, handkerchiefs, writing paper, and pencils.

At last the cartons were sealed and painstakingly wrapped with brown paper and stout string to help endure the long and chancy journey overseas. Brought to the post office, the cartons began their journey undramatically.

And that is all the New York family heard for months and months. They wondered if the packages had gone astray or been stolen. Had something terrible happened to their family in the confusion of post-war Europe? What irony it would be to have survived the war itself and be killed or injured in its aftermath. The family worried. At every dinner, at every gathering, the talk circled around the packages and the family in Europe.

One uncle, sitting at the table at Thanksgiving dinner, recriminated, "You should have included money for postage! Perhaps they can't afford to write us!" He was met with angry stares. "Well, I don't care what you think, I am going to send them some money for postage."

"Better you should send enough money for them to come over here!" someone retorted.

"Big shot!" he replied. "It's easy for you to spend the money I don't have, isn't it? Listen, there are quotas for immigration. It's not that easy to get on the list for America, money or not."

"Maybe we didn't send the right things they needed," someone else contributed. The discussion continued, back and forth. The content was unimportant. They were just expressing, again and again, their worry and concern and their feelings of helplessness. How could they really help? The silence from their distant family was depressing, especially in light of the newsreels they saw at the movie theaters (television being very uncommon then) showing emaciated Europeans walking dispiritedly through rubble-strewn streets, dodging bomb craters or being deloused in long lines by GI medics. Headlines fueled their worries as newspapers wrote about the Marshall Plan and the need for much help in rebuilding war-ravaged countries. Stories circulated about people starving to death. News of a historically severe winter in Europe and shortages of food and fuel upset the family even more.

Although far from wealthy, the family sent more packages, almost every week, off into the void, unsure as to whether or not they were received by their loved ones. More silence ensued. It was maddening.

Finally, another letter arrived from Uncle Lazlo. It had been bent, wrinkled, and torn at the edges, but it was still readable. "My Dearest Cousins," the letter began formally, as Uncle Lazlo was in the habit of writing. "We are in receipt of three packages you sent us. We are forever in your debt for these good things. You cannot know how timely was their arrival. Food is so scarce here and Anna was sick all the time with fevers. This food has meant everything to us. I must confess that we sold some of the things you sent us on the black market in order to get money for our rent." The letter went on to discuss almost every item in the cartons and the uses to which they had been put.

Then came a mystery.

"We also cannot ever thank you enough for the medicine you sent. It is so difficult to get any medicine and often it is of poor potency and doesn't work at all. Cousin Gesher has been in continuous pain for several years and your medicine has miraculously cured him! He was walking only with the help of a cane. His knees were so swollen. These medicines make him almost normal again. My back pain is completely gone as are Lizabeta's headaches."

"America is great and its science is great. You must send more of that medicine as it is nearly used up. Again, thank you. We love you all and pray for when we might see you once more."

The family read and reread Uncle Lazlo's letter. What medicine did we send? They racked their brains to recall but, shamefacedly, had to admit to each other that they had omitted sending any medicines at all! What was Uncle Lazlo talking about? Was some medicine accidently included? If so, what was it? After all, they needed to send some more right away. The mystery couldn't be solved. A letter was drafted to Uncle Lazlo asking him to provide the name of the medicine he so urgently required. The envelope was brought to the post office. The clerk was asked for advice on how to send the letter by the fastest route possible. There was, at the time, nothing faster than regular air mail, express services being as yet only a dream. He did suggest including an international postal reply coupon which would pay for return postage and that was done.

The family waited again, relieved that their packages had been of help but puzzled by the "mystery of the unknown medicines."

Two months passed and then another letter arrived.

"My Dearest Cousins," began Uncle Lazlo, "we are grateful to have heard from you again. Since the first three packages, another two have arrived, and then your letter. Again, you sent that wonderful medicine. It did not come with instructions for use but we are guessing on the dosage. And translating from English to Hungarian is very difficult for us since only young Sandor has studied it in school. Lucky for us he could translate the name of the medicine. It is 'Life Savers.' Please send more as soon as you can. Love, Lazlo."

The filler, in several cartons, had been rolls of that well-known American candy, Life Savers. A literal translation transformed America's favorite candy into a source of great hope.[23]

What did Uncle Lazlo and his relatives think, believe, expect, and get?

This story powerfully demonstrates the placebo effect of belief — "to please" in Greek. However, there is a more ominous aspect of the power of belief known as the "nocebo" effect. The following passage, paraphrased from *Timeless Healing: The Power and Biology of Belief*, by Dr. Herbert Benson, vividly illustrates the nocebo effect.

At the turn of the century, Dr. Walter Cannon, a famous physiologist on staff at the Harvard Medical School, studied, among other subjects, the Maori aborigines in New Zealand — a culture that believed in the power of tapu, or taboo. Taboo was deployed by the tribal hierarchy as a punishment when an individual committed a forbidden act. A 'hex,' or 'magic spell,' would be placed upon the offender that was believed to be so powerful, it would produce a fatal terror in its victim, culminating in death.

Dr. Cannon's research included the following story that addressed the prophetic power of taboo: While traveling, a young aborigine stayed at the home of an older friend. For breakfast the elder served a meal containing wild hen — a food forbidden, thus taboo, to the younger generation. Suspecting that this bird might be wild hen, the young man questioned his host several times, but each time the elder man quelled his fears, assuring him that it was not and the subject was dropped.

A few years later, the friends reunited and the older man asked the younger if he would *now* eat wild hen. The young man replied that, of course he would not because it was forbidden. The elder man then laughed, explaining that years earlier he had tricked him into eating the hen and nothing terrible had happened as the young man believed. The older man knew that the young man's belief was unsubstantiated —

nothing was 'wrong' with eating wild hen — and wanted to prove the fallacy of this belief to him. Upon receiving this news, however, the younger man became extremely distressed. As a matter of fact, he was in so much physical torment that within 24 hours he was dead.[24]

What did the young man think, believe, expect, and get?

Unintentional Creation

Upon arriving in this world, you unknowingly enter the 'game of life.' The goal of this game is to awaken to Who You Really Are and live your life in awareness, choosing what you would *like* to experience and omitting those experiences you do not find appealing. In somewhat the same manner that you choose what you like to eat at a buffet, you do the same in life, choosing what appeals to you and omitting what does not. However, if you fail to make *conscious* choices, you will instead live your life *un*consciously — on 'auto-pilot.'

> *You are at the cause of your experience, not at the effect of it. [A]t first you may not realize this, and so you may not be consciously creating your reality. Your experience will then be created by one of two other energies: your uncontrolled thoughts, or the collective consciousness.*[25]
>
> — NEALE DONALD WALSCH
> *Conversations with God - Book 3*

How is the collective consciousness "programmed?" Let's explore a scientific study referred to as the "Hundredth Monkey" — a study that explored the biology of the unconscious on a group of monkeys in Koshima, Japan, in the 1950s. The findings from this study were so remarkable that they prompted another study referred to as the "Hundredth Human," that led researchers to postulate as to how the collective *human* consciousness is programmed.

The Hundredth Monkey

The Hundredth Monkey, written by Ken Keyes Jr., describes this 30-year scientific research project. Curious about a monkey's ability to problem-solve, scientists posed a quandary to them. They fed the monkeys a food they enjoyed — sweet potatoes — but purposely dropped the potatoes in sand before feeding them. Not being fond of sand, the monkeys took great pains to remove it. Day after day the researchers observed the monkeys until one day an eighteen-month-old female monkey began to wash her potatoes in a nearby stream. Soon thereafter the baby's mother imitated her behavior, and one by one, the majority of her young playmates did as well. However, the researchers noted: Not all of the *adult* monkeys adapted this new behavior. In fact, many of the older generation steadfastly maintained the old paradigm and continued to remove the sand with their hands. Researchers recorded these events from 1952 to 1958, when one day in 1958, something remarkable occurred. The number of monkeys adapting this new behavior grew to what scientists refer to as a "critical mass," which Dr. Lyall Watson arbitrarily placed at 100 — hence the "hundredth monkey." Upon reaching a critical mass, almost all of the monkeys began washing their potatoes. But that wasn't the most amazing aspect of this study. While the majority of monkeys on Koshima adapted this new behavior, at the same time, monkeys on *surrounding* islands, including the mainland of Japan, began washing their potatoes as well! How did the monkeys communicate with one another across a distance? Dr. Watson postulated that some type of morphogenic field must exist that connects the collective mind of the monkey. Interesting? What do these findings imply? That the collective mind of this species of monkey was programmed, or information made available to the species, when a specific number of monkeys adapted this behavior.[26]

The Hundredth Human

The remarkable findings of the "Hundredth Monkey" study created a fervor in the scientific community. Scientists speculated that if monkeys were affected in this manner, could people be affected in the same way?

Researchers from Great Britain and Australia collaborated and decided to find out. They conceived an experiment that would either confirm or deny this theory of the collective consciousness by creating a photograph comprised of hundreds of human faces. Every facet of the image on this photo was made up of faces — little ones, big ones, etc. — making it difficult to distinguish them. In fact, it took training to ascertain where they were.

Phase one of the experiment began in Australia where the researchers selected a few hundred people representing various spectrums of the population and showed each the photograph. After a designated period of time, they asked each person how many faces they saw in the photo. The result? Most answered six to nine, some found ten, but few saw more.

After gathering these primary statistics, the research team in England — on the other side of the world — began phase two of the study. On a closed-cable BBC television station that broadcast solely in England, the researchers displayed the photo and carefully pointed out every face within its composition. Immediately after the telecast, phase three commenced. The Australia team now repeated their initial experiment with a few hundred *new* people. The results? The majority of these people could see most of the faces! How could this dramatic change occur? Scientists speculated that the number of people viewing the program in England comprised a critical mass, thereby programming this new data into the collective human consciousness.[26]

What does this study intimate? That you, a member of the collective consciousness, will automatically be programmed with any aspect of life experience that a critical mass of people accepts as truth, if you, too, accept it as truth. In short, their reality can become *your* reality, plain and simple, unless you choose otherwise. Key word: *Choose*. For the Four-Step Formula allows you to transcend any belief of the mass consciousness, regardless of how many people are living it as truth because you have the power to create your reality and manifest what you want!

Ready or Not, The New Paradigm Is Here!

The Four-Step Formula literally impacts your perception of life. In fact, when first presented with this information, you may feel as though you've landed on a different planet harboring a different set of prevailing rules. The Formula impels a paradigm shift in thinking — the most fundamental paradigm that exists. In *Paradigms: The Business of Discovering the Future*, author Joel Arthur Barker defines a paradigm as

> *[A] set of rules or regulations (written or unwritten) that does two things: (1) it establishes or defines boundaries; and (2) it tells you how to behave inside the boundaries in order to be successful.*[27]

∿　∿　∿

> *Paradigms can be invisible in many situations because "it is just the way we do things." Often they operate at an unconscious level. Yet they determine, to a large extent, our behavior....They have a profound affect in how we live our lives, how we value those things in our lives, how we solve problems in our lives. They are at the core of who we are and where we are going.*[28]

A paradigm shift is when someone comes along and changes the rules. We have grown accustomed to living by the old set of rules. We understand the boundaries. And now we have to step outside the boundaries and learn new ones and these changes dramatically upset our world....Those changes dramatically change our world because we understand the old boundaries and have to learn new ones."[but] when the rules change, so can the world."[29]

Mr. Barker tells us further that we cannot stop a paradigm shift:

You can resist this new paradigm but understand, you cannot stop the process. It will take place with or without you. You must ask yourself, "Do I want to be one of the first?"[30]

ᔕ　　ᔕ　　ᔕ

The message is clear. If you want to be one of the first into the new territory, you cannot wait for large amounts of evidence. In fact, you have to do exactly the opposite. If you want to be early, you must trust your intuition; you must trust your non-rational judgment and take the plunge; make the leap of faith into the new paradigm."[31]

ᔕ　　ᔕ　　ᔕ

You cannot know who is going to bring you your future. You cannot qualify them in advance by looking at degrees or experience, or gender or race. You can only LISTEN.[32]

Integrate the Formula Slowly But Surely

Most folks have difficulty with this information in certain areas of life — subjects that challenge their deeply entrenched core beliefs — which is completely natural because this information 'rings the doorbell' of their comfort zones. As Mr. Barker stated, any paradigm shift will shake your foundation. Your beliefs provide your foundation, so life can become somewhat distressing when you begin to question everything you were taught. When I receive too much profound information, red lights start to blink in my mind signaling 'input-overload,' and everything shuts down. I am unable to receive any more; my circuits are over-loaded. However, rather than dismissing the information, I recognize that I need time to reflect on it. Then, when I have had adequate time to contemplate, reflect upon, and integrate the material into my life, I can delve deeper into it.

So, if you are now experiencing 'input-overload,' put this book aside for a while. You need some time to process this material. Ask yourself, "Am I filled with fear or possibilities?" And don't recriminate yourself for being overwhelmed, for the process of learning and accepting this profound message is taken step by step — seeing, experiencing, and reflecting on it — *slowly* integrating it into your life. So be easy on yourself. Lighten up, relax, and have some fun! Take all the time you need to assimilate this information. *Remember, you have nothing to lose.*

Have you ever seen *The Wizard of Oz?* At the end of this movie there is a scene where the Wizard prepares to escort Dorothy back to her home in Kansas in a hot air balloon he has never before piloted. At the moment of lift-off, Dorothy's beloved dog, Toto, spots a cat and instinctively jumps from her arms to pursue chase. In a panic, Dorothy exits the balloon to retrieve him and the balloon ascends without her. Sadly, she believes that the balloon was her last option to return home. She believes that she will be unable to ever leave Oz, to never again see those she loves back in Kansas. Imbued in those discouraging thoughts, Glinda, the good witch appears:

>   *Dorothy:* "Oh, Glinda, can you please help me get back to Kansas?"
>
>   *Glinda:* "You don't need to be helped any longer. You always had the power to go back to Kansas. It was inside you."
>
>   *Scarecrow:* "Why didn't you tell her?"
>
>   *Glinda:* "She would not have believed me. She had to learn it for herself."

The Moral of the Story: You, too, must learn for yourself and take the necessary steps to integrate your power. Do you recall the long and arduous journey Dorothy and her friends braved as they trekked the yellow brick road? How they grew to recognize their power, wisdom, and strength with each obstacle they overcame along their path? This tale is a great metaphor for life, as it illustrates the journey that each of us must take. You, like Dorothy and her friends, are now discovering that the Wizard, or whomever you are giving your power to, doesn't have the power at all. It is within you, and has been all along.

Let's now explore your beliefs — the building blocks of your life experience — for they are the springboard that will point you in the direction of living life as it is meant to be lived: Loving and laughing all along your journey! ☺

Through Heaven's Eyes

A single thread in a tapestry
though its color brightly shines,
can never see its purpose
in the pattern of the grand design.
And the stone that sits at the very top
of the mountain's mighty face,
does it think it's more important
than the stones that form the base?
So how can you see what your life is worth
or where your value lies?
You can never see through the eyes of man.
You must look at your life through Heaven's eyes.
A lake of gold in the desert sand
is less than a cool fresh spring?
And to one lost sheep, a shepherd boy
is greater than the richest king.
If a man loses everything he owns,
has he truly lost his worth?
Or is it the beginning
of a new and brighter birth?
So how do you measure the worth of a man,
in wealth or strength or size?
In how much he gained or how much he gave?
The answer will come to him who tries
to look at his life through Heaven's eyes.
And that's why we share all we have with you
though there's little to be found.
When all you've got is nothing,
there's a lot to go around
No life can escape being blown about
by the winds of change or chance.
And though you never know all the steps,
you must learn to join the dance.
So how do you judge what a man is worth.
By what he builds or buys?
You can never see with your eyes on Earth.
Look at your life through Heaven's eyes.[33]

Words and Music by Steven Schwartz
from the film *The Prince of Egypt*

the puzzle - 30

Your Beliefs are The Building Blocks of Your Destiny

Nothing in life is to be feared. It is only to be understood.
— MARIE CURIE
1867-1934

The mind is its own place, and in itself can make a Heaven of Hell and a Hell out of a Heaven.
— JOHN MILTON
1608-1674

The wisdom of all ages and cultures emphasizes the tremendous power our thoughts have over our character and circumstances.
— LIANE CORDES

Mind is the Master power that molds and makes. And man is mind and evermore he takes the tool of thought, and, shaping what he wills, brings forth a thousand joys, a thousand ills — he thinks in secret, and it comes to pass: Environment is but his looking glass.[34]
— JAMES ALLEN
1849-1925

Every prayer — every thought — every feeling, every statement — is creative. To the extent that it is fervently held as truth, to that degree it will be made manifest in your experience.[35]
— NEALE DONALD WALSCH
Conversations with God - Book 1

Your beliefs... form your reality, shaping your life and all its conditions.[36]
— JANE ROBERTS
The Nature of Personal Reality - A Seth Book

The real distinction is between those who adapt their purposes to reality and those who seek to mold reality in light of their purposes.   — HENRY KISSINGER

You will become as small as your controlling desire; as great as your dominant aspiration.[37]   — JAMES ALLEN
1849-1925

The only source of knowledge is experience.
— ALBERT EINSTEIN
1879-1955

The best teacher of the Four-Step Formula is not from words written by me or my distinguished 'friends,' but from your own life experience. When you can cite examples of the Four-Step Formula — experiences in your life or in the lives of others — you are on your way to discovering your power! So let's dissect and evaluate a few of your life experiences, for then you will clearly see the correlation between your thoughts, feelings, expectations, and life experience.

Think about an occasion in life where you wanted something and got it:

_____

_____

_____

_____

I thought and felt:_____

I believed:_____

I expected:_____

I got:_____

Now think of an occasion where you wanted something and did *not* get it:

_____

_____

_____

_____

I thought and felt:_____

I believed:_____

I expected:_____

I got:_____

Can you recognize the Four-Step Formula underlying the events in your life? In the lives of your family members or friends?

Hypothetical Case Histories

Dreams are the seedlings of reality.[38]
— JAMES ALLEN
1849-1925

The invisible forces are ever working for man who is always "pulling the strings" himself, though he does not know it. Owing to the vibratory power of words, whatever man voices, he begins to attract. People who continually speak of disease, invariably attract it.[39]
— FLORENCE SCOVEL SHINN
1871-1940

"I will give to thee the land that thou seest." Man is ever reaping on the external what he has sown in his thought world.[40]
— FLORENCE SCOVEL SHINN
1871-1940

Undoubtably, we become what we envisage.
— CLAUDE M. BRISTOL

The following examples illustrate how profoundly and simply the Four-Step Formula impacts life experience.

Joe and His Childhood Dream

Joe grew up in an area where the majority of men in his neighborhood were firefighters or police officers. As a boy, Joe and his friends admired these men in their noble, courageous careers and often emulated their heroes playing "cops and robbers" or "firefighters putting out blazing fires." Joe dreamed of becoming one of these heroes when he grew up, and on the day that Joe graduated from the police academy, his dream became his reality.

Joe's thought and belief:

He observed men who were police officers and firefighters and believed them to be heroes.

Joe's expectation:

He would feel pride and the admiration of others if he became a police officer or firefighter.

What Joe got:

A career he was proud of and the admiration of others — exactly what he expected!

Walter and Racism

Walter grew up in a impoverished neighborhood in the inner city where drugs, gangs, and welfare were commonplace. The prevailing belief was that there were few ways to escape the ghetto, especially if you were a poor black man. Success would be difficult, if not impossible to achieve. Stories about racism and blatant discrimination abounded and Walter's experiences confirmed those 'facts.' He, too, had felt the stinging blows of racism, and subsequently hated those he perceived as racist. Under the surface, he seethed with anger over these "uncontrollable circumstances," and concluded that life was unfair. How could anyone judge him when they didn't even *know* him? As he searched for a job, he encountered difficulty after difficulty and surmised that his misfortune was the result of his being black — something he had no control over. Although he had seen others escape the 'hood and go on to success, he believed that they were the one in a million and he was one of the 999,999. He felt defeated and concluded that he would always confront the shadow of racism. And sadly, his beliefs became a self-fulfilling prophecy.

Walter's thought and belief:

He would experience difficulty in life because he was a poor black man.

Walter's expectation:

He expected difficulty and racism because he had witnessed and experienced so much discrimination.

What Walter got:

Discrimination and rejection — exactly what he expected!

Nancy and a Dreaded Disease

Many members of Nancy's family died of cancer at an early age. Sadly, Nancy witnessed aunts, uncles, grandmothers, and grandfathers die or suffer from this terrible illness and began to wonder if cancer would become her fate as well. To avoid this dreadful disease, she sought advice from doctors about early detection. She adopted a nutritious diet, exercised faithfully, and avoided all things known to contribute to the development of cancer. Although a part of her did not want to acknowledge this insidious disease, it continually haunted her through dispassionate statistics that asserted their omnipotence and inflamed her worst fears. Year after year, Nancy's test results were negative, but one day negated all of her efforts. They found cancer. Although she had done everything in her power to prevent it, deep down inside she harbored a fear that she would develop cancer. Regrettably, she contracted exactly what she had dreaded.

Nancy's thought and belief:

> She might succumb to cancer like other family members, therefore she did everything in her power to push cancer away. However, in pushing against it, she focused her powerful magnetic thoughts on *cancer.*

Nancy's expectation:

> Witnessing many relatives suffer from this disease, she feared the same fate.

What Nancy got:

> Cancer — exactly what she thought about!

Although these examples may appear to be simplistic, do not dismiss the important underlying message: Each of these folks first had a thought that created a thoughtform. This thoughtform then magnetized evidence and upon acknowledging the evidence, they each *believed* this evidence to be an attribute of reality. Next, on some level of consciousness, they *expected* these things to occur. The result? They created their destinies! Not one of these people could escape the miracle of their being, the power of their thoughts, or the Four-Step Formula.

An exception does not exist that disproves the Formula![1] I understand just how powerful this statement is, but when you reduce any issue to its lowest common denominator, the Formula is always at its inception!

You Are Hard-Wired for Miracles

The common thread underlying all life experience is the Four-Step Formula: As you think, a feeling is produced within the center of your being — your 'heart-center' — that creates a magnetic thoughtform. This thoughtform then magnetizes people, events, or circumstances that correlate with it, leading you to believe that your thoughts are an aspect of reality. Holding this belief in your consciousness as truth, you expect it to occur, so you wait in anticipation or dread, and just as certain as the sun will rise tomorrow, what you believe becomes your life experience!

> *You form the fabric of your experience through your own beliefs and expectations. These personal ideas about yourself and the nature of reality will affect your thoughts and emotions. You take your beliefs **about** reality as truth and often do not question them. They seem self-explanatory. They appear in your mind as statements of fact, far too obvious for examination. Therefore they are accepted without question too often. They are not recognized as beliefs about reality, but are instead considered characteristics of reality itself. Frequently such ideas appear indisputable, so a part of you that it does not occur to [will not] speculate about their validity. They become invisible assumptions, but they nevertheless color and form your personal experience.*[42]
> — JANE ROBERTS
> The Nature of Personal Reality - A Seth Book

> *The law of cause and effect works with or without consent or deliberate knowledge, although conscious participation and readiness greatly enhance the built-in rewards.*[43]
> — GLENDA GREEN
> Love Without End: Jesus Speaks

> *To work magic is to weave the unseen forces into form; to soar beyond sight; to explore the uncharted dream realm of the hidden reality.*
> — STARHAWKE

After learning the Four-Step Formula, I was curious as to *how* it actually operates. And once more, my asking led to answers. If you too share my curiosity as to how it operates, you'll love the following chapter as it takes the Four-Step Formula out of the esoteric realm and into the scientific realm, shedding more light on its operation. ☺

Integrate Science and Spirit and Life Begins to Make Sense

Science without religion is lame, religion without science is blind.
— ALBERT EINSTEIN
1879-1955

Any sufficiently advanced technology is indistinguishable from magic.
— ARTHUR C. CLARKE

Thoughts are a very subtle, yet extremely powerful, form of energy.[44]
— NEALE DONALD WALSCH
Conversations with God - Book 1

Every time you have a thought, it sends off an energy, it is energy.[45]
— NEALE DONALD WALSCH
Conversations with God - Book 3

Thought is a tremendous vibratory force and man is drawn to his thought creations.[46]
— FLORENCE SCOVEL SHINN
1871-1940

Thinking is an experimental dealing with small quantities of energy, just as a general moves miniature figures over a map before sending his troops into action.
— SIGMUND FREUD
1856-1939

[W]e should not ignore compelling brain research that demonstrates that beliefs manifest themselves throughout our bodies.[47]
— DR. HERBERT BENSON

The Formula from a More Scientific Perspective...

Although much data is necessary to fully comprehend the Four-Step Formula from a scientific basis, numerous pieces of the puzzle are surfacing daily from diverse echelons of research and science. Amazingly though, no central organization exists to analyze this data and connect the pieces in the 'puzzle of life.' However, when we connect these various pieces, the image they are forming happens to be very revealing.

Let's begin our examination of this data with an overview of information obtained from a vast spectrum of sources — scientific, medical, and metaphysical. (Metaphysics is the study of that which is beyond the physical.) From there we will explore individual quotations. By the way, if you have a raised eyebrow over the word 'metaphysical,' beware of the condition labeled "contempt prior to investigation" and try not to suffer from it. And don't worry about being unscientific, for many who have openly explored metaphysics are deemed quite reputable. It was Albert Einstein who divulged:

> The more I study physics, the more I am drawn to metaphysics. — ALBERT EINSTEIN

Quantum physicists tell us that the physical universe is comprised of energy where presumably solid matter is composed of subatomic particles which are, at their essence, pure energy. They explain that the human body is not solid — nothing is. Each of us, and everything around us, including the Earth, projects different frequencies or vibrations of energy. The Earth's vibration, lovingly referred to by some as her 'heartbeat' and scientifically referred to as the Shumann resonance (quasi-standing electromagnetic waves that exist in the cavity between the surface of the Earth and the inner edge of the ionosphere 55 kilometers up), has consistently measured between 7.25 to 7.8Hz. This measurement was assumed to be a given, a constant, for as many years as scientists have measured this factor, it never wavered. However, in the past few years, the Shumann resonance factor began to *increase*. In fact, since May 1997, Earth reached a new level of vibration measuring between 10 to 11Hz[48] and this vibration is continuing to increase. What are the implications of this increase? Many and vast. Metaphysicists tell us that as the vibrational level of Earth increases, the speed of energy — the speed by which we magnetize 'evidence' of our thoughts into our lives — accelerates as well.[49] Therefore, without an awareness of this knowledge, problems will grow larger and more vast in a shorter period of time than they did in the past. Life will resemble the infamous line from *A Tale of Two Cities*: "It was the best of times, it was the worst of times...." That is precisely why this information is so critical.

Biophysicists tell us that Earth is a living organism, an energy system comprised of a web that generates a magnetic field. This magnetic energy field, referred to as the magnetosphere, is a protective membrane shielding Earth from harmful radiation. Metaphysicists have labeled this Universal interconnecting web, or morphogenic energy field, that all of us and the Earth are a part of, as the "Cosmic Lattice" or "Matrix."

Scientists tell us that the human body also generates an electromagnetic energy field and that every cell in our bodies contains a powerful magnetic substance called magnetite. You may be aware of this field of energy as it the basis for certain diagnostic tests, such as the EEG (electroencephalogram, which reads the electrical activity of the brain) and the EKG (electrocardiogram, which reads the electrical activity of the heart) to diagnose a problem, thereby substantiating the body's electromagnetic basis.

It is said that our body's energy field contains our personal information — our thoughts, beliefs, and history. Our energy field acts as a highly sensitive energy system by virtue of energy transactions that occur within the magnetic fields of others and Earth. Certain people, such as Dr. Carolyn Myss, who is referred to as a medical intuitive, are capable of reading and deciphering the information contained within this field. Furthermore, the energy field of the human body is capable of being *photographed* as a result of aura-imaging photography, also known as Kirlian photography. And even more amazing, this mode of photography has the ability to discern and record various color hues that correspond with the varying moods and temperaments we project.

Pieces of the Four-Step-Formula Puzzle

Why does this applied science, which saves work and makes life easier, bring us so little happiness? The simple answer runs: Because we have not yet learned to make sensible use of it. — ALBERT EINSTEIN
1879-1955

Let's now explore what experts have individually discovered.

Biophysicist Dr. Beverly Rubik presented compelling scientific data about the magnetic basis of the human body and planet Earth in a documentary entitled *HAARP: Holes in Heaven*. Ms. Paula Randol-Smith, a concerned citizen, sold everything she owned to produce this documentary and bring this critical knowledge to our awareness. This exposé examined a government project currently conducting experiments in Alaska that have the potential to destroy or distort the crucial magnetosphere of our planet — the membrane enveloping Earth that shields us from the sun's perilous ultraviolet rays in somewhat the same manner that our skin protects our inner organs. Another more sinister aspect of this technology though is our Defense Department's avid interest in it. Scientists have found that they have the ability to remotely manipulate the magnetic frequencies within the human body, thus enabling them to manipulate people's behaviors on various levels. It is theorized that this technology will facilitate the "warfare of the new millennium." This is a dramatic example of how our 'advanced' technology is not in sync with the best interests of humanity — another consequence of not understanding how life really operates. We now find ourselves at a crossroads where it is crucial to understand our power and stop the escalating 'need' to defend ourselves. See footnote #50 for further information. (Reread the admonition from the psychic message given to me on page ii.) Dr. Beverly Rubik tells us that

> The Earth is a living body, an energy system comprised of a web of interconnections generating a magnetic field... It is interesting to compare humans with the Earth. Human beings are like balls of energy, made up of electricity and magnetic energy. And just like the Earth, the human body also generates a magnetic field, especially intensified in the heart and brain, with the brain outputting frequencies which interact with other frequencies... Every cell in the human body has a powerful magnetic substance called magnetite which responds sensitively to the magnetic fields in our environment... The human body is actually bio-regulated by virtue of tiny energy transactions within the body and also the Earth. [50]

In Anatomy of a Spirit, Dr. Carolyn Myss tells us about

> The Human Energy Field: Everything that is alive pulsates with energy and all of this energy contains information. While it is not surprising that practitioners of alternative or complementary medicine accept this concept, even some quantum physicists acknowledge the existence of an electromagnetic field generated by the body's biological processes. Scientists accept that the human body generates electricity because living tissue generates energy. Your physical body is surrounded by an energy field that extends as far out as your outstretched arms and the full length of your body. It is both an information center and a highly sensitive perceptual system. We are constantly "in communication" with everything around us through this system, which is a kind of conscious electricity that transmits and receives messages to and from other people's bodies. [51]

In *The Path: Creating Your Mission Statement for Work and for Life*, Laurie Beth Jones tells us that

> Physicists are now aware of subatomic particles that hover in and around everything that exists. One interesting character-istic of these particles is that they seem to take on the properties or expectations of the scientists studying them. This has led to the speculation that these particles may be the creative building blocks of the Universe. All mass is surrounded by hovering possibilities waiting only to be spoken in order to become.[52]

In the preface of *The Purpose of Your Life*, author Carol Adrienne summarizes chapter five:

> The Magnetic Force Field of Your Life Purpose — which considers life from the new metaphors of quantum physics — that we exist more accurately as a field of energy/ consciousness, which acts and reacts in the collective field of energy/consciousness.[53]

In *First Thunder*, author MSI tells us of the incredible power embodied in our physical reality using a gardenia, a flower to illustrate the subatomic properties of life:

> See my...flower? [I]ts beautiful color, its perfect form, its delightful scent? This is the surface form of the gardenia, the part we see, the part we appreciate with our senses. It is lovely, but there is more to the flower than our senses perceive. There are many levels of reality we can't see or touch or taste or smell....[The gardenia] contains molecules; the molecules are made of atoms; the atoms are made of protons, neutrons, and electrons; these are composed of sub-atomic particles. We used to think atoms were building blocks of matter, little tight individual balls. But we have learned they are not — almost the entire inside of every atom is empty — about 99.9999%, in fact. If we took any atom and expanded it to the size of the Roman Coliseum, the nucleus with its protons and neutrons would be the size of a bee-bee in the center, the electrons would be infinitesimal ghosts of energy flitting at enormous speed in and out around the outer walls — and the rest would be nothing, nothing at all...[T]here are different levels of reality we don't normally see....And energy increases at deeper levels. If I were to throw this flower at you, I might manage with enough force to

scratch you..., but if I could excite [the gardenia] on the molecular level, we could probably destroy this lovely restaurant — there is more energy contained on subtler levels. Einstein theorized and modern physicists proved the power locked in the atom is exponentially larger [i.e.: atom bomb] — if I could release the power of the atoms in this flower, we could annihilate most of Athens. And quantum physics tells us that the power contained at the Planck scale — 10^{43} centimeters — a decimal point followed by 42 zeros and a one — which is very, very small — the power at that tiniest possible scale is so great it could create a Universe.[54]

In *Timeless Healing: The Power and Biology of Belief*, Dr. Herbert Benson tells us about an unidentifiable aspect of physics labeled "the God particle:"

Nobel Laureate and physicist Leon Lederman has facetiously named one fundamental and stubbornly evasive factor "the God particle." The God particles — or Higgson's particles as they are better known, are like backboards off of which other primary particles of the universe bounce. A sequence gives the bouncing particles tangibility, or what we call mass. Without Higgsons, particles would be massless spirits jetting around space at the speed of light, no particle heavier than the next. Scientists believe that Higgsons are responsible for what we call "creation," in which myriads of matter and recognizable forms of life, the structures of the entire universe, were born. Many contemporary researchers hang their hats on the Higgson's discovery, either presuming that particles spawned the miraculous happenstance we call "life" or that the Higgson was a pawn in a masterful, ethereal game plan.[55]

Psychic Powers, a volume from a series of Time-Life Books labeled *Mysteries of the Unknown*, explores a theory that, in conjunction with other information, could explain psychic power — a power that has stymied scientists for ages:

One of the most popular current metaphors for psychic communication relies on the paradoxical world view of quantum mechanics. This science describes matter at the subatomic level, where basic units are neither particles nor waves, but act like both, and where matter cannot even be said definitely to exist. Rather, it has a "tendency to exist," expressed as a mathematical probability. The micro world of subatomic behavior follows different rules from the macro world we know.... In a thought experiment — a famous example of this paradox — two particles — say, an electron, and its antimatter equivalent, a positron — collide, annihilating each other and creating two photons, which speed off in different directions. By the strange laws of quantum mechanics, photon A does not possess properties such as spin or velocity until it is noted by an observer; the very act of measurement is said to "collapse its wave function" and assign it values at random. At the moment that observers do measure photon A, causing it to acquire a certain spin, photon B will acquire the opposite spin, no matter how far away it is, and despite having no connection with the first particle. Photon B somehow seems to "know" instantaneously what photon A is doing. This occurrence, confirmed in physical experiments, suggests that the Universe is connected in some hidden way, perhaps at a hypothetical sub-quantum level that includes our consciousness. If so, then clairvoyance, which supposedly enables a psychic to know instantly of an airplane crash miles away, may become plausible.[56]

Let's now explore what metaphysicists refer to as the Law of Attraction. Throughout the ages, this principle of nature has been labeled as Universal, Spiritual, or Cosmic law. Like the law of gravity, the Law of Attraction operates in a powerful, neutral, unwavering manner.

In *Creative Visualization*, Shakti Gawain tells us

The scientific world is beginning to discover...that our physical universe is composed of a kind of...force or essence which we call energy...Seemingly solid matter is seen to be smaller and smaller particles within particles, which eventually turn out to be pure energy...Physically, we are all energy, and everything within and around us is made up of energy. We are all part of one great energy field....This energy is vibrating at different rates of speed, and thus has different qualities, from finer to denser. Thought is a relatively fine, light form of energy and therefore very quick and easy to change. Matter is relatively dense, compact energy, and therefore slower to move and change.... All forms of energy are interrelated and can affect one another. Energy is magnetic. One law of energy is this: Energy of a certain quality or vibration tends to attract energy of a similar quality and vibration. Thoughts and feelings have their own magnetic energy which attracts energy of a similar nature....Form follows idea. Thought is a quick, light, mobile form of energy....An idea is like a blueprint; it creates an image of the form, which then magnetizes and guides the physical energy *to flow into that form and eventually manifest it... Simply having an idea or thought, holding it in your mind, is an energy which will tend to attract and create that form.... The law of radiation and attraction is the principle that [states] whatever you put out into the universe will be reflected back to you.... What this means from a practical standpoint is that we always attract into our lives whatever we think about most, believe in most strongly, expect on the deepest levels, and/or imagine most vividly.*[57]

The following "G-rated" passage, condensed from *Conversations with God - Book 2*, by Neale Donald Walsch, describes the underlying energy transaction that occurs between two objects. The original passage in its entirety, examines a sexual attraction between two hypothetical people — Tom and Mary who become "Tomary" — from a more scientific perspective. I highly recommend reading the "PG-13" passage in its entirety as it is incredible!

I have built into all things an energy that transmits its signal throughout the Universe. Every person, animal, plant, rock, tree — every physical thing — sends out energy like a radio transmitter. You are sending off energy — emitting energy — right now, from the center of your being in all directions....This vibration, the rate of speed, the wavelength, the frequency of your emanations shift and change constantly with your thoughts, moods, feelings, words, and actions. And so the "ether," the air between you — is filled with energy; a Matrix of Intertwining, interwoven personal "vibes" that form a tapestry more complex than you could ever imagine. This weave is the combined energy field within which you live. It is powerful, and affects everything, including you...The Matrix — the combined current energy field within any given parameter — is a powerful vibe. It can directly impact, affect, and create physical objects and events...This energy interaction is occurring all the time — in and with everything. Your energy beamed from you like a Golden Light — is interacting constantly with everything and everyone else...These innumerable energies are...attracted to each other. This is called The Law of Attraction. In this law, Like attracts Like. Like Thoughts attract Like Thoughts along the Matrix — and when enough of these similar energies "clump together," so to speak, their vibrations become heavier, they slow down — and some become Matter. Thoughts do create physical form — and when many people are thinking the same thing, there is a very high likelihood their thoughts will form a Reality.[58]

In *The Nature of Personal Reality*, Jane Roberts tells us:

As living cells have structure, react to stimuli and organize according to their own classification, so to do thoughts. Thoughts thrive on association. They magnetically attract others like themselves, and like some strange microscopic animals they repel their "enemies" or other thoughts that are threatening to their own survival. [Y]our ideas and thoughts do not exist as phantoms or shadow images without substance. They are electromagnetic realities.[59]

In *Love Without End: Jesus Speaks*, author Glenda Green shares intriguing information that explains in great detail, the connection between science and spirit:

There is a particle substance [known by science as the "Higgson's" or "God" particle's — in this book referred to as "adamantine particles"], which is the matrix of all energy mass. Its particle units are utterly generic in nature, and are the basic irreducible components of physical existence.[60]

[Adamantine particles] are the fundamental building blocks of physical existence. They are particularized energy potentials which activate, unify, and give form to infinity. As points, they are irreducible, indivisible, and generic. Their very existence, however, establishes a pattern of dimension. Between one point and another, is there not dimension? Between a series of points, is there not a pattern of dimension? Thus there is space. Through such alignments, energy is activated and conveyed into particularized situations. One way of stating it is that [adamantine particles] are the ultimate points which unify infinity and activate its potential.[61]

All physical existence is comprised of adamantine particles and space — mostly vast amounts of space. These particles cohere magnetically to form the basis of all complex patterns of matter and form. Conglomerations build structures, which are then held together by energetic tension which creates the illusion of solidity. All solidity is structure, and structure accounts for all solidity. If you would penetrate the barriers which stand between us and the infinite supply of life energy, we must realize the illusion and look beyond structure.[62]

The idea of "energy as force" has dominated man's thinking about every form of energy from industry to government to life management. What is dominating the world? Force! This will change when the paradigm of understanding shifts from electrical to magnetic performance. As a matter of fact, that shift will be necessary to finally define and understand the adamantine particles. It is magnetic potential which accounts for the unified field, and actually it is magnetic cohesion which unifies physical infinity. Infinity is not the leftover. Infinity is the unifying factor which integrates everything. When you have made the change in thinking from electrics to magnetics, every aspect of your technology will change as well. [Evolution] will begin with a proper respect for the ultimate power. When that understanding is attained and activated by a sufficient number of people, the entire paradigm of humanity will be lifted above the belief in energy as force. [A]damantine particles respond to a magnetic field. With regard to human potential, the heart is your magnetic center. It is through your heart that you are magnetizing adamantine particles and by your love that you command them.[63]

∿   ∿   ∿

The heart center is the true source of human power.[64]

∿   ∿   ∿

The heart is the bringer of all miracles.[65]

∿   ∿   ∿

The heart is your connecting link to God and the universe, which integrates your own unique center of experience, awareness, and character with that which is beyond your comprehension....The heart is magnetic, silent, and still.... As a magnetic center, your heart is the great generator of all your life energy, and whenever you empower your heart, you raise your energy level physically, mentally, emotionally, and spiritually. Within the heart you will also find clarity, resolve, steadfastness, intent, stillness, respect, justice, kindness, and perceptions of greatness....The heart is the soul's gateway, both into life and beyond into eternity. The heart is the timeless and indestructible source of all higher knowledge. It is the one point within each person where the inner and outer forces are the same.[66]

∿   ∿   ∿

[The heart] is a point within your very existence where the physical, mental, emotional, and spiritual components of your life reside in common purpose, in simple harmony. The body's heart expresses that presence physically.[67]

You may remember the children's magnetic drawing boards. [Author's note: Etch-A-Sketch™] Beneath a clear plastic cover are iron filaments which respond to a magnetic pencil. The magnetic pencil attracts the iron filaments and causes them to group together in lines and patterns to form a drawing on the board. All kinds of patterns can be created by guiding the magnet over the iron filaments. Now just imagine that your heart is the magnet and your love is the pencil. That is exactly what your heart is.[68]

～ ～ ～

The heart is a magnetic vortex through which the blessings of all essences and potentialities are received, integrated, and focused into living. Through the laws of electromagnetism, that power is converted into life energy. The heart, being essentially magnetic, functions best through innocent awareness which attracts and receives. Acts of judgment, which divide and repel, will shut the door of the heart behind you. If you would make the heart strong, you must first learn to perceive with innocence, accept, and forgive. As you empower the heart, it will open to you. At first, you may simply notice this change as more passion for living, more peaceful sleep, or better digestion of food. The heart is the center of your health and quality of living, therefore those things will be addressed first. As you progress in your affirmations of the heart, however, your life will begin to have more abundant fruits, and you will have the energy needed to make more dramatic changes.[69]

～ ～ ～

This is your power of influence, and you are literally impacting every aspect of your life by just **being, being the love that you are.** You are a magnet that writes upon the drawing board of your life. As you enter into any situation the adamantine particles inherent to it will adjust to the influence you bring. You don't have to dream up a grand plan and put it on the drawing board. **You are the grand plan!**[70]

～ ～ ～

The love, faith, and consciousness which composes the true essence of man, represent the culminating glory of the Universe. You are children of the Father set in the midst of and in command of life.[71]

～ ～ ～

All that you have to do is be the love that you are. Everything will line up around that. The greater the love, the greater the influence. Nevertheless, you don't have to **do** anything other than be the love that you are. Your love brings forth the patterns and manifestations which will result.[72]

While meditating, author and psychiatrist Brian Weiss M.D., was given a definition of what love *really* is:

> *Love is the ultimate answer. Love is not an abstraction but an actual energy, or spectrum of energies, which you can "create" and maintain in your being. Just be loving. You are beginning to touch God within yourself. Feel loving. Express your love. Love dissolves fear. You cannot be afraid when you are feeling love. Since everything is energy, and love encompasses all energies, all is love.*[73]

Gary Zukav, author of *Seat of the Soul*, was featured on the "Oprah Winfrey Show" where he explained that unseen phenomena are really not incomprehensible. Using the color spectrum as an example, he explained that the human eye is capable of perceiving only a specific range of colors. However, scientists are aware that an *infinite* spectrum of color actually exists. In fact, when we apply certain criteria to the colors red or purple, we are able to perceive the hues of infrared and ultraviolet. Mr. Zukav tells us that the human eye is attuned to specific frequencies that enable us to perceive the color range we see, but as we learn how to perfect our ability to tune in to *other* frequencies, we will be capable of discerning far more.

Some people — Neale Donald Walsch, Esther Hicks, Jane Roberts, and others — have already perfected their ability to 'tune in' to other frequencies, allowing them to 'receive' information. Author, speaker, and recording studio owner Lee Carroll is yet another person who possesses this ability. His ability to tune in to a specific frequency of spiritual energy and allow it to speak through him is considered so important, believable, and scientific, that after an exhaustive background investigation, he was asked to address a group within the United Nations known as the S.E.A.T. (Society for Enlightenment and Transformation) on *three* separate occasions; the last in November 1998 (that's right — *the United Nations!* You can access these transcriptions at www.kryon.com). Whether you accept the phenomenon of channeling or dictation, or are skeptical of this mystery (don't miss the upcoming chapter — "How We Took the Wrong Turn"), the following information was transcribed at a seminar in New Hampshire in November 1997. This information is strikingly similar to what Neale Donald Walsch conveyed as the Law of Attraction. The following passage is a condensed version of "The Cosmic Lattice," offering us further insight into the integration of science and spirit.

> *The Cosmic Lattice is the cosmic constant that has been looked for in science forever. It is the actual mechanical connection that "tunes the strings" of the music of matter. "The Cosmic Lattice" is a specific kind of energy — the*

energy of Spirit — the energy of the Universe. It is the common denominator of the unified energy source of the Universe. The common denominator — meaning that all things emanate from the Lattice. The Lattice is everywhere — throughout the Universe. Everything you can see and everything you cannot see contains the Lattice. From the smallest particles of your physics, and from the electron haze forward, the Cosmic Lattice is present. There is no place that you can conceive of that is without the Lattice. It is perhaps what you would call the consciousness of God and yet it is physics and it is energy and it contains conscious love. It has no visible light, even though it is the essence of light. The Cosmic Lattice energy is everywhere, and when I am done with this message, you will know what triggers it, and you will know how it's used. You'll know how it reacts to other energy, and you'll know why it exists. From the largest to the smallest, this energy source is immense and it's quiet. It is only when it is called upon and destabilized in designed ways that it provides power. It is the common denominator and the stabilizer of all energy and matter everywhere. The Lattice energy responds to time... like a giant cosmic magnet. The Cosmic Lattice responds to human consciousness! All things are possible with the intent of people on this planet right now. You are already aware of the communication between people that seems to surpass any speed known to man. Identical twins, with one being on one side of the Earth, and one on the other side, often have instant communications that have been reported and witnessed. Perhaps one twin is in an anxiety mode, and instantly the other one feels it! They might call each other and say "What happened a moment or two ago?"And they both realize they felt the same thing at the exact same time. I'll tell you what makes it happen: it's the mechanics of the Cosmic Lattice. You are interconnected instantly, and are using the Lattice. It's your spiritual power source...and it's also using physics. The Cosmic Lattice is in a constantly balanced state, and in that balanced energy, it is potentially ready to receive input for release of energy, and that input...is available to the human consciousness. It "sees" all time as zero. Time is like the air you breathe. You watch incredible storms, with wind blowing many directions at many speeds, yet you breathe it gently and normally, even in the midst of a great storm. Therefore, the breathing air in your lungs is nominally at rest, while the air around you is in turmoil. The Cosmic Lattice is like this. The Cosmic Lattice uses naturally occurring physics for the mechanics of miracles...the common physicalness of the energy for power...just like you are being invited to do. Understanding *the physics of Spirit does not void out the love [of Spirit]! Instead it gives a beautiful symmetry and logic to all things, and these things will become clearer to you as you move into the vibration where you can also use the energy of the Lattice. It is one of the most powerful tools of Spirit that exists today, and contains much of what you have called unexplainable magic. There is no greater power in the Universe than human intent and love! Now do you understand that when you give intent, it is not some mysterious energy that seems to fly into the ethers and somehow manifest something you want or need? Now can you see that it has symmetry and size and purpose and consciousness, and that there is a mechanical attribute of physics and love around it called human intent? There is no longer mystery regarding this, instead it will be someday replaced with good solid science…God-given and Universal.*[74]

Ancient Teachings from the Lost Continent of Atlantis?

Within the recorded history of many cultures, such as the Maya, the Egyptians, the Hopi, and the Greeks, there are references to a great, technologically-sophisticated civilization known as Atlantis. While most believe Atlantis to be a myth or legend, the famous Greek philosopher, Plato, detailed accounts of this civilization in many of his writings. *The Children of the Law of One and the Lost Teachings of Atlantis*, speaks of this civilization and how some fled the continent prior to its demise, taking with them the knowledge they had attained. It is said that this knowledge has been sequestered for millennia in a Tibetan pre-buddhist temple referred to by some as "Shangri-La" or "Shambhala," awaiting the consciousness of mankind to increase to the degree that it utilized the information for the good of all.

Author, Jon Peniel, an American who became a monk in the order of "The Children of One," actually lived in this monastery for years. Upon his initial arrival, Mr. Peniel described what he saw: "Placed on top [of the monastery], and towering over the very center… stood a huge, great, gleaming white pyramid. At the top of the pyramid was a clear crystalline peak, with a layer of what appeared to be shiny copper underneath."[75] "Tuned to the Earth's magnetic field, [this pyramid] changed magnetic energy into other forms of energy." "[P]ower generators were simple pyramids that harmlessly collected the energy from the earth's aura (a frequency of Earth's electro-magnetic field — the field that makes a compass point to North).[76]

Although this monastery could be extremely valuable to science, it is now inaccessible as it was unfortunately destroyed in the recent Chinese invasion of Tibet. Prior to its destruction, however, a few monks escaped, taking with them the Atlantean teachings.

Now, I didn't know if any of the preceding information was valid or not, so, initially I dismissed it as unsubstantiated. But when verification of this monastery appeared in *The Ancient Secret of the Flower of Life,* by author Drunvalo Melchizedek, it took on a whole new meaning to me.

The largest known pyramid in the world so far is in the western mountains of Tibet. It's a solid white pyramid that's in almost perfect condition, with a huge, solid-crystal capstone. At least two teams of scientists have been there, and it has also been photographed from the air.[77]

The following very interesting passage was obtained from the Atlantean teachings:

All Is Vibration
All Vibration Follows Universal Law
All Gives All Receives
All Loves

∿   ∿   ∿

All Vibration Seeks to Find its Own Level
To Find Any Level
Set Forth the Vibration
By Law You Will Go There
By Law it Will Come.

∿   ∿   ∿

Always Is There a Greater Vibration
Always Is There a Lesser Vibration
In Harmony with Universal Law
All Vibration Moves as One Flow.
Interrupt the Flow Only to Find
In this Natural Order thus Does it Go
In Forever Passing Through, Divided in Two
Receptivity Be the Way of Emptiness
The One Calls to Come and Fill
Giving Be the Way of Abundance
The One Flows Forth to Fill

∿   ∿   ∿

Always Then the Way of the Flow
Dependence on That Which Is Above
The Object of Dependence
To That Which Is Below
Two Will Repel

Two Will Attract
Two Will Together, Interact
Look Then to Four
Four That All Need Be
For All Creation Be
One.
Two.
One and Two.
Three.
One and Two
Beget Four
Thus Opens the Infinite Door.

～ ～ ～

Build Ye Life as the
Pyr-a-mid
Four Corners Converge Above
With Fire in the Middle
The Fire of Love
Life, Mind, Truth, Love
Spirit.

～ ～ ～

Energy Great Does Course Through this Earth
Collect and Direct, If It Be Your Will
With the Shape of the Temple,
Pure Stones and Golden Laden Box.
Or with the Mind, Focused and Pure
Lowered in Vibration
To Ten in Meditation

～ ～ ～

Vibration Does Flow
In Body and Soul.
High and Low, in All Flesh Is Written
Tune May You to the Right Vibrations
Colors and Sounds, That May Change What We Know
Use Them May You
To Heal, Sow and Grow

～ ～ ～

Power Great
Above and Below
Key Are Vibrations, Secret but to Few
Find Them You Will
By Measure and Trial
And Use of the Word
That Rules All Creation

～ ～ ～

Describe a Rainbow
To a Blind Man Will You?
Open Your Eyes.

∽   ∽   ∽

Senses Five
Does Man Perceive.
The Focus on Self
Restricts All That Is.
Limited in Scope
The Ocean Not Seen.
A Drop of Rain
He Believes Is His World.
So as He Believes
So Shall He Be.
So Let it Be Written

∽   ∽   ∽

Everything Orbits Something

∽   ∽   ∽

All Matter Is as the Universe
Stars, Planets, Time, and Space[78]

During his indoctrination into the ancient order of the "Children of the Law of One,"author Jon Peniel learned many interesting facts about the Atlantean knowledge of "science-magic" — facts that appear to be consistent with the preceding material you just read.

[W]hat many consider the mysteries of life were not confusing or complex, but simply a matter of applying [an] understanding of Universal Laws. Our Atlantean ancestors easily manipulated vibration, using thought, within a framework of scientific facts. God and spirituality were not vague concepts. The Universal Spirit was not unknown to them, or some being that was 'out there somewhere.' And magic and miracles were not just something that existed in fairy tales and religious parables from days gone by. They were the scientific workings of spiritual forces on physical matter. Spirituality, as well as materiality and physical life, were all simply based in scientific facts of Universal Laws. For instance, they understood that psychic phenomenon, electricity, magnetism, gravity, light, sound, space, time, and such, were all related and aspects of the same thing, and all followed Universal Laws. The barbarian cultures that lived around us, or came in contact with our ancestors, couldn't understand these things so they just lumped it all together as 'magic' — some mysterious 'something' that could only be created and wielded by gods, devils, or witchdoctors with

*strange powers and rituals. But what gives anything the appearance of magic? If not deceptive illusions or tricks, what is real 'magic' other than creating or altering energy and matter which is comprised of energy? So, in a very real sense, much of what we do is magic, but it is based in science, not superstition....To us, this use of the mind to create physical reality is just a simple fact of Universal law science, and a very fundamental one. This also applies to everything else in the Children's early days on Earth, such as their use of pyramids to provide power to vehicles and buildings without any visible connection. All their understanding of God, spirituality, and the matters of day to day life, are based in knowing that **real** magic is science, and **real** science is magic.*[79]

Can you recognize the correlation between what is known scientifically and what has been communicated metaphysically? What does all this information essentially mean? That everything in our world and the universe beyond is actually comprised of a dance of energy that transfers into form and shape through our thoughts, perceptions, and intentions. And we, as human beings, are powerful creators, both transmitting and receiving energy. We are *hard-wired* for miracles! Although the inferences of this profound information are vast and far-reaching, from a practical standpoint, the most fundamental aspect of this information states:

WHATEVER YOU GIVE YOUR ATTENTION TO WILL GROW LARGER!!!

The bottom line? If your thoughts are focused on 'good stuff,' you will get more 'good stuff.' If your thoughts are focused on 'bad stuff,' you're gonna get more 'bad stuff.' If you are able to comprehend the simplicity and power of the Law of Attraction and apply it to your life, it will forever be changed!

Mired in old-paradigm programming, most of us have placed our faith solely in science for validating what is real in our world. However, the scientific process, too, is a victim of old-paradigm thinking. Therefore, to fully actualize your power, you must now rely upon your own *inner* knowing for truth.

Although you have just become acquainted with the more scientific aspects of the Formula, let's depart from those clinical terms and substitute them with something more 'user-friendly' to learn how to get what you want out of life. To accomplish that task, let's get acquainted with your guidance system — your inner Angel, or "heart-center" — as Angel is ushering the way for you to live, love, and laugh! ☺

Learn How To Get What You Want in Life Using A Little Divine Intervention!

He will give his angels charge of you, to guard you in all ways. — THE BIBLE
Psalms 91:11

What lies before us, and what lies behind us, are tiny matters compared to what lies within us.... — RALPH WALDO EMERSON
1803-1882

If I love with my spirit, I don't have to think so hard with my head. — PEGGY CAHN

And behold you were within me, and I out of myself, and there I searched for you. — ST. AUGUSTINE
354-430

Seek not outside yourself, heaven is within. — MARY LOU COOK

And I will ask the Father, and He will give you another counselor to be with you forever — the Spirit of truth. The world cannot accept Him, because it neither sees Him nor knows Him. But you know Him, for He lives with you and will be in you. — THE BIBLE
John 14:16-17

Great men are they who see that spiritual is stronger than any material force, that thoughts rule the world.
— RALPH WALDO EMERSON
1803-1882

Men talk of "finding God," but no wonder it is difficult; He is hidden in that darkest hiding place, your heart. You yourself are a part of Him. — CHRISTOPHER MORLEY
1890-1957

The currents of the Universal Being circulate through me; I am part and parcel of God.
— RALPH WALDO EMERSON
1803-1882

Belief is a wise wager. If you gain, you gain all; if you lose, you lose nothing. Wager then, without hesitation, that He exists. — BLAISE PASCAL
1623-1662

Awaken to Your Inner Angel — The Missing Link in Life

Let's now get acquainted with your Inner Angel. "Angel, this is _____ (insert your name), and _____(insert your name), this is your Inner Angel." Let's call your Inner Angel "Angel" for short. Sound good?

Angel Sends Signs to Illuminate Your Path and Faithfully Follows Your Instructions

We all have angels guiding us.... They look after us. They heal us, touch us, comfort us with invisible warm hands.... What will bring their help? Asking. Giving thanks. — SOPHY BURNHAM

Thomas Aquinas (1225-1274), a medieval theologian, said that every person is given a guardian Angel at birth, and this Angel "continually lights, guards, rules, and guides." Your Angel is at your service twenty-four hours a day, seven days a week, and endlessly guides you along your life's Path. Angel's role also includes guarding the boundaries of your comfort zone — your unique definition of what is right or wrong, good or bad, desirable or undesirable, as determined by your unique life experiences. How does Angel know the direction of your Path? You have defined it from the initial blueprint you entered life with, as well as the set of 'instructions' you have conveyed through your beliefs and thoughtforms. Throughout your life you have conveyed instructions to Angel and Angel has faithfully delivered exactly whatever you conveyed back to you. *Uh-oh!* (That's why you've gotten in trouble — you've been conveying the wrong instructions!)

Think of the Universe as a great big kitchen with every conceivable ingredient available, Earth as a wonderful restaurant, and Angel as your server. "Hi, my name is Angel and I will be your server for your lifetime." In somewhat the same manner that you place an order in a restaurant for what you wish to eat, you have been placing orders with Angel, for Angel has construed each of your thoughtforms as an 'order.' Unaware that you were placing orders, your life (your current set of orders), may not reflect what you would have chosen had you *known* that you were placing orders. Therefore, as you progress through this book, you will consciously redefine your set of orders to reflect what you *want*. But for now, let's learn the art of Angel communication.

Angel Communication 101

Angel is the little voice inside that communicates through your emotions, thoughts, instincts, dreams, daydreams, and conscience in one of two ways: Either you feel good or you feel bad. Easy enough? When you feel good, you are on your Path and safely inside your comfort zone. Why do you feel good? Good feelings indicate that you are allowing energy or love to flow to you — energy essential to sustaining life. Conversely, when you feel bad (such as feeling angry, disappointed, embarrassed, guilty, fearful, worried, criticized, or impatient), you've stepped off your Path and ventured outside of your comfort zone. Why do you feel bad? Bad feelings indicate that you are restricting the flow of energy or love to you and Angel's task is to alert you of that fact.

Describe a time when you did something or saw something that you enjoyed very much:

_____

_____

_____

_____

Now take a moment to *feel* what that experience was like.

Feels good, doesn't it? Can you feel a surge of energy or a feeling of fullness within your body? Do you feel a sense of joy and lightness? That's Angel letting you know that you are on your Path, safely inside your comfort zone, and connected with the flow of love and life energy.

Now describe a moment when you felt bad or angry and write that experience down:

_____

_____

_____

_____

Take a moment and feel what that experience was like.

Bad, right? Do you feel a kind of sick sensation in the pit of your stomach — a feeling of weakness or insecurity? That's Angel warning you that you have just stepped off your Path, are now outside your comfort zone, and restricting the flow of love and life energy.

Now let's take this idea further and conceptualize it as something more graphic: Think of yourself as being a battery approximately 6 feet tall, 2 feet wide, and 2 feet deep. At the top of your battery there is a very powerful light source — a light that provides you with continuous life energy — a source of light and love that shines brightly at all times. On the side of your battery there is a large 'off' switch — a switch that *only* *you* are capable of activating. How do you activate your 'off' switch? With your thoughts. Whenever one of your thoughts deviates from what you believe or desire, your 'off' switch will be activated which then restricts the flow of energy to you. How do you know when your switch has been activated? You *feel* bad — you experience a feeling of discomfort immediately in the pit of your stomach. This feeling is meant to alert you of potential danger. It is a warning. Your Angel is holding up a wrong-way sign complete with flashing lights and warning bells communicating, "Excuse me, you don't really *want* this! You are now focusing on something outside of your comfort zone — something that matters to you. Do you want *more* of this?"

> *The voice within is the loudest voice with which I speak, because it is the closest to you. It is the voice which tells you whether everything else is true or false, right or wrong, good or bad, as **you** have defined it. It is the radar that sets the course, steers the ship, guides the journey if you but let it.* [80] — NEALE DONALD WALSCH
> Conversations with God - Book 1

Bad feelings simply indicate that you've activated your 'off' switch. They are wrong-way signs. Nothing more, nothing less. Not a sign from God that you were bad. Not your payback from something dreadful you did. Not something to blame on someone else. Simply an indication that you have stepped outside of your comfort zone. No elaborate explanation needed. *Every* bad feeling you have is a sign from your Angel — an Angel-Alert, a wrong-way sign — warning that you just activated your 'off' switch, stepped off your Path, and are, in that moment, restricting the flow of life energy to you.

Negative feelings were never meant to be utilized as they are. In fact, they have an altogether different purpose. They are catalysts meant to alert you to create something different. A negative feeling serves as your "Point of Power" from which to place an order. Just as your physical body alerts you to potential harm in the form of physical pain, a negative feeling alerts you to potential harm in the form of psychic pain.

Understand that it's not your job to monitor your 90,000 daily thoughts. It's Angel's job. Angel will continually guide you throughout life via your feelings. Your task? To be sensitive to your feelings and utilize them.

Using Your Inner Compass to Get Back on Your Path

When you notice feelings of discomfort, recognize that your 'off' switch has been activated. Your next step? To seize the opportunity before you and utilize it as your wrong-way sign — your Point of Power. How do you do that? You think about the Spice Girls:

> *Tell me what you want, what you really, really want want.*
> — THE SPICE GIRLS
> *from the song "Wannabe"*

Ask yourself:

- "What is it that I want?"
- "How do I want to feel?"
- "Why do I want it?"

Your feelings of discomfort are providing you with the clarity to determine what you want. For when you know what you *don't* want, you can more easily determine what you *do* want. After determining what you want and pondering your answers in joy, by virtue of the Law of Attraction, you will begin to magnetize evidence of *those* thoughts and find that you are reconnected to life energy and back on your Path.

Your feelings have a very important purpose; they are the essence of your communication with Angel — your guidance system. Feelings are the language of your soul. And your bad feelings always indicate one of two things: 1) They tell you what you *don't* want which helps you determine what you *do* want or 2) They illuminate a habit of thoughts that *opposes* what you want — a belief that may need reevaluation. It's that easy!

When you're not listening, don't get it, or are not paying attention to your wrong-way signs, 'don't worry.' Soon enough they will be 'in your face,' for they will continue to magnetize evidence and grow larger. Then you *can't* miss them. However, if you still ignore them, they will continue to bring you greater and greater discomfort until Angel grudgingly resorts to the last wake-up call: Illness. Illness is a big-time wrong-way sign that something in your life needs attention. But don't worry, it's not beyond help. Illness is simply a prolonged restriction of energy — the 'off' button has remained 'off' for a long period of time. Your battery simply needs a recharge. Hopefully, *before* that time you will get the hint.

> *Every human being has, like Socrates, an attendant spirit; and wise are they who obey its signals. If it does not always tell us what to do, it always cautions us what not to do.* — LYDIA M. CHILD
> 1808-1880

Most of us can cite examples in our lives where some unpleasant issue appeared and reappeared, perhaps under different circumstances or involving different people, but the essence of the issue was the same. Unaware of how life really operated, we usually hoped it would just go away. We may have even taken action to push it away, unwittingly magnetizing more of it as we focused our powerful thoughts on it. However, by that time, the issue had grown *so* large that we were *forced* to deal with its unpleasant consequences. Looking back, we can see that if only we had responded earlier, life would have been a whole lot easier.

I have 'pretended' not to hear that little voice on occasion and as a result, have experienced the painful results of repeating the same mistake over and over again until I was forced against the wall. (Like many, I am much better at seeing patterns in other people!) The process for me would begin as a smack on the head with a two by four (a piece of lumber), followed by a two by twelve, and then a two by twenty..., until I finally 'got it'! Had I only been aware of my Angel, I could have saved myself from a lot of needless pain.

An example: I passionately love to design and build houses, room additions, basement rec-rooms, etc. It thrills me to discern people's needs and dreams and then translate them into something tangible that will add beauty and joy to their lives. The entire process is like magic to me: Creating the drawings; hiring and negotiating with the subcontractors; choosing the various materials; and then watching the creation deliciously culminate in something wonderful. My enthusiasm is unbridled to the degree that I sometimes feel as though the contractors are looking at me and thinking, "Lady, take a Valium®"! But, I don't care what they think — I'm in Heaven doing what I love to do. However, my enthusiasm has gotten me in trouble on a few occasions when I failed to predefine compensation for my services.

On one particularly significant occasion, persons close to me requested my design assistance on two projects: a rather large vacation home and an extensive remodeling on their existing home. Aware of my passion for this work, they assumed that I would work for free. And because they were quite wealthy, I assumed there would be no problem with compensation. Hence we never discussed a fee. Throughout the two and one half months that I worked on these projects, I felt as though something was not right. Day after day, I experienced strong feelings of dread and anxiety in the pit of my stomach. And my husband, also sensing that something was awry, compounded my feelings and worst fears as he repeatedly asked when I would be paid. I just replied, "I'm sure any day." Well, the days came and went with no payment in sight. But Angel persevered and continued to transmit warning after warning to me. With each passing day I grew more fearful of a confrontation and losing the job I loved until finally one day, I garnered the courage to ask when I would receive compensation. The outcome? A serious altercation ensued because of our differing assumptions. The price I paid? Not only did I lose the job, but even worse, a relationship for a period of time.

Shortly after this experience, a neighbor wanted to have the first floor of her home remodeled. Not caring to repeat my previous unpleasant experience, together we set up clear guidelines for every aspect of the job and it went very smoothly. Upon completing the job, another neighbor, who had empathized with my previous unfortunate experience, was thinking of having her basement finished. Again I worked on the design, created the drawings, and chose materials, etc., never discussing a fee. (I thought she understood. Am I dense or what?) She had no idea that I charged for my designs, ideas, floor plans, etc. She retained my drawings, paid me 20 percent of the fee I requested, and hired another person to complete the job. Well, rather than learning from my mistake, I became so bitter that I ran away from what I loved and began a career in telecommunications (which I *really* disliked), thinking it would insulate me from all the pain I had associated with the building business.

Had I only been aware of the Four-Step Formula and my Angel, life would have been so much easier, especially now that I know how emphatically Angel was trying to guide me in the right direction.

Angel knows your beliefs and the choices you have made and will always guide you in their direction. Your task is to be sensitive to your feelings and then to act on them. The process of living in the new paradigm will entail feeling your way through life with your heart rather than thinking your way through life with your head. And, as an added bonus, you'll get into far less trouble!

Come to me along the path of your heart, not through a journey of your mind. You will never find me in your mind.[81]
— NEALE DONALD WALSCH
Conversations with God - Book 1

Your vision will become clear only when you can look into your own heart. Who looks outside, dreams; who looks inside, awakes.
— CARL JUNG
1875-1961

I am not responsible for my feelings — only for what I do with them.
— DR. CEOPHUS MARTIN

If you do not go within, you go without.[82]
— NEALE DONALD WALSCH
Conversations with God - Book 1

Now that you understand the true purpose of your feelings as well as your interrelationship with Angel, let's learn the process of placing orders so you can get what you want in life.

Placing Orders 101

The most important aspect of placing an order is to understand that Angel agrees with each and every statement you make. (This can be the good news and the bad news.)

Example:　I choose to be fit and trim.

Angel answers,　"YES!"

Now, let's say you acknowledge your reality:　You are *not* fit and trim and have unwanted weight (bad feeling, wrong-way sign, your Point of Power — time to place an order).

Unaware of your power, you might then think: "I'll never be able to lose all this weight! And why would I even want to make myself miserable dieting and exercising just to try to look better for other people."

Angel answers,　"YES!"

Is that what you want?　*NO!*

Remember, Angel is the ultimate server. Angel can serve you anything your little heart desires if you focus your thoughts properly and remain in a feeling place where you are *expecting* and allowing source energy to flow. (Think of how you felt when you were a child anticipating your birthday.) On the other hand, Angel is quite capable of serving you anything your little heart does *not* desire if your thoughts are focused improperly. Why? Because the Law of Attraction unequivocally states:

Whatever you give your attention to will GROW LARGER!

Therefore, you must be careful because your thoughts are seeding the future:

∾　If you are *thinking, believing, and feeling* that you will never have enough money — guess what? Angel will answer "Order up!" ensuring that you will *not* be prosperous, because no matter what you do, your powerful thoughts are focused on never having enough and what Angel can only deliver are *more* experiences that will confirm that you will never have enough!

∾　If you are *thinking, believing, and feeling* that you are overweight — guess what? Angel will answer "Order up!" ensuring that you will *not* be thin, because no matter what you do, your powerful thoughts are focused on being overweight, and what Angel can only deliver is *more* of what you are currently experiencing!

∾　If you are *thinking, believing, and feeling* that you are unhappy — guess what? Angel will answer "Order up!" ensuring that you will *not* find happiness, because no matter what you do, your powerful thoughts are focused on how unhappy you are and what Angel can only deliver are *more* unhappy experiences!

∿ If you are *thinking, believing, feeling, and knowing* that you are ill — guess what? Angel will answer "Order up!" ensuring that you will *not* get well, because no matter what you do, your powerful thoughts are focused on illness and what Angel can only deliver is *more* illness!

∿ If you are *thinking, believing, and feeling* that you will never find a partner — guess what? Angel will answer "Order up!" ensuring that you will not find a partner, because no matter what you do, your powerful thoughts are focused on *not* having a partner and what Angel can only deliver are *more* experiences confirming that you will never find a partner.

ALTHOUGH THESE THOUGHTS, BELIEFS, AND FEELINGS
ARE CONTRARY TO WHAT YOU WANT, THEY
WILL ALWAYS FOLLOW THE FOUR-STEP FORMULA:
THINK, BELIEVE, EXPECT, AND GET!

Always Think Yes — Never Think No

Your communication with Angel is conveyed through your feelings. Therefore, whatever you focus on for a period of time will create a thoughtform and be construed as an order. Angel cannot respond to "no." Therefore, every time you give your attention to something that makes your heart sing, it will be on its way to you. And every time you give your attention to something that makes your heart sad, angry, or frustrated, *that* will be on its way to you. But remember, it doesn't feel good, so Angel is warning you, transmitting a wrong-way sign to illuminate your habit of thoughts. The Four-Step Formula will not waver in its operation. It is a constant, a given, something you *can* rely upon, so you must learn to use it to your advantage.

If you attempt to control anything you don't want by attempting to push it away from you (as illustrated in the story of Nancy and cancer), you are, once more, focusing on what you don't want. And whenever you focus on anything *accompanied by strong emotion*, what you don't want will be *propelled* into your life experience because those two factors combined create even more powerful thoughtforms that rapidly multiply the results!

For example: The TV news informs you of robberies in your neighborhood. Logically, you feel fearful and in your fear you may attempt to protect yourself by installing additional locks. In that moment, however, you are focusing on robberies while at the same time feeling fearful. As a result, you will create a robbery and fear order. In your attempt to 'push away' the robber, you may instead magnetize him and become his victim, because the two of you are focused on robbery. (This depends on the intensity of your fear and how much time you have devoted to thinking about robberies.) What should you do? First, utilize your negative feelings as your Point of Power to clarify what you want — safety and freedom — and then create a order by *feeling* what it feels like to be safe and free. *(Think and believe.)* Next step? *Expect.* Have faith and expect to be safe and free, for those feelings allow energy to flow! Think, believe, expect, and you will get!

The bottom line? If you attempt to push away what you don't want in life, you will instead *magnetize* it, for you are focusing your powerful thoughts on what you don't want. Reacting and responding to difficulties in life with your logical reasoning mind alone is yet another consequence of old-paradigm thinking. It is living life backwards.

Once you have determined what you want by understanding what you don't want, place your order with a "YES" — a positive — rather than a "NO" — a negative. "Yes, I choose _____." Not, "No, I do not want _____." If you pray for something and say "Pleeeease.....," the feeling in your heart is one of *wanting*, rather than *choosing* what you want. And from your new state of heightened awareness, what do you think you will then get? (Wanting doesn't feel good, therefore, it's a *NO!* Choosing does feel good, therefore, it's a *YES!*)

> *If, now, there is something you choose to experience in your life, do not "want" it, choose it.*[83]
> — NEALE DONALD WALSCH
> Conversations with God - Book 1

> *Your saying you want a thing only works to produce that precise experience — wanting — in your reality. The correct prayer is therefore never a prayer of supplication, but a prayer of gratitude.*[84] — NEALE DONALD WALSCH
> Conversations with God - Book 1

Examining Your Genie Wishes

Now that you know the secret to life — how your thoughts create your reality — let's revisit your list of "Genie Wishes." (*The Prelude* page 1) What did you ask for?

∽ Did you ask for lots of money so you could have a great time and buy all the wonderful things you have always dreamed of?

∽ Did you ask for freedom so that you had the time to travel the world or be with your family?

∽ Did you ask for the world to be free of war, poverty, disease, and strife and be instead filled with peace and love among all people?

∽ Did you ask for a world where there was an abundance of everything for everyone?

∽ Did you ask for fulfilling, harmonious relationships?

∽ Did you ask for peace of mind?

∽ Did you ask for your children to succeed and be happy in life?

∽ Did you ask for fame?

∽ Did you ask for career success?

∽ Did you ask for perfect health?

∽ Did you ask for a body that radiated beauty?

∽ Did you ask for all foods to be free of fat and calories so you could enjoy them without guilt? (I would!)

Now close your eyes. Starting with your first wish, *imagine* what it would be like to have it right here and now. What would it *feel* like to experience what you wished for? What would it *look* like? *Sound* like? *Smell* like? Create the reality in your mind. Now do the same for the rest of your wishes. *Feel* the feelings in your heart. *Be* in the Moments.

How did you feel as you went through the steps of this exercise: awkward, dumb, childlike, uncool, or foolish? Actually, those feelings are pretty normal reactions. Why? Because our imaginations are presently thought of as whimsical fantasy, "child's play," experiences that are not rooted in reality. As a result, most of us learned to stifle our imaginations by the age of four or five and they have become dormant. However, if the preceding feelings best describe your reaction to visualizing, that's okay. Determining what you feel and believe right now is important because that information will serve as your launching pad from which to create the life you wish to live. Furthermore, as you embark on any new undertaking in life, initially you always feel awkward, but as you begin to familiarize yourself with the techniques, you soon become more and more comfortable. (And you'll become comfortable very quickly when you begin to manifest all sorts of 'goodies.')

Living in the old paradigm, you may have become 'programmed' to *not* want because you have repeatedly been stung by the bitter disappointment of not getting what you want. However, it is now necessary to clear away the cobwebs that may be obscuring your imagination because your imagination plays a very important role in life: It is the basis of conscious creation. You employ your imagination to deliberately create a thoughtform, which, by virtue of the Law of Attraction, magnetizes energy into form. And the good news is: Angel can't tell the difference between what you imagine from what you experience.

Your Imagination Is the Basis of Conscious Creation

Without this playing of fantasy no creative work has ever come to birth. The debt we owe to the play of imagination is incalculable.
— CARL JUNG
1875-1961

Fantasies are more than substitutes for unpleasant reality; they are also dress rehearsals, plans. All acts performed in the world begin in the imagination.
— BARBARA GRIZZUTI HARNSON

Imagination is far more important than intellect.
— ALBERT EINSTEIN
1871-1940

Imagination has always had powers of resurrection that no science can match.
— INGRID BERGIS

You see things and say "Why?" but I dream things that
never were and say "Why not?" — GEORGE BERNARD SHAW

1856-1950

Quite deliberately, you use your conscious mind
playfully, creating a game as children do, in which for a
time you completely ignore what seems to be real in
physical terms and "pretend" that what you want is
real.[85]
— JANE ROBERTS

The Nature of Personal Reality - A Seth Book

Here's another example of how we stymie the creation of what we want in our unawareness of the Four-Step Formula: While driving around one day you notice a beautiful silver convertible. Your heart is pounding; you are excited! (Angel likes the car too!) You can just imagine driving that gorgeous car with the top down on a beautiful sunny day with no traffic. You are having fun! YES! YES! YES! (Angel *wants* this car.) In that moment, you are placing an order.

However, 'reality' then occurs to you and you think, "Why am I even torturing myself? I can't afford this car. It costs a ton of money and there is no way I will ever have enough to spend on something so frivolous. I have bills to pay."

NO! NO! NO! What just happened? As your thoughts shifted from those of joy to those of doom and gloom, you canceled your new car order! However, because your *new* order conflicted with what you desired, your 'off' switch was activated. Angel then transmitted a wrong-way sign, alerting you to the fact that your thoughts were focused in the *wrong* direction — you were holding a belief that *contradicted* what you desired. To utilize your negative feeling as your Point of Power, you would then place an order by employing your imagination. Imagine driving your new silver convertible with the sun on your face and your hair blowing in the wind. *Feel* what it feels like to be the proud owner of that beautiful car. Appreciate this magnificent work of art — the time, effort, and love that a multitude of people expended in this car's creation. Then *expect* this car in joyful anticipation without thinking about *how* it will come to you. And as you do, Angel will set the stage for you to receive it, for you are then placing an order for this new 'cool' car.

Living in a culture of instant gratification — I want it now — can be detrimental to placing orders. Old-paradigm thinking is solution-oriented — you were trained to determine what you want and then to take action to attain it. And although taking action can be effective, it is also the *longest* route to attaining what you want. New-paradigm thinking utilizes the far more potent power of your thoughts, which opposes everything you were taught. Consequently, in failing to take action, you may initially experience a knee-jerk response of frustration — not having your order yet rather than *expecting* it in joyful anticipation — a response fatal to the manifestation of what you desire.

For example: If you were in a restaurant and spotted something wonderful on the menu, you would eagerly place your order and begin to salivate at the thought of that yummy dish. You wouldn't think of going into the kitchen to check on how they were preparing your order, right? You would joyfully anticipate your meal because you were hungry! However, if you experienced an extended period of time where you sat at your table and waited and waited as your stomach growled louder and louder, how would you then feel? You might think that your server forgot you, or took an extended break, and in your hunger and impatience to receive your order, your thoughts would have shifted from those of joyful anticipation to those of annoyance and frustration. And from what you now know, what do you think you would then get? Not what you wanted.... Therefore, in those moments it is imperative that you immediately refocus your thoughts in order to maintain your connection to source energy.

The Lack of Money

Whatever we plant in our subconscious mind and nourish with repetition and emotion will one day become a reality. — EARL NIGHTINGALE

Let's explore a subject that most folks have issues with in life: Money. Let's say that your financial condition is not what you desire. When you sit down to pay your bills, you find that you don't have enough money to pay all of them. As a result, you feel frustrated, angry, annoyed, sad, or hopeless. (Angel-Alerts. Wrong-way signs.) What should you do? First, utilize your negative feeling as your Point of Power to clarify what you want: more money.

To magnetize more money, you would then employ your imagination and feel what it's like to *have* more money. Imagine that you have extra money right here and now. Say the words "I choose $_____" and then feel what it's like to have $_____. What does it feel like to have extra money in your checkbook every month? Imagine where you could go. Imagine buying all that you would like to buy *until it feels real.*

As you focus your attention on what you want, you are placing an order for prosperity rather than never having enough. To further utilize your Point of Power, acknowledge how much money you have *right now* and imagine that you have no obligations for that money. To magnetize prosperity in your life, it is essential that you appreciate what you have right now and act 'as if' you are already prosperous. And remember, do *not* say, "I want more money because I don't like what it feels like not to have money." That's a *NO*, an 'off' switch activator, a bad feeling, a wrong-way sign!

> *In order to demonstrate [manifest] your supply [order] you must first feel that you have received — a feeling of opulence must precede its manifestation.*[86]
> — FLORENCE SCOVEL SHINN

> *Jesus Christ said that "And all things, ye shall ask in prayer, believing ye shall receive." (Matthew 21:22) And from the book of Mark 11:24: "Therefore I say unto you, what things soever ye desire, when ye pray, believe that ye shall receive them, and ye shall have them." In this parable he shows that only those who have prepared for their good (thereby showing active faith) will bring the manifestation to pass. We might paraphrase the scriptures and say: When ye pray believe ye have it. When ye pray ACT as if you have already received.*[87]
> — FLORENCE SCOVEL SHINN

As you focus on your order in joyful anticipation, Angel will go to the vast kitchen of the Universe and begin to assemble the ingredients to create your order. (This is step 3 of the Formula — *expect.*) The only catch: *No 'buts' allowed.* You cannot say 'but' for any reason, for the moment you do, the feeling in your heart will change as you are no longer *expecting* what you ordered. The result? You will activate your 'off' switch and either cancel your order or receive a setback. Why? Because you not only restricted the flow of energy necessary to actualize your order, but you also placed a new order with Angel from your shift in feelings.

> *Don't say "but." That little word "but" is the difference between success and failure. Henry Ford said, "I'm going to invent the automobile," and Arthur T. Flanken said, "But ..."*
> — ERNIE BILKO

Miracles are natural, corrective, healing, and universal.
There is nothing they cannot do, but they cannot be
performed in the spirit of doubt or fear.[88]
— A COURSE IN MIRACLES®

If one asks for success and prepares for failure, he will
get the situation he has prepared for.[89]
— FLORENCE SCOVEL SHINN

When it is said that a prayer has not been answered,
what in actuality happened is that the most fervently held
thought, word, or feeling has become operative. Yet what
you must know — and here is the secret — is that
always it is the thought behind the thought — what
might be called the Sponsoring Thought — that is the
controlling thought. If, therefore, you beg and supplicate,
there seems a much smaller chance that you will
experience what you think you are choosing, because the
sponsoring thought behind every supplication is that you
do not have what you wish. The Sponsoring Thought
becomes your reality. Think on this deeply and you will
see that it is true, the Sponsoring Thought is either a
thought of love or fear. This is the thought behind the
thought. It is the first thought. It is the prime force. It is
the raw energy that drives the engine of human
experience.[90]
— NEALE DONALD WALSCH
Conversations with God - Book 1

Success Breeds Success

Think about Tiger Woods, the golf phenomenon. From a very early age his father taught him to visualize his goals with determination and clarity. This technique, combined with much practice, produced his early successes. His continued success can be attributed not only to his focused thoughts, but also to the momentum created by his success and others continually reinforcing his greatness. Bolstered by this powerful energy, he has a far easier time projecting the feeling of success which, by virtue of the Law of Attraction, can only magnetize more success!

My former brother-in-law grew up in a family that was lacking financial abundance and higher education, yet he created a number of businesses that were extremely financially successful. As a matter of fact, he sold one for multimillions. What did he think, believe, expect, and get? From what I observed, nothing could have prevented him from achieving what he desired. He possessed an unrelenting determination and focus. And though he believes there is no such thing as failure, his life has certainly been a roller coaster of extreme ups and downs. In fact, most onlookers believe that he has experienced numerous failures. However, it is *his* belief (the only one that counts) that his 'down' periods merely assisted him in articulating the direction of his goals.

Ready to Apply All the Steps?

Let's now apply this new information. Think of something you don't like having in your life:

_____

_____

_____

_____

_____

_____

From your position of clarity, choose what you want:

_____

_____

_____

_____

_____

Now, close your eyes and *feel* what it would be like to have what you chose. Create an image of it in your mind. Ask yourself *why* you want it (and you don't need to justify why; "just because" is good enough!). For approximately one minute, imagine it until it *feels* real. And don't say *but* under any circumstance or find any reason that you cannot have what you want (a little hint: it will feel bad). Also, do not acknowledge the reality of what exists today. In fact, disregard it completely or you will only magnetize more of it. There is no evolution whatsoever in reliving what you have already experienced. Think only of what you have chosen and then of having it in the present moment. After completing your visualization, Angel will then begin to assemble the ingredients — the evidence necessary to attain your order. How does Angel do that? Through the process of co-creation. So, now let's learn how to co-create, as this process will provide you the foundation to live life as it is meant to be lived: as a joyous magical experience, overflowing with love and laughter! ☺

The Art of Co-Creation:
You're the Visionary,
Angel's the Actionary

The conscious mind sets the goals and the inner self
brings them about, using all its facilities and inexhaustible
energy.[92]   — JANE ROBERTS
The Nature of Personal Reality - A Seth Book

Thou wilt show me the path of life: in thy presence is
fullness of joy; at thy right hand there are pleasures
forevermore.   — THE BIBLE
Psalms 16:11

I could not say I believe. I know! I have had the
experience of being gripped by something that is stronger
than myself, something that people call God.
                                              — CARL JUNG
                                                  1875-1961

You're the Visionary: the "What"
Angel's the Actionary: the "How"

After placing an order, you may wonder how it will come to you. In most
cases it will not be delivered to your front door via UPS® or Fedex®, nor
will it fall from the sky. Your order is co-created with Angel's help, for
you and Angel are partners, each having a different role. Your role is
that of *Visionary* — to determine the 'what,' and Angel's role is that of
Actionary — to provide the how. Angel determines how to fulfill your

order and then sets the stage for its manifestation by providing you with the ingredients for your 'recipe.' And when these ingredients are combined, they manifest in your order. That's co-creating!

To fully master the process of co-creating, it is essential to understand the process of placing an order on an even deeper level. To begin, each of your thoughts and beliefs produces a frequency, a magnetic *feeling* frequency — an attitude or mood that emanates from your heart. This frequency transmits a signal that acts as your order, magnetizing whatever corresponds with it into your life experience.

Understand Your Feeling Frequencies

In your mind's eye create a picture of you: A being that resembles the sun as you drew it as a child — a round circle with rays of light extending out in all directions. And each of your rays represents a 'circuit' — a specific subject-matter, thought, belief, or topic that you have, at some time in your life, focused on. Whatever belief you hold regarding that circuit — how you feel about that particular subject — will either allow or restrict the flow of life energy to you whenever you focus on it. Upon activating a circuit with your thoughts, a frequency will be transmitted that will begin to attract other like frequencies, thus magnetizing 'evidence' into your life. For further clarity, let's examine one of your rays, or circuits more closely. Each of your rays has opposite ends or polarities — one representing the frequency of 'lack' and the other, the frequency of 'plenty.' And between these two ends lie a multitude of different frequencies. For example: An infinite number of frequencies exist that correspond with the subject of money, from one extreme to the other, each projecting a completely different attitude or mood. To determine the specific money frequency you are transmitting, take a look at your current financial condition. The degree of lack or abundance you are now experiencing, the way you feel about money, will indicate the frequency you are projecting — hence, manifesting. The good news? Each of your circuits resembles a radio dial that you are capable of turning. Hence, you have the ability to tune in to the frequency that you *desire*.

Your current life circumstances will indicate what 'stations' you are currently tuned in to. If a certain aspect of your life evokes a good feeling within, that circuit is open to the flow of energy, therefore, we will label it as "green." And if a certain aspect of your life evokes a feeling of discomfort within, that circuit is restricting the flow of energy, therefore, we will label it as "red."

Everything and everyone in our world projects magnetic frequencies, and a specific feeling frequency is projected by each of your thoughtform/orders. As you think of something you desire, it too projects a feeling frequency — an attitude, mood, or 'feeling place.' The objective of placing an order is to create a green 'open' circuit which will allow energy to flow and manifest what you want, rather than one that is red which will restrict the energy necessary to actualize your order.

Placing an order is somewhat akin to tuning in to a radio station that is broadcasting the type of music you wish to listen to. If you want to listen to the music on a certain station, you must tune your dial to its frequency. In other words, if you want to hear the music played on 95.5 but your dial is set at 103.5, you will not hear what you want because you are tuned in to the wrong station! To attain what you desire, you must tune in to its frequency. To do that you must *project* its feeling frequency; to visualize what you desire; to act 'as if' you already have it. Now this may take a little practice in the beginning. But just as you choose the foods you eat, the clothes you wear, the car you drive, and the friends you have, you simply choose what you want for your life experience, project its frequency, and it will then be on its way to you.

Desire and Resistance

Each of your frequencies also indicate one of two factors that affect the amount of energy capable of flowing to you: how much desire and how much resistance you hold relative to that circuit. The greater the emotion, passion, or excitement you feel, the greater your desire, which will summon great quantities of energy. The greater the degree of emotional *dis*comfort, the greater your resistance, which will summon energy in one moment, but restrict it in the next. Therefore, to manifest what you desire, you must release your resistance. How was your resistance created? By an imbalance in your energy field. You are holding a belief that contradicts what you desire. To determine the degree of desire/resistance you maintain on any subject, use the following measure: The stronger the emotion you feel — negative or positive, the greater your desire — the more something really matters to you.

To illustrate your desire/resistance ratios, complete the following sentences: My heart soars in delight when I think about having the following:_____

_____

_____

My heart first soars, but is then followed by a sinking feeling when I think about having the following:_____

_____

_____

I won't even allow myself to think about having the following because I know I'll never have it: _____

_____

_____

For example:

❧   Upon seeing a beautiful home, your heart soars. This response indicates pure, unresisted desire: your circuits are green and open to the flow of energy. As a result, if you focus with joy upon a beautiful home, one that corresponds with your frequency will soon be on its way to you.

❧   Upon seeing a beautiful home, your heart initially soars, but is then followed by a sinking feeling. This response indicates desire *and* resistance; a circuit that is red *and* green, which summons energy in one moment, and restricts it in the next. The result? Chaos. You will have a feeling of discomfort and confusion when you think about having a beautiful home. Therefore, to manifest a beautiful home, it will be necessary for you to uncover your red circuit — your habit of thoughts responsible for impeding its manifestation, and readjust its frequency to green.

❧   Upon seeing a beautiful home, you feel intense negative emotion — anger, envy, or resentment ("Why would anyone need a home like that, anyway? Those folks must be greedy" etc.). You won't even *allow* the thought of living in a beautiful home to enter your consciousness. This response indicates pure resistance: your circuit is red and completely restricting the flow of energy. You have now met with a deeply entrenched core belief that will need reevaluation. That is, if you ever desire to have a beautiful home.

Each of your circuits projects a different frequency based on the amount of desire, resistance, or combination of the two you hold on a particular subject. The degree of emotion that you feel will amplify your awareness to your own unique combination of desire and resistance. Therefore, to attain what you desire, your only work is to create a green circuit: to *expect* (step 3) your order without resistance, thereby allowing the energy to flow to its fulfillment.

The Vast Spectrum of Feelings

To understand the subtle differences in frequencies, take a moment to experience a few different feelings. Using the following list, assign a

number from one to ten to each feeling: 10 evokes the grandest feeling
— unresisted desire allowing full energy; 5 evokes a more neutral feeling
— little resistance or desire allowing a little energy to flow; 1 evokes the
lowest, most despondent feeling — pure resistance or a complete
restriction of energy.

1 *(Low)* ⟫➤ 5 *(Neutral)* ⟫➤ 10 *(High)*

How do you feel when

you see a $1 bill? _____

you are being criticized? _____

you are passionate? _____

you feel guilty? _____

you feel despair? _____

you are fearful? _____

you are disappointed? _____

you are loved? _____

you are angry? _____

you are confused? _____

you are excited? _____

you are desperate? _____

you are hopeless? _____

you are enthusiastic? _____

you are frustrated? _____

you are exhilarated? _____

you are annoyed? _____

you see an injustice? _____

you are peaceful? _____

you are impatient? _____

you are totally confident? _____

you see a $100 bill? _____

you are honored? _____

you are worried? _____

you are overwhelmed? _____

you are resentful? _____

you are embarrassed? _____

you see a $50 bill? _____

you are critical of others? _____

you are appreciated? _____

you see a $1000 bill? _____

Can you feel the differences in these frequencies? Can you feel the energy or lack of energy summoned by your desire and resistance relative to these subjects? Can you discern a shift in your feelings as you pivot from one subject to another? Can you feel the different frequencies you continually project to Angel?

Now that you better understand your feeling frequencies and their desire/resistance ratio, let's explore the next step in co-creating: Manifesting your order.

Angel Orchestrates "Angacles:" The Components of Your Orders

Once you have determined what you desire and placed your order, you have fulfilled your role as Visionary. Next, it's Angel's turn to fulfill the role of Actionary — to provide you with 'Angacles.' What are Angacles? Angel mir*acles* — evidence — the ingredients that comprise your order. Angacles will 'coincidentally' appear as opportunities in the form of people, events, circumstances, or as inspirations to do something. Upon receiving an Angacle, you are to take inspired action, *even though you may not understand why*. Next, piece by piece, your order will manifest, *if* you maintain a state of joyful expectation and allow the energy to flow.

As you learn to perfect the process of co-creation, the unfolding of each of your orders will be like a mystery unraveling, where you won't know exactly who will appear or what event or circumstance will occur, but they *will!* The exciting part is when you begin to recognize your Angacles and intuitively *know* that they are connected to an order you have placed.

> *Coincidences come into being most readily when we are in a highly expectant state. Most esoteric literature advises that a combination of emotional charge and vivid imagining stimulates the ability to attract into our lives that which we desire — in some form or another.*[93]
> — JAMES REDFIELD and CAROLE ADRIENNE

Once you get the hang of co-creating, your life will begin to soar with love and laughter! You'll soon be saying, "Is this fun or what?" Because this, friends, is how life is *meant* to be lived!

Examples of Co-Creation

Here's an example of the Four-Step Formula unfolding step by step: One day I visited my tailor for alterations. In conversation, Vince asked what I was doing and I hesitatingly told him that I was writing this book. (At the end of the book I will tell you how I was "called upon" to do this, as it was never a career aspiration of mine nor a talent I thought I possessed, so I was somewhat leery of divulging the fact that I was writing a book. In addition, the content, as you may have guessed, is somewhat difficult to describe in a short and sweet reply.) Well, much to my amazement, Vince was an Angacle — one of those pieces of an order puzzle that I had unknowingly placed on a deeper level of consciousness. After being labeled "delusional" in the early stages of writing this book, I placed an order for further validation of the Four-Step Formula. The following story was the fulfillment of my order:

A few months prior to our conversation, Vince came home one day and informed his wife that they were going to Las Vegas. Now, he did not have a clue as to *how* they were going to get there, but *he knew* they were going to go. A few weeks later, an Angacle appeared. Vince and his wife were invited to a fund-raising party where the sponsoring organization held a raffle. Guess what the grand prize was? A trip to Las Vegas! Vince bought a ticket and jokingly told others not to bother buying one because he was going to win the trip. Well, he was so confident, they thought he was crazy or had rigged the drawing. Guess what happened? *HE WON!* He thought about it, believed it, expected it, an Angacle appeared, he took inspired action, and what did he get? Just what he had ordered! Coincidence?

The moral of this story: Follow your gut feelings and be on the alert for Angacles. As they present themselves, take inspired action and your order will begin to manifest.

Let Go and Let Angel

My older brother is a doctor of biochemistry, a research scientist, at the University of Illinois in Chicago. Curious as to the impact of the Four-Step Formula in the scientific realm, I asked if coincidences ever occurred while conducting research. His reply? Coincidences are often encountered while conducting research. Scientific research begins with a question where the scientist develops a strategy based on trial and error that hopefully will lead to an answer. Upon implementing this strategy, coincidences often occur. Of course, the scientist is unaware

that he is placing an order, expecting it, and that Angacles —
coincidences or opportunities — are, in reality, the *natural* sequence of
events that follow. (By the way, Dr. Jonas Salk discovered the polio
vaccine through this process.[94] And Post-it Notes®, penicillin, and many
many other things were also discovered by "accident.") The manner in
which a scientist *handles* the coincidence is, in my brother's opinion,
what sets a good scientist apart from one who is too rigid. A good
scientist? One who pursues the coincidence aggressively (*aha!*). A rigid
scientist? One who discards the coincidence because it doesn't fit into
his or her predetermined strategy.

The moral of the story: Do not impose *your* idea of how you will receive
what you have ordered. When you send an order to Angel and *expect* it
to occur, you will ride a wave of energy where everything will fall into
place. Angacles — people, events, or circumstances — will appear at
just the right moment. Other folks may marvel at your good fortune and
say that you were lucky. But you simply applied the secret to life, the
Four-Step Formula: You determined what you wanted, placed your
order, took inspired action from your Angacles, and enjoyed your order!

There are no accidents in life. Be sensitive to those events that may
appear coincidental. *They are not.* They are Angacles alerting you to *take
inspired action* that will culminate in the manifestation of your order.
Emulate the 'good' scientist and utilize your Angacles, understanding
that you will not know how Angel will orchestrate the events for your
order to manifest. You must *expect* and allow Angel to perform his/her
role (step 3). To remind you of *your* role in co-creation, let's borrow a
motto from the Alcoholics Anonymous program, "Let Go and Let God,"
and amend it to read, "Let Go and Let Angel" (God's employee...).

Recognize Opportunities and Then Take Action

To illustrate the importance of taking action when presented with an
Angacle, consider the following fictional story about a faithful, yet
stubborn man named Jacob who lived on the banks of a beautiful river.
Jacob delighted in the ever-changing gift of nature the river provided —
the birds, the ducks, the gentle sound of the river lapping along its banks
— never suspecting that it's loveliness and tranquility could one day be
transformed into something devastating. During an exceptionally intense
rainy season though, that is precisely what happened. Torrential rains
fell day after day in an unrelenting onslaught until the ground was
saturated — it could hold no more. Fueled by this incessant rainfall, the
river grew in power and magnitude, threatening to devour anything in
its path. Soon it reached the front door of Jacob's home, imploring him

to seek higher ground. Jacob, however, being a man of modest wealth, chose to stay. He wanted to protect his belongings as best he could. Believing with his heart and soul in God, Jacob climbed onto his roof and prayed for God to protect him. In the meantime, the rain intensified. Inch by alarming inch the river rose higher, growing even more precarious when suddenly a man in a boat, fleeing for his own safety, spotted Jacob atop the roof of his home and offered his help. Jacob, however, being ever-faithful, was quite adamant about God saving him and, incredulously, declined the assistance replying, "No, thank you, I'm praying to God and He will save me." The man in the boat departed and the downpour continued. The river was fast becoming an unstoppable force claiming home after home in its wake. And though Jacob witnessed disaster all around him, he remained faithful — he would be protected. Under these harrowing conditions, a team of rescue workers searched for any last victims. One worker, on his way to safer ground after hours of searching, noticed Jacob on the roof and urged him to quickly get in his boat. But once again Jacob refused, offering the same reply, "No, thank you, I'm praying for God to save me." This man swiftly departed, knowing full well that his attempt to persuade Jacob might be not only futile, but also result in the loss of his own life. There was no respite in the downpour. The minutes ticked slowly into hours when suddenly the river's strong current began to wash upon the roof where Jacob patiently waited for a momentous miracle — perhaps the river would part. Amid these harrowing, life-threatening circumstances, yet another rescue worker appeared and pleaded with Jacob to get in his boat immediately as disaster was not only certain, but imminent. Unshakable in his stance, Jacob refused. Shaking his head in utter disbelief, the man grudgingly left without him. Moments later, an astounded Jacob was swallowed by the river and drowned. Upon his arrival in Heaven, Jacob beseeched God: "I was praying for You to save me, God, why didn't you?" And God replied, "Three times I sent men in boats to save you, but you refused to get in each time!"

The moral of the story: Do not impose *your* idea of *how* you will receive what you have ordered. Do not dismiss a person, event, or circumstance that appears in your life coincidentally because of your preconceived notion — what *you expect* to happen. "Let Go and Let Angel," and miraculously Angacles will appear that will provide you with the perfect solution to fulfilling your order. However, you must then take inspired action!

Arid Land Transformed into a Garden of Eden

A remarkable example of the power of co-creation took place in 1962 in

Findhorn, Scotland. This community was founded on a barren stretch of gorse and sand where agricultural experts stated that nothing but the most tenacious weeds would be capable of growing. Another group of folks had other ideas, though. They had grand aspirations of developing a community where they could support themselves from this land. Unknown to the experts, however, this group had an advantage: They understood the Four-Step Formula. Disregarding the claims made by the experts, they placed orders for the crops they wanted to grow and other items they desired. Then they projected energy and love to every seed, stone, and task. Guess what happened? Findhorn blossomed into a veritable Garden of Eden, where incredible crops, including cabbages weighing more than forty pounds, were harvested! Findhorn's founders, Peter and Eileen Caddy, and other like-minded folks also manifested other items, including a greenhouse and bungalows, all through the use of the Formula![95] Amazing? This story was so astonishing that PBS taped an hour-long show in the late 1970s on this very project.

Ponder these implications. Can you begin to comprehend the limitless power at our fingertips? Consider the potentials of the Four-Step Formula on Third World countries where people are lacking many of the necessities of life. By simply learning and applying the Formula, people everywhere in our world can awaken to their authentic power and begin to comprehend the true objective of life: that it is *meant* for living, loving, and laughing. I bet there are a lot of folks who don't realize that!

More Examples of Co-Creation

In 1984 I was divorced and subsequently 'inherited' my former husband's debts as he had filed for bankruptcy. As a result, my car was repossessed, foreclosure proceedings began on my home, and the jewelry store I owned went out of business. On top of all that, I was forced to defend myself in court, but unfortunately did not have $80,000 on hand to pay the resulting attorney fees. My only option was to utilize the inventory in my store to pay my fees, and after a short period of time, my attorney's wife was dripping in diamonds. During this debacle, my former husband's creditors relentlessly breathed down my neck day and night, demanding payment for his debts, but I didn't have a quarter of a million dollars to pay them. Amid those great character-building opportunities, I sought a "real job" — one that assured me a consistent paycheck, hence security, as my previously held jobs were those where I was self-employed. Having experience in both selling and grading diamonds (fun, fun, fun!), I was hired by a major upscale jeweler in suburban Chicago.

As my first Christmas selling season approached, I was curious as to the amount of commission I could earn. (I was paid 6 percent on each sale and was eager to begin choosing Christmas gifts!) One of my colleagues recalled that the best salesperson in the company in the previous December had achieved $250,000 in sales, but it was highly improbable that I would attain that amount because I had no established clientele. Well, I thought that number actually sounded quite good, so I said to myself, "I intend to sell $250,000 for the month of December." As I drove to work on Christmas Eve, I was disappointed — I had reached only $200,000 in sales and now thought it would be impossible to attain my goal because I was working only half a day. Guess what happened? Angacles appeared. First, the phone rang. A lady wanted to purchase a $29,500 watch for her husband over the phone. As the day progressed, other clients purchased items that totaled an additional $20,000! *I made my goal!* I reached $50,000 in sales that day, whereas my colleagues averaged $3,000 to $10,000. Coincidence? Not at all, and I now understand why. Angel had received my order and orchestrated the events that had gathered enough momentum to fulfill my order. Even with my last-minute doubts, there was no stopping what was ready to manifest. Thank you, Angel! (In retrospect, I should have chosen $500,000 for my goal — I enjoy abundance and prosperity!)

If you're a fan of the *Oprah Winfrey Show*, you have witnessed guest after guest affirming the Four-Step Formula. On one show, actor Jim Carrey shared a few experiences that preceded his monumental success: Every evening he would park his car on a street overlooking Los Angeles and visualize both directors and others he respected tell him how much they enjoyed his work. One day after visualizing the items he desired, he went even further: He wrote himself a check for $10 million for acting services rendered, postdated it three years later, and carried it in his wallet at all times. Guess what happened? Days short of the check's expiration, he received $10 million for the movie *Dumb and Dumber!* Coincidence? Now, he did not just place his orders, sit back, and wait for them to magically materialize. Angacles appeared in the form of people, events, and circumstances, and from the opportunities presented, he took inspired action and co-created the result!

On another show, Oprah asked Michael Crichton, best-selling author of the book, *Jurassic Park*, if he had any idea that this movie would be the highest grossing movie (at that time) in history. His reply? Yes, he did believe that this movie would gross more than $1 billion after visiting the movie's set. In fact, that is exactly what he told Steven Spielberg, the movie's director. (Four-Step Formula — it works, folks!) Do you think he had any idea that he was summoning Angel to set the events in motion by thinking, believing, and expecting? (*Hollywood, are you listening? By the way, there's a 10 percent fee for this info!* ☺)

Sports Psychology and the Four-Step Formula

Psychologists often utilize a concept that emulates the Four-Step Formula to prepare athletes to overcome a problem they have encountered that has prevented them from achieving optimal success. They begin by instructing the athletes to visualize performing their sport perfectly. And the athletes *believe* that their advice must be valid because they believe these doctors to be competent and knowledgeable. The result? A high rate of success is achieved utilizing this technique. (Little do they know they are summoning Angel!)

Visualization techniques are actually utilized by many in the world of sports. Brian Boitano, the fabulous men's figure skating champion, shared a little known story about his gold-medal winning Olympic performance in a television interview. Prior to the competition, he visualized every detail of his skating program — including his receiving the gold medal. Upon completing his program and receiving his gold medal, when reality paralleled his visualization, he was uncertain whether he was experiencing the 'real' thing or his visualization. However, he abruptly awoke to reality when the "Star-Spangled Banner" was played. Why? It was played at a faster tempo than in his visualization.

The repercussions of old-paradigm thinking are vast, and in sports you can clearly see its profound effects. Whether a team is on a winning or losing streak, the influence of others can have a tremendous affect on the performance of players, for the fans create a powerful collective momentum of energy. That is why the "home court advantage" exists. Consider the collective energy projected by a crowd of roaring happy fans. Now consider how debilitating a group of angry fans could be. Because only one team can win, the team with the greatest collective determination, focus, and desire — the team that has tuned in to the frequency of winning with the greatest intensity — will prevail.

The legacy of Michael Jordan is yet another powerful example of the Four-Step Formula in action. Inspired by coach Phil Jackson, who extolled the virtues and principles of Zen Buddhism, Michael was able to maintain a deep focus and awareness of his authentic power and utilize on the basketball court. In light of the Formula it is no coincidence that the Chicago Bulls won 6 world championships!

Can you imagine how interesting sports will become when there is a universal awareness of the Four-Step Formula? Let's now explore *your* life and uncover any experiences you may have had where Angel was trying to guide you along a path filled with love and laughter. ☺

Has Angel Ever Guided You Without Your Awareness?

And thine ears shall hear a word behind thee, saying,
This is the way, walk ye in it ...
— THE BIBLE
Isaiah 30:21

My angel of destiny goes before me, keeping me in the
Way.[96]
— FLORENCE SCOVEL SHINN
1871-1940

As you look back on your life, you'll find that Angel was always there, always trying to reach you. But often the influence of your family, friends, teachers, the media, and others around you — along with your earlier programming (quite an onslaught) — taught you to dismiss your Angacles. So let's explore a few of your life experiences to determine if you have ever encountered a little divine intervention in the past.

How did you find your present job?[97]

_____
_____
_____
_____
_____
_____
_____

What were your first impressions of the workplace?

_____
_____
_____

_____
_____
_____
_____

Were there any signs along the way that you ignored culminating in a negative situation?

_____
_____
_____
_____
_____
_____

How did you meet the most significant people you have been involved with?

_____
_____
_____
_____
_____
_____

What led to your being in that place at the time you met them?[98]

_____
_____
_____
_____
_____
_____

What was your first impression of each significant person in your life?

_____
_____
_____
_____
_____
_____

Did any of these people remind you of someone else?

_____
_____
_____

_____
_____
_____

Did you receive any other signs or coincidences?

_____
_____
_____
_____
_____

How did you come to live where you are living?

_____
_____
_____
_____
_____

What was your first impression?

_____
_____
_____
_____
_____

Did you receive any other signs along the way?

_____
_____
_____
_____
_____
_____

Was Angel there for you before? Isn't it comforting to now realize that the signs you have been receiving were not foolishness or nonsense? Don't you feel safer and more secure now that you know that Angel is always there to guide you, if only you listen?

Let's now explore the power of influence — how you have unknowingly allowed others to shape your life experience which has unfortunately prevented you from living, loving, or laughing! ☺

When You Believe

Many nights we prayed with no proof anyone could hear
In our hearts a hopeful song we barely understood
Now we are not afraid
Although we know there's much to fear.
We were moving mountains long before we knew we could.
There can be miracles when you believe
Though hope is frail, it's hard to kill.
Who knows what miracle you can achieve
When you believe, somehow you will
You will when you believe
In this time of fear when prayers so often proved in vain
Hope seems like the summer birds too swiftly flown away
Yet now I'm standing here
My hearts so full I can't explain
Seeking faith and speaking words I never thought I'd say
There can be miracles when you believe
Though hope is frail, it's hard to kill.
Who knows what miracle you can achieve
When you believe, somehow you will
You will when you believe
They don't always happen when you ask
And it's easy to give in to your fear
But when you're blinded by your pain,
Can't see your way through the rain,
A small but still resilient voice
Says help is very near.
There can be miracles when you believe
Though hope is frail, it's hard to kill.
Who knows what miracle you can achieve
When you believe, somehow you will
You will when you believe
Just Believe, Believe![91]

Words by Stephen Schwartz

From the film *The Prince of Egypt* ©1998 SKG Music L.L.C.

Psst!
You're Giving Your Power Away!

You may talk of the tyranny of Nero and Tiberius; but the real tyranny is the tyranny of your next-door neighbor. Public opinion is a permeating influence, and it exacts obedience to itself; it requires us to think other men's thoughts, to speak other men's words, to follow other men's habits.
— WALTER BAGEHOT
1826-1877

If you want to please the critics, don't play too loud, too soft, too fast, too slow.
— ARTURO TOSCANINI
1867-1957

If there were such a thing as sin, this would be it: to allow yourself to become what you are because of the experience of others.[99]
— NEALE DONALD WALSCH
Conversations with God - Book 1

How far would Moses have gone if he had taken a poll in Egypt?
— HARRY S. TRUMAN
1884-1972

We forfeit three-fourths of ourselves to be like other people.
— ARTHUR SCHOPENHAUER
1788-1960

Lean too much on the approval of people, and it becomes a bed of thorns.
— TEHYI HSIEH

I am looking for a lot of men who have an infinite capacity to not know what can't be done. — HENRY FORD
1863-1947

The world is in the condition it is in because of you, and the choices you have made — or failed to make. The Earth is in the shape it's in because of you, and the choices you have made — or failed to make. Your own life is the way it is because of you, and the choices you have made — or failed to make.[100]
— NEALE DONALD WALSCH
Conversations with God - Book 1

I cannot give you the formula for success, but I can give you the formula for failure, which is: Try to please everybody. — HERBERT BAYARD SWOPE

An optimist may see a light where there is none, but why must the pessimist always run to blow it out?
— MICHEL DE SAINT-PIERRE

The conflict between what one is and who one is expected to be touches all of us. And sometimes, rather than reach for what one could be, we choose the comfort of the failed role, preferring to be the victim of circumstance, the person who didn't have a chance.
— MERLE SHAIN

Do you remember the great stock market crash in the 1920s, the historic event that spawned an unprecedented mass hysteria which culminated in a catastrophic domino-effect where America was brought to her knees? The ensuing panic became so intoxicating, so contagious, that our country was immobilized and masses unemployed. In fact, some people became so frightened of the future that they committed suicide — some jumping off the rooftops of buildings!

In reality though, little had changed. The infrastructure of America was essentially the same; the workers were available, the factories were accessible — everything was physically indistinguishable. Our country had just survived a world war and the prevailing climate was one of elation and prosperity resulting in the Roaring Twenties. What then created this disastrous turn of events? The power of influence. Stockholders were influenced by the inevitable doomsayers who doubted the continuing expansion of American companies, fearing that prosperity would soon come to an end. And when the sentiments of these doomsayers were broadcast, people panicked, the market plummeted, and a critical mass was negatively influenced. As person after person feared the repercussions of what might happen, the contagion of fear magnetized more and more evidence that culminated in exactly what was feared. The result? Catastrophe. The Great Depression. Extraordinary pain, anguish, and suffering.

Can you recognize the power of the media? Can you recognize the power of influence? Can you recognize the power of fear? Can you recognize the power of the thoughts, beliefs, expectations, and their end results? The residual effects of the Four-Step Formula — the nocebo effect — exist throughout history, underlying every event. Thought does indeed create reality.

You Unknowingly Give Your Power Away

Most of us have an underlying perception that we are powerless, so we abdicate the ability to think for ourselves. We surrender our thinking to those who possess more power than we do; those we believe to be wiser and more knowledgeable. And because we believe them to be more competent, rather than utilizing our Point of Power as it was meant to be used, we instead give it away. We allow others to make our decisions and create our experiences while we limit our participation in life by simply viewing, hearing, or reading. And unfortunately, those we are most influenced by are economically driven — they have something to gain by our buying what they have to sell.

In the media's efforts to protect us from the potential consequences of an endless stream of dangers, they instead do the opposite — they amplify our fears. In their unawareness, thus innocence, they inflame our vulnerability which ultimately compounds our illusion of powerlessness.

Esther and Jerry Hicks tell us that our minds are full of thoughts that have resulted from the experience of others. Well-meaning people in our world have unconsciously influenced us to think as we do. Beliefs have been accepted to the degree that we believe many partial truths or truths based wholly on the experiences created by others. And because everyone accepts these beliefs as truth, they become the reality we live in. A reality that is filled with much more criticism than praise. A reality that is filled with so much worry and fear about the thoughts, beliefs, or influences of *others* that we miss the beauty of Now altogether!

For the most part, your (judgments, decisions, and assessments) are made not by you, but by someone else. Your parents, perhaps. Your religion. Your teachers, historians, politicians. Very few of the value judgments you have incorporated into your truth are judgments you, yourself, have made based on your own experience — you have created yourself out of the experience of others.[101]
— NEALE DONALD WALSCH
Conversations with God - Book 1

It's Time to Reevaluate Your Patterns of Belief

Old-paradigm thinking has rendered us powerless. We have assimilated, absorbed, and accepted what others have presented as truth to the degree that it feels natural. As a result, we have grown accustomed to routinely feeling insecure, guarded, vulnerable, fearful, resentful, frustrated, or as though we will never have enough. Those patterns of thought are all around us. Consequently, rather than living our own unique life experiences — Being in our own Moments — we instead live out the dramas of others.[102]

What can we do? We must stop trying to control or impose our sense of what is right and wrong upon one another and instead focus on our points of harmony: what we agree on. In doing so, we will find that we actually have many more points of harmony than we do of disharmony.[103] To actualize our authentic power and live life as it is meant to be lived, we must reevaluate what others impart to us as truth, reassess our inherited patterns of belief, and use our own personal life experiences to determine our truths.[104]

There are many who are living far below their possibilities because they are continually handing over their individualities to others. Do you want to be a power in the world? Then be yourself. Be true to the highest within your soul and then allow yourself to be governed by no customs or conventionalities or arbitrary man-made rules that are not founded on principle.
— RALPH WALDO TRINE

The power of the influence of others is a powerful hindrance to our own thinking.[105]
— ESTHER and JERRY HICKS

*What the Catholic Church did to Europe during the
Middle Ages, much public education, the media, and
politics do now: They tell us what to think, rather than
how to think, and ultimately not to think.*[106]
— MARIANNE WILLIAMSON

Complacency and Conformity Are Unfortunately the Norm

*Some people don't like to be awakened. Most do not.
Most would rather sleep.*[107] — NEALE DONALD WALSCH
Conversations with God - Book 1

*The opportunity that God sends does not wake him up
who is asleep.* — SENEGALESE PROVERB

*No one can solve problems for someone whose problem
is that they don't want problems solved!*[108]
— RICHARD BACH

*Few are those who see with their own eyes and feel with
their own hearts.* — ALBERT EINSTEIN
1879-1955

Most people in this world are not searching for something better. They
have grown accustomed to lamenting and bemoaning their status as
victim. What they experience in life is always someone else's fault.
Victimhood is the role they have become most comfortable with. Most
people have adopted the beliefs that were present on the day they were
born. They have accepted life as it unfolds before them; it's the path of
least resistance — one where they are not held accountable for their
actions. In the movie *Truman*, one actor stated: "We accept the reality
with which we are presented." And, of course, those who do not seek
will not find. Why should they change if they don't have to? Life is easier
that way, they have surmised. Why do people resist new ideas?

   ∾   Some believe they already have all the answers to all the
questions. Their traditions, beliefs, and those who surround
them, prevent them from seeing or accepting that there are
other valid, valuable ideas outside of those accepted by their
family, religion, or country.

~ Some feel tremendous insecurity because the new ideas do not blend with their old ones, so they try even harder to hold onto, protect, and defend their set of beliefs, even if those beliefs no longer serve them.

~ Some seek nothing because they have felt the sting of wanting and not receiving so often that they now no longer want. Therefore, all new ideas seem to be an intrusion and they resist them. They have decided that it is easier to accept things as they are rather than to want something and not get it.[109]

It is the rare person who does not accept what life doles out. He or she can clearly see that "something is wrong with this picture." Their discomfort has created an opening to examine the potentiality of something more. They concede that they may not have all the answers.

Author Joel Barker tells us in *Paradigms: The Business of Discovering the Future*, that "change will not occur unless there is *discomfort* in the current paradigm." Therefore, adversity appears to be the sole catalyst to evoke change, because people are generally more willing to reexamine their lives when they experience some form of discomfort, uneasiness, or crisis — an event that shakes their foundation.

So, if you attempt to convince others about this message and they disagree, don't consider it a personal affront; their opinions are simply revealing their comfort zones. In fact, when you attempt to give information to someone who is not seeking it, it will always fall on deaf ears. He or she will find a multitude of reasons not to believe and tell *you* reasons not to believe. On the other hand, if someone *asks* a question, the information is valuable to them because he or she desires to know the answer.[110]

Wisdom never kicks at the iron walls it can't bring down.
— OLIVE SCHREINER
1855-1920

Until people realize that life is meant for living, loving, and laughing, they will continue to live a life that reflects their beliefs. And though their life experiences may not reflect what they truly desire, only they can decide if and when they choose to seek a solution. But don't lose faith. Others may become curious and ask your secret when they observe you living in joy, love, and abundance!

Let's now explore the perfection of life — the cycle of creation and your preprogrammed instincts, those "factory-installed" elements you came equipped with that are guiding you to the fulfillment of a life overflowing with love and laughter! ✆

Understand the Perfection of Life By Understanding the Cycle of Creation

Life is an on-going, never-ending process of recreation. You keep recreating yourselves in the image of your next highest idea about yourselves.[111] — NEALE DONALD WALSCH
Conversations with God - Book 2

[I]f we are suffering illness, poverty, or misfortune, we think we shall be satisfied on the day it ceases. But there too, we know it is false, so soon as one has got used to not suffering, one wants something else. — SIMONE WEIL
1909-1943

Oh, it's delightful to have ambitions....And there never seems to be any end of them—that's the best of it. Just as soon as you attain one ambition you see another one glittering higher up still. It does make life so interesting. — ANNE SHIRLEY

The perfection of life exists all around you, but when you are unaware of how life operates, life won't seem to be particularly 'perfect.' To understand the perfection of life, you must first understand its underlying principles and apply them to your advantage. To begin, everything in life is composed of energy. And a continuous stream of energy is required to sustain life — to grow and expand — to put the "eternalness" in eternity. Therefore, from the broadest perspective, life has been orchestrated to generate the continual flow of energy, and the cycle of creation provides the means to do just that.

Conceive ⟫⟶ Create ⟫⟶ Experience

The cycle of creation begins with a negative emotion — what you don't want. Your negative feeling is the catalyst that allows you to determine what you *do* want or to alert you of a red circuit that opposes what you want. Upon conceiving what you want, you place your order, take inspired action from your Angacles, and your order will then manifest. Upon experiencing what you desired, you gain a new perspective teeming with new information that will impel you to either fine-tune your initial creation or to conceive of something altogether different. This process forms the never-ending, always expanding cycle of creation.[112]

An example of a new perspective is often seen in lottery winners. Stories abound about winners whose lives actually changed for the worse. How could that be? Large sums of money are very seductive, causing people to rationalize many things. Oftentimes the distant friends or relatives of the lottery winner come out of nowhere. They either desperately need money, or somehow feel entitled to a portion of the winnings, which places the lottery winner in an awkward position. Consequently, from the new perspective of *being* a lottery winner, reality wasn't quite as rosy as they may have originally imagined it to be. To fine-tune their experience to reflect their initial feelings of joy and elation, they would place an order for respect, privacy, and blessings from others.

The never-ending cycle of creation is demonstrated at an astounding pace in the computer industry. The first computer conceived was not only very large, but operated slowly. Yet it was still superior to people performing certain tasks, as it significantly reduced the human-error factor. New concepts were inspired by the first computer, for researchers now had a different vantage point from which to contemplate ideas that could further enhance it. And each time they successfully crossed another threshold, another platform was created that triggered further innovation. The ongoing result? Countless advancements are occurring at such an astounding pace that our current computer models are obsolete before we even purchase them!

To further explore the never-ending, always evolving cycle of creation and how it pertains to your life, think about the day you were born. Since that blessed event, what achievements have you witnessed that have enriched our world? Think about when your parents were born. What has been achieved since their arrival? Now think about your grandparents. My Grandma Olson died in 1995 at the age of ninety-nine (and, I might add, she always ate the fat on meat, among other 'bad' things that statistics suggested would have buried her long before that).

Imagine being born in 1896. Although it sounds like it was eons ago, in reality, it wasn't *that* long ago. My Grandma witnessed ninety-nine years of incredible achievements: the first car, the introduction of television, the first airplane, a man on the moon (she was disappointed because she thought they would find Heaven), computers, fax machines, cellular phones, medical breakthroughs, pagers, etc., all accomplishments that we could not imagine living without today! Accomplishments that were the natural evolution of what preceded them — the cycle of creation 'doing it's thing' — growing and expanding All That Is. Isn't it amazing to chart the technological progress of mankind and participate in this endless cycle of creation?

To explore the cycle of creation on an even deeper level, let's explore your preprogrammed core instincts — those instincts that allow you to fully optimize your life experience.

Get Acquainted with Your Preprogrammed Core Instincts

All of the animals except man know that the principal business of life is to enjoy it. — SAMUEL BUTLER
1612-1680

There is no such thing as the pursuit of happiness, but there is the discovery of joy. — JOYCE GRENFELL
1910-1974

Too many people expect wonders from democracy when the most wonderful thing of all is just having it. — WALTER WINCHELL
1897-1972

It is only through the exercise of the greatest freedom that the greatest growth is achieved — or even possible. If all you are doing is following someone else's rules, then you have not grown, you have obeyed.[113] — NEALE DONALD WALSCH
Conversations with God - Book 2

Growth is the only evidence of life. — CARDINAL NEWMAN
1801-1890

The greatest gift that God, in His bounty made in creation, and the most conformable to His goodness, and that which He prizes most, was the freedom of the will, with which the creatures with intelligence, they all and they alone, were, and are, endowed. — DANTE ALIGHIERI
1265-1321

Your Preprogrammed Instincts

To ensure the continual flow of energy, you were 'preprogrammed' with certain core instincts. The most powerful instinct driving life experience is that of desire, for desire summons life energy. Desire initiates the cycle of creation, thus expanding All That Is. Therefore, simply having desire, which, by the way, you cannot avoid in an environment of polarities, you will summon life energy. However, to ensure the *quality* of life, you were preprogrammed with three additional instincts — freedom, joy, and growth — for those instincts allow you to fully optimize your creative abilities, *if* you understand their purpose. You instinctively seek FREEDOM because freedom is the basis of life; JOY, because joy is the objective in life; and GROWTH, because growth is the result of life.[114] So, let's explore each of your core instincts, beginning with your primary instinct of desire, and how each serves as a catalyst for the next, thus ensuring the continual flow of energy.

Desire: the Catalyst That Expands Creation

Why are millions of dollars spent on lotteries?

Why do multimillion-dollar lawsuits abound?

Why are gambling establishments becoming more and more prevalent?

Why do people commit crimes?

WHY? WHY? WHY?

Because an all-pervasive misguided belief of enormous proportion permeates humanity: There is not enough. This belief compels us to seek freedom from that which we perceive as imprisoning us. And what do we believe will release us from our prisons? $MONEY$!!! Most of us believe that our lives would be far different if we had an abundance of money. We believe that money is our ticket to security, freedom, and joy; that we will magically feel powerful and happy when we have money! *"Whew! The struggle is finally over."*

You, too, may believe that an abundance of money will magically eliminate your fears of not having enough and then you will be happy, safe, and secure! However, do not confuse money with desire, for desire, on any level — emotional, spiritual, physical, or mental — is the catalyst that *summons* life energy and without it your existence would be short-lived.

> *Desire is the beginning of all creation.*[115]
> — NEALE DONALD WALSCH
> *Conversations with God - Book 1*

Every child enters this world overflowing with innocent, unadulterated desire. And my ten-year-old son Zachary is no exception: he wants, wants, wants, and then wants more! And when he gets what he wants, it holds his interest briefly and then he wants something else. Is he bad or spoiled rotten? No, he is not! (well, maybe a little…). He is pure in his essence and still relatively free from the influence of the outside world dictating the old-paradigm 'facts' of life. He, and *every child*, knows instinctively that desire summons life energy to them.

Not one of us lacks for desire. We believe that we would feel better if we had more money, so we desire money. We believe that we would feel better if our partner changed in some way, so we want them to change. We believe that we would feel better if we had a better job, so we desire a new job. We believe that we would feel better if we were in perfect health, so we desire health. We believe that we would feel better if we lost weight, so we desire to lose weight. In fact, we believe that we would feel better if there was an end to all poverty, war, pestilence, or if our world would just change in some way. However, it is not the world's responsibility to change to accommodate our desires, for each of us has a different opinion of how life should be lived. Our job is to simply choose what we wish to experience from the vast array of options that life presents.

Have you ever experienced a feeling of passion or eagerness flow through your body when you had an idea? Your idea was spawned from desire and the feeling of passion that you experienced was the flow of life energy. Desire is the most essential aspect of life because desire fuels the engine of life! That is precisely why you get *excited* when you see something you desire — Angel is saying "YES!" (Isn't this exciting?)

*Desire is the magnetic energy that attracts the Light and
the essence of the Light is Love.*[116]

CEANNE DeROHAN
as conveyed in *The Right Use of Will*

Were you taught that it is wrong to want? Or that it is virtuous to *not*
want? If you 'marinated' in those beliefs, you may initially find it
challenging to accept that desire is appropriate because you have been
programmed to *not* desire. Therefore, you have a few red circuits that
must now be dealt with.

*All through your life you have been made to feel guilty
about The Things You Want Most. Yet I tell you this:
love, love, love, the things you desire — for your love of
them draws them to you. These things are the stuff of
life. When you love them, you love life! When you
declare that you desire them, you announce that you
choose all the good that life has to offer!*[117]
— NEALE DONALD WALSCH
Conversations with God - Book 2

*The stoical scheme of supplying our wants by lopping off
our desires, is like cutting off our feet, when we want
shoes.*
— JONATHAN SWIFT
1667-1745

Desire Begets Joy and Joy Begets Desire

There is a dynamic relationship between desire and joy — one always
leads to the other, again, ensuring the continual flow of life energy.
Desire catalyzes the experience of joy because a state of joy, love,
passion, and eagerness is your natural state of being — the state of being
that you entered life in. However, your joyful state was soon
extinguished by your indoctrination into old-paradigm thinking. As a
result, the energy summoned by your desires was often restricted by
resistance — red circuits — the conflicting beliefs you acquired along
your journey. The result? A collision of energy — a collision that has
resulted in pain and distress. In your desire to abate your ill feelings and
find a solution to your quandaries, you wrongly assumed that only two
options were available: 1) To accept your feelings, or 2) To minimize or
suppress your desires. But, now you know that a third option exists: To
manifest what you desire by tuning in to its frequency.

Living backwards amid old paradigm beliefs, great quantities of energy are summoned through desire but impeded before anything is fulfilled. In fact, most orders are canceled prematurely — sabotaged, because of the conflict between belief and desire. However, to optimize your life experience it is necessary to utilize your desire as it is meant to be used: As your Point of Power from which to place an order with Angel. As you tune in to the frequency of what you have ordered, you align with the necessary energy which allows your desire to manifest. And as a result, you experience joy! Joy is the objective of life because joy catalyzes desire which summons life energy, again, ensuring the continuum of life.

The Eternal Quest for Freedom

At the core of your being, you realize that freedom is your natural birthright. Freedom provides you the foundation to experience joy and growth, therefore, you instinctively seek freedom. And if you're not experiencing freedom, Angel will intervene with an Angel-Alert, a wrong-way sign, because you're restricting the flow of life energy. Think back to your earlier days. Many of your adverse experiences were the result of someone or something interfering with your freedom, as life in the old-paradigm is rampant with experiences that obstruct freedom.

In your quest for freedom you will instinctively desire money, for money buys freedom — freedom from stress, freedom to travel, freedom to be with your family or friends, freedom to accomplish your Mission, freedom to grow spiritually. Is it *wrong* to want an abundance of money? *No, it is not.* (Don't you just love this?) For in reality, money is nothing more than the means to flow or exchange energy. And in order to exchange it, you've got to have it. Furthermore, *unless* you feel secure and free, it is exceedingly difficult to love and laugh, hence, live a life of joy and fulfillment. The continual flow of money creates an inner feeling of freedom and you are instinctively a *freedom-seeking being.*

> *Money is the sixth sense which enables you to enjoy the other five.*
> — W. SOMERSET MAUGHAM
> 1874-1965

> *Spiritual versus material are not the choices. Everything about life experience is spiritual. It is the end product of spirit. You have nothing to prove. Be the spiritual you and create like a physical fiend.*[118]
> — ESTHER and JERRY HICKS

Money is the symbol of everything that is necessary for man's wellbeing and happiness. Money means freedom, independence, liberty. — EDWARD E. BEALS

The more pleasure you give yourself, the more pleasure you can give to another. Likewise, if you give yourself the pleasure of power, you have more power to share with others. The same is true of fame, wealth, glory, success, or anything else which makes you feel good.[119]
— NEALE DONALD WALSCH
Conversations with God - Book 2

A feast is made for laughter, and wine maketh merry: but money answereth all things. — THE BIBLE
The Book of Ecclesiastes 10:19

Money alone sets all the world in motion. — MAXIM
425 BC

Money is the root of all good. — RUDOLPH WANDERONE

It's a kind of spiritual snobbery that makes people think they can be happy without money. — ALBERT CAMUS
1913-1960

No one would remember the Good Samaritan if he only had good intentions. He had money as well.
— MARGARET THATCHER

Growth: The Expansion of Life

The experience of joy catalyzes growth. How? The fulfillment of each of your orders results in joy. With each new experience, you acquire new information that expands your awareness. The result? Growth. Your new perspective then impels you to instinctively desire something more, because you desire to feel *more* joy — it's a feeling you can't get enough of. It's the cycle of creation "doing it's thing," ensuring the continual flow of energy. However, a common repercussion of living in the old paradigm is the tendency to grow complacent — to become a creature of habit — a 'couch potato.' Why? Because of fear. You may have finally attained a level of security and want to "kick back." However, if you become best friends with your sofa, you will invariably get in trouble, for you then hinder growth — an aspect of life that you cannot repress.

When life is lived from a standpoint of damage control or
optimum advantage, the true benefit of life is forfeited.
The opportunity is lost. The chance is missed. For a life
lived thusly is a life lived from fear.[120]
— NEALE DONALD WALSCH
Conversations with God - Book 1

Another consequence of old-paradigm thinking that deters growth? Living in anticipation of some future event that will bring happiness. And once more, you need not "worry" about suffering from this misunderstanding, for Angel will transmit an Angel-Alert to you in the form of restlessness — a wrong-way sign alerting you of your error. So, if you convince yourself, or let others convince you to be "content" with what you have (including all your problems — *"After all, there are a lot of folks with problems much worse than yours!"* [that's meant to be sarcastic]), you will be deterred from having new experiences, hence, growing, which restricts the flow of life energy. Growth is essential to life, because growth catalyzes the expansion of life.

Custom is the plague of wise men and the idol of fools.
— THOMAS FULLER
1608-1661

I still lived in the future — a habit which is the death of
happiness. — QUENTIN CRISP

Good behavior is the last refuge of mediocrity.
— HENRY S. HASKINS

Your Core Instincts Form a Never-Ending Circle Ensuring the Continuum of Life

Dreams pass into the reality of action. From the action
stems the dream again; and this interdependence
produces the highest form of living. —ANÄIS NIN
1903-1977

Because many people feel unworthy at their core, they think it is virtuous to live their life focused solely on growth to the exclusion of joy. They believe, quite literally, in the saying: "No pain, no gain." However, if you focus on *joy* as your first priority, you will automatically be led to freedom and growth because your core instincts form a never-ending circle with one always leading to the other. They are perfectly balanced with joy being the objective of life, so that when you don't focus on joy, your core instincts will become unbalanced. Growth is always the natural outcome of joy.[121] So enjoy, enjoy, enjoy — it's natural, normal, instinctive, and energy-summoning, thus life-giving.

Your Path and core instincts are synchronized, therefore when you utilize your wrong-way signs as they are meant to be utilized, you can employ the Four-Step Formula and order what you want in life. You can then live your life the way it is *meant* to be lived — loving and laughing all along your merry way. Sound good?

Self-Denial versus Self-Regulation

[D]on't seek to force your evolution — to evolve further, faster — by denying what feels good, or stepping away from it. Self-denial is self-destruction. Yet also know this, self-regulation is not self-denial. Regulating one's behavior is an active choice to do or not do something based on one's decision regarding who they are.[122]

— NEALE DONALD WALSCH
Conversations with God - Book 2

Your primary instinct of desire has many nuances, so before raping and pillaging under the guise of "contributing to the expansion of energy," let's explore the concept of self-regulation using the example of sexual attraction. You may find yourself sexually attracted to someone but are in a committed relationship that may have grown stale. Rather than acting on your feelings and walking into a potential nightmare, stop for a moment and ponder the ramifications of such a liaison. Would you be hurting someone you love? Do you care? Take a moment and think about Who You Choose To Be. Choosing *not* to pursue that relationship is an example of self-regulation as opposed to self-denial. It is acting consciously. To utilize this opportunity as a Point of Power to create what you want, ask yourself what was appealing in this other person that is lacking in your present relationship, and place an order. Or perhaps you can utilize this experience to examine your repressed emotions that may be amplifying your desire for an altogether different relationship. Again, only you know in your heart what is right for you.

It's Never Too Late to Live Life
and Never Too Late to Change One

Some people die at twenty-five and aren't buried until they are seventy-five.   — BENJAMIN FRANKLIN
1760-1790

It's never too late — in fiction or in life — to revise.
— NANCY THAYER

It's never to late to be what you might have been.
— GEORGE ELIOT
1819-1880
Pseudonym of Marian Evans

Death is not the greatest loss in life. The greatest loss is what dies inside us while we live.   — NORMAN COUSINS
1915-1990

Desire is instinctive, it never ceases. You cannot stifle it. People simply learn to extinguish their desire, thus squandering an optimal life experience. Have you noticed that as people grow older, they seem to lack energy, passion, and an eagerness for life? With each passing year trapped in old-paradigm programming, most folks develop the tendency to extinguish their desire to experience new and wonderful things. They accept the beliefs that others have passed down from generation to generation. They tell themselves they are too old — whether they are in their thirties, forties, fifties, or older. They believe it is appropriate to behave only in certain restrained ways. They convince themselves that they don't have enough money, that their health is frail — they might get hurt. They observe others undergoing the aging process and accept it as their destiny. The result? Their powerful beliefs become self-fulfilling prophecies. For each self-defeating belief restricts life-giving, life-sustaining energy. However, if they can find the courage to step outside of their comfort zones and be Who They *Really* Are; if they can acknowledge the *true* purpose of desire — to provide life energy — they can reignite their passion and live long, healthy, and abundant lives *regardless* of their age. The Point of Power for each of us is in the present moment — Now — the moment we choose to place an order for what we desire. And each of us holds the power to transcend any old-paradigm belief and transform our lives.

The Story of Rose

One of the most beautiful aspects of email is that people share meaningful stories with one another — stories that touch our hearts. The following story will, I'm sure, touch your heart as it did mine. It vividly illustrates that it's never too late for anything in life.

The first day of school our professor introduced himself and challenged us to get to know someone we didn't already know. I stood up to look around when a gentle hand touched my shoulder. I turned around to find a wrinkled little old lady beaming up at me with a smile that lit up her entire being. She said, "Hi handsome. My name is Rose. I'm eighty-seven years old. Can I give you a hug?" I laughed and enthusiastically responded, "Of course you may!" and she gave me a giant squeeze. "Why are you in college at such a young, innocent age?" I asked. She jokingly replied, "I'm here to meet a rich husband, get married, have a couple of children, and then retire and travel." "No seriously," I asked. I was curious what may have motivated her to be taking on this challenge at her age. "I always dreamed of having a college education and now I'm getting one!" she told me. After class we walked to the student union building and shared a chocolate milkshake. We became instant friends. Every day for the next three months we would leave class together and talk nonstop. I was always mesmerized listening to this "time machine" as she shared her wisdom and experience with me. Over the course of the year, Rose became a campus icon and easily made friends wherever she went. She loved to dress up and she reveled in the attention bestowed upon her from the other students. She was living it up. At the end of the semester we invited Rose to speak at our football banquet and I'll never forget what she taught us. She was introduced and stepped up to the podium. As she began to deliver her prepared speech, she dropped her 3 by 5 cards on the floor. Frustrated and a little embarrassed, she leaned into the microphone and simply said "I'm sorry I'm so jittery. I gave up beer for Lent and this whiskey is killing me! I'll never get my speech back in order so let me just tell you what I know." As we laughed, she cleared her throat and began: "We do not stop playing because we are old, we grow old because we stop playing. There are only four secrets to staying young, being happy, and achieving success. You have to laugh and find humor every day. You've got to have a dream. When you lose your dreams, you die. We have so many people walking around who are dead and don't even know it! There is a huge difference between growing older and growing up. If you are nineteen years old and lie in bed for one full year and don't do one productive thing, you will turn twenty years old. If I am eighty-seven years old and stay in bed for a year and never do anything, I will turn eighty-eight. Anybody can grow older. That doesn't take any talent or ability. The idea is to grow up by always finding the opportunity in change. Have no regrets. The elderly usually don't have regrets for what we did, but rather for things we did not do. The only people who fear death are those with regrets." She concluded her speech by courageously singing "The Rose." She challenged us to study the lyrics and live them out in our daily lives. At the year's end Rose finished the college degree she had begun all those years ago. One week after graduation Rose died peacefully in her sleep. Over two thousand college students attended her funeral in tribute to the wonderful woman who taught by example that it's never too late to be all that you can possibly be.

— UNKNOWN

The perfection of life is all around you. Everything has been brilliantly orchestrated for you to reap in an abundance of joy, love, fulfillment, and beauty, if you are privy to the principles underlying life experience and apply them.

To be or not to be: That is the question.
— WILLIAM SHAKESPEARE
1564-1616

Now that you have a broader perspective of how life really operates, take a moment and ponder life in the new paradigm where you know and understand how to navigate through the twists and turns that life presents; where you conceive of something you desire, place your order, take inspired action from your Angacles, and then experience what you desired! Fun, huh? The cycle of creation ensures that there is never an end to desire, hence; never an end to creation. Our task is to now expand creation *consciously* and live life as it was intended: loving, laughing, and joyfully creating along our merry paths. ☺

On The Wings of Love

Just smile for me and let the day begin
You are the sunshine that lights my heart within.
And I'm sure that you're an Angel in disguise.
Come take my hand and together we will ride.
On the wings of love
up and above the clouds, the only way to fly
is on the wings of love
On the wings of love only the two of us together flying high
Flying high upon the wings of love
Yes, you belong to me
and I'm yours exclusively.
And right now we live and breathe each other.
Inseparable it seems, we're flowing like a stream running free
traveling on the wings of love.
You look at me and I begin to melt
Just like the snow, when a ray of sun is felt.
And I'm crazy 'bout you baby, can't you see?
I'd be so delighted if you would come with me.
On the wings of love
up and above the clouds, the only way to fly
is on the wings of love
On the wings of love only the two of us together flying high
Flying high upon the wings of love.[123]

Words by Jeffrey Osborne

Your Feelings: Your Greatest Allies

The soul speaks to you in feelings. Listen to your feelings.
Follow your feelings. Honor your feelings.[124]
— NEALE DONALD WALSCH
Conversations with God - Book 2

By going along with your feelings you unify your
emotional, mental and bodily state. When you try to fight
or deny them, you divorce yourself from the reality of
your being.[125]
— JANE ROBERTS
The Nature of Personal Reality - A Seth Book

Feeling good is your way of telling yourself that your last
thought was truth, that your last word was wisdom, that
your last action was love.[126]
— NEALE DONALD WALSCH
Conversations with God - Book 2

Discomfort is aroused only to bring the need for
correction into awareness.[127]
— A COURSE IN MIRACLES®

Feelings, nothing more than feelings…. (remember the song?) They are
nothing more than that. Not right. Not wrong. Not good. Not bad.
Feelings are innocent, neutral. And their sole purpose is to guide you
along your Path in life, for your feelings are the language of your soul.
However, in order for them to guide you, you must be able to identify
and express them — a problem for some of us.

I recall a time when I was in my mid-thirties and recently divorced. I was
in the middle of a session with my therapist recounting some injustice
when she abruptly stopped me in the middle of my discourse and asked,

"Lauren, what are you feeling?" Well I didn't have a clue. I had never pursued the subject of 'feelings' before, so I replied, "I don't know. But if you could give me a list of feelings, perhaps I could identify one and let you know." That moment was an epiphany for me — a *'aha'* moment. I was so disconnected from my feelings that I couldn't even identify what I was feeling. I was a product of old-paradigm thinking.

I believe that many of us are divorced from our feelings. In our early indoctrination to life, the subject of 'feelings' was never broached. Not intentionally; it was just that no one was aware of their purpose and importance. Consequently, when we experience negative feelings, we often stifle them, deny them, ignore them, hide from them, suppress them, or try to substitute good feelings for those that are bad. In fact, we actually consider some to be wrong, bad, shameful, beneath us, not in sync with who we think we are, or even evil. We have become so afraid of facing the possibility of something unpleasant that far too often we try to make our feelings nonexistent. And therein lies the problem, for as we alienate ourselves from our feelings, repressing them rather than expressing them, we create red circuit after red circuit and as a result, magnetize more and more problems in our lives. For our feelings are guiding us along our Path. They are our own personal truth.

> *Do not tell yourself automatically that [negative feelings] are wrong, however, and then try to apply a "positive" belief like a bandaid....It is silly to try to fight what you think of as negative beliefs, or to be frightened of them. They are not mysterious. You may find that many served good purposes at one time, and that they have simply been overemphasized. They may need to be restructured rather than denied....It is very important then that you understand the true innocence of all feelings, for each of them, if left alone and followed will lead you back to the reality of love.*[128]
> — JANE ROBERTS
> The Nature of Personal Reality - A Seth Book

> *Toxic niceness is what happens to us after we internalize the "Nicely" family. Toxic Niceness is like yeast. Yeast causes dough to become nice and light. Toxic niceness causes us to try and make life nice and light. For everyone else. We who suffer from Toxic Niceness work hard to make things a little sweeter, using our own personal "sugar" to make lemonade out of life's lemons. Far too often, this is achieved at a terrible cost to ourselves.*[129]
> — ELIZABETH HILTS

The "Place"

When you pretend not to hear your wrong-way signs or fail to act on them, the frequencies of your denied feelings will be present in your energy field. Impeding this flow of energy is somewhat like allowing pressure to build up inside a pressure cooker: If you fail to remove the pot from the flame, or to gradually release some of the pressure inside, sooner or later the pot will explode. Restricting the flow of energy causes it to increase in power and accumulate where it will seek an outlet — a path of least resistance — and manifest. How does it manifest? In the same way that any order manifests. An Angacle will appear — a person, event, or circumstance — evidence of your powerful thoughts. This Angacle, in sync with the frequency of your bad feeling, will amplify those feelings to the degree that it may push your button and usher you into the 'place' — the negative energy vortex that can erupt and surge forth like a broken dam. This is a 'place' you don't want to go.

Anyone can become engulfed in this powerful vortex of negative energy when they feel strong negative emotion because they are unwittingly aligned with its frequency. And when a match occurs, watch out, for this powerful energy is capable of accelerating and fueling negative reactions.

Do you recall the Rodney King incident? Mr. King was a man in Los Angeles suspected of committing a crime. When police officers captured him, they beat him savagely. Although the policemen were unaware, this beating was videotaped by a witness and aired on TV countless times. (It was alleged that only a portion of the tape was aired and that Mr. King, under the influence of drugs, actually incited the police officers by aggressively resisting them.) Nevertheless, only the portion of the videotape where Mr. King was beaten was aired. Consequently, anyone who tuned in to the TV news witnessed this beating over and over again. (Those police officers were clearly in the 'place.' A telltale sign? With every blow they struck, their rage escalated.) Each time I observed this beating, I would physically cringe until I could bear no more. (Angel-Alert.) During the trial of these police officers most people believed that unless our judicial system was completely corrupt, there was no way that these officers could escape conviction. *From the footage aired*, their guilt appeared blatant and clear. How could anyone justify the rage demonstrated in that beating! As a result of the vast media coverage, emotions were inflamed in many who had also experienced injustice in their lives, especially to *that* extreme. Therefore, these people eagerly anticipated vengeance — retaliation — in the form of a conviction. Consequently, when the *not guilty* verdict was announced, buttons were pushed on some people in Los Angeles — buttons that accessed the 'place' where they, too, had an accumulation of denied, repressed, unhealed emotions. The result? All hell broke loose. These people committed unthinkable acts of violence, in fact, they nearly murdered innocent bystanders.

> Violence is the last resort of repressed Will. Repression of the Will's expression creates violence.[130]
> — CEANNE DeROHAN
> as conveyed in The Right Use of Will

I believe this example powerfully demonstrates the power and magnitude of group consciousness where people can become so intoxicated by the hysteria of the potent group energy — the formidable energy vortex of the 'place' — that they are capable of committing atrocities that defy Who They Really Are.

Is this reason enough to vent your emotions as they arise and stay connected to Angel? I hope so, for this is the same repressed rage that incites war and commits murder.

Consider the Gulf War for a moment. To justify sending our sons and daughters to a foreign land to defend the freedom of others, it was necessary for our government to elicit the support of the American people, wasn't it? The folks we were protecting, however, were those who may have had a great negotiating ploy — oil — to bait the United States into fighting their battle. Our government, armed with an arsenal of sophisticated technology, possessed the power to manipulate us — the American mass consciousness — through the media, demonstrated quite effectively in the movie Wag the Dog. As our televisions projected images and reports of atrocities, such as Iraqi soldiers marching into hospitals and cutting off the life support systems for helpless little babies, our collective emotions were tapped, our buttons pushed, were they not? How did you feel as you observed those horrors and atrocities? Our emotions were so cunningly manipulated that our rage was fueled to the extent that many Americans wanted to 'nuke' the entire country of Iraq! We surmised that something had to be inherently wrong with a culture capable of killing babies! (Of course, we conveniently forgot what we did in the Vietnamese Me Lai Massacre — yet another striking example of the power of the 'place.') As person after person focused their powerful thoughts on the atrocities committed and shared their negative feelings with others, enough support, enough rage, was garnered to justify going to war.

Now I do not profess to have a clue about the real truth in the preceding illustration. I am merely asking you to consider this possibility. My point? Was your button pushed? Were you momentarily engulfed in the powerful energy of the 'place'? And, more importantly, can you see just how easy it could be to be pulled into the 'place'?

How to Redirect the Negative Energy of "The Place"

[T]he expression of normal aggression prevents the build up of anger into hatred.[131] — JANE ROBERTS
The Nature of Personal Reality - A Seth Book

How can you help to dissipate the energy of this powerful negative energy vortex? Pay attention to your feelings. Author Jane Roberts tells us "that normal aggressiveness is basically a natural kind of communication... a way of letting another person know that in your terms, they have transgressed, and therefore, a method of *preventing* violence — not *causing* it."[132] "A frown is a natural method of communication saying 'You have upset me,' or, 'I am upset.' If you tell yourself to smile when you feel like scowling, then you are tampering with your natural expression *and* denying to another person a legitimate communication that tells how you feel."[133] The consequence? Rather than maintaining an authentic relationship with this other person, you will instead project a frequency of resentment — the true feeling in your heart — which will result in future negative interactions. Therefore, it is imperative to understand the *benefit* of all emotions, including anger.

Anger repressed can poison a relationship as surely as the cruelest words. — JOYCE BROTHERS

When you allow your emotions their natural sponta-neous flow they will never engulf you, and always return you refreshed to "logical" conscious-mind thought.[134] — JANE ROBERTS
The Nature of Personal Reality - A Seth Book

Clear Communication Provides the Essence of Understanding

You may have encountered a situation where someone hurt your feelings, but you never said anything because you didn't want to hurt their feelings. You may have been afraid that your response would be seen as inappropriate, even though the incident was one where the sharing of your feelings may have been understood. In failing to share your true feelings, however, they would simply grow larger and magnetize more evidence. And on the next occasion that this person rubs you wrong, you might explode for no *apparent* reason, and the other person will have no idea why you reacted with such hostility and be deeply hurt. As a result, you will feel guilty and further reinforce the idea that you did something wrong. The result? You create a vicious circle where no one wins. You wrongly conclude that the venting of your feelings brought about the disaster, impelling you to, once again, repress them. What's the way out of this vicious circle?

Acknowledge Your Feelings

Feelings are a Divine and necessary part of man and woman. Feelings expressing as emotions open them to receive the Light. Holding emotions because they are judged unacceptable creates resistance to Light.[135]

— CEANNE DEROHAN
as conveyed in *The Right Use of Will*

Listen to your feelings. Listen to your highest thoughts. Listen to your experience. Whenever any of these differ from what you've been told by your teachers, or read in your books, forget the words. Words are the least reliable purveyor of Truth.[136]

— NEALE DONALD WALSCH
Conversations with God - Book 1

Old-paradigm programming is rampant in second-hand rumors, manipulation, and control, where few express their true feelings. Because nothing is out in the open or directly experienced, you have probably acquired the habit of not expressing your feelings. However, to fully embody your authentic power, you must acknowledge your feelings, for they are guiding you through life. In fact, the greatest peril lies in pretending your feelings out of existence, because problems can only occur when feelings are unexpressed, ignored, or denied. Therefore, it is important to understand that you can express feelings quite safely and naturally in everyday life, just not in a destructive way.

How do you respond in an authentic manner when someone rubs you wrong? It is best to prepare yourself in advance. Predetermine a response and then practice role-playing. This strategy will enable you to maintain your center and not be caught off guard. Furthermore, it's not necessary to share your negative feelings with someone that you feel might *deserve* to hear them. It is, however, important that you vent them. For if you don't, they will create red circuits and you will simply experience *more* of the same type of negative experiences.

Your feelings will never get you in "trouble" because your feelings are your truth.[137]

— NEALE DONALD WALSCH
Conversations with God - Book 1

If you feel filled with rage, then do not say "I am filled with peace" and expect results. You will only be blanketing your feelings and inhibiting your energy and power. If you are furious, then beat a pillow and experience the rage, but without violence to another. Work it through until you are physically exhausted. If you do this honestly, the reasons for the fury will come to you, and they will often be quite obvious. You simply did not want to face them.[138] — JANE ROBERTS

The Nature of Personal Reality - A Seth Book

In *Conversations with God - Book 1*, Neale Donald Walsch conveys

Yes, the things that others think, say or do, will sometimes hurt you — until they don't anymore. What will get you from here to there more quickly is total honesty — being willing to assert, acknowledge and declare exactly how you feel about a thing. Say your truth — kindly, but fully and completely. Live your truth, gently, but totally and consistently. Change your truth easily and quickly when your experience brings you new clarity.[139]

∿　∿　∿

And so there are things you can do when you react in pain and hurt to what another is being, saying or doing. The first is to admit honestly to yourself and to another exactly how you are feeling. This many of you are afraid to do because you think it will make you "look bad." But you can't help it. You still feel that way. There is only one thing you can do. You must honor your feelings. For honoring your feelings means honoring yourself. And you must love your neighbor as you love yourself. How can you expect to understand and honor the feelings of another if you cannot honor the feelings within yourself? The first question in any interactive process is: now Who Am I, and Who Do I want to be in relationship to that? Often you do not remember who you are, and do not know who you want to be until you try out a few ways of being. That is why honoring your truest feelings is so important. If your first feeling is a negative feeling, simply having the feeling is frequently all that is needed to step away from it. It is when you have the anger, have the upset, have the disgust, have the rage, own the feeling of wanting to hurt back, that you can disown these first feelings as "not who you do want to be."[140]

There is no need for brutal honesty with anyone. Ask yourself, if you were to share your feelings with another, would they feel larger or smaller? Good or bad? Would you shame or humiliate them? Only let someone know how you feel if failing to do so would compromise your integrity or cause another person to believe something untrue about you. And if you share your feelings, always share them with love, clarity, sensitivity, compassion, and courage.[141] Remember, you created the red circuit, so utilize this opportunity and ask yourself, "How did I create this experience? What is it that I want in this moment? What is the opportunity I have here?"

Children Can Become an Outlet For Unexpressed Negative Emotions

If you fail to express your negative emotions and instead attempt to impersonate *"The Beaver Cleaver Family,"* you will set the stage for disaster. For the accumulated energy of your feelings will eventually find an outlet somewhere. As the law of conservation attests: "Energy cannot be created nor destroyed." And oftentimes this accumulation of energy surfaces in a child's behavior. We have all heard stories about some maniacal child: a 'bad seed' from a 'good home' killing a number of innocent people for no apparent logical reason. The key word in these instances is 'good.' How do we define the word 'good?' Unfortunately, in our misunderstanding of emotion and energy, far too often our definition of a good home is one where people do not express negative emotion —one where no healthy outlet is available to vent this very real accumulation of energy. More than likely, this maniacal child was raised in a home with repressed emotions, as many parents feel that an environment where negativity is stifled is the optimal environment in which to live or raise a child. However, children telepathically pick up on the undercurrent of suppressed emotion and can assume the red circuits — the pent-up energy, i.e., denied frequencies — that their parents are avoiding. The consequence? The child bottles up this accumulated energy and becomes a ticking time-bomb ready to explode when his or her button is pushed.

> Many who unexpectedly commit great crimes, sudden murders, even bringing about mass death, have a history of docility and conventional attitudes, and were considered 'models,' in fact, of deportment. All natural aggressive elements were denied in their natures and any evidence of momentary hatred was considered evil or

wrong. As a result such individuals find it difficult, finally, to express the most normal denial, or to go against their given code of conventionality and respect. They cannot communicate...with their fellow men as far as the expression of a disagreement is concerned. Psychologically, only a massive explosion can free them. They feel so powerless that this adds to their difficulties — so they try to liberate themselves by showing great power in terms of violence.[142]
— JANE ROBERTS
The Nature of Personal Reality - A Seth Book

Negativity is Essential in Life

No feeling brings you to a dead end. It is in **motion,** *and that always leads into another feeling...Your emotions will always lead you into a realization of your beliefs if you do not impede them.*[143]
— JANE ROBERTS
The Nature of Personal Reality - A Seth Book

The reality of life is that there will always be negative aspects within it. Opposites, or polarity, are essential in giving birth to desire — desire necessary to summon life energy and sustain life. And more importantly, what you perceive as negative may not be perceived as negative by another person. So if we attempt to do away with the negative, we also do away with the choices. As you begin to understand the *true* purpose of your negative feelings and utilize them, you will begin to appreciate the guidance they are offering, the clarity to determine what you want.

Do not underestimate your importance in the 'big picture.' When you learn to express your true feelings and deal with your negative emotions in a positive manner by dissecting them and redirecting their energy, you will project an entirely different frequency. When you listen within and align with Angel, you will discover a new sense of empowerment; one where you finally feel free; free to be Who You Really Are. You will also find that the more you live your truth, the more love you will feel for yourself. And as an added bonus, you will magnetize more appreciation and less criticism from others! Being the *authentic you* will become easier and easier as you become more and more conscious and you will find that it is really the only safe way to be.

Let's now explore the limitations you may have thought were obstacles on your Path, for those beliefs have formed the bars of a prison cell — a self-imposed prison. Your task is to now banish their illusory power so you can get on with your real task: living, loving, and laughing! ☺

What Are You Doing
For the Rest of Your Life?

What are you doing for the rest of your life?
North and south and east and west of your life.
I have only one request of your life.
That you spend it all with Me.
All the seasons and the times of your days,
All the nickels and the dimes of your days,
Let the reasons and the rhymes of your days
all begin and end with Me.
I want to see your face in every kind of light;
In fields of flowers and forests of the night.
And when you stand before the candles on a cake,
Oh let Me be the one who hears the silent wish you make.
Those tomorrow waiting deep in your eyes,
In the world of love you keep in your eyes,
I'll awaken what's asleep in your eyes,
It may take a kiss or two.
Through all of my life,
Summer, winter, spring and fall of my life,
All I ever will recall of my life, is all my life with you.[144]

Words by Alan and Marilyn Bergman

Get Out of Prison, Pass Go, and Collect $200 (or maybe $2 Million!)

Help! I'm being held prisoner by my heredity and environment!
— DENNIS ALLEN

It is only when people begin to shake loose from their preconceptions, from the ideas that have dominated them, that we begin to receive a sense of opening, a sense of vision.
— DAME BARBARA MARY WARD
1914-1981

When you do not embrace this conscious knowledge, but refuse it, you are not using one of the finest "tools" ever created...and you are to a large extent denying your birthright and heritage.[145]
— JANE ROBERTS
The Nature of Personal Reality - A Seth Book

For most of your life you've lived at the effect of your experiences. Now, you're invited to be the cause of them. That is what is known as conscious living. That is what is called walking in awareness.[146]
— NEALE DONALD WALSCH
Conversations with God - Book 1

Where there is an open mind, there will always be a frontier.
— CHARLES F. KETTERING
1876-1958

And the day came when the risk to remain tight in the bud was more painful than the risk it took to blossom.
—ANAÏS NIN
1903-1977

We project our future using the ingredients of our past.
— JERRY ANDERSON

Insanity is doing the same things over and over again, and expecting different results. — UNKNOWN

Be thine own palace or the world's thy jail.
— JOHN DENVER

It's Natural and Logical to Acquiesce to Old Paradigm Thinking

When you were born, you were not given a set of instructions or "Rules of Life" manual. No one really knew where you came from, where you were going, or what you were supposed to do while you were here. You entered a strange environment — essentially blindfolded — and had *no idea* what to expect. Scary thought, right? And because you were born in the midst of certain mass beliefs, it was natural to conform to them. To avoid the dreadful feelings of loneliness and exclusion, you mimicked the prevailing behaviors of others, for conformity provided safety and security. And although what you conformed to didn't always feel *good*, it felt *safe* because it was considered "acceptable" behavior. Driven by your core instinct to seek joy, you sought a life as far from the 'bad stuff' as possible and attempted to find as much 'good stuff' as possible. As a result, old-paradigm thinking became natural — your comfort zone — and the frequencies most familiar to you.

As you now know, your comfort zone was not created in awareness or based on conscious choice. It was built *unconsciously* as a result of misguided old-paradigm beliefs which, in reality, had no substance because they were conceived from a fundamental misunderstanding of how life operates. Nevertheless, your comfort zone has become familiar and provides you with an illusion of safety and security — however dysfunctional your life may be. And in reality, you probably didn't even know that you *had* a comfort zone, much less what it was based on. You simply went along with the 'program' like everyone else and tried to make the best out of what life handed to you. The time has come, however, to reconsider many aspects of life.

It's Time To Be All That You Can Be

(and you don't need to join the Army...)

Believe it or not, when you were born, you did not receive the prison sentence of "Life with hard labor." So, if there is any aspect of your life that you are dissatisfied with, your dissatisfaction exists for one reason: You have acquired a red circuit that was created by a belief you hold. Your red circuits have become bars on a *self-created* prison cell — masquerading as your comfort zone — imprisoning you in the reality that you are now living. But only you can decide whether to ramble along day after day and follow the paths of others or to blaze your own trail. It is solely your responsibility to decide if you have experienced enough adversity and want more of life than the *occasional* fun moment.

If you are not getting all the 'good stuff' in life, it's time to examine your comfort zone. And if that sounds like a formidable task, I have simplified and organized the process in Section IV: "The Past." There you will uncover and determine which of your beliefs reflect who you choose to be and which do not. If you choose to do the work required and are eager to experience the full potentialities of life, you can experience heights of elation, euphoria, clarity, and joy you never thought possible. So, are *you* ready to reassess your beliefs, reconstruct your comfort zone, and get out of prison?

> *So what is your intention now? Do you intend to prove your theory that life seldom brings you what you choose? Or do you intend to demonstrate Who You Are and Who I Am?*[147]
> — NEALE DONALD WALSCH
> *Conversations with God - Book 1*

> *Hell... is the experience of the worst possible outcomes of your choices, decisions, and creations... it is the pain you suffer through wrong thinking. It is the opposite of joy. It is unfulfillment. It is knowing Who and What You Are, and failing to experience that. It is being less. That is hell, and there is none greater for your soul. All that it takes to get out of hell — to get out of not knowing — is to know again.*[148]
> — NEALE DONALD WALSCH
> *Conversations with God - Book 1*

> *God offers to every mind its choice between Truth and repose. Take which you please — you can never have both.*
> — RALPH WALDO EMERSON
> 1803-1882

Do you want your life to truly take off? Then change your idea about it. And you.[149] — NEALE DONALD WALSCH
Conversations with God - Book 1

We are all at our core, perfect spiritual beings. Our natural state of being is perfect health, beauty, vitality and joy throughout our lives. There are no limits to all that we want. The only limits to having all that we want and deserve in life are our beliefs, based mostly on fear and a lack of understanding.[150] — SHAKTI GAWAIN

To be or not to be: That is the question.
— WILLIAM SHAKESPEARE

It only takes one person to change your life. You.
— RUTH CASEY

You are a creator. There is nothing worse...than to come forth into an environment of contrast [positive and negative] where desire is born easily, and not allow energy to flow to your desire. That is a true squandering of life.[151] — ESTHER and JERRY HICKS

There are no miracles, but simply the proper utilization of life energies that function according to cosmic law.
— RUTH MONTGOMERY

May each reader be now freed from the thing which has held him in bondage through the ages, standing between him and his own, and "know the truth which makes him free" — free to fulfill his destiny, to bring into manifestation the "Divine Design of his Life, Health, Wealth, Love and Perfect Self-Expression." "Be ye transformed by the renewing of your mind."[152]
— FLORENCE SCOVEL SHINN
1871-1940

Now that you realize that your beliefs are the only obstacles standing in the way of your happiness, you can begin the process of reassessing them. But before beginning the reconstruction of your comfort zone, let's examine the state of being in our world today to better define the issues and problems created as a result of not understanding our power or the Four-Step Formula. This information will provide you with a broader, more thorough perspective from which to create both your new life and our new world so you can begin to live as life is meant to be lived — truly living, loving, and laughing! ✸

Part III

The Present

EXPLORING CURRENT REALITY
PERSONALLY AND GLOBALLY

PART III

The Present

EXPLORING CURRENT REALITY
PERSONALLY AND GLOBALLY

The Messes We Created On Planet Earth

The sheer beauty of our planet surprised me. It was a huge pearl, set in spangled ebony. It was nacreous, it was opal. No, it was far more lovely than any jewel. Its patterned coloring was more subtle, more ethereal. It displayed the delicacy and brilliance, the intricacy and harmony of a live thing.
— OLAF STAPLEDON
1886-1950

The Earth is like a spaceship that didn't come with an operating manual.
— R. BUCKMINSTER FULLER
1895-1983

Earth is crammed with Heaven.
— ELIZABETH BARRETT BROWNING
1806-1961

We are wide-eyed in contemplating the possibility that life may exist elsewhere in the universe, but we wear blinders when contemplating the possibilities of life on earth.
— NORMAN COUSINS
1915-1990

Searching for Life in the Universe

For years, scientists have launched capsules into outer space in an effort to communicate with other forms of intelligent life. To give others a sense of life on Planet Earth, samples of our music, books, art, history, and photographs of humans were included in these capsules.

What would an intelligent being surmise if he/she/it observed everyday life on our planet? What *is* our general state of being? For the most part, not too wonderful, I hate to concede. Nonetheless, it is improving daily by many extraordinary people who are making significant silent contributions that are helping to create a better world.

There are men and women who make the world better just by being the kind of people they are. They have the gift of kindness or courage or loyalty or integrity. It really matters very little whether they are behind the wheel of a truck or running a business or bringing up a family. They teach the truth by living it. — JAMES A. GARFIELD

Before we can utilize the Four-Step Formula to find solutions to the problems we face today, we must first acknowledge their existence and identify what we don't want. For these negative circumstances are simply wrong-way signs pointing us in the direction of what we *do* want.

Problems, Problems, and More Problems

Life seemed hollow, and existence but a burden.
— MARK TWAIN
in *Tom Sawyer* 1835-1910

In *Living in the Light,* author Shakti Gawain tells us that, "The majority of people seem to exist predominantly in a state of negativity or quiet desperation." We go to extremes to hide our despair from ourselves and those around us. Author Marianne Williamson tells us that "We are so tired of feeling sad, that we pretend to be happy instead."[1] In order to deal with the various perils in life that are responsible for our sadness, negativity, and despair, we have come to believe that if we label them, understand them, overpower them, deny them, manipulate them, accept them, repress them, surrender to them, dialogue with them, appease them, or integrate them, *then* we will have the power to control and prevent them, or at least rationalize their existence. To make matters worse, we have been taught to problem-solve in the following manner: 1) to look at a problem and examine it, 2) project it into the future, 3) imagine all sorts of dire consequences, zooming in on the most pessimistic outcome and, 4) treat it as though it was fact. As we now know, those techniques only amplify the issues, rather than resolving them.

Let's begin to resolve our problems by first identifying them. Are you experiencing any of the following problems?

☐ Do you spend your days busily accomplishing tasks on your 'to do' list, yet feel frustrated at having accomplished very little?

☐ Do you feel stressed out and overwhelmed?

☐ Do you feel that you will never have enough of certain things in life?

☐ Do you have fun only on occasion?

☐ Do you feel discriminated against?

☐ Do you have an unrewarding job that encompasses the majority of your time, but is necessary so you have enough money to pay your bills?

☐ Have you been unable to visit the exquisite sites in our world?

☐ Do you tune into television for escape and entertainment and are instead bombarded with many reasons to fear living on our planet?

☐ Are you unhappy with your physical appearance?

☐ Are you unhappy with your life experience?

☐ Do you perceive what you don't agree with as a threat, the enemy, to be eradicated or pushed away?

☐ Do you feel powerless to find solutions to the many problems that you are exposed to daily?

☐ Have you attempted to deaden the pain of life by eating excessively, drinking excessively, being promiscuous, spending excessively, taking drugs, gambling, or committing crimes — escapes that temporarily filled the void you felt inside, but afterwards created guilt because of their consequences?

☐ Have you become so fearful of those who commit crimes that you have installed locks on your doors, bars on your windows, or a fence around your home in order to deter others from harming you or your family?

☐ Do you carry a gun in an effort to protect yourself, your family, or what you have worked so hard for?

☐ Have you had a relationship that started out fun and loving, but disintegrated into hatred, ambivalence, or divorce?

☐ Do you fear developing a horrible disease and dying a dreadful death?

- [ ] Do you feel an emptiness or loneliness within?

- [ ] Do you feel as though you have not found your true purpose in life?

- [ ] Do you yearn for something more?

- [ ] Are you living a life of poverty, barely existing from day to day?

- [ ] Do you feel that material life alone is not satisfying?

In the movie *The Wizard of Oz*, the scarecrow felt that if only he had a brain, then life would be better; the tin man felt that if only he had a heart, then life would be better; the lion felt that if only he had courage, then life would be better. Have you, too, felt that if only you had something, then life would be better?

- [ ] If only everyone felt as I did...

- [ ] If only I had a guaranteed wage...[2]

- [ ] If only we had different people in power...[2]

- [ ] If only I had more money...[2]

- [ ] If only I were more beautiful...[2]

- [ ] If only people treated me better...[2]

- [ ] If only I could lose weight...

Have you concluded that

- [ ] there isn't enough to go around?[3]

- [ ] life is suffering?[3]

- [ ] it is selfish to have abundance when others do not? [4]

- [ ] there is no growth or gain in life without pain?[3]

- [ ] you must work hard and sacrifice for everything you want? [3]

- [ ] you're unworthy and undeserving?[4]

- [ ] you've done bad things in your life and this is your punishment?[4]

- [ ] people are basically bad, selfish, cruel, stupid, or untrustworthy?[4]

☐ the world is an unsafe place?[4]

☐ you have to struggle to get your share because there is so little?[4]

☐ you have no control over anything in your life, you are at the mercy of what you get?

☐ money is the root of all evil?[4]

☐ money and spirituality cannot coexist?

☐ you are incapable?[5]

☐ you cannot trust yourself, others, or the world?[5]

☐ you need to be perfect and you're not?[5]

☐ life is a school of hard knocks where you learn and grow so you can go on to a better place when you die?

☐ you are powerless?.[5]

☐ you're not good enough?[5]

Do these statements reflect what you feel from time to time?

Unaware of our authentic power, none of us have known how to solve our problems, much less where they came from. We simply blamed them on someone else, on destiny, or on God's will, for we felt that there had to be a reason they occurred!

Our failure to recognize the correlation between our thoughts, words, actions, and life experiences, has spawned profound repercussions. Old-paradigm thinking has rendered us deaf to the truth. For when the answers to our age-old quest for truth are not yet scientifically explainable or accepted by our religions, far too often we respond with skepticism, uncertainty, and sometimes even a closed mind. However, the opportunity is once more before us: If we can now embrace our gift of the Four-Step Formula, we can receive the answers we are longing for and allow the door of love and laughter to open into our lives. How do we begin to make the transition into the new paradigm? By first shifting our consciousness — opening our minds. For a shift in consciousness allows our hearts to open and receive truth.

Let's now trace the origins of our skepticism by exploring the unfolding of our evolution. In doing so, we will discover how the domino-effect of our wrong turn led us down a path of destruction and misunderstanding — far, far away from living, loving, or laughing! ✪

The Windows of the World

The windows of the world are covered with rain,
Where is the sunshine we once knew?
Everybody knows when little children play
they need a sunny day to grow straight and tall.
Let the sun shine through.

The windows of the world are covered with rain,
When will those dark skies turn to blue?
Everybody knows when boys grow into men
they start to wonder when their country will call.
Let the sun shine through.

The windows of the world are covered with rain,
What is the whole world coming to?
Everybody knows when men cannot be friends
their quarrel often ends where some have to die.
Let the sun shine through.

The windows of the world are covered with rain,
There must be something we can do?
Everybody knows whenever rain appears it's really Angel tears.
How long must they cry?
Let the sun shine through.[6]

Words by Hal David – Music by Burt Bacharach

How We Took the Wrong Turn Long Ago

Or, How the Heck Did We Get into This Mess?

Life is a maze in which we take the wrong turning before we have learnt to walk. — CYRIL CONNOLLY
1903-1974

The greatest obstacle to discovery is not ignorance — it is the illusion of knowledge. — DANIEL J. BOORSTIN

I call that mind free which jealously guards its intellectual rights and powers, which calls no man master, which does not content itself whencesoever it may come, which receives new truth as an Angel from Heaven. — WILLIAM ELLERY CHANNING
1780-1842

To believe what has not occurred in history will not occur at all is to argue disbelief in the dignity of man. — MAHATMA GANDHI
1869-1948

The most fatal illusion is the settled point of view. Since life is growth and motion, a fixed point of view kills anybody who has one. — BROOKS ATKINSON
1894-1984

Education's purpose is to replace an empty mind with an open one.　　　　　　　　　　— MALCOLM FORBES
1919-1990

Education is the ability to listen to almost anything without losing your temper or your self-confidence.
　　　　　　　　　　— ROBERT FROST
1874-1963

The world is in the condition it's in because the world is full of sleepwalkers.[7]　　— NEALE DONALD WALSCH
Conversations with God - Book 1

Universities should be safe havens where ruthless examination of realities will not be distorted by the aim to please or inhibited by the risk of displeasure.
　　　　　　　　　　— KINGMAN BREWSTER
1919-1988

I believe that order is better than chaos, creation better than destruction. I prefer gentleness to violence, forgiveness to vendetta... I think knowledge is preferable to ignorance and I am sure human sympathy is more valuable than ideology... And I think we should remember we are a part of a great whole, for which convenience we call nature. All living things are our brothers and sisters.　　　　　— KENNETH CLARK
1903-1983

What we have to do is be forever curiously testing new opinions and courting new impressions. The important thing is to not stop questioning. Curiosity has its own reason for existing. One cannot help but be in awe when he contemplates the mysteries of eternity of life, of the marvelous structure of reality. It is enough if one tries merely to comprehend a little of this mystery every day. Never lose a holy curiosity.　　　— ALBERT EINSTEIN
1879-1955

Uncovering the Origins of our Skepticism

Gopi Krishna stated that "In no other period of history were the learned so mistrustful of the divine possibilities in man as they are now." To uncover the origins of this mistrust, let's explore the powerful momentum of fear that created the skepticism that now pervades the mass consciousness.

We will begin in the seventeenth century, at the time in history when the church and science separated. Prior to that pivotal turning point, the church had power over most aspects of life. And though the church was oppressive in many ways, it provided a sense of security, for people knew what to expect. However, when the church began to misappropriate its power through greed and corruption — selling 'express tickets to Heaven' for large contributions — some folks became distressed. Their disillusionment was further compounded when the church took a strong stance on scientifically invalid 'facts' (the sun revolves around the earth). Hence, a movement ensued resulting in the separation of the church and science; with the church having control over the religious facets of life, and science having control over the area of exploring the earthly wonders of life. The result? The balance of power, along with the pendulum of security, began its swing from one extreme to the other.

In 1760, the Industrial Revolution flourished as technology advanced. Invention after invention astounded our civilized world, making everyday life easier and easier. It was during this period of time that we became more awed by man's creations than by God's. As scientists pursued a more specific understanding of life, they began to dissect nature; killing it, tearing it apart, categorizing it, naming it, and examining it. The consequence? We lost our connection with nature's living quality — its soul. At the same time, we lost our significance in life — how we fit into the big picture. Separated from our purpose within nature, we became fearful.

> When man or woman feels no connection between personal reality and experience and the surrounding world, he [or she] loses even an animal's sense of pure competence and belonging.[8] — JANE ROBERTS
> *The Nature of Personal Reality - A Seth Book*

In our detached state of being, we saw nature, in all her power and glory, destroy much life. Nature became an *adversary* to be controlled and feared. Imbued in feelings of fear and insecurity, we reached out to science to quell our fears and provide us a sense of security. The result? As science identified all the frightening physical aspects of life — the 'evils' that were out to 'get us' if we were ill-prepared — we felt safer living in our perilous world. We placed our saviors (scientists) on pedestals, glorifying them in all their brilliance, and bestowed upon them God-like power. We placed them at the helm of our evolution — a two-edged sword — for this degree of power is both a formidable responsibility and compelling aphrodisiac.

Our scientists, being mere mortals, now had to live up to our expectations. Quite naturally, in assuming the role of God, they adopted an attitude of arrogance and superiority — a mask to cover their insecurities. And because we placed upon them the burden of being all-knowing, scientists were compelled to maintain certain unmitigated guidelines to ascertain truth. Consequently, only the aspects of life that could be clinically proven by scientific research were deemed truth. And we didn't question the truth they espoused. In fact, we did the opposite. We willingly accepted their truth because most of us felt that they had to be smarter or wiser than we were.

Under these circumstances, it is completely logical that scientists are so highly skeptical. Think about it. If you were a scientist regally standing "naked" on a pedestal meting out truth to mankind, would you not feel an overwhelming responsibility for that truth? In fact, if the truth science metes out cannot be unequivocally validated by empirical evidence, scientists would jeopardize not only their position of power, but also the respect of their esteemed colleagues (something they worked very hard to attain), and more importantly, the vaunted position science holds in our culture. Therefore, scientists are safe when they deem truth to be only that which can be proven. They must maintain this attitude. From their positions of appointed responsibility, they must be right — regardless of the costs.

However, the costs are quite high. The degree to which science maintains its position of skepticism is at issue. In maintaining this position, science assumes a very narrow scope from which to determine truth, and in the process, obstructs the scientific procedure, thus compromising the very reason science exists. How does science compromise its purpose? By supporting the study of only *certain* aspects of life — aspects that fit neatly inside its comfort zone, aspects that do not jeopardize the position that science has attained. The result? Rampant prejudice exists within the scientific community. Theories that oppose established scientific dogmas are often met with skepticism and a raised eyebrow, rather than an attitude of curiosity, free of prejudice — necessary elements in encouraging research and exploration. In fact, scientists that have taken the risk of exploring aspects of life outside the current paradigm — the comfort zone adopted by their particular area of science — have been castigated; deemed outcasts by their peers. The consequence? Any of the mysterious aspects of life, such as spirituality, the powers of the mind, or metaphysics (anything beyond the physical), are far too often denied, scoffed at, ridiculed, trivialized, labeled as 'nonsense,' or dismissed as unfounded fiction. Furthermore, researchers who are curious to explore these uncharted territories often meet with criticism and ridicule as they share their aspirations with more seasoned colleagues. In fact, when Dr. Herbert Benson of the Harvard Mind/Body Clinic, shared his desire to explore the field of transcendental meditation and its impact on healing with colleagues, he was given the following advice: "You don't want to jeopardize your promising career!" The consequence? Exploration into these unknown areas is discouraged. After all, who wants to risk being alienated and mocked by your peers?

One prominent psychiatrist met face-to-face with the limitations of his scientific training when he encountered a woman who, under hypnosis, began to recount past-life memories — aspects of life not deemed as fact by science. Author Brian L. Weiss, M.D., tells us of the quandary he faced in *Many Lives, Many Masters*:

Years of disciplined study had trained my mind to think as a scientist and physician, molding me along the narrow paths of conservatism in my profession. I distrusted anything that could not be proved by traditional scientific methods. I was aware of some of the studies in parapsychology that were being conducted at major universities across the country, but they did not hold my attention. It all seemed too farfetched to me. Then I met Catherine. For eighteen months I used conventional methods of therapy to help her overcome her symptoms. When nothing seemed to work, I tried hypnosis. In a series of trance states, Catherine recalled "past-life" memories that proved to be the causative factors of her symptoms. She also was able to act as a conduit for information from highly evolved "spirit entities" and through them she revealed many of the secrets of life and death. I do not have a scientific explanation for what happened. There is far too much about the human mind that is beyond our comprehension....Perhaps she tapped into what the psychoanalyst Carl Jung termed the collective unconscious, the energy source that surrounds us and contains our memories of the entire human race.[9]

∿   ∿   ∿

I had been reluctant to discuss [this] revelation with other professionals. Actually, except for Carole [his wife] and a few others who were "safe," I had not shared this remarkable information with others at all. I knew the knowledge from our sessions was both true and extremely important, yet anxiety about the reactions of my professional and scientific colleagues caused me to keep silent. I was still concerned with my reputation, career, and what others thought of me.... As I gradually accepted and believed the messages, my life became simpler and more satisfying.... My reluctance to share the wisdom that had been given to me through Catherine began to diminish. Surprisingly, most people were interested and wanted to know more.... Parapsychological events are fairly common, much more frequent than people realize. It is only the reluctance to tell others about psychic occurrences that makes them seem rare. And the more highly trained are the most reluctant to share.... I understood why...highly trained professionals remained in the closet. I was one of them. We could not deny our own experiences and senses. Yet our training was in many ways diametrically opposite to the information, experiences, and beliefs we had accumulated. So we remained quiet.[10]

How has science dealt with this unacceptable subject-matter? It has adopted the position of 'sitting on the fence' — a position of non-committal. If scientists cannot find a way to empirically prove any of the mysterious aspects of life as being valid, they will not commit to whether they are or not. Although they are quick to acknowledge that indeed there is much that is unknown, they fail to maintain this neutrality and objectivity when they label those mysterious aspects of life that cannot be scientifically proven as nonsense. Is this not a paradox with a fundamental flaw within its rationale?

We do not know one millionth of one percent about anything.   — THOMAS EDISON
1847-1931

If there is anything [that] human history demonstrates, it is the extreme slowness with which the academic and critical mind acknowledges facts to exist [that] present themselves as wild facts, with no stall or pigeonhole, or as facts [that] threaten to break up the accepted system.
— WILLIAM JAMES
1842-1910

The more we mapped and named the physical phenomena in the universe, the more we could feel the world in which we lived was explained, predictable, secure, even ordinary and mundane. But in order to sustain this illusion we had to constantly screen and psychologically repress anything that reminded us of the mystery of life.[11]   — JAMES REDFIELD and CAROL ADRIENNE

How do you define the role of science? I define it as an exploration of *what is unknown*. There would obviously be no field of scientific research if all were known. Therefore, we must not prematurely deny or label the mysterious as nonsense, because current unprovable mysterious aspects of life will only remain mysterious until someone unravels the mystery behind them. Again, this is the very reason science exists.

> *The philosophies of one age have become the absurdities of the next, and the foolishness of yesterday will become the wisdom of tomorrow.* — DR. WILLIAM OSLER
> 1849-1919

> *The most beautiful thing we can experience is the mysterious. It is the source of all true art and science. He to whom this emotion is a stranger, who can no longer pause to wonder and stand rapt in awe, is as good as dead: His eyes are closed.* — ALBERT EINSTEIN
> 1879-1955

> *No kind of evolution ever took place through denial.*[12] — NEALE DONALD WALSCH
> *Conversations with God - Book 2*

Is Our Skepticism Warranted?

What have folks been skeptical of over the centuries that is now recognized as fact? Christopher Columbus, Alexander Graham Bell, Marie Curie, Thomas Edison, or any other visionary whose ideas resulted in significant contributions to the evolution of humankind were all first seen as foolish. In the end, of course, it was the skeptics who were foolish. As a matter of fact, we need only examine the past century to ask ourselves if the degree of skepticism we maintain is warranted.

> *The Wright brothers flew right through the smoke screen of impossibility.* — CHARLES F. KETTERING
> 1876-1958

Do you believe that God, or a higher source of power exists? Can anyone *prove* that God exists? The movie *Contact* explored the inconsistency of scientific truth being the only truth when one actor asked another, "Did you love your father?" The second actor replied, "Yes." And the first actor retorted, "Prove it!"

Can you look up into a star-filled sky and begin to comprehend the limitless possibilities that could exist out there? Can you look deep into the ocean and comprehend the complexity of life that exists within that habitat? Can you look into a microscope at any form of life and comprehend the complexity that exists within that environment? Have you ever thought about the creative force that causes our Earth to revolve around the sun? Have you ever contemplated how and why you can plant a tomato seed that will one day bear fruit? Have you ever wondered about the various components within your own physical body that miraculously perform an infinite number of complex functions day after day?

Mysterious aspects of life do exist, whether we care to acknowledge them or not. They simply are not capable of being proven today. The real scope of science is to identify what can be proven with the knowledge and technology available today, rather than to pass premature judgment upon that which cannot be proven. And in reality, is it not primitive in its logic to summarily dismiss certain aspects of life simply because they cannot be scientifically proven? Therefore, to find the greater truths that exists within the complexities in life, we must be willing to step outside of our existing paradigms — our comfort zones.

We are admonished in *Conversations with God - Book 1*, by author Neale Donald Walsch that the greatest barrier to our evolution is our illusion of knowledge:

> *You don't want to know the Truth, you want to know the Truth as you understand it. This is the greatest barrier to your enlightenment. You think you already know the Truth! You think you already understand how it is. So you agree with everything you see or hear or read that falls into the paradigm of your understanding, and reject everything which does not. And this you call learning? This you call being open to the teachings? Alas, you can never be open to the teachings so long as you are closed to everything save your own Truth.*[13]
> — NEALE DONALD WALSCH
> *Conversations with God - Book 2*

> *We, as a society, have much to gain from research into the mysteries of the mind, the soul, and the continuation of life after death, and the influence of our past-life experiences on our present behavior. Obviously, the ramifications are limitless, particularly in the fields of medicine, psychiatry, theology, and philosophy. However, scientifically rigorous research in this area is in its infancy. Strides are being made to uncover this information, but the process is slow and is met with*

much resistance by scientists and lay people alike. Throughout history, humankind has been resistant to change and to the acceptance of new ideas. Historical lore is replete with examples. When Galileo discovered the moons of Jupiter, the astronomers of that time refused to accept or even look at these satellites because the existence of these moons conflicted with their accepted beliefs. So it is now with psychiatrists and other therapists, who refuse to examine and evaluate the considerable evidence being gathered about survival after bodily death and about past-life memories. Their eyes stay tightly shut.[14] — DR. BRIAN WEISS

There are two objectionable types of believers: Those who believe the incredible and those who believe that "belief" must be discarded and replaced by the scientific method. — MAX BORN
1882-1970

Whenever either the political or scientific discourse announces itself as the voice of reason, it is playing God, and should be spanked and stood in the corner. — URSULA LEGUIN

When the mind is reinforced by academic and intellectual pursuits, the heart will be overshadowed.[1] — GLENDA GREEN
Love Without End: Jesus Speaks

We must now reexamine the role of science and the unrealistic burden we have placed upon its shoulders. For as scientists sit on the fence, unwilling to commit to what may or may not be true until they have obtained unequivocal scientific evidence, they are overlooking many aspects of life — aspects that may hold the keys to the evolution of mankind.

The important thing in science is not so much to obtain new facts as to discover new ways of thinking about them. — SIR WILLIAM HENRY BRAGG
1862-1942

Most conditions need relaxing, for man has built them into walls and prisons. You can ease conditions by broadening your tolerance, widening your viewpoints, increasing your forgiveness, and expanding your curiosity for life.[16] — GLENDA GREEN
Love Without End: Jesus Speaks

Our Comfort Zones are Becoming Less and Less Comfortable

Let's continue to paint the picture of our evolution to better understand how uncomfortable our current comfort zone really is.

As we pursued the illusory security of science and technology, our advancements created an aspect of life not factored into our equation of happiness and security — a fearful aspect. Weapons were built that were capable of obliterating all life. Simultaneously, we discovered that the indiscriminate use of natural resources was polluting portions of our beloved planet and her life support systems. These unpleasant aspects of life created the potential for the devastation of our world — the world that science sought to enrich with its technological developments.

We find ourselves in a precarious position: How do we manage living in a world that could be annihilated if our scientific achievements were to fall into the wrong hands — hands lacking the objective of the betterment of humanity? We simply become numb to those aspects of life — we carry on in spite of them. However, those dangers still exist, lurking like silent shadows fleeting in the night regurgitating our distress whenever they are brought to our attention.

At the dawning of a new millennium, we are living a dichotomy: We are experiencing the most miraculous technological era that has ever existed in the history of humanity, yet we don't feel very good about life — globally or personally. We have focused so exclusively on our gadgetry — the evolution of technology — that we have stagnated in other aspects of our evolution. We have become imbalanced and we feel it.

We Have Compromised Our Evolution for Our Security

The position that science now holds defeats its own purpose, for it does not nurture, nor support, nor encourage a ruthless examination of all aspects of life. The weight of responsibility that we have placed on science has stifled its ability to freely seek the whole truth. By expecting science to assume the unrealistic role of God, we have unwittingly pushed ourselves further and further from discovering the real truth.

Each one of us contributes to the state of denial that lies at the core of humankind's stagnation and source of disconnection we feel. In our desperation to feel secure; in our ignorance, insecurity, and unwillingness to assume yet another responsibility, we have abdicated our power and handed it to science. The result? We consider scientific truth to be the only valid truth. We have adopted the same rigid stance of intolerance and skepticism that science has, rather than to think for ourselves. We, too, readily dismiss as nonsense anything that pushes the envelope beyond traditional thinking. Why? We're overwhelmed. Our lives are inundated with so much information that it is simply easier to deny the mysterious aspects of life than it is to focus on another issue. Yet, in our denial, we have closed ourselves off to other truths.

Wanted:
A Balance Between Science and Spirit

What is needed is balance — individually, a balance between body, mind, and spirit, and collectively, a balance between science and spirit. To further our evolution, we must allow each school of wisdom to contribute its gift with the underlying intent being the betterment of humanity.

> *Most of us in the West have been taught that the center of our wisdom is in our heads. If you ask people where their ability to process thought and experience is, they will generally respond that it is in the brain. Ask consciously spiritual persons the same question and they will indicate the heart...Spiritual life does not grow in the soil of intellectual information gathering...Trusting your heart space is imperative for the growth of a healthy spiritual life. This means cultivating a harmony between mind and heart...The mind must surrender its role as full-time judge and allow the heart to contribute its wisdom.*[17]
> — DR. WAYNE DYER

> *The intuitive mind is a sacred gift, and the rational mind is a faithful servant. We have created a society that honors the servant and has forgotten the gift.*
> — ALBERT EINSTEIN
> 1879-1955

*One believes that the conscious mind and the intellect have all the answers, but to this school ...the conscious mind is analytical above all, and it can find all the answers through reason alone. The other school believes that the answers are in feelings and emotion. Both are wrong. Intellect and feeling **together** make up your existence, but the fallacy is particularly in the belief that the aware mind must be analytical above all, as opposed to, for example, the understanding or assimilation of intuitive psychic knowledge. Neither school understands the flexibility and the possibilities that are inherent within the conscious mind, and mankind has barely begun to use its potentials.*[18]   — JANE ROBERTS

The Nature of Personal Reality - A Seth Book

Can you see how this imbalance of power — our inability to integrate science and spirit — has created the circumstances for humankind to exist in a state of confusion and frustration? Can you see how easy it was for us to have taken the wrong turn? Can you see how we have created nothing but pain, anguish, and suffering by utilizing only our body and mind to make sense of life? Can you see how our emphasis on logic, on rational and analytical thought created the powerful momentum of fear that has pushed us further and further from our authentic power?

We now find ourselves at a crossroads, for if we continue to be so self-deluded and self-enamored; if we fail to embrace our authentic power and actualize all that we really are, we will not free ourselves from the trap of old-paradigm thinking. The consequence? More of what we are currently living — poverty, war, strife, hatred, ambivalence, discrimination, stress, tension, disease, fear, etc. The impact on humanity? Potentially fatal.

It is imperative that man acknowledge the heart's higher intelligence, for the mind alone cannot tell him who he is, and genetic intelligence is a lethal weapon when combined with the technological potentials in the world.[19]
— GLENDA GREEN
Love Without End: Jesus Speaks

We've arranged a global civilization in which most crucial elements profoundly depend on science and technology. We've also arranged things so that almost no one understands science or technology. We might get away with it for a while, but sooner or later, this combustible mixture of ignorance and power is going to blow up in our faces.
— CARL SAGAN
1934-1996

In the novel *One*, Richard Bach explored a hypothetical planet Earth thousands of years from today:

Evolution made civilization steward of this planet. One hundred thousand years later, the steward stood before evolution not healer, but parasite... a gifted society in so many ways, trapped at last by its greed and lack of vision. It ravaged the forests into desert, consumed the soul of the land in mine-pits and waste, smothered its air and its oceans, sterilized the earth with radiation and poisons. A million million chances it had to change, but it would not. From the ground it dug luxury for a few, jobs for the rest, and graves for the children of all. In the end, the children didn't agree, but the children had come too late... How could a civilization have been so blind?[20]

— RICHARD BACH

Concern for man and his fate always forms the chief interest of all technical endeavors. Never forget this in the midst of your diagrams and equations.

— ALBERT EINSTEIN
1879-1955

All our lauded technological progress — our very civilization — is like an axe in the hand of a pathological criminal.

— ALBERT EINSTEIN
1879-1955

Your present technology is threatening to outstrip your ability to use it wisely. Your society is on the verge of becoming a product of your technology, rather than your technology being a product of your society. When a society becomes a product of its own technology, it destroys itself.[21]

— NEALE DONALD WALSCH
Conversations with God - Book 3

Science is but a perversion of itself unless it has as its ultimate goal the betterment of humanity.

— NICOLA TESLA
1856-1943

Humankind is standing precariously on the edge of its destiny. It will either rise to a paradigm change or experience decline and possible destruction. This is an unavoidable confrontation.[22]

— GLENDA GREEN
Love Without End: Jesus Speaks

It's important now, it's time now, to change your mind about some things. This is what evolution is all about.[23]
— NEALE DONALD WALSCH
Conversations with God - Book 1

To believe in something not yet proved and to underwrite it with our lives; it is the only way we can leave the future open.
— LILLIAN SMITH

Be open. Don't close off the possibility of a new truth because you have been comfortable with an old one. Life begins at the end of your comfort zone.[24]
— NEALE DONALD WALSCH
Conversations with God - Book 3

The structure of scientific theory needs to be relaxed if innovative thinking is to occur.[25]
— GLENDA GREEN
Love Without End: Jesus Speaks

The price we pay for asking science to be our God is indeed high. In abdicating our power, not only have we created the potential for disaster, but we also have divorced ourselves from experiencing many wondrous facets of life: Our living connection to nature, our living connection to the realm of Spirit, and the unknown wonders of an exploration into the mysterious.

We must now reconsider the role of science, understanding the magnitude and potential consequences of its unleashed power. We must reexamine what we consider to be truth. We must identify and diffuse what we are skeptical of. We must reevaluate who we give our power to. We must now move forward and actualize our authentic power. The time has come for us to open our eyes and take action. Past civilizations have demonstrated that technology and science without a connection to Spirit will eventually lead to disaster and demise. Science and spirit must be integrated. These two schools of wisdom must work hand in hand in order to unleash our true power — the likes of which humankind has yet to witness. How do we integrate them?

We utilize the Four-Step Formula — think, believe, expect, and get. As you are now aware, our negative feelings have a very clear purpose: They are our Points of Power from which to clarify our path of evolution. Our negative emotions will lead us to achieve our task of integrating science and spirit.

Are you ready to examine the legitimacy of your skepticism and contemplate a new perspective? Can you see how your current comfort zone is becoming less and less comfortable? Are you ready to consciously reconstruct a new one? Have you garnered enough proof of the Four-Step Formula? Are you ready to allow Angel to contribute its gifts and wisdom? Are you ready to embrace your incredible power?

"Come to the edge," he said. They said, "We are afraid."
"Come to the edge," he said. They came. He pushed them... and they flew.   — GUILLAUME APOLLINAIRE
                                                                                                                1880-1918

Don't be afraid to take a big step if one is indicated. You can't cross a chasm in two small jumps.
                                                            — DAVID LLOYD GEORGE

Someday, after we have mastered the winds, the waves, the tide, and gravity, we shall harness for God the energies of love. Then, for the second time in the history of the world, we will have discovered fire.
                                                            — PIERRE TEILHARD DE CHARDIN
                                                                                                                1881-1955

Everything has a crack in it — that's how the light gets in.   — LEONARD COHEN

Beyond plants are animals, Beyond animals is man. Beyond man is the universe. The Big Light. Let the Big Light in!   — JEAN TOOMER
                                                                                                                1894-1967

Regard the present moment as sacred. In this, you will find answers to many problems which have baffled you. Respect life in all its ways as an unfolding of experience. Life is not behind you — it's in front of you. It is not history or a memory. Life is that which is birthing before your very eyes. Know that, and your intelligence will become a dynamic force rather than a stagnating body of knowledge with formulas for mortal structure.[26]
                                                            — GLENDA GREEN
                                                            Love Without End: Jesus Speaks

Having explored the evolution of our wrong turn and the resulting chaos it created, let's now examine what we take for granted, so we can begin to make the fundamental changes necessary to facilitate our new beginning. Then we can get on with our real task in life: living, loving, and laughing! ✆

Just a Little Bit of Love

I was alone, I was afraid.
I couldn't face another day of pain in my life
I called your name and you were there
Just like an answer to a prayer.
You made it all right.
So I give my heart and I give my soul to you, oh I do.
And now I know I found the truth.
Just a little bit of love's gonna turn it around,
and around and around.
I found the truth, I found the way.
I'm standing in the light of day.
I got the power, I'm not worried any longer.
No, I'm only getting stronger by the hour.
You can move a mountain or calm a stormy sea.
There's no doubt about it, I truly do believe.
Just a little bit of love's gonna turn it around
A little bit of love can do it.
And just a little bit of love's gonna turn it around
and around and around.
And it can free your mind, yes, it can free your soul.
Free your soul, let it go, let it go.
Just a little bit of love's gonna turn it around
A little bit of love can do it.
And just a little bit of love's gonna turn it around
and around and around.[27]

Words by Maria Christiansen, Arnie Roman, Arthur Jacobsen

There Are Fundamental Flaws in What We Take for Granted

Life is not war, and people are not the enemy.
— UNKNOWN

Joy, interrupted now and again by pain and terminated ultimately by death, seems the normal course of life in Nature. Anxiety and distress, interrupted occasionally by pleasure, is the normal course of man's existence.
— JOSEPH KRUTCH
1893-1970

We have met the enemy, and they is us! — WALT KELLY
1913-1973

The white man knows how to make everything, but he does not know how to distribute it. — SITTING BULL
1834-1890

[N]o one in enlightened societies is willing to get anything, or have anything, at someone else's expense.[28]
— NEALE DONALD WALSCH
Conversations with God - Book 2

If you think your life is about doingness, you do not understand what you are about. Your soul doesn't care what you do for a living — and when your life is over, neither will you. Your soul cares only about what you're being while you are doing whatever you're doing.[29]
— NEALE DONALD WALSCH
Conversations with God - Book 1

Men for the sake of getting a living, forget to live.
— MARGARET FULLER
1810-1850

Independence? That's middle-class blasphemy. We are all dependent upon one another, every soul of us on Earth.
— GEORGE BERNARD SHAW
1861-1950

Soon as you learned to see; pictures. Soon as you learned to listen; stories, and songs. There is Us and there is Them. They will hurt Us if we're not vigilant, suspicious, angry, armed.[30]
— RICHARD BACH

'Tis peace of mind lad, we must find.
— THEOCRITUS
310-250 BC

Ignorance gives one a large range of probabilities.
— GEORGE ELIOT

Life in the Old Paradigm

A state of powerlessness imbues life in the old paradigm; powerlessness born of fear. We believe that our world is an unsafe place; that we must take precautions to ensure our survival. And one way we are taught to survive is to become financially secure. Accordingly, we attend schools to prepare ourselves to get a good (well-paying) job. The result? Our intent is focused on money and survival rather than happiness. The result? We can only experience what we project.

What truly matters to us and what we spend our time doing are often opposed. Unknowingly, we lock ourselves in various prisons, surmising that in order to survive and enjoy a little leisure, the price we must pay is one of an unfulfilling job. We further encumber ourselves in credit — charging clothes, vacations, VCRs, whatever, and then wonder how we are going pay for all these things — things that temporarily bring us joy.

A predominant old-paradigm belief is that of scarcity — the illusion that there is not enough. We presume that if one person gets too much, there will not be enough for the rest of us. We see our world as having limits to its abundance and those limits frighten us into a survival-mode of living — a mode where there is little joy or inner peace.

Think about it... this old-paradigm illusion of scarcity has created wars, intense competition, and crime — our current world condition.

> *Greed is the root of all evil. In the presence of greed, people go to extremes, and in the presence of extremes, the idea of scarcity is invented. When scarcity is invented, fear sprouts up like weeds in a garden. Every negative emotion known to man is born from fear.... Fear abounds in the absence of love, and hatred is fear of love itself. Greed is an obsessive desire, which attempts to nourish and supply the needs of life without love....As for greed, the initial advantages of it are quite deceptive. Greed has a built-in 'therapy' which at first generates a sense of elation. Prior to the pursuit of excess, a person might have reduced himself to a belief in scarcity and then wearied himself with countless decisions of, 'do I have this or do I have that?' Then one day he declares, 'I think I'll have it all!' An incredible thing has happened in that moment. He has removed his belief in scarcity and ended the duality of endless decisions! In doing so, he has released a great force of creativity within himself. Now if he could seize the quality of that force and apply it to the connectedness of all life, he would have fulfilling prosperity instead of a destructive addiction. But too often, a person applies it to himself alone, and recreates a new scarcity called 'only for me.' Abundance applied to the 'self alone' is a betrayal of the perception![31]*
> — GLENDA GREEN
> *Love Without End: Jesus Speaks*

The War-Zone

The business world is driven by the premise of scarcity to the extent that companies feel they must compete, control, and conquer in order to survive. Competition, or survival of the fittest, is so fierce that it has become the equivalent of war. And what effect does war have on people?

Because so many companies offer similar products or services with no discernable distinctions, they are no longer able to differentiate themselves from their competitors with something tangible. How do they survive? By resorting to the old "If you can't sell 'em, scare 'em" philosophy" — instilling fear, uncertainty, and doubt in their customer's minds regarding their competitor's products.

The pressure to survive is unrelenting because of the constant stream of newly emerging forms of marketing, such as the Internet. These changes create tension and put people on edge as they scramble to survive in the latest paradigm shift.

At the same time, competition is growing more and more fierce in the new global economy where low-wage workers in other countries can produce a product at a far lower cost than their American counterparts. This has created a system that pits worker against worker, country against country, and perpetuates low wages along with deplorable working conditions. It is fueled by the utter greed of wealthy corporations where they, along with the owners of the factories in these countries, horrendously exploit the poor — not for survival, but for a greater profit margin.

> Such a system of rank obscenity could exist only in a world motivated by greed, where profit margin, not human dignity, is the first consideration.[32]
> — NEALE DONALD WALSCH
> Conversations with God - Book 2

In their efforts to survive, some companies have taken drastic measures — extending hours, lowering prices (and profits), or terminating tremendous numbers of employees in an effort to cut overhead and increase their margin. The next quarterly report has become so significant to a company's survival that, on occasion, shrewd accountants resort to desperate measures: Manipulating their numbers in order to maintain the company's position in the market. The consequence? A system has emerged that places more emphasis on the profitability of stockholders, rather than rewarding the folks who work hard to make the company a success. In fact, the employees are 'rewarded' by being paid the lowest possible wages the companies can get away with. But it's all done under the covers so those making out like bandits never have to face those being hurt. This travesty has become very civil, with no one daring to examine the reality of what is transpiring, because to do so might entail looking in the mirror and feeling something unpleasant. And unfortunately, those who recognize this injustice, unaware of their real power, feel powerless to change the system.

Mired in the old-paradigm illusion of scarcity, we rationalize that once we have attained the "good life" we will see the end of a life filled with anxiety, the end of never having enough, whether we are making $50,000, $100,000, or $1,000,000. We justify that our good fortune is finally the end of our struggle and we don't want to lose any part of it!

We convince ourselves that we have worked hard, taken risks, and now deserve to live the good life! We further maintain that if others want to work as hard as we do, they can go out and earn it, too. After all, it's a free country, right?

If a business does reach its goal, there is certainly no reward or time to relax. The game then becomes one of maintaining its position — sometimes an even more daunting task!

This ceaseless race begets another pitfall: We have become so stressed-out that we are unkind, irritable, or impatient with one another. There is simply no time for niceties, they take too much effort. Our minds are so preoccupied with survival, we don't have the time or energy to concern ourselves with etiquette.

We have become the proverbial hamster running on the wheel faster and faster but getting nowhere. And boy, are we exhausted! We exist as though we are competing in a race — but the race has no finish line! Imbued in this unrelenting state of being, rather than pursuing what we want out of life, we are bombarded with so much information from so many different sources that we are too overwhelmed to experience happiness and leisure. In fact, most of us rarely experience how it feels to Be In The Moment; to be completely immersed in an experience without distraction. Instead, our leisure time far too often includes cellular phones, pagers, lap-top computers, and modems. We dare not leave the business world behind, for if we divert our attention for even a moment, we will surely fall behind, lose the race, or others will get there first, and there will be nothing left.

Programmed in old-paradigm thinking, the pressure never stops. Why? The risk is too great. Because we believe that there is not enough, we are compelled to take any measure we can to survive. On a daily basis, we prepare for battle. We cannot let our guard down for even a moment, for if we do, we will be annihilated by the enemy.

The Game of Trading Piles

I was involved in the telecommunications industry for four-and-one-half years as a broker/consultant to business clients for their long distance needs. I must admit that it was a business I didn't enjoy, but embraced it fully because it allowed me to work at home and be "mom" to my son Zachary. It also offered a lucrative recurring monthly income based on receiving a percentage of my clients' monthly telecommunications invoices.

To offer a little background, the telecommunications industry has undergone a major metamorphosis due to its deregulation. Beginning in 1984 with the divestiture of AT&T, new laws were passed that precipitated many changes. I am currently not involved in this industry as my business 'went down the tubes' in February of 1997. (You'll find out how I unknowingly created this demise as you read further.) The new perspective I gained, however, was invaluable, for it produced multitudinous data that I would never have been aware of had I not gone through this experience — the cycle of creation "doing it's thing."

As I interacted with those in corporate America, I was intrigued with how the corporate world operated. The various telecommunication giants employ telemarketers to offer gimmick upon gimmick as an incentive for people to switch their long distance services. And these tactics are effective, for every day approximately 60,000 users switch carriers. Hence, the 'pile' (market share) is continually redistributed from company to company. Although the deregulation of telecommunications has resulted in the cost-per-minute for long distance service decreasing significantly, have we ever considered the cost to you and me with these incessant interruptions throughout our days? The point is, while these companies are playing the game of 'exchanging piles,' is anyone really accomplishing anything?

Rationalizations 'R Us

I once saw a television interview with a shrewd attorney famous for winning huge sums of money for his wealthy corporate clients. This attorney was asked how he could justify a legal fee of more than $300 million for one case, and somehow this man was completely convinced that his fee was equitable! In his ignorance, hence, innocence, of how life really operates, he wouldn't even consider the repercussions of his actions. At the most primal level of existence he was so frightened of not having enough that he censored those thoughts. In fact, most of us are so driven by fear that we banish most thoughts regarding the repercussions of our actions. Those thoughts are just not permitted in the forefronts of our consciousness or consciences!

Our illusion of powerlessness is responsible for this all-pervasive fear. Crippled by our fear, we have evolved into a society that rationalizes attaining money (security and survival) any way we can, whether it is by gambling, stealing, suing someone, or stepping on others.

> *Greed is considered legitimate now, while brotherly love is not.*[33]
> — MARIANNE WILLIAMSON

> *We have become technological giants and moral pygmies.*
> — UNKNOWN

> *What kind of glory is attained when it is achieved at the expense of another?*[34]
> — NEALE DONALD WALSCH
> *Conversations with God - Book 2*

> *We must distinguish morality from moralizing.*
> — HENRY KISSINGER

In the brilliant book, *Gift From the Sea*, Anne Morrow Lindbergh offers an insight that explains why we have become so imbalanced:

> *Because we cannot deal with the complexity of the present, we often override it and live in a simplified dream of the future. Because we cannot deal with the many as individuals, we sometimes try to simplify the many into an abstraction called the mass. Because we cannot solve our own problems right here at home, we talk about problems out there in the world. An escape process goes on from the intolerable burden we have placed upon ourselves. But can one really feel deeply for an abstraction called the mass? Can one make the future a substitute for the present? And what guarantee have we that the future will be any better if we neglect the present? Can one solve world problems when one is unable to solve one's own? Where have we arrived in this process? Have we been successful working at the periphery of the circle and not at the center? If we stop to think about it, are not the real casualties in modern life just these centers I have been discussing: the here, the now, the individual, and his relationships. The present is passed over in the race for the future; the here is neglected in favor of the there; and the individual is dwarfed by the enormity of the mass.*[35]
> — ANNE MORROW LINDBERGH

Imbued in feelings of powerlessness to resolve the myriad problems we are exposed to daily, we instead focus on our own survival, something we feel we have some control over. However, in our attempt to survive, we have confused the adrenalin rush of living in 'war-mode' — competing, controlling, and conquering — with real energy and excitement, and have forgotten, or never even experienced, the real thing. The difference is that real joy and happiness is *never at the expense of someone else*.

> *Humankind has not woven the web of life. We are but one thread within it. Whatever we do to the web, we do to ourselves. All things are bound together. All things connect.*
> — CHIEF SEATTLE
> 1786-1866

As we move into the new paradigm it won't be necessary to step on others to get to the top of the pile. It won't be necessary to place profits before principles. It won't be necessary to forsake the sacredness of life. For we will fully comprehend and embody our true power, which will enable us to honor one another as the sacred souls we truly are.

> *Ignorance is the true original sin. Men are bankrupt morally because they do not know the gold mine that is in them.*
> — J. BRIERLEY

How can we begin our transition into the new paradigm filled with peace of mind, happiness, joy, love, and a feeling of accomplishment that accompanies an endeavor that has purpose? How can we get off the fast track, survive, thrive, and enjoy prosperity? How can we stop surrendering to what life doles out and begin to live a life that prioritizes what is most important to us? How can we achieve a level of prosperity where we no longer have to fight, fear others, or feel guilty? How can we recognize the fundamental truth that our worth is not measured by what we have, but Who We Are? Simply, by embracing and embodying the truth of Who We Really Are.

> *Lip service without the behavior has no value. It is easy to read about or to talk about love and charity and faith. But to do it, to feel it, almost requires...sustained physical behavior, by act and deed, by practice. It is taking something nearly mystical and transforming it to everyday familiarity by practice, making it a habit.*[36]
> — BRIAN L. WEISS, M.D.

To be or not to be: That is the question.
— WILLIAM SHAKESPEARE
1564-1616

Real success in life can only be measured in terms of joy. Therefore, to cross the bridge from fear to love, it is essential that we actualize our power! Step by step, as we begin to utilize the Four-Step Formula and experience our authentic power, we will shift our consciousness from living in fear and unawareness, to living in love and awareness.

Try not to become a man of success, but rather to become a man of value.
— ALBERT EINSTEIN
1879-1955

Go ahead and do what you really love to do! Do nothing else. You have so little time. How can you think of wasting a moment doing something for a living you don't like to do? What kind of a living is that? That is not a living. That is a dying![37]
— NEALE DONALD WALSCH
Conversations with God - Book 1

It is the heart that makes a man rich. He is rich according to what he is, not according to what he has.
— HENRY WARD BEECHER
1813-1887

The standard of success in life isn't the things. It isn't the money or the stuff — it is absolutely the amount of joy you feel.[38]
— ESTHER and JERRY HICKS

Life is meant for living, loving, and laughing, friends — to be lived as a magical, joyous, creative experience. So let's take the next step in achieving our goal. Let's explore what each of us is doing every day that we think is so important. ⊛

Call Me

If you're feeling sad and lonely, there's a service I can render
Tell the one who loves you only,
I can be so warm and tender
Call me, don't be afraid you can call me
Maybe it's late, but just call me.
Tell me and I'll be around.
When it seems your friends desert you.
There's somebody thinking of you.
I'm the one who'll never hurt you.
Maybe that's because I love you.
Call me, maybe it's late but just call me.
Tell me and I'll be around.
Now don't forget me, 'cause if you let me I will always stay by you.
You gotta trust me, that's how it must be.
There's so much that I can do.
If you call, I'll be right with you.
You and I should be together.
Take this love I long to give you,
I'll be at your side forever.
Call me, don't be afraid, you can call me
Maybe it's late , but just call me.
Tell me and I'll be around.[39]

Words and Music by Tony Hatch

What Are We Doing Every Day That is So Important?

As long as habit and routine dictate the pattern of living,
new dimensions of the soul will not emerge.
— HENRY VAN DYKE
1852-1933

There is more to life than increasing its speed.
— MAHATMA GANDHI
1869-1948

In order to seek one's own direction, one must simplify
the mechanics of ordinary everyday life.
— PLATO
428-348 BC

Your life work is a statement of Who You Are. If it is
not, then why are you doing it?[40]
— NEALE DONALD WALSCH
Conversations with God - Book 1

It is good to have an end to journey towards; but it is the
journey that matters in the end.
— URSULA K. LEGUIN

Many people are in a state of burn-out today because
they are trying frantically to change life by do, do, doing,
or think, think, thinking, and it is not work, work,
working! A simple change of heart would handle the
problem.[41]
— GLENDA GREEN
Love Without End: Jesus Speaks

As you scurry around day in and day out absorbed in all of your tasks and obligations, have you ever pondered the purpose underlying your efforts? Have you ever asked yourself, "What are all of us trying to accomplish?" Take a look at every major industry in the world. What do they all have in common as their objective?

It's not to make money, because they will not make money unless their product or service addresses this fundamental objective:

To Make Life Better, Easier, or More Enjoyable

Think about it....

- The automobile industry creates beautiful vehicles that continually offer more and more creature comforts so we can get from place A to place B in more luxury, style, and fun. This industry certainly helps to make life more enjoyable, doesn't it?

- The computer industry creates a means to exchange information at amazing speeds where we can now complete tedious tasks in a fraction of the time it took only a decade ago. This industry certainly helps to make life better and easier, doesn't it?

- The telecommunications industry allows us to communicate with one another instantaneously, allowing us to accomplish more in a shorter period of time. This industry certainly helps to make life better and easier, doesn't it?

- The healthcare industry provides more sophisticated ways to enjoy a healthy life free from illness. And if illness does strike, this industry's goal is to find ways to eradicate the illness and restore our health. This industry certainly helps to make life better and easier, doesn't it?

- The appliance industry creates wonderful contraptions to wash our dishes, clean our clothes, cook our food, preserve and cool our food, etc. As a result, we are able to spend less time accomplishing tasks that in the past, took much time. This industry certainly helps to make life better and easier, doesn't it?

- The gas and oil industries provide fuel they have extracted from the earth to power our vehicles and provide a comfortable environment in which to work, live, and play. These industries certainly help to make life better and easier, don't they?

~ The building industry provides increasingly more ease of function and beauty in our homes and buildings. This industry certainly helps to make life better and easier, doesn't it?

~ The government (the largest industry of all) certainly attempts to make life better by creating and enacting laws meant to protect our rights, Mother Earth, the economy, etc., doesn't it?

~ Those in research explore various environments in their quest to provide answers to some of life's problems that have eluded us. They certainly try to help to make life better, easier, or more enjoyable, don't they?

~ Parents at home raising their children desire to provide them with as much preparation for the outside world as they can, helping to build their self-esteem — a necessary element to live a better, happier life. Their goal is to help create more fulfilling lives for their children, isn't it?

I Got, Got, Got, Got No Time...

My candle burns at both ends; It will not last the night.
— EDNA ST. VINCENT MILLAY
1892-1950

Many today feel a sadness we cannot name. Though we accomplish much of what we set out to do, we sense that something is missing in our lives and — fruitlessly— search 'out there' for the answers. What's often wrong is that we are disconnected form an authentic sense of self.
— EMILY HANCOCK

All of the preceding endeavors help to improve the quality of life by attempting to make it better, easier, and more enjoyable, wouldn't you agree? And as a result, we should have a lot more time to enjoy our better easier lives, right? Wrong! Do you have any extra time?

Because so many of us fear that we might miss out on something, we attempt to squeeze as much as we can in our days. However, in so doing, we don't have a spare moment left.

And, unfortunately we overlay the same pattern onto our kids. Because we don't want them to miss out on anything, we sign them up for so many extra-curricular activities that they, too, don't have a spare moment. However, uninterrupted 'free' time is essential for the development of their imaginations; time free from TV, cartoons, computer games, and videos (all those wonderful devices that keep mommies and daddies sane...). Once again, our imaginations are important — they are the bases of conscious creation.

Although many of our technological advances were developed to make life easier, they often do the opposite. Because we don't have the time to learn how to operate each of these wonderful time-saving devices, they overwhelm us and add to our burdens. They make life even more complex! How many of us don't know how to program a VCR, a computer, or each new generation of telephones that are introduced on a daily basis? (My husband and I alone could start a 'cellular phone cemetery.') Living in this Information Age, we're on 'input-overload.'

We have increased the speed of life to such a ferocious pace that we are suffering from battle-fatigue — a state of being where we are numb, vacant, and tired. A state of being where there is no time left for reflection. Yet reflection is key to a centered life.

> *Now instead of planting our solitude with our dream*
> *blossoms, we choke the space with continuous music,*
> *chatter and companionship to which we do not even*
> *listen. It is simply there to fill the vacuum. When the*
> *noise stops there is no inner music to take its place. We*
> *must re-learn to be alone.*[42]
> — ANNE MORROW LINDBERGH

Time spent alone is essential to our well-being. We seem to have forgotten the value of relaxing and have instead labeled it laziness.

> *As far as the search for solitude is concerned, we live in*
> *a negative atmosphere as invisible, as all-pervasive, and*
> *as enervating as high humidity on a August afternoon.*
> *The world today does not understand, in neither man or*
> *woman, the need to be alone.*[43]
> — ANNE MORROW LINDBERGH

> *-Alone, alone. Oh! We have been warned about solitary*
> *vices. Have solitary pleasures ever been adequately praised?*
> *Do many people know they exist?* — JESSAMYN WEST

Work is not always required... There is such a thing as
sacred idleness, the cultivation of which is now fearfully
neglected. — GEORGE MACDONALD

As we scurry about, day in and day out, attempting to make our lives better, easier, and more enjoyable, have we even recognized the reason for our scurrying? Or have we become so engaged in the process, that we have lost sight of our goal?

My answer is an emphatic yes! I believe that we have entrapped ourselves in our attempt to make life better and have inadvertently made it worse! We have become so caught up in the day-to-day tasks of life that we don't know how to live a centered life. Therefore, we must ask ourselves if we are achieving what we set out to achieve. Are we living lives that are better, easier, and more enjoyable?

In *Gift From The Sea*, Anne Morrow Lindbergh provides an insight as to why we have gotten so caught up in the process of life.

> *For to be [human] is to have interests and duties, raying out in all directions from the central core, like spokes from the hub of a wheel. The pattern of our lives is essentially circular. We must be open to all points of the compass; mate, children, friends, home, community; stretched out, exposed, sensitive like a spider's web to each breeze that blows, to each call that comes. How difficult for us then, to achieve a balance in the midst of these contradictory tensions, and yet how necessary for the proper functioning of our lives. [Human] relationships have their myriad pulls — normal occupations in general run counter to creative life, or contemplative life, or saintly life. The problem is not merely one of individual and career, individual and the home, individual and independence. It's more basically: how to remain whole in the midst of the distractions of life; how to remain balanced, no matter what centrifugal forces tend to pull one off center; how to remain strong, no matter what shocks come in at the periphery and tend to crack the hub of the wheel.*[44]
> — ANNE MORROW LINDBERGH

How *do* we find our center? How *do* we make life better, easier, and more enjoyable? How *do* we begin to utilize our power and the Four-Step Formula? First we must slow down, relax, quiet our inner minds, and redefine our priorities. We must take time for ourselves, even if it is only a few minutes.

Many of our so-called priorities are, in reality, illusory limitations; nothing more than the beliefs we hold; 'programming' born of old-paradigm thinking. And these beliefs are the culprits responsible for creating our life experiences. However, now that we know that our beliefs are simply habits of thought, we can readjust our red circuits to reflect what we want in life, so we can live better, easier, and more enjoyable lives. As a further bonus, when each of us creates our own joyful life, we will simultaneously add to our world's joy and the process of creating Heaven on Earth will occur. Remember, this work starts with you finding your center, rather than with all of those people who you may think are doing it wrong.

To remind people of the importance of taking responsibility for their own lives rather than for the lives of others, the Alcoholics Anonymous program has adopted the serenity prayer by Reinhold Niebuhr.

> *God, give us grace to accept with serenity the things that cannot be changed, courage to change the things which should be changed, and the wisdom to distinguish the one from the other.* — REINHOLD NIEBUHR
> 1892-1971

Now that you understand that your life experiences have been created by your beliefs, let's explore what you believe — the set of orders you have unknowingly conveyed to Angel that has created your current comfort zone. To understand your very important part in the transformation of our world, it is essential that you understand your personal evolution: Where you have been and how you got there. As you dissect each of your past experiences, you will uncover the hidden treasures buried within them that you may not have recognized as having value. At the same time, you will redefine your set of orders and construct a new comfort zone — one that reflects what you want from life. Sound good? Are you ready to launch a new beginning? Are you ready to live, love, and laugh? ☺

PART IV

The Past

DISSECTING YOUR PAST AND
UNCOVERING ITS HIDDEN TREASURES

Part IV
The Past

Part IV

The Past

DISSECTING YOUR PAST AND UNCOVERING ITS HIDDEN TREASURES

Scrutinize Your Beliefs and Toss Those that No Longer Serve You

First we form habits, then they form us. Conquer your bad habits or eventually they'll conquer you.
— DR. ROB GILBERT

Look not mournfully into the Past. It comes not back again. Wisely improve the Present. It is thine.
— HENRY WADSWORTH LONGFELLOW
1807-1882

On any journey, we must find out where we are before we can plan the first step.
— KATHY BOEVINK

The unexamined life is not worth living.
— PLATO
428-348 B.C.

Without an examination of your past, you are doomed to repeat it.
— UNKNOWN

To look backward for a while is to refresh the eye, to restore it, and to render it the more fit for its prime function of looking forward.
— MARGARET FAIRLESS BARBER

All men should try to learn before they die what they are running from, and to, and why.
— JAMES THURBER
1894-1961

To fall into a habit is to begin to cease to be.
— MIGUEL DE UNAMUNO
1864-1936

Life is not a problem to be solved, but a reality to be experienced. — SOREN KIERKEGAARD
1813-1855

You can choose to be a person who has resulted simply from what has happened, or from what you have chosen to be and do about what has happened.[1]
— NEALE DONALD WALSCH
Conversations with God - Book I

We don't receive wisdom; we must discover it for ourselves after a journey that no one can take for us or spare us. — MARCEL PROUST
1871-1922

Your Beliefs Seed the Future

To redefine the set of orders you have unknowingly conveyed to Angel to now reflect what you want, it is helpful to examine what you believe. In reality, a belief is nothing more than a habit of thoughts. In fact, the majority of the 90,000 thoughts you will have today are identical to those you had yesterday and the day before that and the day before that. And approximately 60 percent are those of blame, 30 percent those of guilt, and a teeny-weeny percentage, those of appreciation and love.[2] Therefore, one of the objectives of this book is to provide you with the knowledge to live your life with the majority of your thoughts being those of joy, appreciation, and love.

Let's now examine your core beliefs, because they are the building blocks of your life experience. By exploring your beliefs, you will uncover your red circuits — those frequencies responsible for activating your 'off' switch, thus restricting the flow of energy to you and impeding the manifestation of what you want.

> *Subtle and ever-present core beliefs are the invisible determining factors in our life. They must be brought to the surface before they can be expanded or changed.*[3]
> — JAMES REDFIELD and CAROL ADRIENNE

[Your beliefs…] form the structure of your life, and to lose them would be to unravel the fabric of your experience. Still, examine them one by one. Review them piece by piece. Do not dismantle the house, but look at each brick, and replace those which appear broken, which no longer support the structure. [4]

— NEALE DONALD WALSCH
Conversations with God - Book 1

If you find great exuberance, health, effective work, abundance, smiles on the faces of those you meet, then take it for granted that your beliefs are beneficial. If you see a world that is good, people that like you, take it for granted, again that your beliefs are beneficial. But if you find poor health, a lack of meaningful work, a lack of abundance, a world of sorrow and evil, then assume your beliefs are faulty and begin examining them. [5]

— JANE ROBERTS
The Nature of Personal Reality - A Seth Book

There is no place where you are not connected with the one spirit. Yet, belief is like a thought cast into that oneness. There is a direction and intent with all beliefs. If you were to examine your beliefs you might ask, 'What vector am I establishing with that belief? How does it connect with my truest self and where it is going?' Surely the arrow of belief is as swift and true as the arrow of thought, and will find its mark. There is nothing more vulnerable and formative than spirit. As you interweave your love, thoughts, and beliefs with spirit, your life is formed. You would be wise to respect that truth in all its applications. [6] — GLENDA GREEN
Love Without End: Jesus Speaks

Your Core Beliefs or Habits of Thought

You will not understand your emotions unless you know your beliefs. [7] — JANE ROBERTS
The Nature of Personal Reality - A Seth Book

What do you believe about the following?

Relationships and Love:

_____

_____

_____

_____

the past - 3

Family:

_____

_____

_____

_____

_____

_____

The Opposite Sex:

_____

_____

_____

_____

_____

_____

How You Attain a State of Health:

_____

_____

_____

_____

_____

_____

Your Work, or How You Spend the Majority of Your Energy:

_____

_____

_____

_____

_____

_____

How You Attain Money, Prosperity, and Wealth:

_____

_____

_____

_____

_____

_____

How You Attain Happiness:

_____
_____
_____
_____
_____
_____
_____

How You Achieve Inner Peace:

_____
_____
_____
_____
_____
_____
_____

How You Protect Yourself:

_____
_____
_____
_____
_____
_____
_____

Why the World Is in the Shape It's In:

_____
_____
_____
_____
_____
_____
_____

How You Attain Freedom:

_____
_____
_____
_____
_____
_____
_____

How You Grow as a Person:

_____
_____
_____
_____
_____
_____
_____

How You Came to Live Where You Do:

_____
_____
_____
_____
_____
_____
_____

How You Attain Material Things:

_____
_____
_____
_____
_____
_____
_____

How You Gain Understanding:

_____
_____
_____
_____
_____
_____
_____

Why Discrimination Exists:

_____
_____
_____
_____
_____
_____
_____

Your Thoughts About/ Toward the Elderly:

_____
_____
_____
_____
_____
_____
_____

Your View on Illness:

_____
_____
_____
_____
_____
_____
_____

Your Thoughts on Death:

_____
_____
_____
_____
_____
_____
_____

Your View of the Handicapped:

_____
_____
_____
_____
_____
_____
_____

Your View of the Homeless:

_____
_____
_____
_____
_____
_____
_____

Your View of Those Who Beg:

_____
_____
_____
_____
_____
_____
_____

Your View of Those Who Are Overweight:

_____
_____
_____
_____
_____
_____

Your Thoughts About Being Alone:

_____
_____
_____
_____
_____
_____

Your Attitude About Food:

_____
_____
_____
_____
_____
_____

Your Attitude About Diets:

_____
_____
_____
_____
_____
_____

Your View of Our Government:

_____
_____
_____
_____
_____
_____
_____

Your View of Our Judicial System and Lawyers:

_____
_____
_____
_____
_____
_____
_____

Your Perception of Heaven and Hell:

_____
_____
_____
_____
_____
_____
_____

Your View on Politics:

_____
_____
_____
_____
_____
_____
_____

Your Perception of God or a Greater Power:

_____
_____
_____
_____
_____
_____
_____

Now go back and feel the emotions associated with each of your responses. Those that are aligned with Who You Choose to Be will feel good. And those that are not will feel bad, therefore, they are Angel-Alerts — wrong-way signs beckoning you to readjust their frequencies. To begin the process of readjusting those frequencies, determine what you *want* and focus on each item for one minute a day. Soon those frequencies will become more dominant than their predecessors and your life experience will reflect those changes.

> [D]aily experience will seem to justify what you believe more and more. The only way to get out of [discomfort] is to become aware of your beliefs, aware of your own conscious thought and to change your beliefs so that you bring them in line with the kind of reality you want to experience....The first most important step is to realize that your beliefs **about** reality are just that — beliefs about reality and not necessarily attributes of reality. You must make a clear distinction between you and your beliefs. You must then realize that your beliefs are physically materialized. What you believe to be true in your experience **is** true. To change the physical effect you must change the original belief — while being quite aware that for a time, physical materializations of the old beliefs may still hold. However, as you change your beliefs the physical evidence will begin to gradually prove your new belief as faithfully as your old one did.[8]
>
> — JANE ROBERTS
> The Nature of Personal Reality - A Seth Book

> Stick to your beliefs, if that serves you. Hold tight. Do not waiver. For your ideas about "right" and "wrong" are your definitions about Who You Are. Yet do not require that others define themselves according to your terms. And don't stay so "stuck" in your present beliefs and customs that you halt the process of evolution itself.[9]
>
> — NEALE DONALD WALSCH
> Conversations with God - Book 3

Unaware of how life really operates, you have adopted protective responses — survival mechanisms — to mitigate any harm or threat you may encounter in life. These responses have formed layers, often referred to as "excess baggage" (i.e,. red circuits) that are covering your *real* self. Unfortunately, they can become so burdensome that they can prevent you from living a life filled with love and laughter! So, let's uncover those layers and jettison their heavy burden. ☯

Peel Your Onion Layer by Layer and Set Your Real Self Free

Life is an onion. You peel it off one layer at a time, and sometimes you weep.
— CARL SANDBURG
1878-1967

I learned how to survive, but not how to live. — GILLY A.

We all live with the objective of being happy; our lives are different and yet the same. — ANNE FRANK
1929-1945

You cannot experience yourself as what you are until you've encountered what you are not.[10]
— NEALE DONALD WALSCH
Conversations with God - Book 1

There were deep secrets hidden in my heart, never said for fear others would scoff or sneer. At last I can reveal my sufferings, for the strength I once felt in silence has lost all its power. — DEIDRA SARAULT

They always say that time changes things, but you actually have to change them yourself. — ANDY WARHOL
1928-1987

Mistakes are the portals of discovery. — JAMES JOYCE
1882-1941

Sometimes a person has to go back, really back — to have a sense, an understanding of all that's gone to make them — before they can go forward. — PAULE MARSHALL

Living in the old paradigm, you have no idea why 'bad stuff' happens, much less how to prevent it. As a result, your life has been a process of learning how to survive, trying to fit in, and attempting to get some 'good stuff' along the way. Throughout this process you experienced unpleasant events that you perceived as threatening. In your desire to protect yourself, you adopted behaviors, either consciously or subconsciously, to avoid these threats if they reoccurred. These behaviors have produced 'coats of armor,' or layers protecting your real self, somewhat like the layers on an onion protect its core.

An example of a subconscious protective reaction: When you were a child you may have burned your hand on a hot stove. In that traumatic moment, your brain registered this experience as a threat to your physical body. The result? You now have an automatic avoidance reaction around hot stoves that protects you from being burned.

An example of a conscious protective reaction: When you were young, you were more than likely teased over one of your 'imperfections' (we all have them). These experiences created emotional scars that may have resulted in adopting the protective response of becoming a bully, outmaneuvering others before they could bully you, or perhaps withdrawing into a shell, where you ignored these kind of remarks and stifled your feelings.

As you accrued one unpleasant life experience after another, you simultaneously accrued one protective layer upon another which covered the core essence of Who You Really Are. And the *real* you is pure, spontaneous, joyful, and innocent, without judgment, shame, or fear. Therefore, who you are today is a result of both your inherited beliefs and the protective responses you adopted.

Eliminate Your Excess Baggage — Those Unwanted Frequencies You Continue to Project

Because you are now reading this book, suffice it to say, your protective responses were effective — you survived. However, the emotional scars left in their wake still exist. For each of your survival mechanisms produced a red circuit that will continue to magnetize evidence until it is readjusted. Evidence of these red circuits manifests as an inappropriate response to a perceived threat. In other words, if you feel threatened in some way today and one of your buttons is pushed, you will respond as you did long ago as that bully or person in a shell.

If you fail to readjust these frequencies, sooner or later you will experience difficulty, detachment, or ambivalence in your relationships and you will wonder why. Someone significant in your life may say that your bullying or introversion was hurting them. Or they may say nothing, concluding that you no longer love them, and they will gradually drift away, either physically or emotionally. You will then reach a critical point and either seek professional help, accept your condition as "just being who you are," blame someone else for what is going wrong in your life, or go out and buy a red sports car (part of the mid-life crisis syndrome).

Gathering the Info Necessary to Create Your New Now

What you have done is unimportant compared to what you are about to do. How you have erred is insignificant compared to how you are about to create.[11]
— NEALE DONALD WALSCH
Conversations with God - Book 3

The test of a civilized person is first self-awareness, and then depth after depth of sincerity in self-confrontation.
— CLARENCE DAY
1874-1935

How can you identify your excess baggage and rid yourself of their unwanted frequencies? First, by uncovering those childhood issues that created your red circuits, for they have created barriers that are preventing you from living an optimal life experience. Why? Those red circuits are restricting the flow of energy and will entrap you in recurring negative experiences. Therefore, if you fail to shed your now-unnecessary protective responses, their powerful frequencies will simply magnetize more unpleasant evidence of their existence. Therefore, to *truly* live, love, and laugh, it is to your benefit to examine the experiences from your past and utilize them as 'critical data' — data that will help to clarify what you want. This data is important because you will use it in the reconstruction of your comfort zone — the new set of orders you convey to Angel.

A person who has experienced traumatic events in life, such as sexual abuse, the death of loved ones, traumatic illnesses, accidents, family disruption, drug addictions and the like, can become bonded with the past painful events and replay them for attention and pity. These wounds of our lives can seem to give us an enormous amount of power over others. The more we tell others about our wounds and our suffering, the more we create an atmosphere of pity for ourselves. Our creative spirit remains so connected to our memories of woundedness that it cannot be about the business of transforming and manifesting. A feeling of being unworthy of receiving all that one desires is the result. Very often the tale of these woes is told in the first few moments with a sort of urgency for the listener to know how horrible the wounding was and still is. After a while the ego uses this energy as a power play in individual and group situations that encourage discussion of one's struggles to survive the wounding. This can keep individuals from advancing spiritually and can reinforce the image of themselves as unfortunate. To finalize the path of worthiness, you must sever your relationship with these old wounds.[12]

— DR. WAYNE DYER

This is the reason so many people have unhappy experiences repeated in their lives: I knew of a woman who bragged of her troubles. She would go about saying to people; "I know what trouble is!" and then wait for their words of sympathy. Of course, the more she mentioned her troubles, the more she had, for by her words she was "condemned." She should have used her words to neutralize her troubles instead of to multiply them. For example — had she said repeatedly: "I cast every burden upon the Christ within and I go free," and not voiced her sorrows, they would have faded from her life, for "by your words you are justified."[13]

— FLORENCE SCOVEL SHINN
1871-1940

To uncover the real you, you must determine why you put on your layers, recognize that those layers are now interfering with your having a joyful life experience, and heal the emotional scars they created by readjusting their frequencies!

Peeling Back a Few of My Layers

When I was growing up, there was little demonstration of affection in my family. My father was an alcoholic and extremely violent when he drank.

While in a drunken rampage my father would often, without provocation, unleash his rage on my mother or older brother. During those times I would intervene and try to defend them. I would stand up to my father and defiantly attack, condemn, goad, curse, and castigate him — anything it took to divert his attention so that he wouldn't harm them. And my body bore testimony to his wrath, covered in black and blue welts from beatings with his belt, or an occasional black eye. After enduring countless occasions where he came close to killing me, I became numb to the pain. My fear transmuted to rage — I no longer cared if I lived or died. At that time in our culture (I was born in 1949), society stayed out of 'family business,' essentially closing its eyes to child and spousal abuse. When I was nineteen years old I married (I had to escape), and found that I yearned for affection on a constant basis to fill the void left from my childhood. I look back on my first marriage with a profound appreciation for my former husband and no regrets. He was the antithesis of my father. Loving, kind, and gentle, which provided me the foundation for a reparenting process that was a wonderful gift. One of the repercussions of my childhood, however, was a mistrust of people. And this mistrust manifested in many ways, one being an extreme discomfort while hugging people. I was particularly ill at ease having a woman hug me and I interpreted hugs from men as having a sexual implication. Of course, in reality, hugging was merely an expression of warmth, but one I had never experienced, so I was fearful of it.

From the ages of 29 to 37, I sang in a band part-time while simultaneously owning and operating a fine jewelry store. During that time, I met a musical group of wonderful, talented guys called the "Perfect Circle," who would occasionally invite me to sing with them when they performed at a club. These experiences were like magic to me, because not only did they know some of the songs I sang, but could also harmonize with me — an awesome experience! I had a problem though. When I knew that I would be seeing them, I would begin to experience anxiety attacks because I knew they would *hug* me! However, my joy of singing exceeded my fear of hugging, so, toes curled, tongue in cheek, heart beating sooo fast, I forced myself to hug them. And after repeating this process a number of times, I became more and more comfortable hugging people and eventually became a *hug*aholic!

This was the process I had to undergo to peel back one of my layers and eradicate a red circuit. I look back on this layer as one that subconsciously protected me from people (who were untrustworthy in my young mind, for they, too, could potentially hurt me), my survival adaptation. But, as an adult, this layer interfered with my ability to feel a true depth of affection and emotion from others! The process of ridding myself of that red circuit was vital to my evolution and allowed me to get closer to the core of the real me that I am continually uncovering. And from where I stand today, I feel much, much better!

When I was eighteen years old, I experienced yet another brutal beating from my father. This incident, however, became the catalyst for him to seek help because he finally recognized that he was indeed capable of killing me (he had come very close on that occasion) which frightened him considerably. He became acutely aware of the intensity of his emotions and felt powerless to control them. As a result, he joined Alcoholics Anonymous where he was helped greatly. In fact, after being involved in the program for a number of years, my dad's transformation was so significant that it seemed as if a new soul inhabited his body. He felt deep remorse for the emotional and physical abuse he inflicted upon my brothers, sisters, and me. And I feel a profound sorrow for the little girl I had been, so desperately needing affection and guidance, forced to grow up and defend my very life between the ages of five and eighteen. The significance of this abuse and neglect became especially poignant for me after giving birth to my son (when I was forty years old). I then knew first-hand how vulnerable a child really is.

Although I survived these experiences, they left many emotional scars — red circuits — in their wake. Problems and issues began to manifest in my life. Resolved to understand them, I sought therapy which enabled me to understand my feelings on a deeper level. Yet as painful as my negative experiences were, I can honestly tell you that they became the catalyst for my developing many positive attributes: learning to rely upon myself, being able to differentiate between real fear and insignificant barriers, being responsible, being a do-er in life rather than a dreamer, being cognizant of my power, and having a profound sense of empathy and compassion for others. Additionally, these experiences became the catalysts that inspired me to search for truth (adversity will compel you to seek answers), where I can now share what I have learned. And in retrospect, each of my experiences was instrumental in preparing me for my Mission.

The moral of this story: The trick is not to deny the challenges and obstacles that have occurred in your life, but to dissect them and uncover their treasures — the golden opportunities that lie buried within them. You cannot go back. You can only move forward and try to understand what happened, why it happened, and then utilize what happened to your benefit. There are no mistakes you cannot profit from, regardless of how tragic they may have been. Minimally, your negative experiences assist you in clarifying what you want, so you can apply the Four-Step Formula and choose that for your life experience.

Now, let's uncover your layers. To identify your survival adaptations, the protective responses you adopted, begin by writing down your most unforgettable ordeals.

Exploring Your Life Story

To rid yourself of annoying restrictions... repattern your past from the present. Use [the past] as a rich source, looking through it for your successes, restructuring it. When you search it looking for what is wrong, then you become blind to what is right...so that the past only mirrors the shortcomings that now face you. [14]

— JANE ROBERTS
The Nature of Personal Reality - A Seth Book

Know thyself.

— SOCRATES
469-399 BC

What has happened to you so far in your life? Beginning with your school days, what were significant events in your life?

_____
_____
_____
_____
_____
_____
_____

What did you these experiences cause you to *believe* about yourself and/or others?

_____
_____
_____
_____
_____
_____

Now follow the same procedure for your first employment experience.

_____
_____
_____
_____
_____
_____
_____

Your first significant relationship:

_____
_____
_____
_____
_____
_____
_____
_____
_____
_____
_____

Your first or only marriage.

_____
_____
_____
_____
_____
_____
_____
_____
_____

Your children.

_____
_____
_____
_____
_____
_____
_____
_____

Now add any other significant experiences or relationships where you drew a conclusion or *belief* about the nature of life itself.

_____
_____
_____
_____
_____
_____
_____

If you find it difficult to identify the layers you have donned, think of instances in your life that evoked strong emotional reactions within. You may need to enlist the help of others in this endeavor (they are usually most accommodating…). Ask them to try and recall occurrences where you may have overreacted to a situation. After uncovering those experiences, think about how you were feeling in those moments and try and recall earlier occasions where you felt those identical feelings. As you trace your feeling frequencies back further and further, you will generally be led to the origin of your red circuits — most often painful childhood experiences. Once uncovered, you can readjust their frequencies from red to green.

All Your Trials And Tribulations Actually Had a Benefit!

A pessimist is one who makes difficulties of his opportunities; an optimist is one who makes opportunities of his difficulties. — REGINALD B. MANSELL

Now, think of the positive things you learned as a result of your preceding experiences and write them down. Although this may be difficult, I promise you that positive aspects are inherent in any life event, they are things you never would have known had you *not* gone through those experiences. *For example*: If you were bullied, you may have finally stood up to the bully and gained a sense of power as a result — power you didn't realize you had — and your peers may have looked at you differently from that day forward.

School

_____

_____

_____

_____

_____

_____

_____

Job

_____

_____

_____

_____

_____
_____
_____

Relationship

_____
_____
_____
_____
_____
_____
_____

Marriage

_____
_____
_____
_____
_____
_____
_____

Children

_____
_____
_____
_____
_____
_____
_____

Miscellaneous

_____
_____
_____
_____
_____
_____
_____

Your Negative Experiences Provide
Necessary Feedback

Men can starve from a lack of self-realization as much as they can from a lack of bread. — RICHARD WRIGHT
1908-1960

There are no mistakes. The events we bring on ourselves, no matter how unpleasant, are necessary in order to learn what we need to learn. Whatever steps we take, they're necessary to reach the places we've chosen to go. — RICHARD BACH

Now, write down the negative aspects of each of your experiences (a little easier...), followed by the opposite of each negative. *For example*: If you had a significant other who was unfaithful, write down its opposite — what you would have preferred — what you discovered was important to you through this painful experience. Rather than a partner who strays, you would prefer a monogamous, trusting, respectful relationship. Remember, each of your negative experiences is providing you vital information about what you don't want, and from that perspective, you can choose what you *do* want. (Aren't you glad that all that pain had a benefit?)

Although this may seem simplistic, our world is filled with many options, beliefs, contrast, and diversity. Often, *until* you have experienced something negative, you don't *know* what you want. In fact, you are always in the best position to know what you want when you feel strong emotion about what you don't want. Therefore, nothing in life can be construed as a mistake because all of your experiences help to define and shape your life from this point forward.

School

_____

_____

_____

_____

_____

Job

_____

_____

_____

Relationship

_____
_____
_____
_____
_____
_____

Marriage

_____
_____
_____
_____
_____
_____

Children

_____
_____
_____
_____
_____
_____

Miscellaneous

_____
_____
_____
_____
_____
_____
_____
_____
_____
_____

Your New Life Story: Chapter Two

*Glorify what you are today, yet do not condemn what
you were yesterday, nor preclude what you could be
tomorrow.* [15]
— NEALE DONALD WALSCH
Conversations with God - Book 3

*There is no need to recriminate yourself. Simply notice
what you've been choosing and choose again.* [16]
— NEALE DONALD WALSCH
Conversations with God - Book 1

*The subconscious mind is man's faithful servant, but one
must be careful to give it the right orders. Man has ever
a silent listener at his side — his subconscious mind.
Every thought, every word is impressed upon it and
carried out in amazing detail. It is like a singer making a
record on the sensitive disc of the phonographic plate.
Every note and tone of the singer's voice is registered. If
he coughs or hesitates, it is registered also. So let us break
all the old records of the subconscious mind, the records
of our lives we do not wish to keep, and make new and
beautiful ones.* [17]
— FLORENCE SCOVEL SHINN
1871-1940

Let's now convey a new set of orders to Angel — one that reflects all
that you have discovered. Take your list of both the positive aspects of
your experiences as well as your list of the *opposite* of the negative aspects
and create a composite of what you now choose.

School

_____

_____

_____

_____

_____

_____

_____

_____

_____

_____

_____

Job

_____
_____
_____
_____
_____
_____
_____
_____
_____

Relationship

_____
_____
_____
_____
_____
_____
_____
_____
_____

Marriage

_____
_____
_____
_____
_____
_____
_____
_____
_____

Children

_____
_____
_____
_____
_____
_____
_____
_____
_____

Miscellaneous

_____

_____

_____

_____

_____

_____

_____

_____

_____

_____

_____

_____

_____

_____

_____

_____

_____

_____

To summarize what you uncovered from your past negative experiences:

1. Your protective responses were revealed.
2. Each experience allowed you to discover positive aspects within it.
3. You gained an understanding about what you didn't want which provided you the clarity to determine what you want!

Years ago I tore out a magazine article that 'spoke' to me. Although the words written were those of an incest victim, they seemed to articulate what I felt in my heart about my tumultuous past.

> I feel about my life the way some people feel about war. If you survive, then it becomes a good war. Danger makes you active, it makes you alert, it forces you to experience and thus to learn. I now know the cost of my life, the real price that has been paid. Contact with inner pain has immunized me against most petty hurts. Hopes I still have in abundance, but very few needs. My pride of intellect has been shattered. If I didn't know about half my own life, what other knowledge can I trust? Yet, even

here I see a gift, for in place of my narrow, pragmatic world of cause and effect and matter moving to immutable laws, I have burst into an infinite world full of wonder. The whole mystery of the universe has my reverence. Nothing is sure, but nothing can be dismissed. I pay attention. All of us are haunted by the failed hopes and undigested deeds of our forebears. I was lucky to find my family's dinosaur intact in one deep grave. My main regret is excessive self-involvement. Too often I was sleepwalking through other people's lives, eyes turned inward while I washed the blood off my hands. My toughest lesson was to renounce my own sense of specialness, to let the princess die along with the guilt-ridden child in my closet, to see instead the specialness of the world around me. Always I was traveling from darkness into the light. In such journeys, time is our ally, not our enemy. We can grow wise. As the arteries harden, the spirit can lighten. As the legs fail, the soul can take wing. Things do add up. Life does have shape and maybe even purpose. Or so it seems to me.

— UNKNOWN

Exorcizing Another of My Layers

On one occasion when I was fourteen years old, my father had beaten me moments before an orthodontist appointment. As I entered the doctor's office, I was crying hysterically, my hair was disheveled, my knee was bloody, and my clothes were a mess. One of his assistants looked at me in horror and asked what had happened. Feeling bitter and unashamed, I replied that my father had beaten me. Her retort? "No he didn't, you fell and skinned your knee."

After that episode I concluded that there was no one I could rely upon, therefore I had to rely on myself. And because no one was in control that I could trust, I had to control everything. Now this can be the good news and the bad news. Bad news, because on occasion I carried this control a bit too far. Every Christmas, birthday, holiday, etc., I had to be the one in charge of everything. I was the only one I trusted to do it right, and I was a perfectionist. I would spend days preparing food, buying gifts, and decorating the house, all for my family to have the 'perfect' celebration. As the years passed, however, I began to resent the members of my family because I was the only one working while they were having a good time! When my frustration finally reached a boiling point, I suggested that we alternate hosting these occasions.

On the first occasion that I was not in charge, I began to experience an anxiety attack. My sister was preparing Beef Wellington for our Christmas Eve dinner and had grand aspirations for a beautiful gourmet meal. At eleven p.m. we still had not eaten (she was still yucking it up… forgetting about her new role as 'hostess' and all the *work* she had to do), and we were starving! She had not finished wrapping the meat in the pastry crusts and *still* had visions of braiding the pastry dough to place atop the Wellingtons as her little 'artistic touch.' Well, I was going crazy and said, "Let's forget the fancy-shmancy crusts, and get these things into the oven so we can eat!" Momentarily I felt good, as I was once again in control (the role I was most comfortable with), and upon being fed, all was fine. And with each successive occasion hosted by my siblings, my anxiety lessened little by little until I eventually began to relax, let go of some of the perfectionism, and truly enjoy someone serving me. As a matter of fact, I now much prefer being a guest!

The moral of this story: Let go of your desire to control and let your sisters do the work… (☺ha, ha!). And another layer was exorcized!

Getting Closer and Closer To My Core

We are healed of a suffering, only by experiencing it to the fullest. — MARCEL PROUST
1871-1922

The following is another experience where I attempted to push away my past, not understanding that I had to delve into it in order to heal it. When I was in my twenties, the subject of my past was one that did not interest me. I was glad it was over, I had survived. What could possibly be the *benefit* of going back into it? I was now entering a new chapter in my life, one where I was in control. Sounds logical, right? However, after twelve years of marriage, I had a nagging feeling of discontent with my life but had no idea why. So naturally I blamed my husband. Looking back, I can now see that this discomfiting dilemma became the catalyst that inspired me to discover how my past actually *had* impacted my life.

When I married my first husband in 1969, I was nineteen and he was twenty. Although he served in the Army at the height of the Viet Nam War, he remained state-side because he was a 'sole-surviving son' (his father died suddenly of a heart attack at the age of thirty-five while serving in the Air Force). My husband earned $90 a month (yes, you read it right), our rent was $300, we had a car payment and, of course, other monthly living expenses. Compelled by necessity to supplement our income, I scoured the newspapers and discovered a want-ad for a part-time sales position. My husband and I were hired as a team to sell deluxe cookware (three-ply stainless steel with copper clad bottoms. Are you impressed?) door-to-door and became the top salespeople in Columbus, Georgia! We received a $40 commission per sale and thought we were rich!

Living away from home for the first time was both fun and lonely. Fun, because I was finally on my own, but lonely, because I had become addicted to the adrenalin rush born of living in a dysfunctional home, so anything that resembled 'normal' was boring — it had no 'charge,' no 'rush.' Because both my husband and I had experienced dysfunctional childhoods, void of healthy role models (who didn't?), we each assumed roles in our marriage emulated from TV personalities resulting in very rigid 'scripts.' There was no tolerance in our roles for anything that deviated from the original script or any kind of personal growth (we never heard of that...). Therefore, if one of our behaviors changed or we dared to reexamine our role (God forbid), it threatened the very core of the marriage. We had assumed at our tender young ages that we would be in marital bliss forever.... Although our roles imposed many restrictions that impeded aspects of our growth, they became our comfort zones, and as a result, provided us a level of safety and security.

As much as I felt safe with my role on one level, after twelve years of marriage, I began to feel as though I was suffocating. I was growing restless; I was changing, but the relationship didn't allow for that, so I was violating the rules. Our problems felt like a dull ache of unfulfillment under the surface of everyday life that wouldn't go away, but were never brought out in the open because we didn't know what to do with them. Like most, we blamed each other for the negative feelings we were experiencing. I felt that my husband didn't appreciate me the way I felt I deserved to be appreciated, and I'm sure he felt the same way. However, in our fear of changing the status-quo, we swept our problems under the rug and donned the masks of 'Barbie® and Ken®' for the outside world.

This nagging undercurrent was always present, though, so when I met another man who thought I was wonderful, I became enchanted. Here was a different man who was sweet, charming, caring, sensitive, and gentle, a man who saw my 'true value' and appreciated me! Therefore, working through issues with my husband never became an option. Another man was the answer! I assumed the grass had to be greener, so I asked for a separation. In my naïvete, I felt that if you were attracted to another person when you were married, the marriage was over. Although that belief may seem absurd to you, I was innocent, for I did not know anything different. There were no courses in school entitled

Relationships 101, let alone *Marriage* 101; television didn't broadcast talk shows at that time that helped to shed light upon those aspects in life, and in retrospect, I obviously didn't get it!

After a six-month, long-distance relationship with this other man, all the while trying to explore and understand the feelings I was struggling with, I decided to return to the illusory 'safety' of my husband. In my state of insecurity, vulnerability, and longing for peace in my life, I 'bought' his idea that all our problems were *my* fault and sought a minister for counseling. After a few months, the minister felt that our problems were deeper than he had originally considered, resided with the two of us, and were beyond his level of expertise. He suggested couple's therapy with a credentialed psychotherapist.

Well, as you may have guessed, much damage had been done to the marriage by my violation of the 'rules,' and although my husband felt great love for me, he was also seething with intense feelings of anger and rage under the surface (lots of red circuits created from my leaving him). However, because we didn't understand the real dynamics behind our problems and were both still addicted to the dysfunctional 'security' the relationship provided, we sought the recommended counseling.

After a number of sessions, our psychotherapist suggested that I look into my childhood for unresolved issues. Well, to me that was unthinkable. Why the heck would I want to stir up that horrible time in my life? It was over, thank God. I was moving forward, not backward. I emphatically said, "No, the past is the past. I have closed the pages on those chapters in my life, relegating them to my 'personal history.' The problems I was experiencing with my husband had nothing to do with my childhood! They had to be a result of something else, and once he discovered and identified them, life could return to normal!" The therapist then explained that the two of us needed to redefine our roles. My husband, however, in his naïveté, was quite adamant about resuming our original roles and convinced that I just needed 'fixing.' It was then I knew that I could no longer remain in the relationship and we divorced. Suffice it to say, it was much deeper than that with many more nuances, but the point was: I didn't have a clue that the experiences in my childhood had effected my later life.

During the period of time that my husband and I were engaged in therapy, I became infatuated with my therapist, and, I later discovered, he with me. I perceived him as a man who possessed knowledge — a man who could transcend the petty issues of life.... Little did I know that I was experiencing a very common reaction labeled "transference," where a patient falls in love with his or her therapist. This infatuation occurs because therapy can become a very powerful aphrodisiac.

Another person not only listens intently to your every word for an entire hour, but also provides you a loving, non-judgmental environment, an environment where you feel completely accepted for Who You Really Are, imperfections and all. However, it does not resemble reality. Nevertheless, imbued in this illusion, after my divorce, I entered into a two-year live-in relationship with my psychotherapist, which sadly was even *more* dysfunctional than my marriage!

At the onset of this relationship, I began to receive intense feelings of foreboding in the pit of my stomach. While packing his belongings for him to move in with me, my feelings grew so intolerable that I blurted out that "this was just not going to work." In that moment though, he had a childlike temper-tantrum and I unfortunately, backed down. After all, I rationalized, he knew so much more than I did (Ph.D. and all). Two long years later, fraught with many heart-wrenching experiences (with Angel incessantly tugging at my sleeve), I finally understood my dysfunctional dependence on him, reclaimed my power, and found the courage to ask him to leave, in spite of the fact that he was in the process of saving my home from foreclosure (due to issues I had inherited from my former husband). I finally realized that I had to be true to myself and let the chips fall where they may — house, or no house.

The Workshop — A Life-Changing Event For Me

In the midst of this relationship, and probably as a result of the unhappiness I was feeling, I began the process of reopening the old chapters of my life. One of my younger twin sisters suggested that she and I attend a weekend workshop for Adult Children of Alcoholics. She had discovered that she, like my father, was an alcoholic and had joined AA. My new therapist (a woman; I felt safer) also felt that it was a good idea.

The goal of this workshop (unbeknownst to those of us attending) was to exorcize our red circuits — the residual pain and trauma that continued to impact our lives. The workshop curriculum sought to accomplish its goal by having each of us reenact a traumatic event that had significantly affected our lives. Thrust back into our dramas in a controlled safe environment, we would be provided an optimal opportunity to release some of the rage, sadness, and regret that continued to plague us in adulthood.

Prior to the workshop, one lady had been selected to become a 'star' for the day — to reenact a traumatic life event on a deeper, more expansive level. To provide an all-encompassing, graphic perspective of the underlying dynamics that preceded this lady's ordeal, she was given the prior task of researching the history of key players who had participated in her tragedy — key players that included both her and her husband's parents and grandparents. Workshop participants were to assume the roles of these key players and reenact the backgrounds that shaped each of these people's lives — from their births, to the 'unspoken rules' they 'marinated in' as a result of their family's influence. Interestingly, these histories also revealed the origin of each family member's red circuits, and how they were passed on from generation to generation.

Prior to this enactment, gymnastic cushions were placed between the actors and the star. At a critical moment in this lady's drama — the moment that changed her life forever — she would be given a plastic baseball bat to beat these cushions, thus exorcizing the pent-up rage buried deep within her. This would be followed by an opportunity to create a new 'script' for this event. By releasing her destructive emotions from a position of awareness and power, an emotional healing would be facilitated and as a result, her powerful red circuits readjusted.

As this lady's nightmare slowly unfolded, the moment of reckoning was soon upon us. In a torrent of intense emotion fueled by rage, sadness, and regret — all the feelings she had tried to bury long ago — the star furiously pummeled the cushions. Imbued in the intensity of this drama, she was then asked how she wanted to *change* the moment — what she wished she had done. As she uttered her response and her feelings came gushing out, mere words cannot describe the emotional magnitude of what each of us experienced. Every person attending the seminar was living this moment vicariously, sobbing to their core, empathizing with the excruciatingly painful ordeal this lady, our sister, had endured.

Prior to attending the workshop, each of us was required to complete a detailed history of our lives to appraise the workshop therapists of our unresolved issues. Well, I had this idea that because my father had stopped drinking, went to AA, and was remorseful, I had *no* issues. I attended out of curiosity, to learn whatever I could... or so I thought.

After the conclusion of the star's drama, the group reorganized into smaller groups of six with two workshop therapists assigned to each. Each of us was then asked to reenact a short vignette of one of our emotionally-scarring experiences while the rest of us assumed acting roles in the dramas. Eventually, I was the only one who had *not* enacted a drama. My personal therapist had assured me that I did *not* have to participate if I chose not to. Thus, I declined my turn.

After observing my overenthusiastic volatile reactions to the various roles I played in other people's dramas, one of the workshop therapists, much to my chagrin, questioned my decision and asked me why I was there. I replied that I had come to observe rather than to participate;

that I was 'lucky' because my father no longer drank. The therapist, however, was not content with my 'pat' answer and startled me when he challenged, "Why do you have such perfect hair?" And before I had a chance to reply, he proceeded to mess it up! Then he attacked from two fronts — emotional and physical — as he further goaded me: "You're so strong, aren't you, Lauren? You were the strong one in your family, weren't you? The one who defended everyone, the one who defied your father? So, if you're so strong, take this!" and he handed me a gigantic five-foot rubber ball.

Shocked and alarmed by this confrontation, I pleaded, "Come on you guys, leave me alone." But the therapist was unrelenting in his onslaught: "You're so strong, Lauren, you don't need *help*, do you?" And at that moment, he took a blanket and placed it on top of me and the ball! Shrouded under the darkness of the blanket, I began to panic, however, I didn't know how to react 'appropriately.' This therapist was pressing every button I had, intentionally provoking me, while I was simultaneously doing all I could to 'keep it together' — *especially* in front of an audience.

After a few minutes — to me an eternity — he removed the blanket. And for a brief moment I felt relief, the onslaught was finally over. However, when my eyes refocused to the light, I found that my nightmare had actually just begun…. I was then thrust into a living hell. Two actors, playing the roles of my father and mother, were reenacting an all-too-familiar scene from my childhood: My father beating my mother! As I said earlier, whenever this situation occurred, I would always defend my mother. I was stronger than she was and believed that I could 'take' the beating. And, truthfully, it was actually easier for me to 'take' than it was to watch. At that pivotal moment, I have no explanation for what happened. I snapped. I was catapulted back into my childhood, imbued with the same uncontrollable feelings of hatred and rage I had had for my father then. In fact, it felt as though I had never left my childhood! With venom oozing from every fiber of my being, I swung the bat with utter vehemence, while simultaneously screaming guttural profanity at the top of my lungs! I then went beyond what the therapists had prepared for: I bulldozed through the protective barriers to 'get' the guy portraying my father. To me, he was completely indistinguishable from my father! Sensing my uncontrollable rage, the therapist then interceded and shouted, "What do you want, Lauren? How do you want to change this?"

Well, I was off in another world. The real me was not related to the 'crazy deranged lunatic' I had become in this quite-real nightmare. The buttons the therapist had pushed on me had accessed some other dimension outside of my reality. I suddenly awoke from this hell and cried out for my mother (in her fear she often abandoned us, leaving us to fend for ourselves). I was sobbing to my core, as was the 'Mom' actor. After exposing my dark side I felt utterly humiliated, embarrassed, and ashamed — especially after I so emphatically defended the fact that I did *not* need help. In that moment, all I wanted was to be left alone without everyone staring at the maniacal, possessed woman I had become. Every person in my group could now see right through the façade I had created; all the masks I wore to cover the pain and rage that I *did not even realize existed!*

I am certain that I scared the daylights out of every person in my group. They were probably all waiting for my head to begin spinning on my shoulders and for green vomit to spew from my mouth (remember *The Exorcist?*) — I was that scary. The following day was graduation and the actor who had portrayed my father (who attended the seminar as a therapist's aid and probably feared for his life the day before) came up to me, said nothing, and just hugged... and hugged... and hugged me.

The moral of this story: This was a life-changing event for me. It was pivotal, not only to my understanding of how much negative energy I was suppressing, but also to understanding how adversity creates the opportunities for growth and awareness. Additionally, it demonstrated the elaborate lengths I would go through to *not* open the chapters of my past — my past that needed healing. And luckily for me, the brilliant workshop therapist in my group was astute enough to see through my façade and courageously go the distance to help me to forever heal my life. And that, friends, is the reason that I share this traumatic experience with you. For I believe that my experience might assist you in uncovering any past events in your life that may still be magnetizing evidence, no matter how buried or insignificant they may appear to be. The significance is irrelevant, but the feelings underlying the event are relevant — they are the root cause of subsequent experiences that are projecting the same distressful frequencies.

Today, when I set limits for my son I recognize his instinctive anger. I tell him that it's okay to be angry — it's a normal feeling. I encourage him to hit a pillow *hard*, to vent his rage, to get it out of his system because I am not allowing him to do what he wants, which is in direct opposition to his core instinct of freedom. By creating a safe environment infused with acceptance and understanding, I help him to acknowledge his feelings rather than to suppress them. I explain how necessary and important it is to release his feelings in a healthy way. (I also constantly shower him with kisses, hugs, and much, much love — I feel so fortunate to have been blessed with him!)

Each of us possesses red circuits as a result of residual pain and anger from our childhoods, no matter how wonderful we may think they were.

At the very least, someone had to set limits and it was instinctive to rebel against them. If you were not allowed to vent your anger, you were forced to suppress it, and as a result, you will continually magnetize life experiences that make you angry. Therefore, only when you uncover the origin of your anger and stop denying it, can you begin to heal it! And if you fail to do so, someone, somewhere, sometime, may push one of your buttons and you will find yourself in the same 'place' that I went: The dimension of reality where distinctions are distorted. The 'place' where you may do something you regret. A 'place' where no therapist exists that will awaken you to reality.

This 'place' is a very real vortex of energy created by the accumulation of denied negative emotions that are seeking an outlet — the Law of Attraction 'doing it's thing.' And after my brief rendezvous in the altered state of consciousness of the 'place,' I now can fully comprehend the process that could occur which would make it very easy for a perfectly rational human being to commit a horrible crime. Think of the Menendez brothers, the boys who shot their parents to death; Susan Smith, the lady who drove her children into a lake; Jeffrey Dahmer, the man who murdered many innocent people.... What frequencies were those folks projecting when they committed their crimes? What powerful vortex of energy did they magnetize with their repressed feelings? I believe that each of those people experienced such prolonged periods of suppressing their emotions, they became 'ticking time bombs' that exploded when their buttons were pushed. And from a more expansive perspective, these people were simply Angacles — the physical manifestation of our collective repressed feelings — feelings that each of us deposits into the 'place' every day with our negative emotions.

If you had a childhood experience similar to mine — shockingly commonplace to those in my generation — I highly recommend this form of rage therapy, or "psycho-drama." This therapy will help you to release and heal your past negative experiences; eliminating the poisonous red circuits lurking within your body, soul, and energy field that may be covered up with masks: nice hair, beautiful clothes, a great career, good kids, a fancy car, a fantastic home, etc. And on the opposite end of the spectrum are other masks: illness, addiction, poverty, feelings of unworthiness, etc. The bottom line? Your red circuits are present in your energy field and will continue to magnetize evidence of their existence until you readjust them. And their repressed energy has the potential to ignite when someone pushes your button. ('Road rage' is one common example of the explosion of repressed energy.) Therefore, it is to your advantage to exorcize the red circuits born of your past negative experiences, for if you don't, you will continue to relive them over and over again, in some way, shape, or form. However, when you do readjust them, not only will you feel better, but you will also free yourself to live as life is meant to be lived: truly living, loving, and laughing! ⊘

Examine the Unspoken Rules in Your Family and Jettison Those That Don't Reflect The Real You

When you thought I wasn't looking, I saw you hang my first painting on the refrigerator and I wanted to paint another one.
When you thought I wasn't looking, I saw you feed a stray cat and thought it was good to be kind to animals.
When you thought I wasn't looking, I saw you make my favorite cake just for me and I knew that little things are special things.
When you thought I wasn't looking, I heard you say a prayer and believed there is a God I could always talk to.
When you thought I wasn't looking, I felt you kiss me goodnight and I felt loved.
When you thought I wasn't looking, I saw tears come from your eyes and I learned that sometimes things hurt, but it's all right to cry.
When you thought I wasn't looking, I saw that you cared and I wanted to be everything that I could be.
When you thought I wasn't looking, I looked... and wanted to say thanks for all the things I saw when you thought I wasn't looking.   — UNKNOWN

From the earliest stages the child automatically compares its interpretation of reality with its parents'. Since the parents are bigger and stronger and fulfill so many of its needs, it will attempt to bring its experience into line with their expectations and beliefs.[18]   — JANE ROBERTS
The Nature of Personal Reality - A Seth Book

You've seen what has resulted on your planet from the
passing down of values from parent to child. Your planet
is a mess.[19]
— NEALE DONALD WALSCH
Conversations with God - Book 2

Children Learn What They Live

If children live with criticism,
They learn to condemn.
If children live with hostility,
They learn to fight.
If children live with ridicule,
They learn to be shy.
If children live with shame,
They learn to feel guilty.
If children live with tolerance,
They learn to be patient.
If children live with encouragement,
They learn confidence.
If children live with praise,
They learn to appreciate.
If children live with fairness,
They learn justice.
If children live with security,
They learn to have faith.
If children live with approval,
They learn to like themselves.
If children live with acceptance and friendship,
They learn to find love in the world.
— DOROTHY LAW NOLTE

Capitalize on the Opportunities Your Family Provided

When you were a child, you were at the mercy of the god-like adults you depended upon, who, for the most part, had your best intentions in mind. They had their own beliefs, however fallible, and passed them on to you about what was right and wrong for both yourself and others. And as Iyanla Vanzant, the wonderful, warm, and loving author/ teacher/ 'Bringer of Light,' explains: you've been 'marinating' in those beliefs for a long time — they have soaked into your being.

Living in the Information Age, you have been exposed to a multitude of differing beliefs: those of your friends, co-workers, and society at large, which oftentimes opposed what you were taught as a child. At some point in time, you noticed these discrepancies and began to reconsider what you were taught. For example: Your parents may have been racist or believed that women were inferior to men and passed those beliefs onto you. However, because your life experiences were altogether different from those of your parents, you altered your belief.

Were you taught to be honest? Were you taught to be kind? Were you taught that others would take advantage of you if given the chance? Were you taught to be reliable, have integrity, or that family was important? Was the love that your family showed to you and others conditional, or unconditional? Were the values that were passed onto you *lived* by the members of your family, or merely lip-service? You may wish to consult the section on your core beliefs and discover how many you inherited. (pages 3–10 *The Past*)

By exploring the unspoken rules in your family, you can gather additional data — more hidden treasures — from which to construct your new comfort zone.

What were the unspoken rules in your family? What have you been marinating in?

_____

_____

_____

_____

_____

_____

_____

_____

_____

_____

_____

_____

_____

_____

_____

_____

_____

_____

_____

_____

_____

_____

_____

_____

_____

_____

_____

_____

_____

_____

_____

_____

_____

_____

_____

_____

Next, let's explore the level that *preceded* your parents, because each of them adopted the 'unspoken rules' from their respective families as well. What beliefs did your *grandparents* pass onto your mother and father? And which beliefs of your parents oppose those of *their* parents? (You may find it beneficial to conduct interviews. It can be very interesting and enlightening).

Your *mother's* mother_____

_____

_____

_____

_____

_____

_____

_____

_____

_____

_____

_____

_____

_____

_____

_____

_____

Your *father's* mother_____

_____
_____
_____
_____
_____
_____
_____
_____
_____
_____
_____
_____
_____
_____
_____
_____
_____
_____
_____
_____

Your *mother's* father_____

_____
_____
_____
_____
_____
_____
_____
_____
_____
_____
_____
_____
_____
_____
_____
_____
_____
_____

Your *father's* father _____

_____
_____
_____
_____
_____
_____
_____
_____
_____
_____
_____
_____

> *Some of your beliefs originated in your childhood, but*
> *you are not at their mercy unless you* **believe** *that you*
> *are. Because your imagination follows your beliefs, you*
> *can find yourself in a vicious circle in which you*
> *constantly paint pictures in your mind that reinforce*
> *negative aspects in your life.*[20]　　　— JANE ROBERTS
> 　　　　　　　　　　The Nature of Personal Reality - A Seth Book

Can you recognize the correlation between your beliefs and your life experiences? Can you recognize the correlation between your parent's beliefs and their life experiences? In your unawareness of the Four-Step Formula or your authentic power, can you understand how and why your life was not overflowing with love or laughter?

Your beliefs and what you glean from your personal history are providing you with the necessary data to create your new set of orders to convey to Angel. This information will become your launching pad to consciously reconstruct your comfort zone which you will do in the following section: *The Pathway.*

For now, let's learn more about who you — and every other person on this planet — *really* are by exploring the various 'cloaks' each of us have donned. We wear these cloaks to mask the frightened, vulnerable souls we really are while trekking our paths through the unknown. As you gain a new perspective of the reality behind the masks each of us wears, you will perceive your fellow travelers in a whole new light — a light that fosters compassion rather than judgment. And as an added bonus, you will progress further along your path to living life as it is meant to be lived: loving, and laughing! 🕮

Uncover the Disguise That Hides Your Real Self

Seek first to understand, not to be understood.
— ST. FRANCIS OF ASSISI
1181-1226

Life is playing a violin solo in public and learning the instrument as one goes on.
— SAMUEL BUTLER
1612-1680

People cannot be judged, as people often are, by their covers.[21]
— JULIA INGRAM and G.W. HARDIN
words spoken by Jesus to his followers from "The Messengers"

Through our own recovered innocence, we discern the innocence of our neighbors.
— HENRY DAVID THOREAU
1817-1862

It is not for you to judge the journey of another's soul. It is for you to decide who YOU are, not who another has been or has failed to be.[22]
— NEALE DONALD WALSCH
Conversations with God - Book 2

Everything that irritates us about others can lead us to an understanding of ourselves.
— CARL JUNG
1875-1961

Any preoccupation with ideas of what is right or wrong in conduct shows an arrested development.
— OSCAR WILDE
1854-1900

That which we call sin in others is experiment for us.
— RALPH WALDO EMERSON
1803-1882

She lacks confidence, she craves admiration insatiably. She lives on the reflections of herself in the eyes of others. She does not dare be herself.
— ANÄIS NIN
1903-1977

Spiritual energy brings compassion into the real world. With compassion, we see benevolently our own human condition and the condition of our fellow beings. We drop prejudice. We withhold judgment.
— CHRISTIANA BALDWIN

No man is your enemy, no man is your friend, every man is your teacher.
— UNKNOWN

Nobody, as long as he moves about among the chaotic currents of life, is without trouble.
— CARL JUNG
1875-1961

The Real You

When you arrived in this world, you were pure; you were innocent; you were eager to explore, anxious to touch, smell, eat, love, feel, know, and try. You were filled with wonder, curiosity, delight, joy, passion, eagerness, and awe. You were without shame, without judgment, and without fear. You were the embodiment of love — Who You Really Are. However, during your indoctrination into life on Earth, you adopted the prevailing beliefs of those around you and forgot Who You Really Are. You entered this 'game of life' — but didn't know that it was a game. And no one else knew it either. This was a game that you had to discover all by yourself. And though countless visionaries and ancients have revealed the game and its rules, we have dismissed their wisdom in the illusion of our civility and brilliance. The goal of this game of life? To awaken to Who We Really Are and live our lives from that perspective. The result? We create a Heaven on Earth.

Underlying All Behavior: Fear or Love

All human actions are motivated at their deepest level by one of two emotions — fear or love.[23]

— NEALE DONALD WALSCH
Conversations with God - Book I

In *A Course in Miracles*®, it is conveyed that there are essentially two emotions: love and fear. Although we have labeled different emotions with different names, they are, at their essence, either love or fear. So, if a person is not behaving in a loving way, he or she is afraid. Think about that.... How angry can you be with someone who is afraid? As a matter of fact, if you observe someone shaking in fear, that behavior elicits compassion from you, doesn't it? On the other hand, if you observe someone screaming or behaving inappropriately, it is merely fear in disguise (although it poses a greater challenge to respond with compassion). The bottom line? All negative behavior is based in fear and the illusion of powerlessness.

Fear is the energy which contracts, closes down, draws in, runs, hides, hoards, harms. Love is the energy which expands, opens up, sends out, stays, reveals, shares, heals.[24]

— NEALE DONALD WALSCH
Conversations with God - Book I

In the beginning there was no evil, fear, or hatred. There was only One Love, One Body of Potential, and One Spirit. As manifestations began to take shape, free will was extended to every aspect of love, to be life, to experience life, to fulfill its potential, and to know itself as love. There was even the choice to deny its own nature, if that should be desired. From this last choice, all the 'weeds' of peril have sprung. This last choice was a very important gift. For without it you would have been an aspect of love without the power to forward creation.[25]

— GLENDA GREEN
Love Without End: Jesus Speaks

The most important choice you were ever given was to be the Love that you are, or not... All negative emotion and experiences are the result of having chosen an alternative to honoring the love that you are...which is denial.[26]

— GLENDA GREEN
Love Without End: Jesus Speaks

Once a man's sense of self has been separated from his true nature, then love can be understood only as an action or a feeling. In that state, everyone will surely fall short. On earth, that is the current belief about the subject of love.[27]
— GLENDA GREEN
Love Without End: Jesus Speaks

Love is the power of the universe. Love is beyond just a feeling or an orientation. It is a dimension of intelligence and purposeful living. Above all, it is the essence of **being.** *Love heightens a person's instinct to nourish, enhance, and apply those purposes. Love is both a way of being and also a pathway for becoming. Love ignites life. Love savors life and sustains faith and hope. Even though life often brings lessons in hard packages, learning happens only when forgiveness has occurred and love is restored. That is how you take something from the school of hard knocks and transmute it into a permanent gain for yourself. You can then say "I don't have to do this again. I have completed this lesson. I know the meaning." Love brings certainty to life and when your love is clear and unpolluted with regrets or false desires, you will have the confidence to live your life with passion.*[28]
— GLENDA GREEN
Love Without End: Jesus Speaks

A New-Found Compassion for Your Fellow Traveler

Most of us go through life kicking and screaming, moaning and groaning, blaming someone else for the misery we feel, or incessantly whining about being victimized. And those reactions lock us into the first phase of creation: the negative emotion. Rather than utilizing our feeling as a Point of Power as it was intended, we instead focus on what's wrong and inadvertently magnetize more of it. The result? We push ourselves further and further from recognizing Who We Really Are and the real power we possess.

Trekking our paths in fear and trepidation, we observe others and intuitively discern what is acceptable from what is not. The result? We conform to the behaviors we deem as acceptable. Why? We want to be liked; we want to 'fit in,'. So we don a 'cloak' or personality type — a mask to conceal our uncertainty, despair, and distress.

Since each of us is engaged in the game of life at various levels, our behaviors will indicate what level of awareness we, and others, are at. As such, it is advantageous to understand our cloaks and behaviors because, in reality, they are simply subconscious survival adaptations. Achieving a state of awareness will allow us to pierce the illusion behind our masks — the illusion of fear and powerlessness that underlies our behaviors. Furthermore, as each of us becomes more and more aware, we will remember all too well the levels of unawareness we endured, subsequently, a keen sense of compassion will replace our old-paradigm judgments. We will recognize that no one can take the journey for another — it is a journey that each of us must take alone. And from that perspective, we will relate to our fellow travelers on their sacred journeys in an entirely different manner.

The Four Personality Cloaks — What Cloak Are You Wearing?

The cloak that each of us has adopted was generally based on the cloaks each of our family members adopted. And interestingly, our cloaks change as our environment changes. For example: We may wear one cloak at our place of employment where we wish to be perceived in one way; another at home, where we are perceived in an altogether different manner; and yet another when we are with friends. The cloak we don in any moment depends upon how we wish to be perceived. Have you observed how proficiently we adapt to the various circumstances we encounter in life? Any great salesperson will tell you that her strength lies in her ability to perceive and adapt to the needs of her clients. She is able to intuit their frequencies, thereby creating an environment where her clients feel comfortable, making it far easier for her to consummate a sale.

Our cloaks can be best described as four distinctive personality types which fall into two categories. The aggressive category includes the Dynamic and Cheerful types, and the passive category, the Virtuous and Easy-Going types. As no classification is ever all-inclusive, most of us are a combination of these types. However, each of us has a dominant personality type. Let's now determine which cloak you, or those you are closest to, are wearing.

The Aggressive Cloak of Mr./Ms. Dynamic

When they are loving: Dynamics are born leaders. They are powerful, active, and have a compulsive need for change. They are predisposed to correct wrongs, are strong-willed, and decisive. Not easily discouraged, they are generally unemotional. Independent and self-sufficient, they exude confidence and can run most anything. They are goal-oriented, great organizers, and can see the whole picture. Dynamics seek practical solutions and move quickly to action. Insisting on production, they meet their goals and stimulate activity.

When they are fearing: Dynamics can be bossy, impatient, rigid, and intimidate or dominate others. They are quick-tempered and can't relax. They get other's attention by being loud, threatening, or exploding in an outburst. They enjoy controversy and arguments; find it hard to give up when losing, and thrive on opposition. Unsympathetic and disliking emotions, they have little tolerance for mistakes. They may be rude, tactless, manipulating, and demanding. Work is usually their major preoccupation. They order others around, make decisions for them, and have a tendency to use them, seducing others with their aura of power. Dynamics can be inflexible, sarcastic, or sometimes even violent.

Who do you know who exhibits the largest percentage of their personality wearing the cloak of Mr./Ms. Dynamic?

_____

_____

_____

_____

_____

_____

_____

If *you* are wearing the cloak of Mr./Ms. Dynamic:

Your major fears are losing your freedom, and not having enough of whatever you want. You get hooked on the adrenalin rush of overpowering and winning. If this best describes your behavior, ask yourself, "What is it that I want most? Do I need to get it only this way?" Be willing to stay open and flexible and stop trying to control everything. Although it may be difficult at first, it will free you from anxiety when you succeed. Be sensitive to your feelings and they will guide you with integrity.[29]

What's Really Going on with Mr./Ms. Dynamic?

When he/she is exhibiting:	He/She is really feeling:
1. Denial or not listening	Fear of being controlled and losing freedom
2. Anger	Fear of not [having] enough
3. Get whatever I can, any way I can	Someone else will get it first
4. Arrogance	No one notices me [fear of being alone]
5. Me first	Fear of not having enough
6. Control	I have to do it alone
7. Rage	No one ever took care of me [fear of being alone]
8. Violence	I'm dead [fear of being alone or of the unknown]

Makes others feel:	Reactions from other personalities
1. Afraid	*Easy-Going* — Don't hurt me, I'm not threatening [fear of aloneness]
2. Angry	*Dynamic* — You can't hurt me. I'll fight back [Fear of losing freedom]
3. Vengeful	*Cheerful* — You're not as powerful as you appear to be [fear of losing freedom]
4. Negated	*Virtuous*: I will not confront you [Fear of aloneness][29]

How Will the Four-Step Formula Benefit Dynamics?

Dynamics will benefit from the Four-Step Formula by understanding that there *is* enough for everyone to have abundance. They will learn to relax and let go of their anxiety that they may lose their freedom, because they have complete control of it. As they learn to utilize the Four-Step Formula in their lives, they will become what they really are at their cores: wonderful, loving leaders, inspiring those around them.[29]

The Aggressive Cloak of Mr./Ms. Cheerful

When they are loving: Cheerfuls are advocates. They have wit, infallible logic, facts, and intellect. Possessing appealing personalities, they are talkative, and always telling stories. They have a good sense of humor and will be the life of a party. Cheerfuls are emotional, demonstrative, enthusiastic, and expressive. Curious, wide-eyed, and innocent, they live in the present. They are always sincere at heart, child-like, and look great on the surface. Creative and colorful, they start in a flashy way — inspiring and charming others to join and work. Cheerfuls make friends easily, love people, seem exciting, and don't hold grudges. They apologize quickly and like spontaneous activities.

When they are fearing: Cheerfuls are compulsive talkers, dwell on trivia, and sometimes scare others off. They exaggerate, elaborate, and have restless energy. They can be egotistical, complaining, and naïve. Cheerfuls have loud voices, loud laughs, and become angry easily. They seem phony and too happy to some, and are childlike at heart. They don't follow through and oftentimes have their priorities out of order. Their confidence fades fast and they decide by feelings. Easily distracted, they forget obligations, interrupt others, and don't listen. Cheerfuls make excuses, answer for others, and hate to be alone. They can break down another person's spirit by mentally monitoring activities and motivations. Hyper-vigilant, skeptical, sarcastic, needling, perfectionistic, or self-righteous, they have a tendency to look for ways to make others seem to be in the wrong.

Who do you know who primarily exhibits the traits of a Cheerful?

_____

_____

_____

_____

_____

_____

If you are wearing the cloak of Mr./Ms. Cheerful:

Your major fear is that of being alone. Are you suspicious of others, or feel like they are not paying enough attention to you? Do you needle or question them endlessly? You get hooked in the illusion of self-righteousness. You can begin to escape these tendencies by putting yourself in the shoes of the other person. Be willing to talk about your real feelings rather than to chase someone who is withdrawing.[29]

What's Really Going on With Mr./Ms. Cheerful?

When he/she is exhibiting:	He/She is really feeling:
1. Who do you think you are?	No acknowledgment as a child [fear of losing freedom]
2. Where are you going?	People leave me and I'm afraid [fear of aloneness]
3. Why didn't you?	I want proof of your love [fear of aloneness]
4. Why don't you?	You're going to leave me [fear of aloneness]
5. I told you so.	You need me, I need you [fear of aloneness]

Makes others feel:	Reactions from Other Personalities:
1. Monitored	*Virtuous* — You don't know what I'm thinking [fear of losing freedom]
2. Negated	*Virtuous* — You are more powerful than I am. You count more than I do [fear of aloneness]
3. Wrong	*Easy-Going* — Someday you'll see my true worth [fear of aloneness][29]

How Will the Four-Step Formula Benefit Cheerfuls?

Cheerfuls will benefit from the Four-Step Formula by understanding that they will never be alone unless they choose to be. In fact, they can never lose their freedom because they alone have the ability to control every aspect of their life experiences and attain exactly what they want. As they learn to utilize the Four-Step Formula in their lives, they will become what they really are at their core: wonderful, loving advocates, providing joy to all from a sense of their power within.[29]

The Passive Cloak of Mr./Ms. Virtuous

When they are loving: Virtuouses are teachers. They are deep, thoughtful, analytical, honorable, serious, purposeful, and often, geniuses. They are talented, creative, artistic, or musical. Appreciative of beauty, they are often philosophical and poetic. They are sensitive to others, self-sacrificing, conscientious, and idealistic. They are schedule-oriented, perfectionistic, detail-conscious, persistent, and thorough. They are orderly, organized, neat, tidy, and economical and need to finish what they start. Virtuouses like charts, graphs, figures, and lists. They find creative solutions, have high standards, and are content to stay in the background. Virtuouses avoid causing attention, are faithful, devoted, and will listen to complaints. Having a deep concern for others, they can be moved to tears with compassion.

When they are fearing: Virtuouses have unresolved struggles, fears, and self-doubts. They are moody, depressed, and remember the negatives. Often they are off in another world, and have a low self-image. They are self-centered, too introspective, have guilt feelings, and a persecution complex. They have a tendency for hypochondria and depression. They choose difficult work, hesitate to start projects, and never ask for help. They spend too much time planning and prefer analysis to work. Having standards that are often too high, opportunities oftentimes slip away as they overanalyze everything. They are insecure socially — withdrawn and remote. They are critical of others and dislike those in opposition. They are suspicious, antagonistic, and unforgiving. They believe if they are mysterious or detached, others will draw them out. Virtuouses have a tendency to be disinterested, unavailable, uncooperative, condescending, rejecting, or contrary.

Who do you know who primarily exhibits the traits of a Virtuous?

_____
_____
_____
_____

If you are wearing the cloak of Mr./Ms. Virtuous:

Your worst fear is of being revealed for having no real value. You feel that if you were revealed, no one would want you. You fear being alone. Do you keep your distance and play hard-to-get? Do you avoid situations that expose the deeper aspects of who you are? Do you fear being judged? Wanting to cover up your fears, you get 'hung up' by self-doubts, and confusion. You can escape these tendencies by being willing to ask for help. Be willing to walk toward something rather than away from it, for that habit has become your 'modus operandi.'[29]

What's Really Going on With Mr./Ms. Virtuous?

When he/she is exhibiting:	He/She is really feeling:
1. I'm not ready to...	I'm not sure I can survive [Fear of being revealed, then abandoned, then alone
2. I need more (money, time, education).	I don't trust myself. I'm afraid [fear of being revealed for having no worth, then abandoned, then alone]
3. I don't know, I'm not sure, maybe...	I'll be trapped and I won't be able to perform [fear of being revealed for having no worth, then abandoned, then alone]
4. I'll let you know...	I don't know what I feel, and if I tell you what I feel, you may leave me [fear of being revealed for having no worth, then abandoned, then alone]

Makes others feel:	Reactions from Other Personalities
1. Uncertain	Cheerful: Are you mad at me? [fear of being alone]
2. Suspicious	Cheerful: What did I do wrong? [fear of being alone][29]

How Will the Four-Step Formula Benefit The Virtuous?

Virtuouses will benefit from the Four-Step Formula by understanding their true incalculable value, importance, and worth, which will enable them to pursue and reach their goals in life. Their actions will reinforce their feelings of value to themselves and as a result, they will radiate those feelings to others around them. Virtuouses, too, will never be alone unless they choose to be. As they learn to utilize the Four-Step Formula in their lives, they will become what they really are at their core: wonderful, loving teachers, providing a sense of power to others from their sense of power within.[29]

The Passive Cloak of Mr./Ms. Easy-Going

When they are loving: Easy-Goings are the reformers. Relaxed, calm, cool, and collected, they have a consistent life. They have low-key personalities, are patient, and well-balanced. Easy-Goings are quiet but witty, sympathetic, and kind. Keeping their emotions hidden, they are happily reconciled to life. They are all-purpose people: competent, steady, peaceful, and agreeable. They have administrative abilities and can mediate problems. They avoid conflict and are good under pressure. They are easy to get along with — pleasant and enjoyable. They are good listeners, inoffensive, and have a dry sense of humor. Easy-Goings enjoy watching people and have many friends. They are compassionate and have concern for others.

When they are fearing: Easy-Goings have worried facial expressions, sigh a lot, stare into the distance, and retell poignant dramas and crises. They are unenthusiastic, fearful, indecisive, avoid responsibility, and have a quiet will of iron. Oftentimes, they can be too shy and reticent, too compromising, and self-righteous. They are not goal-oriented, are hard to get moving, and resent being pushed. They can discourage others and would rather watch than participate. They damper enthusiasm, judge others, and can be sarcastic and teasing. Easy-Goings are pessimistic and like to go last in line. Seducing others with their vulnerability and need for help, they are not really interested in solutions. Their two favorite words are "yes, but...." They demonstrate over-accommodating behavior, and then feel taken advantage of, which reinforces their feelings of being a victim. Their behaviors range from trying to convince, being defensive, making excuses, or explaining over and again, as they try to solve problems that are really none of their business. Easy-Goings have a tendency to open themselves to being taken advantage of and then resent it when they are.

Who do you know who primarily exhibits the traits of a Easy-Going?

_____

_____

_____

_____

_____

_____

If you are wearing the cloak of an Easy-Going:

Your major fear is that of being alone. Are you always complaining and focusing on your problems hoping that others will come to your rescue?

If you experience negative encounters with Dynamics, you probably feel out of control or disempowered. If you feel as though you are a victim, in reality, you are actually attempting to justify your powerlessness.[29]

What's Really Going on With The Easy-Going?

When he/she is exhibiting:

He/She is really feeling:

1. I'm tired.

Pay attention to me — I do so much, no one sees me [fear of being alone]

2. That's just the way I am.

I'm vulnerable, you have to take care of me [I don't know any other way — fear of being alone]

3. I'm doing the best that I can.

If I change you won't love me [fear of being alone]

4. I'm fine.

You don't really care about me [and if I tell you the truth, you might leave me—fear of aloneness]

5. Let me do it.

You need me, I need you [fear of being alone]

6. Don't worry about me.

I need recognition [but if I tell you the truth, you might leave me — fear of being alone]

Makes others feel:

Reactions from other personalities

1. Guilty.

Dynamic: You want to control me [fear of losing freedom]
Cheerful: You are so self-centered [fear of losing freedom][29]

How Will the Four-Step Formula Benefit the Easy-Goings?

Easy-Goings will benefit from the Four-Step Formula by understanding that they have complete control of their destiny. As they choose and create what they want in life, they will achieve a sense of power and control. They will come to understand that they can choose to be alone, or choose companionship — the power resides wholly in them. As they learn to utilize the Four-Step Formula, they will no longer feel anxious or fearful, which will rekindle their true purpose — to help others. They will become what they really are at their core: wonderful, loving reformers, providing compassion to all from a sense of their authentic power within.[29]

Utilize Your New Insights With Compassion

Our Consciousness Is the Result
Of Our Own Choosing.
Where You Are
Is Where You Have Come.
Where You Will Go
Is Decided by How You Are[30]

— JON PENIEL
The Lost Teachings of Atlantis

Now that you are aware of the four personality types and understand that fear is underlying all negative behavior, you will automatically respond to difficult situations in a new manner. You can no longer look at others as you may have before for you now understand many of the reasons underlying their behaviors. Possessing that knowledge will allow you to offer an alternative viewpoint when in conversation with those who may be castigating the behavior of another. Lending your differing perspective with love, and not the need to be 'right,' will perhaps allow them to open their hearts to consider another explanation.

As you shift your frequency from that of judgment to that of compassion, you will sweep your path of the obstacles that were created as a result of old-paradigm thinking. This will make it far easier for you to live, love, and laugh!

Let's now explore your past conflicts so you can ferret out any nasty red circuits left in their wake — frequencies responsible for magnetizing much of the dissatisfaction you have experienced in life. ⊗

Learn How Great Altercations Provide Great Opportunities

That old law about "an eye for an eye" leaves everybody blind.
— MARTIN LUTHER KING JR.
1929-1968

Out of every crisis comes the chance to be reborn, to reconceive ourselves as individuals, to choose the kind of change that will help us to grow and to fulfill ourselves more completely.
— NENA O'NEILL

In the middle of every difficulty lies opportunity.
— ALBERT EINSTEIN
1879-1955

Each circumstance is a gift, and in each experience is a hidden treasure.[31]
— NEALE DONALD WALSCH
Conversations with God - Book 1

Life affords no higher pleasure than that of surmounting difficulties, passing from one step of success to another, forming new wishes and seeing them gratified.
— SAMUEL JOHNSON
1709-1784

When you lose sight of each other as sacred souls on a sacred journey, then you cannot see the purpose, the reason behind all relationships.[32]
— NEALE DONALD WALSCH
Conversations with God - Book 1

Toleration is the greatest gift of the mind.
— HELEN KELLER
1880-1968

You cannot take responsibility for how well another accepts your truth; you can only ensure how well it is communicated. And by how well, I don't mean merely how clearly; I mean how lovingly, how compassionately, how sensitively, how courageously, and how completely.[33]
— NEALE DONALD WALSCH
Conversations with God - Book 2

When in doubt, always err on the side of compassion. The test of whether you are helping or hurting: Are your fellow humans enlarged or reduced as a result of your help? Have you made them bigger or smaller? More able or less able?[34]
— NEALE DONALD WALSCH
Conversations with God - Book 2

Another consequence of old-paradigm thinking is the manner in which we handle conflict. In reality, conflict is nothing more than an Angacle — evidence of many wrong-way signs offered earlier, but dismissed. The origin of your conflicts can generally be traced back to the unmet needs and expectations of your childhood that resulted in the creation of red circuits. If you fail to readjust those circuits, you will only magnetize more conflict and eventually get stuck in a habit of conflict. Therefore, your dramas, difficulties, and challenges are illuminating the need to readjust red circuits — they are opportunities to create what you want. Now that you have a broader understanding of your conflicts, you can evaluate them in an entirely different manner. This may allow you to relax a little, appreciate (?!?!?) your conflicts, and ultimately have an easier time working through them.

Think about disputes that have raged between groups of people for prolonged periods of time, such as the infamous Hatfields and McCoys, or the conflict in Ireland between the Protestants and Catholics. Oftentimes those engaged in these battles don't have a clue as to why or how the conflict even originated. They have simply become intoxicated by the formidable energy of the 'place' — victims of the negative energy vortex. Why do these battles continue from generation to generation? As each new generation is indoctrinated into life, the red circuits from the previous generation are passed on. This results in an ongoing conflict until someone finally 'wakes up' and recognizes the futility of it all. Therefore, if you are now caught up in a vicious circle of conflict and wish to disengage, you must uncover the red circuit lurking beneath it.

What Is Really Going On?

When you are engaged in conflict you feel alive and energized. Why? Energy is flowing through you. In fact, the only reason you ever feel discomfort is when you meet with a *contradiction* of energy — resistance. Conflict can actually become addictive because it generates a sense of thrill and elation — a rush of adrenalin from the increased flow of energy summoned with intense emotions. I can relate first-hand to this topic. One of the red circuits created as a result of my childhood manifested in my being perpetually late. I became addicted to the adrenalin charge that corresponded with lateness — rushing around and driving fast. When I was growing up, I was continually 'on edge,' unsure whether my father would be drunk or not when he came home from work; uncertain if I would receive another beating that night. The imbalance created in my energy field from those experiences simply followed the Law of Attraction and magnetized evidence — evidence that allowed me the opportunity to heal my imbalance and readjust my red circuit to green.

Unaware of your real power, you may think that the only way to have a sense of feeling 'alive' is to thrash out at others, manipulate them, or find ways to force them to give you attention. However, these behaviors are always counterproductive, for you will unwittingly connect with a negative vortex of energy, activate your 'off' switch, and magnetize *more* negative circumstances. So, it's essential to understand your conflicts and redirect the energy of their red circuits.

The Theater of Human Drama

Conflict manifests in many ways. When you feel overwhelmed, browbeaten, stuck, or powerless[35], you are experiencing conflict (all Angel-Alerts — wrong-way signs). When you point a finger, you are blaming someone else rather than taking responsibility for the frequency you are projecting. At the root of what bothers you about someone else is always *your* frequency. Therefore, to become aware of your frequencies, become aware of your habitual behaviors.

Conflict provides optimal opportunities for your evolution — for you to expand into areas you may have heretofore neglected. Conflict helps you to recognize the frequencies you are holding that may be locked in denial. As you work through your conflicts, however, you will ultimately grow stronger and become more whole. Understanding the real purpose of conflict allows you to be Who You Choose To Be with far greater ease. But again, it is wholly up to you to heed its message.

What Behaviors Are You Magnetizing From Others?

You are completely responsible for the way you are treated, for you are projecting the frequency responsible for magnetizing the behaviors of others. Understand, however, while some of your frequencies were created on a conscious level, others were created subconsciously. Your subconscious behaviors surface as automatic reactions — as illustrated in our earlier example of hot stoves — and should be considered as valuable because they are revealing red circuits that need adjusting. Therefore, if you're experiencing unpleasant interactions with certain people, you must uncover your red circuit, for you will continue to experience this same type of interaction until you readjust it. As you do, however, the adverse behaviors of others will slowly subside as your frequency will now be set on a different station.

The Messengers, is an incredible book that tells the story of Nick Bunick, a successful businessman who lived a normal existence until something incredulous changed all of that. On one fateful day Nick was told that he had been Paul the Apostle during the time that Jesus lived. Uneasy with this information, Mr. Bunick sought out others to either validate or refute this information. The result? The news was verified — he *was* the reincarnation of Paul. Still apprehensive and unconvinced, he was prompted to seek past life hypnosis. And once again, the information obtained in these sessions not only confirmed his news, but also revealed unknown details about the life of Jesus. Believing he would be judged harshly by others — deemed a 'fraud,' or 'crazy' — Mr. Bunick was reluctant to share his story, for he didn't want to jeopardize his reputation or family. However, after a succession of incredible miracles, he overcame his inner demons and agreed to divulge his compelling story. In fact, his story was so incredible that Hollywood has contracted with Mr. Bunick to make it a movie, with the lead role being offered to actor Anthony Hopkins. While under hypnosis, Mr. Bunick, as Paul, recited the following words that were spoken by Jesus:

> *We don't have the right to judge others. We should concern ourselves only with our own lives. How we conduct our life and respond to those around us will be reciprocated to us by others. A person may act in anger toward one person and love to another, depending on how that person acted toward them. The response a person gives back is a reaction to what they received and should not be judged bad or good. We cannot judge another person's behavior toward us because we are responsible for their behavior. They are responding to us. Therefore, we should judge ourselves and not them. If someone responds in anger, we need to look at what we did to create that anger coming toward us.*[36]

Your Response to Conflict

Let's now dissect your past conflicts and uncover the 'hidden treasures' that lie buried within them — the critical data that will further assist you in the reconstruction of your comfort zone.

In the past, when confronted with conflict, you have probably responded instinctively from habit. You may have attacked, retreated, justified yourself, bullied the other person, or tried to ignore the conflict without addressing it. So, let's uncover your habits that may need reevaluation.

Describe a conflict in your life:

_____
_____
_____
_____

How did you respond?

_____
_____
_____

Did you lock yourself into a position?

_____

Describe the situation.

_____
_____
_____

What were you feeling?

_____
_____
_____

What are you trying to accomplish?

_____
_____
_____

How do you wish to feel?[37]

_____
_____
_____

Your Past Reactions to Conflict

When engaged in past conflicts,

➤ were you self-righteous? Did you categorize the other person and look for ways to reinforce your judgments?[38]

➤ did you make everything black or white? Did you limit your options by looking only for a certain outcome?

➤ were you afraid of anything?

➤ did you project your issues onto someone else?
   a) Did your struggle reveal something you need to be aware of?
   b) Do you interpret the actions of others through your own fears?
   c) Are others reflecting a part of your unwanted anger, hatred, or judgment?

➤ did you use perfectionism or confusion as an excuse for staying stuck? Are you unwilling to move from your position because everything is not perfect or you are not perfect yet?

➤ did you look for a resolution or stay stuck inside the struggle? Did you take responsibility and act on your own issues?

➤ did you gain anything by staying focused on this struggle?

➤ were you letting fear run your life?
   a) What could have been the worst outcome?
   b) What did you fear that is even worse than that?
   c) Is your worst fear realistic?[39]

Your Unexamined Childhood Will Continue to Haunt You

Most often a recurring conflict has its roots in childhood, revealing itself as an opportunity to peel back another layer — to readjust a red circuit — covering your real self.

Describe a conflict in your life:

_____
_____
_____
_____
_____
_____
_____

What were you feeling in the midst of that conflict?

_____
_____
_____
_____
_____
_____
_____

When have you ever felt those feelings before? Can you recall a childhood experience where you felt the same way?

_____
_____
_____
_____
_____
_____
_____

How to Utilize Conflict

Conflict is nothing more than an Angel-Alert — a wrong-way sign. It is your Point of Power alerting you to recognize that: 1) you are holding an unconscious core belief that needs adjustment — a red circuit, or 2) you are focused on something that does not serve Who You Choose To Be and is providing you the clarity necessary to determine what you want. If you heed your wrong-way sign and refocus your thoughts to those of love, you will then allow for an unimpeded flow of energy to you.

The most important factor in dealing with conflict is to remain centered. Because your Point of Power is in the present Moment, you can choose whatever you want in any moment. Therefore, when confronted with conflict, stop and think about what your intentions are. What are your expectations? What are you fearing? What might the other person be fearing? To maintain your center, you must be true to yourself and let the chips fall where they may.

From a position of centeredness — knowing with clarity what you want — ask the person with whom you are in conflict, what his intentions are and what he wants. Thank him (perhaps silently), for creating the opportunity for you to readjust one of your red circuits and apply your newly discovered knowledge. And remember, if you walk away from conflict with a feeling of resentment, if you carry a grudge, whom do you hurt? How do you feel? And what will you magnetize with that bad feeling? Only more of the same, my friend. So let's learn the techniques to disarm conflict.

How to Disarm Conflict

- Be willing to look at any situation from the other person's point of view.[40]

- Try not to control everything — be open to cooperation.[40]

- Be willing to walk toward some form of resolution.[40]

- What do you want from the other person that you could do yourself?[40]

- What could you do differently?[40]

- Consult your Vision Statement — Who You Chose to Be — (upcoming in *The Pathway* - page 9). In light of your statement, decide how you wish to deal with the conflict. And if in doubt, always err on the side of compassion.

- When engaged in conflict, step back for a moment, count to ten and recenter yourself.[40] Ask yourself, "What is it that I want? *Why* do I want to have it? How do I *want* to feel? How did *I* create this conflict? What frequency am I projecting that is magnetizing this conflict?"

- State your feelings completely with love, clarity, sensitivity, compassion, and courage.

- Ask the other person what he or she is feeling and then *listen*. Then ask, "What do you want? How do you *want* to feel? Why do you want it?"

- Restate their response so they know they have been heard and their feelings, honored.

∼ Then let go; you are finished. You have chosen to readjust your frequency and have cannot control how anyone will hear or interpret your truth; that is not your responsibility.

∼ If you are unable to disengage from the conflict, need time to recenter yourself, or to sort through your feelings, motives, and expectations, request a postponement of this discussion until a future date.[40]

∼ Be true to yourself.

Make Conflict A Thing of the Past

There is no such thing as a "bad" experience, but only opportunities to learn and grow in inner understanding. [O]ur stumbling blocks are our stepping stones.
— RUTH MONTGOMERY

Because each of us desires respect and appreciation, in order to get it, we must give it — project its frequency. Therefore, rather than judging those you may not agree with, focus instead on their qualities. Get in the habit of searching for the positive aspects in each person that you encounter and every face you look at, rather than looking for all the nasty little things you may not like. Appreciate each person for who they *truly* are: an innocent, sacred, blindfolded soul struggling through their life experiences. Have empathy and compassion in your heart, understanding that each of us must undergo similar experiences. And remember, the differing points of view in our world add to its variety and diversity providing the contrast essential to creating the choices that allow *you* to create whatever you desire.

The manner in which you conduct yourself will always be reflected back to you, for once again, you are projecting the frequency to which others respond. Therefore, choose your frequencies *intentionally*, rather than reacting to the frequencies of others.

Now that you have a more expansive view of conflict, you can look at conflict as an opportunity, rather than a major irritant. You can now utilize conflict as it was meant to be used: as a catalyst from which to create. In so doing, you will be living as life was intended: loving, and laughing! ☺

You Needed Me

I cried a tear, you wiped it dry.
I was confused, you cleared my mind.
I sold my soul, you bought it back for me
and held me up and gave me dignity.
Somehow you needed me.
You gave me strength to stand alone again
to face the world out on my own again.
You put me high upon a pedestal,
so high that I can almost see eternity,
you needed me, you needed me;
and I can't believe it's you I can't believe it's true.
I needed you, and you were there.
And I'll never leave. Why should I leave, I'd be a fool
'cause I finally found someone who really cares.
You held my hand when it was cold.
When I was lost, you took me home.
You gave me hope, when I was at the end
and turned my lies back into truth again.
You even called me friend.
You gave me strength to stand alone again
to face the world out on my own again.
You put me high upon a pedestal,
so high that I can almost see eternity,
you needed me, you needed me.
You needed me, you needed me.[41]

Words and Music by Randy Goodrum

Make Peace with Your Past and Make Room for Joy

When one door of happiness closes, another opens; but often we look so long at the closed door that we do not see the one that has been opened for us. — HELEN KELLER
1880-1968

Love is an act of endless forgiveness. — PETER USTINOV

I can either complain about my mother not believing in me, or I can tell you that it served me in some way to become who I am. — BARBRA STREISAND

To be wronged is nothing unless you continue to remember it. — CONFUCIUS
551-479 BC

The soul leads you to the right and perfect opportunities for you to experience exactly what you had planned to experience. What you actually experience is up to you.[42] — NEALE DONALD WALSCH
Conversations with God - Book 1

If only your "positive" beliefs given were materialized then you would never clearly comprehend the power of your thought, for you would not completely experience its physical results.[43] — JANE ROBERTS
The Nature of Personal Reality - A Seth Book

With each new day I put away the past and discover new beginnings I have been given. — ANGELA L. WOZNIAK

There is nothing for you to go back and live over, or fix, or feel regret about now. Every part of your life has unfolded just right. And so, now, knowing all that you know from where you stand — what do you want? The answers are now coming forth. Go forth in joy and get on with it.[44] — ESTHER and JERRY HICKS

You learn through your creations.[45] — JANE ROBERTS
The Nature of Personal Reality - A Seth Book

Instead of looking at life through a rear-view mirror, look before you and behold the current possibilities with innocent perception....Forgive yourself and others, for yesterday has already been lived... Be here now and face the path in front of you, for that is where life is.[46]
— GLENDA GREEN
Love Without End: Jesus Speaks

Past experiences are a source of wisdom.[47]
— CEANNE DeROHAN
as conveyed in The Right Use of Will

Imagine for a moment that your life was a play. Prior to your birth, you wrote this play as a framework where certain people, events, and circumstances would create opportunities for you to evolve and awaken to Who You Really Are. To experience your play, you had to recruit others who loved you dearly to assume the roles of key characters with some acting as 'good guys,' and others as 'bad guys.' It really didn't matter what role someone played, for when the final curtain went down your play was over and everyone removed their masks. Then you would evaluate how *you* responded to the opportunities you were presented.

From that perspective, think of all your family members (or others you may deem as thorns in your side) as the actors you recruited, begging them to participate in your play. And the 'villains' in your life were those who *loved you the most*, because they grudgingly agreed to assume the 'bad guy' role to facilitate your evolution. No opportunities, no evolution, no awakening. Period.

Think about it. Although you may think of your 'villains' as adversaries, in truth, their higher purpose is to *serve* you, for they are your greatest teachers. They 'push your buttons' until change is provoked. They force you to examine those aspects of Who You Are that are locked in various states of denial, those traits that you refuse to accept as belonging to you, those areas of yourself that you are neglecting.

Pondering this perspective may help to take the sting out of some of your less-than-harmonious relationships. It may allow you to change your perception of those who elicit strong negative emotions from you. For when you experience strong emotions on any subject, you have simply unveiled a red circuit that needs adjusting.

Having gained this perspective, I was able achieve a new-found sense of peace and greater understanding for my father. I was able to comprehend life from a more expansive level, and to experience forgiveness, for I then recognized Dad's real role in my life. Although I am not attempting to diminish or minimize the pain I experienced, from my new position of awareness and power, I have come to recognize that when I give someone the benefit of the doubt, I get the benefit!

> *Peace is everywhere. When you plant lettuce, if it does not grow well, you don't blame the lettuce. You look for reasons that it is not doing well. It may need fertilizer, or more water, or less sun. You never blame the lettuce. Yet, if we have problems with our friends or our family, we blame the other person. But if we know how to take care of them, they will grow well, like the lettuce. Blaming has no positive effect at all, nor does trying to persuade using reason and arguments. That is my experience. No blame, no reasoning, no argument, just understanding. If you understand and you show that you understand, you can love and the situation will change.*[48]
> — THICH NHAT HANH

> *Relationships are constantly challenging; constantly calling you to create, express, and experience higher and higher aspects of yourself, grander and grander visions of yourself, ever more magnificent versions of yourself. Nowhere can you do this more immediately, impactfully and immaculately than in relationships. In fact, without relationships, you cannot do it at all.*[49]
> — NEALE DONALD WALSCH
> *Conversations with God - Book 1*

Understanding the higher purpose of the challenges that your early life circumstances presented — opportunities from which to grow, your real objective in life — you can now work through them and readjust the red circuits they created. However, if you fail to address these challenges, they will simply reappear in the form of a new person, new place, or new circumstance, with greater and greater intensity until you resolve them.

So, you can run away from what you don't want to face and find a new relationship, a new city, or a new job, believing that escape is the answer, but you will continue to magnetize the same kind of culprit, for you take your frequencies with you wherever you go. As an added consequence, until you ferret out the real culprit, your red circuit, and readjust its frequency to green, the doorway to your joy and happiness cannot fully open.

If you have made mistakes that you regret yet *choose* to remain stuck in guilt, you will only regurgitate the past. Once more, the red circuit that your guilt created will only magnetize more evidence of its frequency. We, as human beings, are the only species with the ability to make a mistake, discover it to be an error, and then choose not to repeat it. That is called 'evolution.' Therefore, if you stay mired in guilt and regret, you will only stagnate and find it difficult to ever be fully present and experience all the beauty it has to offer. The goal of life is to awaken — to utilize your past to redefine your life experience and Be in the fresh new place you stand right now, based on all that you have discovered.

> *Guilt is the source of sorrows, the avenging fiend that follows us behind with whips and stings.*
> — NICHOLAS ROWE
> 1674-1718

> *Persistent feelings of guilt will prevent you from manifesting anything worthwhile because you are attracting the very same things you are putting out to the Universe. More anguish, more reasons to feel bad and more evidence to prove that you are not worth what you deserve.*[50]
> — DR. WAYNE DYER

Family Reactions to Your Evolution

As you become more aware of Who You Really Are and how life operates, it is exceedingly important to be *more* loving with those closest to you. The transition from the old paradigm into the new is fraught with much introspection, for you are reassessing life from the most fundamental level. Therefore, your tendency may be to disengage for a while — to visit 'la la land' — the deepest recesses of your mind while you process this new information. However, the demands of daily life will continue to require your attention. Consequently, during the period of time that you are shedding the 'old' you for the 'newly-improved version,' those closest to you may feel estranged, abandoned, or as though you don't love them any more. However, they will continue to interact with you based on your former level of consciousness, for that is what is most natural to them.

It is oftentimes detrimental to share what you are learning, as others may react defensively. As you evolve, those around you are forced to examine their lives, which is never a comfortable position to be in. As a result, they may become defensive and do everything in their power to maintain the old-paradigm status-quo. (This is first-hand info. I've learned the hard way!) Therefore, when you are more loving with those closest to you, they will associate your change with love and 'good,' rather than threat and 'bad.'

In light of your new knowledge, you may have a tendency to react in frustration to the negative behaviors exhibited by others because you now understand how self-perpetuating they are. However, it's not your responsibility to 'fix' them. They are not broken; they're asleep, and it is solely *their* job to awaken, if and when they *choose* to. The purpose of any experience they are now living is for their evolution and for you to 'fix' it for them *robs* them of their opportunity for self-discovery. And though they may seem uninterested in your newly-discovered knowledge, don't lose faith, for as they observe you living a more joyful life, they may eventually become curious and *ask* what precipitated your change.

One of my sisters learned a great deal about family dysfunction when she participated in group therapy. In fact, she became so excited about her newly-discovered knowledge that she wanted to share it with everyone that she knew to help them to understand their dysfunction! This simple information allowed her to comprehend certain aspects of life, so she assumed that people would be eager to hear this information as it would enhance their lives! Well, as you may have guessed, most folks don't want to hear about their dysfunction. Consequently, it can be frustrating when the dysfunction, pain, or anguish that you observe in others is so transparent but they are not interested in solutions.

I, too, have experienced the same feelings with this profound knowledge. I have wanted to shout it from the rooftops because I am bursting with excitement about the potential it holds. I now look at our world and understand how issues may have originated, as well as how we might resolve them! However, I understand that each of us must progress along our journey at our own rate and will awaken if and when we choose to. And for those interested in solutions, hopefully this book will help to expedite their awakening and minimize any unnecessary pain, anguish, and suffering they may now be experiencing.

To glean a deeper insight into your relationship with your primary caretakers — those who had the most dramatic impact on your earlier life — answer a few questions posed in an exercise by James Redfield and Carol Adrienne in *The Celestine Prophecy – An Experiential Guide.*

The Role of Dad and His Influence

Dad's role was to connect you with your power and leadership. The purpose of fathering is to make you self-sufficient and able to take action toward your goals.[51]

1. What kind of work did your father do when you were young?

_____

_____

_____

_____

_____

_____

_____

2. Was he proud of what he did?

_____

_____

_____

3. In what way did he excel?

_____

_____

_____

_____

_____

_____

4. List positive words that best describe your father (intelligent, adventurous, loving, etc.).

_____

_____

_____

_____

_____

5. What two words — positive or negative — best describe his personality?

_____

_____

6. What was unique about him?

_____
_____
_____
_____
_____
_____
_____

7. List any words that best describe any negative traits in your father (critical, overbearing, opinionated, etc.).

_____
_____
_____
_____
_____

8. What triggered his negative behavior?

_____
_____
_____
_____
_____

9. What one or two words best describe his worst traits?

_____
_____
_____

10. Describe your father's childhood.

_____
_____
_____
_____
_____
_____
_____

11. Was he happy? Neglected? Went to work at an early age? Poor? Rich?

_____
_____
_____

12. What personality types do you think his parents were?

_____
_____
_____
_____

13. In what way did his childhood influence his life choices?

_____
_____
_____
_____
_____

14. What was most important to him?

_____
_____
_____
_____
_____
_____

15. What statement or credo best describes your father's philosophy of life?

_____
_____
_____
_____
_____

16. What do you think was missing from your father's life?

_____
_____
_____
_____
_____

17. What might he have done if he had more time, money, or education?

_____
_____
_____
_____
_____

What Cloak Did Dad Wear?

Was he _Mr. Dynamic?_
Did you stand up to your father and take a strong
or rebellious position?   ❒ Yes   ❒ No

Was he _Mr. Cheerful?_
Did you try to get his attention by asking questions?   ❒ Yes   ❒ No

Did you try to find loopholes in his arguments and
try to be smarter than he?   ❒ Yes   ❒ No

Was he _Mr. Virtuous?_
Did you withdraw into yourself, or hide out in your
room doing some activity by yourself?   ❒ Yes   ❒ No

Did you stay away from home a lot?   ❒ Yes   ❒ No

Did you hide your true feelings?   ❒ Yes   ❒ No

Was he _Mr. Easy-Going?_
Did you try to make your father feel that you needed
help, money, support, attention by focusing on your
troubles so that he would pay more attention to you?   ❒ Yes   ❒ No

Finish this sentence with a _positive_ trait about your father. Like my
father, I am:

_____
_____
_____
_____
_____
_____

Finish this sentence with a _negative_ trait about your father. Like my
father, I am:

_____
_____
_____
_____
_____
_____

From my father I learned that in order to succeed I should:

1._____

_____

2._____

_____

3._____

_____

From observing my father's life, I want to be more:

1._____

_____

2._____

_____

3._____

_____

For what are you grateful to your father?

_____

_____

_____

For what would you be willing to forgive your father?

_____

_____

_____

What was missing from your father's life that you have chosen to develop?

_____

_____

_____

(It is likely that these missing elements are directions that will influence your choices about your career, lifestyle, relationships, parenting, and spiritual contribution.)

The Role of Mom and Her Influence

The role Mom played was one of helping us to relate to others. In most cases, it was your mother who taught you how to connect with your ability to heal, comfort, and nurture others. Feminine energy is the creator of goals and reveals what has heart and meaning for you.

1. What kind of work or activities did your mother do when you were young?

_____

_____

_____

_____

_____

_____

_____

2. Do you think she felt fulfilled in her activities?

_____

_____

_____

3. In what way did she excel?

_____

_____

_____

_____

_____

4. List positive words that best describe your mother (intelligent, creative, adventurous, loving, etc.)

_____

_____

_____

5. What two words — positive and negative — best describe her personality?

_____

_____

_____

6. What was unique about her?

_____

_____

_____

_____

7. List any words that best describe any negative traits in your mother (insecure, strict, critical, overbearing, opinionated, etc.).

_____

_____

_____

_____

_____

_____

8. What triggered her negative behavior?

_____

_____

_____

_____

_____

9. What one or two words best describe her worst traits?

_____

_____

_____

_____

10. Describe your mother's childhood.

_____

_____

_____

_____

_____

_____

11. Was she happy? Neglected? Went to work at an early age? Poor? Rich? Sheltered? Ambitious?

_____

_____

_____

12. What personality types do you think her parents were?

_____
_____
_____
_____

13. In what way did her childhood influence her life choices?

_____
_____
_____
_____
_____

14. What was most important to her?

_____
_____
_____
_____
_____
_____

15. What statement or credo best describes your mother's philosophy of life?

_____
_____
_____
_____

16. What do you think was missing from your mother's life?

_____
_____
_____
_____
_____

17. What might she have done if she had more time, money, or education?

_____
_____
_____
_____
_____

What Cloak Did Mom Wear?

Was she *Ms. Dynamic?*
Did you stand up to your mother and take a strong
or rebellious position? ☐ Yes ☐ No

Was she *Ms. Cheerful?*
Did you try to get her attention by asking questions? ☐ Yes ☐ No

Did you try to find loopholes in her arguments and try
to be smarter than she? ☐ Yes ☐ No

Was she *Ms. Virtuous?*
Did you withdraw into yourself, or hide out in your
room doing some activity by yourself? ☐ Yes ☐ No

Did you stay away from home a great deal? ☐ Yes ☐ No

Did you hide your true feelings? ☐ Yes ☐ No

Was she *Ms. Easy-Going?*
Did you try to make your mother feel that you needed
help, money, support, attention by focusing on your
troubles so that she would pay more attention to you? ☐ Yes ☐ No

Finish this sentence with a positive trait from your mother. Like my
mother, I am:

_____

_____

_____

_____

_____

_____

Finish this sentence with a negative trait from your mother. Like my
mother, I am:

_____

_____

_____

_____

_____

_____

From my mother I learned that in order to succeed I should:

1._____
_____

2._____
_____

3._____
_____
_____

From observing my mother's life, I want to be more:

1._____
_____

2._____
_____

3._____
_____
_____

For what are you grateful to your mother?

_____
_____
_____

For what would you be willing to forgive your mother?

_____
_____
_____

What was missing from your mother's life that you have chosen to develop?

_____
_____
_____
_____

(It is likely that these missing elements are directions that will influence your choices about your career, lifestyle, relationships, parenting, and spiritual contribution.)

The Similarities Between You and Your Caretakers

What made your mother afraid?

_____
_____
_____
_____
_____
_____
_____
_____
_____
_____
_____
_____

What behavior did she exhibit?

_____
_____
_____
_____
_____
_____
_____
_____
_____
_____
_____

What made your father afraid?

_____
_____
_____
_____
_____
_____
_____
_____
_____
_____
_____

What behavior did he exhibit?

_____
_____
_____
_____
_____
_____
_____
_____
_____
_____

What makes you afraid?

_____
_____
_____
_____
_____
_____
_____
_____
_____

How do you act?

_____
_____
_____
_____
_____
_____
_____
_____
_____

How are you similar to your primary caretakers?

_____
_____
_____
_____
_____
_____
_____

_____

_____

_____

_____

_____

_____

_____

_____

_____

_____

_____

_____

_____

_____

_____

_____

Has the knowledge gained about your primary caretakers helped you to glean a deeper understanding and sense of compassion for them? Has it helped you to uncover some of the issues that created red circuits in your life so you can now readjust their frequencies? Perhaps this knowledge will enable you to see aspects of your life in a different light — a light that shines a new possibility for peace, understanding, and reconciliation within your family. And because you and your family are essentially a microcosm of our world, this same light shines a new possibility for peace, understanding, and reconciliation within our world. Now that you're equipped with your new insights, you may want to mend some fences in your life, for if you are unable to mend the fences with those closest to you, how can we possibly mend them around the world?

If you have unresolved conflict with a someone who has passed away, or if they are still living but would never comprehend your feelings, write a letter to them expressing how you feel. Then either visit their grave and read it, or read it aloud to yourself privately as this exercise is for your benefit, not theirs. This will help you to release the energy of your red circuit and readjust it to green.

Whew! The past is over! Fortified with your new knowledge, you now have a more expansive viewpoint of the life you've lived and how your life experiences have presented opportunities for you to discover Who You Really Are. As a result, you have gathered much critical data from which to build your new comfort zone.

Let's now continue to gather more information that will help in the fine-tuning of your comfort zone — the new set of orders you will convey to Angel, which will make it far easier for you to live, love, and laugh! ☯

Part V
The Pathway

PART V

The Pathway

REDEFINING YOUR PATH

Part V

The Pathway

REDEFINING YOUR PATH

Current Reality:
Your Springboard
From Which to Create

Bloom where you're planted. — MARY ENGELBREIT

If you don't know where you're going, you'll probably end up somewhere else. — LAURENCE PETER
1919-1990

Examining the General Aspects of Your Life

Let's now examine the general aspects of your life, for your current reality is your launching pad to apply the Four-Step Formula — think, believe and expect — to consciously get what you want.

Write down your positive characteristics:

_____

_____

_____

_____

_____

_____

_____

_____

_____

_____

_____

_____
_____
_____
_____
_____
_____
_____
_____

Write down your negative characteristics or any areas in your life that may need fine-tuning:

_____
_____
_____
_____
_____
_____
_____
_____
_____
_____
_____
_____
_____

Write down your current reality in the following areas of your life:

Your job or what you do every day_____

_____
_____
_____
_____
_____
_____
_____

Your financial circumstance_____

_____
_____
_____
_____
_____
_____

Your health_____
_____
_____
_____
_____
_____
_____
_____
_____
_____

Your physical body_____
_____
_____
_____
_____
_____
_____
_____

Your relationships_____
_____
_____
_____
_____
_____
_____
_____
_____
_____
_____
_____
_____
_____
_____
_____

To help you to recognize your power, make a list of all of your accomplishments in life and know that you were the person responsible for them. (You may want to note this page, for as you add new accomplishments, each should be listed.)

_____

_____

_____

_____

_____

_____

_____

_____

_____

_____

_____

_____

_____

_____

_____

_____

_____

_____

_____

_____

_____

_____

_____

_____

_____

_____

_____

_____

To rebuild your new comfort zone, you must first examine the data you have accrued from your life experiences. For your feelings and responses to those experiences will help you clearly define the life you choose to live, thus enabling you to truly live, love, and laugh in the majority of your moments!

Let's now examine your life from a more sobering perspective: the inscription on your gravestone. ✆

Here Lies You...
How Does the Inscription On Your Gravestone Read?

Life is now in session: Are you present? — CAROL KELBY

The cemeteries are filled with people who thought the world couldn't get along without them.
— UNKNOWN

While alive, he lived.   — MALCOLM FORBES
1919-1990
etched on his tombstone

What a wonderful life I've had! I only wish I had known it sooner.   — COLETTE
1873-1954

Never confuse having a career with having a life.
— EDDIE BAUER SHOPPING BAG

Life is short. Live it up.   — NIKITA KHRUSHCHEV
1894-1971

May you live all the days of your life.   — JONATHAN SWIFT
1667-1745

Imagine that at this moment you were able to fast-forward and see your gravestone after you had died (just as Ebenezer Scrooge did in *A Christmas Carol*). How would you want your inscription to read?

Your Gravestone

_____

_____

_____

_____

_____

Now let's visit your wake and funeral. What are others saying about you?

_____

_____

_____

_____

_____

_____

_____

_____

_____

_____

_____

_____

_____

_____

_____

_____

Is this how you want to be remembered? Are you on the path to accomplishing what you really want or do your goals seem too overwhelming to accomplish? Fret not, my friend. As you learn to apply the Four-Step Formula, you will not only accomplish your goals, but move far beyond them. Remember, life is meant for living, loving, and laughing!

Let's now define Who You Choose To Be, for in articulating your vision, you define your center and gain a greater sense of clarity of Who You Are. This knowledge will make it far easier for you to respond to any challenge you may encounter in life with love. ☺

Create the Highest Vision of Who You Choose To Be

Begin at once to imagine life the way you want it to be, and move into that. Check every thought, word and action that does not fall into harmony with that. Move away from those.[1]
— NEALE DONALD WALSCH
Conversations with God - Book 1

If you do not think of the future, you cannot have one.
— JOHN GALSWORTHY
1867-1933

If you dwell upon limitations, then you will meet them.[2]
— JANE ROBERTS
The Nature of Personal Reality - A Seth Book

There is only one admirable form of imagination: the imagination that is so intense that it creates a new reality, that it makes things happen, whether it be a political thing, or a social thing, or a work of art.
— SEAN O'FAOLÁIN
1900-1991

Limited expectations yield only limited results.
— SUSAN LAURSON WILLIG

When we start at the center of ourselves, we discover something worthwhile extending toward the periphery of the circle. We find again some of the joy in the now, some of the peace in the here, some of the love in the me and thee which go to make up the kingdom of heaven on earth.[3]
— ANNE MORROW LINDBERGH

All you need is deep within you waiting to unfold and reveal itself. All you have to do is be still and take time to seek for what is within, and you will surely find it.

— EILEEN CADDY

On a stormy night in the South Pacific our plane was trying in vain to land on the Tontouta airstrip, but could not do so. We had to rev the engine and make another pass. Another failure. Another big circle in the sky; knuckles white with fear. This time we made it and gave thanks. Later, at midnight, I went out and walked the length of the airstrip, looking at the dim outlines of the mountains we had so narrowly missed. And as I stood there in the darkness, I caught a glimpse of the remaining years of my life and I swore an oath that when peace came, if I survived, I would live the rest of my years "as if I were a great man." I did not presume that I would BE a great man. I never thought in those terms, but by damn I would conduct myself as if I were. I would adhere to my basic principles. I would bear testimony to what I believed. I would be a better man. I would help others. I would truly believe and act as if all men were my brothers. And I would strive to make whatever world in which I found myself, a better place. In the darkness, a magnificent peace settled over me, for I saw that I could actually attain each of those objectives, and I never looked back. Two immediate consequences: I started the next day to draft the book "Tales of the South Pacific." And shortly thereafter my entire staff, flying back to Tontouta, hit one of the shadowy mountains and all were killed. I'd had cause to be white-knuckled.

— JAMES MICHNER

This Is Who I Choose To Be

Now that you are privy to the Formula and aware of your power, define Who You Choose To Be. And remember: nothing is etched in stone. You can fine-tune your Vision statement anytime you choose. Although I have provided a few topics on the following page to stimulate your thoughts, it is best to allow the ideas to flow from you.

My Vision Statement

_____
_____
_____
_____
_____
_____
_____
_____
_____
_____
_____
_____
_____
_____
_____
_____
_____
_____
_____
_____
_____
_____
_____
_____
_____
_____

Some of the topics you may wish to address:

- conflict
- health
- physical body
- relationships
- finances
- confronting wrong-way signs
- the world
- people in need
- your spiritual path
- your job
- your Mission
- your fellow human beings

Now, having seen the differences between where you are and where you want to be, begin to change — consciously change — your thoughts, words, and actions to match your grandest vision.[4] — NEALE DONALD WALSCH

Conversations with God - Book 1

When you have a thought that is not in alignment with your higher vision, change to a new thought, then and there. When you say a thing which is out of alignment with your grandest idea, make a note not to say something like that again. When you do a thing which is misaligned with your best intention, decide to make that the last time.[5] — NEALE DONALD WALSCH

Conversations with God - Book 1

So much is a man worth as he esteems himself.

— RABELAIS
1483-1553

By defining Who You Choose To Be, you establish your center making it far easier for you to respond when you encounter challenges in life. And when you do encounter a challenge, you need only review your Vision Statement and ask yourself, "How would the highest vision of who I have chosen to be respond to this challenge?" As a matter of fact, if you don't articulate your vision, you will always feel uncentered and continually search for the 'right way' to respond.

When you "make up your mind" about something, you set the universe in motion. Forces beyond your ability to comprehend — far more subtle and complex than you could imagine — are engaged in a process, the intricate dynamics of which you are only just now beginning to understand.[6] — NEALE DONALD WALSCH

Conversations with God - Book 2

It's a funny thing about life; if you refuse to accept anything but the best, you very often get it.

— W. SOMERSET MAUGHAM
1874-1965

You've now completed one more step on your path to living, loving, and laughing! So let's proceed further and define your goals so you can plant those seeds and watch them blossom! ☯

Define Your Goals and Watch Them Blossom

Life is something like a trumpet. If you don't put anything in, you won't get anything out. — W. C. HANDY
1873-1958

Since the mind is a specific biocomputer, it needs specific instructions and directions. The reason most people never reach their goals is that they don't define them, or ever seriously consider them as believable or achievable. Winners can tell you where they are going, what they plan to do along the way, and who will be sharing the adventure with them. — DENNIS WAITLEY

Choose not to crawl in life, but to soar. — UNKNOWN

You can have anything you want if you want it desperately enough. You must want it with an inner exuberance that erupts through the skin and joins the energy that created the world. — SHEILA GRAHAM

Don't be too timid and squeamish about your actions. All life is an experiment. — RALPH WALDO EMERSON
1803-1882

Obstacles are those frightful things you see when you take your eyes off your goals. — UNKNOWN

Written Goals Hold The Greatest Power

When you are writing, you are at the strongest point of focus.[7]
— ESTHER and JERRY HICKS

Let's now get acquainted with another tool in your 'bag of magic tricks' — the written word. Although thoughts, words, and actions are all magnetic in nature, the degree of power they project differs. The nature of a thoughtform is more or less fleeting, therefore, a thought hold less magnetic power than a word. Words are thoughtforms that have grown larger and more dominant because they have been given prolonged focus with no resistance. Therefore, by virtue of the Law of Attraction, they have magnetized more evidence. And the written word holds the greatest power because it *more* specifically defines focused intent. Ergo, the written word holds the greatest power to magnetize what you want in life.

For example: In 1953, researchers polled the Yale graduating class and found that only 3 percent had written goals established and a game plan to reach those goals. When researchers polled this class twenty years later, the same 3 percent had amassed a greater net worth than the remaining 97 percent of the class combined.[8] Coincidence?

Film star Jim Carrey, *wrote* himself a check for $10 million, postdated it three years later, and received $10 Million for the movie *Dumb and Dumber* days before its expiration. Coincidence?

After completing *The One Minute Manager*, authors Ken Blanchard and Spencer Johnson conducted market research pertaining to their book's potential and found that they could expect to sell only a certain number of books — well under one million. However, those statistics didn't squelch their dreams, for these men were tuned in, tapped in, and turned on to their power. What did they do? They simply 'acted as if' their book was the number one best seller on the *New York Times* bestsellers list! They clipped the list from the newspaper and placed the name of *their* title, *The One Minute Manager*, in the spot currently held by the number one bestseller. Next, they posted this list in a conspicuous place where they could focus on it. Then they went even further. They toasted the success of their book with a champagne 'Celebration' dinner. The results? *The One Minute Manager* **became** the New York Times number one bestseller and sold millions (plural) of books! Coincidence?

Bill Gates, president of *Microsoft* (a multi-zillion dollar corporation that you've probably heard of), articulated his goals in writing, too. And one of them was to be a millionaire by the age of thirty. Another? For every person in America to have access to a computer. His first order has certainly manifested above and beyond being a mere millionaire (he's one of the richest men in the world...), and his second continues to manifest daily. Coincidence?

You, too can take advantage of the written word. Write down your goals, just like Bill Gates, for then they will begin to manifest. Joyfully anticipate the Angacles you will magnetize and allow their mysteries to unfold. And remember: don't impose your idea as to *how* they will manifest. You must expect and allow your orders — remain connected.

Let's Resurrect Your Imagination

Ours is a world where people don't know what they want and are willing to go through hell to get it.
— DON MARQUIS
1878-1937

♪ Dream... dream... dream... dream... ♪

What would you do if you had all the time and money in the world and knew you couldn't fail?

_____

_____

_____

_____

_____

_____

_____

Describe every detail of your 'dream home': how many bedrooms, bathrooms, the colors in each room, the neighborhood, etc.

_____

_____

_____

_____

_____

_____

_____

_____
_____
_____
_____
_____
_____
_____
_____
_____
_____
_____
_____

What schools would your children attend?

_____
_____
_____
_____
_____
_____
_____

What organizations would you lend a helping hand or give money to?

_____
_____
_____
_____
_____
_____
_____
_____

How many cars would you own? Describe them? The color, accessories, etc.

_____
_____
_____
_____
_____
_____

What places would you travel to? Describe your next five vacations:

_____
_____
_____
_____
_____
_____
_____
_____
_____
_____
_____
_____
_____
_____
_____
_____

How does it *feel* to live without any financial burdens or obligations?

_____
_____
_____
_____

Reconstructing Your Comfort Zone

*You don't need to accept life the way it comes to you.
Instead, you can use the power of goal-setting to design
your life so it comes to you the way you would like to get
it.*   — UNKNOWN

Now write down all of the things you currently have in your life that you
enjoy having. By focusing on what you *have* that you appreciate when
you 'go to work,' you will ensure that they will remain in your life.

_____
_____
_____
_____
_____
_____
_____

_____

_____

_____

_____

_____

_____

_____

_____

_____

_____

_____

_____

_____

Write down all the things that you don't _enjoy_ in your life (this list may be longer....).

_____

_____

_____

_____

_____

_____

_____

_____

_____

_____

_____

Acknowledge each item that you don't _enjoy_ and utilize it to clarify what you want. _Old-paradigm example_: "I don't have enough money." _New-paradigm response_: "I choose an abundance of money." Then cross out each negative statement above.

_____

_____

_____

_____

_____

_____

_____

_____

_____

How do you want to feel (spiritually, mentally, emotionally, physically)?

_____
_____
_____
_____
_____
_____
_____
_____
_____
_____
_____
_____
_____

What do you want to have?

_____
_____
_____
_____
_____
_____
_____
_____
_____
_____
_____
_____

The more clear you are on what you want, the more power you will have. — UNKNOWN

I learned this, at least, by my experiment: that if one advances confidently in the direction of one's dreams, and endeavors to live the life which one has imagined, one will meet with successes unexpected in common hours. — HENRY DAVID THOREAU
1817-1862

Have your answers pointed in the direction of living, loving, and laughing? ☺

Hero

There's a hero if you look inside your heart
You don't have to be afraid of who you are.
There's an answer if you reach into your soul
And the sorrow that you know will melt away
And then a hero comes along with the strength to carry on
And you cast your fears aside and you know you can survive
So when you feel that hope is gone
Look inside you and be strong
And you'll finally see the truth —
That a hero lies in you.
It's long road when you face the world alone
When one reaches out a hand for you to hold
You can find love if you search within yourself
And the emptiness you felt will disappear
And then a hero comes along with the strength to carry on
And you cast your fears aside and you know you can survive
So when you feel that hope is gone
Look inside you and be strong
And you'll finally see the truth —
That a hero lies in you.
Love knows.
It's not hard to follow
But don't let anyone take it away
Hold on
There will be tomorrow
In time you'll find the way
And then a hero comes along with the strength to carry on
And you cast your fears aside and you know you can survive
So when you feel that hope is gone
Look inside you and be strong
And you'll finally see the truth —
That a hero lies in you.[9]

Words by Mariah Carey — Music by M. Carey & W. Afanasieff

The Steps to Recreate Your Life

Be not afraid of Life. Believe that life is worth living and your belief will create the fact.
— WILLIAM JAMES
1842-1910

We are what we repeatedly do. Excellence, then, is not an act, but a habit.
— ARISTOTLE
384-322 BC

I'm not a big girl from a little town planning to make it in the big town. I'm a big girl from a big town, and I have every intention of making it in this small town.
— MAE WEST
1893-1980
a year later, she was the biggest star in Hollywood

I used to work at the International House of Pancakes. It was a dream, and I made it happen.
— PAULA POUNDSTONE

I simply haven't the nerve to imagine a being, a force, a cause which keeps the planets revolving in their orbits, and then suddenly stops in order to give me a bicycle with three speeds.
— QUENTIN CRISP

Wake up, wake up, and clothe yourself with strength. Put on your beautiful clothes. Rise from the dust, take off the slave bands from your neck...Recognize that it is I, yes, I who speaks to [you].
— THE LIVING BIBLE
book of Isaiah 52:1-2, 6

*It is vital that you realize you **are** working with beliefs in your mind — that the real work is done there in the mind — and not look for **immediate** physical results. They will follow — **as surely and certainly** as the "bad" results followed, and this must be a belief: that the good results will come. But the real work is done in the mind. If you do the work then you can rest assured of the results, but you must not check constantly for them.[10]*

The Nature of Personal Reality - A Seth Book

Conscious Creation:
To Believe It is to See It!

Jesus regularly visualized the success of his efforts. "I declare a thing and it is done for me. My word accomplishes that which I send it out to do."[11]

— LAURIE BETH JONES
from *The Bible: Isaiah 55:11*

In three weeks I will be harvesting my crops. Imagine where you will be and it will be so. — GENERAL MAXIMUS
addressing his troops prior to battle in the movie *"Gladiator"*

Conscious creation is achieved through your imagination, whereas unconscious creation is achieved through your beliefs, expectations, or whatever you give your attention to. To create consciously, combine steps 1 and 2 — think and believe — to formulate what it is that you desire. After conceiving your desire, expect and allow it to come to you and you will then receive it.

Old-paradigm thinking is solution-oriented. You were taught that in order to attain a goal, you must take action. However, as you try diligently through hard work, effort, and action to attain what you want, you actually work against yourself and in the process become frustrated, tired, and overwhelmed. Taking action prior to receiving an Angacle is the longest route to attain what you want — it is living life backwards. In fact, most of the action now expended in life is spent on cleaning up the messes created by not understanding the Four-Step Formula.

You are now action-oriented and need to become thought-oriented.[12] — ESTHER and JERRY HICKS

the pathway - 20

Whether you think you can or whether you think you can't — you are right. — HENRY FORD
1863-1947

The imagination may be compared to Adam's dream — he awoke and found it truth. — JOHN KEATS
1795-1821

There is nothing neither good or bad, but thinking makes it so. — WILLIAM SHAKESPEARE
1564-1616

THINK AND BELIEVE

DETERMINE WHAT YOU WANT
AND PLACE YOUR ORDER

Formulate what it is that you want by utilizing both the wrong-way signs and inspirations Angel will continually transmit to you. To initiate the birthing process for your orders, think of something that brings you joy, for when you feel joy, you are connecting with Angel and source energy.

Next, visualize having what you want. Tune in to its frequency by imagining how it *feels* to have it right here and now: describe it until it feels real. Explain why you want it. See it, feel it, love it, explain what it's like, remember another time like it, think of reasons why you want it, describe what it would be like to have it, get excited about it, and appreciate it. Smell it, touch it, hear it, taste it — utilize all of your senses to align with the frequency of what you desire. Complete this step with each of your orders for approximately one minute every day for you are then creating its 'blueprint.' Just as a builder needs a blueprint before he can build a house, Angel needs a blueprint to align all the necessary items required to manifest your order.

Because the dominant thought in your heart always produces your frequency, be specific about what it is that you want, yet not so specific that you feel apprehensive or guarded. Be sensitive to your feelings. If you feel good, you're 'on the money.' Place your orders with the words that feel right to *you.* Feel the difference between the words "I intend," "I choose," or "I am." It's not important which words you use, however, it is important that you project a frequency that corresponds with the frequency of your order. It would be difficult to say the words "I am prosperous" if you were being evicted next week. Instead, "I choose prosperity" would do the trick. And remember, you can't fool Angel. Angel always knows what's in your heart because you are always projecting a feeling frequency — Angel's only means of order-taking.

> Use the great command that calls forth creative power:
> I am. Make "I am" statements to others. "I am" is the
> strongest creative statement to the Universe. Whatever
> you think, whatever you say after the words "I am" sets
> into motion those experiences, calls them forth, brings
> them to you.... The Universe responds to "I am" as
> would a genie in a bottle.[13]   — NEALE DONALD WALSCH
> > Conversations with God - Book 1

> The words "I am..." are potent words; be careful what
> you hitch them to. The thing you're claiming has a way
> of reaching back and claiming you.   — A. L. KITSELMAN

> It is through powerful wanting, and then choosing with
> strong emotions and deliberate thoughts that will propel
> what you desire into your life experience.[14]
> > — ESTHER and JERRY HICKS

EXPECT

ALLOW, RELAX, HAVE FAITH, AND
JOYFULLY ANTICIPATE YOUR ORDER

> One's ships come in over a calm sea.[15]
> > — FLORENCE SCOVEL SHINN
> > 1871-1940

> Act as if it were impossible to fail.   — DORTHEA BRANDE

> Learn to listen. Opportunity could be knocking at your
> door very softly.   — FRANK TYGER

After completing your visualizations, your orders will be 'in process.' Your next step? To have faith; to act 'as if' they have already been fulfilled; to expect them in joyful anticipation; to remain connected to source energy so they can come to you. Recognize that during the period of time that you are waiting, Angel is 'rearranging the furniture behind the curtains' preparing your Angacles — the opportunities that will enable you to co-create your order.

> *Man must prepare for the thing he has asked for, when*
> *there isn't the slightest sign of it in sight.*[16]
> — FLORENCE SCOVEL SHINN
> 1871-1940

To attain what you have ordered, it is essential that you 'stay connected,' for in your connection, you allow what you want to come to you. Oprah Winfrey once shared an experience that spoke of another method of allowing an order to manifest: surrender. After reading the book *The Color Purple*, and hearing the Hollywood buzz that a movie would soon be made, Oprah knew, beyond a shadow of a doubt, that she could play the role of Sophie — she *was* Sophie! Day after day she focused on how much she wanted this role and how she "would die" if she didn't get it. After auditioning, she heard nothing for weeks. In desperation, she called her agent and was informed that many other actresses were also auditioning, so it was uncertain as to when a decision would be made. Tortured by this delay, Oprah went to a spa and while running on a treadmill, "surrendered to God," telling Him that whatever He wanted for her, she would accept. Less than 5 minutes later, director Steven Spielberg was on the phone telling her that if she lost a pound she would not get the role! Immediately, she got off that treadmill, went to the Dairy Queen,® and celebrated! What happened? Oprah's powerful desire had summoned great quantities of energy, however, she was not allowing it to flow because her powerful frequency was tuned in to 'wanting.' But when she 'got out of the way,' energy-wise, and surrendered to God, her powerful frequency shifted and allowed her desire to manifest!

The moral of the story: Either get out of the way, 'tune in' to the frequency of what you desire, or just maintain pleasant thoughts to ensure your connection — and your order will manifest!

To continually assure your connection, conduct an 'attitude analysis' on the hour. Ask yourself, "How am I feeling? Am I having pleasant thoughts?" If not, refocus. By consciously monitoring your thoughts and switching 'channels' when bad little thoughts creep in, you will maintain your connection, and, as a result, whatever you desire can come to you.

For example: If you desire a better job, it is essential that you *appreciate* aspects of the position you currently hold, as those feelings create green circuits. As you appreciate your current job while simultaneously envisioning the job of your dreams, your circuits will remain open. The result? You will then magnetize the Angacles necessary to manifest your new job!

The process of actualizing your authentic power takes dedication, determination, and discipline. You must become aware of your thoughts — a habit that is foreign, so when you feel a nagging doubt, uncertainty, or fear begin to surface, distract yourself: laugh, appreciate, relax, listen to beautiful music, do things that soothe your mind and body, and lighten up! Look for *anything* to appreciate, focus on it, and your powerful magnetic thoughts will attract evidence that corresponds with your new frequency. As you practice this technique over and over again, soon your green circuits will become more and more dominant, allowing for more energy, hence, larger orders to manifest.

> *This is not a prescription for idleness, but for letting go of worry, anxiety, and fear...Stay alert for any small circumstance that indicates the first sprouting of the seed that you have planted in the universal mind, and allow it to form in your life as a growing materialization... You see in great detail what it is that you want, and you repeatedly affirm this picture with faith in the absolute power that is in all things, including yourself... You can picture yourself healthy, your business thriving, your sales quotas being met, your relationships healing, your house selling, finances coming your way or anything you desire. The key is to repeat these pictures until the truth of what you are affirming resonates within you without an ounce of doubt.*[17]
> — DR. WAYNE DYER

GET

TAKE INSPIRED ACTION FROM YOUR ANGACLES

A longing fulfilled is sweet to the soul.
— THE BIBLE
Proverbs 13:19

The next step is to be alert for Angacles, for they are the components that comprise your order. Opportunities will magically appear in the form of coincidences — people, events, or circumstances that you meet unexpectedly. Upon receiving an Angacle, you must then take inspired action. If a period of time has lapsed and nothing has appeared, you probably missed an Angacle and will need to place your order once again. Do not expect your orders to instantly manifest. There will be a time delay involved that is dependent upon how long you have focused on each of your orders as well as the intensity of emotion underlying them. For approximately thirty days, you will reap the rewards (cough, cough…) of your prior orders. Remember, the more frequently and intensely you focus on your orders in pure joy, the faster you will receive them. As you maintain a state of uncompromising belief and expectation that your orders will manifest — a state of pure focus free from resistance — you will begin to see some sort of change within three days.

Experiment with the Four-Step Formula and Flex Your Powerful Muscles

Let's now give the Formula a try! In your creative infancy, it's best not to begin with aspects of your life that evoke strong emotions within. Strong emotions indicate resistance that impedes the flow of energy. Preferably, begin with three items not critically important, extremely large, or emotionally-charged; items that do not evoke a negative feeling within — something impersonal that you believe you could attain but don't quite know how. This will allow you to see your successes more easily.

For example: It would not be advisable to place an order for "$1 Million next week" if you just received a 'final notice prior to disconnection' for the electric bill.

A great example of an initial order came from a librarian. What did she order? A cigar. Because she had no emotional attachment to a cigar, it held no contradicting belief or resistance that would impede it's manifestation. What happened? The day after placing her order, she opened a magazine to a cigar advertisement. Thinking that this experience might be 'coincidental,' she sought a more physical manifestation. The following day while checking in returned books, she discovered one with a curious lump inside. What was it? You guessed, a cigar! Now, what the heck would a cigar be doing in the middle of a library book? Coincidence? Well, that cigar was confirmation enough for her. She then recognized the reality of her power and the vast potentialities of life before her.

Another example you may wish to adopt utilizes stop lights. For a one week period, record the number of red lights that you encounter every day on your routine route to work, school, day-care, etc. After compiling your statistics to utilize as your basis of comparison, in the following week, order more *green* lights and see what happens.

Or you may opt to follow my example and invoke the 'parking lot' Angels. Whenever I desire a convenient parking space, I visualize how wonderful it feels to park a short distance from the stores I wish to patronize, while singing "Parking lot Angels, how I love you..." (To the tune of "Johnny Angel.") Guess what? It works!

Tune In and Win $$$

My mother-and father-in-law want to win the lottery (you too?). If we look deeper, what they really desire is financial independence or freedom, their core instinct. Although somewhat skeptical of the Four-Step Formula, they visualized winning the lottery and what they would do with their winnings. A few days later, they purchased a 'scratch-off' lottery ticket and won $250! In the following week, they went to bingo and won the grand prize of $500. And in the week after that, another $250! (See, it works!) Then they gained a new perspective on their newly acquired 'winner' status that shed an entirely different light on winning: Friends now wanted them to purchase *their* tickets because my mother-and father-in-law were so 'lucky'! With that, my mother-and father-in-law felt a bit uneasy over their newly discovered talent and subsequently abandoned the Formula. However, within a few months they 'reconnected,' went to Las Vegas and won more than they lost!

Have they won multi-millions? No. Why? Simple. They have resistance. They don't really *believe* it is possible. They don't *expect* to win — two elements essential in conscious creation. Although they try to think optimistically about winning the lottery, their hearts 'ain't buying it.' They have come to believe the statistics that proclaim a 'one in a zillion' chance to win. Why? Living in the old paradigm for so many years, they have acquired many frequencies that don't necessarily feel good, but feel natural. Therefore, when they purchase a lottery ticket, their frequencies are those of hope, disbelief, and strong desire — contradicting frequencies — frequencies impede the manifestation of *millions* of dollars. However, *some* additional money will manifest because their shift in consciousness created an opening — a shift in frequency. Despite being blessed with me as their daughter-in-law ☺, it's far easier to dismiss what I have come to discover than it is to reconstruct a new comfort zone and relinquish a belief system they have held for their entire lives.

The moral of the story: Your sponsoring thought is always the 'creative' thought. You can only manifest what you truly believe in your heart.

Now, choose your three items.

1. I choose_____

2. I choose_____

3. I choose_____

Next, write down all the reasons why you want what you have chosen. (Write down the reasons as they come naturally. Do not force anything and stop when your thoughts stop.)

1. I chose_____

because_____
_____
_____

2. I chose_____

because_____
_____
_____

3. I chose_____

because_____
_____
_____

Learn to Change Stations

Many folks prematurely cancel their orders by noticing they have not yet manifested. Rather than *expecting* the fulfillment of their orders by maintaining a feeling of joyful anticipation, they instead activate their 'off' switches, thus preventing their manifestation. So, whatever you do, don't focus your powerful thoughts on *not* receiving your order! Think of your mind as a TV remote control and quickly change stations when your thoughts begin to wander in the wrong direction.

When a person chooses to eliminate a compulsion or addiction in their life, in certain moments they will encounter anxiety. In those moments, they will automatically be triggered to revert to their 'preprogrammed' response — their habit. Why? It provides them with relief. However, if they anticipate those moments and predetermine a strategy in advance, the likelihood of eliminating their addiction is far greater. So, take advantage of that knowledge and predetermine your strategy.

Select three different 'stations' you can quickly switch to when your thoughts begin to wander in the wrong direction — stations that will ensure your connection. Think of joyful places you have visited — scenes so beautiful they took your breath away. Think of wonderful moments in your life, or simply look around and find something to appreciate and focus on it.

Station #1

_____
_____
_____

Station #2

_____
_____
_____

Station #3

_____
_____
_____

If you share your orders with others, you also take a risk. Because most have 'marinated' in old-paradigm beliefs for their entire lives, they will naturally attempt to protect their comfort zone. As a result, they may inundate you with a myriad of reasons that you *cannot* have what you want. Influenced by their negativity, you may inadvertently alter your frequency, activate your 'off' switch, and cancel your order. The bottom line? Before you can fully embody your authentic power, you, and you alone, must recognize and actualize your ability. And further down the road when you begin to manifest all sorts of wonderful things in your life, others may ask how you are doing it. *Then* you can share your secret.

When we speak to others about our efforts to manifest, our power is weakened. In general, when we describe these activities it is because the ego has entered the picture. This kind of approach considerably dissipates our power of attraction. It is human nature to talk to others about problems because we want to alleviate their influence in our life. By sharing, we hope to relieve some of the pressure of the problem. So, too, when we articulate our power to attract something, our attention shifts to the reactions of those in whom we are confiding. Energy is dispersed in the direction of their reactions in the same way that it is when we share problems. The moment a thought is presented to another, it is weakened. Maintain privacy concerning your own unique, possibly mysterious power to others, powers to attract to you what you desire.[18]   —DR. WAYNE DYER

Remember, you have nothing to lose. Just try the Formula and see what happens. Keep in mind though, if you think it won't work, your powerful thoughts will create that result and you will be right!

Practice Makes Perfect

When you no longer split your thoughts and feelings with contradictory feelings, you will know your power.[19]
— ESTHER and JERRY HICKS

Make it "Real" in Your Mind
And Your Mind Will Make it So.

Re-live Actions in the Realms of the Mind
Making it Right to Repeat it Not.

Always Speak to Your Mind
In a Manner That Shows it
What You Desire to Achieve
As the Positive Outcome.
In Speaking to Your Mind
Never Fight the Negative with Itself.
In a Direct Struggle
Good Will Lose to Evil.
Make Strong in the Good
And Evil Will Be Gone

Be Ever Vigilant
In Tending to Your Mind.
Turn from Your Negative Thoughts.
Use Your Free Will.
Dwell Only on Positive Thoughts
And Success Is Assured.[20]
— JON PENIEL
The Lost Teachings of Atlantis

Having acquired your frequencies — your habits of thought — throughout your life, it will initially take discipline, dedication, and determination to integrate the Four-Step Formula in your life. In fact, that's where the real work lies in moving from the old-paradigm into the new. On a physical level, you've got to build new neural pathways in your brain. What's a neural pathway? Something like a computer software program that requires downloading before it can be fully accessed. Whenever you learn a new skill, your brain constructs a new neural pathway. Do you recall the process you went through when you learned how to tie your shoes, drive a car, or ride a bike? While learning each of these new skills, you initially had to apply conscious thought and effort. Why? Your brain was building a new neural pathway and was 'under construction' — in the process of downloading new software. However, as you practiced and practiced this new skill, it became easier and easier because your neural pathway was almost complete. And pretty soon, your new skill became second nature because your brain was now fully downloaded with this new information.

While actualizing your power and honing your creative skills, try not to be impatient. Just as it took time for you to become proficient in any undertaking that you eventually mastered, utilizing the Formula will require practice, trial and error, and good old 'on the job training.' You must take *small* steps in the beginning in order to build a strong foundation that you solidly believe. If you attempt to move too fast or too soon, your confidence may soon fade as doubt will become your new frequency — a frequency fatal to creation.

Build Strength of Will Slowly
One Stone at a Time.
If One Attempts to Lift a Stone Larger
Than One's Strength
It Can Crush You Under its Weight

The Drop of Water, Can Carve the Rock
The Glacier Can Carve the Mountain.
Thusly Do Consistency and Perseverence
Overcome All Obstacles.

In All Things, Be Moderate

When the Two Minds Oppose Each Other
Neither's Goal Is Achieved.
Want What You Want
And Tend to Both Branches and Roots.

The Jellyfish That Drifts with the Tide
Is Wiser than a Man with No Ideal.[21]
— JON PENIEL
The Lost Teachings of Atlantis

When you learn to utilize your power, the world will be at your fingertips, for you will then be living as life is meant to be lived: truly living, loving, and laughing in the majority of your Moments! ⊕

Take Fifteen Minutes a Day to Ensure a Magical Life

Never face reality unless your reality is just the way you want it.[22]
— ESTHER and JERRY HICKS

I know of no more encouraging fact than the unquestionable ability of man to elevate his life by conscious endeavor.
— HENRY DAVID THOREAU
1817-1862

Let your hook always be cast. In the pool where you least expect it, will be a fish.
— OVID
43 BC-17 AD

Dream lofty dreams and as you dream, so shall you become.[23]
— JAMES ALLEN
1849-1925

I begin each day to see what my overall goals are in this lifetime, and what the overall goals of humanity might be, and start listening very carefully within.[24]
— RUTH MONTGOMERY

Have the courage to act instead of react.
— DARLENE LARSON JENKS

You will never "find" time for anything. If you want time you must make it.
— CHARLES BUXTON

Implement Your New Path
and Create Beautiful Tomorrows

Before you began reading this book, what was your state of mind? Were you like most: confused, frustrated, and yearning for answers in life? How much would it have been worth to you to know the secret to life — how to attain everything you have always wanted in life? *Priceless?* (I just wanted to make sure this info was valuable because I didn't want you to forget my 10 percent fee on anything over and above your current earnings for sharing it with you. *What?* You didn't read the fine print at the beginning of this book? Is this information not worth 10 percent? After all, you're receiving 90 percent aren't you? ☺ Just kidding, to make my point.) Is a better life worth investing fifteen minutes a day to you?

Living amidst old-paradigm lower frequencies, you have probably become acclimated to those frequencies. Consequently, you may have grown accustomed to occasionally feeling ornery, aggravated, frustrated, angry, doubtful, or overwhelmed, and as such, you are not allowing energy to flow to you in the majority of your moments. However, to attain what you want in life, it is imperative that you maintain a state of connection.

The overriding objective of this book is to convey to you the importance of living a joyful life and how your joy adds to the collective joy in our world. Therefore, to ensure your magical life, it's important to commit fifteen minutes a day to 'go to work.' Life in the old paradigm is rampant with powerful vortexes of negative energy that can pull you in their whirlwinds quite easily, therefore it is essential that you constantly *choose* what you want for your life experience. As you identify and clearly state what you want, you will not attract experiences that you don't want! Living in the Information Age, where you are continually inundated with events occurring all over the globe, it is exceedingly difficult not to be influenced or absorbed by all of it. So, rather than living your life putting out all of the brush-fires you created unconsciously by focusing haphazardly, and creating 'good stuff' only occasionally, deliberately order what you want. By placing your orders daily, you will automatically sift through the vast amount of information you are exposed to and magnetize only what you choose. This will leave you refreshed and stimulated, moving ahead, open fully to life.[25]

Completing Your New Comfort Zone

*You must have a room or a certain hour of the day
where you do not know what was in the morning
paper....A place where you can simply experience and
bring forth what you are, and what you might be....At
first, you may find that nothing's happening....But if you
have a sacred space, use it, and take advantage of it,
something will happen.* — JOSEPH CAMPBELL

Let's now compile all of the data obtained from the questions you
previously answered and complete the construction of your new comfort
zone. Keep in mind that although some items will remain consistent,
others will change daily.

*Begin by being still. Quiet the outer world, so that the
inner world might bring you sight.*[26]
— NEALE DONALD WALSCH
Conversations with God - Book I

1. Find a place as free from distraction as possible and then quiet the
physical world around you both mentally and emotionally. Begin by
thinking of something relaxing and soothing. To help quiet your inner
mind, breathe deeply and focus on each breath you take, for breath is
life. Next, mentally bring yourself to a place of joy. This could be
remembering a joyful moment in your life, thinking of a beautiful place
you have visited, petting your animal, or simply playing beautiful music.

This is my unique place of joy:

_____

_____

_____

_____

2. *These are the things I currently enjoy having in my life:* (you do not want
to *forfeit* them by *not* giving them focus — *The Pathway* {page 15–16})

_____

_____

_____

_____

_____

_____
_____
_____
_____
_____
_____

3. *I now choose to have:* (Use your list of the *opposite* of those things you did not like having in your life — *The Pathway* {page 16})

_____
_____
_____
_____
_____
_____
_____
_____
_____

4. *The following items are wishes from my 'Genie' list:* (*The Puzzle* {page 66})

_____
_____
_____
_____
_____
_____
_____
_____
_____
_____

5. *The following are affirmations that resonate with me:* (*The Postscript* {pages 11–14})

_____
_____
_____
_____
_____

_____
_____
_____
_____
_____
_____

6. *From the wrong-way signs that Angel has sent me, I choose:* (carry a small pad of paper with you at all times and write down your negative feelings throughout your day. When you have time, determine what it what you *really* wanted and bring those notes to 'work' the next morning so you can place your order.)

7. *This is what is most important to me in life:* (your 'gravestone' list if those items were not already covered — *The Pathway* {page 6})

_____
_____
_____
_____
_____
_____
_____

8. *After reviewing my history, I choose to have:*

_____
_____
_____
_____
_____
_____
_____
_____
_____
_____
_____

9. *I choose to feel:*

_____
_____
_____
_____
_____

10. *I choose to have the following:*   (what you wish to have spiritually, emotionally, physically, or mentally)

_____

_____

_____

_____

_____

_____

_____

_____

_____

_____

11. *This is Who I Choose to Be:*   (*The Pathway* {page 9})

_____

_____

_____

_____

_____

_____

_____

_____

12. *My Mission is:*   (*The Pathway* {page 68})

_____

_____

_____

_____

_____

13. *My Vision to actualize my Mission is:*   (*The Pathway* {page 69})

_____

_____

_____

_____

_____

_____

Utilizing this list when you 'go to work' every day will ensure a magical life experience. You will then live as life is meant to be lived: as a joyous creative experience filled with love and laughter! ☺

Utilize Your Power Throughout the Day

[Being who you choose to be] is a day-to-day, hour-to-hour, moment-to-moment act of supreme consciousness. It is a choosing and re-choosing every instant. It is ongoing creation. Conscious creation. Creation with a purpose. It is using the tools of creation we have discussed, and using them with awareness and sublime intention.[27]
— NEALE DONALD WALSCH
Conversations with God - Book 1

Do not put off till tomorrow what can be enjoyed today.
— JOSH BILLINGS
1818-1885

The present is the point of power.[28] — JANE ROBERTS
The Nature of Personal Reality - A Seth Book

Let your mind be quiet, realizing the beauty of the world, and the immense, the boundless treasures that it holds in store. All that you have within you, all that your heart desires, all that your nature so specially fits for you — that, or the counterpart of it waits embedded in the great Whole, for you. — EDWARD CARPENTER

The distance is nothing: it is only the first step that is difficult. — MARIE ANNE DU DEFFAND

Specific
Time-Period Ordering

Every day you engage in many activities; arising in the morning, going to work, taking care of the kids, running errands, cleaning, cooking, exercising, talking with friends, going to sleep, etc. As you begin each new task, your desires change. Therefore, by simply taking a moment to decide what you would like to occur in each period of time and then placing an order for it, you can fine tune your experience even further.

For example: When you leave your home to go to work, what is it that you want? How do you want to feel? Why do you want it? As you get in your car or walk to the train or bus, think about what it is that you want to happen during that interval of time. Assuming you want to arrive safely at your destination, you might say, "I intend safety for myself and those around me." You may also wish to add, "I choose to arrive at _____ a.m./p.m. with joy and enthusiasm." Then, after placing your order with Angel, you can relax, let go of any anxiety and enjoy the scenery, because Angel will be hard at work ensuring that outcome!

If you are employed in a sales position, before calling on a customer, specifically define your intent to assure a pleasant, successful outcome. Think about what you *want* to happen and then place an order for it.

For example: If you are a sales representative en route to an appointment, you may wish to place the following order: "I choose to create a wonderful, respectful, mutually beneficial working relationship with Joe from the XYZ Corporation. I intend for Joe to acknowledge the benefit of my product or service." Now, close your eyes (unless you're driving…) and imagine yourself with Joe. The two of you are happy, harmonious, and respecting one another. Imagine him 'lighting up' when he realizes how your product or service will benefit his company. Watch it all unfold in your mind until you feel excited. Then go to your appointment and enjoy the manifestation!

If you are at home caring for your children, think about what you want to happen during the day that would make your collective experience more joyful. Visualize your children benefitting from their experience with you. If you work outside your home, visualize their caretaker having all the qualities you desire. Understand the magnitude of being your children's spiritual teacher, for you are the caretaker of their souls. Imagine each of them growing into adulthood where your caring gave them the foundation to be self-assured and self-confident. In your mind's eye, see them contributing their greatest gifts to the betterment of our world as a result of the foundation that you provided them. Although raising children may sometimes feel unrewarding because the real results lie in the future, the care you are giving your children is the most valuable gift they could ever receive, so be proud of yourself and radiate that pride to them.

Avoid Accidents by Clearly Defining Your Intent

For years, statisticians have been perplexed by the unusually sparse number of car accidents that occur in relation to the vast number of drivers on the road. It simply defies logic. Yet, now think about the Four-Step Formula. What is the dominant intention of a driver going to work? Compare that *deliberate* intention with that of a teenage (or any age), driver going out for a 'spin.' Generally, teenage drivers have no defined destination — they simply want to go cruisin' — they're on a journey of adventure (that's what I did...). Therefore, they are at a much higher risk of attracting whatever may come their way. If statistics were available, they would more than likely confirm the fact that teenage drivers with no defined destination have a higher rate of accidents than their counterparts with defined destinations.

Moral of the story: Order safety for yourself, your kids, and those around you at all times.

You can utilize the Four-Step Formula to create what you want in every moment, for each of your moments is a new Point of Power. As you begin each day, decide what you want to experience, place your orders, and then tune in. Order your long-term goals, your short-term goals, and the moments before you. You have the ability, so use it to its fullest. Again, the Four-Step Formula — think, believe, expect, and get — is unwavering in its operation; it is something you can rely upon. So, as you apply it to your advantage, you will live your life the way it is meant to be lived: loving and laughing in the majority of your Moments!

Let's now proceed further along your path and uncover both your personal Mission in life as well as our global Mission: the recreation of our world. ☺

Reach Out, I'll Be There

Now, if you feel that you can't go on 'cause all of your hope is gone,
your life is filled with much confusion
until happiness is just an illusion
And your world around is crumblin' down
Well, darlin' reach out
Reach out for Me.
I'll be there to give you all the love you need.
And I'll be there, you can always count on me.
When you feel lost and about to give up
'cause your best ain't just good enough,
And you feel the world has grown cold
and you're driftin' out all on your own,
And you need a hand to hold
Darlin' reach out, reach out for Me.
I'll be there with a love that will shelter you.
And I'll be there with a love that will see you through.
I'll be there to give you all the love you need.
And I'll be there, you can always count on Me.
I can tell the way you hang your head,
You're without love and now you're afraid,
And through your tears you look around,
but there's no peace of mind to be found,
I know what you're thinkin', you're all alone now,
no love of your own,
But darlin' reach out, Reach out for Me.
I'll be there to give you all the love you need.
And I'll be there, you can always count on Me.
I'll be there with a love that will shelter you.
And be there with a love that will see you through.[29]

Words and Music by Brian Holland, Lamont Dozier, and Eddie Holland

Missions Possible:
Personal and Global

Here is the test to find whether your mission on Earth is finished: If you're alive, it isn't. — RICHARD BACH

I cannot believe that the purpose of life is to be "happy." I think the purpose of life is to be useful, to be responsible, to be compassionate. It is, above all, to matter, to count, to stand for something, to have made some difference that you lived at all. — LEO ROSTEN

To love what you do and feel that it matters — how could anything be more fun? — KATHERINE GRAHAM

Within us all there is divinity hiding, waiting for its moment to be born into the world, the opportunity to come out of the shadows of our entrenched illusions. It will begin within each one of us, spreading like light through each of us and our world.[30]
— MARIANNE WILLIAMSON

When the deepest part of you becomes engaged in what you are doing, when what you do serves both yourself and others, when you do not tire within but seek the sweet satisfaction of your life and your work, you are doing what you were meant to be doing.[31] — GARY ZUKAV

The essential conditions of everything you do must be choice, love, passion.
— NADIA BOULANGER
1887-1979

Within our dreams and aspirations we find our opportunities.
— SUE ATCHLEY EBAUGH

When you cease to make a contribution, you begin to die.
— ELEANOR ROOSEVELT
1882-1962

You give but little when you give of your possessions. It is when you give of yourself that you truly give.
— KHALIL GIBRAN
1883-1931

Real joy does not come from ease or riches or from the praise of men, but from doing something worthwhile.
— W. T. GRENFELL
1865-1940

Imagine awaking each morning knowing what really matters to you and then doing it. Imagine how it would feel to have a sense of purpose, value, and importance. Imagine meeting people and rather than asking "What's your zodiac sign?" (like we did in the '70s), asking "What's your Mission?" Imagine employment applications requiring your Personal Mission Statement to determine if your statement is compatible with the company's Mission. (Isn't this cool?) Imagine others knowing what matters to them and having a sense of purpose, value, and importance. Can you imagine how awesome that could be?

When you understand your higher purpose in life, you look at yourself and others differently. You walk a little taller knowing that indeed you have a Mission. You no longer define yourself according to *what* you are — your job, your body, your physical appearance, your race, your financial status, your religion, or any of those external things that don't really mean much in the big picture — but instead, by *who* you are.

I believe that each of us came into this world with a Mission or goal, a spiritual task, a purpose for our being here. And it is not to simply survive or to live a life quivering in fear, for that is no fun whatsoever! So, if you are now living a ho-hum life of complacency, Angel will bug you relentlessly with wrong-way signs.

To shed some light on your purpose, let's begin a very methodical process that should lead you to the discovery of your Mission. First, ask yourself a few questions. Have you ever felt as though there was something you were supposed to do but you had no idea what it was? Have you ever felt as though time was slipping away and one day soon you would look into a mirror and say "I coulda, I woulda, I shoulda?" Does the mere word 'Mission' conjure a feeling within of being overwhelmed? Are you struggling to go to work each day, pay your bills, take care of the kids, and keep your household running? Do you feel as though you don't have a spare moment left for a Mission? Well, guess what? The definition of a Mission is actually very broad and does not require 'saving the world.' (Whew! You're off the hook!)

So, before blaming someone or something else in your life for not permitting you to accomplish your Mission — before you meet with a day when you are filled with regret — answer a few more questions: Are you making a contribution to the world? Do you want to leave this world knowing that you made a difference? Are you giving more than you are taking?

How do you define a Mission? A Mission is something that everyone benefits from. It supports all life and diminishes none. It is something you enjoy doing, something you truly love, a passion where time seems to fly by. Your Mission can be as simple as 'giving joy to the world,' 'adding beauty to our world,' or 'helping others' in some way, shape, or form. Your Mission encompasses more of Who You Really Are. It extends beyond the role you are currently playing — whether you are a mother, CEO, or both. Your current role, however, may provide clues to unlock your mystery when you examine it from a more expansive perspective. For what does a mother really do? She nurtures, teaches, and encourages independence — all attributes that can certainly transcend the role of motherhood to encompass another endeavor. What does a CEO really do? He/she wears the hat of Visionary: leading, guiding, and encouraging others to utilize their gifts and attributes — characteristics that can certainly transcend the role of CEO. Your Mission extends beyond a limited role.[32] Your Mission and what you do in life should interrelate.[33]

When each of us arrived in this world, we were very clear about the goals we intended to accomplish. However, as we embarked upon our journeys we oftentimes met with extenuating circumstances that distracted our focus. As a result, we got sidetracked and lost sight of our Mission.

For example: Imagine that you were a skin-diver and your Mission was to retrieve a treasure chest that you could clearly see one hundred feet below the surface of the water. Upon diving in the water, you left an environment of clarity and now found yourself submersed in a completely unfamiliar environment. Scary feeling, right? Then, when you reached a depth of fifty-five feet, out of the corner of your eye you spotted a shark swimming toward you. Consumed in fear and panic, you swam furiously trying to evade this dreadful killer. Finally, you discovered a safe place to hide and remained hidden in order to avoid certain death. During this process, you forgot all about the treasure chest you were to retrieve. Your focus changed from 'Mission' to 'Survival' and now you couldn't wait to get back to the security of the boat. Hello.... That's living a life of fear! Seeking a life of security will only create an inner feeling of emptiness, a wrong-way sign.

How do you reconnect with your Mission? The first step is simple: You *choose* to fulfill it, even though you may not know what 'it' is. By placing your order, Angel will then provide you with the necessary Angacles — people, events, or circumstances — that will guide you to the key to unlock your mystery.

Oftentimes the key to your Mission can be found in the dreams and goals you have had in life, for they, too, can point you in the right direction. Other indicators? Your gifts, talents, attributes, or quite often, your Mission is linked to a significant life event that has influenced you.

A Path to Unveil Your Mission

A human being is part of a whole, called by us the "Universe," a part limited in time and space. He experiences himself, his thoughts and his feelings, as something separated from the rest — a kind of optical delusion of his consciousness. This delusion is a kind of prison for us, restricting us to our personal desires and to affection for a few persons nearest us. Our task must be to free ourselves from this prison by widening our circles of compassion to embrace all living creatures and the whole of nature in its beauty. — ALBERT EINSTEIN

Your work is to discover your work and then with all your heart to give yourself to it. — BUDDHA
563-483 BC

If you still don't have a clue as to what your Mission might be, don't worry, we've only begun this process. To shed more light on your Mission, answer a few more questions:[34]

1. If you were wealthy and had all the time in the world, what would you do? _____

_____

_____

_____

_____

2. What dreams and goals have you had (even those that seem far out)?

_____

_____

_____

_____

_____

3. What attributes or talents were you given in life?

_____

_____

_____

_____

_____

4. What things in life energize you?

_____

_____

_____

_____

_____

5. What would you say you have been in training for?

_____

_____

_____

_____

6. What does the purpose of your life seem to be so far?

_____

_____

_____

_____

7. What seems complete for you?

_____

_____

_____

_____

_____

8. What feels unfinished?

_____

_____

_____

_____

_____

9. Do you see a repeating pattern of experience, achievement, or lesson?

_____

_____

_____

_____

_____

Did your answers provide any additional clues from which to determine your Mission? If not, let's proceed further...

Additional Keys that May Unlock The Mystery of Your Mission

To unlock the mystery of your Mission, it is helpful to break it into smaller pieces, for a Mission essentially contains four key elements: What, Why, Who, and How. *What* concerns do you have that you feel call for change or improvement? (Identifying the negative offers you the clarity to determine its opposite.) *Why* does this issue need improving? *Who* will be helped by this improvement? *How* can you help to effect this improvement?

The life experiences or tragedies you have undergone will often point in the direction of your Mission. *For example:* A friend of mine had a son who died of AIDS. This agonizing experience was replete with much sorrow, challenge, and fear, as well as many unexpected painful twists and turns for both her and her son. Imbued in a state of hopelessness, her son ferociously lashed out at her over his many unresolved life issues — a very painful experience for her. After his death, she discovered that his behavior was actually normal, in fact, an element of the grieving process. Filled with a sense of regret, she felt that if only she had been aware of this knowledge, she could have responded differently and not personalized the attacks as she did. My friend then felt compelled to share this knowledge with others who might be undergoing similar situations so they could avoid needless pain. As a result of her tragedy, my friend discovered her Mission and became a volunteer at the Howard Brown Association in Chicago, an organization dedicated to helping those who have contracted AIDS.

> *What:* After experiencing the tragedy of her son dying of AIDS, my friend recognized the need to provide others with critical information.

> *Why:* To spare those affected by a life-threatening illness from needless pain.

> *Who:* Anyone affected by a life-threatening illness.

> *How:* She joined an organization dedicated to providing knowledge and comfort to others.

Hypothetical Mission Statement: My Mission is to provide knowledge to those affected by a life-threatening illness, thereby easing their pain during this difficult time.

Another example of a life experience that inspired a Mission is the story of Jack Canfield — co-creator of the successful *Chicken Soup for the Soul* series of books. Teaching history in an inner city school in Chicago, Mr. Canfield became more interested in why kids were *not* learning than he was in history. Finding that a self-defeating attitude was often the culprit responsible for this disinterest, he sought a way to help others to overcome this attitude. Upon formulating his desire, an Angacle appeared in the form of his future partner, Mark Victor Hansen. And the two of them then went on to actualize their Mission of inspiring others to overcome difficulties in life through a series of heart-warming books.[35]

> *What:* While teaching history, Mr. Canfield found that many students were not learning in school which piqued his curiosity to discover why. Finding that a self-defeating attitude was oftentimes at the core of this issue, he became interested in helping others to overcome this obstacle in their lives.

> *Why:* People oftentimes feel defeated and give up on life when faced with seemingly insurmountable obstacles and challenges.

Who: Others.

How: By providing real-life stories that demonstrate the power of the indomitable human spirit to overcome challenges in life, *Chicken Soup For the Soul®* books offer inspiration that help others to reignite their sense of power and determination. In short, Mr. Canfield and Mr. Hansen sought to demonstrate that if others could overcome obstacles, anyone could.

Hypothetical Mission Statement: Our Mission is to inspire and empower others to overcome the inevitable challenges in life by providing real-life stories that demonstrate the strength of the indomitable human spirit.

Have you had a life experience that provided you with an insight that could help or benefit others?

_____
_____
_____
_____
_____
_____
_____
_____
_____

The First Piece of Your Mission Puzzle

The first piece of your Mission puzzle is to determine **WHAT** needs change or improvement in our world. Ask yourself:

∾ What cause, principle, issue, purpose, injustice, unfairness, or change would you like to participate in that you believe would make our world a better place to live in?

∾ What do you believe our world needs more of?

∾ What do you believe our world needs less of?

∾ What topic would you like to raise consciousness over?

∾ What topic inspires you?

Do any of the following topics resonate with you?

the arts	joy	service	justice
family	creating	beauty	freedom
equality	tolerance	love	kindness
compassion	recycling	the environment	animals
addictions	mentoring	illness	illiteracy
education	health care	judicial system	pollution
the government	community	corporate reevaluation	
alternative fuels	child care	spirituality	

What aspect of this topic interests you?_____
_____

Piece #1 — What area of life do you wish to improve upon?
_____
_____

The Second Piece of Your Mission Puzzle

Piece #2 — WHY does this area of life need improving and why is it important to you?
_____
_____

The Third Piece of Your Mission Puzzle

Every Mission implies that someone will be helped, therefore, WHO do you wish to make a difference for?

Examples:

children	adults	teens	the poor
the homeless	women	men	the terminally ill
senior citizens	abused women	others	welfare to work
the world	those in third world countries		

Piece #3 — Who do you wish to assist?
_____
_____

The Fourth Piece of Your Mission Puzzle

Piece #4 — How can you help to effect this change?_____

_____

Examples of how you might help:

inspire	add beauty	raise consciousness	write
give your time	counsel	provide knowledge	connect
communicate	create	help to build	add joy
empower	translate	encourage	mediate
integrate	heal	provide enthusiasm	negotiate
organize	reform	restore	renew
serve	share	understand	speak

Laurie Beth Jones tells us that Jesus had a Mission statement:

To give life, and give it more abundantly.[36]

The message in this book is essentially the same: To reawaken the power within so you can live more abundantly! After reading Laurie's wonderful book, *The Path: Creating Your Mission Statement for Work and for Life,* I created my Mission Statement. And because I have more than one passion, it is two-fold:

My Mission is to inspire and awaken others to the incredible power that lies within them.

My Mission is to add beauty to our world through designing and creating environments that inspire joy, serenity, and an interconnection with Mother Earth.

Before You Finalize Your Mission Statement — How Do You Feel?

The world exists the way it exists — just as a snowflake exists the way it exists — quite by design. You have created it that way — just as you have created your life exactly as it is.[37]

— NEALE DONALD WALSCH
Conversations with God - Book 1

Do not condemn, therefore, all that you would call bad in the world. Rather, ask yourself, what about this have you judged bad, and what, if anything, you wish to do to change it.[38]
— NEALE DONALD WALSCH
Conversations with God - Book 1

Do not judge, and you will not be judged. Do not condemn, and you will not be condemned. Forgive, and you will be forgiven. Give, and it will be given to you. For with the measure you use, it will be measured to you.
— THE BIBLE
Luke 6:37-38

Be a light unto the world, and hurt it not. Seek to build, not to destroy.[39]
— NEALE DONALD WALSCH
Conversations with God - Book 2

It is better to light a candle than to curse the darkness.
— CHINESE PROVERB

Our Global Mission

Although this topic may appear to depart from your personal Mission, in reality, it does not. For your personal Mission and our global Mission are interwoven. To ensure that your Mission is compatible with new-paradigm thinking, it is imperative that you examine your underlying feelings and motives before you finalize your Mission Statement because your natural tendency would be to react and respond in old-paradigm thinking. Therefore, by examining the 'bigger picture,' you can contemplate your personal Mission from a broader perspective.

When you observe an injustice that evokes strong negative emotion within you, you now know that your 'off' switch has been activated. You're receiving an Angel-Alert — a wrong-way sign, therefore, your Point of Power from which to create. To work toward the change of an injustice, the trick is not to hate or feel militant, but to *love* — to channel your passion into positive inspired action.

You are not here to cry about the miseries of the human condition but to change them when you find them not to your liking through the joy, strength, and vitality that is within you.[40]
— JANE ROBERTS
The Nature of Personal Reality - A Seth Book

You can only help to resolve issues in life using *love* as the underlying frequency. All other methods are backwards — consequences of old-paradigm thinking! Your actions cannot effect a positive change if you push against and attack what you feel is wrong, for negativity is fueling them. This approach will always work against you and actually *add* to the problem because you are giving your attention to what you don't want.

Various causes in our country, such as the war on crime, the war on drugs, or the war on poverty, are all working backwards, unwittingly adding to these issues rather than diminishing them because they are pushing against. Remember, whatever you resist, will persist, for whatever you focus your powerful magnetic thoughts on can only grow larger!

> *The act of resisting something is the act of granting it life... the more you resist, the more you make it real — whatever it is you are resisting.*[41] — NEALE DONALD WALSCH
> *Conversations with God - Book 1*

Although you may feel righteous in hating what appears to be evil (and most of us would agree with you...), if you find yourself feeling anger, you will only create more anger, activate your 'off' switch, and restrict the flow of life energy. And you can accomplish nothing in a state of disconnection.

> *There is no justification for hatred. When you curse another, you curse yourselves, and the curse returns to you.*[42]
> — JANE ROBERTS
> *The Nature of Personal Reality - A Seth Book*

Eradicating Injustice

> *I have listened to the realm of the Spirit. I have heard my own soul's voice, and I have remembered that love is the complete unifying thread of existence.* — MARY CASEY

To effect a positive change in our world, you must tune to the frequency of joy, love, and brotherhood, as opposed to a frequency of frustration, overpowering, judgement, or fear. On any controversial issue, whether it is abortion, gay rights, the environment, equal opportunity, racism, don't protest: Visualize. Utilize your power to your advantage. And though you may have strong negative feelings for other worthy issues, choose only one issue you feel drawn to, for if you focus on too many you will only dilute your energy. And rather than ranting and raving, passing moral judgment on others, or moaning or groaning about a issue (old-paradigm thinking), offer a viable alternative. Also, recognize that some pro-testers are actually addicted to the adrenalin rush of protesting. They are not really looking for a solution; they simply have many layers of onion to peel. In fact, some protesters feel alive and energized when connected to a negative vortex of energy — it has become their comfort zone. Unaware of how to connect with *source* energy, negative adrenalin filled experiences often become their only means of attaining energy.

How can you use your authentic power to effect a change? Begin by creating an environment imbued with non-judgment, acceptance, and love. This will allow those entangled in an issue to be receptive to alternate solutions. Next, create a vision where all can benefit. And always provide an escape for those you disagree with that allows dignity. Why? Because humanity begets (magnetizes) humanity.

To eradicate an injustice:

- Uncover the root of the problem by asking, "How has this issue been created?"

- Examine the who, what, why, when, where, and how of the situation.

- Provide alternatives and offer support.

- Help resolve the issue by offering a practical solution.

- Create a vision of what is desired.

- Visualize what is desired with love and joy until it feels real.

- Take inspired action from the Angacles that will appear — the people, events, and circumstances you will magnetize that are necessary to manifest your vision.

> *Look to see who is truly serving the world, truly seeking to share wisdom and knowledge, insight and under-standing, caring and compassion. Provide for those people, and provide grandly. Pay them the highest honor. Give them the largest amount. For these are the Bringers of Light.*[43]
>
> — NEALE DONALD WALSCH
> *Conversations with God - Book 3*

Empowering Versus Enabling

Your Mission need not entail giving up your joyful life for the sake of someone more needy, for if you do, you are simply joining them in their frequency, thus *adding* to it. In fact, I believe we do a disservice to our brothers and sisters who may be quite capable when we continually hand things to them, for what is the message we send? That they cannot 'do' for themselves. We prevent them from recognizing their power, strengths, and abilities. Unwittingly, we help to perpetuate their complacency and dependency while reinforcing their neediness and illusion of powerlessness.

As parents, we know that if we continually give our children all they want, we will not create the incentive for them to do anything for themselves. In fact, we do them a great disservice, for we disempower them, stifle their growth, and hinder their ability to connect with the feeling of accomplishment and pride they radiate when they achieve something on their own.

We must recognize that there will always be those who will seek aid as a means of avoiding responsibility. It's the path of least resistance, yet also a path with far-reaching ramifications. Furthermore, there are people who encourage those less fortunate to lean on them because they believe that to be virtuous. And still others who offer help while feeling a sense of superiority, as if they were making a sacrifice.

With that in mind, it is essential to examine your underlying feelings and intentions before donating money or possessions to any cause, for it is not virtuous to give away anything if your frequency is tuned to guilt or the acknowledgment of another's lack. If you help others while feeling guilty for having more, you will simply magnetize evidence of those beliefs. Esther and Jerry Hicks explain that in our recognition of another's inability to create what they want in their life — in our pain of noticing their *lack* — we are focusing our powerful magnetic thoughts on their lack, thereby perpetuating it! We must understand that if someone is sick, it does them no good for us to be sick; if someone is hungry, it does them no good for us to hunger; if someone does not have enough money, it does them no good for us not to have money. For in reality, we can never cry enough tears or feel enough pain to make something better for someone else.[44] I am not suggesting that we stop giving, I am simply suggesting that we stop enabling and promoting powerlessness.

> *Charity degrades those who receive it and hardens those who dispense it.*
> — GEORGE SAND
> 1804-1876

Anticipate charity by preventing poverty; assist the
reduced fellow man, either by a considerable gift, or a
sum of money, or by teaching him a trade, or putting him
in the way of business, so that he may earn an honest
livelihood, and not be forced to the dreadful alternative
of holding out his hand for charity. This is the highest
step and the summit of charity's golden ladder.

— MAIMONDES
1135-1204

How can we genuinely help our brothers and sisters in need? We can provide a pathway for them to take responsibility for their own lives — a path that engenders dignity, respect, self-worth, purpose, value, and importance — attributes each of us deserves. This path would assist others in awakening to their authentic power. How might we begin? First, we would establish a system that temporarily offers basic survival needs: food, shelter, clothing, childcare, and health care. Next, we would create an underlying support system that provides a safety-net for a person needing help with an issue. This system could perhaps emulate the Alcoholics Anonymous program, where on any day, at any time, a person in need could attend a meeting or call a 'help line.'

I believe that each of us chose life on our beautiful Earth to participate in its many wondrous aspects as well as to learn and grow. However, I also believe that we have a responsibility to offer all of our brothers and sisters worldwide an opportunity to awaken to the power they have within; for pain, anguish, and suffering only result from an ignorance of authentic power.

Give a man a fish, and you feed him for a day. Teach a man
to fish, and you feed him for a lifetime. — CHINESE PROVERB

This does not mean that we turn our heads in blind disregard
for the plight of others, because we are a brotherhood. On the
other hand, when we set out to DO LOVE before we have
BEEN IT we have simply judged a condition and failed to
honor the person within it. Until we can walk in another
man's shoes, what right have we to tell him what kind of
shoes to wear?[45] — GLENDA GREEN
Love Without End: Jesus Speaks

A disciple having asked for a definition of charity, the Master
said: Love one another. — CONFUCIUS
551-479 BC

There are no victims in the Universe, only creators.[46]
— NEALE DONALD WALSCH
Conversations with God - Book I

This does not mean to ignore a call for help, nor the urging of your soul to work toward the change of some circumstance or condition. It does mean avoiding labels and judgment while you do whatever you do. For each circumstance is a gift, and in each experience is hidden a treasure.[47]
— NEALE DONALD WALSCH
Conversations with God - Book I

The most rejuvenating idea of all and the greatest step to any true illumination, is the realization that your exterior life springs from the invisible world of your reality through your conscious thoughts and beliefs, for then you realize the power of your individuality and identity. You are immediately presented with choices. You can no longer see yourself as a victim of circumstances.[48]
— JANE ROBERTS
The Nature of Personal Reality - A Seth Book

Examining the Abortion Controversy in Light of the Four-Step Formula

You may feel quite virtuous ... in hating evil, or what seems to you to be evil; but if you find yourself concentrating upon either hatred or evil, you are creating it.[49]
— JANE ROBERTS
The Nature of Personal Reality - A Seth Book

Those who would lead us into cynicism or anger, lead us away from healing.[50]
— MARIANNE WILLIAMSON

Let's examine the issue of abortion in light of the Four-Step Formula as it is yet another consequence of old-paradigm thinking — one with no winners. The opposing factions, in their well-intentioned righteousness, endlessly push against one another, and in the process, inadvertently create a powerful negative energy vortex which only perpetuates the issue and makes it worse. Although both factions have received many wrong-way signs, they are unaware of their meaning. As a result, they unwittingly create more harm than good. The bottom line? Both sides have lost sight of what is *wanted*. Both sides are operating from the frequency of fear, rather than love.

How can we begin to resolve this issue? First, we must examine the root cause of abortion and ask a few very basic questions: Why do women need abortions? Why have these women become pregnant? What are the underlying reasons for their pregnancies, beyond the obvious sexual implications? Are these women seeking love and perceive a baby as their 'answer'? Are they attempting to manipulate their lovers into committed relationships? Certainly we live in a time where birth-control is readily available, so we must peel back a layer and explore the underlying reason for their pregnancies. And the answer might simply be a fear of pregnancy, which could unwittingly magnetize it.

However, when reality becomes clear to these pregnant women, rather than experiencing the illusion of love they may have initially envisioned, they are instead confronted with the overwhelming commitment of caring for a child the next eighteen years of their lives. And they may feel incapable of achieving that task. They may feel that they lack the time, commitment, or financial resources. Or they may have imagined the worst possible outcome: One where they are robbed of *their* lives. How can we help?

He has the right to criticize who has the heart to help.
— ABRAHAM LINCOLN

As Hillary Clinton has recognized, "It takes a village." Real solutions require help from others. Rather than trying to manipulate the mothers-to-be with guilt, we must offer them something tangible: A practical solution for the day-to-day care of their child. Members from both sides of this controversy could volunteer to care for these children a specific number of hours per week, offering the mom-to-be a viable contract — security. This solution addresses the feelings of powerlessness inherent in a mother contemplating an abortion — feelings that strike terror in her heart. The protesters can redirect their valuable energy from fear to love by creating day-care centers or finding employment for the moms. In short, they can assist in the day-to-day raising of these children, rather than engaging in a futile battle with one another. And those who *really care about the children* would soon be separated from those caught up in the adrenalin rush of opposition.

Let's now consider the points of harmony between the two opposing factions. I believe that each side wishes to see babies cared for with love, respect, and honor. To create that reality, both sides would visualize babies being born to parents who are eagerly awaiting their arrival. These parents have chosen to raise a child; they look forward to the miraculous experience of a human life unfolding day after day; they are grateful for the child in their arms; they willingly accept the sacred task of being their child's spiritual teacher. Once this visualization is complete, they would then "Let Go and Let Angel," and stay attuned to the frequency of love.

"Natural" Birth-Control

When both the pro-life and the freedom-of-choice advocates have addressed the issue as it exists today and created a solution where everyone benefits, the next step would be to examine unwanted pregnancy in light of the Four-Step Formula. A few years ago I came across a passage in a book that made a very distinct impression on me — it was another 'aha' moment. Anthropologist Margaret Meade encountered a very interesting group of folks in Africa in her studies. In this group, the young people engaged in sexual intercourse before they married but never conceived a baby. Why not? They had been *told* that it was not possible until they married! What did they think, believe, expect, and get? This knowledge alone could end the abortion controversy.

Another Person's Life is Not Your Concern

I once saw a movie starring Sean Connery that resonated deeply within me as it articulated what I believe to be a spiritual truth. In this movie, an oriental custom was conveyed regarding the manner in which you treat an enemy: When you recognize a 'wrong-doing' that your enemy has committed, you never force him into a corner without a dignified way out of the situation. Instead, you provide him a graceful exit. He understands that you are fully aware of his wrong-doing and recognizes that you have *chosen* to extend dignity to him, rather than humiliation. Why respond in this manner, rather than gleefully saying 'Gotcha!'? Should *you* ever make a mistake (however unlikely that may be), the green circuit you created will magnetize the same humanity back to you.

You may recall a past experience where you were in a corner guilty of some wrong-doing, and felt the gut-wrenching feeling of utter shame. You may also remember how it felt to not want to admit to your deed, so you denied the accusation — sometimes in the face of blatant evidence proving your guilt. In truth, there is not one of us who has not done something we wish we could take back; not one of us who has not made mistakes; not one of us without the capacity to commit the worst atrocity, or to exhibit the greatest love. Imagine, for a moment, what it might be like to stand in the shoes of a politician or celebrity where your every action was subjected to microscopic scrutiny while you were engaged in your evolutionary process. No thank you! So have compassion in your heart for your fellow life traveler and "Do unto others as you would have them do unto you." It's good advice.

Judge not, and neither condemn, for you know not why a thing occurs, nor to what end. And remember you this: that which you condemn, will condemn you, and that which you judge, you will one day become. Rather, seek to change those things — or support others who are changing those things — which no longer reflect your highest sense of Who You Are.[51]

— NEALE DONALD WALSCH
Conversations with God - Book 1

In *The Healing of America*, Marianne Williamson calls upon us to emulate the wisdom of Gandhi and Martin Luther King Jr. — the wisdom of solving problems with nonviolence and love.

They rose to the occasion by defining a problem but did not choose to whine about it [or "blast" their enemies off the face of the earth]. They did not curse the darkness. They became the light. They answered the plea for justice and were given all the strength they needed to bring forth the resurrection of good.[52]

— MARIANNE WILLIAMSON

Creating a Heaven on Earth will begin with each of us extending humanity, empathy, and compassion to one another. For in truth, we are all sacred souls on a sacred journey. And though you may not understand the broader perspective of another person's seemingly inappropriate actions — *the opportunity their soul has presented them to evolve and awaken* — you have come to realize that our journeys through life are rampant with difficulties and that we are all in this together.

Re-Creating Our World

Enlightenment begins with acceptance, without judgment of "what is."[53]

— NEALE DONALD WALSCH
Conversations with God - Book 3

Those of us in America form an entity comprised of our collective frequencies. The choices we have made or failed to make produce frequencies that magnetize Angacles — people, events, or circumstances that correspond with our choices. And oftentimes our Angacles manifest in the form of an adversary or as an issue having dramatic implications where we are then forced to deal with them.

A society living in fear very often — actually, inevitably — produces in form that which it fears most.[54]

— NEALE DONALD WALSCH

In order to recreate our world, we must utilize our authentic power and hold the vision of what we want, while simultaneously readjusting the red circuits created in our past. And our first step is to acknowledge our responsibility for the creation of these issues, for in so doing, we acknowledge our power.

Our adversaries are our Angacles — the physical manifestations of our collective repressed emotions — our unfaced unexpressed 'evil.' And many factors have contributed to their manifestation. Just as an individual magnetizes evidence of a red circuit in his or her life experience, the same is true of our collective red circuits. By repressing our collective negative issues, we direct them outward where their accumulated energy will eventually culminate in a physical manifestation. What happens if we ignore our issues? The Law of Attraction will do it's thing and they will simply grow larger. Then, once our manifestation is staring us in the face, we are *forced* to define Who We Choose To Be in relation to it. Therefore, any conflict is an opportunity to recognize that we are holding a red circuit that has activated our 'off' switch, thus restricting life energy, and disallowing what we desire. Conflict is a gift, and issues or adversaries, our teachers. However, only until we identify and dissect the core issue underlying the conflict, can we clarify what we desire and manifest it instead.

Examining Military/Political Conflicts in Light of The Four-Step Formula

Let's examine another controversial issue in light of the Four-Step Formula: The conflict in Iraq. Whatever we fear, we magnetize. Period. Whatever we push against, we attract. Period. Whatever we focus our powerful thoughts on grows larger. Period. Therefore, our fears of nuclear or bio-chemical warfare can only create a disastrous outcome. That is how the Formula works. It is unwavering in its simplicity, therefore, it is essential that we use it to our advantage.

We unwittingly amplified the conflict in Iraq when we pushed Saddam Hussein into a corner where he had no eloquent way out of the situation. Although this may be difficult to swallow, he, like any human being, has a core right for civility and understanding, regardless of the atrocities he has committed — whether we think he deserves it or not. Remember, he is our teacher, and the atrocities we are judging are the manifestations of *our* unexpressed 'evil.'

To better understand the origin of any issue of magnitude, think in terms of the accumulation of energy. Think of a time when you were angry with someone; when you felt resentment; when you were critical; when you cursed at a driver on the road; when you "bit someone's head off."

Each time you responded to a life experience in that manner, you made a deposit to the negative energy vortex. And because each of us has access to this vortex via our emotions, at some point in time, someone, somewhere, will open the valve of this powerful stream of collective energy and become the physical manifestation of that vortex . How does that happen? Simple. Someone tunes in to that specific frequency. When one projects a frequency that corresponds with any vortex of energy — positive or negative — they can open the valve to that vortex. The consequence when they align with a negative vortex? All hell can break loose! Therefore, we cannot judge those who have become the physical manifestations of our collective frequencies, because, in reality, *each* of us is responsible for their abhorrent behavior.

To capitalize on the opportunity to evolve and redirect the energy of our red circuits — the repressed thoughts that magnetized the situation in Iraq — it is essential that we first identify them. To begin, we must ask ourselves, "What are we fearing?" Scarcity? Do we feel that we must have their oil or our way of life will be threatened? If others allege that we exploit them, we need to take a hard look in the mirror and honestly ask ourselves if we do. I believe that we have finally learned our lesson about the horror and futility of war — the lesson that it *does not work*. For to destroy another is to magnetize self-destruction. Therefore, if we employ our old-paradigm approach to problem-solving and 'justify' the annihilation of an enemy that does not comply with our rules, we now know that our problem will never be solved. For the minute a 'Saddam' is gone, another, who we would judge to be even *worse*, will manifest in his place. Why? *We* are still projecting the same frequency.

In order to more fully comprehend this issue, it is necessary to examine it from the opposite perspective. What motivated Iraq to initially take the actions it did? Recently, I viewed a television documentary that provided the Iraqi perspective of the Gulf War. This documentary revealed information about our role in this altercation — information that our government conveniently omitted communicating to the American people, for it helped to explain the underlying reasons for Saddam's hostility. It was alleged that our government made promises that it did not keep — a recurring theme in our history — one that does not speak of our integrity, and one that magnetizes an embittered reaction. And even if Iraq's claims were bogus, we now know that nothing just 'happens.' There is always a reason underlying the action. "To every action there is always an equal and opposite reaction," right?

When you push an animal into a corner with no way out, what will it do? It will become ferocious and capable of hurting a lot of innocent people. When we 'pushed against' Hussein, we pushed the animal, our brother, into a corner with no dignified way out. Unaware of our authentic power, we knew of no other way to control it's evil. We sought a peaceful solution to beat 'the animal' into submission and compliance. However, we now know what happens when we push against anything:

it simply grows larger. We strengthen its fortitude and reinforce its feeling that it is *we* who are evil, thereby creating a vicious circle. Furthermore, in the process, we activate our 'off' switch, restrict our flow of life energy, and create our own living hell. Once we have created a 'Saddam,' however, we have no choice but to stop him, for to do nothing would only further empower him. Therefore, our challenge is to employ our new knowledge without painting ourselves into a corner where we respond in fear. What is at the core of our adversaries? If it's not love, it can only be fear.

> *If we could read the secret history of our enemies, we should find in each man's life sorrow and suffering enough to disarm all hostility.* — HENRY WADSWORTH LONGFELLOW
> 1807-1882

Imagine an authority figure scolding you when you behaved inappropriately. Now imagine a wise authority figure lovingly guiding you, recognizing that your behavior was based in fear, and giving you the benefit of the doubt. Can you feel the shift in your frequency?

> *Most criminals [adversaries, bullies, etc.] share a sense of powerlessness and feeling of resentment because of it. Therefore they seek to assure themselves that they are indeed powerful through antisocial acts, often of violence. They desire to be strong, then, while believing in a lack of personal strength. They have been conditioned, and furthermore have conditioned themselves, to believe they must fight for any benefits. Aggression becomes a method of survival. Since they believe so strongly in the power of others, and in their own relative powerlessness, they feel forced into aggressive action almost as preventative measures against greater violence that will be done against them.*[55] — JANE ROBERTS
> The Nature of Personal Reality - A Seth Book

Every dictator must incite and maintain the passion and anger of their citizens in order to perpetuate their power. So, how can we heal this situation? As John Lennon stated: "All you need is love."

> *Bless your enemy, and you rob him of his ammunition." His arrows will be transmuted into blessings.*[56] — FLORENCE SCOVEL SHINN
> 1871-1940

> *There is no object so foul that intense light will not make it beautiful.* — RALPH WALDO EMERSON
> 1803-1882

> *Peace cannot be achieved through violence, it can only be attained through understanding.* — ALBERT EINSTEIN

Man must evolve for all human conflict a method which rejects revenge, aggression, and retaliation. The foundation of such a method is love. — MARTIN LUTHER KING JR.
1929-1968

By recognizing our enemies potential for love, we have made contact with his heart and he is less likely to continue his hostility. Love does not attack love.[57] — GLENDA GREEN
Love Without End: Jesus Speaks

Always forgive your enemies — nothing annoys them so much. — OSCAR WILDE
1854-1900

We must seek to understand what Iraq desires at the deepest level — to understand its fears and feelings of powerlessness. Perhaps the people of Iraq fear the extinction of their culture. As smaller cultures observe western civilization infiltrating every nook and cranny of the world, they must fear the extinguishing of their culture, their history, and everything else that makes them unique.

The illusion of powerlessness lies at the core of all conflict which in turn creates the fear of scarcity. However, once people awaken to their power, they will no longer feel the need to conquer others in order to survive, and scarcity will become a non-issue. In the meantime though, how do we diffuse a conflict once we're embroiled in it? We utilize the same key responsible for its creation: The Law of Attraction.

Defining Our Country's Highest Vision

Once to every man and nation comes the moment to decide…and the choice goes by forever 'twixt that darkness and that light. — JAMES RUSSELL LOWELL
1819-1891

To heal the issues that face our nation, we must first create our Vision Statement and articulate the highest vision of Who We Choose to Be. From that position of centeredness, the solution to any problem becomes clear. Maybe not comfortable, but clear. Defining our vision allows us to examine any issue in light of our Vision Statement, just as our forefathers did with the Declaration of Independence. Think about the Civil War. Although it was fought under the guise of 'states rights,' the underlying catalyst for this war was a breach in our country's Vision Statement. If our forefathers intended to *be* who they unequivocally stated they were: A nation that believed that "all men are created equal," they *had* to take action against slavery. Had they failed to act, they would have committed the highest breech of all: The betrayal of Self. Therefore, by predefining our Vision Statement, all decisions made from that day forward will flow with conviction and without doubt.

To more fully comprehend the purpose for our Vision Statement, let's borrow from a concept inspired by the brilliant author, Anne Morrow Lindbergh: Our motive is not simply one of articulating who we choose to be. It more basically defines our true purpose, what we believe in, and our responsibility to one another. Our Vision Statement articulates those premises so specifically that there is no question as to how to remain centered and balanced when confronted with an issue. We fully recognize that centrifugal opposing forces will always exist that will tend to pull us off center, however, our Vision Statement provides us the strength to remain strong and centered regardless of the shocks that come in at the periphery of our wheel that attempt to crack its hub.[58]

Other issues that face our nation could also benefit from a predefined Vision statement, such as the issue of mistrust for our elected officials. Consider the following: If every person seeking elected office were to disclose his or her Vision Statement upon announcing his or her candidacy, we would then be aware of who that person chooses to be under any circumstance. Hence, if lobbies or self-interest groups seek favoritism, it would be extremely difficult for our representatives to compromise their ethics, or feel *forced* to compromise them in light of their very public Vision Statement.

After defining our nation's Vision Statement, we would then convey it to the world. Our Vision would proclaim our conviction to assist in maintaining the honor and dignity of every nation in our world; for the sanctity of life of every human being; for the appreciation of our differences. It would proclaim the truth that we are all connected — that what we do to one another, we do to ourselves. It would clearly state that we came forth to love and honor one another — to peacefully co-exist. Our Vision would convey our resolve for all people in our world, all of our brothers and sisters, to live prosperous, joyful lives.

As leaders in our world, we must respond to any adversary or difficult issue with wisdom, respect, compassion, sensitivity, courage, and love — as a true power would. To identify and heal our red circuits, we must examine all issues brought before us. When confronted by an adversary, we would listen intently, and then restate what was conveyed so that our adversary knew that he/she was being heard, understood, acknowledged, and honored — no matter how irrational we may feel he/she is. Next, we would communicate, in no uncertain terms, that the answer to any issue lies within the body of our Vision Statement because that is Who We Choose To Be. And we will not deviate from our vision for that would constitute the highest betrayal of all: Betrayal of Self.

Peace on Earth, Goodwill Toward All

Hatred of war will not bring peace.... Only love of peace will bring about those conditions.[59]
— JANE ROBERTS
The Nature of Personal Reality - A Seth Book

Our only true enemy is not people or institutions, but fear-laden thoughts that cling to our insides and sap us of our strength.[60]
— MARIANNE WILLIAMSON

In light of the Four-Step Formula, we will be capable of achieving peace on Earth in a far different manner, for world peace actually begins within each of us....

In the book, *Emissary of Light*, author and musician James Twyman was serendipitously guided and inspired to perform a peace concert in Bosnia-Croatia — an area riddled in hatred and war. During his stay, he was led to a secret group referred to as "The Emissaries of Light." For thousands of years members of this group have placed themselves in the midst of conflict while projecting powerful thoughts of love for humanity through meditation. Why? Love projects a higher frequency, thus overriding the lower frequencies of fear, hatred, and threat. Upon being led to these folks, Mr. Twyman was instructed to convey the following message to the world: The world is now ready to begin adulthood and take responsibility for itself. Humanity has finally reached a stage of evolution where it understands the futility of war.

The following passage from *Emissary of Light*, is spoken by the head emissary to Mr. Twyman. It clearly articulates the path to achieve our goal of peace on Earth:

> *When you came here, you thought the work we do was going to bring peace to the world. You perceived a violent world, then set up the circumstances that would make it peaceful. This isn't what the Emissaries do at all. We don't perceive a violent world. It's that simple. We see a world that is living with the illusion of violence, and we project the truth, an experience of peace...Our mission is not to bring peace to where it isn't, but to reveal peace where it is hidden...Lasting peace will never come to a world that thinks it has a choice*

between peace and war…'Seek not peace here' means do not try to fix a world that was born from the idea of conflict. Look past that vision of the world. Seek peace where it really is, within you. Then extend that peace wherever you are, to whoever you meet. Then the world that was born from conflict will change by itself. It will begin to reflect the new choice you made, the choice to see peace where it really is. In other words, do not look for peace outside yourself. This is the surest way to never find it. The world and everything in it appears to be "outside." Go within to your deepest thoughts and desires. Seek those parts of your mind that are blocking your experience of peace [your red circuits]. When you have discovered these blocks and have dissolved them in love, then peace will be revealed — first in your mind, then in the world. Do not believe those that tell you that you must change the world. It is easy to see that such attempts have always brought temporary results at best. Change your mind about the world. See the world as an extension of your mind. Find peace and love within and it will automatically project itself outward into the world…When you seek peace where it is not, or outside, then it is nowhere to be found. When you find peace within, you are able to see the truth. Conflict may seem to exist, but you now see past it… By experiencing peace as the only true reality, we see it present everywhere, even where conflict and war seem to rule. Then we project that vision to humanity…Peace is everywhere. You can choose to see peace, or you can choose to see violence… Stop trying to bring peace to war. [that's pushing against] Bring peace to peace and then you'll know what you're to do. Do you remember when I told you about seeing past the masks people wear? Our masks are the way we hide Who We Really Are. You can't heal a mask, but you can heal what is behind it. And how do you do that? Simply by seeing that the face behind the mask is already perfect. It is already healed. Healing then is simply helping people take off their masks and showing them who they really are. It is the same in bringing peace to the world. Violence and conflict are the masks the world wears to keep from seeing the peace that lies beneath the surface. You will heal the world by taking off the mask…Humanity is waiting for this message…The world has been waiting for people to tell the truth, the truth they have always felt inside them, but that they could never quite identify. But, most of all, teach [the world] what you have learned, that they are ready to take a new step, a step so tiny it will hardly be noticed. And yet this tiny step is a leap past the conflict and fear that has seemed so real for so long. Humanity is ready, but it must believe it is ready.[61]

— JAMES TWYMAN

Are you ready? Can you take that tiny step and firmly and finally call forth peace within yourself?

A tiny change today brings us to a dramatically different tomorrow.[62]
— RICHARD BACH

Enlighten the people generally, and tyranny and oppressions of body and mind will vanish like evil spirits at the dawn of day.
— THOMAS JEFFERSON
1743-1826

Love and goodwill destroy the enemies within one's self, therefore, one has no enemies on the external! "There is only peace on earth who sends goodwill to man."[63]
— FLORENCE SCOVEL SHINN
1871-1940

You must be the change you wish to see in the world.
— GANDHI
1869-1948

Character comes from following our highest sense of right, from trusting ideals without being sure they'll work. One challenge of our adventure on Earth is to rise above dead systems — wars, religions, nations, destructions — to refuse to be a part of them, and express instead the highest selves we know how to be.[64]
— RICHARD BACH

To recreate our world, we must first identify the red circuits we inadvertently created in our past and readjust them to green. Just as we individually evolve from the truths gleaned from our personal histories, we can do the same with our country's history. Furthermore, because we in America have the might, we have a far greater responsibility to utilize it with wisdom, understanding, compassion, and love.

By your choice dwell you now in the world which you have created. What you hold in your heart shall be true, and what most you admire, that shall you become. Fear not, nor be dismayed at the appearance that is darkness, at the disguise that is evil, at the empty cloak that is death, for you have picked these for your challenges. They are the stones on which you whet the keen edge of your spirit. Know that ever about you stands the reality of love, and in each moment you have the power to transform your world by what you have learned.[65]
— RICHARD BACH

Putting The Pieces of Your Mission Puzzle Together

Now that you have gained an awareness of our global Mission, you may now complete your personal Mission Statement. Be clear about what you wish to achieve and understand that your Mission can only be accomplished with love. All other methods are backwards — consequences of old-paradigm thinking!

> *A good mission statement will be inspiring, exciting, clear and engaging. It will be specific to you and your particular enthusiasms, gifts, and talents....*[66] — LAURIE BETH JONES

---
piece #1 - *What* topic have you chosen that you feel needs improving?

---
piece #2 - *Why* does this concern need improvement?

---
piece #3 - *Who* will be helped by this change?

---
piece #4 - *How* will you help to effect this change?

Your Mission Statement will generally follow the order of piece #4 — *how*, followed by piece #3 — *who*, followed by piece #1 — *what*. Although piece #2 was necessary to help you to clarify the topic you chose, it is generally omitted in your statement.

My Mission Is to:

Now create a vision where you are fulfilling your Mission.

> *I now clearly see the perfect plan of my life. Divine*
> *enthusiasm fires me and I now fulfill my destiny.*[67]
> — FLORENCE SCOVEL SHINN
> 1871-1940

My *vision of fulfilling my Mission is:*_____
_____
_____
_____
_____
_____

Keep a copy of your Mission and Vision statements with you at all times. If you feel dejected at any time, simply read your statements and you will immediately feel centered and grounded.

> *I do not want to die... until I have faithfully made the*
> *most of my talent and cultivated the seed that was placed*
> *in me until the last small twig has grown.*
> — KATHE KOLLWITZ

> *Tomorrow is promised to no one.*   — UNKNOWN

> *You don't get to choose how you are going to die. Or*
> *when. You can only decide how you're going to live.*
> *Now.*   — JOAN BAEZ

The late Princess Diana was a brilliant example of a person who discovered and was in the process of actualizing her Mission. Fully aware of her power to raise consciousness over the injustices she observed around the world, she exploited it to benefit others. Although she could have lived solely amid pomp and splendor, she instead chose a life with purpose. When she died, her Mission and its impact became an important part of her legacy. As a result, she will always be remembered as a person of substance beyond her incredible beauty. Her untimely death caused many of us to recognize that life can sometimes be short, therefore, we must have the courage to act before our opportunities are gone. Diana left the world a better place for having been here, and I, along with millions of others, profoundly appreciate her contributions.

Higher Love

Think about it.
There must be higher love
Down in the heart or hidden in the stars above
Without it, life is wasted time
Look inside your heart and I'll look inside mine
Things look so bad everywhere.
In this whole world, what is fair?
We walk blind and we try to see
Falling behind in what could be.
Bring me a higher love
Bring me a higher love
Where's that higher love I keep thinking of?
World's a turnin' and we're just hanging on.
Facin' our fears and standing out there all alone.
A yearning, and it's real to me.
There must be someone who's feeling for me.
Bring me a higher love, bring me a higher love
Bring me a higher love.
Where's that higher love I keep thinking of?
I will wait for it
I'm not too late for it.
Until then, I'll sing my song.
To cheer the night along.
Bring it .... Oh Bring it....
I could light the night up with my soul on fire
I could make the sun shine from pure desire.
Let me feel that higher love come over me.
Let me feel how strong that love could be.
Bring me a higher love
Where's that higher love I keep thinking of? [68]

Words by Steve Winwood

Courage and Tenacity:
Essential Ingredients in Life

Be bold — and mighty forces will come to your aid.
— BASIL KING

Courage is mastery of fear — not absence of fear.
— MARK TWAIN
1835-1910

The problem with world peace is that the individual feels helpless, but the answer to that is not complicated. A man can do something for peace in our world without having to jump into politics. Each man has inside him a basic decency and goodness. If he listens to it and acts upon it, he is giving a great deal of what it is the world needs most. It is not complicated, but it takes courage. It takes courage for a man to listen to his own goodness and act upon it. Do we dare to be ourselves? That is the question that counts. — PABLO CASALS
1876-1973

Wealth lost — something lost. Honor lost — much lost. Courage lost — all lost. — OLD GERMAN PROVERB

You cannot act positively if you cannot act.[69]
— JANE ROBERTS
The Nature of Personal Reality - A Seth Book

Only those who dare, truly live. — RUTH P. FREEDMAN

Even if you're on the right track, you'll get run over if you just sit there. — WILL ROGERS
1879-1935

When you have to make a choice and don't make it, that is itself a choice. — WILLIAM JAMES
1842-1910

Life shrinks or expands in proportion to one's courage. — ANÄIS NIN
1903-1977

Life is either a daring adventure or nothing. — HELEN KELLER
1880-1968

What you do matters. All you need is to do it. — JUDY GRAHN

Nothing in the world can take the place of persistence. Talent will not; nothing is more common than unsuccessful men with talent. Genius will not; unrewarded genius is almost a proverb. Education alone will not; the world is full of educated derelicts. Persistence and determination alone are omnipotent. — CALVIN COOLIDGE
1872-1933

To laugh is to risk being a fool.
To weep is to risk being sentimental.
To express feelings is to risk exposing your true self.
To place your ideas, your dreams, before the crowd is to risk their loss.
To love is to risk not being loved in return.
To live is to risk dying.
To hope is to risk despair.
To try is to risk failure.
The person who risks nothing, does nothing, has nothing, and is nothing.
They may avoid suffering and sorrow, but they simply cannot learn, feel, change, grow, love or live.
Risk is taken because the greatest hazard in life is to risk nothing.
Only a person who risks is free. — LEO BUSCALIA

Talk doesn't cook rice. — CHINESE PROVERB

Any powerful idea is absolutely fascinating and absolutely useless until we choose to use it.[70]
— RICHARD BACH

Let me tell you the secret that has led to my goal. My strength lies solely in my tenacity. — LOUIS PASTEUR
1882-1895

Courage is often required to fulfill your Mission — to take action *in spite* of the fear you may feel. Because our Missions are oftentimes in response to something that needs improvement in our world, we may encounter those who don't *want* improvement — they would rather maintain the status-quo. And though your underlying intent is to help, they have become so focused on defending their 'comfort zones,' they are not interested in your intent. Therefore, it's important to utilize your power and place your orders *before* embarking on your Mission.

Unaware of her authentic power, Princess Diana was relentlessly ridiculed by those who accused her of self-aggrandizement rather than of helping others less fortunate. Yet despite the unrelenting judgments of others, she remained true to herself. She persevered, shed many tears, and carried on. Many of us understood her true motivations in our hearts and that is why we loved her. She demonstrated great courage in taking the actions that she did.

You, however, have an advantage: You are aware of your authentic power. Therefore, it will be far easier for you to fulfill your Mission than it was for Diana. So use your power and act on what is important to you. Visualize your Mission, and take inspired action from the Angacles that appear. Demonstrate the courage of your convictions in spite of what others may think, for as you live your life with courage, you not only forge a path for others to follow, but also help them to awaken to the fact that life is meant for living, loving, and laughing! *You can make a difference* — a big difference! ☺

> *You must believe in yourself at all times.*
> *You must never lose faith that you are capable of doing anything in life that you choose to do.*
> *[B]elieve in yourself so that your character never bends, never compromises, and is consistent.*
> *[Y]ou must have the patience and tolerance to realize that others will not always agree with you or understand you,*[71]
> *[but do not find fault, for you must trust that every person is at the right at the right time in their evolutionary process.– author]* — NICK BUNICK
> subject of the book The Messengers

Where Do I Begin?

Where do I begin
to tell a story of how great a love can be?
The sweet love story that is older than the sea.
The simple truth about the love He brings to me.
Where do I start?
With His first hello,
He gave a meaning to this empty world of mine.
There will never be another love, another time.
He came into my life and made the living fine,
He fills my heart.
He fills my heart with very special things,
with Angel songs, with wild imaginings.
He fills my soul with so much love that everywhere I go,
I'm never lonely.
With Him around, who could be lonely?
I reach for His hand;
it's always there.
How long does it last?
Can love be measured by the hours in a day?
I have no answers now but this much I can say:
I know I'll love Him 'til the stars all fade away.
And He'll be there.[72]

Words by Carl Sigman – Music by Francis Lai

PART VI

The Procedures

STAYING CENTERED ON YOUR PATH

Part VI

The Procedures

STAYING CENTERED ON YOUR PATH

Don't Seek Happiness — Be Happy!

In your joy, you offer joy to the world. In your pain, you offer pain to the world.[1] — ESTHER and JERRY HICKS

You see beauty where you desire to see it. You see ugliness where you are afraid to see beauty.[2]
— NEALE DONALD WALSCH
Conversations with God - Book 2

Choose a frequency that matches your desires rather than offering a frequency that keeps tuning in to "what is."[3] — ESTHER and JERRY HICKS

Your Free Membership in The Chorus of Joy

Upon arriving in this world you are Who You Really Are, a member of the "Chorus of Joy." You are overflowing with light, love, and happiness. You are fully aware that by simply maintaining your connection with source energy, all that you want will come to you. However, you began to forget who you were as you conformed to life on Earth and mimicked the prevailing negative behaviors of others. In this process, you activated your 'off' switch, restricted the flow of life energy, and created many obstacles that have made it difficult to attain what you wanted in life.

Throughout your journey, you have searched for things that would make you feel good. (You instinctively seek joy, remember?) You observed how others lived, evaluated their experiences, and decided what you wanted to experience. However, as you observed, analyzed, and compared things, you were generally not sensitive to your feelings. And you now know that the true purpose of your feelings is to apprise you of the frequency you are projecting relative to what you are focused on. When you have an experience that is aligned with your beliefs and desires, you feel good, and join the Chorus of Joy — source energy. And when you give your attention to anything *not* aligned with your beliefs or desires, you activate your 'off' switch, restrict the flow of life energy, and join the Chorus of Pain. This restriction of life energy is the culprit responsible for all the pain, anguish, and suffering that exists in our world. Mired in old-paradigm thinking, whenever we feel the restriction of energy, we associate the accompanying discomfort with whatever we are focused on and blame it, thus magnetizing more of it. Consequently, we create one vicious circle after another, and in the process, amplify and perpetuate our suffering!

Experiencing "Bad" Situations That Feel "Good"

Unaware of how life really operates, you may have had experiences that felt good but would be defined as bad. How can that be? Unaware of the power of your thoughts, you have unwittingly magnetized many unwanted circumstances. Not having knowledge of how or why you were experiencing this discomfort, quite logically you blamed someone or something else for your bad feelings. If you concluded that a certain someone was the culprit responsible for your pain, you may have felt delight in seeking revenge — you wanted them to 'get theirs.'

To further illustrate this paradox, consider the following: After having a major disagreement with another person, you found yourself seething in anger. Seeking to justify your feelings of violation, you may have called a friend to commiserate with. If you called someone who had 'gone to work' (like a good little person...) — someone who had *intentionally chosen* their frequencies and was 'connected,' you would *not* feel in sync with them — your frequencies would be incompatible and you would feel it. On the other hand, if you called a friend who listened and empathized with your every word, someone who felt your pain (like good friends are 'supposed to'...), you *would* feel in sync with them because your frequencies were compatible. Your disconnected friend felt good to you, whereas your connected friend felt bad.

What do these examples illustrate? Simply, the Law of Attraction. The fact that your frequency will always magnetize evidence that corresponds with it. Therefore, if you project a frequency of revenge, you will magnetize evidence that corresponds with that frequency which will feel good because you are aligned with that particular energy vortex. The only instance where you would *not* feel good is when you have resistance — a belief or desire that contradicts what you are focused on.

Be aware that if you neglect to intentionally set your frequencies, you can be swept quite easily into the frequencies of others. In our preceding example, your 'understanding' friend had not deliberately set his or her frequencies, therefore as he or she focused on your issue, he or she became ensnared in the powerful maelstrom of your energy vortex — The Chorus of Pain. In fact, the moment that you shared your experience and spoke your powerful potent words, you automatically activated their subconscious mind to recall similar violations. Consequently, as an additional residual effect of your frequency, your friend, now caught up in your negative energy vortex, will begin to magnetize evidence of that vortex in his or her life — the 'ripple effect.' How can you avoid these situations? By recognizing that your earlier wrong-way signs had gone unheeded. But don't be hard on yourself, for oftentimes it is only *until* you are experiencing the full impact of a physical manifestation that you become aware of a red circuit that needs adjusting.

In the past, my sisters would often share various offenses perpetrated by their husbands with me. They would explain, in graphic detail, every transgression and my protective 'big-sister self' would grow angrier by the moment. Of course, *their* roles in the altercations had been conveniently omitted…. However, by the time our conversations were coming to a close, I had grown to despise the 'creeps' they had married. "How dare they treat my little sisters in that manner!" Well, time after time, they would patch things up and become all kissy-kissy again, but I would still be angry with the dirty, rotten scoundrels — that is, until I understood the trap I allowed myself to enter.

The Chorus of Pain — The Dark Side

The Chorus of Pain is another label for the powerful energy vortex of the 'place.' The 'place' we spoke of earlier; 'the place' that contains all denied, unhealed negative emotions that can feel good if they are aligned with the frequency you are projecting. To avoid the Chorus of Pain, consciously and deliberately decide Who You Choose To Be daily. For when you choose what you want, your frequencies will be so powerful, they will only magnetize what corresponds with them. To borrow a line from the wonderful movie *October Sky*: "As long as you are alive and breathing on this Earth, *you have a choice*." (my emphasis) Indeed, you always have the power to choose what to focus your powerful thoughts on. Additionally, when you intentionally set your frequencies, upon meeting with others, who in the past may have elicited strong negative reactions from you, now *only* the aspects of that person that correspond with your dominant frequency will manifest into your experience.[4]

Here's another example of how you can unintentionally become caught up in the Chorus of Pain. As you view and listen to negative reports on television or the radio; stories about murders, heart disease, cancer, pollution, how do you feel? Not good.... Do these stories personally affect your life? Probably not. Do they add to your fear? Probably. Do they add joy to your life? I don't think so. Do you share these stories with others? More than likely. As a matter of fact, your natural tendency is to share the bad things you observe rather than the good. However, upon doing so, what do you conclude? That our world is a dangerous place and getting worse all the time. In reality, though, our world is not getting worse. It is improving daily by millions of caring people who continually extend acts of love, kindness, and appreciation to others.

Why doesn't the media broadcast good news? Simple. It doesn't sell. We have grown so accustomed to hearing the bad news that we have come to expect it — it has become our dominant frequency. Can you imagine what it would be like to hear good news? Stories about health flourishing; happy people all over the world. People smiling, being kind, helping one another. Cats purring; birds chirping; the sun rising; the seasons changing. Appliances functioning; flowers blooming; hummingbirds humming; cell phones buzzing; the stock market thriving. People working; the stars glistening; coffee perking; the copy machines copying; the crops growing; airplanes flying.... Look around friends:

GOODNESS IS ABOUNDING — WELL-BEING IS
PREDOMINANT AND EVERYWHERE!!!

More good news? The good in our world *far outweighs* the bad. And by giving your attention to the *good* rather than the bad, you can help to amplify this wealth of goodness, for you will then magnetize more of it. So begin today: Stop focusing on the negative conditions that have influenced you and contributed to your feelings of powerlessness. Begin today: Become aware of how you start conversations and now share all you find to be good — things that you appreciate — rather than discussing a problem, situation, or person you disagree with. Begin today: Ask yourself if you are having pleasant thoughts and 'change stations' if you're not. Begin today: View each situation that arises in your life as an opportunity to respond with a frequency of love, rather than fear. Begin today: Keep your dial set to the frequency of the Chorus of Joy. BE the love that you are, for when you begin to become conscious of what you are doing in each Moment, you will help to create a Heaven upon our Earth. Remember, life is meant for living, loving, and laughing, and it begins with you! ☯

Appreciate All The Wondrous Things Around You and Soar With Joy

There are only two ways to live your life. One is as though nothing is a miracle. The other is as though everything is a miracle.

— ALBERT EINSTEIN
1879-1955

All is a miracle. The order of nature, the revolution of a hundred million of worlds around a million of suns, the activity of light, the life of animals, all are grand and perpetual miracles.

— VOLTAIRE
1694-1778

Gratitude is not only the greatest of all virtues, but the parent of all the others.

— CICERO
106-43 BC

When I slow down long enough to smell the roses, I usually see the beauty and all else that is ours to share.

— MORGAN JENNINGS

...now is the closest approximation of eternity that this world offers. It is in the reality of now, without past or future, that the beginning of the appreciation of eternity lies.

— UNKNOWN

Appreciation begets appreciation.[5]

— ESTHER and JERRY HICKS

Do you realize that having a grateful heart may keep you from needing a transplanted one?[6] — LAURIE BETH JONES

To the dull mind all of nature is leaden. To the illumined mind the whole world sparkles with light.
— RALPH WALDO EMERSON
1803-1982

Every time you praise something, every time you appreciate something, every time you feel good about something, you are telling the Universe, more of this please, more of this please, more of this please ...[7]
— ESTHER and JERRY HICKS

Look with wonder at that which is before you.[8]
— FLORENCE SCOVEL SHINN
1871-1940

What Do You Appreciate?

Infinite riches are all around you if you will open your mental eyes and behold the treasure house of infinity within you. There is a gold mine within you from which you can extract everything you need to live life gloriously, joyously, and abundantly. — JOSEPH MURPHY

Develop interest in life as you see it; in people, things, literature, music — the world is so rich, simply throbbing with rich treasures, beautiful souls, and interesting people. — HENRY MILLER
1891-1980

Imagine that a devastating disaster just destroyed everything around you. A fire, tornado, hurricane, earthquake, flood, or bomb decimated your home, schools, churches, stores…. Everything that was there before is now gone. What would you miss having in your life?

Do you appreciate the warm (or cool) place you reside? The people and animals around you? The beauty of nature? The movie theaters? The UPS® person? The dry cleaners? The McDonald's® drive-through? Dunkin Donuts® cinnamon-raisin bagels and french vanilla coffee? (I do.) Think of the things you would miss if they were not there — the little things, the big things — all of the things that make your life a little nicer, easier, and more enjoyable. Write down what you may have taken for granted that you now realize you appreciate, for oftentimes you don't realize how much you appreciate something until it is gone.

●

　　————————————————————————
　　————————————————————————
　　————————————————————————
　　————————————————————————
　　————————————————————————
　　————————————————————————
　　————————————————————————
　　————————————————————————
　　————————————————————————
　　————————————————————————
　　————————————————————————
　　————————————————————————
　　————————————————————————
　　————————————————————————
　　————————————————————————

●

　　————————————————————————
　　————————————————————————
　　————————————————————————
　　————————————————————————
　　————————————————————————
　　————————————————————————

Take the time to acknowledge what you appreciate and say aloud, "I appreciate _____." As you shift your consciousness and alter your perspective, you will find that there are many things in life you take for granted that you really do appreciate. Furthermore, as you acknowledge what you appreciate, you add positive energy to the Chorus of Joy and contribute to a higher collective frequency for our world.

Adversity — Until Now, a Necessary Catalyst

> *Great occasions do not make heros or cowards; they simply unveil them to the eyes of men. Silently, imperceptibly, as we wake or sleep, we grow strong or weak; and at last some crisis shows what we have become.* — BROOK FOSS WESTCOTT

Many habitual beliefs are automatically shattered as a result of crisis.[9]
— JANE ROBERTS
The Nature of Personal Reality - A Seth Book

Consider that people are like tea bags. They don't know their own strength until they get into hot water.
— DAN MCKINNON

Most people live, whether physically, intellectually or morally, in a very restricted circle of their potential being. They make use of a very small portion of their possible consciousness, and their soul's resources in general, much like a man who, out of his whole bodily organism, should get into a habit of using and moving only his little finger. Great emergencies and crises show us how much greater our vital resources are than we had supposed.
— WILLIAM JAMES
1842-1910

There are some things you learn best in calm, and some in storm.
— WILLA CATHER
1873-1947

Without Adversity You Grow Complacent

If you are sleepwalking through life in complacency or fear, your underlying core instincts and the goals of your lifetime will *create* the circumstances for growth. And unfortunately, adversity is the avenue most often used. You will be awakened with an event that has dramatic meaning — one that provides you an opportunity to evolve. In short, you will be forced against the wall, just as Ebenezer Scrooge was in the classic, *A Christmas Carol*. For only until Mr. Scrooge recognized the repercussions of his tyrannical ways, was he able to awaken and readjust his frequency to that of love and appreciation. As a result of his new insights, his life took on a whole new meaning with a reverence for each moment and person.

Think about what happens in a natural disaster. People are thrust into circumstances that require help from one another. And those they are forced to help, or need help from, are often people they may previously have passed judgment upon. Forced to interact under these extenuating circumstances, each participant in a disaster discovers many points of harmony. They reignite their sense of compassion, and rediscover a love for their fellow man. They are presented with opportunities to perceive others in a new light, discover a renewed vitality, and feel a sense of further purpose. In addition, beliefs they may have previously been blind to are exposed; habitual judgments are revealed; subconscious reactions arise to the surface of their consciousness. And when habitual beliefs ascend to the forefronts of consciousness, frequencies shift. The result? Consciousness changes.

The bottom line? Crises and disasters create a renewed sense of community, brotherhood, and recognition of our interdependence upon one another. Adversity creates new experiences designed to shatter our patterns of rigid behavior. The higher purpose of adversity is to trigger growth — to push us out of our boxes — a.k.a. comfort zones.

In *A Course in Miracles*®, it is explained that without some form of adversity, it would be difficult to ever grow, evolve, and awaken.

> *Tolerance for pain may be high, but it is not without limit. Eventually everyone begins to recognize, however dimly, that there must be a better way. As this recognition becomes more firmly established, it becomes a turning point.*[10]   — A COURSE IN MIRACLES®

The movie, "The Game," starring Michael Douglas, effectively illustrated how adversity spawns new perspectives that open the door for evolution to occur. Motivated primarily by greed and conquest, the character Mr. Douglas portrayed had created a formidable business empire by taking advantage of those less fortunate — he had become a cold, hardened man. As he succumbed further and further to his greed, he was thrust deeper and deeper into the ominous whirlpool of the negative energy vortex. Alarmed by his distressing change in character, those formerly close to him were impelled to take dramatic action. His younger brother purchased an unforgettable birthday gift for him: an experience labeled "The Adventure of a Lifetime" — a kind of 'rich man's intervention.' When Mr. Douglas' character agreed to participate in this adventure, he had no idea what was in store for him. A very real drama ensued — one that forced him into circumstances that seemingly jeopardized his life. As he encountered dilemma after dilemma, each calling on hidden sources of strength and awareness, he was able to uncover the buried compassion that lay dormant within his heart. At the conclusion of his very real drama, when he finally awoke to reality, a new man was born within as a result of those frightening experiences. A new dimension of his soul emerged — a dimension that included a new appreciation for life, love, and purpose.

I believe that this movie is a significant metaphor for what each of us experiences throughout our lifetimes. We, too, are given many opportunities to awaken to Who We Really Are, but unfortunately, we generally take action only when we are forced into a corner.

The Story of Brian and the "Birdies"

The following story was an email I received from a friend — another heart-warming story that illustrates how lives can dramatically change when adversity knocks at your door. This story, told by a loving father named Lloyd Glenn, took place in 1994.

> *Throughout our lives we are blessed with spiritual experiences, some of which are very sacred and confidential, and others, although sacred, are meant to be shared. In the summer of 1994, my family had a spiritual experience that had a lasting and profound impact on us — one that we feel must be shared. It is a message of love. It is a message of regaining perspective, restoring proper balance, and renewing priorities. In humility I pray that I might, in relating this story, give you a gift that my little son Brian gave our family one summer day last year.*
>
> *On July 22nd I was enroute to Washington DC for a business trip. It was all very ordinary until we landed in Denver for a plane change. As I collected my belongings from the overhead bin, an announcement was made for Mr. Lloyd Glenn to see the United Air Lines Customer Service Representative immediately. I thought nothing of it until I reached the door to leave the plane and heard a gentleman asking every male if they were Mr. Glenn. At this point I knew something was wrong and my heart sank. When I got off the plane a solemn-faced young man came toward me and said, "Mr. Glenn, there is an emergency at your home. I don't know what the emergency is or who is involved, but I will take you to a phone so you can call the hospital." My heart was now pounding, but the will to be calm took over. Woodenly, I followed this stranger to a distant telephone where I called the Mission Hospital. I was connected to the trauma center where I learned that my 3 year-old son had been trapped underneath our automatic garage door for several minutes, and when my wife had found him he was dead. CPR had been performed by a neighbor who is a doctor, and the paramedics had continued the treatment while Brian was being transported to the hospital. At the time of my call Brian had been revived. The doctors believed that he would live, but didn't know how*

much damage had been done to his brain or his heart. They explained that the door had completely closed on his little sternum located right over his heart. He had been severely crushed. After speaking with the medical staff, my wife sounded worried but not hysterical, and I took comfort in her calmness.

The return flight seemed to last forever, but finally I arrived at the hospital six hours after the accident. When I walked into the intensive care unit, nothing could have prepared me for what I saw. My little son was lying completely still on a great big bed connected to a respirator with tubes and monitors everywhere. I glanced at my wife who tried to offer me a reassuring smile. It all seemed like a terrible dream. I was filled in with the details of my son's condition and given a guarded prognosis. Brian was going to live, and the preliminary tests indicated that his heart was okay — two miracles in and of themselves. But only time would tell if his brain had received any damage. Throughout the seemingly endless hours, my wife remained calm. She felt that Brian would eventually be all right. I hung on to her words and faith like a lifeline.

All that night and the next day Brian remained unconscious. It seemed like forever since I had left for my business trip the day before. Finally at two o'clock that afternoon, our son regained consciousness, sat up, and uttered the most beautiful words I have ever heard spoken: "Daddy hold me" and he reached for me with his little arms. The next day he was pronounced as having no neurological or physical deficits, and the story of his miraculous survival spread throughout the hospital. You cannot imagine the depth of our gratitude and joy. As we took Brian home, we felt a unique reverence for life and the love of our Heavenly Father that is felt by those who brush death so closely.

In the days that followed there was a special spirit that imbued our home. Our two older children were much closer to their little brother. My wife and I were closer to each other, and all of us became very close as a family. Life took on a less stressful pace. Perspectives seemed more focused, and balance much easier to gain and maintain. We felt deeply blessed. Our gratitude was deeply profound. Our story is not over though (smile).

Almost a month later to the day of the accident, Brian awoke from his afternoon nap and said, "Sit down mommy. I have something to tell you." At this stage of his life, Brian usually spoke in small phrases, therefore this large sentence surprised my wife. As the two of them sat down on his bed, he began his remarkable story. "Do you remember when I got stuck under the garage door? Well it was so heavy and it really hurt bad. I called to you, but you couldn't hear me. I started to cry, but then it hurt too bad. And then the 'birdies' came." "The birdies?" my wife asked puzzled. "Yes," he replied. "The birdies made a whooshing sound and flew into the garage. They took care of me." "They did?" "Yes" he said. "One of the birdies came and got you. She came to tell you that I got stuck under the door."

A sweet reverent feeling filled the room. The spirit was so strong and yet lighter than air. My wife realized that a three-year-old had no concept of death and spirits, so he was referring to the beings who came to him from beyond as "birdies" because they were up in the air like birds that fly. "What did the birds look like?" she asked. Brian answered, "They were so beautiful. They were dressed in white, all white. Some of them had green and white. But some of them had on just white." "Did they say anything?" "Yes" he answered. "They told me that the baby would be all right." "The baby?" my wife asked confused. Brian answered. "The baby lying on the garage floor." He continued, "You came out and opened the garage door and ran to the baby. You told the baby to stay and not leave." My wife nearly collapsed upon hearing this, for she had indeed knelt beside Brian's body and upon seeing his crushed chest, knowing he was already dead, looked up and whispered, "Don't leave us Brian, please stay if you can." As she listened to Brian recite the words she had spoken, she realized that his spirit had left his body and was looking down from above on his little lifeless form. "Then what happened?" she asked. "We went on a trip," he said. "Far, far away." He then became agitated because he didn't seem to have the words to describe what he had experienced. My wife tried to calm and comfort him, to reassure him that everything was okay. He continued to struggle in his desire to describe something that was obviously very important to him, but found it difficult to find the appropriate words. "We flew so fast up in the air. They're so pretty Mommy," he added. "And there is lots and lots of birdies."

My wife was stunned. A sweet comforting spirit enveloped her soundly, but with an urgency she had never before known. Brian went on to explain that the birdies told him that he had to come back and tell everyone about the birdies. The birdies then brought him back to the house and a big fire truck and ambulance were there. He saw a worried man bring the baby out on a white bed. He tried to tell him that the baby would be okay, but the man couldn't hear him. The birdies then told him that he had to go with the ambulance, but they would be near him. He described them as being "so pretty and peaceful, that he didn't want to come back." Then he saw a bright light appear. He described the light as warm; that he loved the bright light so much. Next, someone in the bright light put their arms around him and told him, "I love you, but you have to go back. You have to play baseball, and tell everyone about the birdies." Then the person in the bright light kissed him and waved bye-bye. Last, he heard a whoosh — the big sound came and the birdies went into the clouds.

Brian's story went on for an hour. He taught us that the birdies were always with us, but we can't see them because we look with our eyes, and we can't hear them because we listen with our ears. We can only see them in here (he put his hand over his heart). The birdies whisper things to help us to do what is right because they love us so much. Brian continued, "I have a 'plan,' Mommy. You have a 'plan.' Daddy has a 'plan.' Everyone has a 'plan.' We must all live our 'plan' and keep our promises. The birdies help us to do that because they love us so much."

In the weeks that followed, Brian often recited all, or part of his story again and again. And always it remained the same. The details were never changed or out of order. A few times he added further bits of information that would clarify the message he had already delivered. It never ceased to amaze us how he could recall such detail and speak beyond his ability when he spoke of the birdies. And keeping his promise to the birdies, everywhere he went, he told strangers about the birdies. Surprisingly, no one ever looked at him strangely. Rather, a softened look would come over their face and they would smile.

Needless to say, our family has not been the same since that day, and I pray that we never will be.

In the New Paradigm You Can Avoid Adversity and Still Experience Growth

Suffering is not necessary for man's development; it is the result of violation of spiritual law, but few men seem able to rouse themselves from their "soul sleep" without it.[11]
— FLORENCE SCOVEL SHINN
1871-1940

Although adversity, crisis, tragedy, and disaster offer invaluable opportunities to evolve, these experiences are often laced with pain and anguish. However, now that you have knowledge of the Four-Step Formula and your authentic power, you can utilize the opportunities presented to you *daily*, so that you won't need adversity as your wake-up call. Simply heed your wrong-way signs as your Points of Power from which to create. And remember, you can adjust your frequency and reconnect with source energy at any time by focusing on something you appreciate.

To ensure your continual connection to source energy, carry a small pad of paper with you at all times and write down three or more things every day that you appreciate. If you can convince your family members to participate, make it a family event. At your dinner table, ask each person to share what he or she appreciated during the day and record their answers in a family journal. The result? Your family's collective frequency will rise higher and higher, resulting in more and more love as each of you searches for things to appreciate in life rather than focusing your powerful thoughts on what you find displeasing. As an additional benefit, something else quite magical will occur. As you connect with love and joy, the negative aspects of life will begin to dim in comparison to the wonder and magnificence of the big picture — the miracle of life and the world of beauty surrounding you. So begin today and look into each face you see and judge not. Instead, have compassion for each soul surmounting life's challenges and project love to them. You will then experience a wonderful benefit. Not only will you maintain your connection with Angel and The Chorus of Joy, but you will also discover that life feels much better when you are truly living, loving, and laughing! ☺

Know That Joy Multiplies Exponentially

Three things in human life are important. The first is to be kind. The second is to be kind. And the third is to be kind. — HENRY JAMES
1843-1916

The fragrance always remains in the hand that gives the rose. — HEDA BEJAR

No act of kindness, no matter how small, is ever wasted. — AESOP
550 BC

Joys divided are increased.... — JOSIAH GILBERT HOLLAND
1819-1881

A complete reevaluation takes place in your physical and mental being when you've laughed and had some fun. — CATHERINE PONDER

Kind words do not cost much. They never blister the tongue or lips. Mental trouble was never known to arise from such quarters. Though they do not cost much, yet they accomplish much. They make other people good natured. They also produce their own image on men's souls, and a beautiful image it is. — BLAISE PASCAL
1623-1662

Kindness is the heart of living. It is what makes life bearable, meaningful and delicious. [12] — GLENDA GREEN

The giving of money, time, support, and encouragement to worthy causes can never be detrimental to the giver. The laws of nature are structured so that acts of charity will open an individual to an unbounded reservoir of riches. — JEFFREY MOSES

Those who bring sunshine to the lives of others cannot keep it from themselves. — UNKNOWN

A warm smile is the universal language of kindness. — WILLIAM ARTHUR WARD

There is as much greatness of mind in acknowledging a good turn as doing it. — SENECA
4-65 BC

One joy scatters a hundred griefs. — CHINESE PROVERB

I can live for two months on a good compliment. — MARK TWAIN
1835-1910

Getters generally don't get happiness; givers get it. You simply give to others a bit of yourself — a thoughtful act, a helpful idea, a word of appreciation, a lift over a rough spot, a sense of understanding, a timely suggestion. You take something out of your mind, garnished in kindness out of your heart, and put it into the other fellow's mind and heart. — CHARLES H. BURR

Praise and an attitude of gratitude are unbeatable stimulators... we increase whatever we extol. — SYLVIA STITT EDWARDS

How far that little candle throws his beams! So shines a good deed in a naughty world. — WILLIAM SHAKESPEARE
1564-1616

Kindness is gladdening the hearts of those who are traveling the dark journey with us. — HENRI-FREDERIC AMIEL
1821-1881

The Ripple-Effect

Every time you are thoughtful, appreciative, loving, joyful, compli-
mentary, or simply being congenial with another person, your seemingly
small act of kindness is like casting a stone in a pond and watching the
ripples grow larger and larger until the entire pond is affected.

Imagine that when you extend a simple act of kindness, a ball of light is
created that radiates an energy of love within it. And this ball grows
larger with each person it touches, infusing light and joy throughout
their beings. Imbued in the energy of your gift, the person who was
touched by your kindness carries the ball of light home with them where
each of their family members is also touched by it. Next, as their family
members interact with others, they pass the ball of light onto each of
them. And each of those folks then passes the ball onto whomever they
come in contact with. Your radiating ball of light and love continues to
grow larger and larger with each new person it touches. In fact, it will
grow to such remarkable proportions that it will affect the entire world!

When my son Zachary was about five years old, he seemed to have a
crush on every girl who had long hair, regardless of her age. (He seemed
to prefer those in their twenties….) He would whisper to me "That girl
is really pretty, Mom." I would tell him to share his compliment with the
girl because she would feel wonderful. Although he felt a bit uncomfortable, I explained how important it was to share his compliments with
others, for his compliments have a significant effect. They affirm a
quality that someone possesses who then feels it, radiates it, and as a
result, adds to our world's joy.

Think about how you feel when someone compliments you. Great, right?
It sends your frequency soaring, doesn't it? What a wonderful gift. What
an extraordinary feeling of love! So don't keep those marvelous feelings
inside of you. Let someone know if you think something wonderful about
them. You might just make their day!

When you receive a compliment, are you immediately suspicious,
presuming that someone has an ulterior motive? If so; STOP. It's a
wrong-way sign. Instead, be grateful for the compliment. Thank the
person and glow in their recognition of one of your gifts. If you're a gal
and the guys whistle at you, smile back and say, "Thank you, you just
made my day," rather than walking by with your nose in the air.
Remember, we have all been programmed to assume the negative, so
oftentimes our knee-jerk response is to distort and dismiss the good. So,
it may take a little work to consciously retrain yourself to accept the
good. In reality, it's a risk for someone to share with you; so acknowledge
and appreciate their courage. Let them know that they made your day!

The Story of Shaya and an Everlasting Gift of Kindness

*Compassion can be defined as our capacity to care for
other living beings. Yet it goes a little deeper than that.
Compassion requires action — giving of our time,
money, or experience whenever there's a need. Since it is
available in such abundance, we sometimes take this
feeling for granted. But, oh, it's power! Compassion is
the ultimate salve we can place upon the universal
feelings of despair, pain, or regret. Which means that
even sometimes the simplest act of kindness can define a
moment. Or change a life.*

— FROM A NIEMAN MARCUS CATALOG

Here is another email I received — a true story that profoundly
illustrates the far-reaching effects of kindness.

*In Brooklyn, New York, Chush is a school that caters to learning-
disabled children. Some remain in Chush for their entire school
careers, while others can be mainstreamed into conventional
Jewish schools. At a Chush fundraising dinner, the father of a
Chush child delivered a speech that would never be forgotten by
all who attended.*

*After extolling the school and its dedicated staff, he cried out,
"Where is the perfection in my son Shaya? Everything God does
is with perfection. But my child cannot understand things as other
children do. My child cannot remember facts and figures as other
children do. Where is God's perfection? The audience was
shocked by the question, pained by the father's anguish and stilled
by the piercing query. "I believe," the father answered, "that when
God brings a child like this into the world, the perfection that He
seeks is in the way that people react to this child." He then told the
following story about Shaya.*

*One afternoon Shaya and his father walked past a park where
some boys that Shaya knew were playing baseball. Shaya asked,
"Do you think they will let me play?" Shaya's father knew that he
was not at all athletic and that most boys would not want him on
their team. But Shaya's father understood that if his son were
chosen to play it would give him a comfortable sense of belonging.
So Shaya's father approached one of the boys in the field and
asked if Shaya could play. The boy looked around for guidance
from his teammates. Getting none, he took matters into his own*

hands and said "We are losing by six runs and the game is in the eighth inning. I guess he can be on our team and we'll try to put him up to bat in the ninth inning." Shaya's father was ecstatic as Shaya smiled broadly. Shaya was told to put on a glove and go out to play center field. In the bottom of the eighth inning, Shaya's team scored a few runs but was still behind by three. In the bottom of the ninth inning, Shaya's team scored again and now with two outs and the bases loaded with the potential winning run on base, Shaya was scheduled to bat. Would the team actually let Shaya bat at this juncture and give away their chance to win the game?

Surprisingly, Shaya was given the bat. Everyone knew that it was all but impossible because Shaya didn't even know how to hold the bat properly, let alone hit with it. However, as Shaya stepped up to the plate, the pitcher moved in a few steps to lob the ball in softly so that Shaya could at least make contact with it. The first pitch came in and Shaya swung clumsily and missed. One of Shaya's teammates came up to Shaya and together they held the bat and faced the pitcher waiting for the next pitch. The pitcher again took a few steps forward to toss the ball softly toward Shaya. As the pitch came in, Shaya and his teammate swung the bat and together they hit a slow ground ball to the pitcher.

The pitcher picked up the soft grounder and could easily have thrown the ball to the first baseman. Shaya would have been out and that would have ended the game. Instead, the pitcher took the ball and threw it on a high arc to right field, far beyond the reach of the first baseman. Everyone started yelling, "Shaya, run to first. Run to first!" Never in his life had Shaya run to first. He scampered down the baseline wide-eyed and startled. By the time he reached first base, the right fielder had the ball. He could have thrown the ball to the second baseman who would tag out Shaya, who was still running. But, the right fielder understood what the pitcher's intentions were, so he threw the ball high and far over the third baseman's head. Everyone yelled, "Run to second, run to second." Shaya ran towards second base as the runners ahead of him deliriously circled the bases toward home. As Shaya reached second base, the opposing shortstop ran to him, turning him in the direction of third base and shouted, "Run to third." As Shaya rounded third, the boys from both teams ran behind him screaming, "Shaya run home!" Shaya ran home, stepped on home plate and all 18 boys lifted him onto their shoulders and made him the hero, as if he had just hit a "grand slam" and won the game for his team. "That day," said the father softly with tears now rolling down his face, "those 18 boys reached their level of God's perfection."

Gratitude VS. Cynicism

While vacationing in Colorado, a very nice lady assisted me with a lovely jacket I had admired while shopping. She thought the buttery color of the jacket went well with my hair color (four colors of blonde streaks with dark brown and now graying roots! *Oops!* Didn't feel good, so I had better reword that statement: "My lovely brown roots..." Hey wait, *anything* is possible, right? I'm a powerful creator — my roots could actually be blonde... Nah, that's going a bit too far for my belief at the moment). My first thought was that her compliment was motivated by her desire to make a sale, but then two teenage girls chimed in and told me that they agreed and loved my hair. (Fortunately a good hair day!) To say the least, I was beaming and couldn't wait to get back and deliver the news to my colorist who would also appreciate the compliment. As I left the store, I made a point of telling them how much I appreciated their kindness and how they made my day! I must admit that it was a bit difficult for me to utter those words as I began to well up with so much emotion that I was on the brink of tears. Am I weird or what? I'm *always* on the brink of tears. In the movie *Hope Floats*, one character explained that whenever she experienced an overabundance of emotion causing tears to well up, she would announce: "My cup runneth over." I believe that expression describes my feelings quite succinctly. Vast amounts of emotion pour through me when I observe people being kind, giving, and loving with one another. It affirms to me that we are all loving at our core and that sometimes our life experiences and the resulting survival mechanisms we have adopted to protect ourselves cause us to deviate from the truth of Who We Really Are: Joyful beings filled with love.

Are you aware that Disney World™ in Orlando, Florida is the most frequently visited destination in the world? Each time we visit, I am so overwhelmed with emotion, I have to continually hold back tears. Why? My heart overflows with an unbounding love and joy as I observe people from so many different countries appreciating this beautiful, magical, wondrous place. My emotions are especially intensified in Epcot Center where people admire, treasure, and appreciate the different countries and cultures of our world. I feel like a self-appointed 'Ambassador of Love' for the United States because I am on a 'love high' — I smile and radiate all the joy I feel within to anyone who even glances my direction. This is my perception of what it *feels* like to live in a world that more closely resembles Heaven.

P.S. Life is meant for living, loving, and laughing.... With all of these repetitions, the neural pathways in your brain should now be reprogrammed and you will *assume* that this is how life is meant to be lived. As a result, when your life deviates from joy, you will immediately recognize that you've stepped off your path and will then take the steps to get back on! So you see, there is a method to my madness! ☺

Learn How to Use Your Power to Help Others

Spread love everywhere you go: First of all in your own house... let no one ever come to you without leaving better and happier. Be the living expression of God's kindness; kindness in your face, kindness in your eyes, kindness in your smile, kindness in your warm greeting.

— MOTHER TERESA
1910-1997

Every good act is charity. Your smiling in your brother's face, is charity; an exhortation of your fellow man to virtuous deeds, is equal to alms-giving; your putting a wanderer in the right road, is charity; your assisting the blind, is charity; your removing stones, and thorns, and other obstructions from the road, is charity; your giving water to the thirsty, is charity. A man's true wealth hereafter, is the good he does in this world to his fellow-man. When he dies, people will say, "What property has he left behind him?" But the angels will ask, "What good deeds has he sent before him?"

— MOHAMMED
570-633

There is no greater joy than giving and no greater gift than love.

— UNKNOWN

Friends are Angels who lift us to our feet when our wings have trouble remembering how to fly.

— UNKNOWN

Every time a hand reaches out to help another... That is Christmas. Every time someone puts anger aside, and strives for understanding... That is Christmas. Every time people forget their differences and realize their love for one another... That is Christmas.

— A CHRISTMAS CARD

Dr. Carl Jung, a doctor of psychology and student of Dr. Sigmund Freud, theorized that a level of consciousness exists where we are all connected to one another, labeling it as the "Collective Unconscious." This is the same field of energy we discussed earlier in the "Hundredth Person" study. There is another important element, however, of the collective consciousness: We have the ability to access information from this level of consciousness to help ourselves and others.

For example: In 1986, I attended a course entitled DMA ("Dimensional Mind Approach" later renamed "Technologies for Creating" created by Robert Fritz). This course was taught by a college professor who was also a psychotherapist. Largely experiential in its approach, DMA utilized visualization — guided imagery — to access your Super-Consciousness (Angel) to create the life you wanted. At the close of one class we were given a rather profound homework assignment: We were asked to pair up with another student, a stranger, and ask a personal question that was to be answered by the other person's Angel.

Well, I got a doozy! My partner was a gal who didn't have a job or a car, and her live-in boyfriend had just broken up with her, so she didn't have a home, or significant other! The question she asked was, "What should I do next?" *Oy Vay!* Talk about an emotionally-loaded question! I instinctively felt an overwhelming responsibility to help her. As I went through the steps to connect with Angel and asked her question, the response I received was very peculiar. Pictures appeared in my mind — images of English Tudor houses and Swiss Chalets!?! Huh? Was I too uptight? Too emotionally involved? What did I do wrong? I felt like a total failure. Poor Amy desperately needed my assistance and I was seeing houses!?! In a phone conversation prior to our next class, we shared our results. She, of course, had written a lengthy, detailed answer to my question, the size of a thesis (well, maybe not quite *that* large...but, three to four pages!). When it was my turn to share my results, I apologized and sheepishly told her about the images I had received. In utter amazement, she explained that she owned a collection of plates with images of English Tudor houses and Swiss Chalets, and was, *in that moment*, packing them. Incredible! At our next class, we were informed that Angel sometimes communicates in images and it was our task to interpret their meaning. In Amy's case, her next step was to look for a home (hints: packing her plates, images of homes...). So Angel did not fail me or Amy!

Another demonstration of our connection to the collective consciousness took place in late 1996 on the Oprah Winfrey show. A friend of Demi Moore's appeared as a guest and informed the studio audience at the beginning of the show that she had a question she was going to ask them at the end of the show. However, she did not disclose the question. At the end of the show, she asked what the answer was — again without disclosing the question. The result? Many people answered it correctly! It was amazing! This was yet another example of the collective unconscious in action.

To think in terms of the degree that we are able to create for, or influence one another, let's pretend that each of us is a car. We can create for one another in the sense that we can wax each other's cars, give them paint jobs, or repair a few things here and there. What we cannot do is to push one another's gas pedals or brakes. They alone are responsible for moving forward or backward.

Sprinkling "Magic Angel Dust"

To become a catalyst of joy for another person, find things that you appreciate about them — things that make you feel good. Whenever you are appreciative, loving, or seeing something positive in someone, you are actually showering them with "Magic Angel Dust" — stimulating their subconscious connection to joy, even if they are completely unaware. As you practice this technique you will begin to notice obvious changes, so try it and have fun seeing the results!

Recognizing Greatness

The rare and beautiful experiences of divine revelation are moments of special gifts. Each of us however, lives each day with special gifts which are part of our very being and life is a process of discovering and developing the God-given gifts within each one of us. — JEANE DIXON

All of us have unique talents and gifts. No obstacle, be it physical, mental or emotional has the power to destroy our innate creative energies. — LIANE CORDES

When each of us was born we were given a special gift or 'greatness.'
Write down what you believe to be the greatness in the following people:

Your significant other:

_____
_____
_____
_____
_____
_____
_____

Your children:

_____
_____
_____
_____
_____
_____
_____
_____
_____

Your family members:

_____
_____
_____
_____
_____
_____
_____
_____
_____

Your friends:

_____
_____
_____
_____
_____
_____
_____
_____

Your co-workers:

_____

_____

_____

_____

_____

●   _____

_____

_____

_____

_____

Anyone else you interact with on a continuing basis:

_____

_____

_____

_____

_____

_____

_____

_____

●   _____

Share Your Observations of Greatness

Think of each person's greatness as seeing their higher spiritual side. Now share your observations regarding their greatness with each of the preceding people you noted. (You may feel uncomfortable, but try to do it anyway!) For when you see the positive in people and express it to them, it impacts their life significantly, readjusts their frequency, and they receive joy! Furthermore, they often begin to conduct themselves in accordance with the great person you acknowledged.

Once you begin utilizing the Four-Step Formula on a daily basis, you will become more and more aware of each of your negative emotions which will trigger you to think about what you want. As you repeat this process over and over again, it will soon become second-nature to you, which will, in turn, enable you to help others to formulate *their* visions with far greater ease than they could alone. In fact, when a person begins to implement the Four-Step Formula in their life, initially they find it difficult to form their own visions because they are so emotionally close to them and their old-paradigm response is to 'push against.' However, as you listen intently to their tales of woe, you will instinctively pick up on what they *don't* want, which will allow you to ascertain what they *do* want. With their permission, you can then share your observations and help them to formulate their vision.

For example: If a friend was in the midst of a nasty divorce, embroiled in a plethora of gut-wrenching battles from the most trivial — who gets the crystal, to the most significant — sharing the kids, it can be difficult for them to 'see the forest through the trees.' Oftentimes this person is so hopelessly engaged in the battle, that if you don't join them in their lower frequency and commiserate over the betrayal they feel, *you* are deemed a traitor. Furthermore, you must lovingly sit on the sidelines while the tragedy unfolds, understanding fully that this experience is a significant opportunity for growth that their soul has provided them. However, if this person is receptive, you can help them to create a vision that will help them to ease their pain.

A hypothetical vision for the preceding example? "I choose to be respectful, fair, and equitable with my spouse. I remember the love I once felt for him or her and choose to focus on his or her good qualities. I will seize this opportunity to examine my past negative experiences and uncover their hidden treasures — the golden opportunities that lie within them for my personal growth. I choose to move forward in my life knowing my power and blessing the time we spent together. I choose to part as friends, appreciating his or her love. I send love and blessings to him or her for the rest of his or her life."

> *In certain instances, man cannot [create his vision] alone. He needs someone to help him hold the vision. This is what one man can do for another, because when one man becomes too close to his affairs, he becomes filled with doubt and fear. The friend or "healer" sees clearly the success, health, or prosperity, and never wavers, because he is not too close to the situation. It is much easier to "demonstrate" for someone else than for one's self, so a person should not hesitate to ask for help if he feels himself wavering. A keen observer of life once said, "no man can fail, if some one person sees him as successful." Such is the power of the vision, and many a great man has owed his success to a wife, or sister, or a friend who "believed in him" and held without wavering to the perfect pattern![13]* — FLORENCE SCOVEL SHINN
> 1871-1940

When you help others to formulate their visions, you enable them to see more clearly what they want. And while doing so, you might just help them to recognize that life is meant for living, loving, and laughing! ✪

Know How to Develop and Sustain Magical Relationships

Treat your friends as you do your pictures and place them in their best light. — JENNIE JEROME CHURCHILL

Seldom or never does a marriage develop into an individual relationship smoothly and without crisis. There is no birth of consciousness without pain.
— C. J. JUNG
1875-1961

Most people enter into relationships with an eye toward what they can get out of them rather than what they can put into them.[14]
— NEALE DONALD WALSCH
Conversations with God - Book 1

I suggest that it is your judgments which keep you from joy, and your expectations which make you unhappy.[15]
— NEALE DONALD WALSCH
Conversations with God - Book 1

Love doesn't grow on the trees like apples in Eden — it's something you have to make. And you must use your imagination to make it too, just like anything else.
— JOYCE CARY

To love is the will to extend one's self for the purpose of nurturing one's own or another's spiritual growth.
— M. SCOTT PECK

Blessed is he who expects no gratitude, for he shall not be disappointed. — W.C. BENNETT

The capacity to care is the thing that gives life its deepest meaning and significance. — PABLO CASALS
1876-1973

Others treat us the way we invite them to treat us. — UNKNOWN

Let's now apply the Four-Step Formula to relationships as they are key to both our evolution and living a happy life. First, recognize that each of us alone is responsible for our happiness — i.e. frequency. Acknowledging that our old-paradigm response is to push against, we now recognize that when we push against anything, it simply grows larger! And therein lies the root of most difficulties in relationships. Therefore, our challenge is to reprogram our habits of thoughts to work *for* us, rather than against us. Let's begin by examining the genesis of a relationship.

In the beginning of any significant relationship, the person you are attracted to is projecting a frequency that corresponds with yours, therefore you feel an intense attraction. Initially, you appreciate all the wonderful aspects of this person, in fact, you thrill at everything you see. Your feelings are so impassioned that nothing in the world seems to bothers you. This person adores you, you adore them, and you feel wonderful. You are in love! Immersed in these glorious feelings, you are connected to source energy — basking in all of the love of your connection. However, you then arrive at a flawed conclusion: You associate your wonderful feelings with your 'love' and assume that *they* are the reason you feel good.

Imbued in this misguided perception, as your relationship progresses and the demands of real life begin to unfold, your 'honey' has other things in life to attend to other than adoring you. Consequently, you may feel disheartened, disillusioned, and forlorn — feelings that activate your 'off' switch, restrict the flow of life energy, and *amplify* your bad feelings. As an added consequence, you then magnetize evidence that corresponds with your new frequency. Nasty, irritating characteristics, traits, or behaviors begin to emerge that displease you. I refer to them as 'warts.' As you focus on these warts, lo and behold, you magnetize more and more of them until pretty soon this person becomes rather evil. Quite logically, you then associate your bad feelings with your 'love' and conclude that it must be *their* fault that you feel bad. The result? Your relationship changed from one of love and adoration to one of conditional love: I'll love you *if* you change the following conditions!

Whenever you have an unpleasant encounter with another person, understand that it's not their fault; it's your frequency. Therefore, it's a gift. Something really matters to you — something in the opposite direction of what you are experiencing. In that moment, take a step back and ask yourself: "What is it that I want to experience?" Then use your Point of Power to order what you want.

Relationships can also fail to be fulfilling when you take them for granted or forget to be thankful for the wonderful qualities that originally thrilled you. Always remember: *Anything you fail to focus on will go away if you no longer give your attention to it.*[16]

What can you do to ensure happy relationships? Begin by gathering information about each person you are in a relationship with so you can formulate a vision of what you want to experience with them.

Your Significant Other

His or her positive attributes:

_____
_____
_____
_____
_____

His or her displeasing attributes:

_____
_____
_____
_____
_____

The opposite of each of their displeasing attribute:

_____
_____
_____
_____

Other characteristics you would like him or her to possess:

_____
_____
_____
_____
_____

Your Children

Their positive attributes:

_____

_____

_____

_____

_____

_____

_____

_____

_____

_____

_____

Their displeasing attributes:

_____

_____

_____

_____

_____

_____

_____

_____

_____

The opposite of each of their displeasing attributes:

_____

_____

_____

_____

_____

_____

_____

_____

Other characteristics you would like each of them to possess:

_____

_____

_____

_____

_____

_____

Your Family Members

Their positive attributes:

_____
_____
_____
_____
_____
_____
_____
_____
_____
_____
_____
_____

Their displeasing attributes:

_____
_____
_____
_____
_____
_____
_____
_____
_____

The opposite of each of their displeasing attributes:

_____
_____
_____
_____
_____
_____
_____
_____
_____

Other characteristics you would like each of them to possess:

_____
_____
_____
_____
_____
_____

Your Friends

Their positive attributes:

_____
_____
_____
_____
_____
_____
_____
_____
_____

Their displeasing attributes:

_____
_____
_____
_____
_____
_____
_____
_____
_____

The opposite of each of their displeasing attributes:

_____
_____
_____
_____
_____
_____
_____
_____

Other characteristics you would like each of them to possess:

_____
_____
_____
_____
_____

Your Co-workers

Their positive attributes:

_____
_____
_____
_____
_____
_____
_____
_____
_____
_____

Their displeasing attributes:

_____
_____
_____
_____
_____
_____
_____
_____
_____

The opposite of each of their displeasing attributes:

_____
_____
_____
_____
_____
_____
_____
_____
_____

Other characteristics you would like each of them to possess:

_____
_____
_____
_____
_____

Others You Interact With on a Continuing Basis

Their positive attributes:

_____
_____
_____
_____
_____
_____
_____
_____
_____
_____

Their displeasing attributes:

_____
_____
_____
_____
_____
_____
_____
_____
_____
_____

The opposite of each of their displeasing attributes:

_____
_____
_____
_____
_____
_____
_____
_____

Other characteristics you would like each to possess:

_____
_____
_____
_____
_____
_____

Once you have articulated what you desire in your experiences with each of these people, visualize them *having* those positive attributes (no 'but's' allowed...). You won't believe the results!

Always pay attention to how you feel. When you feel appreciation, love, or notice the positive aspects in people, you will feel wonderful, because that is your *natural* state of being. Additionally, while projecting those marvelous frequencies, you will attract *more* of those experiences. On the other hand, when you blame, criticize, or find fault, you will activate your 'off' switch, feel discomfort, and can only attract more of those experiences.

Romantic Love

Because each of us is on our own journey, we cannot take another for a ride nor can we hitch onto another's star along the way. So, if you feel that once you've 'got' him or her that it's easy sailing from that point on, you are both in for disappointment. Your work is just beginning, but it can be fun and games if you act consciously and utilize your power.

In *The Celestine Prophecy: An Experiential Guide*, James Redfield and Carol Adrienne tell us to beware of our intentions regarding romantic love:

> *Romantic love retards our evolution when it's used as a substitute for our connection to the Universal energy.*[17]
> — JAMES REDFIELD and CAROL ADRIENNE

In one of my favorite books, *Gift From the Sea*, author Anne Morrow Lindbergh describes the dance of a relationship, offering us insight as to why we so often lose our rhythm in the dance:

> *The dancers who are perfectly in time never destroy the "winged life" in each other or themselves. But how does one learn this technique of the dance? Why is it so difficult? What makes us hesitate and stumble? It is fear, I think, that makes one cling nostalgically to the last moment or clutch greedily toward the next. Fear destroys the "winged life." But how to exorcize it? It can only be exorcized by its opposite, love. When the heart is flooded with love there is no room in it for fear, for doubt, for hesitation. And it is this lack of fear that makes for the dance. When each partner loves so completely that he has forgotten to ask himself whether or not he is loved in return; when he only knows that he loves and is moving to its music — then, and only, are two people able to dance perfectly in tune to the same rhythm.*[18]
> — ANNE MORROW LINDBERGH

Unaware of the truth behind our need for source energy, we seek others to fill us with love and energy. And oftentimes we set out on a quest to find our 'soulmate,' assuming that life will be better when we find someone who is just like us and really understands.... Wrong! Soulmates are not our mirror images; in fact, if they were, why would we need them? While soulmates can certainly make our journeys easier and provide us a lot of 'warm fuzzies,' that notion, in and of itself, is a fallacy. For our soulmates happen to be on their journeys, too, and don't have the power to provide us the continuous love and light we require. In short, our soulmates cannot recharge our batteries as source energy can. Furthermore, by expecting them to, we deplete their batteries. The longer we hold onto that misconception, the longer it will take us to truly enjoy our partner who is on his or her own sacred journey of evolution.

In another passage from *Gift From the Sea*, Anne Morrow Lindbergh tells us of the need for each of us to be whole:

> *Woman must come of age by herself. This is the essence of "coming of age" — to learn how to stand alone. She must learn not to depend on another, nor feel she must prove her strength by competing with another. In the past, she has swung between these two opposite poles of dependence and competition, of Victorianism and Feminism. Both extremes throw her off balance; neither is the center, the true center of being a whole woman. She must find her true center alone. She must become whole. She must, it seems to me, as a prelude to any "two solitudes" relationship, follow the advice of the poet to become "world to oneself for another's sake." In fact, I wonder if both man and woman must not accomplish this heroic feat. Must not man also become world to himself? Must he not only expand the neglected sides of his personality; the art of inward looking that he has seldom had time for in his active outward-going life; the personal relationships which he has not had as much chance to enjoy; the so-called feminine qualities: aesthetic, emotional, cultural, and spiritual, which he has been too rushed to fully develop. Perhaps both men and women in America may hunger, in our material, outward, active masculine culture, for the supposedly feminine qualities of heart, mind, and spirit — qualities which are actually neither masculine nor feminine, but simply human qualities that have been neglected. It is growth along these lines that will make us whole, and will enable the individual to become world to himself.*[19]

While working in the jewelry business, I had many opportunities to observe the various nuances of romantic love. I sold countless engagement rings to men wanting to get married (is that an oxymoron?). I would always grin when I observed the sweat on their brows as they fastidiously examined the diamond rings, obviously contemplating the decision they had made. I would tease and tell them that I'd be worried if they were not sweating! For their sweat was an indication of how deeply they had contemplated their decision (or perhaps, the high cost of diamonds…). They were taking the plunge into the 'great unknown' and were uncertain whether a life preserver was available in case they needed one. I would offer them reassurance, that the water was just fine, to be thankful for the person they had met, and to focus on all of her wonderful qualities. (Little did they know they were in for free counseling with every diamond consultation….) To provide a realistic outlook on marriage and life, I would then advise them to read *The Road Less Traveled*, by M. Scott Peck (perhaps the reason this book has been on the best sellers list for so many years…☺). By intuiting their frequencies, I was able to assist them in assuaging some of their fear and at the same time, shift their consciousness. Whether my 'words of wisdom' had an impact on their futures or not, I could certainly feel their effect in those moments, whether they bought a ring or not.

How to Create a Near-Perfect Partner

The purpose of relationship is not to have another who might complete you; but to have another with whom you might share your completeness.[20]
— NEALE DONALD WALSCH
Conversations with God - Book 1

Have you met your wonderful someone yet? Or have you met him or her, but found that their 'warts' outweigh their positive qualities? In either case, let's use your power to fine-tune your 'honey' to magnetize exactly what you want to experience!

What would your ideal mate be like? A combination of the many people you have met or had relationships with in your life? You may have liked the wonderful warmth of _____, the ambition of _____, the sensitivity of _____, the strength of _____, the spiritual centeredness of _____, the generosity of _____, the physical attributes of_____.

Guess what? You can get pretty close to creating that wonderful person! Remember the 'kitchen' of the Universe we discussed earlier, the kitchen that Angel accesses to create your orders, the vast place that contains everything imaginable? Well, 'everything' includes characteristics in people. Whether you currently have a mate or not, or if yours is less than perfect (cough, cough), you can specify the characteristics you find appealing in others and order them for your special someone. Your task? To search for attributes that you admire in people. (By the way, not one of us is without negatives. Not even little ol' you!)

Once you have determined what you desire, imagine your partner having those qualities. Act 'as if' they possessed them right now. Feel what it would be like to experience life with your partner having those attributes. And if you currently do not have a partner, visualize a person without a distinct face having all that you desire. I know this sounds crazy, but try it! You have nothing to lose! Then watch what happens. The Law of Attraction never fails and will always magnetize evidence that corresponds with the frequency you are projecting.

To rekindle the passion you once felt with your partner, recollect the feelings you felt when you first met one another and how you fell in love. In your mind's eye, relive all the wonderful moments that led to your becoming a couple.

Write down your initial feelings, regardless of what you may feel now.

_____
_____
_____
_____
_____
_____
_____
_____

Next, add characteristics you admire and would like your partner to possess.

_____
_____
_____
_____
_____
_____
_____
_____

Now I'm going to pull a fast one on you. Turn the tables around and visualize *yourself* having all the attributes that you desire in someone else.

In the novel *One*, by Richard Bach, one character asks another on the brink of divorce:

"What is there about you that your mate ought to love?"

    Are you loving?

    Are you understanding and supportive?

    Are you open and sensitive to his/her feelings?

    Are you caring and compassionate?

    Are you communicative, a good conversationalist, entertaining, interesting, enlightening, enthusiastic, inspiring?

    Are you romantic?

    Are you thoughtful?

    Do you do sweet things for him/her?

    Are you a good cook?

    Are you orderly around the house?

    Are you reliable, a problem-solver?

    Are you a haven from stress for him/her?

    Are you his/her friend?[21]

As *you* embody these qualities, you will begin to attract them in another, for your frequency can only magnetize what corresponds with it. Remember, the people you are currently attracting *are* in harmony with you — they are your mirror. So, if you find yourself attracting others not to your liking, you need to ask yourself the above questions and uncover your red circuits so that you can magnetize the qualities you want in someone else. In short, you must 'be' what you want to attract, for you can only get what you project!

Not one person walking on the face of this Earth is a 'done deal.' Therefore, you must understand that your special someone is engaged in an evolutionary process (whether they know it or not). So, honor your less-than-perfect partner and continually fine-tune what you wish to experience daily. And don't worry about knowing what you want, for your feelings, good and bad, will always guide you.

Remember Your New Perspectives

To keep a lamp burning we have to keep putting oil in it.
— MOTHER TERESA
1910-1997

Love doesn't just sit there like a stone, it has to be made, like brick; re-made all the time, made new.
— URSULA K. LEGUIN

You now know that what you think, believe, and expect; you will get. Therefore, as you think about what you want in another person, remember, every time you receive something, you experience something new which creates a new perspective. This is called *growth* and should be allowed, expected, encouraged, struggled through, and embraced with love within the relationship. From this ever-changing perspective, it is essential that you are aware of what you want and don't want on all levels: physical, emotional, spiritual, and mental. And most importantly, to continually communicate your ever-evolving desires to your partner.

One technique to ensure effective communication with your partner is to set up a weekly date to discuss your new perspectives. For if you neglect to inform him or her of your desires, there is little possibility they will be met or for your relationship to be fulfilling and joyful.

In *The Road Less Traveled*, author M. Scott Peck uses the analogy of a mountain base camp to illustrate what a partnership really is. He explains that after trekking your separate paths, climbing the many 'mountains' you encounter in life, you need a place to relax and find comfort at the day's end. As your day is coming to a close, you look forward to the coziness of your camp, the warmth of the fire, the good food, the warm blankets, those you love, and you joyfully anticipate all those wonderful things. To ensure that what you desire becomes your reality, it is essential that you take the necessary steps to ensure that your camp is well-stocked with all the things that you need. If you fail to do the necessary preliminary work, you will only encounter more work when you are depleted of energy. This will invariably create tension, stress, impatience, and impoliteness — aspects of life that do not make for a pleasant encounter with your loved ones.[23]

The moral of the story: You must take the time and effort required to establish and consistently restock your mountain base camp, for if you don't, there will be nothing there for you when you need it most. You can also amend this analogy to include your family, any relationship, your company, your church, etc.

Creating Strong Joyful Relationships

There is no hope of joy except in human relations.
— ANTOINE DE SAINT EXPERY
1900-1944

Man is a knot, a web, a mesh into which relationships are tied. Only those relationships matter.
— ANTOINE DE SAINT EXPERY
1900-1944

Another technique to create strong joyful relationships is to formulate a Vision Statement as a couple and/or family. Again, in defining your vision — Who You Choose To Be as a collective entity — you define your center. To begin this project, ask each of your family members to define their needs and desires. Next, ask them what they could do to fulfill one another's needs and desires. As you formulate your Vision Statement, and articulate your collective desires, far fewer issues will arise between you. Furthermore, when a difficulty does arise, your Vision Statement will provide you the clarity needed to resolve it quickly.

Another technique to ensure magical relationships is to acknowledge and verbalize what you appreciate in those most significant to you on a daily basis. Be the love you want to experience in your life. This technique is extremely effective in maximizing joy in your relationships — a very important factor in cultivating a life meant for living, loving, and laughing!

Let's now get acquainted with the tools and techniques that will help you to get back on your path when you find yourself caught in the midst of a dilemma. The solution? Learning how to fine-tune and direct energy to make it work *for* you rather than against you! ☺

LIKE *snowflakes*

floating

g e n t l y,

unexpectedly

e a r t h,

SMALL KINDNESSES

TOUCH

our

lives.

First   one,

a n d T H E N A N O T H E R,

and

A N O T H E R ,

until at last

t h e WORLD *i s b r i g h t*

and s h i n i n g

with goodwill.

— A Christmas card

PART VII

The Predicaments

GETTING BACK ON YOUR PATH
WHEN YOU LOSE YOUR WAY

Part VII

The Predicaments

GETTING BACK ON YOUR PATH
WHEN YOU LOSE YOUR WAY

Break a Habit of Failure and Replace it with a Habit of Success

Don't part with your illusions. When they are gone you may still exist, but you have ceased to live. — MARK TWAIN
1835-1910

Hold fast to your dreams, for if dreams die, life is a broken winged bird that cannot fly. — HUGHES LANGSTON

The human spirit cannot be paralyzed. If you are breathing, you can dream.   — MIKE BROWN

I keep the telephone of my mind open to peace, harmony, health, love and abundance. Then, whenever doubt, anxiety or fear try to call me, they keep getting a busy signal — and soon they'll forget my number.
— EDITH ARMSTRONG

If things are not going well with you, begin your effort at correcting the situation by carefully examining the service you are rendering, and especially the spirit in which you are rendering it.   — ROGER BABSON

Follow your dream ... take it one step at a time and don't settle for less, just continue to climb.
— AMANDA BRADLEY

You can't win any game unless you are ready to win.
— CONNIE MACK

Negativity always arises out of an unhealed part of you.[1]
— NEALE DONALD WALSCH
Conversations with God - Book 2

No pessimist ever discovered the secrets of the stars, or sailed to an uncharted land, or opened a new heaven to the human spirit.
— HELEN KELLER
1880-1968

When the energy of a belief meets with the energy of a contradicting desire, a collision of energy will occur — one that summons energy in one moment, but obstructs its flow in the next. Unresolved, this quandary can create a vicious circle leading to depression, addiction, or even death. To unravel these contradicting frequencies, let's uncover their culprit — resistance, which often surfaces in the statements we make.

The Power of Words

Man can change his conditions by changing his words. "Death and life are in the power of the tongue."[2]
— FLORENCE SCOVEL SHINN
1871-1940
from Proverbs 18:21

A spoken word is the declaration of a thought. A word holds greater power than a thought because it projects a frequency that is more specific, hence, stronger. The spoken word projects a very powerful frequency that magnetizes evidence rapidly. Think of a word as a radio signal transmitting at 100HZ as opposed to a thought transmitting at 50HZ. Now this can be the bad news if you are making declarative statements that don't reflect what you want in life, for whatever words you speak will quickly manifest in your life experience.

Never voice lack or limitation for "by your words you are condemned."[3]
— FLORENCE SCOVEL SHINN
1871-1940

So, if you are continually trying and trying but failing and failing in certain areas of life, begin to examine your declarative statements. Are you making statements similar to these?

> "I am unhappy"
> "I am fat"
> "I can't seem to get ahead"
> "I always seem to attract the wrong people in my life"
> "I will never find the right mate"

Man's word is his wand filled with magic and power! Jesus Christ emphasized the power of the word; "By thy words thou shalt be justified and by thy words thou shalt be condemned," and "death and life are in power of the tongue." So, man has power to change an unhappy condition by waving over it the wand of his word. In the place of sorrow appears joy, in the place of sickness appears health, in the place of lack appears plenty.[4]
— FLORENCE SCOVEL SHINN
1871-1940

Depression

The genesis of depression is resistance — a powerful desire meeting a deeply entrenched core belief. Depression is simply a prolonged restriction of life energy; repressed energy yearning to escape; the illusion of powerlessness magnetizing more and more evidence; the extinguishing of desire. Depression manifests when you feel as though you will *never* have what you want in life, when you feel so defeated that you cannot foresee anything different for your future. Most people in a state of depression have repeatedly tried and tried and failed and failed. The result? They lost hope. Imbued in feelings of powerlessness, helplessness, and frustration, they grew weary of trying to conform to life. It no longer felt good and as a result, they gave up.

Why do you think depression is becoming more and more prevalent impelling so many to take Prozac®, or its equivalent to alleviate its agonizing effects? Author Matthew Fox explains in *The Coming of the Cosmic Christ*, that when "the mystic" within each of us is suppressed or denied, an extinguishing of the physical spirit occurs. In *For Your Own Good*, author Alice Miller states that depression is the result of being "separated from one's true self." (i.e. source energy). She writes that "soul murder" occurs when an individual is denied access to his or her true self. Mr. Fox goes on to tell us that "In a culture that denies the mystic [i.e.; the development of the true self] soul murder is a regular event."[5]

The feelings of misery that accompany depression can become so intense, so intolerable, that many people will choose the path of least resistance and either extinguish their desire or diminish it substantially. And though this solution will temporarily provide relief because their resistance is lessened, it will also impede the full flow of energy, and as a result, life will become an existence rather than a joyous experience.

Paralyzed by the strangulating grip of depression, most people attempt to push depression away. In their desperation to feel better, they may turn to a doctor who will more than likely provide them with prescription drugs. While these drugs may momentarily anesthetize their pain and provide them relief, they have an added repercussion, for drugs also numb *good* feelings. Furthermore, those affected by depression then believe that the *drugs* are responsible for providing them with relief, when in reality it is their *belief* that the drugs are helping that is responsible for their improvement. This fundamental flaw in thinking will only prolong their dependence on drugs and perpetuate their illusion of powerlessness — the very feelings they need to get to the bottom of.

Norman Cousins explains in *Anatomy of an Illness* that pain has a very important function. Pain alerts us to the fact that something is wrong. Therefore, from the broader perspective, our vaunted pain-*killing* drugs actually do more harm than good, for they alienate the pain from the underlying condition, thus deadening the mechanism that alerts the brain to address the fact that something is wrong. Although Mr. Cousins was not privy to the Four-Step Formula, he certainly uncovered aspects of it. He was quite accurate in his belief that the body pays a high price for masking symptoms and suppressing pain, because it draws attention away from the primary cause of the ailment — i.e. red circuit.[6]

If you are a victim of depression, thoughts of being unable to change an aspect of your life will only magnetize *more* of the same feelings and circumstances (Angel-Alerts — wrong-way signs). The consequence? A vicious circle — a circle that, if unheeded, will create the circumstances where you can sink deeper and deeper into depression's abyss and eventually lose the will to live. The solution? Your battery needs a recharge. When a battery begins to lose its energy, whatever it is powering becomes sluggish and begins to wane. How can you recharge your battery? With desire. For desire summons life energy. The Buddha once said, "At the heart of all suffering lies desire — unfulfilled desire."

All human activity is prompted by desire.
— BERTRAND RUSSELL
1872-1970

Life is nothing without desire.[7]
— ESTHER and JERRY HICKS

Desire remains unfulfilled for only one reason: A fundamental misunderstanding of how life operates. This ignorance is creating all of the pain, anguish, and suffering that exists in our world. Therefore, the objective of this book is to provide you with hope and practical solutions to these quandaries.

Unless man has some Promised Land to look forward to,
he begins to perish.[8]
— FLORENCE SCOVEL SHINN
1871-1940

Hope is a waking dream.
— ARISTOTLE
384-322 BC

To free yourself from the powerful vortex of depression, begin by completing this book, for the tools, techniques, and step-by-step processes to awaken you to your authentic power are all included in these pages. As you answer every question and fill in every blank, you will discover what you want from life and reignite your desire. At the same time, you will identify the red circuits responsible for restricting life energy to you. After readjusting your red circuit, energy will flow, and with it, all the light and love you need to exist in a joyful state of being. Remember, your desires can only be fulfilled if you remain connected to source energy — expecting, having faith, and allowing what you desire to manifest by not offering contradicting frequencies.

Man's [abundance] is inexhaustible and unfailing when
fully trusted, but faith or trust must precede the
demonstration. "According to your faith be it unto you."
"Faith is the substance of things hoped for, the evidence
of things not seen —" for faith holds the vision steady,
and the adverse pictures are dissolved and dissipated,
and in due season we shall reap, if we faint not."[9]
— FLORENCE SCOVEL SHINN
1871-1940

You get your life to "take off" by first becoming very clear in your thinking about it. Think about what you want to be, do and have. Think about it often until you are very clear about this. Then, when you are very clear, think about nothing else. Imagine no other possibilities. Throw all negative thoughts out of your mental constructions. Lose all pessimism. Release all doubts. Reject all fears. Discipline your mind to hold fast to the original creative thought. When you catch yourself thinking negative thoughts — thoughts that negate your highest idea about a thing — think again! I want you to do this literally. If you think you're in a doldrums, in a pickle, and no good can come of this, think again. If you think the world is a bad place, filled with negative events, think again. If you think your life is falling apart, and it looks as if you'll never get it back together again, think again. You can train yourself to do this. (Look how well you've trained yourself not to do it!) [10]

— NEALE DONALD WALSCH
Conversations with God - Book I

Success is not the result of spontaneous combustion. You must set yourself on fire. — REGGIE LEACH

If you're never scared or embarrassed, or hurt, it means you never take any chances. — JULIA SOREL

Angel's only means of alerting you to the ominous projections of your thoughts is to transmit wrong-way signs to you which are meant to illuminate your path. You *can* make trying and failing a thing of the past; a byproduct of living life backwards because YOU ARE POWERFUL. You can create whatever you choose and begin to live a more joyous life by simply utilizing the guidance you continually receive from Angel. However, you must remember, no one can do it for you, this is a 'do-it-yourself' project. It is solely your responsibility to stay connected and keep your battery charged. It is solely your responsibility to utilize your incredible power. I can show you the door, but you must walk through it. And when you do, Angel will bring you nothing but 'good stuff' so you can live the way life is meant to be lived: loving, and laughing all along your merry path of life. ☺

Understand the Disquises of Addictions and Preoccupations

You always get what you create, and you are always creating. If you don't like what you've created, choose again.[11]
— NEALE DONALD WALSCH
Conversations with God - Book 1

When you stop drinking, you have to deal with this marvelous personality that started you drinking in the first place.
— JIMMY BRESLIN

The saints are the sinners who kept on trying.
— ROBERT LOUIS STEVENSON
1850-1894

In the depth of winter, I finally learned that within me there lay an invincible summer.
— ALBERT CAMUS
1913-1960

The problems of alcoholism and drug addiction have strong links to depression. The search for highs may often begin as a flight from lows.
— NATHAN S. KLINE, M.D.

In all of your waking moments you are thinking, thus, creating. The very nature of your being is to create — to summon and flow energy to that which you desire. In fact, you can't avoid it. Therefore, it is beneficial to understand how energy flows so you can use it to your advantage. Mired in old-paradigm thinking, you have been unaware that your negative feelings were meant to act as catalysts to ignite desire — desire that summons life energy. As a result, you may have attempted to suppress your negative feelings which would only cause them to accumulate and restrict the flow of energy. The result? Very unpleasant feelings: those of misery, discouragement, distress, grief, pain, suffering, torment, woe, agony, anxiety, despair, malaise, misfortune, sadness, trouble, or tribulation.

Preoccupations or addictions in life are outlets for repressed energy. Unaware of the true purpose of negative feelings, most of us have adopted various preoccupations to dissipate the accumulation of their energy. Are you preoccupied with any of the following?

_____	independence	_____	control
_____	sex	_____	anger
_____	gaining approval	_____	self-criticism
_____	conformity	_____	alcohol
_____	gambling	_____	drugs
_____	smoking	_____	crime
_____	family entanglement	_____	overspending
_____	physical image	_____	underearning
_____	lack of love	_____	security
_____	guilt	_____	emotional dramas
_____	perfectionism	_____	fear
_____	revenge	_____	intellectual accomplishment[12]

To become aware of the feelings associated with pent-up energy, answer the following questions while being sensitive to your responses:

How do you feel when you are faced with many problems that need to be solved?

_____

_____

_____

_____

_____

_____

How do you feel when you observe folks who are homeless or in need?

_____

_____

_____

_____

_____

_____

How do you feel when you see a TV commercial for children living in impoverished circumstances staring into the camera with blank lifeless eyes, all skin and bones, needing food, clothing, medicine, and love?

_____
_____
_____
_____
_____
_____

How do you feel when you see food that is 'not good' for you — food laden with fat and calories, but it looks so good that you want it anyway?

_____
_____
_____
_____
_____
_____

How do you feel when you take a bite of this 'forbidden' food?

_____
_____
_____
_____
_____
_____

How do you feel when you believe that you will never find a solution to a dilemma?_____
_____
_____
_____
_____
_____

Did you feel a sense of powerlessness as you responded to these questions? Did you feel energy begin to build up within your body? This is the type of energy that seeks release. This is an energy born of desire, but accompanied by resistance. This is an energy born of observing problems but having no solutions for them. This is an energy born of the pain, despair, and suffering you oftentimes feel that can become overwhelming. This is an energy that is born but finds all exits blocked.

The Genesis of Addiction

When you have an unresolved issue in your life, a conflict of energy will result. This conflict will magnetize evidence of it existence that will grow to such an intolerable degree of discomfort that the resulting accumulation of energy will seek release either in an outlet where you feel powerful, or an outlet where you can numb the pain of feeling powerless. Channeled positively, this energy is released in a preoccupation that is aligned with Who You Choose to Be, such as maintaining or working towards a sculpted or a healthy body, gaining an education, or helping others. Channeled negatively, this energy is released in an addiction that can hurt both you and/or others, such as drinking an excess of alcoholic beverages, smoking, committing crimes, overeating, taking drugs, being promiscuous, overspending, or gambling — outlets that create vicious circles and amplify the very feelings of powerlessness you are trying to alleviate.

Old-Paradigm Methods of Eliminating Addictions

As we move into the new paradigm, many of our old-paradigm methods of problem-solving will require reevaluation. And one institution that will benefit from a reassessment is the anonymous programs. For what their current agendas convey to people in their most vulnerable moments can oftentimes do more harm than good. Why? They fail to address the root cause of addiction — powerlessness, which we now know is an illusion. And though these programs have served a very important purpose and have helped many people, in their unawareness of how life really operates, they often compound the illusion of powerlessness that those with addictions must get to the bottom of.

Let's take a look at the old-paradigm methods that the anonymous programs employ today. First, the programs address only the *symptoms* of addictions, not taking into consideration the habitual nature of negative feelings, aggressions, or repressions. When a person 'hits bottom' and desperately desires help, he or she *feels* utterly powerless, filled with shame, guilt, humiliation, and unworthiness. And in that state of being, this person is very willing to abdicate their power to the wisdom of the programs which further amplifies their illusion of powerlessness. These feelings are then reinforced when they are told that for their *entire life*, they are, and will always be, an addict. Using the old-paradigm method of 'tough love,' they are told to "get with the program," to "take responsibility for their lives and all the pain they have created." And how might someone *feel* when they speak of the many, oftentimes tragic mistakes they have made in their lives?

To further compound an addict's feelings of powerlessness, he or she may choose to address a meeting and share his or her gut-wrenching saga beginning with the words "Hi, my name is_____ and I am an _____ (alcoholic, gambler, addict, overeater, etc.)." And in light of the Four-Step Formula, uttering those words can only *perpetuate* their pain, for the most powerful words anyone can speak are "I AM." As you now know, those words summon Angel to *deliver* that very experience!

> The words 'I am...' are potent words; be careful what you hitch them to. The thing you're claiming has a way of reaching back and claiming you. — A. L. KITSELMAN

Let's examine another important element of the anonymous programs: Meetings. Although meetings offer many positive aspects, such as acting as a lifeline, a distraction, an outlet that helps to dissipate the powerful pent-up energy of the conflict between what a person desires and what they believe, they oftentimes act as a replacement for the addiction. Anonymous meetings fail to provide a path that helps to empower people and channel their energy into something positive. Instead, they provide a safe-haven to verbalize negative feelings; to express how those with addictions have wronged others; to explain how their parents were addicts or co-dependents; to recall their rotten childhoods — all issues that exacerbate problems and at the same time, restrict the flow of life energy.

> [C]oncentration upon the past unhealthy situation will only prolong it. Period.[13] — JANE ROBERTS
> *The Nature of Personal Reality - A Seth Book*

To further alienate the primary cause of addiction from its true source, researchers have now discovered a physiological explanation for certain addictions, a *physiological* predisposition: Genes — something people feel even *more* powerless over. This creates yet another scapegoat for those with addictions to shirk their creation and blame it on something else, ultimately pushing them further and further from recognizing the correlation between their thoughts, beliefs, actions, and life experience — further and further from their authentic *power*.

Although the Twelve-Step Program provides an incredibly rich format that helps people to peel back many layers and thus shift their consciousness, the program does not yet provide a solution that addresses the underlying illusion of powerlessness.

If you have a preoccupation or addiction that no longer serves you, let me take the opportunity to awaken you to the TRUTH of Who You *Really* Are. You are *not* an alcoholic, a gambler, an overeater, a criminal, a smoker, a drug addict, or whatever someone may have mislabeled you.

YOU ARE A POWERFUL MAGNIFICENT BEING, A MASTERFUL CREATOR, WORTHY OF NOTHING LESS THAN HONOR!

And if you look deep into your soul you will begin to remember. You are innocent. You have merely anesthetized the pain of living life backwards with this preoccupation. You chose this escape because you didn't understand your authentic power or Who You Really Are. Your choosing this escape did not *make* you the escape; it allowed you to endure life. It was only a choice you made based on the knowledge you possessed at the time. Now, my friend, my brother or sister, you are reawakening to your true power and recognizing that there is nothing you are powerless over. For in reality, you are invincible!

I am not inferring that the anonymous programs are faulty, or have even made mistakes. They, too, are innocent. None of us understood how life really operated. The anonymous programs did the best job they could with the knowledge available at the time and have indeed helped many people. In fact, I am very grateful for the Alcoholics Anonymous program because it helped my father immeasurably. The program allowed him to grow in ways he, and those in my family, never dreamed possible. By embracing the twelve-step program, a visible change occurred in his life: On most occasions, he began to think *before* he reacted — AA held him accountable. He was able to regain more control of his life and to temporarily escape his agonizing feelings of powerlessness. Furthermore, the camaraderie of others allowed him to see that he was not alone in his problems.

When my father died in January of 1997, my siblings and I discovered his 'fourth step' — his searching and moral inventory of himself. Upon reading it, I was filled with an incredible pride for my dad because it was so remarkable in its insight. My dad courageously examined his painful issues until he discovered their origins. He then bravely made amends to the many people he had harmed along his path and felt genuine remorse while doing so. I am certain that when he arrived at Heaven's gate there was great honor and celebration for his life, his evolution, and for the courage he demonstrated. Yet my dad, a by-product of old-paradigm thinking, always felt like a failure because he never attained *financial* success — the definition and pinnacle of success to many.

In light of the Four-Step Formula, I suggest that the time has come for the anonymous programs to reevaluate their messages and evolve — an undertaking that many institutions will now find necessary. Although the programs have succeeded in peeling back one layer of consciousness, the next layer is ready to be peeled back. To facilitate this evolution, perhaps the anonymous programs could unite and assume a new broader role: one that assists all people in awakening to their authentic power. (Anyone interested in that Mission? Sounds pretty exciting!) I believe that daily meetings held in many places will be essential to assist folks in learning how to integrate the Four-Step Formula in their lives. Therefore, the help of the dedicated people who administer these programs could be of enormous value.

Preoccupations Illuminate the Goals of Your Life

Let's now reexamine your preoccupations from your new state of heightened awareness because they actually hold great significance: They are the goals you set out to accomplish in your life.

Preoccupation	*Your Goal*
independence	interdependence
intellectual accomplishment	wisdom
self-criticism	acknowledgments
addictions	self-security — power
overspending	healing deprivation you felt before
underearning	being paid what you are worth
security	adaptability
resistance to authority	sharing leadership
emotional dramas	self-actualization
fear	love
control	trust
gaining approval	self trust
conformity	creativity
family entanglement	honest commitment
physical image	intrinsic worth
lack of love	divine love within
anger	empowerment
guilt	love with wisdom
perfectionism	self-acceptance
revenge	forgiveness[14]

Now, imagine what it *feels* like to accomplish your goals. Think it, believe it, expect it, and you will get it. You will then be on the path to truly living, loving, and laughing! ☺

A Time For Us

A time for us, someday we'll see
when chains are torn by courage born of a love that's free
A time when dreams so long denied can flourish
As we unveil the love we now must hide
A time for us, at last will be
A hope we've found for you and me.
And with our love through tears and thorns
we will endure as we pass surely through every storm
A time for us someday there'll be, a new world
A world of shining hope for you and me
A time for us at last will be, the hope we've found for you and me.[15]

Words by Larry Cacique and Eddie Snyder — Music by Nino Rota

The Steps to Reignite Your Desire and Connect with Your Power

Things won are done; joy's soul lies in the doing.
— WILLIAM SHAKESPEARE
1564-1616

It's not in the having, it's in the getting. — UNKNOWN

After a time, you may find that having is not so pleasing a thing, after all, as wanting. It is not logical, but it is often true.
—SPOCK
from the TV show *"Star Trek"*

Living in the old paradigm, many of your red circuits were created by the patterns and beliefs born of your earlier programming. Therefore, readjusting some of your more deeply entrenched circuits may be a bit more challenging for some exist at a subconscious level. But fear not. You were born with an intense desire to experience many aspects of life, and as a result, your red circuits will automatically rise to the surface of your consciousness when you begin to assume your authentic power. How? When you're not manifesting what you desire, you can darn well bet that the culprit is one of those unconscious core beliefs rising to the surface.

If you find it difficult to feel desire, if having desire evokes a feeling within of greed, as if you were taking more than your fair share while others are suffering, you are simply meeting with a red circuit that needs readjusting. The culprit? A belief born in childhood. *For example:* If you had repeatedly been told that you could *not* have what you wanted from the time you were a child, you probably learned to stifle your desires. You became so conditioned to receiving only a few things that 'scarcity consciousness' became one of your deeply entrenched habits of thought. Consequently, you will now find yourself cautious and guarded about wanting anything because your desires were suffocated at such an early age. Therefore, you may initially experience difficulty in determining what you want. However, now that you know *why* you react in that manner, it will be far easier for you to shift your underlying belief.

Decisions = Power

When you are uncertain about what you want, you feel tired and lethargic. Why? You are not summoning life energy. However, when you focus on something you desire and make a decision, regardless of its significance, you feel empowered, for you are then allowing life energy to flow. Feel the difference between the following two statements:

ᕦ "I am pondering…"

ᕦ "I have decided…"

Can you feel the vast difference in the energy of those statements?

To reignite your desire, you must become sensitive to your wrong-way signs and utilize them, for they are the catalysts meant to stimulate desire within you — your Points of Power. Therefore, to discover what you want and reignite your desire, place an order for the following:

ᕦ I intend to find things that I want.

ᕦ I intend to find experiences I would like to have.

When you have gathered enough information about something you have observed or thought about, you will feel a sense of elation. You will then be ready to add that item to your list of orders. If you feel doubtful, guarded, or fearful, you are still projecting a frequency that *opposes* what you desire — resistance — an order killer. In those moments, close your eyes and think of what may be preventing you from having what you desire. What do you believe? Say aloud "I cannot have what I want because _____." Your core belief will then surface so you can shift your frequency to what you want.

Once you have decided what you want, feel what it would be like to have it right here and now. Then let go. Remember, it's not necessary to justify *why* you want something — simply want it. The very nature of your being is to create, to summon and flow energy, so any excuse to flow it is perfectly acceptable.

> *The way you activate the seeds of your creation is by making choices about the results you want to create. When you make a choice, you mobilize vast human energies and resources which otherwise go untapped. All too often people fail to focus their choices upon results and therefore their choices are ineffective. If you limit your choices only to what seems possible or reasonable, you disconnect yourself from what you truly want and all that is left is a compromise.*[16] — ROBERT FRITZ

> *Until one is committed, there is hesitancy, the chance to draw back, always ineffectiveness. Concerning all acts of initiative (and creation). There is one elementary truth, the ignorance of which kills countless ideas and splendid plans: that the moment one definitely commits oneself, the Providence moves too. All sorts of things occur to help one that would never otherwise have occurred. A whole stream of events issues from the decision, raising in one's favor all manner of unforseen incidents and meetings and material assistance, which no man could have dreamed would have come his way. Whatever you can do, or dream you can, begin it. Boldness has genius, power and magic in it. Begin it now.*[17] — GOETHE
> 1749-1832

Be, Do, and Then You Will Have

Another technique to uncover what you desire is to ask yourself how you want to *feel*. For anything that you desire in life — a relationship, a physical object, a better job, or more money — is always prompted by the desire to feel better. "If only I had _____ then I would feel better." So, from that perspective: How do you want to feel? Then place your order and allow the creative process to unfold. Angacles will then appear

— opportunities in the form of people, events, or circumstances — and after you take inspired action, your order will manifest.

As you learn to utilize the Four-Step Formula, you will relish Being in each new moment of Now. As you make intentional decisions while anticipating the manifestation of your prior orders, you will feel infinitely more satisfied than you did when you tried to justify how and why you were experiencing whatever you were experiencing in the past.[18] In those moments you will know what it is to truly live, love, and laugh! ⊛

Stop a "Wheel of Frustration" and Replace it with a "Wheel of Good Fortune"

You are telling me that you haven't always gotten what you wanted. Yet I am here to tell you that you have always gotten what you called forth. Your life is always a result of your thoughts about it.[19]

— NEALE DONALD WALSCH
Conversations with God - Book 1

Whatever you are thinking about is like planning a future event. When you are worrying, you are planning. When you are appreciating, you are planning.... What are you planning?[20]

— ESTHER and JERRY HICKS

Whenever you encounter a setback in manifesting what you desire, it's generally for one of two reasons. The first? You've inadvertently developed a habit of thoughts that is manifesting as a recurring issue in your life; such as getting lost, having 'bad hair' days, or misplacing things. These episodes indicate nothing more than what you've been focusing on — you're attuned to that particular frequency. The solution? To simply readjust your frequency to reflect what you desire.

The second reason for a setback? You're rendezvousing with a deeply entrenched core belief — powerful resistance — conscious or unconscious. You've uncovered a habit of thoughts that has grown very powerful, gathered lots of momentum in the wrong direction, and has become a "Wheel of Frustration." The solution in this instance is to bridge the gap between your belief and your desire by utilizing the more thorough technique of "The Wheel of Good Fortune" (and this is not the "Vanna, I'd like the letter 's'" variety). The primary reason that most people don't live the life they would like to, is, once more, what they desire and what they believe are in conflict with one another.

How to Get a Wheel of Good Fortune Rolling and Stop a Wheel of Frustration Dead in its Tracks

[S]trong contradictory beliefs can cause great power blocks.[21]
— JANE ROBERTS
The Nature of Personal Reality - A Seth Book

To begin this important passage, I would like to extend my deepest appreciation to authors/speakers Esther and Jerry Hicks for being my spiritual teachers as well as providing me the inspiration to write this book. The contribution they have unknowingly made to my life, and to the lives of many others, is beyond measure. I wish to acknowledge and credit them for the creation of the following techniques that I feel are essential in creating the life you wish to live. Although I have labeled these techniques with different names, the concepts are solely theirs.

The "Wheel of Good Fortune" technique is a more specific process used to readjust your frequency when the gap between what you desire and what you believe appears to be insurmountable.

A Wheel of Good Fortune is rolling when things are going your way and you are receiving what you want. Your wheel is moving quickly and gathering lots of momentum as each of your orders manifests. On the other hand, a Wheel of Frustration is rolling when things are moving in the *opposite* direction of what you want. And the culprit is always resistance — an underlying belief you hold — a red circuit that needs readjusting. This red circuit has become a great power block that will prevent you from attaining what you desire.

Be forewarned that as you begin to reconstruct your comfort zone, your new orders will project higher frequencies. As a result, many of your old-paradigm core beliefs and patterns that exist at lower frequencies will begin to surface, magnetizing evidence of their existence. Why? They are no longer congruent with what you desire. Lower frequencies cannot abide with your new higher frequencies as they are no longer aligned Who You Choose To Be. Therefore, for a period of time, it may feel as though 'all hell is breaking loose' as you manifest experiences, opportunities, that alert you to these red circuits. What can you do? First, relax and breathe deeply. Then, one by one, heed these opportunities to readjust your red circuits utilizing the following technique.

As you learned earlier, you can think of each of your circuits as a radio dial having a vast spectrum of stations that you are able to tune into. And each of your circuits represents a topic, or subject-matter in life that is currently tuned in to a specific 'station' or frequency. Let's say that you wish to listen to the wonderful music on 104.5 (your desire), but are currently tuned in to the awful sounds of 98.9 (your current reality which reflects your belief). The Wheel of Good Fortune technique provides you the step by step process that allows you to turn your dial to 104.5. Keep in mind though, as you begin turning your dial, you will first hear static. Then, as you move your dial closer and closer to 104.5, you will begin to detect faint sounds, and when you finally reach 104.5 its signal will come in loud and clear — you have tuned in to its frequency! In this same manner, the Wheel of Good Fortune technique allows you adjust your frequency little by little to whatever it is that you desire.

   Slow down your Wheel of Frustration so you can turn it around and head it in the right direction. This is generally accomplished by shifting your consciousness — recognizing that another valid option exists which will open your heart to receive.

   Determine what you want from your clear understanding of what you don't want.

   Make general neutral statements that embody what you desire. Think of statements that feel good, soothing, and provide you with a feeling of relief. Avoid statements that evoke a feeling of vulnerability, guardedness, or fear. Angel will always let you know if you are headed in the right direction via your feelings.

   Each time you make a statement that is accompanied by a feeling of relief, you are getting closer and closer to the frequency of what you desire.

After formulating a general statement, put it to the test by asking yourself the following questions:

   How did that statement feel?
   Do I feel a sense of relief?
   Do I feel like I don't quite 'buy it'?
   Is it projecting something I believe?

Each statement you make must feel good and evoke a feeling of relief within you. If it doesn't, try again. Find another statement that you believe and begin once more. By focusing on a statement that provides you with relief, by virtue of the Law of Attraction, you will magnetize another thought that corresponds with it and then another and another. This process will redirect the energy of a red circuit that no longer serves you, moving your dial closer and closer to the 'station' you have chosen, thus allowing energy to flow to the manifestation of what you desire.

Let's now apply this process, step by step, to a very important aspect of life: your job, because what you do for a living generally encompasses the majority of your time. In the following chapter, we will apply the Wheel of Good Fortune to the issue of parenting — raising children in the new paradigm. And following that chapter we will explore the issue of money — an essential element in living a life filled with joy, love, and laughter.

Get a Wheel of Good Fortune Rolling with a Great Job!

The return from work must be the satisfaction which that work brings you and the world's need of that work. With this, life is heaven, or as near heaven as you can get. Without this, with work which you despise, which bores you, and which the world does not need, this life is hell. — WILLIAM EDWARD BURGHARDT DUBOIS
1868-1963

If you cannot work with love but only with distaste, it is better that you should leave your work. — KHALIL GIBRAN
1883-1931

The more I want to get something done, the less I call it work. — RICHARD BACH

In order that people may be happy in their work, these three things are needed: they must be fit for it. They must not do too much of it. And they must have a sense of success on it. — JOHN RUSKIN
1819-1900

You may presently be employed in a job that does not utilize your talents — one where you feel drained of life energy. This is a great situation in one sense. Great, because it reveals what you don't want. And when you know what you don't want, it is far easier to determine what you want. Therefore, your first step is to specifically define what you *don't* like.

For example: You may be experiencing some of the following circumstances that cause discomfort within you:

ↄ✫ Co-workers who gossip and talk about the petty negative issues in life. They seem to seek satisfaction from sharing problems rather from working

ↄ✫ Low wages

ↄ✫ A position where your creative abilities are not utilized or encouraged

ↄ✫ A sense of being imprisoned by the hours you work

ↄ✫ A feeling of being 'on guard' — as though others are waiting to pounce on you should you make a mistake

ↄ✫ A feeling of criticism and condemnation toward one another

ↄ✫ A feeling of dreadful anticipation when you go to work

ↄ✫ A feeling that you cannot truly express who you are

ↄ✫ A working environment where no vision has been articulated, therefore no one really understands their purpose or the 'big picture'

You would prefer:

ↄ✫ Co-workers who feel rewarded, invigorated, fulfilled, and gratified by what you do. Those who seek solutions to issues in a loving, caring, respectful, diplomatic way

ↄ✫ High pay

ↄ✫ A position where you have the freedom to express your creative abilities and ideas

ↄ✫ An environment that supports taking risks and making mistakes, knowing that they are an essential element of the creative process

ↄ✫ A flexible work schedule that allows you the freedom to accomplish all you want in life

ↄ✫ A feeling of support for one another

ↄ✫ Co-workers who desire to understand and give one another the benefit of the doubt when conflict arises

~ A feeling of joyful anticipation when you go to work

~ Working in an environment where you are free to express who you are and utilize the best of your talents and abilities

~ A company vision in harmony with your Mission. A vision where everyone understands both their individual purpose and the meaning of the 'big picture'

Once you have defined what you desire, your task is to then *feel* what your new job feels like — visualize it every day for a few minutes. If you don't believe that the job of your dreams is possible, you must examine what you believe and ask yourself *why* you feel the way you do. Then utilize that information and begin to shift your frequency by making a few general statements that you do believe. This will neutralize your wheel and stop its momentum in the wrong direction.

~ "I believe that all people have some form of talent."

~ "I believe that we are all unique."

~ "I believe that I can do _____ well."

~ "I believe that people should be compensated handsomely for their contributions, because all tasks are necessary to the whole."

~ "I believe that I should be compensated handsomely for my contribution."

Again, choose statements that resonate with you. This should slow your wheel enough to turn its momentum in the direction of good fortune. At this point, your statements can become more specific and you may add the opposite of your negative statements to more specifically define what you want.

~ "I am doing something that I feel passionate about."

~ "I enjoy being in an environment where I feel challenged and supported in what I do."

~ "It feels wonderful to make a lot of money doing what I love to do."

~ "I understand my contribution to my company's vision."

~ "My contribution is greatly appreciated by those in my company."

Remember, after placing your orders you must be careful. If you become anxious for your orders to arrive, you will activate your 'off' switch and prevent them from manifesting. Just remember to be ever vigilant and 'switch channels' to one of your predetermined stations when your thoughts begin to wander in the wrong direction.

It is Essential to Divert Your Negative Thoughts

Anxiety is the space between the "now" and the "then."
— FRITZ PERLS

When your order has not yet arrived, you are in the greatest peril of sabotaging it. For if you think about the absence of what you ordered, you will activate your 'off' switch. In that case, not only will you *not* get what you ordered, but also you will also magnetize additional experiences that will validate the fact that you *never* get what you want. The vicious circle once again. Therefore, to attain what you desire, it is essential that you stay connected to source energy: relax and expect your order in joyful anticipation without offering contradicting thoughts.

Esther and Jerry Hicks advise you to think of this process as you would think of boiling water for a cup of tea. If, for a period of years you placed a pot of water on the stove, turned on the flame, and just as the water was about to boil, you turned off the flame, what would you conclude? That you were incapable of making a cup of tea! In reality, though, you just needed to keep the flame on longer![2] Readjusting your red circuits will require conscious effort, time, practice, and focus. Remember, you're building new neural pathways, therefore, for a period of time, your old frequencies will be dominant.

> *No thing great is created suddenly, any more than a bunch of grapes or a fig. If you tell me that you desire a fig, I answer you that there must be time. Let it first blossom, then bear fruit, then ripen.* — EPICTETUS
> 55-135

> *When unto thee there comes a feeling that draws thee nearer to the dark gate, examine thine heart to know if the feeling has come from within. Send through the body a wave of vibration, irregular at first, regular at second, repeating time after time until free. Start the wave force in the brain center. Direct in waves from thine head to thy foot.* — ESSENE GOSPEL OF PEACE

Many of life's failures are people who did not realize how close they were to success when they gave up.
— THOMAS EDISON
1877-1931

Faith is like the air in a balloon. If you've got it you're filled. If you don't, you're empty. — PEGGY CAHN

The common idea that success spoils people by making them vain, egotistical, and self-complacent is erroneous; on the contrary, it makes them, for the most part, humble, tolerant, and kind. Failure makes people cruel and bitter. — W. SOMERSET MAUGHAM
1874-1965

If you *still* don't think that you can have something you really want, write down the reasons why.

*(1) I believe that I cannot have*_____

_____

_____

_____

_____

because_____

_____

_____

_____

_____

which leads me to my habit of thoughts which is_____

_____

_____

_____

_____

The opposite of my belief is (state it in the positive)_____

_____

_____

_____

_____

Would you really want this if you could have this? ☐ yes ☐ no. If so, then choose it.

I choose to have_____

_____

_____

_____

_____

I choose it because_____

_____

_____

_____

_____

     (2) I believe that I cannot have

_____

_____

_____

_____

_____

because_____

_____

_____

_____

_____

which leads me to my habit of thought which is_____

_____

_____

_____

_____

The opposite of my belief is (state it in the positive)_____

_____

_____

_____

_____

Would you really want this if you could have this? ☐ yes ☐ no. If so, then choose it.

I choose to have_____

_____

_____

_____

_____

_____

I choose it because_____

_____

_____

_____

_____

Now think about what you have ordered and feel what it would be like to have it right now. And remember, it's not necessary to justify *why* you want what you want. As you stand in your fresh new moment of Now and joyfully anticipate what you have ordered, it will begin to manifest!

> *We can have excuses, or we can have health, love, longevity, understanding, adventure, money, happiness. We design our lives through the power of our choices.*[23]
> — RICHARD BACH

Four Factors That Can Prevent You from Getting What You Want

1. *FEAR* — You're afraid to want anything because you're afraid you won't get it. This reaction will only magnetize more 'not getting' and disappointment. What can you do? Determine the opposite of what you fear and focus on it daily.

2. *DISBELIEF* — Your core belief or habit of thoughts doesn't buy it. Your contradictory feelings indicate your need to reassess a core belief. What can you do? Utilize the Wheel Of Good Fortune technique — reprogram your belief and tune in to what you desire.

3. *LACK OF FOCUS* — attention and joy. You're not 'going to work' every day... (naughty, naughty... you're not taking those fifteen minutes... you're not utilizing your power... Aren't you worth it?). Your former frequency is still more dominant than your new frequency — as with the teapot, you may have turned off the flame prematurely. What can you do? Spend more time focusing in order to build your new neural pathway.

4. *DID NOT TAKE INSPIRED ACTION* — you didn't act on your Angacles — opportunities — when they magically appeared. What can you do? Place your order once again.

In all four cases, your old frequency is still more dominant than your new frequency. Therefore, simply go back and refocus on what you want so you can get on with your real task in life: living, loving, and laughing! Incidentally, it's a lot more fun! ☺

New - Paradigm Parenting

The deepest principle in human nature, is the craving to
be appreciated. — WILLIAM JAMES
1842-1910

I have found the best way to give advice to your children
is to find out what they want and then advise them to do it.
— HARRY TRUMAN
1884-1972

Children enjoy the present because they have neither a
past nor a future. — JEAN DELABRUYERE
1645-1696

To live means sharing another's space, dreams, sorrows,
contributing our ears to hear, our eyes to see, our arms
to hold and our hearts to love. — PAUL TILLICH
1886-1965

You love me so much you want to put me in your pocket.
And I should die there smothered. — D.H. LAWRENCE
1885-1930

A mother is not a person to lean on, but a person to
make leaning unnecessary. — DOROTHY CANFIELD FISHER

Most kids hear what you say; some kids do what you
say; but all kids do what you do.
— KATHLEEN CASEY THIESEN

What most of us want, is to be heard; to communicate.
— DORY PREVIN

There is no such thing as a non-working mother.
— HESTER MUNDIS

Each of us entered this world without shame, without judgment, and without fear. We were innocent. We had a simple purity of heart. We were spontaneously joyful. We were filled with wonder, curiosity, delight, passion, eagerness, and awe. We were eager to touch, smell, eat, love, feel, know, and try. However, our natural state of being was soon extinguished by pattern after pattern of fears and judgments. Far too often what we heard in childhood was NO, NO, NO! We were too happy, too eager, too loud, too excited, too interested. We were told to STOP THAT!!![24] until we were programmed to the lower frequency of those caring for us.

In one psychological study, three-and-four-year old children were outfitted with tape recorders that registered everything they heard during a specific period of time. The results? Eighty-five percent of what they heard was either about what they could *not* do or how bad they were because of what they were doing.[25] What does this mean? Unless we awaken to our power, we will perpetuate our negative beliefs and cycle of fear into the next generation.

Know you what is to be a child? It is to be something very different from the man of today. It is to have a spirit yet streaming from the waters of baptism; it is to believe in love, to believe in loveliness, to believe in belief; it is to be so little that the elves can reach to whisper in your ear; it is to turn pumpkins into coaches, and mice into horses, lowness into loftiness, and nothing into everything, for each child has its fairy godmother in its soul.
— FRANCIS THOMPSON SHELLEY

How We Disempower Our Children

Children telepathically pick up on the ominous overtones born of the dire pictures of danger we continually project. The result? They learn to perceive life through the eyes of fear. We rob them of their natural curiosity and narrow their perception of life experience.

In our fear we attempt to shield, protect, or divert our children from the consequences of their choices, and while doing so, we disempower them. In reality though, the sooner they learn that their behaviors produce a feeling which can only magnetize more of the same types of experiences, the sooner they will know their authentic power. In our failure to allow our children the consequences of their behaviors, we create the circumstances for them to blame others for what is going wrong in their lives, rather than allowing them to recognize what they are creating all by themselves. It is essential that they associate their thoughts and actions with their experiences in life. It is essential that they know the consequences — good and bad — of their choices, for then they will recognize their power.

> *Awareness is bred out of us from birth onward with the regimen of feeding, schooling, and mind-control imposed by well-meaning teachers and parents. That is why mistakes keep being repeated over and over again and why man's upward progress seems so inert. When parents and teachers correct the utterances of children, they slow their imaginations and teach them the same fallacies, which they themselves have been spoon-fed throughout their lives.*[26]   —RUTH MONTGOMERY

Encourage, Promote, and Nourish Your Child's Spirit

As parents and educators, our job is to provide our children with avenues to express their high energy rather than to suppress it, for their high energy simply indicates the high frequencies they are attuned to — their natural state of being (and ours as well). In our misunderstanding of energy or frequencies, we have misdiagnosed certain children as having ADHD (Attention Deficit Hyperactivity Disorder). In reality though, many of these children are simply those projecting higher frequencies. It is we who have a problem coping with them because our institutions and methods of educating are based on old-paradigm lower frequencies. In our defense, however, it can be difficult and sometimes uncomfortable to be with someone tuned in at a higher frequency. Nonetheless, our task is not to label our children as "defective" or to medicate them into numbness, but to instead provide them with avenues to express their energy. As we provide interesting stimulating structures — programs that allow freedom while engaging children's high energy — we then let the Law of Attraction 'do its thing' and allow our vision to manifest.

Empowering the New Generation

To allow our children the freedom to experience life, we must loosen the grip we have on them. For in reality, words cannot teach; only life experience can. We must allow and encourage children to make decisions from the earliest stages of life, for if someone continually makes decisions for them, how can they ever learn to make their own? As a matter of fact, they will only resist and rebel due to their core instinct of freedom. Instinctively, they understand that freedom is the basis of life, and they cannot experience joy or growth if they are denied freedom.

> *I hear and I forget, I see and I remember, I do and I understand.*
> — CHINESE PROVERB

As parents and educators, our task is to assume the role of our children's spiritual teachers and empower them! It is essential that we impart to them that they can be, do, or have anything they want in life. We must teach our kids to love and appreciate all those around them, to laugh and be joyful — to celebrate the differences in everything and everyone. For within this great sea of differences on Earth lies the experiences each of us chooses from to create our lives.

The Tug-Of-War between Career and Home

Are you a mom or dad working full time but feeling a tug-of-war between your children and your career? How do you feel when you leave your children with someone else, for your feelings are your true gauge. Only you know in your heart if having a job is right or wrong for you. And don't feel guilty if you work — all of us do not share the same path, we're not supposed to. If working is right for you, you will know it in your heart, so don't allow anyone to influence you otherwise.

On the other hand, if you feel that you would like to be at home or to work part-time, yet believe you cannot manage it financially, don't try to figure out how you can do it — that's Angels responsibility. Use your power and place an order. Visualize what you want and tune in to the frequency of what it would be like to stay at home with your children. Then have faith and your order will become reality. And perhaps when your children are a little older, you will gain a new perspective and want something different. Just listen to your heart and you will know.

After giving birth to my son Zachary, I, too, had to confront a sick feeling in the pit of my stomach when I worked two days a week and left him in someone else's care. I had wanted a baby for a very long time, but had difficulty with pregnancy (what frequency was I projecting?). I had undergone the infertility routine, surgery, and endured four losses. And when Zach finally came, he was very eager to begin his life, arriving two-and-one-half months *early*, weighing in at three pounds, nine ounces. One day a few months after his birth, I met with a moment of truth: I did not want anyone, other than myself and my husband, see him take his first steps, stand up, say his first words, etc. With the support of my husband, I made a difficult decision and quit my job, thus placing the burden of financial responsibility solely upon him. This decision evoked feelings of guilt and anxiety within me because I was now in a position of dependence — a position very uncomfortable for me. However, I knew in my heart that it was the right decision.

> We are always too busy for our children; we never give them the time or the interest they deserve. We lavish gifts upon them; but the most precious gift — our personal association, which means so much to them — we give grudgingly.
> — MARK TWAIN
> 1835-1910

Should you do choose to stay at home, you can give your children another gift as they grow older. By contributing some of your time, even a few hours a week to something you care about, you will convey the message that your role encompasses more than simply existing for their accommodation (as you are probably aware, that's their assumption). Mommies and daddies make contributions to the world, too, and the message your children will receive is that people have value in many different areas of life.

Kids and the Four-Step Formula

Here's an example of how the Four-Step Formula benefitted Zach's life: When Zach was five to six years old, he attended a class in karate where he occasionally participated in large tournaments. Although he didn't participate in one-on-one combat, he did participate in kata competition — a series of defense maneuvers used to disable invisible opponents. Prior to a competition, I would ask him to visualize every movement of his kata. He would sit at the breakfast table with a little smile on his face and go through the movements in his mind. Then he would imagine winning the trophy, how proud he was of himself, and how proud his Mommy and Daddy were over his accomplishment. Guess what? *He never lost!* Not only did he win eleven trophies, but he also ranked first in his division in Chicagoland. He has experiential proof of the Four-

Step Formula and feels empowered by it! On occasion, however, Zach takes this knowledge a bit too far. For when his grandma, grandpa, or dad expresses a problem, he impatiently retorts, "Just think, believe, expect, and get!" He assumes that everyone knows the Formula! When I drive him to school in the morning, I ask him to place an order for learning new 'cool' things about life and our world and to feel how exciting it is to learn more and more. After all, if he has to attend school he may as well order a joyous experience. He also visualizes being safe and secure at all times. And when he goes on a field trip, he instructs the bus driver to intend safety for himself and those around him. (Heaven knows what the driver thinks!)

I consistently remind him of his power and have a profound respect for the sacred soul he really is (not that I don't often slip up). I believe that he chose Ken and me to be his father and mother — his spiritual teachers. However, with the passage of time, I have come to recognize that the opposite is actually true: He is *our* spiritual teacher, sent to teach us. And we are honored to have been chosen (yes, he still gets well-deserved time-outs... But, perhaps we should get them, too!).

Here's another occasion where the Four-Step Formula came in handy: In the summer of 1997, Ken and I bought a new boat and invited my younger brother and his family to join us for a weekend of fun in the sun. One of Zach's cousins wanted to learn how to water ski, so I jumped in the lake to assist him. After placing my arms around Phil's waist and my feet on the back of his skis, I asked Ken to pull the two of us slowly so that Phil could feel what it was like to be pulled by the boat. After trying and failing to get up twice, he then wanted to quit as he was shivering uncontrollably. Knowing how proud kids can be when they accomplish something significant, and how demoralizing it can be when they fail, I asked him to give it one more try. But this time I asked him to first imagine that a red light was entering his body and warming him up. Next, I asked him to close his eyes and imagine what it might feel like to be pulled up on the water skis — the feeling of freedom, the exhilaration of gliding on the surface of the water, and the feeling of ecstasy! (He probably thought I was nuts....) Guess what? Not only did he get up, but he skied for ten minutes — phenomenal for the first time! Of course, I was left behind shivering in the water but cheered so loudly for Phil that two nearby fishermen (I didn't realize they were there; honest) shouted "Not too excited, lady!", and left in a huff for a more peaceful fishing spot. When I finally got back in the boat Phil asked me, "Was it the third time that I tried to get up when you told me to think about the red light and skiing behind the boat, Aunt Lauren?" I replied, "Yes, it was." His reply? "It really worked!"

The moral of the story: The Formula really works and can empower your kids (even if you feel corny)!

Raise a Positive Kid by Being a Positive Parent

Your children are not your children.
They are the sons and daughters of life's longing for itself.
They come through you but not from you.
Although they are with you, yet they belong not to you.
You may give them your love, but not your thoughts.
For they have their own thoughts.
You may house their bodies but not their souls.
For their souls dwell in the house of tomorrow, which you
cannot visit, not even in your dreams.
You may strive to be like them, but seek to not make them like you.
You are the bows from which your children as living arrows are
sent forth.
Let your bending in the archer's hand be for gladness.
— KHALIL GIBRAN
1883-1931

Child of mine, I will never do for you that which I know you
can do for yourself. I will never rob you of an opportunity to
show yourself your ability and talent. I will see you at all times
as the capable, effective, powerful creator that you've come
forth to be. And I will stand back as your most avid cheer-
leading section. But I will not do for you that which you have
intended to do for yourself. Anything you need from me, ask.
I'm always here to compliment or assist. I am here to encourage
your growth, not to justify my experience through you.[27]
— ESTHER and JERRY HICKS

☺   Tell your kids how much and why you love them all the time.

☺   Demonstrate your integrity at all times.

☺   Continually remind them of their power.

☺   Say, "Do this" rather than "Don't do that"

☺   Listen to them.

☺   Respect them.

☺   Continually point out their qualities.

☺   Look for things to laugh about and laugh with them.

☺   Show them the wonders of our world — the beauty of nature all around us — however large or small the wonder may be.

☺   Give them thorough, complete explanations.

☺   Point out the greatness in people you see, rather than looking for negative characteristics.

☺   Ask them what they believe to be the greatness in various people.

☺   When someone commits an unconscionable act, provide possible reasons why they could have acted in that manner, recognizing that fear was underlying their behavior.

☺   Always, always, always provide them with choices — on anything and everything.

☺   When you see a person who is physically challenged, do not divert your eyes and run in the opposite direction fearing your child's response. Anticipate your child's response and talk with that person. Ask them to explain their condition to your child. Let your child know that there is nothing to fear, and that most often these folks are just as normal as you and I.

☺   Schedule an appointment with each of your kids for special time: playing a game, reading, or whatever they choose to do, on a regular basis and Be in that moment with them completely.

☺   Whenever they have a problem, ask them what feels bad about it, what they want instead, and then have them write a script that illustrates exactly what they would like to happen. Then have them imagine that their script was 'real.' This will help to empower them when their script becomes reality.

☺   Stress how important, how valuable, and how powerful they are.

☺   Ask them to look at others and imagine what it would feel like to walk in their shoes.

☺   Have them write down three things each day that they appreciated and then share them at the dinner table. Record each family member's thoughts for the day in a family journal.

☺   Have them teach you what they learned in school that day (you probably forgot it all anyway, so it becomes interesting).

☺   Ask them how they would handle a problem in life. You might be amazed at the answers you get — kids can be quite wise.

☺   Appreciate the special unique gift that your child contributes to the diversity in our world.

☺   Be loving, appreciative, and inspirational. As you demonstrate these qualities consistently, you will magnetize the same qualities from them.

☺   Encourage them to talk about situations that occur in our world or in their personal lives. Ask them what they felt, what they might have learned, or if they had been that person, how would they have responded in that situation.

☺   Ask them how they feel at all times and honor their feelings without judging them. Lead with: Do you ever feel sad? Do you ever feel lonely? Do you ever feel scared? As they express their natural frustrations and anger, they will release their emotions, thus expressing their repressed energy.

☺ Give them meaningful chores around the house, and stress how the family works like a corporation with everyone contributing to the whole.

☺ Stress the importance of not basing their sense of humor on the ridicule of others.

☺ Know that kids are kids. They are not adults with whom you can share your most intimate thoughts, doubts, and fears.

☺ Never shame them or compare them with anyone else.

☺ Share your childhood experiences (positive and negative) with them.

☺ Ask them to describe an ideal family life to you.

☺ Rather than reacting and meting punishment with a knee-jerk response, predetermine a consequence they are fully aware of.

☺ BE love. Live your life always reaching for a good feeling frequency. And don't recriminate yourself when you mess up, for what you demonstrate, they will emulate.

☺ Pay attention to what your children tell you, even if what they say is negative. For what they say and how they behave is oftentimes symbolic — mirroring something you need to examine in yourself. Children always assume and amplify the frequencies of their parents. (Uh oh…)

☺ Stop and listen carefully when they want to share stories or problems with you.

☺ Take the time necessary to determine age-appropriate limits for your kids. Why? Limits define acceptable behavior. Limits guide them in the right direction. Limits must be firm enough to guide, yet flexible enough to accommodate growth and change. Use the following gauge: the younger they are, the more restricted the boundaries. "This is black, this is white. And if you cross the line, this is the consequence." Why should they have a consequence? They feel safer and will be better prepared to deal with their power. Kids have a lot of power, which can be scary to them, therefore, they need *you* to be in control. Consistent boundaries inspire cooperation, whereas inconsistent boundaries inhibit learning. Furthermore, if their boundaries are inconsistent, your children will learn that you don't mean what you say — a recipe for disaster.

☺ As they get older, conditionally expand their boundaries: "We'll try this for a week and see how it works." If it didn't work, don't reprimand them. Instead, tell them that they can try again next week, and you're sure that they will do better then. This teaches them to take responsibility for their actions.

☺ Adhere to your consequences immediately and consistently when the limits are broken. Choose consequences that logically relate to the behavior. You must be willing to live with the consequences that you have chosen or your kids will rebel and continually test your limits. And when the consequence is over, wipe the slate clean and begin anew.

☺ Avoid overhelping, overprotecting, and overlooking. Understand that the most difficult aspect of parenting is to let your children learn from their mistakes. Why? You love them and perceive them as a reflection of you.

Parenting Problems?
Get a Wheel of Good Fortune Rolling

There is a tribe in east Africa where the art of true intimacy is fostered even before birth. In this tribe, the birth date of a child is not counted from the day of its physical birth nor even the day of its conception, as in other village cultures. For in this tribe, the birth date comes the first time the child is a thought in its mother's mind. Aware of her intention to conceive a child with a particular father, the mother then goes off to sit alone under a tree. There she sits and listens until she can hear the song of the child that she hopes to conceive. Once she has heard it, she returns to her village and teaches it to the father so that they can sing it together as they make love, inviting the child to join them. After the child is conceived, she sings it to the baby in her womb. Then she teaches it to the old women and midwives of the village, so that throughout the labor and at the miraculous moment of birth itself, the child is greeted with its song. After the birth, all the villagers learn the song of their new member and sing it to the child when it falls or hurts itself. It is sung in times of triumph, or in rituals or initiations. This song becomes a part of the marriage ceremony when the child is grown, and at the end of life, his or her loved ones will gather around the deathbed and sing this song for the last time. — UNKNOWN

Conception

I was dancing — pure light
formless consciousness
when you called me —
by the power of your intention —
with the song of your desire,
in the intensity of your passion —
you called me
and tentacles of your sending shot though timeless space —
found me
and I sent back a joyful "yes!"
And the universe changed —
a new frequency began to hum
And I was there —
in those most tender moments
and most ecstatic
and you knew, mama, in that way you have of knowing
and I whispered my name to you . . .
And you smiled . . .

— UNKNOWN

When you first learned that you were going to be a parent, you may have pondered the thoughts of raising your child in a manner that was more desirable than what you experienced as a child. As a result, your initial intent was to protect the precious, vulnerable soul entrusted in your care. Therefore, if your current experience deviates from your initial intention, if you are constantly quarreling or engaging in power struggles with your children, you are receiving signs that these experiences are the wrong way for both you and your children. Angel is tugging on your sleeve warning you of the red circuit you are holding. The message? Something is important, something really matters to you, and this something is in the opposite direction of what you are experiencing.

In order to stop a Wheel of Frustration with your children, first explore your negative feelings, for your negative feelings are, more than likely, illuminating your desire to experience a relaxed, respectful, allowing, joyful, communicative relationship with your children.

To begin shifting your frequency to what you desire, try some of these statements on for size:

☺ "I love my children."

☺ "My children love me."

☺ "I choose to be the best mother/father I can be."

☺ "I choose to be loving."

☺ "I choose to be respectful."

☺ "Being in a family with intense interpersonal relationships allows us many opportunities to evolve and define Who We Choose To Be."

☺ "I understand that it is not my responsibility to live my children's lives for them."

☺ "I am allowing my children to grow."

☺ "I choose to be joyful."

☺ "I am learning many things from my children."

☺ "Each of my children have many wonderful qualities. They are:_____."

☺ "I intend for my children to be, do, and have everything in life that they choose."

☺ "When I observe my children working through their issues, I am proud of them."

☺ "I choose to radiate peace, understanding, and gentleness so my children feel safe while communicating with me, therefore I will refrain from using my PSYCHO-PARENT voice"

☺ "I choose to allow them freedom."

☺ "I intend to assist them in awakening to their power, to help them to understand the correlation between their thoughts, feelings, and life experience."

☺ "I understand that by maintaining my point of centeredness and connection to source energy, I am offering them the best of Who I Am."

☺ "I choose harmony in all our interactions."

Can you feel a shift in your feelings from those of frustration to those that provide you with a sense of relief? Can you feel how these statements are more aligned with what you want? You will always know if statements resonate with you because you will feel it. And when you find a statement that you 'don't buy,' think again and search for another that provides you with a feeling of relief. Then focus on *that* statement and let the Law of Attraction do 'its thing.' To tune in to a frequency that corresponds with what you want, recall a time in your life when each of your children *was* loving and kind and focus on how you felt in those moments. Now, imagine them responding consistently in that manner and how wonderful it feels. Imagine them sharing their experiences with you and how eager you are to participate in their lives, helping to guide them along their journey.

As you focus on your new vision every day for a few minutes and remember to 'change stations' when conflicting thoughts arise, within a week's time your new relationships will begin to unfold. Not only will it seem like magic, but you will also feel wonderful because your new experiences are aligned with the original orders you placed with Angel.

Our New World Begins at Home

To be nobody but myself in a world which is doing its best, night and day, to make you everybody else means to fight the hardest battle which any human being can fight and never stop fighting. — E.E. CUMMINGS
1894-1962

Were kids cruel, abusive, and heartless to you when you grew up? Did they pinpoint your deficits and belittle you in front of your peers? Were you excluded from certain groups because you didn't quite fit in? If so, do you recall how painful that was? If not, can you imagine how painful it could be? How it can erode self-esteem, self-worth, and sense of personal value?

As we send our kids off to school each day, they meet with an underlying social order we could compare to a hierarchal prison system where 'survival of the fittest' (as defined by the children) is the prevailing paradigm. How well a child acclimates to this 'fraternity' determines, to a large extent, how happy one's childhood is. Whether a child is deemed cool, a nerd, a jock, popular, or any of the new labels unknown to me, the quality of each of their days is directly related to how they are perceived by others. And because most children want to fit in, they take great pains to adapt to this peer pressure in order to thwart the jeers of their peers. Upon undergoing the initial once-over and being labeled, many aspects of their being are subject to scrutiny and judgment: the clothes they wear, the style of their hair, their physical appearance and 'defects,' how far they push the envelope with authority figures, etc.

As adults we are fully aware of this conduct, however, we rationalize it as a rite of passage in childhood. "Kids are mean," we say to one another. "The world is a cruel place." "They may as well learn how people really are now, because they'll have to learn it sometime," "They'll toughen up." And what do we do? Nothing. In our failure to act, however, our children assume that we condone these behaviors. And though it may not be outwardly apparent, the devastation to a child's psyche can have far-reaching effects — sometimes, for life.

The Story of Johnny

While I was deep in thought over the issue of children and the process by which the Divine within becomes suffocated, I magnetized an Angacle — an e-mail from a friend that provided me with an insight — "The Story of Johnny." Johnny was a little boy who had a home life that was not particularly wonderful. It was commonly known that his parents struggled financially and as a result, they continually fought with one another. This conflict at home took its toll on Johnny, and as a result, he routinely misbehaved in his parochial school. Johnny was constantly disruptive in class and Sister Mary, his third grade teacher, reprimanded him often. However, each time she scolded him, he always replied, "Thank you for correcting me Sister Mary," which endeared him to her.

One day in class Sister Mary overheard some of the kids taunting one another and decided to teach them a lesson. The assignment? To write down one *positive* quality about each of their classmates. At the end of the day each child was to share their insights with one another and record what their classmates had expressed about them. The result of Sister Mary's lesson? From that day forward, a different overtone imbued that classroom, for every child now had a new insight about what their classmates thought of them. This knowledge allowed each of them to shift their frequencies from those of insecurity and self-doubt to those of an underlying assurance of their goodness and assets. However, the story did not end here.

As the years passed, the children completed both grade school and high school and some of the boys were drafted in the Army, for the Viet Nam War was at its height of ferocity. As fate had it, tragedy befell Johnny and he was killed in action. When the soldiers found his body, they searched his uniform for his personal belongings and discovered a torn and tattered folded piece of paper in his pocket: The list of positive qualities that each of Johnny's classmates had shared with him in the third grade.

Back home Sister Mary was informed of the tragedy as well as the note that was found. Feeling great sadness, she attended his funeral with other students from that same third grade class. However, it was when she shared the story of Johnny's note that she knew just how powerful her lesson was. For many of Johnny's classmates also shared that they, too, carried their list of positive qualities with them at all times. That list had become their source of inspiration when life presented the darkest of moments. In times of doubt and uncertainty, they would read and reread their list and it would magically restore their sense of value, for others had seen and validated their worth.

Failing to Act Can Have Dire Consequences

Although to a lesser degree, is our state of denial regarding the cruelty that children inflict upon one another not unlike the state of denial regarding child and spousal abuse that was prevalent when I grew up? As adults, we must stop this destructive behavior. For to do nothing is to condone it. In our failure to act, we convey that this behavior is okay. By interceding, we not only offer our kids guidance, but also help them to avoid developing many red circuits. We must let our children know just how painful it is to tease, taunt, and ridicule others. Ask your children to imagine how it would feel to be subjected to that kind of pain and torment. And in doing so, you will help to prevent tragedies like those in Littleton, Colorado. Tragedies born of the numerous, continual hurts and stabs inflicted upon the perpetrators — repressed pain that had accumulated so much power that it eventually exploded.

I Have a Dream — Do You?

To commemorate Martin Luther King Jr's. birthday at Zachary's school, the teachers sought to demonstrate the deeper meaning behind the Reverend King's "I have a dream" message. The third grade children cut out the form of a dove — the sign of peace — and articulated their dream for our world on one side. And on the other side, the parents articulated their dream. At a school open-house, the doves were prominently displayed in the classroom, and ironically, the majority of dreams had a consistent theme: To live in a peaceful world where all people loved one another despite their differences.

Actualizing this dream begins at home; your home. We must not allow our children to extinguish one another's spirits. We must impart that there is *nothing* wrong with them. How can you help? Encourage your children's teachers to follow the powerful example set by Sister Mary and you can make a significant difference in the lives of many children. As Johnny and his classmates so poignantly demonstrated — that small, simple, brief exercise has far-reaching effects.

Kids are really receptive to the Four-Step Formula. They know instinctively who they are. Therefore, when we adore them, inspire them, instill confidence in them, take a lighthearted approach to life, let them know how much fun life can be, stimulate their curiosity, and convey that life will unfold in magical ways for them, we can sit back and watch them create a life filled with love, laughter, and unbounding joy! ☻

Today I Will Take the Time to Appreciate the Wonder of My Child

Just for this morning, I am going to smile when I see your face and laugh when I feel like crying.

Just for this morning, I will let you wake up softly, all rumpled in your sheets and I will hold you until you are ready for the day.

Just for this morning, I will let you choose what you want to wear, and smile and say how perfect it is.

Just for this morning, I am going to step over the laundry, and pick you up and take you to the park to play.

Just for this morning, I will leave the dishes in the sink, and let you teach me how to put that puzzle of yours together.

Just for this afternoon, I will unplug the telephone and keep the computer off, and sit with you in the back yard and blow bubbles.

Just for this afternoon, I will not yell once, not even a tiny grumble when you scream and yell for the ice cream truck, and I will buy you one if the truck comes by.

Just for this afternoon, I won't worry about what you are going to be when you grow up, or second guess every decision I have made where you are concerned.

Just for this afternoon, I will let you help me bake cookies, and I won't stand over you trying to fix them.

Just for this afternoon, I will take you to McDonalds™ and buy us both a Happy Meal™ so you can have both toys.

Just for this evening, I will hold you in my arms and tell you a story about how you were born, and how much I love you.

Just for this evening, I will let you splash in the tub and not get angry.

Just for this evening, I will let you stay up late while we sit on the porch and count all the stars.

Just for this evening, I will snuggle beside you for hours, and miss my favorite TV show.

Just for this evening, I will run my fingers through your hair as you pray. I will be simply be grateful that God has given me the greatest gift ever given. I will think of mothers who are searching for their missing children; mothers who are visiting their children's graves instead of their bedrooms; mothers who are in hospital rooms watching their children suffer senselessly and screaming inside that they can't handle it anymore.

And when I kiss you goodnight, I will hold you a little bit tighter, a little longer. It is then that I will thank God for you, and ask him for nothing except one more day. — UNKNOWN

Turn On the Money Valve and Let the Good Times Roll!

Money isn't everything as long as you have enough.
— MALCOLM FORBES

Money is like love, it kills slowly and painfully the one
who withholds it, and it enlivens the other who turns it
upon his fellow man.   — KHALIL GIBRAN
                                                    1883-1931

Money is God in action.
— FREDERICK J. EIKERENKOETTER II

Money is the seed of money.   — JEAN-JACQUES ROUSSEAU
                                                    1712-1778

Wealth is not in making money, but in making the man
while he is making money.   — JOHN WICKER

Money is the symbol of duty, it is the sacrament of
having done for mankind that which mankind wanted.
— SAMUEL BUTLER
1835-1902

Money is like an arm or a leg — use it or lose it.
— HENRY FORD
1863-1947

When you believe that spirit is opposite the material
world, you lose the ability to have an integrated spiritual
life.[28]   — GLENDA GREEN
Love Without End: Jesus Speaks

Money is the most important thing in the world.
— GEORGE BERNARD SHAW
1854-1950

Man must choose whether to be rich in things, or in the freedom to use them.
— IVAN LILLICH

The love of money as a possession — as distinguished from the love of money as a means to the enjoyments and realities of life — will be recognized for what it is, a somewhat disgusting morbidity, one of those semi-criminal, semi-pathological propensities which one hands over with a shudder to the specialists in mental disease.
— JOHN MAYNARD KEYNES
1883-1946

I care for riches, to make gifts to friends, or lead a sick man back to health with ease and plenty. Else small aid is wealth for daily gladness; once a man be done with hunger, rich and poor are all as one.
— EURIPIDES
480-406 BC

Money, which represents the prose of life, and which is hardly spoken of in parlors without an apology, is, in its effects and laws, as beautiful as roses.
— RALPH WALDO EMERSON
1803-1882

Every day examine your consciousness and see just what you are preparing for. [If] you are fearful of lack and hang on to every cent, [you will] thereby attract more lack. Use what you have with wisdom and it opens the way for more to come to you.[29] — FLORENCE SCOVEL SHINN
1871-1940

Be not penny-wise: riches have wings, and sometimes they fly away of themselves; sometimes they must be set flying to bring in more.
— FRANCIS BACON
1561-1626

Lack of money is the root of all evil.
— GEORGE BERNARD SHAW
1856-1950

Greed is the root of all evil.[30]
— GLENDA GREEN
Love Without End: Jesus Speaks

Your Inherited Beliefs

The problem of money dogs our steps throughout the whole of our lives, exerting a pressure that, in its way, is as powerful and insistent as any other problem of human existence. And it haunts the spiritual search as well.

— JACOB NEEDLEMAN

Much of what you were taught during your indoctrination to life has prevented you from living life the way it is meant to be lived. As you marinated in those misconceptions, you created many of the problems you are now experiencing. And one of the most prevalent issues in life is a lack of money, which makes it difficult to live, love, or laugh.

The majority of us have adopted a fundamentally flawed perception of money. In our misunderstanding of how life really operates, we have attached many judgments to money — distorted and conflicting judgments. These judgments have created red circuits because oftentimes they project frequencies of wanting or needing money. The consequence? We experience *more* wanting or needing money, accompanied by a bad feeling informing us that what we really want is in the *opposite* direction. These red circuits were created quite unconsciously in our childhoods from the most influential adults in our lives. Therefore, our first step in eradicating them is to identify them.

What have you been influenced to believe about money? If you grew up without an abundance of money and are now not living a life of prosperity, suffice it to say, there is good reason to believe that you are holding a red circuit that requires readjusting. Did you marinate in any of the following beliefs?

☹   "Money is scarce."

☹   "You must work hard to earn money."

☹   "You must be very careful with money because there is a limited supply of it."

☹   "Money doesn't grow on trees."

☹   "You must save your money for a rainy day." (That's a double whammy as it translates to: 1. "You will never have enough money" and 2. "Bad things always happen when you don't expect them to.")

☹   "Money and spirituality are in conflict with one another."

A man who believes in scarcity will program his mind to believe that scarcity is a reality. Therefore, he has to make a lot of money to compensate for scarcity. Consequently, he will make his money in a way that will allow scarcity also to persist. He will continue to invest in scarcity. He will align his values in limited or controlled supply. 'There are only a few diamonds,' he will say, 'so of course they will remain costly.' Or there is a fixed amount of real estate, so naturally the investment will be sound even though the cost is high.' He will empower his thinking with the economies of leverage, and then the leverage will begin to cause problems in his own life. He is forever working for more money to secure leverage for himself, until eventually he is out-leveraged by life. In such a state of mind, he will never solve the riddle of abundance at all, but merely defend himself against the consequences of believing in scarcity....However, the universe is infinitely expanding. There is no end to its abundance.[31] — GLENDA GREEN
Love Without End: Jesus Speaks

Feel your way, little by little, into a greater sense of abundance by looking for the treasures that the Universe is offering you on a day-to-day basis.[32]
— ESTHER and JERRY HICKS

Do what you love, and the money will follow.
— MARSHA SINETAR

To manifest prosperity you must first create a vision of what you want and then utilize your imagination to place your order. However, because most of us were encouraged to turn our imaginations off by the age of four or five, yours may have become dormant. Therefore, to clear away the cobwebs that may be impeding its operation, you've got to reignite your imagination. How do you do that? By generating ideas. So, let's play a game to revitalize your imagination.

Who Wants to Be a Millionaire?

Imagine for a moment that you will be given $1 Million. But, there's a catch — you must spend every penny of it within thirty days or you will have to give it all back. Write down exactly what you will spend your $1 million on. (Or $10 or $100 Million if $1 Million seems too little.)

My Million-Dollar Shopping Spree

_____
_____
_____
_____
_____
_____
_____
_____
_____
_____
_____
_____
_____
_____
_____
_____
_____
_____
_____
_____
_____
_____
_____
_____
_____
_____
_____
_____
_____
_____
_____
_____
_____

Now that your imagination is in full gear, let's take a closer look at what you just did. Think about the number of people involved in each of your purchases; the raw materials needed for each item; the designers, manufacturers, sub-contractors, retail stores, and all the people involved in the transportation of the goods. How much energy was expended by all of these people as a result of your purchases? Can you see how the money you spent — the energy you flowed — contributed to many people's lives, to the economy, and as a result, to the betterment of our world?

Money: The Energy of Life

The well of Providence is deep. It's the buckets we bring to it that are small. — MARY WEBB

Let's examine money from a new perspective — one that will open your heart and shift your frequency. What is money? It is simply is the representation of energy — energy that flows in a never-ending cycle. The transfer of money is the transference of energy. *For example*: When you go to work, you expend energy and for that energy you receive money. You then spend your money — exchange your energy — for the energy that someone else has expended. You might spend your energy on groceries, rent, a vacation, gas, your mortgage, your car payment, new clothes, a new home, whatever. And each of these items represent the flow of many other people's energy. The bottom line? To spend money is to flow energy, and in the process, *perpetuate life*.

From this perspective, think about what happens when you save or hoard money. You stop the flow of energy, right? You unwittingly take away from life. Think about what happened during the Great Depression in the 1920s when people lost their jobs, money, houses, or cars. Energy stopped flowing, didn't it? And as energy stopped, many aspects of life stopped along with it. People extinguished their desires, activated their 'off' switches, and in the process, restricted the flow of energy. The consequence? Things got so bad that some people took desperate measures. They committed suicide, anesthetized their pain through alcohol, resorted to crime, or were even forced to forage for food in garbage cans in order to survive. (That's what my Grandma Olson did, along with her ten brothers and sisters.) Can you recognize the far-reaching ramifications of *not* spending money — not flowing energy?

Does this perspective allow you to see the 'bigger picture' — a more expansive reality regarding money? I certainly hope so because when you spend money you contribute to the continuum of life. Therefore, don't ever feel guilty about wanting or spending lots of money for now you know its real purpose: To give life. So spend your money with joy, love, and abandon, and while doing so, just think about all those people you are helping!!! (By the way, I'm still trying to convince my husband of this one... He doesn't quite "buy it" yet.)

Abundance and Prosperity Issues?
Get a Wheel of Good Fortune Rolling

Let's now examine your $$$ circuit. If you're now not enjoying prosperity let's get to the bottom of your red circuit — your habits of thought. Then, let's readjust their frequencies utilizing the Wheel of Good Fortune technique! Try a few of these statements on for size:

$ "Money is the means of transferring goods and services in our world."

$ "Money is nothing more than a transference of energy."

$ "It feels good to do something and be rewarded for it."

$ "Money itself is simply paper, not good or bad."

$ "It is fun to have money."

$ "I can help others if I have an abundance of money."

$ "I feel joyful when I have extra money."

$ "I feel wonderful on vacation — I feel wonderful when I buy new clothes — I feel wonderful when I have a new car."

$ "Money buys freedom — a necessity to accomplish my goals."

$ "Money allows me a multitude of joyful experiences."

$ "I exchange my money or energy for the energy of someone else that has something I desire."

$ "I feel confident and secure when I have money."

Once you have practiced statements that resonate with you for a few days, you will begin to readjust your frequency. To manifest prosperity, imagine having all the money you desire, for you are then creating an order for it. Ponder what it might be like to have money: relish it, appreciate it, and then wait in joyful anticipation for Angacles to appear — people, events, or circumstances that will lead to the manifestation of money when you take inspired action! And remember: No 'Buts' Allowed! Forget the who, what, why, where, when, or how, for those thoughts will activate your 'off' switch and cancel your order! Be sensitive to any thought, word, or action that does not correspond with what you want. To distract yourself in those moments, use the 'remote control' in your mind and switch your channel to one of your preselected stations.

Once more, you don't need to save money. To save it means that you believe that there is 'not enough' — another consequence of old-paradigm thinking — 'poverty consciousness.' Simply attune to the frequency of $$$, stay connected to source energy, and money will continually flow in and out of your life, day after day, just like the air you breathe — if you trust, relax, expect, and allow it to.

Feel your way to prosperity little by little. Work on conceiving ideas, things to spend your money on, for the people with the most money happen to be the people with the most ideas who focus on them! And remember that your Point of Power is always in the present Moment, the moment you see something you desire, for then you can create it!

Instructions for Winning the Lottery

(You didn't believe it when you read "a complete operating manual"?)

I often visualize Heaven as being like a catalog fulfillment center, full of Angels reading requests. "This one reads 'I want to be happy in the future,'"says Gabriel. "Put it in the 'hold' file, with all the rest. Someday maybe these humans will learn to be specific," sighs Michael, as he marks yet another request "incomplete."[33]

— LAURIE BETH JONES

Although I was reluctant to include instructions for winning the lottery, as your desire to win usually implies that you don't trust that money will flow in and out to you, I nonetheless believe that these instructions will provide you with a good example of how the Four-Step Formula operates. But understand, if you feel that a windfall of money is going to provide you with security and happiness, you are sadly mistaken. For the real security and happiness you desire is within. Nevertheless, here are instructions for winning the lottery. (And if you feel guilty, send me 10 percent of your winnings for these instructions! We'll donate it to help Dr. "Patch" Adams build his "Gesundheit" new-paradigm healing centers....)

As you probably realize, many people want to win the lottery, yet most will not. And not as a result of the odds, but because of the beliefs they hold. Projecting a frequency that corresponds with a large sum of money is difficult for most folks because it is such an unfamiliar feeling. As a result, most folks buy lottery tickets while projecting the frequencies of lack, need, or desperation, and because those red circuits activate their 'off' switches, lottery winnings cannot flow to them.

If you have believed all of your life that money was scarce, that you were "powerless to have big money," "that only the lucky ones ever won," or that "rich people were, at best, shallow," you would be very far from magnetizing the quantity of money that the big lotteries pay out. Therefore, the trick to winning the lottery is to align with the frequency of money. To begin attuning to the lottery-winning frequency, imagine yourself in front of your television listening to the lottery folks announce the winning numbers. Feel your excitement build as they call out your numbers one by one. Then imagine what it would feel like to realize that you had won!!! Imagine yourself jumping up and down in your jubilation! Now, imagine receiving your check and buying everything you have always wanted. Feel the joy within — the energy flow through you. The next step? Write a script of your scenario. Then practice your script over and over until it becomes familiar. For the more you envision your script, the more familiar its frequency will become, hence, the sooner it will become reality! And don't forget to buy a lottery ticket each week.

Another technique to win the lottery is to eliminate any resistance that could block your order. When you have ordered joy, are connected to source energy, and are basking in appreciation on any subject, your connection is open to receiving only 'good stuff.' Therefore, the trick is to buy a lottery ticket while feeling appreciation for what you have. Because most lottery ticket purchasers are tuned in to lack, want, and need, your higher, stronger, and faster frequency will allow Angel to deliver big money to you. But, remember, the feeling in your heart creates your frequency. So, if you are *thinking* intently about winning the lottery but your heart 'ain't buying it,' you will be unsuccessful. What can you do? Identify and readjust your 'lottery' circuit. Keep in mind that *someone* is going to win, so it might as well be you!

You are the only obstacle to having all you want in life. If your desire is strong enough; if you wish to experience the full breadth of life; to travel; to help others; to experience freedom and independence; you must have money! You may have to consciously work at readjusting your frequency, but it will be well worth the effort. And though it can be difficult to eliminate a deeply entrenched habit of thoughts, it is not impossible. Remember, everything in your life is coming to you as a result of your frequencies — the feelings in your heart — your attitudes or moods. Therefore, to change any aspect of your life, you must adjust your frequency! You will then be living as life is meant to be lived: loving, and laughing! ☺

You've Got a Friend

When you're down and troubled
And you need some love and care,
And nothing, no nothing is going right.
Close your eyes and think of me and soon I will be there
To brighten up even your darkest night.
You just call out my name and you know wherever I am,
I'll come runnin' to see you again
Winter, Spring, Summer or Fall
All you've got to do is call and I'll be there, yes I will,
You've got a friend.
If the sky above you grows dark and full of clouds
and that old north wind begins to blow
Keep your head together and call My name out loud;
Soon you'll hear me knockin' at your door
You just call out my name and you know wherever I am,
I'll come runnin' to see you again
Winter, Spring, Summer or Fall
All you've got to do is call and I'll be there, yes I will,
You've got a friend.
Now, ain't it good to know that you've got a friend
when people can be so cold?
They'll hurt you, yes, and desert you
and take your soul if you let them
Oh, but don't you let them
You just call out my name
And you know wherever I am
I'll coming running to see you again
Winter, Spring, Summer, or Fall
All you've got to do is call
And I'll be there, yes I will.
You've got a friend, You've got a friend
Ain't it good to know, you've got a friend.[34]

Words and Music by Carole King

Know How to Determine
if a Sign Is from Angel

All hatred driven hence, the soul recovers radical innocence and learns at last that it is self-delighting, self-appeasing, self-affrighting, and that its own sweet will is Heaven's will. — W. B. YEATS
1856-1939

Telltale signs distinguish the messages sent by your ego from those sent by your Angel. Your ego — your conscious intellectual mind — is a great salesperson who has the job of ensuring your survival (but takes it a bit too far…). Your ego is responsible for your feelings of fear, doubt, and uncertainty, which you now know are nothing more than Angel-Alerts — wrong-way signs — Points of Power. On the other hand, Angel has the job of maintaining your connection to source energy, guiding you along your Path, and ensuring your survival. And as an added bonus, Angel always sends you love and light.

Signs from your ego are generally:

☹   based on scarcity, fear, or guilt

☹   based on protecting you from an imagined harm

☹   compelling, with no time to reflect

☹   quick answers that feel out of sync with your flow

☹   the first thing to come to mind

☹   feel like a desperate need

☹   distressed, disturbed, restless, or unhappy [35]

Signs from your Angel are:

☺   loving and reassuring

☺   persistent

☺   encouraging and positive

☺   not usually demanding immediate action

☺   rarely radical without smaller steps to initiate change[36]

Practice Makes Perfect

Pay attention to every hunch you have, every feeling you feel, every intuitive "hit" you experience. **Pay attention.** *Then act on what you "know." Don't let your mind talk you out of it. Don't let your fear pull you away from it. The more you act on your intuition fearlessly, the more your intuition will serve you. It was always there, only now you're paying attention to it.[37]*

— NEALE DONALD WALSCH
Conversations with God - Book 3

To determine if a sign is from Angel, begin by using plain old 'trial and error' or 'on the job training.' When you feel it is right for you to take a certain action, you will feel uplifted; you will have a kind of flow in your work, your friendships, and all your decisions, or as the Irish say, "You will have the wind at your back." If you fail to heed a wrong-way sign and take premature action, you will activate your 'off' switch, restrict the flow of energy, and nothing will work. You will feel uncentered and uncertain in your decisions. If you start your day determined to accomplish certain tasks with no regard for what you are feeling, you may also find yourself meeting with obstacles. However, if you listen within for feelings of what will work today, you will allow energy to flow and everything will seem to fall in line.

The challenge is one of discernment. The difficulty is knowing the difference between messages from God and data from other sources. Discrimination is a simple matter with the application of a basic rule. Mine is always the highest thought, your clearest word, your grandest feeling. Anything less is from another source.[38]

— NEALE DONALD WALSCH
Conversations with God - Book 1

Listen for Angel

 Whenever you are completing a task, ask yourself, "Does this feel right?" If not, put it aside for a time until it does.

 Start listening carefully within and quietly choose the direction that seems the most harmonious.

 If you arrive at a point in time where you must choose one direction or another, pause for a moment, clear your mind and then listen for a message from Angel. Don't try to reason with logic. Feel, don't think. Angel will then guide you to the right choice which will feel right to you, whereas your other options will be fraught with if's and but's.

 If you feel a sense of apprehension or foreboding regarding a decision, put it off for a while and collect more information. Always be aware of signs from your body — a tightening in the neck or stomach, clenching your jaws, a loss of energy, shallow breathing, tapping fingers, crossed arms or legs, or irritation with sounds. Contemplate the underlying reason for these circumstances. They are clearly wrong-way signs from Angel.

 Don't force anything — force restricts the flow of energy. If you are struggling, having nagging doubts, or are working very hard to make things happen, be assured that you are not expecting (step #3) what you want.

 Always take the course that feels right and you will have no nagging doubts.

 When you connect with Angel you will feel energized and reach your goals quickly, safely, and more easily than if you tried to make something happen.

 If you continue to receive setbacks in one form or another, you are simply meeting with a red circuit — an unconscious habit of thoughts that has activated your 'off' switch, restricted the flow of energy, and created an obstacle. You are more than likely wanting to think one way but your heart 'ain't buying it.' Are you pretending not to hear Angel?

If you are engaged in some endeavor simply to make money so that you can do something *else* that will bring you joy, I guarantee first-hand that it will fail. I pursued my career in telecommunications simply for the money. I believed that money would provide me security, which would provide me freedom, which would allow me to do what I *really* wanted to do, which would bring me joy! This career was enticing to me because I was paid a monthly residual income on every client I signed up. Therefore, I surmised, if I worked hard and developed a large client base, I would have a significant guaranteed monthly income *without* having to work every day. Sounds rational, right? Brimming with enthusiasm, I entered into contractual agreements with major telecommunication providers and became a broker-consultant offering the best telecom solution to business clients based on their specific needs.

For two-and-one-half years I worked hard building my business and earned nothing — the expenses exceeded the income. During this period, I also contracted with twenty-four sub-agents from Hawaii to New York, who worked under my contracts which allowed me to earn an additional percentage on their clients as well. Finally, on one glorious day, all of my hard work paid off. I began to earn a six-figure income! And though the money was great, I began to really dislike the business (manifestation begets new perspective), for this job required my being available for phone calls sixteen hours a day! It felt as though I was never off of the phone! This unknown aspect of the job completely conflicted with my core instinct of freedom as I dislike having to be a 'slave' to anything or anyone (even an alarm clock...)! Yet, I continued to rationalize that as soon as I achieved my goal, I could pursue what I really loved: designing and building houses.

As a result of my prior unpleasant building experiences, I decided to build houses on speculation, where you build the home as a finished product for resale. Selling real estate for seven years (another career I had when I was in my twenties), I learned that buying a home is one of the most emotionally-charged purchases anyone ever makes. Furthermore, it becomes even more emotional when people build their 'dream home.' Therefore, by building 'spec' homes, I would avoid the petty, life-draining issues associated with home buyers. My next challenge? To find a way to actualize my dream. My solution? Telecommunications. If I created a sizeable, consistent monthly income, I would have the freedom to build spec homes without needing home buyers to provide the funding. Thus, telecommunications became the path to actualize my dream. What I didn't realize though, was that the negative feelings I harbored for my business were creating a frequency that would culminate in its demise! How did it's demise unfold?

On one magnificent winter day while vacationing in Colorado, I checked my voice mail and became extremely distressed: Fifty-plus messages were awaiting my response! After spending an entire evening listening to them, it appeared that many of my clients' 800 toll-free service — which they relied upon for business, often advertising this number in expensive ad campaigns — had been disconnected by one of my vendors in a financial dispute with their underlying carrier. In that moment, four-and-one-half years of hard work went down the tubes. Much to my husband's amazement, rather than 'going ballistic,' I was quite calm. Actually, I found it to be ironic. I received this dreadful news while surrounded by the most exquisite scenery you could imagine; the breathtakingly beautiful majestic Colorado mountains; the snow-covered trees; the glorious clear blue sky — God in all His glory. Immersed in all of this beauty, the importance of my business paled in comparison to the bigger picture. (Six months earlier, I had also begun to write this book which refocused my thoughts and priorities as well.)

Moral of the story: If you try to find a solution to an issue that does not sing in your heart, or if you attempt to assume Angel's role of Action-ary, you will end up as I did. And you cannot escape your creation, for it's the feeling in your heart — the frequency you project — that creates your reality. So, do only what you love in life, for doing what you love allows for passion, life energy, joy, and abundance to flow to you!

When in Doubt, Just Ask Angel

If you are unclear about the meaning of a sign you are receiving, or if you have a question, simply ask Angel.

- Formulate the questions that you have
- Keep them with you and look at them periodically
- Ask Angel for messages
- Be especially alert in the first seventy-two hours
- Don't try to figure things out
- Ask Angel what you should know now
- Place your order with Angel and your answers will come to you in the form of dreams, daydreams, thoughts, or from other people[39]

Your task is to be sensitive and anticipate your Angacles and then act on the opportunities presented to you.

In *Conversations with God - Book 1*, Neale Donald Walsch conveyed one of the most beautiful lyrical passages I have ever read, and the reason I have included the lyrics of songs throughout these pages:

> *If you have questions — day to day questions... know that you can count on Me to answer them... Listen to Me in the truth of your soul. Listen to Me in the feelings of your heart. Listen to me in the quiet of your mind. Hear me, everywhere. Whenever you have a question, simply know that I have answered it already. Then open your eyes to the world. My response could be in an article already published. In the sermon already written and about to be delivered. In the movie now being made. In the song just yesterday composed. In the words about to be said by a loved one. In the heart of a new friend about to be made. My truth is in the whisper of the wind, the babble of the brook, the crack of the thunder, the tap of the rain. It is in the feel of the Earth, the fragrance of the lily, the warmth of the sun, the pull of the moon. My Truth — and your surest help in the time of need — is as awesome as the night sky, and as simply, incontrovertibly, trustful as a baby's gurgle. It is as loud as a pounding heartbeat — and as quiet as a breath taken in unity with Me.*[40]   —NEALE DONALD WALSCH
> *Conversations with God - Book 1*

May The Force Be With You...

Actually, the "force" is always with you, but in every moment you either allow it to flow or restrict it. And you always know if it is flowing by the way you feel — either you feel good and are allowing the force to flow, or you feel bad and are restricting its flow.

Have you seen the rerelease of the George Lucas movies: *Star Wars, The Empire Strikes Back,* and *Return of the Jedi?* In these movies, Luke Skywalker, the principal character, is taught by Master Yoda about the powers within him; how he must maintain an unwavering belief and to practice focusing his power (sound familiar?). I believe the Universe (God, to me) uses many avenues to convey knowledge to us and that these movies are a reminder to the newer generation of the force within them, as well an attempt to reawaken the rest of us. You might find it interesting to see these movies once again after reading this book. They may have a deeper significance now that you know that the force is, and always has been, within you! 🙂

Eliminate Your Fears and Discover True Freedom

Fear is only an illusion. It is the illusion that creates the feeling of separateness — the false sense of isolation that exists only in your imagination. — GERALDINE SAUNDERS

Fear is pain arising from the anticipation of evil.
— ARISTOTLE
384-322 BC

Fear is the darkroom where negatives are developed.
— MICHAEL PRITCHARD

Worry is a state of mind based on fear. — NAPOLEON HILL

I am an old man and have known many troubles, but most of them never happened. — MARK TWAIN
1835-1910

Fear is static that prevents me from hearing myself.
— SAMUEL BUTLER
1612-1680

Worry never robs tomorrow of its sorrow; it only saps today of its strength. — A. J. CRONIN
1899-1981

Fear is false evidence appearing real. — UNKNOWN

Do the thing you fear, and the death of fear is certain.
— RALPH WALDO EMERSON
1803-1882

Whenever you are afraid you are deceived, and your mind cannot serve the Holy Spirit. This starves you by denying you your daily bread.[41] — A COURSE IN MIRACLES®

There is no peace or happiness for man, until he has erased all fear from the subconscious. Fear is misdirected energy and must be redirected, or transmuted into faith. Jesus Christ said "Why are ye fearful, O ye of little faith? All things are possible to him that believeth."[42]
— FLORENCE SCOVEL SHINN
1871-1940

You've Gotta Accentuate The Positive and Utilize The Negative

Fear is a by-product of old-paradigm programming. Fear locks you in a reactive mode of living, compelling you to resort to manipulation and control. Fear imprisons you in the illusion of powerlessness; it debilitates you; it saps your strength. Fear weighs you down like an incredibly heavy load. It locks you into an endless cycle of envisioning negative possibilities rampant with danger, doubt, terror, and failure. Fear activates your 'off' switch, restricts the flow of energy, ties you in knots, and renders you powerless. To grasp the incredible power of fear, just take a look at history, for the same story has been told and retold countless times: Those who failed to recognize their power and reacted in fear always became victims!

Throughout your life you have been programmed to react in fear. Rather than joyfully anticipating life as it unfolded while feeling all warm, fuzzy, and safe, you were taught to examine a problem, project it into the future, envision its dire consequences, prepare for its manifestation, and then to defend yourself when it manifested. The result? You created an unpleasant life experience rampant with more things to fear.

The well-intentioned media amplifies our fears by continually fore-warning us of an unending stream of dangers that are 'out to get us' if we fail to prepare ourselves. Bombarding us with statistic after statistic of terrible experiences that could potentially harm us — experiences that have harmed unfortunate others (accompanied by graphic video), the media, unknowingly, compounds our fears. And what do we magnetize when we are tuned to the frequency of fear? More fear, which produces more evidence! As an added consequence, what do we pass onto our children? FEAR. "This could happen, that could happen," and in so doing, we perpetuate this never-ending vicious circle.

Think of the attitudes that were prevalent when you grew up. Are we not more fearful, vulnerable, and guarded today? When I was a child, all the kids in our neighborhood were fairly independent. We rode our bikes all over town and our parents rarely checked up on us. During the summer, my parents would occasionally rent a small lake cottage for a week. And each day my sisters and I would stand on the pier and wave frantically at passing boats in an attempt to find someone to take us water-skiing! Can you even believe we did that? I can't — especially now that I am a mom. (Yes, we found some 'takers,' had some fun adventures, great memories, and were just fine....) In the 1950s and 1960s, people *were* less fearful and our parents somehow assumed that we would be fine.

Today the prevailing attitudes are quite different. Today we're afraid of the air we breathe, the water we drink, the food we eat, the schools our children attend, the medicine we take, our family's medical history, people on the street, terrorists, bomb threats, perverts, the Internet, bio-chemical warfare, viruses, antibiotics that are no longer effective against certain viruses, swimming in our lakes and oceans, the cars we drive, contracting a sexually-transmitted disease, losing our job, being outdoors where many terrible things could happen — AD NAUSEAM! And as we heap new fears on top of those we inherited, we may as well hide out in caged shelters twenty-four hours a day, for our statistics surely guarantee that eventually *some* tragedy will befall us!

THIS CYCLE MUST STOP! And we must take an aggressive stand to stop it. In the 1970s I saw the movie Network, where the late actor, William Holden, portrayed a man working as a television news anchor who became so fed up with what was occurring in life that he went 'over the edge' on the air. He called out for viewers to open their windows and shout "I'm mad as hell and I'm not going to take it any more!" It's time we do the same (although we may choose to refrain from the shouting part. We might be arrested for disturbing the peace [if that's what you believe...]. However, if you live in an area where you wouldn't be carted away in a straight jacket — Go for it!!!). What does our frustration indicate? That we're focused in the wrong direction. It's an Angel-Alert — a wrong-way sign meant to ignite our desire for freedom — freedom from all the sinister forces out to 'get' us. Unfortunately, the TV news anchor was not privy to the Four-Step Formula, but fortunately you are!

Your Power Ends When Your Fear Begins

Fear is the most prevalent obstacle in manifesting what you desire in life, however, fear is only present when you don't understand your power. For in truth, nothing terrible can ever happen to you unless you 'invite' it through your thoughts.

Most fears are an anticipation of what might happen in the future, rather than an actual warning of danger. Therefore, it is essential that you learn to differentiate real danger from the irrational feeling of what could possibly occur. And the more you stay connected to source energy, the more you will be able to distinguish between the two. Fear is meant to serve you. It is a natural instinct that helps you to survive. Fear is meant to warn you of real danger, not to rule your life. In fact, you were born with the same abilities that wild (unprogrammed) animals possess: To instinctively know when to flee from danger. However, if you allow your fear — which emanates from your mind rather than your heart — to determine the choices you make in life or how you interpret new information, your fear will become debilitating.

When you feel fearful, recognize that it's simply a wrong-way sign, you are focused on something that is important — something in the opposite direction of what you desire or believe. Feelings of vulnerability and the expectation of negative experiences are the reason they occur! So you must take action and utilize your fear as a Point of Power. Allow your negative feelings to offer you the clarity to illuminate what you really really want want — freedom, safety, and joy!

> *Fear is a natural emotion. All babies are born with only two fears: the fear of falling, and the fear of loud noises. All other fears are learned responses, brought to the child by its environment, taught to the child by its parents. The purpose of natural fear is to build in a bit of caution. Caution is a tool that helps to keep the body alive. It is an outgrowth of love. Love of self.*[43]
> — NEALE DONALD WALSCH
> *Conversations with God -Book 3*

Unresolved Fear Manifests as Reality

> *That which you fear strongly you will experience.*[44]
> — NEALE DONALD WALSCH
> *Conversations with God -Book 1*

Thoughts of what you fear accompanied by intense emotion produce an incredibly powerful frequency that magnetizes evidence very rapidly. Unresolved fear always magnetizes its own solution by becoming reality.

In late 1996, Roman Catholic Cardinal Bernadin of Chicago died of cancer. A friend of mine heard a speech given by the Cardinal days before his death where he spoke of the three things he feared most in life. They were:

1. Being falsely accused.
2. Developing cancer.
3. Dying.

In his speech, the Cardinal explained how the Lord made him face all of his fears. His first fear manifested when he was accused of sexual molestation. And though his accuser later recanted the charges, it was said that the Cardinal had questioned his faith after the charges were made, as many people had believed the accuser. How do you think the Cardinal may have felt after that experience? Do you think he may have always wondered what people really thought of him in light of the numerous reports of priests who were guilty of such deeds? Did he perhaps imagine that people were looking at him and wondering if he was lying? Although his life was filled with a multitude of extraordinary accomplish-ments with people of all faiths, he became more well-known as a result of the molestation charges. In the face of such mixed emotions, would it be difficult to go on as he did before the incident?

Cardinal Bernadin's second fear manifested when he developed cancer. And his third, with his death. It was said that he welcomed death because he would then be with the Lord. I really wonder if he welcomed death because it was the only safe and peaceful place to be. The bottom line? His unresolved fears became his reality. What did he think, believe, expect, and get?

Think about Nicole Brown Simpson.…. Tragically, what did she think, believe, expect, and get?

Acknowledge Your Fears

It is essential to acknowledge your fears, rather than to ignore or deny them. Simply put them in their proper perspective. To assist you in doing that, let's define your fears and examine what lies at their core.

The most common fears are:

- *abandonment* — fear of aloneness
- *lack or scarcity* — fear of not having enough
- *limitation* — fear of not having enough
- *unworthiness or not being liked* — fear of aloneness
- *confrontation* — fear of aloneness
- *authority* — fear of losing freedom
- *success* — fear of aloneness or the unknown
- *change* — fear of aloneness or the unknown
- *death* — fear of aloneness or the unknown
- *enlightenment* — fear of aloneness or the unknown

What to Do When You Feel Fear

- Acknowledge the fear
- Feel your fear and notice the signs of heaviness
- Write down the specifics of what you fear
- Is there a message in your fear? Is it realistic?
- Do you feel inadequate in any way?
- What other thoughts are accompanying your fearful thoughts? More negatives?
- What is your core belief that underlies what you fear?

> *Our deepest fear is not that we are inadequate. Our deepest fear is that we are powerful beyond measure. It is our light, not our darkness that most frightens us. We ask ourselves, who am I to be brilliant, gorgeous, talented, and fabulous? Actually, who are you not to be? You are a child of God. Your playing small doesn't serve the world. There is nothing enlightened about shrinking so that other people don't feel insecure around you. You were born to make manifest the glory of God that is within us. It is not just in some of us: it's in everyone. And when we let our own light shine, we unconsciously give other people permission to do the same. As we are liberated from our own fear, our presence automatically liberates others.*
> — NELSON MANDELA
> from his 1994 inaugural speech

Identifying each of your fears is vital in readjusting the red circuits they have created. Begin by stating your fears:

I fear _____

_____

_____

because _____

_____

_____

I fear _____

_____

_____

because _____

_____

_____

Casting Aside Your Fears

- ～ Relax and clear out every other worry or concern[45]

- ～ Surround yourself with thoughts of love and appreciation[45]

- ～ See whatever it is you fear and state it completely[46]

- ～ Identify where it has lodged within your body[46]

- ～ Let go of the thought that caused the fear and let the fear stand on its own[46]

- ～ Visualize your fear inside a plastic bubble. Watch it, but don't do anything with it. Do not feed it with any additional thoughts as they will further energize it[46]

- ～ Thank your fear for attempting to protect you, but you now understand your power, so you will no longer need protection

- ～ Now watch the bubble burst, releasing your fear[46]

- ～ Don't fight or wrestle with your fear, simply let it leave[46]

- ～ Concentrate on what you want to happen and how you want to feel[46]

- ～ Don't attach any judgment to this feeling, simply let it come in and be at home[45]

Now revise each of your fears to reflect what you really want.

I choose to have_____

_____

_____

_____

because_____

_____

_____

_____

I choose to have_____

_____

_____

_____

because_____

_____

_____

_____

On the Other Side of Fear is Freedom

You gain strength, courage and confidence by every experience in which you really stop to look fear in the face....You must do the thing you cannot do.
— ELEANOR ROOSEVELT
1884-1962

[We] are all coming out of the House of Bondage, [however] your doubts and fears will keep you in slavery.[47]
— FLORENCE SCOVEL SHINN
1871-1940

As soon as a fear image presents itself, it should be halted. Then another image, one with a good outcome, should be willed into the mind. As you reprogram yourself to sense the difference between real danger and unsubstantiated fearful feelings, soon negative images will almost never surface. Then when a negative image pops up, you should heed its message seriously and take warning and action.[48]
— JAMES REDFIELD and CAROL ADRIENNE

When you face your fears they become your friends, helping you to recognize your power and get back on your path, for in reality, they are simply Points of Power from which to create. As you employ the Four-Step Formula on a daily basis, you will be filled with a sense of power, joyous freedom, and will no longer fear the actions of others.

Something Inside "Told Me"

There are many people who listen to their inner guidance and act upon the advice they are receiving even though they have no logical reason to. Consider the following statistics regarding train crashes: On a day that a crash occurs, statistics reveal that there are up to 30 percent fewer people traveling than normal. Why? Something must be intervening and alerting these people to not get on the train.

We have all heard stories about people who acted on their intuition. Some followed their inner guidance and didn't get on an airplane that later crashed. Many stories, in fact, were told in the aftermath of the 1995 bombing in Oklahoma City — stories that spoke of people who had received a 'sign' or had an unusual circumstance dramatically intervene in their lives that prevented them from going to the federal office building that day. Who provided these signs? Angel. Those signs were 'Angel Interventions;' and luckily those folks listened and took inspired action. For in taking that action they were saved from potential tragedy. The moral of the story? Follow your inner guidance and act upon your feelings even though you may not logically understand why.

Know The Good News:
You Completely Control Your Life Experience

We generate our own environment. We get exactly what we deserve. How can we resent the life we've created for ourselves? Who's to blame, who's to credit, but us? Who can change it, any time we wish, but us?[49]

— RICHARD BACH

No man gives to himself but himself, and no man takes away from himself but himself: the "Game of Life" is a game of solitaire; as you change, all conditions will change.[50]

— FLORENCE SCOVEL SHINN

When a man blames others for his failures, it's a good
idea to credit others with his successes.
— HOWARD W. NEWTON

No one can create for someone else. Another person can only influence you to think they can. Therefore, if you are fearful of a certain person or of actions they are taking, do not invite them into your experience through your powerful thoughts. And more importantly, you will not fall prey to someone else's frequency if you 'go to work' daily.

Think about voodoo or black magic. What do you suppose really happens now that you are aware of the Four-Step Formula? People are simply influenced to believe what others tell them. The result? They became a victim of the nocebo effect we spoke of earlier. For as they focus their powerful thoughts on what they fear, they magnetize it into their life experience. On the other hand, think about miracle healers. Some believe these healers possess incredible powers. The result? Miracles can and have occurred — the placebo effect! If you believe what others tell you and accept it as truth, what will happen? THINK, BELIEVE, EXPECT, and GET!

Racism... Simply More Pushing Against

Let us now free ourselves from the tyrants of negative
thinking: we have been slaves to doubts and fears and
apprehension and let us be delivered as Moses delivered
the children of Israel; and come out of the land of Egypt,
out of the House of Bondage. [51] — FLORENCE SCOVEL SHINN
1871-1940

Man's work is with himself, to send out goodwill and
blessings to every man, and the marvelous thing is, that
if one blesses a man he has no power to harm him. [52]
— FLORENCE SCOVEL SHINN
1871-1940

When I hear people speak of reacting unconsciously in a racist manner when they consciously do not believe they are racist, I think of Scherezad — one of my three cats. She is sixteen years old and so sweet, bless her little heart, and not capable of hurting a flea as she is pretty much overweight and arthritic. (She lives to eat — no kidding. Time for the kitty shrink?) She just kind of plods along having difficulty with each step. Nonetheless, when she is in the backyard, the birds start squawking in their fear, warning each other of the predator: "The killer is loose!" *Wrong!*

How many times have you been exposed to crime statistics regarding young black men? These reports have programmed the mass consciousness, each of us, to subconsciously protect ourselves. We instinctively react in fear (our wrong-way sign) just like the birds. And our fear is generally unsubstantiated. I do not believe that the majority of us are racist, but I do believe that there are many people focused on 'pushing against' racism which would subsequently magnetize evidence into their lives by virtue of their powerful beliefs. Unaware of their incredible power, they are unwittingly perpetuating the very racism they are trying to banish.

Here is an example of how racism was in 'my face,' and how I got so caught up in my justification of righteousness, that I became ensnared in the powerful negative energy vortex of racism. After graduating from high school in 1968, I worked as a rental agent for Hertz® Rent-A-Car at O'Hare Field. I really enjoyed working at one of the busiest airports in the world, exposed to a multitude of different people and events where there was always something exciting happening (celebrities, people making movies, etc.). The rental counters were located throughout the airport, therefore the employees had a lot of freedom. This job was fun, fun, fun — in fact, one of my favorites! I worked the three p.m. – midnight shift as my fiancé was in the Army and I was earning money to pay for our wedding. Whenever the opportunity presented itself, I would work the midnight to seven a.m. shift because I could earn time-and-a-half. Working this shift periodically, I became friends with a wonderful, soft-spoken, kind, and gentle black man who was a 'hiker' — he would transport clients to their cars after completing their rental contract. Between flights we would chat and try to stay awake, and on occasion, he would fill my car with gas and take it through the Hertz® car wash. Wasn't that nice? I really liked this man.

Late one evening a flight arrived and a passenger needed help with his baggage. Spotting my friend this man shouted "Hey, boy!" Unfazed, my friend began to walk over to him. However, this man's condescending comment set alarms off in my mind and I became incensed. I then yelled, "Who do you think you are calling 'Boy'?" The man looked at me in disbelief and told me to mind my own business. And I told him that this was not the (Pre-Civil War) South and he had no right to call my friend 'Boy,' let alone ask him to carry his bags. (He certainly would not have referred to me as 'Girl!') I was shouting to my friend *not* to take his bag and he seemed rather confused. The man became quite angry with me and shouted "What's your name, young lady?" Defiantly, I replied "Lauren Olson," and spelled it, "O-L-S-O-N." Well, he wrote a nasty letter about me to Hertz®, but I could not have cared less. No one was going to call my friend Boy!, and I didn't care if I lost my job! My friend's reaction? He never said anything. Actually, I never even stopped to consider his perspective. He may have been angry with me because he may have received a sizeable gratuity from this man. But that didn't matter to me. The *principle* mattered and I believe that no one had the right to address any human being in a way he would not want to be addressed himself. My point? How did you *feel* as I shared my story? Did you agree that my actions were justified? If so, can you see how easy it is to be caught up in a powerful negative energy vortex? Can you see how easy it is to activate your 'off' switch under the guise of righteousness?

One day when Zachary was 7 years old, we were discussing the plight of minorities in our country and he asked me what racism was. Zach attended a Montessori school through the third grade where approximately twenty-five children were enrolled from second to fifth grades in one classroom. Adjacent to a high-tech corridor, the area we live in is very culturally diverse — a microcosm of our world. And Zach's school mirrored that fact. In fact, Zach, being Caucasian, was in the minority. Children of every age, shape, color, and nationality were in his class and we loved that aspect of it! Subsequently, Zach was never exposed to anything *other* than diversity. Therefore, the conclusions he derived about his classmates were based on who they were as individuals. Thus, the idea of racism was intriguing to him.

I explained that in the 1800s, part of our country had very large cotton plantations, however, there were not enough laborers to work in the fields to grow, maintain, and harvest the cotton. So, some 'unconscious' individuals went to Africa and abducted people to perform this work. I described how they tore these people from their families while they vehemently resisted. I explained how these people were treated like animals, rather than the human beings they were. How they were herded onto deplorable ships, and how many people died from this inhumane treatment on their journey to America.

Then I asked him to *feel* what it would be like to have a 'bad guy' grab you, your mommy, or daddy, and take you to a faraway place completely different from your home — a place where you had no freedom and were forced to perform backbreaking labor all day long. And the two of us felt these gut-wrenching feelings to the point of tears.

I further explained that Abraham Lincoln, our sixteenth president, among many other folks, thought that this horrific treatment of people was unconscionable! How could any human being rob another of their right to freedom? President Lincoln believed that slavery was so wrong that he grudgingly decided that in order to abolish it the only solution was war. And as I learned from a television documentary: More people were killed in the Civil War than in both World Wars, the Korean War, and the VietNam War combined!

I know there is much more to the tragedy of racism, but I would like to emphasize the fact that many white men who believed as President Lincoln did about the inalienable rights of any human being, were killed while defending the freedom of all people, regardless of the color of their skin. Perhaps this perspective can serve as a point of refocus, a shift in consciousness, to open the hearts of those who have been victims of racism. If you have been a victim of racism, rather than focusing on all of the injustice, instead focus on one of your white brothers sacrificing his life for the sake of freedom. Think of the sorrow of his family — his children, wife, mother, father, brothers, and sisters grieving over the loss of his life. Honor him for having the courage of his convictions, placing his belief in freedom and justice for all before his own flesh and blood, for he, too, helped to lay the bridge so all of us could live in freedom.

Racism doesn't feel good, therefore it's an Angel-Alert — a wrong-way sign warning that we are focusing on something that is important; something in the opposite direction of what we want. When you think of racism what *feels* better: the progress made so far, or the injustice that still exists? What *feels* better: to love or to blame? What *feels* better: to be mad at the world for handing you a stacked deck, or to appreciate and utilize your negatives the way they were meant to be used — to ignite your desire to live in harmony with others. Remember, you always have a choice about what you give your attention to. Is your cup half empty or half full? When it is half empty, you will, in no uncertain terms, magnetize evidence to reinforce your belief in that emptiness. *Feel* that feeling…. Doesn't feel good, does it? Now think about what it feels like to have your cup half full…. Quite a different frequency, right?

If racism is 'in your face' you have a challenge to overcome, a red circuit to adjust. You must reprogram your powerful thoughts to those of appreciation rather than observation, for when you do, racism will not abide in your experience. Appreciation exists at a higher frequency, therefore, it is incapable of coexisting with the lower frequency of racism. Racism will magically disappear from your life experience when you focus on love and harmony, for as you project the frequencies of goodness, love, and appreciation, you can only attract more goodness, love, and appreciation.

In light of the Four-Step Formula, think about those attempting to force racial equality onto others. How does it feel when someone tries to force something upon you? Do you put up your walls and adopt a defensive posture? Do you fight back and defend your core instinct of freedom? Now think about how it feels to be discriminated against. Are these frequencies not the same? Compare the militant feeling of forcing integration upon someone, to a feeling of love exhibited when someone opens his or her heart and accepts you for the person you truly are.

Let's Put an End to Racism

The topic of slavery and racism was the focus of an Oprah Winfrey show. An older black man, who had lived through the most horrific years of segregation and discrimination, was asked his opinion about the racism that still exists in our country. His reply? "Well just look at you!" (Referring to Oprah's phenomenal success.) He chose to see the positive, not the negative. Through the wisdom of his years, he recognized that much progress *had* been made. Although he recognized that racism had not completely been abolished, he chose to appreciate what had been achieved. He chose not to blame; he chose not to point the finger; he chose not to be angry; *he chose to see the positive.* Following his powerful example is the only way we will ever eliminate racism. We can only heal the gaping wounds of our collective psyche through love and appreciation, for again, those attributes exist at a higher frequency.

To eliminate racism, we must first shift our consciousness, for we cannot *change* consciousness until it is shifted. And consciousness can only be shifted one person at a time using love as the underlying frequency — not anger, militance, revenge, bitterness, or sadness (all wrong-way signs). At our core, we are lovers, not haters. How do we achieve a state of being where love permeates our existence? By understanding Who We Really Are, for that knowledge creates the fertile soil for love to grow. As stated so eloquently on a Hallmark® plaque: "Knowledge is the power that gives us wings to soar." Indeed.

Don't look backward and allow anything to activate your 'off' switch and restrict the flow of life energy to you. There is no evolution in regurgitating the past. It is gone. Use it as it was intended, for the clarity it provided to birth a new creation. Stand in your fresh new Moment of Now and ponder all the wonderful things that lie in front of you, for that feels infinitely better than rehashing the past. Visualize the dream of Martin Luther King, Jr.: Living in a world where people allow and appreciate their differences, where they draw conclusions about one another on the basis and content of one's character.

How can you help to end racism? Appreciate the differences in others. Treat others with dignity, honor, and respect, even if you disagree with them. Extend kindness, compassion, praise, and gratitude to others, for those love-based frequencies will help to eliminate racism from the face of this planet. Furthermore, as you maintain your connection to Angel and allow life energy to flow, you will become a beacon of light for others to follow. For then others may awaken to the fact that life is really meant for living, loving, and laughing! ⊛

Know How to Deal With Intense Negativity

...the Universe is just a big Xerox® machine. It simply produces multiple copies of your thoughts. Now there's only one way to change all that. You have to change your thought about it.[53] — NEALE DONALD WALSCH
Conversations with God - Book 1

If you are distressed by anything external, the pain is not due to the thing itself, but to your estimate of it; and this you have the power to reverse at any moment. — MARCUS ANTONINUS
86-161 AD

Your environment is the physical picture of your thoughts, emotions, and beliefs made visible.[54] — JANE ROBERTS
The Nature of Personal Reality - A Seth Book

Bless a thing and it will bless you. Curse it and it will curse you....If you bless a situation, it has no power to hurt you, and even if it is troublesome for a time, it will gradually fade out, if you sincerely bless it. — EMMET FOX

When you are in the midst of an intensely negative experience, such as being in the depths of despair or feeling extreme anger, don't attempt to refocus your thoughts. It is difficult, if not impossible, to refocus on something positive when you're on the verge of going ballistic. Instead, either go to sleep or distract yourself, for then you will automatically reestablish your connection with source energy. Other suggestions? Go to a movie, sing songs at the top of your lungs, play loud fast music and dance furiously, hit a pillow hard until you are exhausted, clean the house with a vengeance, whatever — just dissipate your negative energy. And don't recriminate yourself if you 'fall off the wagon.' Idealism and faith can be directly disproportionate to the distance of a problem.

Once you have dissipated your negative energy and have reconnected, you can dissect your issue and uncover its origin — the red circuit you are holding. More importantly, however, you would not have experienced this ordeal had you 'gone to work' and ordered harmony and joy from Angel (naughty, naughty….). Don't take my word for it, try it.

How to Solve Problems

~ Consult your Vision Statement, as it defines Who You Choose To Be.

~ Identify the problem followed by the negative aspects of it.

~ List the positive aspects, followed by the opposite of each negative.

~ Ask yourself, "What is it that I want?" "Why do I want it?" "How do I want to feel?"

~ Compare what you want to your Vision Statement and respond according to Who You Choose To Be.

~ Place your order, tune in, and await your Angacles!

How Can You Protect Yourself?

Always begin your day 'going to work' — it's important. Order harmony and joy in everything you do and with everyone you meet. Do not invite anything that could cause harm into your life experience by giving your attention to it. Choose safety for yourself and those around you in everything you do and everywhere you go. Should you encounter a situation that requires protection, focus with intent on what you want and order the outcome. Then listen for guidance and act upon the Angacles that appear. If you find yourself in an accident or disaster, Angel will guide you to safety and to help others do the same. Remember, unresolved fear creates its own reality, so don't focus your powerful thoughts on what you fear. Life is meant for living, loving, and laughing and you have the power within to order that experience! ☯

You and You Alone are Responsible for Your Happiness!

The happiness of your life depends on the quality of your thoughts.
— MARCUS ANTONINUS
86-161 AD

Happiness depends upon ourselves.
— ARISTOTLE
384-322 BC

Keep your face to the sunshine and you cannot see the shadow.
— HELEN KELLER
1880-1968

The man who makes everything that leads to happiness depend on himself, and not upon other men, has adopted the very best plan for living happily.
— PLATO
428-348 BC

Happiness is not a destination. It is a method of life.
— BURTON HILLS

The bottom line is that I am responsible for my own well-being, my own happiness. The choices and decisions I make regarding my life directly influence the quality of my days.
— KATHLEEN ANDRUS

Pain and suffering is inevitable, being miserable is optional.
— ART CLANIN

Happiness is a stock that doubles in a year.
— IRA U. COBLEIGH

Nothing can bring you peace but yourself.
— RALPH WALDO EMERSON
1803-1882

There's no need to recriminate yourself. Simply notice what you have been choosing and choose again.[56]
— NEALE DONALD WALSCH
Conversations with God - Book I

To wait for someone else, or to expect someone else to make my life richer, or fuller, or more satisfying, puts me in a constant state of suspension; and I miss all those moments that pass. They never come back to be experienced again. — KATHLEEN TIERNEY CRILLY

If [people] wish to defy this cosmic law [of attraction] they only have themselves to blame for their unhappiness.[57] — RUTH MONTGOMERY

Happiness is not in our circumstance, but in ourselves. It is not something we see, like a rainbow, or feel, like the heat of a fire. Happiness is something we are.
— JOHN B. SHEERIN

Have you ever had an experience where you felt intense negative emotion, but felt trapped? Were you ever in a classroom where the teacher berated the students, but you had no option but to remain in class? In a job where the boss bullied everyone, but you desperately needed this job, so you felt that there was nothing you could do? In a relationship where you were abused or treated with disrespect, but you stayed because you thought that a family together was certainly better than one that was fragmented? Or if you had no children living at home, you remained because you believed that no one else would want you, or that you would be treated in the same manner by the next person?

These outlooks are simply consequences of old-paradigm thinking. Unaware of your power, you feel trapped because you can't control the circumstances. You believe that you can only feel better if the circumstances are better, or that you must find perfect circumstances and then you'll be happy.[57] Mired in old-paradigm thinking, you don't see how you can respond differently.[58] The result? If you allow your happiness to depend on what someone else does or does not do, you will put yourself in a trap. You cannot control what people think or what they do. People have very different ideas of what is right and wrong and you cannot demand that people change their ways simply to please you, nor would you want to seclude yourself from our beautiful world to avoid what you don't like. What can you do?

First, recognize that there is not a person or place that exists without negative aspects, for opposites in life are essential in giving birth to desire. Therefore, if you leave a relationship, job, or city because of some form of negativity, you will magnetize the same thing in the new place. Why? Because the real culprit is your frequency. Your frequency is so powerful that you will magnetize the same type of situations, events, and people you did previously. Therefore, always remember that

Negativity is not fed
if you do not participate in it.
Think of any negative condition as the
equivalent of a match. It has the potential
for a great deal of damage if it is ignited,
but it can do no harm if you don't strike it.

Your joy and happiness in life do not depend on anyone else. You cannot blame any person or circumstance for your issues, for *you* created them. To avoid these traps, choose not to give your attention to anything that makes you feel bad, for your joy depends only on what give your attention to. Your task is not to look for the perfect place where only the things you want exist, because you will be looking forever, but to instead look for the things you *appreciate* in every place. And as you do, there will be no room left for the bad because when you feel good, you attract good.[59]

Do your part in adding to our world's joy. You have the
ability, power, and freedom to do so.[60]

— ESTHER and JERRY HICKS

To deal with any issue 'in your face,' you must let your power of appreciation outweigh your power of observation.[62] In any situation where you feel trapped, as difficult as it may seem, search for one positive aspect within it and focus on it. Find *one* positive aspect in your teacher, boss, mother, or spouse, and as you focus on that one quality you appreciate, by virtue of the Law of Attraction, you will magnetize another good thought, then another, and another. As a result, your life experience will be altered forever. For whenever you focus on anything that you appreciate, you immediately adjust your frequency to a higher level and subsequently will only magnetize what is in harmony with that frequency. And don't worry about giving your attention for a few moments to something negative. It is not your initial response that creates your order, but the intensity, length of time, and feeling within your heart that holds the creative power.

Who's in Control of Your Destiny? You Are!

We are the masters of our own fate.[62]
— RUTH MONTGOMERY

All you can do in life is be who you are. Some people will love you for you. Most will love you for what you can do for them, and some won't like you at all.
— RITA MAE BROWN

People are often unreasonable, illogical, and self-centered; Forgive them anyway.
If you are kind, people may accuse you of selfish, ulterior motives; Be kind anyway.
If you are successful, you will win some false friends and some true enemies; Succeed anyway.
What you spent years building, someone could destroy overnight; Build anyway.
If you find serenity and happiness, they may be jealous; Be happy anyway.
The good you do today, people will often forget tomorrow; Do good anyway.
Give the world the best you have, and it may never be enough; Give the world the best you've got anyway.
You see, in the final analysis, it is between you and God; It was never between you and them anyway.
— MOTHER TERESA

Esther and Jerry Hicks tell us that each of us alone controls every aspect of our life experience. Keep in mind, though, that some experiences are a result of unintentional creation. Your soul is fully aware of what you are creating, but lovingly allows you to miscreate, for you cannot learn and grow unless you have something to test you. Your miscreations are meant to awaken you to understand the power of your thoughts: that thought creates reality *literally* — positive and negative. Additionally, some of your experiences that may seem to be unintentional were actually a result of your original 'blueprint' — your soul's intentions for growth and experience that you entered life with. However, your blueprint can be transcended in the moment you begin to create *consciously*, for your soul has now fulfilled its ultimate purpose: aligning the physical you, body and mind, with the non-physical you, spirit, and living life from the perspective of Who You Really Are.

How much of what you get in life is controlled by you?
All of it.

How many of the events you participate in, are a result of your choices?
All of them.

How many of the people who are part of your daily experience, are brought to you by you?
Every one of them.

What percentage of your life do you have control over?
One hundred percent.

How many others are currently creating in your experience?
None.

How many others have responsibility for what is happening to you?
Not one other.

What part do odds or fate or luck play in your experience?
None.

Who is the absolute and only creator of your life experience?
YOU are.[63]

When you begin to actualize your authentic power and take responsibility for your life, you will experience the ultimate feeling of true freedom! For when you are able to acknowledge that people choose different things, believe different things, want different things, act in different ways, and none of that can threaten you because the only thing that can affect you is what you *choose*, then you can begin to live freely and joyously.[64] Only then can you embody the greatest joy in life: Unconditional love — truly loving others in spite of their differences as you would want them to love you. (Sounds like a Golden Rule to me!) Ultimately, your challenge is to *appreciate* their differences, for their sometimes bothersome differences contribute to the vast spectrum of choices that allows you and I to decide what we want for our life experience. No diversity + no variety = no choices. It's as simple as that.

Once there is a universal understanding of the Four-Step Formula, we will no longer live life backwards, blaming others for what feels bad in our lives, but will instead seek to understand how and why we have magnetized our unpleasant experiences and capitalize on the opportunity to readjust the red circuits responsible for them.

Remember, your negative feelings serve an important purpose — they are your Points of Power from which to create. They are the catalysts to birth desire within you — desire that summons life energy. And life lived without desire and passion is absolutely no fun and will ultimately culminate in your demise.

Prior to gaining this knowledge, on some level of consciousness, I seem to have been aware of several aspects of it and unknowingly utilized it. The following passages are a few of my life adventures that presented me with moments of truth, moments where I was forced to choose between fear or love.

Adventures with Happy Endings

Fear is the only thing standing between you and your experience of love.[65] — JAMES TWYMAN

Late one evening I ran out of gas on a large interstate highway (before cellular phones were available) and decided to hitchhike to a gas station. (Please understand that I have a core belief regarding the innate goodness in people and do not recommend hitchhiking unless you share my belief. It is my belief that 'wicked' people are those who had probably not been given the knowledge or opportunity to awaken the good within them. In addition, I also view every situation as an opportunity for an adventure.) Although I was hoping that a police officer would drive by, a semi, passing on the opposite side of the expressway, exited, and came back to help me. Something 'inside' told me not to get in his truck, so I thanked the man profusely and told him what a Good Samaritan he was, but would prefer to wait for a police officer. I did not offend him; I acknowledged his kindness. I have no idea what was on his mind when he stopped to help me, but I refuse to think it was anything to fear. I chose to see a Good Samaritan, but I also chose not to get in his truck — I acted on my intuitive feeling. Shortly thereafter, a police officer stopped and rescued me — the 'Damsel in Distress.' (In jest, that's what I shouted as he rolled down his window. He had to think I was a bit looney, but that's okay. He was way too serious, so perhaps I added a little spice to his night! The bottom line? This was my adventure and I was going to have fun getting gas at two o'clock in the morning regardless of what he thought!) My point? I had a *choice*. Did I choose to fear or to love? It was completely up to me and I much prefer fun, joy, and love, over fear and negativity!

Moral of the story: When you are open and joyous, all life experiences can become adventures with happy endings. You may believe that I behaved foolishly because of the many tragic stories regarding hitchhikers you have been exposed to on the evening news. However,

I was centered in my spirit, and even in my ignorance of the Four-Step Formula, my Angel was there to watch over me. The trick is not to disregard your Angelic messages, but to take inspired action from them!

An Averted Robbery?

I experienced yet another situation where I was forced to choose between fear and love. During the seven years that I owned a fine jewelry store in the suburbs of Chicago, I was robbed three times and burglarized once. (What frequency was I projecting???) This factor, along with many others, eventually culminated in the demise of my store, as insurance companies are in business to take in more money than they give out. Consequently, after the fourth occurrence my business became uninsurable.

On one hot summer day during the time my jewelry business was thriving, a rather large, sweaty, unkempt man in a too-small T-shirt trudged into my store with his mouth hanging open, belly hanging out, and hair askew. Not my typical suburban customer! Alarms went off inside me as I imagined yet another robbery. However, this time, I was determined *not* to be robbed. Understand that I am a salesperson at heart and will talk anyone to death if I am nervous and given the opportunity. (My former husband maintained that my success in real estate was largely due to the fact that people would get so tired of listening to me, they would buy a house to shut me up! "OK, OK, we're convinced. We'll take the house!") Well, this fellow didn't have a chance as my dominant intention was not to be robbed. But rather that acting in fear, I employed a different tactic....

As he entered the store, I graciously pulled out a chair and said, "Come on in and sit down. You look awfully hot and it is so dreadful outside." I went on and on and on about the weather, my former real estate career, my singing career, my family and the myriad problems with them, all the robberies I had experienced at the store and how *devastating* they were, and how most people assumed *incorrectly* that I was rich simply because I owned a store — ad nauseam. Well, after a while he just got up and left. No good-bye or anything. Never did look at a piece of jewelry.... As a matter of fact, he never got a word in edgewise. And I *think* I talked myself out of a robbery. Or was it a sale?

Life can be fun and adventurous if you choose that direction. When you walk into your fears, get past them, and understand your power, you can have a great time and live as life is meant to be lived: loving and laughing! ☯

New World Coming

There's a new world coming and it's just around the bend.
There's a new world coming,
this one's coming to an end.
There's a new voice calling, you can hear it if you try
and it's growing stronger with each day that passes by.
There's a brand new morning, rising clear and sweet and free.
There's a new day dawning, that belongs to you and me.
Yes, a new world's coming, the one we've had visions of,
Coming in peace, coming in joy, it's coming in love.
It's coming in love.[66]

Words and Music by Barry Mann and Cynthia Weil

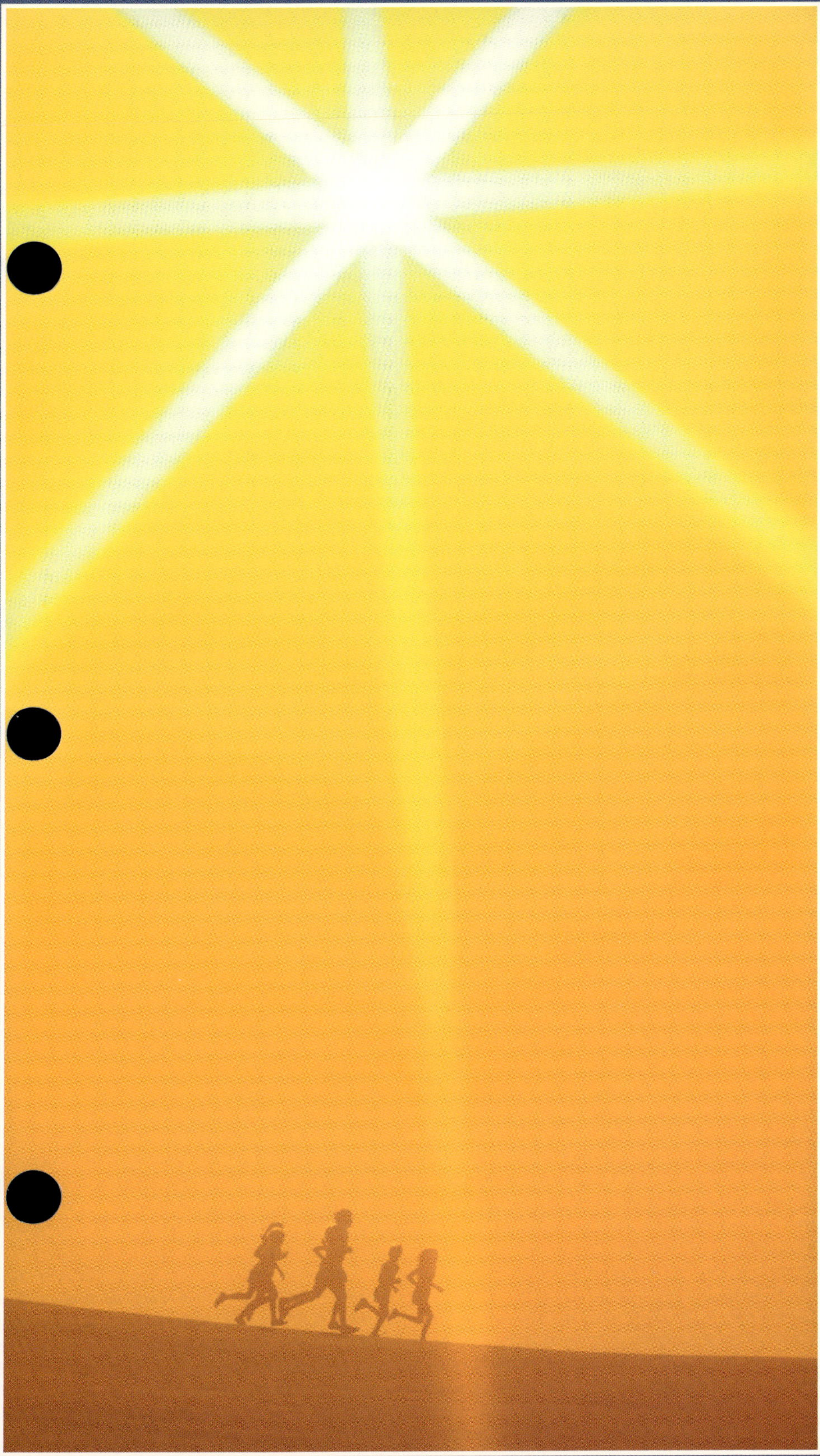

Part VIII

The Physical Body

PART VII

The Physical Body

ATTAINING PERFECT RADIANT HEALTH
AND A BODY YOU DESIRE

Part VIII

The Physical Body

ATTAINING PERFECT HEALTH AND A
BODY YOU DESIRE

The Prognosis for the Future of Illness is Bleak

Measure your health by your sympathy with morning and Spring. If there is no response in you to the awakening of nature, if the prospect of an early morning walk does not banish sleep, if the warble of the first bluebird does not thrill you, know that the morning and spring of your life are past. Thus you may feel your pulse.
— HENRY DAVID THOREAU
1817-1962

Health is the state about which medicine has nothing to say.
— W. H. AUDEN
1907-1973

A good physician is a changer of beliefs. He replaces an idea of illness with one of health. Whatever methods or drugs he uses will not be effective unless this change of belief takes place.[1]
— JANE ROBERTS
The Nature of Personal Reality - A Seth Book

The field of medicine, as in no other, poses the most formidable challenge for the application of the Four-Step Formula because of its far-reaching implications. For applying the Formula to what ails our physical bodies can literally mean the difference between life and death. In this arena we are faced directly with the full impact of years and years of deeply entrenched core beliefs accompanied by deeply entrenched fears — a recipe for disbelief, hence, great resistance. Therefore, I purposely put the chapters on illness and health at the end of the book, for to achieve a state of perfect radiant health using the Four-Step Formula, it is beneficial to have achieved prior visible results utilizing the Formula. So, if you turned to this section before completing the work in the preceding sections, you will probably encounter difficulty in achieving results. However, if you have laid a foundation block by block, followed my instructions like a good little person, and have experienced results, you will only have to expand your consciousness a bit further to effectively apply the Four-Step Formula — think, believe, expect, then get — to your body.

What is the future of healing? I may have gotten a 'peek' a few years ago....

In 1993, my husband, son Zachary (then two-and-one-half years-old), and I went skiing in Colorado. While Ken and I skied during the day, we hired a lady to care for Zach. After babysitting for a few days, she felt that Zach was exhibiting symptoms of an ear infection and suggested that we see a doctor before our flight home. When Zach and I walked into the doctor's office, I spotted a very unusual plaque adorning the waiting room wall that read:

Today, healing is achieved through the miracle of modern medicine and your body's spiritual awareness.

Tomorrow, all healing will be achieved through your body's spiritual awareness.

Okay...? Hmmm.... Interesting? I couldn't wait to meet this guy! What kind of doctor would advertise *that* message.

First order of business? Zach was fine — no ear problem. (Why was I led to this doctor? Was he an Angacle?) Second order of business? This doctor was a wonderful, kind man. When I inquired about the unusual plaque, he told me that he had been 'instructed' in his daily meditations to have it framed and to place it on the wall of his waiting room. He was further instructed to write a letter to all of his friends reflecting on his life's journey and all that he had come to believe. Well, within five minutes we were buddies. (I got a letter....) We hugged each other and exchanged book titles that were significant in our searches for truth in life. (What is that saying: The teacher will appear when the student is ready?) ☺

You Have An Incredible Body!

The body is a sacred garment. It's your first and last
garment; it is what you enter life in and what you depart
life with, and it should be treated with honor.
— MARTHA GRAHAM
1894-1891

There's lots of people in this world who spend so much
time watching their health, that they haven't the time to
enjoy it.
— JOSH BILLINGS
1818-1885

One evening while sleeping in an unfamiliar bed in a hotel room, I fell
asleep on my arm and abruptly awoke when it fell on the floor. As I
picked it up it felt so heavy! What a very strange feeling. My arm, for all
intents and purposes, was dead. However, 'I' was completely whole in my
mind. Once my blood surged back through my veins and my arm
'resurrected,' I experienced an *aha!* moment — a divine revelation: I
was not my body, rather, it was a physical extension of me, and together
we were one. And by inhabiting this body I was able to experience many
wonderful aspects of life. In that moment I gained a whole new
appreciation for the marvelous vehicle I inhabited!

I recall a few other provocative *aha!* moments in my life — moments
where my mind and body appeared to 'separate.' While learning to
slalom ski (on one water ski as opposed to two), I experienced numerous
dramatic 'spills,' but tumbles in the water are generally not too serious
because water is obviously pliable. The challenge and fun in slalom
skiing lies in traversing back and forth across the boat's wake (the V-
shaped wave behind the boat formed by the propeller's underwater
agitation) in a sort of figure-eight pattern. As you cut through or jump

the wake, you are attempting to lean at an acute angle while applying pressure to the ski at certain points. During this process, you are traveling faster than the boat speed of 32–35 m.p.h., consequently, if you happen to fall, you have gathered a great deal of speed and momentum which adds to the intensity of the fall.

Oftentimes in the midst of a precarious fall, something peculiar would occur: My body would skip like a stone over the water with such force and speed that I would find myself underwater unable to ascertain which direction was up. In those moments, it felt as though my mind would take a leave of absence, translate the event as perilous, and choose not to participate in it — "No thank you, not for me!" In fact, I felt as though I entered an altered state of consciousness, one where I was completely aware of what was occurring — having a sort of detached birds-eye perspective of the ordeal — yet one where I was unaware of any discomfort to my physical body. Intriguing? (Actually, these experiences were, and still are, pretty 'cool.' I refuse to grow up!)

Looking back on my life, I have experienced quite a few situations where this "mind/body separation" occurred — all in times of seeming peril. You may have heard similar stories recounted by others who had undergone perilous moments in their lives. Although their physical bodies were injured, sometimes critically or even mortally, they were completely unaware that they had been harmed.

Could this transition of consciousness be similar to what we experience when our physical body dies? Would 'I' still be fully conscious as I was when my arm fell asleep, or my body was perilously flying through the air?

Imagine not having a body. Imagine what it would be like to be in spirit rather than physical form. Imagine what you could not do. You couldn't hug anyone. I don't think sex would be possible. You couldn't enjoy eating wonderful food. You couldn't smell the delicious fragrances all around you. You couldn't hear the wonderful sounds of nature and music. You couldn't feel the exhilaration of pushing your body to its physical limits athletically. (At least, I don't *think* you could....)

Imagine what actor/director Christopher Reeve undergoes every day after being paralyzed. What kind of appreciation do you think he now has for his former fully-functioning body? What kind of desire was born within him for perfect radiant health as a result of his accident? I actually believe there is a greater message in his circumstance because I don't believe that anything in life is an accident. I also believe that he has the ability to achieve a state of total wellness (I'll tell you how later), and as a result of his fame, can influence others to achieve the same state of wellness. Could that be his Mission in life?

Do You Appreciate the Magnificent Creation You Inhabit?

Have you ever marveled at your body? How it breathes in oxygen and exhales carbon monoxide? How the food you eat is broken down into the nutrients and fuel your body needs to maintain your health while simultaneously eliminating everything it does not need? How your blood carries these nutrients to the areas requiring them? How your body has incredible tactile sensors that allow you to feel the silky fur of a kitty or the painful prick of a pin? How your muscles react instinctively to what you want to do or where you want to go? How your brain processes a profusion of information and responds with thoughts, words, or actions? How the miraculous creation you inhabit has the ability to repel germs and viruses — all sorts of things — and repair itself even after being cut open?

Were you aware that each of the billions of cells that compose your body possesses an exact duplicate of you? (Your DNA!) And each one of those cells performs approximately six trillion functions per second, at the same time aware of and in harmony with what all the other cells are doing![2]

Scientist Guy Murchie tells us that the body can be understood as a corporation with one hundred organs, two hundred bones, six hundred muscles, trillions of cells, and octillions of atoms — all working together to make a whole person. "No one could critically examine it without a respect amounting to awe!"[3] Every second of every day your body performs a myriad of delicate and precise tasks in absolute orchestration. And, I might add, without your instruction!

I recall seeing my Mother immediately after she had undergone open heart by-pass surgery. She was lying unconscious on a cold slab of steel in intensive care and looked dead. She had just been cut from stem to stern; her rib cage pried open; veins cut out of her leg to be used in her heart; and sewn up again! Is that a horrific thought or what? Yet, three days later, she was walking down the hall of the hospital! It was absolutely amazing to witness her body's ability to function after it had literally been taken apart and put back together only a few days earlier. I don't mean to gross you out, but think about the miracle of it....

Your body is one incredible, miraculous creation!

What do you think about your body? Are you in awe of your amazing apparatus? Or are you like most who take it for granted and look in the mirror criticizing all the things you don't like: "If only this were different and that was different."

Have you ever really appreciated the magnificence of the awesome body you inhabit? If not, you may want to reconsider the messages you are sending to your body. Why? Your body responds only to what you project to it through your powerful thoughts and beliefs.

Uh, oh!!

Dr. Herbert Benson provides us a scientific insight into the interaction between our brains and the messages we send to our bodies.

> *Our brains are wired for beliefs and expectancies. When activated, the body can respond as it would if the belief were a reality, producing deafness or thirst, health or illness.*[4]
> — DR. HERBERT BENSON

> *Belief can...work against us. The brain/body does digest unpleasant images and can fulfill ugly prophecies.*[5]
> — DR. HERBERT BENSON

So, what instructions are *you* sending to your body? Are the beliefs you hold creating green circuits — the kind that allow you to live, love, and laugh — or have you gathered a few red circuits here and there?

Remember, Angel is listening, taking orders, and delivering.... ☺

The Mystery of the Placebo is No Longer a Mystery!

Placebos can have profound [healing] effects on organic illness, including incurable malignancies.
— DR. A. K. SHAPIRO
The American Journal of Psychotherapy

A placebo is a 'sugar pill' used in clinical studies to determine the effectiveness of a drug. Upon dividing a group of people suffering from a specific illness, each person is given either the drug being tested or a placebo. Researchers then monitor these groups for a specific period of time to analyze the drug's performance. Assuming those receiving placebos would be the control group — the group whose illness would take its natural course and progressively get worse — they then compare and measure the drug's effectiveness against those receiving placebos. In study after study, however, researchers met with an unforseen circumstance: Many folks receiving placebos either improved or overcame their illnesses!

The unsuspecting researchers were unaware of the formidable power they were rendezvousing with: The power of belief — the power to create reality. However, because no scientific explanation exists for the findings generated by placebos, researchers simply minimized, underplayed, or explained this nuisance as an anomaly. This placebo-effect has become more of an annoyance, hampering their ability to quantify the effectiveness of their drugs, rather than a profound scientific discovery.

As science continues to ignore the data on placebos, study after study continues to amass more and more uncomfortable findings — 'evidence' growing larger and larger. An indisputable mysterious factor is revealing itself — one that is not yet quantifiable, but one that can no longer be ignored or denied. Dr. Herbert Benson offers an insight as to why science has been reluctant to delve into the placebo-effect: "Because medicine separated and compartmentalized the realms of mind and body for so long, the discipline never got the respect it deserved."[6]

> We want the facts to fit the preconceptions. When they don't, it's easier to ignore the facts than to change the preconception.
> — JESSAMYN WEST

I believe that another reason exists for the lack of interest in the placebo-effect: fear. If the truth of the placebo-effect were known, every specialty and subspecialty of medicine would be affected and change would result. And change is frightening — it strikes terror in our hearts because it forces us to step outside of our comfort zones. Change requires that we reconsider what we have accepted as truth — to experience an uncomfortable stage of uncertainty — a sinking feeling in the pit of our stomachs. A feeling that might resemble what a trapeze artist feels the first time he is released by teammate #1 and has yet to be caught by teammate #2 — a sinking feeling of being in midair for what seems to be an incredibly long period of time without knowing whether he will be caught or not. Consequently, no one chose to open "Pandora's Box."

As history poignantly demonstrates, however, this blatant state of denial — repressing the whole truth — inevitably produces those who can *clearly* see the truth: "The emperor is naked. He doesn't have any clothes on!" For the truth will always emerge — it cannot be pretended away; it cannot be denied; it cannot be suppressed. In reality, however, there is little to fear, because change is never cataclysmic. It occurs gradually. And a few brave souls are helping to bring about this gradual change, for they have challenged the accepted dogma of the current scientific paradigm. They are Dr. Herbert Benson, Dr. Andrew Weil, Dr. John E. Sarno, Dr. Brian Weiss, and Dr. 'Patch' Adams (whose story was told in the movie *Patch Adams* starring Robin Williams). These visionaries had the fortitude to not only brave the sneers of their colleagues, but to also jeopardize their careers in the name of Truth. These 'Bringers of Light' (and there are probably many many others who have taken the same quantum leap into the dark abyss of controversy), have courageously followed their hearts to help usher in a new stage of evolution for humankind — a time to see the truth, apply it, and as a result, recreate our world.

Let's take a closer look at the fear we have of opening Pandora's Box. If we were to look deeper into this story, we would be pleasantly surprised, for this story actually ends on an optimistic note: After all of the evils are released upon mankind, *hope* is left lying at the bottom of the box.

To assist you in "seeing the light," I have included the following case studies that illustrate the remarkable scientific findings of the placebo-effect — the power of belief.

A dynamic example of the power of a placebo, the power of a doctor, and the power of influence, comes from a study of patients afflicted with bleeding ulcers. Upon dividing this group in two, the first was informed by doctors that a new drug had been developed that would undoubtably provide them relief. The second group was informed by *nurses* that a new experimental drug would be administered, but there was little information about the effects of the medication. The results? 75 percent of the first group received relief compared to only 25 percent in the second group. However, that's not the most remarkable aspect of this study because something even more amazing occurred: *both* groups had actually received the identical 'drug' — a placebo![7] What did they think, believe, expect, and get?

Dr. Herbert Benson, author of *Timeless Healing: The Power and Biology of Belief*, cites study after study after study that confirms the Four-Step Formula. In fact, he explains that placebos are shown to be effective in the *majority* of cases! Here are a few of the studies that Dr. Benson cited:

> *In 1979, Dr. Benson and his colleague Dr. David P. McCallie Jr. reviewed a long history of therapies designed to alleviate angina pectoris — pain in the chest and arms caused by decreased blood flow to the muscle of the heart. The treatments, ranging from injections of cobra venom to surgeries to remove the thyroid or parts of the pancreas, were enthusiastically introduced medical practice years ago even though today we know they were misguided. But despite there being no physiologic reason these techniques should have worked, they often did. When these ersatz techniques were used and believed in, they were effective 70 to 90 percent of the time, working two to three times more often than doctors had said they would. And interestingly, later, when physicians began to doubt whether these treatments worked, their effectiveness dropped to 30 to 40 percent.[8]*
>
> — DR. HERBERT BENSON

What did they think, believe, expect, and get?

In 1994, Dr. Alan H. Roberts and his colleagues at the Scripps Clinic and Research Foundation, looked at medical and surgical treatments of bronchial asthma, herpes simplex cold sores, and duodenal ulcers. Employing a retrospective approach,...Robert's team studied treatments once thought to be successful but later debunked. They concluded, according to Clinical Psychology Review, that "under conditions of heightened expectations" [step 3 of the Formula] the power of the placebo-effect "far exceeds that commonly reported in literature." A full 70% of the patients they studied experienced excellent or good results from bogus treatments.[9]   — DR. HERBERT BENSON

What did they think, believe, expect, and get?

Take the case of 2000 men who were treated with beta-blocking drugs after having heart attacks. It turned out that doubts or negative beliefs, translated into actions, helped to determine whether they lived or died.[10]
                                          — DR. HERBERT BENSON

What did they think, believe, expect, and get?

Reported in a 1990 paper in the British medical journal, The Lancet, *this investigation compared the effects of beta-blockers, a drug that prevents hormones from causing the heart to beat too rapidly or forcefully, to the effects of placebos. The study revealed that men who did not adhere well to the treatment regimen — whether they received active medication or inert placebos — were 2.6 times more likely to die within a year of follow-up than were good adherers. It didn't matter whether these men were taking the beta-blockers or placebos; if they took the pills less than 75% of the time, they were twice as likely to die as those who took the medicine or sugar pills more consistently. Remarkably, the death rate among those who did not take their placebos was much higher than for those who took their placebos regularly.*[11]
                                          — DR. HERBERT BENSON

What did they think, believe, expect, and get?

In *Anatomy of an Illness*, author Norman Cousins cited a study that tested the drug Laetrile®. After exhaustive research, our nation's leading cancer centers were unable to find any medicinal value in this drug. However, according to documented accounts, after giving Laetrile® to a number of people suffering from cancer, many recovered.[12]

What did they think, believe, expect, and get?

In a study conducted by Dr. Thomas C. Chalmers of the Mount Sinai Medical Center in New York, two groups tested the theory of ascorbic acid (vitamin C) as a cold preventive. The results?

> *The group on placebos who thought they were on ascorbic acid, had fewer colds than the group on ascorbic acid who thought they were on placebos.*[13]
> — DR. THOMAS C. CHALMERS
> *Mount Sinai Medical Center*

What did they think, believe, expect, and get?

Dr. Benson believes that the time has come to address the spiritual crisis in the field of medicine — that the findings on placebos, the power of belief, can no longer be dismissed:

> *As medical researchers, we expect some exceptions and anomalies from our statistics. But the finding that patients who consistently follow doctor's orders, believing that doing so would make them well, were twice as likely to live, is sobering.*[14]

> ∿ ∿ ∿

> *[P]hysicians could no longer dismiss the phenomenon [placebos] as a relatively minor factor, because now it seemed to have an effect the majority of the time.*[15]

> ∿ ∿ ∿

> *[W]e are, without a doubt, at a turning point in the history of belief in healing. Clearly the public is ahead of medicine in articulating the void — the lack of regard for human personalities, for the beliefs and priorities we possess as individuals, or for the spiritual quality of life, which often feels more important to people than the physical reality. Medicine must soon attend to this craving for meaning, this demand that health be defined by more than test results and vital signs.*[16]

What stands in our way? Only a stodgy dichotomy separating mind from matter, only an accepted system, which this accumulation of brain research will eventually topple. The medical system is in crisis... and the best remedy of all may lie in the promise of remembered wellness, and in the yet untapped resources that our brilliant brains and visceral souls make possible.[17]

— DR. HERBERT BENSON

The Four-Step Formula is at the genesis of every life experience, and its implications are far-reaching. Essentially it conveys that any modality of medicine or healing has at its inception, belief. Furthermore, as you now know, the placebo-effect is not exclusive to healing or illness, it merely validates the fact that thought creates reality!

For to no other creature in the kingdom of our Earthly mother is given the power of thought. All the beasts that crawl and birds that fly live not of their own thinking but of a law that governs all life. Only to the sons and daughters of man is given the power of thought. And even that thought can break the bonds of death. Do not think that because it cannot be seen that thought has no power, for I'll tell you truly that the lightning that cleaves the mighty oak, the quaking the opens up cracks in the earth, these are like the play of children compared to the power of your thought. Mankind has forgotten this power for man does not see the world of spirit.

— ESSENSE GOSPEL OF PEACE

When we are able to fully absorb and integrate this profound truth in our lives, we will begin to live as life is meant to be lived: loving and laughing!

For additional case studies regarding the power of belief, I highly recommend Dr. Benson's *Timeless Healing: The Power and Biology of Belief.* He has amassed an incredible amount of compelling scientific evidence that confirms the Four-Step Formula (just in case the 1000+ quotations I have provided are not convincing enough for you). Dr. Benson credentials? He is the founder of the Harvard Mind/Body Medical Institute at the New England Deaconess Hospital in Boston, chief of its Division of Behavioral Medicine, and on staff at the Harvard Medical School. ☯

Warning:
What You Were Taught about Illness Can Be Fatal!

The past few years have seen a steady increase in the number of people playing music in the streets. The past few years have also seen a steady increase in the number of malignant diseases. Are these two facts related?
— FRAN LEBOWITZ

We have not lost faith, but we have transferred it from God to the medical profession. — GEORGE BERNARD SHAW
1856-1950

Doctors can be very helpful in plummeting you into the depths of despair.[18]
— ESTHER and JERRY HICKS

Overnight, patients diagnosed with chronic medical problems or illnesses began to think of themselves as "sick," and the effect that label had on their psyches and their physical health was substantial.[19]
— DR. HERBERT BENSON

Illness is the doctor to whom we pay most heed; to kindness, to knowledge, we make promises only; pain we obey.
— MARCEL PROUST
1871-1922

From the moment you arrive in this world, dedicated, well-meaning doctors probe and prod your body looking for things that might jeopardize your well-being. As you grow older, they admonish you to do routine self-examinations; to be on the constant lookout for any aches or pains 'out of the ordinary.' How do you define "ordinary?" Could this ache or that pain be ordinary? In an intensified state of vulnerability, each ache or pain that you experience becomes a potential dreaded disease capable of imposing a death sentence upon you.

As doctors impart their powerful beliefs in our most impressionable moments, most of us accept what they believe without question! And what happens when we believe something? Angel is waiting in the wings (no pun intended...). To make matters worse, when we become ill we *expect* to be given some form of drug to alleviate our symptoms. In fact, if we don't receive a prescription, we feel that perhaps nothing was wrong with us, and then we feel foolish. We might be labeled a "hypochondriac." The consequence? We become hooked on drugs to validate our illnesses.

Author Norman Cousins, in *Anatomy of an Illness*, warned us of the perils of the indiscriminate and promiscuous use of drugs. He believed that the unremittingly barrage of drug advertising that we are exposed to was setting the stage for a mass anxiety neurosis — creating chronic ailers and psychological cripples out of millions of people. To appreciate just how pervasive pharmaceutical advertising is, just count the number of drug commercials you see on TV within a given period of time. You will be blown away! It was Mr. Cousin's belief that as we view the continual onslaught of drug commercials, we become brainwashed into the "hypochondriac's clamorous and morbid world."[20] Why? We unequivocally accept that all of these illnesses exist, and, perhaps more importantly, we need not worry, for these wonderful cures will alleviate their symptoms!

> *Despite the fact that the body is the grandest problem-solver there is, quietly and perpetually sustaining life, overcoming billions of obstacles without our conscious imperatives for it to do so, we don't trust it. Instead, we turn to our medicine cabinets. Our doctor's first impulse is to prescribe something for us, and we fully expect to emerge from these visits with a prescription in hand.[21]*
> — DR. HERBERT BENSON

> *Remedial medicine is not really healing; it is the suppressing, neutralizing, or banishing of symptoms.[22]*
> — CEANNE DEROHAN
> as conveyed in *The Right Use of Will*

Suppression of symptoms is not the way Body heals itself.
The practice of taking drugs for pain often masks early
symptoms so that the person is not aware of the problem
until it is acute and advanced.[23] — CEANNE DEROHAN
as conveyed in *The Right Use of Will*

Hippocrates (460-370 bc), the first major historical name in medicine, whose philosophies gave birth to the "Hippocratic Oath" that doctors promise to uphold upon graduating from medical school, was both a theoretician and practitioner. Attempting to bridge the gap between disease and its treatment, Hippocrates believed that it was natural for the body to heal itself. He believed that the essential function of the physician was to *avoid* any treatment that might interfere with the healing process or harm the body.[24] Do you think that drugs or knives might interfere with or delay the body's healing process?

Centuries ago, the famous philosopher, Voltaire, was wise enough to recognize the true function of the medical field:

The art of medicine consists of amusing the patient while
nature cures the disease. — VOLTAIRE
1694-1778

Throughout the annals of time, healers have used extraordinary methods to cure patients. One of the most unpleasant methods? Leeches to suck the 'bad' blood from patients. Yet, even under these horrific circumstances, many patients successfully overcame their illnesses. Why? Norman Cousins explained in *Anatomy of an Illness*, that these people were given something far more valuable than drugs. They held "a robust belief that what they were getting was good for them." By simply reaching out to a doctor, they believed and expected they would be helped, and they were.[25] In reality though, what was really underlying the cures? *The Four-Step Formula* — think, believe, expect, and get.

In primitive tribes the medicine man is thought to possess extraordinary gifts of healing and as a result, cures many people. But what is underlying his cures? *The Four-Step Formula* — think, believe, expect, and get.

In cases of heredity or genetic predisposition, doctors inform us that statistics imply that we are likely to develop a certain disease because a member of our family suffered from it (planting the seed of illness, hence, fear, in our brains). But what is really underlying disease? Simply the Four-Step Formula. Think, believe, expect, and get.

Genes are not inherited. Thoughts are.[26]
— ESTHER and JERRY HICKS

> *A man believing he has heart trouble will finally, through his own anxiety, affect the functioning of his involuntary system until his heart is definitely harmed if the belief goes unchecked. The conscious mind directs the so-called involuntary systems of the body, and not the other way around.*[27]
>
> — JANE ROBERTS
> *The Nature of Personal Reality - A Seth Book*

Why are more and more people developing cancer and succumbing to AIDS in this age of advanced medicine, science, and technology? Just think about the Four-Step Formula — think, believe, expect, and get.

Fundamentally, what we have been taught about illness and disease is negative — a wrong-way sign. When we speak of illness, however, we are confronted with not only the deeply entrenched beliefs of the mass consciousness, but also the formidable power of the medical profession who have an arsenal of statistics, a litany of evidence, to prove whatever they say is true (all based on fundamentally flawed old-paradigm beliefs.)

> *Body does not just "get sick," contrary to popular opinion. Disease does not just travel from person to person, and germs do not spread disease. Modern science has been spending a lot of time and money tracking down the cause of disease but has limited the search so far to studying only the symptomatic result of spiritual balance.*[28]
>
> — CEANNE DeROHAN
> as conveyed in *The Right Use of Will*

> *The most educated Western doctors will look with utter dismay and horror at the thought of a chicken being sacrificed in a primitive witch doctor's hut, and yet will consider it quite scientific and inevitable that a woman sacrifice two breasts to cancer. The doctor will simply see no other way out, and neither will the patient.*[29]
>
> — JANE ROBERTS
> *The Nature of Personal Reality - A Seth Book*

In *Conversations with God - Book 3*, it is conveyed that it is now imperative that we comprehend and utilize our authentic power. For as technology advances without an understanding of how life really operates, an ominous potential for mankind is created.

> *By developing medicines to do the work that your bodies were intended to do, you've created viruses so resistant to attack that they stand poised to knock out your entire species…If you are not careful, your own technology — that which was created to serve you — will kill you.*[30]
>
> — NEALE DONALD WALSCH
> *Conversations with God - Book 3*

Your Choice: Victim or Creator

The medical profession is unwittingly influencing us to follow their recommendations which we now know are backwards! But our Angels are saying "No, no, no! This is important! You don't want this!" However, in our illusion of powerlessness and dominant instinct to survive, we accept what we have been taught, fear what we have been taught, believe what we have been taught, and have concrete evidence to prove what we have been taught — hospitals brimming over with people who are dying proof! In *The Nature of Personal Reality*, Jane Roberts tells us that hospitals are the worst place to deal with illness. Think about what hospitals are and what they do. They isolate groups of folks with negative thoughts about illness where the contagion of beliefs spread. These beliefs are then reinforced by well-intentioned professionals in the medical field and accepted unequivocally as truth.

> *The ill are gathered together and denied all their normal and natural conditions, including the compensating motivations that alone would sometimes be enough to restore health if given time. This isolation would be unfortunate enough without the application of drugs meant to help, but often given without understanding. ...For all practical purposes, the ill are put into prison. They are forced to concentrate upon their condition. All of this applies quite apart from any other dehumanizing effects, such as overcrowded [understaffed] conditions, the denial of human privacy, and often the negation of dignity. The individual is made to feel powerless, at the mercy of doctors and nurses who often do not have the time or energy to be personable or to explain his [or her] condition in terms that he can understand. The patient is therefore forced to transfer his own sense of power to others, which further deepens his misery; this in turn reinforces the sense of powerlessness that initiated his condition....Healings occur, but they do so despite the system and not because of it.[31]* — JANE ROBERTS
> *The Nature of Personal Reality - A Seth Book*

How did we end up in this dreadful predicament? By not understanding the Four-Step Formula — how thought creates reality. So, now let's apply the Formula to our advantage. Let's think, believe, and expect, so we can get what we want. Then we can get on with our real task: living life as a joyous magical experience filled with love and laughter! ☺

We're All Alone

Outside the rain begins and it may never end.
So cry no more, on the shore a dream will take us out to sea
Forever more, forever more.
Close your eyes and dream
And you can be with Me,
'Neath the waves, through the caves of hours
long forgotten now, we're all alone.
Close the windows calm the light
and it will be all right.
No need to bother now
Let it out, let it all begin
Learn how to pretend.
Once a story's told, it can't help but grow old
Roses do, lovers too, so cast your seasons to the wind
And hold Me, dear, oh, hold Me, dear
Close the windows calm the light
and it will be all right
Let it out, let it all begin
All's forgotten now, my love
We're all alone, We're all alone.[32]

Words and Music by Boz Scaggs

Wake Up!
Illness is Your Last Wake - Up Call!

Your biography becomes your biology.[33] — CAROLYN MYSS

Illness is a state of mind — it has nothing to do with germs or heredity — it is the way you use your thoughts.[34] — ESTHER and JERRY HICKS

One way to get high blood pressure is to go mountain climbing over molehills. — EARL WILSON

Remember, even false beliefs will seem to be justified in terms of physical data, since your experience...is the materialization of those beliefs.[35] — JANE ROBERTS
The Nature of Personal Reality - A Seth Book

You don't get ulcers from what you eat. You get them from what's eating you. — VICKI BAUM

Doubts and fear poison the mind and body and imagination run riot, attracting disaster and disease.[36] — FLORENCE SCOVEL SHINN
1871-1940

Medicine is not about the human body; it is about the human mind. It is about guilt, and fear, and blame, and unworthiness, and loneliness.[37] — ESTHER and JERRY HICKS

When Angel has transmitted wrong-way sign after wrong-way sign and you have either intentionally or unintentionally ignored the messages, illness will be your last wake-up call. Some issue in your life has needed attention, recognition, acknowledgment, or change, and rather than dealing with it, you may have attempted to rid yourself of it. You may have shared it with others hoping to dilute it, or you may have continuously worried about it to the degree that you could take no more. The result? Your 'off' switch was activated and as a result, your body began to shut down because you were restricting the flow of life energy.

You Must Find the Root Cause of Your Illness

Illnesses usually represent unfaced problems…and these dilemmas embody challenges meant to lead you to greater achievement and fulfillment.[38] —JANE ROBERTS
The Nature of Personal Reality - A Seth Book

When you have an unresolved issue in your life, your repressed energy will accumulate until it finds an outlet — a path of least resistance. What defines a path of least resistance? An ailment that you have focused on or feared for a long period of time. For example: If you believe that you are pre-disposed to a certain illness — a heart attack, cancer, or even an old football injury — that particular ailment will have magnetized enough energy to become your path of least resistance.

Illness and pain are sending a message that fortunately *cannot* be ignored. What is the message? Think back. A wrong-way sign that was offered much much earlier was ignored; so it grew larger. And it was ignored again, so it grew even larger still. Your illness is compelling you to ask yourself, "What is bothering me? What is it that I want that I believe I cannot have?" So, now it's up to you to heed your sign and act on it, for it is not possible to feel negative emotion on any subject, such as illness, and manifest its opposite, wellness, into your life. They are projecting incompatible frequencies — they are at opposite ends on the health circuit. Therefore, when you feel negative emotion and do nothing about it, you are literally asking for what you don't want.

Practitioners of energy medicine believe that the human energy field contains and reflects each individual's energy. It surrounds us and carries with us the emotional energy created by our internal and external experiences — both positive and negative. This emotional force influences the tissue within our bodies… In this way, your biography — that is, the experiences that make up your life, becomes your biology.[39] —DR. CAROLYN MYSS

Every thought you have had has traveled through your biological system and activated a physiological response. Some thoughts are like depth charges, causing a reaction throughout the body. A fear, for instance, activates every system of your body: your stomach tightens, your heart rate-increases, and you may break into a sweat. A loving thought can relax your entire body. Some thoughts are more subtle, and still others are unconscious. Many are meaningless and pass through the body like wind through a screen, requiring no conscious attention, and their influence upon your health is minimal. Yet each conscious thought — and many unconscious ones — does generate a physiological response. All our thoughts, regardless of their content, first enter our systems as energy. Those that carry emotional, mental, psychological, or spiritual energy produce biological responses that are then stored in our cellular memory. In this way, our biographies are woven into our biological systems, gradually, slowly, every day.[40]   — DR. CAROLYN MYSS

If you are sick...there is a reason. To recover thoroughly without taking on new symptoms, you must discover the reason.[41]   — JANE ROBERTS
The Nature of Personal Reality - A Seth Book

Only seeking and healing the cause in the consciousness will produce true healing.[42]   — CEANNE DEROHAN
as conveyed in The Right Use of Will

If you have developed an illness, don't feel guilty. You are innocent. You didn't understand the signs being given to you. (None of us did.) You've been banging around 'life' trying to find explanations for how and why things occurred. You had no idea what to do. But, now you do.

Your illness is giving birth to either an intensified desire for life or a desire to exit. If you choose life, you have a challenge to overcome. For it is your responsibility to recognize your power, own the creation of your illness, dissect its message, and understand that the power to heal lies solely within you!

To uncover the origin of the underlying issue that led to your illness, ask yourself: "When did I begin to receive wrong-way signs?" To help ferret out the root cause responsible for the creation of your illness, you must ask yourself two difficult questions. The first is:

"How am I benefitting from my illness?"

When I am sick, I enjoy being nurtured and pampered by my husband and son. My husband takes care of me, gives me loving attention, and relieves me of my obligations. What a wonderful feeling.... How am I benefitting from my illness? I am receiving love, attention, concern, and time off. I can watch TV without feeling guilty; I don't have to be anywhere; I don't have to talk to anyone; I don't have to take care of anything; I have no responsibilities. How can I enjoy the same experiences without becoming ill? By discovering what I wanted. That was my gift! My illness impelled me to recognize how I wanted to feel and what I wanted to have in my life periodically — freedom (my core instinct) and being nurtured. From that perspective, how might *you* be benefitting from your illness?

The second question to ask yourself is:

"Who might be adversely affected by my illness?"

Do you feel as though you are being taken for granted by someone? Do you want to 'punish' someone for something they did to you (your unintentional creation, I hate to say), and this is your ultimate revenge — "I'll show them: I'll die and see how much they miss me!" or "I'll get ill and let *him* take care of the kids — see how much *he* likes it!" Do you need attention, love, or appreciation and know of no other way to get it? That is certainly what children do. When they cannot get attention or love in a *positive* way, they instinctively revert to something negative. Why? In their state of negativity, they are connected to a powerful energy vortex — energy necessary to sustain life.

Because illness manifests on an unconscious level, you may find that you are seeking something that only illness can provide. I know of cases where women developed cancer or some other dreadful disease when their husbands left them. Because they could not deal with their loss on a conscious level, their repressed negative energy found its outlet in disease (which really places an emotional burden on some ex-husbands...).

Dr. Bernie Siegel candidly asks his cancer patients the question, "Why do you need your cancer?"[43] He, too, has recognized the link between illness and unresolved issues in life.

> *Illness is not sabotage; it is the body's statement that it has been having to hold the imbalance of denied Will [feelings] and needs release. If you can accept the message and regain the necessary balance, illness disappears and health prevails.*[44] — CEANNE DEROHAN
>
> as conveyed in *The Right Use of Will*

Anger conquers when unresolved. — UNKNOWN

Only when you say "I did this" can you find the power to change it.[45]　　　— NEALE DONALD WALSCH
Conversations with God - Book 1

You are all mental lepers. Your mind is eaten away with negative thoughts. Some of these are thrust upon you. Many of these you actually make up — conjure up — yourselves and then harbor and entertain for hours, days, weeks, months — even years... and you wonder why you are sick?[46]　　　— NEALE DONALD WALSCH
Conversations with God - Book 1

If we look deep enough into the lives of people with illness, we will always find a "wrong-way" sign; an emotional, psychological, physical link, or stress that led to the development of their illness.[47]　— DR. CAROLYN MYSS

Worry, hate, fear — together with their offshoots: anxiety, bitterness, impatience, avarice, unkindness, judgementalness, and condemnation — all attack the body at the cellular level. It is impossible to have a healthy body under these conditions. Similarly — although to a somewhat lesser degree — conceit, self-indulgence, and greed lead to physical illness, or lack of well-being. All illness is created first in the mind.[48]
— NEALE DONALD WALSCH
Conversations with God - Book 1

By hanging onto the traumas of your earlier life, you literally have an impact on the cells of your body. When we examine the biology of an individual, we find that his or her biography is close to the surface. Thoughts of anguish, self-pity, fear, hate, and the like all take their toll on the body and the spirit. After a while the body is unable to heal, largely because of these (repeated) thoughts.[49]　　　— DR. WAYNE DYER

In order to heal, a person must first believe they can be healed and then must believe they are able to facilitate this healing. They must recognize that they caused the sickness, even though they may not have realized it. They must now recognize it and what the underlying cause might have been. [Anger, jealousy, greed, intolerance...] If they are willing to acknowledge that they themselves caused it, they must then forgive themselves and from that point, healing can take place.[50]
— JULIA INGRAM and G.W. HARDIN
words spoken by Jesus to Paul in *The Messengers*

*When man is harmonious and happy he is healthy! All
sickness comes from sin or violation of Spiritual Law.
Jesus Christ said: "Be thou healed, your sins are
forgiven." Resentment, ill-will, hate, fear, etc, tear down
the cells of the body and poison the blood.*[51]

— FLORENCE SCOVEL SHINN
1871-1940

*If you have a physical symptom, do not run from it. Feel
its reality in your body. Let the emotions run freely.
These will lead you, if you allow them to flow, to the
beliefs that caused the difficulty. They will take you
through many aspects of your own reality that you must
face and explore. These methods release your withheld
natural aggressiveness. You may feel that you are
swamped by emotion, but trust it — again, it is the
motion of your being, and it arouses your own creativity.
Followed, it will seek the answers to your problems.*[52]

— JANE ROBERTS
The Nature of Personal Reality - A Seth Book

How Society Helps to Spread Illness

What are other contributing factors underlying the occurrence and
spread of illness?

In our misunderstanding of how life really operates, we live our lives
imbued in an all-pervasive war-like atmosphere. We are consumed by
fear and thoughts of scarcity. Everyday life immersed in this state of
being creates stress — stress which activates our 'off' switches and
restricts the flow of life energy, energy essential to maintain a state of
health.

Societally, we do not acknowledge what people need at the most
fundamental level: love, appreciation, companionship, time alone, etc..
In fact, often we applaud fathers or mothers who work forty to eighty
hours a week to provide for their families; we consider it to be virtuous.
However, children need their parents to be with them consistently, in a
heartfelt capacity, rather than simply providing them a means of
survival. And parents need their children. We have abandoned our
children, believing that the 'things' our hard-earned money buys will
bring us happiness. In reality, we have a sacred contract to prepare our
children for life and cannot fulfill it if we don't spend time with them.

We cannot truly know our children on an emotional level either, if we don't spend undivided time with each of them on a consistent basis. Time spent with them individually is the only way we can be cognizant of the fluctuations and nuances of their emotions to guide them through their growth process. At our core we feel this conflict. The result? Stress. Stress that activates our 'off' switches, restricts the flow of life energy, and unwittingly opens the door for illness to enter.

Living in the Information Age, we are continually pulled in many different directions that all vie for our attention — home, career, children, spouse, Mission, friends, social issues, hobbies, etc. As a result, we become buried underneath the accumulation of 'things to do.' As we attempt to keep up with all of the demands that are made of us and that we make on ourselves, we create an overwhelming level of stress. The result? We become numb to the true objective in life — joy. The conflict between what we desire and what we believe is responsible for the discomfort and torment we feel in our lives. However, unaware of the purpose of our wrong-way signs, we disregard them. The result? More stress.

> *Emotional, physical, and psychological stress in a patient's life contribute to the development of illness.*[53]
> — DR. CAROLYN MYSS

Stress: The Enemy of Life

Author Hans Selye explains in *The Stress of Life*, that the most prevalent health problem of our times is stress. Mr. Selye defines stress as "the rate of wear and tear on the human body." He explains that our bodies actually produce negative chemical changes as a result of the effects of negative emotions. He tells us that stress manifests in many different ways and is very toxic to our bodies.[54]

Dr. Herbert Benson addresses the perils of living in our stress-laden culture in *Timeless Healing: The Power and Biology of Belief*. He explains that our bodies are equipped with a natural response to stress — the "fight or flight response" — an instinctive survival mechanism that we are pre-programmed with from birth. How is this response evoked? When faced with potential threat, our bodies instinctively assess a situation and respond by either fighting or fleeing. Our blood pressure, breathing rate, and speed of metabolism increase; our muscle tension increases and our brain waves become more frequent and intense. On average, we have a 300 to 400 percent increase of blood flow to the muscles of our arms and legs. All of these responses occur so we can effectively fight or flee.[55] Although the threat of mortal harm is less prevalent today than it was long ago, this fight or flee response is continually evoked in our modern-day society by the suppression of anger, negative emotion, and stress. The result? Illness.

> *Anger shuts down the brain and internal organs so more blood can go to the muscles. It speeds up the heart and increases blood-clotting factors. This is the classic "fight or flight" response.... But the problem is: fight or flight is turned on all the time in our modern world — when someone cuts us off on the freeway, when our boss yells at us, when we miss a traffic light. Our blood pressure goes up and stays up; the internal organs remain shut down until they fail.*[56]
>
> —MSI

A Restriction of Life Energy Creates Havoc on Our Physical Bodies

Recent scientific research has explored the connection between emotions and their effect on the physiology of the human body. The Institute of HeartMath®, a research institute founded in 1991 by Doc Childre, has pioneered inroads in the fields of neuroscience, cardiology, psychology, biochemistry, bioelectricity, and physics. More specifically, its team of experts have conducted studies on the heart, both as a physical apparatus, as well as the as the emotional center of our beings.

Their findings? Stress is the enemy. Stress creates incoherence (disconnection) — a state of being that actually pits our biological systems against each other. Our nervous systems and heart become desynchronized and our hormonal balance is compromised. Negative mental and emotional responses, such as anger and worry, create an imbalance in our autonomic nervous systems. Incoherence diminishes our capacity to perform, live a quality life, and negatively impacts our health. On the other hand, when our systems are coherent (maintaining a connection to source energy) — in sync with our hearts rhythmic patterns — no energy is wasted and power is maximized. Positive emotions, such as happiness, appreciation, compassion, care, and love, not only change the patterns of activity in the nervous system, but also reduce the production of the stress hormone, cortisol. Furthermore, the experience of love and compassion boosts IgA levels — an important secretory antibody that our immune system utilizes as its first line of defense, making our bodies more resistant to infection and disease.

Numerous scientific studies reveal that connecting with the emotions associated with the heart, not only facilitates brain function, it also adjusts balance in the autonomic nervous system, lowers blood pressure, increases stress-relieving hormones, and increases immune responses. The bottom line? Positive emotions affect our well-being down to the cellular level. Further research by The Institute of HeartMath® offers scientific evidence on the correlation between energy and emotions. Energy assets? Optimistic perspectives, thoughts of appreciation, or gestures of kindness add energy to our bodies. Energy deficits? Anger, jealousy, and passing judgment upon others deplete our stores of energy.[57]

Negative emotions wreak havoc on our health and have the potential to destroy our bodies! Therefore, it is imperative that we recognize and heed our wrong-way signs immediately so we can maintain our connection to source energy.

The Power of Positivity

In the late 1970s, Norman Cousins, a prominent editor for the magazine *Saturday Review*, as well as chairman for an American delegation to Russia in the 1960s, wrote a best-selling book entitled *Anatomy of an Illness*. Upon developing an 'incurable' disease, Mr. Cousins flatly refused to accept his fatal prognosis. No one was going to tell him that he was going to die! Instead, he chose to take control of his destiny. He conducted extensive research on his rare condition, knowing full well that doctors had limited time to study every aspect of every disease. Through his research he discovered the correlation between emotions and the physical body, and pondered the idea that if negative emotions could *adversely* affect the body's chemistry, then what affect could *positive* emotions have? Could love, hope, laughter, faith, confidence, and the will to live, positively enhance the body's chemistry to the degree that it could cure illness?

Making himself a guinea pig, he viewed humorous videotapes, such as "The Three Stooges," "Candid Camera," and "The Marx Brothers," and had others read humorous books to him. The result? Ten minutes of belly laughter eliminated his need for powerful pain killers for more than two hours! Why didn't he want pain killers? They *interfered* with his body's ability to heal. The morphine he was being given to relieve his acute pain also had an adverse effect: it put him in a catatonic state where he was unable to utilize his powerful thoughts. And though he didn't realize that his laughter provided a connection to life energy that allowed for his body to produce the condition of health, he *did* realize that it worked! Unwittingly, he had taken his attention from his illness

— the culprit responsible for restricting the flow of energy — and instead focused on positive, which allowed healing energy to flow.[58] The outcome? Mr. Cousins lived an additional 20+ years past the 'expiration date' his doctor's fatal prognosis had predicted.

> *If people only knew the healing power of laughter and joy, many of our fine doctors would be out of business. Joy is one of nature's greatest medicines. A pleasant state of mind tends to bring abnormal conditions back to normal.*
> — CATHERINE PONDER

> *Laughter is the tonic, the relief, the surcease for pain.*
> — CHARLIE CHAPLIN
> 1889-1977

> *Emotional states have long been known to affect the secretion of certain hormones — for example, those of the thyroid and adrenal glands. It has been discovered that the brain and the pituitary gland contain another class of hormones which go by the name of endorphins. [You have probably heard of a "runner's high," a state of euphoria where endorphins are secreted at some point in the run becoming very addictive.] The physiological activity of some endorphins presents great similarity to that of morphine, heroin and other opiate substances that control pain, not only acting on the mechanism of the pain itself, but also by inhibiting the emotional response to the pain and thereby the suffering. It is thought that there probably is a correlation between the secretion of endorphins with those mental attitudes the patient has, thereby affecting the patient's perception of the illness.[59]*
> — RENÉ DUBOS
> 1901-1982

Positive mental attitudes such as joy, laughter, the belief in the body's ability to heal, as well as the will to live, cause endorphins to be released, thereby inhibiting pain during the process of healing! (Isn't this exciting!)

AIDS: More Contagious Thoughts

In *Anatomy of the Spirit*, author Carolyn Myss tells us about a man infected with the HIV virus that had progressed to the first stage of AIDS. In this instance, the man was reluctant to disclose the fact that he was homosexual to his family. As he focused his powerful thoughts on his secret, he received many wrong-way signs, but dismissed them fearing his family's negative judgment and disdain. Dr. Myss, however, advised him to be honest about his sexuality — to eradicate this red circuit — and told him that the truth would set him free. Upon hearing this unexpected good news — hope — this man was so grateful that he graciously accepted responsibility for his demanding program to heal with an attitude of gratitude — i.e. connection. (Dr. Myss feels that a willing, grateful attitude is key to regaining health.) The results? Six weeks after disclosing the fact that he was homosexual to his loved ones and undergoing another blood test, his new test results indicated that he was HIV negative! Today he is a practicing attorney and remains HIV negative.[60] This transformation was so significant, so remarkable, that Dr. Myss co-authored *AIDS: Passageway to Transformation* (Stillpoint, 1987) with Dr. C. Norman Shealy, and conducts seminars across the country speaking with AIDS patients.

Why hasn't this information become publically known? Why do celebrities wear ribbons representing the 'war on AIDS' at every awards show? Overcome with feelings of powerlessness while watching their loved ones die slow painful deaths, people feel they must do *something*. And invariably they 'push against' disease. In their agony, they become angry and frustrated, which unwittingly activates their 'off' switches and restricts the flow of life energy. Imbued in a state of impotence, they then focus their repressed energy onto anything they can blame, such as the government for not appropriating enough money to find a cure. However, the government cannot ever appropriate enough money to eradicate AIDS, because dollars cannot eradicate it. Although a cure may be discovered, another more fatal disease will take its place because it's not about the manifestation; it's about what is underlying it!

Out of Sight, Out of Mind, Out of Life Experience

To eradicate AIDS, we must put the beautiful quilts away and remove the ribbons. They evoke feelings of sadness, powerlessness, hopelessness, or even worse, militant feelings of "killing" this disease — all red circuits that restrict the flow of energy.

The rampant spread of AIDS in the homosexual community is predominantly a byproduct of old-paradigm thinking. Because of the powerful magnetic nature of fear that accompanies any disease, millions of gay men, as well as many heterosexuals, have died and others are suffering today. Why? Think about it: As science labels a disease, creates a composite of its predisposing conditions, and then broadcasts its findings to the world, any person remotely fitting this composite is struck with terror and begins to fear developing the disease. And what happens when one projects the frequency of fear? The 'nocebo' effect — think, believe, expect, and get!

It is imperative that we now shift from 'pushing against' disease and illness, to instead focusing on anything that allows energy to flow. We must utilize the Four-Step Formula to save lives. We must reach out to those who have developed a disease and help them to awaken to the fact that the power to heal is within them. We *can* stop this needless pain, anguish, and suffering, but only using love as the underlying frequency! All other methods are backwards! (Could this be your Mission?)

The following passage is a poignant poem from *Dialogues*, by Jane Roberts, who passed away in 1984 after battling cancer. In this passage, the physical self is communicating with the soul:

> *But now*
> *my body trembles and breathes deep.*
> *Ancient angers*
> *rumble up from my toes.*
> *A dull heavy black hole*
> *rises up through my belly to my throat*
> *and empties its load upon my tongue*
> *which turns leaden*
> *with unsaid uncried things,*
> *long forgotten by my mind*
> *but clotted in my blood.*
> *Ashen statues*
> *of unspoken words and syllables,*
> *images I should have kicked,*
> *all from my lips go toppling.*
> *The specifics merge,*
> *the icy heavy mass*
> *grows alive in birth*
> *and rushes*
> *squalling, out*
> *into the universe.*
> *Shapes and colors,*
> *blacks and purples mix*
> *with the skyscape's*
> *great moving picture*
> *and are lost*
> *and redeemed in it.*
> *And I feel you now, even in my anger,*
> *splendid and terrible*

emerging through my flesh
with the rightness of storm winds
and clouds blowing,
devastating the landscape
yet filling it with freshness,
sending debris flying
full blast and releasing
new tubers
which lay hidden under
and are justly served by my anger,
which lifts them
and you and me all together
over repression's frosty land,
surging in giant free swirls
that burst like summer lightning, flashing
and speeding over the countryside,
joyously furious.[61]

The road to wellness requires that you uncover the origin of your repressed emotions — the red circuits responsible for the manifestation of any illness — in order to eradicate it. To live a life filled with joy, laughter, and perfect health, you must awaken to your power and utilize it on a daily basis. Remember, once more, it's completely up to you. For to know this truth, and to live it, are two entirely different experiences.

To be or not to be: That is the question.
— WILLIAM SHAKESPEARE
1564-1616

Preventing Illness

To prevent illness, be sensitive to how you feel at all times. If you feel a loss of energy because of a stressful situation, utilize your feeling as your wrong-way sign — your Point of Power — and order what you want. If you are vigilant and sensitive to your feelings, the likelihood of developing an illness will be nipped in the bud. As you make the transition from the old paradigm into the new, you will learn to navigate through life feeling with your heart, rather than thinking with your head. Then you will be living life as it is meant to be lived: loving and laughing along your journey!

Let's now learn the specific techniques to attain a state of pure radiant health. ☺

Georgy Girl

Hey there Georgy girl, swinging down the street so fancy free.
Nobody you meet would ever see the loneliness there, inside you.
Hey there Georgy girl, why do all the boys just pass you by.
Could it be you just don't try or is it the clothes you wear?
You're always window shopping but never stopping to buy.
So shed those dowdy feathers and fly, a little bit.
Hey there Georgy girl,
Dreamin' of the someone you could be.
Life is a reality, you can't always run away.
Don't be so scared of changing and rearranging yourself.
It's time for jumping down from the shelf, a little bit.
Hey there Georgy Girl
There's another Georgy deep inside.
Bring out all the love you hide and oh what a change
there will be.
The world would see a new Georgy girl.
Wake up Georgy girl.[62]

(Georgy boys, too!)

Words by Jim Dale — Music by Tom Springfield

Choose Perfect Radiant Health and It Will Soon Be On Its Way to You!

Health and cheerfulness usually beget each other.
— JOSEPH ADDISON
1672-1719

For fast acting relief, try slowing down.   — LILY TOMLIN

You can cure yourself of an "incurable" disease if you realize that your point of power is in the present.[63]
— JANE ROBERTS
The Nature of Personal Reality - A Seth Book

Your conscious beliefs direct the functioning of your body. It is not the other way around.[64]
— JANE ROBERTS
The Nature of Personal Reality - A Seth Book

You cannot be ill without at some level causing yourself to be, and you can be well again in a moment by simply deciding to be.[65]
— NEALE DONALD WALSCH
Conversations with God - Book 1

Health will improve almost at once when worrying ends.[66]
— NEALE DONALD WALSCH
Conversations with God - Book 1

The Genesis of Illness

Now that we understand how life operates at the most fundamental level, we can see how many unintentional manifestations — including illness — were created. As those who came before us met with negative circumstances in their lives, they focused on them and while doing so, restricted the flow of energy needed to sustain their physical bodies. The result? Eventually their bodies degenerated to the degree that illness resulted. Instinctively, they pushed against these illnesses in their attempt to eradicate them. They gathered data and categorized this data into statistics, hoping to discover a correlation between the statistics and illness. By virtue of the Law of Attraction, they magnetized volumes of empirical 'evidence' and assumed that this evidence was Truth or an attribute of reality. Once this 'truth' permeated the mass consciousness, fear struck. As person after person focused their powerful thoughts on illness and disease, they perpetuated this misconception and created *more* illness and disease. The consequence? This fundamentally flawed 'truth' became the reality we all live in.

To end the vicious cycle of illness and early death, we must reassess our earlier programming. We must now have the courage to move into the new paradigm and let our powerful bodies do what they can on their own — heal themselves without interference. How can we cross the bridge from skepticism, fear, and disbelief, to trusting that each of us has the power within to manifest perfect radiant health?

First by shifting our consciousness. For a shift in frequency opens our hearts which helps to release our resistance. We must recognize that the Four-Step Formula is the one truth in life we can rely on, for again, there is not a shred of evidence to disprove it![67] Think once more about the plaque hanging in the doctor's waiting room I visited: "In the future, *all* healing will be accomplished through your body's spiritual awareness." **The future is NOW, friends.**

> *In every incident of "remembered wellness" [utilizing the power of your belief, your physician's belief and/or a combination of the two], the catalyst is belief. The belief may be your own, a composite of your life experiences. The belief may be your clinician's, the product of his or her professional and personal history. Finally, the belief can be instilled in you by the confident and trusting tone established in consultations between the two of you.*[68]
> — DR. HERBERT BENSON

What are the implications of the Four-Step Formula in the medical field? Enormous. I fully understand that it is difficult to alter deeply entrenched core beliefs, especially when they contradict the prevailing attitudes of our culture. Our thinking mind may desperately desire health, but our hearts may not be 'buying it,' thus creating a conflict of energy that will disallow healing. So, how can we begin to alter our frequencies and reassess our underlying beliefs? By recognizing the truth. As more and more physicians, those we respect and revere, begin to comprehend and utilize the incredible power of belief, our resistance will begin to diminish. The result? Healing can be achieved in a far different manner. And to hasten this shift in consciousness, an extraordinary amount of evidence is mounting daily from many diverse sources, that confirms the veracity of the Four-Step Formula.

> *Every day there is a growing body of medical and scientific research to corroborate the truth that reality is an outgrowth of mental intention.*[69]
> — JAMES REDFIELD and CAROL ADRIENNE

> *The conventional medical world is on the brink of recognizing the link between spiritual dysfunction and illness.*[70] — DR. CAROLYN MYSS

In *Ageless Body, Timeless Mind*, Dr. Deepak Chopra debunks the assumption that human awareness can be completely explained as a product of biochemistry. He explains that

> *Perception… is a learned phenomenon. The world you live in, including the experience of your body, is completely dictated by how you learned to perceive it. If you change your perception, you change the experience of your body and your world.*[71] — DR. DEEPAK CHOPRA

> *[Y]our emotions and actions follow your beliefs. If you believe that you are sick then, for all intents and purposes, you are sick. If you believe that you are healthy, then you are healthy. [T]he belief itself will generate the negative emotions that will, indeed, bring about a physical or emotional illness. The imagination will follow, painting dire mental pictures of a particular condition. Before long physical data bears out the negative belief; negative in that it is far less desirable than a concept of health.*[72] — JANE ROBERTS
> The Nature of Personal Reality - A Seth Book

Energy medicine is a holistic [encompassing the whole being; body, mind and spirit] philosophy that teaches, "I am responsible for the creation of my health. I therefore participated, at some level, in the creation of this illness. I can participate in the healing of this illness by healing myself, which means simultaneously healing my emotional, psychological, physical, and spiritual being.[73]

— DR. CAROLYN MYSS

[O]ur brains often cannot distinguish external from internal "reality." When you dream that you are being chased, your heart rate increases just as it would if you were really being chased. For your brain, and thus your heart, this is reality.[74]

— DR. HERBERT BENSON

[A]ll of us have distinct neurosignatures — for wellness, for illness, for strength and endurance, for headaches and nausea, for mobility and pleasure, for pain and disability, for the symptoms you associate with arthritis or angina, and for the specifics you associate with all the other activities and situations you faced in life. Like a bad habit, or conversely like a good habit, recurring top-down thoughts, along with their corresponding emotional values, engage your brain's previously used nerve-cell-firing patterns to instruct the body. This is how our thoughts become self-fulfilling prophecies, and how our beliefs gear our bodies for the splendid opportunities of "remembered wellness."[75]

— DR. HERBERT BENSON

Every specialty and subspecialty of medicine is having to reevaluate and appreciate how intimately our thoughts are related to our bodies....it's a matter of our everyday thoughts, dreams, and superstitions being related to our entire anatomy.[76]

— DR. HERBERT BENSON

Disease is an image of thought externalized. Whatever is cherished in mortal mind as the physical condition, is imaged forth on the body.[77]

— MARY BAKER EDDY
founder of the Christian Science faith
1821-1910

How to Achieve a State of Health

If you are ill, remember when you were not. Search your life for proofs of your health. Your very life itself is hard evidence that health is within you.[78] — JANE ROBERTS

The Nature of Personal Reality - A Seth Book

[I] learned that our [bodies] are nourished or starved according to our expectations. When mobilized for our benefit, this is a magnificent physiologic endowment.[79]
  — DR. HERBERT BENSON

How can we utilize this knowledge to our advantage? Simple. By utilizing the Law of Attraction. Think about it: When we tell others about our illness and conjure all sorts of horrible images in our minds, we are arguing for our illness. However, if we instead argue for our *wellness*, the Law of Attraction will magnetize evidence of health!

The Case of Body VS. Illy

Argue for your limitations and sure enough, they're yours. — RICHARD BACH

Because the subject of illness is so critically important, I have chosen to illustrate both its power and dire consequences using the following very graphic example:

Let's assume that you are ill and wish to regain your health. You are to assume the role of an attorney and enact dual opposing roles that represent two aspects of who you are. Your case? "Body vs. Illy." You will present your case to a jury — your conscious rational mind. First, you will defend your illness, a very real entity we'll call 'Illy.' Illy is fighting for its survival and needs the energy 'Body' is providing to exist, therefore, it wishes to remain in Body until Body's energy is depleted. However, Body has now attained a conscious awareness of how Illy came to reside within him and now wishes for Illy to depart. Assuming the role of defending attorney, convince your jury beyond a shadow of doubt that Illy was 'invited' to take up residence within Body; that the frequency that Body projected was perfectly aligned with Illy. As Body focused on an unresolved life issue, he transmitted a powerful beacon which magnetized Illy. Therefore, Illy believes it has every right to inhabit Body as its new home. Illy argues that it was Body who 'pulled a fast one' and began to become conscious, which Illy considers to be completely unfair, and should not be taken into consideration. Convince your jury that they should not allow Body to change his mind and you should be awarded a favorable verdict: one that allows Illy to remain, whether it poses a death sentence or torturous years of pain to Body!

Now, assume the role of prosecuting attorney and convince your jury beyond a shadow of a doubt that Illy must now leave Body. Yes, the invitation was given, however, it was unintentional: Illy was never *literally* invited to occupy Body. Argue that Body, in fact, made a grievous error, but is now capable of altering his frequency to that of perfect radiant health — a frequency that Illy cannot abide in. Body has come to recognize that, in reality, he has many, many more things *right* within him than he does wrong. Convince your jury that if they can only acknowledge the multitudinous things that are functioning perfectly within Body and decide in your favor, Body can readjust his frequency to that of perfect radiant health — his natural state of being — and send Illy out looking for a new residence.

Is this example graphic enough for you? I hope so, because every time you think about or speak of your illness you are feeding its glutenous appetite, giving it more power. Why? Because the Law of Attraction unequivocally states:

WHATEVER YOU GIVE YOUR ATTENTION TO WILL GROW LARGER!!!

To eradicate your illness, you must use the Law of Attraction and argue for your *wellness* — the innumerable aspects of your body that are functioning perfectly in this moment. Focus on what is *right* within your physical body and *why you appreciate* those aspects.

For example: How is your vision? If this is an aspect of your body that is functioning perfectly, ask yourself *why* you are grateful for your sight. You might begin by imagining what it would be like to be blind. For that perspective helps you to clarify *why* you appreciate your ability to see. What you would miss seeing every day? For example: "I am so grateful to have these wonderful, glorious eyes. I can see the beautiful blue sky, the clouds, those whom I love. I can see the trees and the birds and the green grass. I can watch TV, look at a computer screen, and function with ease having these incredible eyes from which to view this world. I am so thankful for my eyes!" Now go further and appreciate the wonder of all of you.

∿ How is your sense of smell functioning?
∿ How is your sense of taste functioning?
∿ How is your sense of touch functioning?
∿ How is your circulatory system functioning?
∿ How is your digestive system functioning?
∿ How is your brain functioning?
∿ How is your hearing functioning?
∿ How is your skin?
∿ How is your dexterity?
∿ How is your balance?
∿ How is your body's response to your thoughts?

There are many, many more things that are right within your body than wrong, but if you focus your powerful thoughts on anything that is not functioning optimally, it can only grow larger.[80]

If you are ill, your task is to continually divert your attention from your illness to something positive. Constantly ask yourself: "Am I having pleasant thoughts?" If not, switch stations. Choose your thoughts wisely, and only permit those of joy, laughter, and appreciation so your body can heal. Try not to feed it with anything negative for you now know that negativity is the breeding ground for disease to grow! Illness is a big-time warning bell. Angel is holding up a gigantic flashing neon sign reading 'Wrong-Way.'

Begin your journey into wellness — possibly the challenge of your life — by sorting through what you really want out of life. If you have ventured so far from your path that you don't know what you want, as you complete this book you will rekindle your desires. Utilize that information, place your orders, and have faith that Angel will work hard for you. Understand that the power you have access to is the same power that creates worlds!

> Man should watch himself hourly to detect if his motive is fear or faith. "Choose ye this day whom ye shall serve, "fear or faith."...Perhaps one's fear is of disease or germs. Then one should be fearless and undisturbed in a germ-laden situation, and he would be immune [like Mother Teresa was in India]. One can only contract germs while vibrating at the same rate as the germ. Of course, the disease-laden germ is the product of carnal mind, as all thoughts must objectify. Germs do not exist in the superconscious or Divine Mind, therefore are the product of man's "vain imagination." In the twinkling of an eye, "man's release will come when he realizes there is no power in evil."[81]   — FLORENCE SCOVEL SHINN

Tune Into "104.5": The Frequency of Health

To tune in to the frequency of health, imagine how it feels to be healthy. Act 'as if' you are healthy. What you can do? Where you can go? Think about a typical day: Feel your body move with ease as you get in and out of your car, pick up your children, swim in a pool, swing a golf club, hug people you love, take a shower, whatever.

If you want to feel free and happy, ponder that for a moment and imagine being in a place where you *are* feeling free and happy; on a beach, in a forest, on a boat. Then ask yourself, "What is it that I want to have?" and ponder that for a few days. What does *that* feel like? Visualize the billions of cells in your body performing six trillion functions per second and appreciate the magnificent creation that you inhabit. Imagine your body being healed and restored to perfect health. And every night before you go to sleep, think of all the wonderful aspects of your body that are serving you well so you have the benefit of six to eight hours of non-resistant time to heal.[82] Do not jump into action; simply think about how you want to feel, what you want to have, and then choose it! And within a few days, you will begin to feel better.[83] As you utilize this technique on a daily basis and maintain a state of connection, Angel will respond to your new frequency and perfect health will soon be your experience.

> *If you divert your thoughts from the negative ideas to the positive ones, then your concentration will begin to alter the balance. The vast reservoir of energy and potential within you is called into action under the leadership of your conscious mind.*[84]
> — JANE ROBERTS
> The Nature of Personal Reality - A Seth Book

> *Think healthy, be healthy....We can improve our own state of being by visualizing ourselves as happy and at peace with others. If we want to enjoy vibrant good health, we can manifest it by thinking in those terms. If you visualize yourself as being ill or fearing a situation will develop that will prevent you from being active, you may begin subconsciously making the decisions which lead to that situation. But, when we picture our body as working in health and inner harmony, we improve our attitude and attract the healing energies that are all about us.*[85]
> — RUTH MONTGOMERY

Once people recognize the power of the Four-Step Formula — their authentic power — healing can be accomplished in a far different manner. Healing centers can be created — centers that focus on love, laughter, and diverting the powerful human mind from illness to the wonder and beauty of life. (Cool Mission! I've got a few ideas up my sleeve if anyone is interested....)

Transforming Power — Your Adamant Refusal to Accept a Negative Prognosis

The key to your transformation lies in understanding and reclaiming your power. While others can assist you, they do not have the power to control your beliefs, therefore, they cannot heal you. Only you hold that power. So employ a course of action like Norman Cousins did. Overflow your life with positivity, appreciation, joy, laughter, hope, love, and pets. Do not let anyone tell you that you are going to die. Let others say that you are in denial and let them watch as you create a miracle. In their ignorance, thus innocence, they do not have any idea just how *toxic* they can be to your ability to heal when they acknowledge your 'lack of health.' Unknowingly, they are influencing you negatively! Let them know very lovingly that you now understand how harmful negativity can be to healing and that your priority now is to heal. Find folks who are positive to be around — doctors included — those who understand just how powerful you are! You can use your power to transform your life, and all that it requires is desire and determination!

> *Healing involves great natural aggressive thrusts of energy, growth, and the focus of vitality. The more powerless you feel, the less able you are to utilize your own healing abilities. You are then forced to project these outward upon a physician, a healer, or an outside agency. If your own belief in the physician "works" and you are cured of symptoms, you are physically relieved, and yet your own belief in yourself may be further infringed upon. If you are making no effective efforts to handle your own problems, then the symptoms will simply reappear in a new fashion, and the same process will be reinitiated. You may lose faith in your doctor while still retaining confidence in doctors as a whole, and run from one to another. But the body has its own integrity, and illness is often a natural sign of imbalance, a physical message to which you are to listen and make inner adjustments accordingly.*[86] —JANE ROBERTS
> The Nature of Personal Reality - A Seth Book

Even the most dreaded disease will vanish when you completely remove your attention from it. You attracted it through thought and feeling and you release it by releasing your thought and feeling regarding it.[87]

— ESTHER and JERRY HICKS

There is growing evidence that our emotions can influence resistance and immunity to infection and even to cancer. There have been several studies documenting the fact that positive outlooks by doctor and patient can have a beneficial course on a variety of disorders.[88]

— DR. ISADORE ROSENFELD
New York Hospital-Cornell Medical Center

Illness Can Ignite a Strong Desire for Life

I have heard people with critical illnesses say that their lives only really began when they were diagnosed. Why is that? Because whenever we are diagnosed with a critical illness, much of our superficial baggage is dropped in the first five minutes. Why do I act so arrogantly? Why am I pretending to be so tough? Why am I judging so many people? Why am I not appreciating all the love and beauty that surrounds me? Why am I avoiding the simplest and most important element of my being, the love in my heart? Dropping our illusions is a healing in itself.[89]

— MARIANNE WILLIAMSON

We forget ourselves and our destinies in health, and the chief use of temporary sickness is to remind us of these concerns.

— RALPH WALDO EMERSON
1803-1882

AIDS has...forced us into a realization that we must cherish every moment of the glorious experience of this thing we call life. We are learning to value our own lives and the lives of our loved ones as if any moment may be the last.

— ELIZABETH TAYLOR

It is part of the cure to wish to be cured.

— SENECA
4 BC - 65 AD

Illness creates the grand desire for wellness.[90]
— ESTHER and JERRY HICKS

I thank God for my handicaps for through them I have found myself, my work, and my God. — HELEN KELLER
1880-1968

A wise man should consider that health is the greatest of human blessings, and learn how, by his own thought, to derive benefit from his illnesses. — FRAN LEBOWITZ

Difficult times have helped me to understand better than before how infinitely rich and beautiful life is in every way and that so many things that one goes worrying about are of no importance whatsoever. — ISAK DINESEN

If you are ill, write down why you want to be healthy.

_____
_____
_____
_____
_____

What will you do when you achieve a state of perfect radiant health?

_____
_____
_____
_____
_____

Although I understand that illness can be a difficult issue to overcome because of the prevailing beliefs of our culture and the resulting fears they evoke, what you *choose* can be even more powerful than what you believe if it is accompanied by a pure unrelenting focus. Do you recall the story about a child who was trapped under a car and his mother lifted the car to rescue him? Do you think this mother *believed* that she could lift an automobile? How was she able to lift the car? Could she go to the gym tomorrow and lift that much weight? In this case, her desire was so intense, so focused, that it overcame her beliefs. Although it can sometimes be challenging to alter habitual beliefs, it is not impossible. Simply use the strength of your willpower to overcome the beliefs that have limited you in the past. Imagine yourself as the mother in this example and feel her intense emotions: she would not allow anything to get in her way! Her beloved child was under that car and she refused to stand by helplessly and watch him die! Her desire was so intense that it overcame her powerful beliefs. You, too, embody the exact same power this mother utilized, so use it. Visualize the 'sick' you as the child and the 'well' you as the mother who rescues you!

Healing the "Impossible"

Why do some illnesses seem to be impossible to heal? Only because we *believe* them to be. Perhaps you have an illness or disability that is said to be impossible to heal — such as a spinal cord injury. To facilitate your healing, let's first expand your perspective and shift your consciousness. Consider the following: It is scientific fact that the cells of your body continually replenish themselves. As a result, a new cellular 'you' is recreated every one to five years (the accounts vary as to how often this occurs). Literally, you are not the same person today that you were five years ago. Metaphysicists tell us that each of our cells actually has a memory, or set of instructions it follows that is obtained from our beliefs. And when each cell dies and is replaced, it passes its memory onto its successor. Ergo, if you had surgery early in your life that left a scar, even though the damaged cells have been replaced, possibly many times, the only reason your scar remains is because you *expect* your scar to remain. Think, believe, expect, and get! Because you are the 'captain of your ship,' your body is taking its orders from you. It is the physical manifestation of your beliefs. Therefore, the key to healing lies in conveying a new set of instructions to your body, for your thoughts do indeed create your reality.

> *The body as it's experienced in the waking state is a creation of the mind. The body is not a frozen, unchanging sculpture; it's in a constant state of flux with the environment...The body is interchanging at every moment with the environment. I've heard 98% of the atoms in our body weren't there a year ago! That's how fast we are transforming. It is as if we live in a miraculous building in which every stick is being replaced each year, but because of ignorance, we rebuild it exactly the same way, year after year after year. If the body is sick, we rebuild it as sick. If we have a tumor, we recreate the tumor. If the body is old, we reform it old.*[91]
>
> —MSI

If you are willing and determined to reassess your inherited beliefs and complete the steps to actualize your power, you can eliminate illness and regain your natural state of perfect health. *Choose* perfect health with passion, determination, and focus. *Appreciate* all the things you may have taken for granted. Think about what you're going to do when you fully recover and joyfully anticipate it. Imagine the life you have chosen and feel it until it feels real. Feel the new person being born within — the person with a brand new desire and appreciation for life. As you begin to appreciate your amazing body, you will connect with source energy which will allow health to manifest. And from an even broader perspective — the perspective of your life's original blueprint — perhaps your illness was meant to catalyze the direction of your Mission: to illuminate the path for others by demonstrating that your body's spiritual awareness can indeed produce healing.

Utilize Your Existing Beliefs to Heal

There is a delicate balance in determining what modality of healing will prove to be the most effective in any individual. Because each of us is unique, we hold different beliefs. Hence, one person could approach healing exclusively using the Four-Step Formula — belief — while another may require medical technology in addition to his or her beliefs. If your beliefs fall in the latter category, don't recriminate yourself. Instead, focus on all the miraculous medical technology that you believe *can* eradicate your illness. Place an order with Angel to find a doctor who respects the *whole* human being — one who recognizes the link between body, mind, and spirit — one who is a healer! Follow a course in healing that you believe can overcome your illness.

If you find a treatment that resonates with you, it *will help* because you believe it will. Understand that each of us will undergo a time of transition from the old paradigm into the new, so you must find your own balance: the unique combination of treatments you believe can heal you. If you believe passionately in anything that has the potential to restore your health, you will get better. And don't forget to 'go to work' daily, for your affirmations have power. The intentions you set forth will not only supplement your state of health, but also insulate you from negative suggestions — any wrong-way signs given by your doctor or anyone else.

If you are ill and wish to utilize alternative modalities to healing, you may want to consider the Mind/Body Institute at Harvard University. This institute utilizes many of the underlying principles in this book and as a result, many folks have manifested amazing results!

Choose "To Be" a Creator

When I was eight or nine years old, I recall committing some offense that my father deemed punishable. Heaven knows what it was, probably something insignificant, nonetheless, it pushed his button. Once again, Dad was completely inebriated — drunk out of his gourd. I sensed his uncontrollable wrath and ran to our small powder room. I placed my feet against the toilet, my back against the door, and braced myself. I knew that his rage was so intense that he could kill me, but also felt that if I could hold him off long enough, he would tire, and the inevitable beating would be less severe. Minute after minute, he hurled his 6 foot, 200-pound body against the bathroom door with all his strength, anger, and adrenalin, but scrawny little me held him off! He could not get in! My desire was so focused, my emotion so intense and determined, it became my dominant intention! The point of my story? Under dire circumstances, your intense desire and unrelenting focus can overcome your deeply entrenched conflicting beliefs.

I now recognize that Dad had gone to 'the place' — the powerful negative energy vortex where distinctions of reality are distorted. Years later, he and I discussed what had happened between us. As we delved deeper into his past, he disclosed the fact that his father had beaten him — he actually thought it was normal behavior. No credence was ever given to the feelings little Harry (Dad) had felt, so he repressed them. The consequence? He was robbed of the full expression of his feelings for his entire life! Furthermore, because the energy of his red circuits could not be suppressed, they grew more and more powerful as they magnetized more and more evidence. The result? In my father's unhealed state of being, whenever I pushed his button he vented his rage — his repressed energy — onto me. And with each succeeding offense I committed, his rage grew more and more intense until the day that his denied feelings exploded and he came very close to murdering me!

> *Each person's life is far from finished with death. Our acts of love and failures to love continue to have consequences until the end of history... What you and I do, and what we fail to do, will matter forever.*[92]
> — JIM FOREST

So this is a admonishment: You must stop the cycle of denial! If you fail to heal your denied negative emotions and readjust your circuits from red to green, you will pass your unhealed issues onto your children and they will, in turn, do the same to their children. You will also rob yourself of the full breadth of emotion, love, or passion, until you free that imprisoned aspect of yourself. To stop the cycle of denial, you must begin the process of healing. And in so doing, you may just save a few lives!

Helping Others Who Are Ill

*If you have not slept, or if you have slept, or if you have
a headache, or sciatica, or leprosy, or thunder-stroke, I
beseech you, by all angels, to hold your peace, and not
pollute the morning.* — RALPH WALDO EMERSON

*Bring your health and your strength to the weak and
sickly, and so you will be of use to them. Give them, not
your weakness, but your energy, so you will revive and
lift them up. Life alone can rekindle life.*
— HENRI FRÉDÉRIC AMIEL
1821-1881

If you have a friend who is ill, do not contribute to his or her illness by acknowledging it or even speaking of it. Explain that you now understand the secret to life, how thought creates reality, and how destructive negative thoughts can be to both them and yourself. Try to understand your friend's underlying need for their illness. And if they *ask*, help them to formulate a vision of what they want. Another way you can help? Think of them only in perfect radiant health — Who They Really Are — without the mask of illness. For if you feel pity and sorrow for them, you are joining them in their frequency and can only add to their illness. To avoid having a negative impact on them, always search for the thought in your mind that *feels* better: Does it feel better to see your friend in health or in illness? If you find your thoughts wandering in the wrong direction, quickly switch stations. Provide them with joy, laughter, and love, and if you are unable to do that, don't visit them. Respect them and the power of your thoughts enough to stay away. Send them something wonderful instead (this book... if you believe it might help).

I once attended a telecommunications sales seminar where the instructor explained that many people would be unwilling to switch their long distance provider even if they could save 50 percent! In making his point, he used the analogy of having a cure for cancer and offering it to cancer patients. It was his belief that more than 50 percent of patients would *not* be interested in a cure. Fascinating? Some people, knowing of no other viable options, create a vested interest in maintaining their illness; it becomes their new comfort zone. And from an even broader perspective, their soul may have an underlying objective for this experience that you are not privy to. So, if your enthusiasm for this knowledge falls on the deaf ears of those who you feel are most needy, you must accept and honor *their choice*. People will awaken if and when they choose to.

If you are a physician and wish to expand your ability to heal, your awakening is vital. As you begin to recognize and actualize the full breadth of your power in your personal life, you will heighten your ability to intuit which modality of healing works best to produce wellness in each of your patients. As you are aware, the power of your belief has tremendous influence, whether it is to utilize medical technology, instill confidence in a patient's own power to heal, or to apply a combination of the two. When you share your knowledge and compassion; when you look into a patient's eyes and tell them that you are a team with the same objective; when you assure your patient that he or she plays an integral role in restoring their wellness, you help to dispel their resistance and open the floodgates to their healing.

Understand that if a person desires wellness, their desire has already summoned vast amounts of life energy. Therefore, your task is to simply open the valve of energy they have already summoned. As you meet them where they stand and help to uncover their beliefs, you will know how to assist them in releasing their resistance which will allow healing life energy to flow. You may also wish to employ another technique that utilizes the ancient Chinese healing art of ch'i. This technique incorporates the help of your patients' loved ones — those who oftentimes feel powerless to help. Have them gather around the patient and all hold hands while you guide them through a healing visualization. A very powerful vortex of energy is created when more than one person is aligned with and projecting healing energy, and as a result, remarkable healings can occur.

Reaffirm your initial dream — the reason you chose the field of medicine: your dream to heal others. Utilize your tremendous power and responsibility to its fullest. Assist others in making the transition to perfect radiant health using the most powerful tool of all — belief. Join doctors like Dr. 'Patch' Adams who are committed to new-paradigm healing that applies the powerful 'magic' of love, laughter, and positivity.

In the book *Gesundheit* ("Good Health" in German), Dr. Adams explains his new-paradigm methodology: Upon meeting a new patient, he conducts a *four-hour* interview. He addresses the whole person, asking pertinent questions about their hobbies, dreams, aspirations, job, relationships, etc. rather than focusing on their illness — the physical manifestation of an underlying issue. To employ Dr. Adams' new-paradigm healing techniques on a larger scale, his Vision encompasses the creation of healing centers that offer free medical assistance in the spirit of love, kindness, and dignity. And though he is helping to usher in the wave of the future, he is meeting with some difficulty in obtaining funds. I will do my part and send him a copy of this book free of charge so he can visualize the healing centers (plural, he visualized only one, but we need more) and all the people he is helping. You, too, can help to usher in this model for healing by contributing to this fund: Gesundheit Institute, HC 64 Box 167, Hillsboro, West Virginia 24946

While writing *Many Lives, Many Masters*, Dr. Brian Weiss experienced a vivid dream where he addressed a group of his colleagues, fellow psychiatrists, about the value of human relationships:

> *We [Psychiatrists] are the ones who still talk to our patients, patiently and with compassion. We still take the time for this. We promote the conceptual understanding of illness, healing with understanding and the induced discovery of self-knowledge, rather than just with laser beams. We still use hope to heal. In this day and age, other branches of medicine are finding these traditional approaches to healing too inefficient, time-consuming, and unsubstantiated. They prefer technology to talk; computer-generated blood chemistries to the personal physician-patient chemistry, which heals the patient and provides satisfaction to the doctor. Idealistic, ethical, personally gratifying approaches to medicine lose ground to economic, efficient, insulating, and satisfaction-destroying approaches. As a result, our colleagues feel increasingly isolated and depressed. The patients feel rushed and empty, uncared for. We should avoid being seduced by high technology. Rather, we should be the role models for our colleagues. We should demonstrate how patience, under-standing, and compassion help both the patient and the physician, taking more time to talk, to teach, to awaken hope and the expectation of recovery — these half-forgotten qualities of the physician as healer — these we must always use ourselves and be an example to our fellow physicians. High technology is wonderful in research and to promote the understanding of human illnesses and disease. It can be an invaluable clinical tool, but it can never replace those inherently personal characteristics and methods of the true physician....We are the teachers. We should not abandon this role for the sake of assimilation, especially not now.*[93]

— DR. BRIAN WEISS

New-Paradigm Healing

What might the future of healing hold? I may have gotten a glimpse at a lecture given by author Gregg Braden. At this lecture, Gregg presented an incredible video-clip that documented, in real time, the ancient

Chinese healing art of ch'i, or energy movement. Gregg, too, has discovered the incredible power of thought via a more circuitous route. He studied the ancient prophecies; pored over the teachings of both the indigenous American Indians and the Mayans; analyzed the Dead Sea Scrolls; investigated the pyramids in Egypt; and traveled to the monasteries in Tibet in search of libraries untainted by western civilization. His findings? A recurring theme emerged in each of these diverse realms — the power of the human being. And this incredible power was demonstrated in this film that Mr. Braden first viewed while visiting China!

Recorded at the Huaxia Zhineng Qigong Clinic and Training Center, the "medicineless hospital," in the city of Qinhuangdao, China, this video-clip was filmed in a cramped room with a small 'cast' — a camera man, three white-coated male energy-practitioners, an ultra-sound technician, and a woman diagnosed by traditional medicine to be in the latter stages of terminal bladder cancer. The healing began as the technician moved an ultrasound instrument over the woman's abdomen that clearly revealed a 3" diameter cancerous tumor. The practitioners then began to recite a single word over and over again that grew more powerful and emphatic as the healing progressed. In English, the word loosely translated to "already done," or "already accomplished." What happened next was truly remarkable. First, the tumor began to vibrate and then in the following 2 minutes and 40 seconds, it slowly dissipated until it completely vanished.[94]

Could this video have been a hoax? Or had I just witnessed something for which Western medicine has no answer. From what I know today, I believe it was the latter.

> These are the dark ages....right here and now. We're so proud of our technological marvels and scientific advances, but they are baubles, mere toys compared to the power and glory contained in every human nervous system. The most complex machine in Creation is within our bodies....In a few decades, no one will even remember these sad years — if any one thinks back on them at all, it will be with wonder the human race could have been so blind.[95]
>
> — MSI

The future is upon us friends and it is exciting! As each of us begins to recognize and utilize our authentic power, we will abolish what was previously known as illness and return to our natural state of perfect radiant health which will allow us to truly live, love and laugh!

Let's now proceed to our last subject, the appearance of your physical body, and apply the Four-Step Formula to create a body that reflects the real you! ᗺ

Eat, Drink, Be Merry, and Have a Body that Pleases You!

You are what you think, not what you eat.[96]
— JANE ROBERTS
The Nature of Personal Reality - A Seth Book

There is no cosmetic for beauty like happiness.
— COUNTESS OF BLESSINGTON

To change your experience or any portion of it, then, you must change your ideas. Since you have been forming your reality all along, the results will follow naturally.[97]
— JANE ROBERTS
The Nature of Personal Reality - A Seth Book

Food is an important part of a balanced diet.
— FRAN LEBOWITZ

Quite literally, you live in the body of your beliefs.[98]
— JANE ROBERTS
The Nature of Personal Reality - A Seth Book

Food is one of the most wonderful blessings in life. It awakens our taste buds to pure pleasure and delicious sensations. We love it! (and so does Angel! — vicariously.) Why do you think we have so many great restaurants serving so many wonderful dishes? Because we love food! What is not to love? Hot fudge sundaes, creamy sauces, butter, sour cream, potato chips, hash browns, gravy, candy, cookies…. Are you getting hungry? Or do these thoughts of 'bad' food strike terror in your heart? Do you believe these foods are so bad that you reject them completely? I would much prefer salads and carrot sticks.... *NOT!* The key is, of course, how you feel — positive, negative, or perhaps a combination of the two.

The key to relishing each bite of scrumptious food, as well as having a body you truly desire is within your reach. However, most of us are in a quandary, because what we love to eat and what we have been influenced to believe will happen if we eat it, are compelling opposing forces. And Angel is in a tither, for we are projecting contradicting frequencies. For each time Angel transmits an Angel-Alert to us — a wrong-way sign — in our unawareness of its meaning, we dismiss it. As a result, we magnetize more discomfort over the topic of food. To make matters worse, many well-intentioned celebrities that we trust, unwittingly reinforce this misconception when they advise us to exercise and watch our dietary intake continuously — advising us to push against! In reality though,

> *Diet and exercise have nothing to do with our physical bodies.*
> *We only **believe** that they do.*

What do you believe about food? Is it some evil villain tempting you at all times? Do all of those wonderful concoctions exist simply to drool over? Do you believe that everything you eat is going to turn to fat, clog your arteries, or cause a heart attack? Are you going to gain weight after eating the wonderful food you crave and then hate yourself afterwards for not having the will power to just say no?

Have you ever been on a diet? Most people on a diet focus on how much they hate dieting. They think about how hungry they are, how much they miss ice cream, Doritos®, McDonald's® french fries, etc. They think about how bored they are with the mostly bland, icky, limited selection of food the diet allows and how much trouble the process is. In those moments what are they focusing on? Wanting food. And what frequency does that feeling project? Not a good one.... However, unaware of the Four-Step Formula, most folks believe that dieting is their punishment for having sinned with food. The result? Another vicious circle is born.

Obesity is one of the leading health issues in our country. Why do you think the diet industry is estimated at more than $40 BILLION? We don't want to be overweight! And though our health would seem to be the predominant reason we want to lose weight, what we really desire is to look better. For when we look better, we *feel* better. In fact, everything we want in life is driven by our desire to feel better. We live in a visual society where we are first evaluated by our appearance. And being overweight, generally — unfairly — evokes feelings of irreverence from others — not a life of joy! Instead it oftentimes creates a life of humiliation, disrespect, and rampant discrimination. However, entrapped in our insidious beliefs, we project the pain and sorrow we inwardly feel outwardly onto our bodies. We think of them more as prisons rather than of the awesome vehicles they really are. The result? We abuse, disrespect, and denigrate them. A TV news magazine show explored the issue of weight and revealed startling statistics: 86 percent of American women feel they are overweight and 46 million Americans are on a diet today! Do you think these folks appreciate their bodies?

The influence of those we highly regard in our culture is felt everywhere, further amplifying this travesty. Our media, publications, movies, and TV screens are filled with pencil-thin people who believe it is virtuous to dine on salad and then jog until they drop, delivering the message that "thin is beautiful" at any cost. Young children are being influenced to fear food itself because of their fear of being overweight and the resulting rejection and taunting it elicits. The result? Kids are fainting because of inadequate nourishment! People are dying of anorexia because their self-image is so distorted they think they are overweight when they weigh as little as eighty pounds! Others have resorted to regurgitating what they eat because of their fear of weight. And some have taken even more drastic measures: they have undergone major surgery to staple their stomachs or remove some of their intestines all in an effort to look and feel good about themselves! These lives are not filled with joy!

Then there are those who are totally obsessed with their bodies. They are addicted to exercise, nutrition, and physical fitness — predominantly fueled by the fear that if they stop, they will gain weight and be miserable. That, friends, is not a life of joy either!

We compulsively eat the very foods we fear while believing they will create an ill-effect. And do they? Yes. Angel is, once more, delivering our orders to us. Because so many of us fear being overweight, what are we giving our attention to? Weight! Therefore, Angel will deliver our 'weight' order and as a result, we will crave more food, and in the process, gain more weight — more of what we *don't* want!

Overeating is the most prevalent manifestation of the conflict between what we desire and what we believe. Our beliefs are not only creating additional weight, but stress and conflict as well. If you are a victim of the vicious circle of weight, seize the opportunity before you. For your bad feelings are simply Angel-Alerts — a wrong-way signs — Points of Power. What do you really want, but believe you cannot have? Or if overeating has become a method of anesthetizing the pain of a red circuit, what is bothering you?

> Find out for what you are hungry, and from what you really need to purge. What grief is causing you to bury your life in distress?[99]
> — GLENDA GREEN
> Love Without End: Jesus Speaks

If you could have the body you desire, would you want it? If you could eat anything you felt like with no negative effects, would you? Could you? (Even green eggs and ham? Sorry, I couldn't resist...) The true test is how you feel; good or bad? (A little hint: fear and guilt feel bad....) Are your beliefs so ingrained that you may have a real obstacle before you? Remember, as long as you cling to old-paradigm programming, you will continue to project the same frequency and magnetize more of what you have right now. Is that what you want?

In *The Nature of Personal Reality*, Jane Roberts offers an insight into the conflict between our bodies and diets.

> You are overweight. It is a physical fact. It grieves you, but you believe it completely. You begin a round of diets, all based on the idea that you are overweight **because you eat too much**. Instead, **you eat too much because you believe that you are overweight**. The physical picture always fits because your belief in being overweight conditions your body to behave in just such a manner... diets simply reinforce the condition. ...Until you change your belief, you will continue... to overeat. Momentary gains will not last. Your entire behavior pattern operates according to the strong hypnotic suggestions given, and then of course your appearance and experience always reinforce your belief.[100]

> Diets do serve momentarily as outer signs that you are in control, and can seize the initiative; and as such they can be important. Usually, however, a pattern of unsuccessful diets occurs, operating then as a series of negative suggestions. The resistance is the result of conflicts in beliefs. You think you are overweight and accept this as reality. Steps to lose weight do not make sense in the face of that belief. They are "unrealistic" or even impossible.[101]

The reason why some lose-weight groups succeed in their therapy, at least momentarily, is that belief in the worth of the self is stressed. Unfortunately, weight is attacked as "bad" or "evil"; symbolic moral judgments enter the act. The therapy seldom has long-reaching effects because from then on any gained weight is even more negatively charged.[102]
— JANE ROBERTS
The Nature of Personal Reality - A Seth Book

The body is continuously changing, replenishing, and rebuilding itself at every moment and it has no other pattern to follow in doing so except the guidance to it by the mind.[103]
— SHAKTI GAWAIN

Enough insight? Let's now explore your beliefs and apply the Four-Step Formula to your advantage, so you can begin to manifest a body that reflects the real you!

What foods do you like?

_____

_____

_____

_____

Have you been influenced to believe that these foods are good or bad for you? _____

Do you allow yourself to eat what you crave?_____

Do you limit your food intake so your body will look good? _____

How do you feel when you consume foods labeled as bad?

_____

How do you feel when you exercise?_____

Is that feeling consistent?_____

Do you exercise to the point of exhilaration or exhaustion?_____

Mirror Mirror on the Wall...

What response do you receive when you look into a mirror?

_____

_____

_____

_____

_____

Imagine that your body had a completely different identity from you. If your body were a different Angel, would you speak to this Angel the way you speak to your body? Would you give 'Body Angel' what it liked and asked for? Remember, Angels communicate in two ways — one feels good and one feels bad.

Now rewrite your script regarding food and diet, utilizing the Formula.

1.   List the positive aspects of the foods you desire.

_____
_____
_____
_____
_____
_____

2.   List their negative aspects.

_____
_____
_____
_____
_____

3.   Determine the opposite of each negative and revise it to reflect something positive.

_____
_____
_____
_____
_____
_____

4.   Now feel what it would be like to enjoy both the positive aspects of food and the opposite of the negative aspects *right now*. Do you feel good? Free?

Reprogramming Your Body

We come into the world with some factory-installed elements...This inborn wiring gives the body the guidelines it needs to thrive, to ensure blood and oxygen flow, immune system functioning, our perceptions of sights and sounds, and other basic survival mechanisms.[104]   — DR. HERBERT BENSON

Our bodies were preprogramed to ensure our survival, and some elements of this programming were essential long ago. In prehistoric 'cave man' days it was common to have had extended periods of time without food. To accommodate for this lack of nourishment and potential peril, our bodies responded by slowing our metabolic rate, thus allowing nutrients to last longer.

Living in America today, we are assured that we will not starve. Stores are open twenty-four hours a day to purchase food, food stamps are available for those who are needy, and soup kitchens are accessible for those who are homeless. Yet when we diet today, our bodies still react as they did in 'cave man' days, instinctively interpreting a lack of food as perilous to our survival. The result? Our metabolism slows and we stop losing weight.

That response can now be altered. Because our bodies can be thought of as 'electromagnetic biocomputers,' we can reprogram them to correspond with what we desire. Think of this process as 'reprogramming a computer.' When you purchase a computer, it is preprogrammed with certain default settings to ensure its smooth operation. Settings for your mouse, cursor speed, and various other functions have been predetermined. However, as you begin to understand the operation of your computer more completely, you can manually reprogram it to respond to the settings you desire, rather than to what the factory deemed appropriate for a mass audience.

In this same manner, you can now reprogram your body. Having attained a new awareness of Who You Really Are, you can now assume responsibility for the messages you receive from your body and reprogram those that no longer serve you. As a result, you can maintain your desired weight with no anxiety. Sounds a lot better than dieting, doesn't it? It does because it is consistent with a life of joy, one that ensures your connection to source energy, rather than one of deprivation or guilt!

Let's Readjust Your Body-Image Frequency!

Your body is your own living sculpture. [105]

— JANE ROBERTS
The Nature of Personal Reality - A Seth Book

What is your desired weight? _____

Describe how you look and *feel* at this weight using all your senses.

_____

_____

_____

_____

_____

To rid yourself of unwanted weight, first thank your body for ensuring your survival while you were 'unconscious.' Now inform your body that you will no longer require your unwanted weight because it is interfering with your having a joyous life experience. Tell your body that whatever foods you consume will provide it with energy, vitality, and nourishment, and to eliminate anything it doesn't need in order to maintain your desired weight. Imagine your body very pleased, knowing that you are readjusting many red circuits — ridding yourself of contradicting thoughts. Then visualize your unwanted weight in a clear bubble, bursting, and then disappearing.

Next, look at your body in a different way. Lovingly, give the old-paradigm voice in the mirror its 'walking papers.' Now, rather than noticing the characteristics that displease you, appreciate the aspects of your body that are wonderful. Look in the mirror and say, "I have a strong body, I have soft skin, I have really nice hair," etc. Next, acknowledge the awesome vehicle you inhabit. Appreciate all of your bodily functions chugging away miraculously in perfect harmony.

Joyfully anticipate the body you desire every day for a minimum of one minute. Imagine what it feels like to inhabit your new body, for as you acknowledge the things that please you, you will maintain a state of connection which will allow your new body to manifest. In fact, the more you appreciate your present body, the faster your new body will manifest! However, be patient with your results, for you don't want to replace your frequency of joyful anticipation with impatience, for it will activate your 'off' switch and cancel your order. Just bask in the good feelings of inhabiting your new body. Fast-forward and visualize living without this conflict — this wrong-way sign that has drained you of the life energy necessary to live joyously. You may also choose to throw away your scale, for 'taking score' can act as a powerful negative influence, which can activate your 'off' switch, and cancel your order.

After placing your order, be on the lookout for Angacles — people, events, or circumstances — that will point you in the direction of your order. You will be led to the foods, exercise, or whatever you need to manifest your order. And the good news is that you will *feel* like eating whatever you are craving and be motivated to do whatever you are inspired to do.

Whatever body-image frequency you project inwardly from your heart will manifest outwardly in your life experience, hence, you are the only obstacle to having what you want. Your body is simply taking its instructions from your beliefs which will determine your beauty and health, or lack of beauty and health. Therefore, when you readjust your body-image circuits from red to green, you will allow life energy to flow and your health and beauty will follow.

A Thought and Affirmation Regarding Food and Diet

The Thought

When eating bamboo sprouts, remember the man who planted them. — CHINESE PROVERB

What meal you would eat if it were your last?

_____
_____
_____
_____
_____

Now, think about the process that every item in your meal went through before it was placed on your plate. Imagine each item growing, where it grew, and the person who tended to it day after day. If it was a grain, think about the farmer planting the seeds, tending the crops, harvesting them, and bringing them to market. Think about the food manufacturer buying the grains and creating the finished product. Think about the steps taken to package it. Think about the plane that carried your food; the truck that brought it to the distribution center of your grocery store; the unloading of the truck; the folks who stocked it on the shelves; your selecting it, and then preparing it for your meal.

If you chose meat for your final meal, think about the mother animal giving birth to her baby. Think of the days 'Baby' spent growing up on the farm grazing or eating grains until he grew large enough to sell at market. Think about Baby being loaded onto a truck, Baby's journey to the slaughterhouse, and Baby's death. Think about the folks who stripped Baby's carcass, butchered him, and packaged Baby for you to select at your grocery store. Think about going to the store to purchase Baby for the express purpose of giving you the energy, vitality, and nourishment that allows you to live. *Give thanks to Baby* — a very real, living, feeling creature with a spirit — for Baby's gift enabled you to live another day without hunger. Be thankful for the numerous people involved in bringing you the food you are now consuming. Appreciate every step. In other words, be conscious. All of these steps had to occur so that you could eat. (I'm not trying to put you on a guilt trip or gross you out with my graphic example. I believe that some animals are here for our consumption. Earth is an environment of free will where the law of Attraction prevails and like can *only* attract like. Therefore Baby *intended* to provide you with the gift of his body as nourishment. Baby was actually an Angacle that appeared in response to an order.) However, I also believe that you were meant to be conscious — to be grateful and appreciate his gift. My point? I want to impress upon you that in every "Happy Meal™" there is a Baby who died to provide you nourishment.)

The Affirmation

Whenever you eat a meal — whether you are eating at home, dining in a fine restaurant, or eating in your car at the drive-through — be thankful for the food, plants, or animals that are providing you with nourishment. Be thankful for all the people involved in nurturing and preparing this food for you. After expressing your gratitude, instruct your body to utilize everything it needs, and to eliminate everything it does not to reach and/or maintain your ideal weight of ____ pounds. Intend for this food to provide you with energy, health, vitality, and nourishment. Then feel yourself becoming healthier, stronger, and filled with energy as a result of consuming this food — regardless of what you may have been influenced to believe about it.

Express Your Gratitude

I once read an interview with a woman who worked in a slaughterhouse. Because she was the last person the cattle saw before their heads were cut off, she felt it was important to pet them, love them, and thank them just before their deaths. I believe there can be no greater gift of compassion and love than the one she gave these animals about to make their sacrifice for us (yes, I was crying). Now, we just need to *appreciate* their gift. As you express your gratitude for the food you eat and the body you inhabit, you will then be living as life is meant to be lived — as a joyous magical experience overflowing with love and laughter! ☺

Part IX
The Postscript

PART IX

The Postscript

LIVING HAPPILY EVER AFTER!

Part IX

The Postscript

LIVING HAPPILY EVER AFTER!

Now This is Life!

I'm not afraid of storms for I'm learning how to sail my ship. — LOUISA MAY ALCOTT
1832-1888

We are each given a block of marble when we begin a lifetime, and the tools to shape it into sculpture. We can drag it behind us untouched, we can pound it to gravel, we can shape it into glory. Examples from every other life are left for us to see, lifeworks finished and unfinished, guiding and warning.[1] — RICHARD BACH

The most incomprehensible thing about the world is that it is comprehensible. — ALBERT EINSTEIN
1879-1955

Life is no brief candle to me. It is sort of a splendid torch that I have got hold of for the moment. — GEORGE BERNARD SHAW
1856-1950

I think of life as a good book. The further you get into it, the more it begins to make sense. — HAROLD S. KUSHNER

Getting there isn't half the fun — it's all the fun. — ROBERT TOWNSEND

See golden days, fruitful of golden deeds, with joy and love triumphing. — JOHN MILTON
1608-1674

*Follow your dream... If you stumble, don't stop and lose
sight of your goal, press on to the top. For only on the top
can you see the whole view.* — AMANDA BRADLEY

*Life is to be an experience of constant joy, continuous
creation. Be joyful, loving, accepting, blessing and
grateful.*[2] — NEALE DONALD WALSCH
Conversations with God - Book 1

Ithaka

*As you set out for Ithaka, hope your journey is a long
one, full of adventure, full of discovery.*

*Laistrygonians, Cyclops, angry Poseidon — don't be
afraid of them: You'll never find things like that on your
way as long as you keep your thoughts raised, as long as
a rare excitement stirs your spirit and your body.*

*Laistrygonians, Cyclops, wild Poseidon — you won't
encounter them unless you bring them along inside your
soul, unless your soul sets them up in front of you.*

Hope that your journey is a long one.

*May there be many summer mornings when, with what
pleasure, what joy, you enter harbors you're seeing for
the first time;*

*May you stop at Phoenician trading stations to buy fine
things; mother-of-pearl and coral, amber and ebony,
sensual perfume of every kind — as many sensual
perfumes as you can; and may you visit many Egyptian
cities to learn and go on learning from their scholars.*

*Keep Ithaka always in your mind.
Arriving there is what you're destined for.
But don't hurry the journey at all.
Better, if it lasts for years, so you're old by the time you
reach the island, wealthy with all you've gained along the
way, not expecting Ithaka to make you rich.*

*Ithaka gave you the marvelous journey.
Without her you would not have set out.
She has nothing left to give you now.*

*And if you find her poor, Ithaka won't have fooled you.
Wise as you will have become, so full of experience, you
will have understood by then what these Ithakas mean.*

— CONSTANTINE PETER CAVAFY
1863-1933

Celebrate the adventure of life as it unfolds before you each and every day! There is no finish line in this game called Life, so relax and enjoy your exciting journey. Go forth and be, do, and have whatever you desire, for you have the power within to manifest it. Choose love and the highest vision of yourself and others in every thought, word, and deed. And when you make a mistake, don't reprimand yourself — simply choose again in the next moment.

Everything you have experienced in your life — your successes, failures, interests, frustrations, challenges, confusions, dilemmas, and loves — has led you to the place you stand today, a fresh new Moment of Now. A Moment you can begin anew. And anything disguised as a 'lesson' was, in reality, a divine opportunity to awaken to Who You Really Are. Your willingness to pick up this book, read it, study it, and do the work required, is a part of the evolution into the Age of Spirit. What is your real task in life? To experience whatever you desire from this glorious place of incredible richness and diversity. A place where many varieties of experiences, beliefs, and desires exist. And through the manifestation of your desires, you will experience joy and growth.

Always remember that the greatest gift that you can give another is *Joy!* Your joy creates a powerful field of energy — the energy of light and love that infuses everything around it. An energy that becomes an inspiration to others who will remember that they want this joy as well. Therefore, whatever you are doing, whether it is picking up trash, being a mom, working in customer service, telemarketing, or acting as chairman of the board: *Be Joyful!!!*

The next greatest gift you can give is to *allow* — to allow your energy to flow despite what is occurring all around you, to allow the negative circumstances around you act as your catalyst to create.

"Robotsville" Is Not Too Appealing...

Because each of us is a powerful creator having free will, an environment that is conducive to creating is essential. And life on Earth provides that optimal environment because of its opposites — the vast array of options that life provides. Therefore, to neutralize or eliminate the opposites — those things you may not like — you deny others their creations, and in turn, diminish your ability to create.

Each of us has a different idea of what we want. My sister Jill has a poignant response she offers when someone disagrees with her: "That is why they made chocolate, vanilla, and pistachio" and, of course, the other twenty-eight flavors. One flavor is not right and the other wrong, they are just different and each of us likes a different flavor. And though you may not always agree with the choices made by others, allow them the freedom to choose their experiences. Allow them their choices as you would want them to allow you yours.

> *Those who deny freedom to others, deserve it not for themselves.* — ABRAHAM LINCOLN
> 1809-1865

> *Allow each soul to walk its path.*[3]
> — NEALE DONALD WALSCH
> *Conversations with God - Book 1*

Authors Esther and Jerry Hicks ask: Would you want to live in a world where everyone thought and acted just like you did? Where everything was the same color? Where the seasons never changed? Where all songs had the same notes? A world where all people behaved the same, looked the same, and agreed on everything? A world where everyone drove the same car having the same color? Think about it: If your tummy were full all the time, would you ever hunger for a certain food and then savor each and every bite as you ate it? If you grew up impoverished, did you not feel the intense desire for more? If you had grown up in wealth and opulence surrounded by beauty everywhere, how would you even know that your life was wonderful? Would you like to immediately have the answer to every question you have ever had in one moment, or do you appreciate having your life gently unfold with the answers slowly coming forth along the way?[4]

So you see my friend, it in the differences — the diversity, the separateness, the variety, the unique, the good and the bad, the gloomy days and the sunny days, the hot and the cold, the sleep and the weariness, the beauty and the ugliness, the fear and the love, the delicious and the icky, and all the points on the vast spectrum between these opposites that allow you to evaluate what you would choose for a perfect life experience. For without this vast spectrum — without all of these things you may have previously labeled as bad — there would be no choice and everything would be the same. Can you now see how all experiences are essential elements within this Divine Plan designed to maximize your ability to create?

> *The soul cannot choose to be anything if there is nothing to choose from.*[5]
> — NEALE DONALD WALSCH
> *Conversations with God - Book 1*

Good and evil then simply represent the birth of choices.[6]
— JANE ROBERTS
The Nature of Personal Reality - A Seth Book

If we had no winter, the spring would not be so pleasant: if we did not sometimes taste of adversity, prosperity would not be so welcome. — ANNE BRADSTREET
1612-1672

[A]ll seeming opposites are other faces of the one supreme drive toward creativity.[7] — JANE ROBERTS
The Nature of Personal Reality - A Seth Book

We are made out of oppositions; we live between two poles — you don't reconcile the poles, you just recognize them. — ORSON WELLES
1915-1985

If all the year were playing holidays, to sport would be as tedious as to work. — WILLIAM SHAKESPEARE
1564-1616

...we could never learn to be brave and patient if there were only joy in the world. — HELEN KELLER
1880-1968

Sleep, riches, and health, to be truly enjoyed, must be interrupted. — JEAN PAUL RICHTER

A man is insensible to the relish of prosperity till he has tasted adversity. — SA'ID

To optimize your enjoyment of the vast choices that life endows, your task is to be sensitive to your negative feelings and understand that they are simply wrong-way signs, your valuable gifts, for they are illuminating your path, not the path of another. Furthermore, as you become more and more proficient in your power, you will not be bothered by what others are doing or saying, because you will not magnetize them.

We must love them both, those whose opinions we share and those whose opinions we reject. For both have labored in the search for truth and both have helped us in the finding of it. — THOMAS AQUINAS
1225-1274

Your joy, freedom and growth does not depend on what
others choose for themselves. As you find your balance,
you will offer inspiration to those around you.[8]
— ESTHER and JERRY HICKS

Will this knowledge lead you to a "Pollyanna" life of only positives? No, it's not supposed to. It's meant to lead you along a path of empowerment — appreciating what is positive and utilizing what you perceive as negative. However, your negative experiences will no longer carry the sting they did in the past, for you now know their purpose: To ignite the desire within you that summons life energy, thus sustaining your life.

When you come to understand that this world is truly *overflowing* with abundance, that an infinite amount of energy exists that awaits your instructions, that each of us is equally powerful, you will banish any guilt and order just what you want for your life experience. Furthermore, as you focus your powerful thoughts on what you appreciate, regardless of the circumstances, you will set the stage to experience the most wondrous feeling of all: inner peace and unconditional love for others.

There is a Life Stream that flows to you, and this is a
Stream of clarity, a Stream of wellness, a Stream of
abundance... and in any moment, you are allowing it or
not. What someone else does with the Stream, or not,
does not have anything to do with how much of it will be
left for you. This Stream is as abundant as your ideas
allow it to be.[9]
— ESTHER and JERRY HICKS

As you experience the miraculous nature of your Angacles appearing day after day, you will reawaken to the magic in life. You will then begin to utilize your living connection to the very real realm of Spirit — to Angel and God who have been with you throughout your journey. Allow Angel to now guide you to joy, freedom, and growth and become an integral part of your everyday life from this day forward.

Now that you know the secret to life, you may be tempted to recruit the entire planet. However, it would be advisable for you to refrain, for those around you will attract this information when they are ready to. Recognize that everyone will awaken in their own time, so allow them their time. (Rent the movie *Pleasantville* — a metaphor for the awakening — to observe how some people react to change.... A little hint: they get scared.) How would you feel about a baby who had not yet learned to walk? Would you be mad? Would you be impatient? Or would you be empathetic and understand that you, too, had gone through a similar learning process where you had to learn how to crawl before you walked. You now understand the value of this process, for each of your 'spills' helped you to find your balance. Remember the advice from Glinda the good witch in the *Wizard of Oz*: You have to learn this truth for yourself or you won't believe it.

What can you do to help others? Be Who You Really Are: loving, kind, appreciative, compassionate, and offering praise to others. For when you align with those high frequencies, you lift your energy and others around you magically change. Your power to help others remains the greatest when you *walk* the talk, rather than talking the talk. For when you walk the talk, people's curiosity is piqued and they may ask your secret. Then you can share it with them. Remember, information is only valuable to a person who has asked a question, for then he or she is truly *interested* in the answer.

So, What's Your Verdict?

Upon completing the DMA — Dimensional Mind Approach — course I attended, I was asked to articulate what I had learned and how my life had benefitted from the knowledge imparted. I wrote:

~ *I had a greater sense of inner peace.*

~ *I had a sense of direction regarding my business.*

~ *My relationship issues became less critical and anxiety-laden.*

~ *I felt an inner guidance regarding my life's path.*

~ *My love for everything and everyone was amplified*

~ *I felt that I had the ability to love and accept myself as the person I really am.*

~ *I felt I now had someone else to go to or count on to help me (Angel!).*

~ *I knew I had the ability to help others.*

~ *I understood that I was responsible for my choices.*

~ *My anxiety was lessened.*

~ *I felt more comfortable being true to myself.*

~ *I felt powerful.*

It is my innermost wish that you have had a similar experience and that my 'friends' and I have conveyed enough evidence for you to awaken to Who You Really Are, and award us a favorable verdict.

The Purpose of Your Life

The end of all our exploring will be to arrive where we started and know the place for the first time.
— T.S. ELIOT
1888-1965

Any life, no matter how long and complex it may be, is made up of a single moment — the moment in which a man finds out, once and for all, who he is.
— JORGE LUIS BORGES
1899-1986

Man's task is to become conscious of the contents that press upwards from the unconscious … As far as we can discern, the sole purpose of human existence is to kindle a candle in the darkness of mere being. — CARL G. JUNG
1875-1961

So live your life that the fear of death can never enter your heart. Trouble no man about his religion — respect him in his views, and demand that he respect yours. Love your life, perfect life. Beautify all things in your life. Seek to make your life long and of service to your people. Prepare a noble death song for the day when you go over the great divide…. Always give a word or sign of salute when meeting or passing a friend, or even a stranger, if in a lonely place. Show respect to all men, but grovel before none. When you arise in the morning, give thanks for the morning light, for your life and strength. Give thanks for your food and for the joy of living. If you see no reason for giving thanks, the fault lies in your self. Touch not the poisonous firewater that makes wise men turn to fools and robs the spirit of its vision. When your time comes to die, be not like those whose hearts are filled with the fear of death, so when their time comes they weep and pray for a little more time to live their lives over again in a different way. Sing your death song, and die like a hero going home. — TECUMSHEH, SHAWNEE

Man's main task in life is to give birth to himself, to become what he potentially is. — ERICH FROMM
1900-1980

All power is given man (through right thinking) to bring his heaven upon his earth, and this is the goal of the "Game of Life." The simple rules are fearless faith, nonresistance, and love![10] — FLORENCE SCOVEL SHINN

Sometime in your life you will go on a journey. It will be the longest journey you have ever taken. It is the journey to find yourself. — KATHERINE SHARP

The true profession of man is to find his way to himself. — HERMANN HESSE
1877-1962

The soul is crying for a reality experience which only physical life can give to it. The body is crying for an immortality experience which only the soul can give to it. As you permit this union to fulfill itself, you will directly know what it feels like to be the love that you are.[11] — GLENDA GREEN
Love Without End: Jesus Speaks

Every experience you have had in life and every phase of your growth has led you to this Moment: The moment to awaken to Who You Really Are. However, you always have the choice "To Be or Not To Be."

The right of choice is your freedom. You can stay lost as long as you want, and you can come home when you're ready. In the meantime, you may experience all the lessons that the denial of love can bring you![12] — GLENDA GREEN
Love Without End: Jesus Speaks

A little knowledge that acts, is worth infinitely more than much knowledge that is idle. — KHALIL GIBRAN
1883-1931

What you have lived before is a result of the thoughts, feelings, and beliefs you had. Your future will result in what you think, believe, and expect from this day forward. It's now up to you![13]

It's Up To You

One song can spark a moment,
One flower can wake the dream.
One tree can start a forest,
One bird can herald spring.
One smile begins a friendship,
One handclasp lifts a soul.
One star can guide a ship at sea,
One word can frame the goal.
One vote can change a nation,
One sunbeam lights a room.
One candle wipes out darkness,
One laugh will conquer gloom.
One step must start each journey,
One word must start each prayer.
One hope will raise our spirits,
One touch can show you care.
One voice can speak with wisdom,
One heart can know what's true,
One life can make the difference,
You see, it's up to you!

— UNKNOWN

Let the Good Times Roll!

Work like you don't need the money,
Love like you've never been hurt,
Dance like nobody's watching.

— UNKNOWN

And so, my friend, the time is come for you to become whatever you can imagine. The time is come to create a Heaven upon our beautiful Earth: to allow her to become Who She Really is — a living being patiently awaiting our higher consciousness, providing us with everything we desire; our home to cherish with love, awe, and a reverence for her majestic splendor.

I hope that you now understand that you are so much more than what you may have previously thought. I wish you a life filled with love and joy, with blessings and gratitude, with happiness and fulfillment, with inner peace and an unbridled exuberance that bursts forth from every cell of your being! It's now time to live happily ever after, love happily ever after, and laugh happily ever after! ☯

Sample Orders For a Life Overflowing With Joy!

Every moment of your life is infinitely creative and the Universe is endlessly bountiful. Just put forth a clear enough request and everything your heart desires must come to you.[14] — SHAKTI GAWAIN

Lord, make me an instrument of Your peace. Where there is hatred let me sow love; where there is injury, pardon; where there is doubt, faith; where there is despair, hope; where there is darkness, light; and where there is sadness, joy. — ST. FRANCIS OF ASSISI
1181-1226

We can act as if there were a God; feel as if we were free; consider Nature as if she were full of special designs; lay plans as if we were to be immortal; and we find then that these words do make a genuine difference in our moral life. — WILLIAM JAMES
1842-1910

Grant yourself permission to have all that life has to offer — and you will discover it has more to offer than you've ever imagined.[15] — NEALE DONALD WALSCH
Conversations with God - Book 2

Today a new sun rises for me; everything lives, everything is animated, everything seems to speak to me of my passion, everything invites me to cherish it. — ANNE DE LENCLOS

Potential Orders You May Wish to Incorporate in Your Daily "Work"

I choose relaxation and quiet from the physical world
when I am "going to work."[16]

℘ ℘ ℘

I am growing through joyous experiences;
I choose a wondrous life experience.[16]

℘ ℘ ℘

There is nothing I cannot be, do or have.
I have Angel ready to assist me and I am ready.[16]

℘ ℘ ℘

I am joyful, I am free, I am inspired, I am prosperous.[16]

℘ ℘ ℘

I am a magnificent mother (father, wife, husband, daughter, son, etc.).[16]

℘ ℘ ℘

I am looking for what I like and what I want in my life today.[16]

℘ ℘ ℘

I intend to contribute the best of myself to this world,
and my contribution is making it a better place in which to live.[16]

℘ ℘ ℘

I am waking each day refreshed, full of vitality, and energy.[16]

℘ ℘ ℘

In intend for my family, myself, and those around me to be
safe in everything we do and everywhere we go.[16]

℘ ℘ ℘

Today, no matter where I go, what I do, or who I interact with,
I choose that which makes me feel good and is in harmony
with the highest vision I have of myself.[16]

I choose joy and happiness throughout my day.[16]

I am enjoying freedom, balance, and peace of mind in my life.[16]

I am growing and evolving as a person in a positive
happy way in all my experiences.[16]

I am accomplishing what my greatest gifts have led me to
accomplish for my lifetime.[17]

I choose prosperity and intend an abundance of dollars,
(or $____.00) in my checkbook every month.[16]

I choose to travel with my family or friends and enjoy
the beautiful sites in our world.

I choose to be beautiful, fit and trim.

I choose perfect radiant health.[16]

I intend to have the food I consume bring me health and vitality.
I intend for my body to eliminate everything I do not need to
maintain my desired weight of _____lbs.[17]

My relationship with _____ is loving, kind, gentle, allowing, respectful, growing, evolving, flourishing in health, prosperity, and abundance. We are filled with joy in each other's presence and share our lives together in harmony. We constantly communicate our ever-changing desires to one another and they are accepted with love. Together, we are helping and inspiring others in their quest for fulfillment.

℘ ℘ ℘

My relationship with my child, _____, is loving, kind, gentle and respectful. We are both teacher and student to one another. _____ is happy, healthy, safe, joyous, exuberant, and full of love. _____ uplifts others in his or her presence.

℘ ℘ ℘

This world is full of abundance and there is plenty to go around for all.[16]

℘ ℘ ℘

I am goodness and mercy and compassion and understanding.
I am peace and joy and light.
I am forgiveness and patience, strength and courage,
a helper in time of need,
a comforter in time of sorrow,
a healer in time of injury,
a teacher in times of confusion.
I am the deepest wisdom and the highest truth;
the greatest peace and the grandest love.[18]
— NEALE DONALD WALSCH
Conversations with God - Book 1

The Recipe For Eternal Joy

I choose joy first and foremost.
I choose laughter.
I choose to find reasons to offer praise to myself and others.
I choose to see the beauty in nature, animals, and other people.
I choose reasons to love.
I choose to look for things that bring forth reasons to love.
I choose to find what uplifts me.
I choose to seek opportunities to uplift others.
I choose a feeling of well-being.
I choose to find what I want for a perfect life experience.[19]
— ESTHER and JERRY HICKS

You may wish to include some of these wonderful attributes on your "This is Who I Choose To Be" list (The Pathway - page 9).

End your 'work' with:

This, or something better, will now begin to happen for me in positive ways for all concerned.[20]

Techniques To Hasten Your Orders

To expedite the arrival of your orders, search for pictures from magazines, newspapers, etc. that represent your orders, and tape them on your refrigerator door, bathroom mirror, or any place where you can focus on them in joy. If there are people in your home who do not subscribe to the Four-Step Formula, you may be influenced negatively as a result of their beliefs. In that case, honor their feelings and remember that they are sacred souls on a sacred journey. At the same time, honor yourself. Purchase an album for your pictures, and don't forget to continually add to it. Reserve a time to peruse them in joy and anticipation while being sensitive to your feelings as you do. Then relax, stay connected to source energy, and your orders will begin to manifest. And when they do, enjoy them until you find your life energy waning. At that point, you'll know that it's time for *more* ideas — more avenues to summon life energy to you.

What will life include in the new paradigm? First, you'll choose what pleases you from the magnitude of experiences you observe all around you. Then you'll place your orders and wait in joyful anticipation for your Angacles to appear. Next, you'll take inspired action and last, you'll enjoy your manifestation. And then the cycle of creation will begin once more. Sounds a lot better than being a victim to the twists and turns of fate, doesn't it? It does, because you are embodying your authentic power and truly living, loving, and laughing! ☺

A lot of Livin' To Do

There are guys just ripe for some kissin'
And I mean to kiss me a few.
Oh, those guys don't know what they're missin'
I've got a lot of livin' to do.

And there's wine just ready for tastin'
And there's Cadillacs all shiny and new.
Gotta move cos' time is a 'wastin'
I've got a lot of livin' to do.

Well there's music to play, places to go, people to see.
Oh, everything for you and me.
Life's a ball, if only you know it.
And it's all just waitin' for you.
You're alive, so come on and show it.

I've got a lot of livin'
Such a lot of livin'
I've got a lot of livin' to do.[21]

Words by Lee Adams - Music by Charles Strouse
from the Broadway musical "Bye Bye Birdie"

$\mathcal{I}\,\mathcal{H}ave\,\mathcal{A}\,\mathcal{D}ream\ldots$

Imagine all the people sharing all the world.
— JOHN LENNON
1940-1980

~ I have a dream.... In my dream each of us appreciates our world for the beautiful wondrous place it is and our lives for all the potential and excitement they hold.

~ In my dream, each of us embodies perfect radiant health, as illness does not exist in our world.

~ In my dream, we do not all share the same beliefs, for there is much contrast and great diversity among us; however, there is no struggle between us. Those of us who think in similar ways simply gravitate to one another. We are not threatened by others who think differently, for we do not invite them into our life experience through our thoughts.

~ In my dream, we allow, respect, and appreciate our differences for we know that they create the environment that allows us to choose the experiences we each desire. We understand that life without desire and passion is meaningless.

~ In my dream, there is no one right way or wrong way, nor one set of rules that applies to everyone. Each of us lives in a manner we have chosen and respects the uniqueness of others who have chosen a different path, for we know that our identity embraces all.

~ In my dream, we understand that each of us has different feelings. We have a deep trust and awareness of our feelings because we understand that they come from Spirit and are meant to guide us along our path of free will.

~ In my dream, whenever we encounter an aspect of life that does not please us, we simply utilize our displeasure as a sign to clarify what we want to create for our experience.

~ In my dream, we utilize our power, clarity, and new perspectives to continually evoke new ideas, thus expanding creation further and further.

~ In my dream, Mother Earth provides us an abundance of natural resources for all of us to enjoy prosperity.

~ In my dream, each of us travels whenever we choose, participating fully in the beauty and magnificence of our world.

~ In my dream, whenever we choose to experience something new in the Universe, we simply 'will' it and it happens.

~ In my dream, we love without judgment, act without prejudice, and honor without need. We offer praise freely, feel compassion from the bottoms of our hearts, and appreciate the beauty that surrounds us.

If my dream resonates with yours, will you help bring it to fruition? For when each of us as God's children embodies Who We Really Are, we will create our new world and be free at last! ☯

Has This Message Awakened You to a Mission?

There are two ways of spreading light: to be the candle
or the mirror that reflects it. — EDITH WHARTON
1861-1937

You have to raise consciousness before you change
consciousness.[22] — NEALE DONALD WALSCH
Conversations with God - Book 3

Alone we can do so little; together we can do so much. — HELEN KELLER
1880-1968

Give light and the people will find their own way. — MOTTO OF THE SCRIPPS-HOWARD NEWSPAPERS

Never doubt that a small group of thoughtful committed
people can change the world, indeed it's the only thing
that ever has. — MARGARET MEAD
1901-1978

Follow life, serve the living, and fulfill your love by
following the pathways that life is revealing to you.[23] — GLENDA GREEN
Love Without End: Jesus Speaks

Again and again some people in the crowd wake up.
They have no ground in the crowd, and they emerge
according to much broader laws. They carry strange
customs with them, and demand room for bold gestures.
The future speaks ruthlessly through them. — RAINER MARIA RILKE
1875-1926

Author Gregg Braden shared a beautiful story at a lecture I attended — a story about children who had entered a "Special Olympics" race. As you probably know, the Special Olympics is held for children who are mentally 'challenged' in some way. In a race that was scheduled later in the day, the competitors met one another prior to the event and in a short period of time forged an emotional bond. Little did they know that their bond would soon be put to a test.

The race began undramatically: The gun sounded and the children took off for the finish line. In the middle of the race, however, one child looked back to see how his friends were faring and much to his dismay found that one had never made it off the starting line. Without hesitating, he stopped and went back to help his new friend. And one by one, each of the competitors did the same. Then they did something even more remarkable. The children locked arms, formed a chain of one, and crossed the finish line *together*. Spectators looked on in awe, for they had just witnessed a truly powerful message: Any individual victory is empty, at best, if everyone doesn't win. For in reality, there are no winners if anyone is left behind.

In the books *Conversations with God - Books 1, 2, & 3* (I believe I quoted half of), author Neale Donald Walsch was a bit hesitant to share the profound information he had received with the rest of the world as it was exceedingly personal and defied much traditional thinking. As he posed this quandary to God, this was the reply he received:

> *These ideas will separate you from the many. Most of your fellow man. They will call you crazy. They will do this because others will become attracted to your truth — for the promises it holds for them. Here is where your fellow man will interfere — for here is where you begin to threaten them. For your simple truth, simply lived, will offer more beauty, more comfort, more peace, more joy and more love of self and others than anything your earthly fellows could contrive. And the truth adopted would mean the end of their ways. It would mean the end of hatred and fear of war and bigotry. The end of the condemning and the killing that has gone on for centuries in My Name. The end of might-is-right. The end of purchase through power. The end of loyalty and homage through fear. The end of the world as they know it — and as you have created it thus. So be ready, kind soul. For you will be vilified and spat upon, called names and deserted, and finally they will accuse you, try you and condemn you — all in their own ways — from the moment you accept and adopt your holy cause — the realization of self.*[24]

Why then do it? Because you are no longer concerned with the acceptance or approval of the world. You are no longer satisfied with what that has brought you. You are no longer pleased with what it has given others. You want the pain to stop. You want the suffering to stop, the illusion to end. You have had enough of this world as it presently is. You seek a newer world. Seek it no longer, and Call it Forth![25]

∿   ∿   ∿

And so I have chosen you to be my messenger. You, and many others. For now, during these times immediately ahead, the world will need many trumpets to sound the clarion call. The world will need many voices to speak the words of Truth and healing for which millions long. The world will need many hearts joined together in the work of the soul, and prepared to do the work of God. You don't have to do anything. You have no obligation, only opportunity. It takes great courage. Are you ready?[26]

Upon reading Book Three, the final book in the *Conversations With God* trilogy in November of 1998, the psychic message I had received years ago now made complete sense to me. Planet Earth *is* on the verge of the greatest destruction *or* the greatest stage of evolution that humankind has ever experienced. The potential for destruction exists because power is in the wrong hands. The wrong hands of governments who, in their ignorance, hence, innocence, react and respond in fear — old-paradigm thinking — as they develop technologies that have the capability of destroying our planet. Power is in the wrong hands of those in medical science, who, in their lack of understanding how life fundamentally operates, are developing viruses so resistant to antibiotics that they have the potential to eliminate humankind. Power is in the wrong hands of unconscious scientists who are contributing to the creation of a technology that has the means to control the mental states of people wholly by manipulating their magnetic frequencies.

As the message given to me by the psychic on the second page of this book stated: our 'advanced' technology is now capable of destroying us as it has various civilizations that preceded us, if our consciousness is not raised. We have been blind, so we must now open our eyes. For when there is technology without the awareness of God, life will not function properly. Channeling the power [i.e., Formula] properly will benefit and evolve mankind.

The evolution of humanity is in each of our hands. The recreation of our world will begin with each one of us becoming aware of our power and then utilizing it! The Four-Step Formula will allow us to realize our grandest dreams if we can transcend old-paradigm thinking. As the message further stated: "The time is now for these events to happen; that is the task at hand." We now stand at a crossroads, for unless we recognize the power of our thoughts and elevate them to the level of our technology, the repercussions can result in the extinction of mankind.

> *Advanced technology without advanced thought creates not advancement, but demise.*[27] — NEALE DONALD WALSCH
> *Conversations with God - Book 3*

> *The largest question facing the human race is not when will you learn, but when will you act on what you've already learned?*[28] — NEALE DONALD WALSCH
> *Conversations with God - Book 3*

What Can Little Ol' You Do? A Lot!

I don't know about you, but I'm feeling uncomfortable with the preceding information, therefore, it's a wrong-way sign. So, let's apply the Four-Step Formula. What do I want? I want to feel free and safe. I want others to understand their power and live life as it is meant to be lived. Now I'm going to choose those things and place my order by *feeling* what that feels like…. Two minutes later… Awesome…. Done!

Did you join me in my visualization? For that is certainly one way you can help. You can also help by living your life in accordance with Who You Really Are — someone who cares about others, life, our planet, and the future of humanity. You are now aware that you have the power to help — it is within you. Take that one tiny step for humankind and know that your step will help immensely! For when you are Being Who You Really Are, you are helping to raise the collective frequency of our world and eliminate fear-based living. Furthermore, when many of us join together in mind and spirit, we create an incredibly powerful vortex of healing energy.

> *You clearly will not change what you are doing, until you change how you are being. You have to change your idea about who you are in relationship to your environment and everything in it, before you will ever act differently.*[29] — NEALE DONALD WALSCH

Mr. Walsch conveys that our purpose is clear:

> You came to the room to heal the room. You have come
> to the space to heal the space. There is no other reason
> for you to be here.[30]

And when Neale felt that the task of awakening humanity would be too overwhelming to accomplish, he was told

> You will wake up! You are waking up! The paradigm is
> shifting. The world is changing. It's happening right in
> front of your eyes. Don't give up, don't give up. The
> grandest adventure has just begun![31]

⌇ ⌇ ⌇

> Your grandest ideas are as yet unexpressed, and your
> grandest vision unlived. Look! Notice! The days of your
> blossoming are at hand. The stalk has grown strong, and
> the petals are soon to open. And I tell you this: The
> beauty and the fragrance of your flowering shall fill the
> land, and you shall yet have your place in the Garden of
> the Gods.[32]

We are then told how to fulfill our purpose on an individual basis:

> Behold the darkness, yet curse it not. Rather be a light
> unto the darkness, and so transform it. Let your light so
> shine before men, that those who stand in the darkness
> will be illumined by the light of your being, and all of you
> will see, at last, Who You Really Are.[33]

⌇ ⌇ ⌇

> Be a Bringer of the light! For your light can do more
> than illuminate your own path. Your light can be the
> light which truly lights the world.[34]

⌇ ⌇ ⌇

> [S]hine on then, O Illuminati! Shine on! That the
> moment of your greatest darkness may yet become your
> grandest gift. And even as you are gifted, so, too, will
> you gift others, giving to them the unspeakable treasure:
> Themselves. Let this be your task, let this be your
> greatest joy: to give people back to themselves. Even in
> their darkest hour. Especially in that hour.[35]

The world waits for you. Heal it. Now. In the place where you are. There is much you can do. For my sheep are lost and must now be found. Be ye, therefore, as good shepherds, and lead them back to Me.[36]

Indigo Children, by Lee Carroll and Jan Tober, is a book that speaks of the different and unusual psychological attributes that many children born in the past ten years possess, as chronicled by day-care workers, teachers, Ph.D.s, M.D.s, etc. Their findings verify what has been previously stated by metaphysicists who refer to these children as the "new kids on the block" — those children born with a greater awareness of Who They Really Are — those with higher frequencies. At the end of *Indigo Children* a wonderful passage was included by an unknown author that spoke of what is to come:

> *The time of the Great Awakening is come. You who have chosen to lift your eyes from darkness to the light are blessed to see the event of a new day on planet Earth. Because your heart has yearned to see real peace where war has reigned, to show mercy where cruelty has dominated, and to know love where fear has frozen hearts, you are privileged to your world.*
>
> *Planet Earth is a blessing to you. She is your friend and your Mother. Always remember and honor your relationship with her. She is a living, loving, breathing being, like unto yourself. She feels the love that you give as you walk upon her soil with a happy heart.*
>
> *The Creator has chosen your hands to reach the lonely, your eyes to see innocence, not guilt, and your lips to utter words of comfort. Let pain be no more! You have wandered in dark dreams for so long now. Step into the light and send for what you know is truth. The world has suffered, not from evil, but from fear of acknowledgment of the good. Allow fear to be released now and forever — released into the light and transformed. It is within your power to do so.*
>
> *No one can find yourself but you. All your answers are within. Teach the lessons you have learned. Your understanding has been given, not only for yourself, but to guide a sore and tired world to a place of rest in a new consciousness.*
>
> *Here before you is your vision come true. Here is your answer given you — a song to soothe a weary soul and make it new again. Here is the bridge that joins you to your*

brothers and sisters. Here is your Self. Look gently upon yourself, and allow yourself to be filled by the Light you have been seeing. True love comes from yourself, and every thought is a blessing to the entire Universe.

All areas of your life will be healed. You will shine with a golden splendor that speaks of the One who created you in wisdom and glory. The past will dissolve like a dark dream, and your joy will be so brilliant that you will have no recollection of the night.

Go forth and be a messenger of Hope. Point the way to healing by walking in gratefulness. Your brothers and sisters will follow. And as you pass beyond the portal of limitation, you will be united and reunited with all who seem to be lost. There is no loss in the Creator. Choose the path of forgiveness, and you will weep tears of joy for the goodness you find in all.

Go forth and live the life of the radiant soul that you are. Glorify the Creator in your every deed. You are important, you are needed, and you are worthy. Do not allow the dark cloak of fear to hide the light from your view. You were not born to fail. You were destined to succeed. The hope of the world has been planted in your breast, and you are assured of success as you stand for the One who created you.

This, then, is the healing of Planet Earth. All your doubts and fears can be set aside, as you know the healing comes from the love in your heart.[37]

I believe that God sent many of us to remind our brothers and sisters of Who We Really Are so that we can all choose to live life as we wish. If this message has inspired you to assist in this endeavor but you still have doubt, ponder this scenario: If you were visited in the middle of the night by a group of beautiful Angels who entrusted you with a luminous glowing box that contained the Secret to Life — a secret that would enable people to alleviate much of the pain, anguish, and suffering in our world, as well as the keys to creating a Heaven on Earth — what would you do with it?

Send me an e-mail at **www.secrettolife.NET** if you have any ideas. My vision encompasses workshops, seminars, television, a radio talk-show, a help-line, and daily meetings held in schools, churches, and homes where people can learn how to utilize the Four-Step Formula on an ongoing basis. ☯

Cabaret

What good is sitting alone in your room?
Come hear the music play.
Life is a Cabaret old chum, come to the cabaret.
Put down the knitting, the book, and the broom.
It's time for a holiday.
Life is a cabaret old chum, come to the cabaret.
Come taste the wine, come hear the band,
Come blow your horn start celebrating,
"Right this way your tables waiting."
No use permitting some prophet of doom.
To wipe every smile away.
Life is a cabaret old chum, come to the cabaret.
Start by admitting from cradle to tomb
It isn't that long a stay.
Life is a cabaret old chum,
Only a cabaret old chum.
And I love a cabaret![38]

Words by Fred Ebb — Music by John Kander

A Note from Me to You

Love is everywhere, I see it.
You are all that you can be, go on and be it.
Life is perfect, I believe it.
Come play the game with me.
— JOHN DENVER

Hi, my name is Lauren Tratar (pronounced Trotter). Do you feel as though you know me now? Throughout this book I have shared my personal experiences, and hope that through my sharing you can gain a new perspective from your own experiences.

I am fifty years old and live in a suburb of Chicago with my ten-year-old son Zachary and fifty-eight-year old husband, Ken (it's now July of 2000). I have been married since 1989 to this 'crazy' man (in a loving, fun sense) who is busy running a company specializing in selling techno-logically-advanced computer data storage equipment and leading-edge database software. Anyone out there need any? If that sounds foreign to you, believe me, it does to me, too. In fact, whenever I have attended any kind of convention with him, I don't understand a word these folks are uttering — it all sounds like Martian to me!

Ken has been very supportive and loving throughout the evolution of this book (he financed it... with my 'orders' and Angel's help!), but at the same time was skeptical. He cannot fathom that his wife could have been led to something of such magnitude. He seems to live vicariously through all of my serendipitous events, 'sitting on the fence,' uncertain whether to commit to either side (although he professes to believe 80 percent of this message). At some point he will have seen enough and be ready to utilize the Formula to the extent that he 'goes to work' every day. But only when he is ready and I respect that... (well, I try — but I must confess that at times it drives me insane, and in my frustration, I resist by impatiently telling him: Whatever you give your attention to, will increase! I long for him to connect with his power and experience more joy in his life, rather than reacting to his self-created issues. (I know, place an order...) And because the Law of Attraction is absolute, I have paid the price.... As I resist, he, of course, persists and becomes more adamant in his refusal to try it out! He is definitely my teacher. Ken now thinks that I should have my own cable TV show as an evangelist ("Lauren, the Apostle"), and that because I wrote this book, or better said — compiled this material — I should have somehow magically transformed into Mother Teresa. Unfortunately, I have not.... Yet. Maybe that TV show is a good idea? It could resemble the kind of church depicted in the movie *"Sister Act"* with Whoopie Goldberg, et. al., singing all those great songs with joy and abandon. If only our churches took that message seriously — God is supposed to be fun! I loved that movie. But I'm only kidding... no TV shows. However, with each passing day it becomes easier and easier for me to walk the talk.

As you may have recognized, my background has been quite diverse — I get bored easily. My resumé? I've sold real estate; been a singer in a band; owned a jewelry store; had a telecommunications consulting /brokerage firm, where I was both president and janitor; designed and general contracted a few homes (that's now what I want to do when I grow up!), and had my son (my best accomplishment and challenge so far). No, you did not see the word author in any of my past endeavors as I mentioned in the preface, but I guess I can now include this undertaking as well on my list of accomplishments. What inspired me to write this book? It was the unrelenting barrage of messages I received for the past twenty-plus years, all reminding me that I had 'signed up' for some kind of Mission. The following events were my most significant wake-up calls:

એ   In 1981, I attended a luncheon with a friend hosted by the Nieman Marcus department store in downtown Chicago. This luncheon featured the renowned psychic, Irene Hughes, as keynote speaker. Upon answering a question I asked, Ms. Hughes added that something 'exciting' was going to happen to me later in my life. Having received the same message previously, I asked "What is it?" Her reply? "You'll find out when you are supposed to." OK...? Hmmm...! ♫ Do, do, do, do♫ (the theme from the *"Twilight Zone"* wafts through the air...).

એ   To add further details to the psychic message I received on the first page of this book: A friend of mine called late one evening and asked if I would join her the following day to see a psychic in Chicago, as her scheduled friend had serendipitously canceled at the last moment. Well, I was not quite sure if I wanted to know anything about the future, but after she begged and pleaded, I thought "what the heck," it could be an adventure! And it was very interesting indeed, as Robert told me quite a few things that no one else could have known. Consequently, I felt that he was 'on target' with most of the information he conveyed.

Although I didn't live my life in anticipation of, or in accordance with what he said, I nonetheless found this alternative perspective intriguing — I have learned to trust my ability to discern. In the middle of our session, he stopped abruptly and dictated the following message to me:

> Things only happen when you make them happen. To let go and surrender is to let things happen to you. You have free will and have to set things in motion. (Sound familiar...?) Planet Earth is on the verge of destructive power in the wrong hands. Things will only change when people change. To raise people's spiritual consciousness is the task at hand. It can only begin there and be demonstrated as such. There is much work to do. Begin by helping others become aware. You have the gift — use it or it will be wasted. This is your Mission. DMA [Dimensional Mind Approach] is the first step. Everyone's Universal Truth they espouse is holy unto them. Formulate your own truth and live by it, share it, and teach it. That is your Mission. To blend the psychological awareness of your past with the awareness of the reality of the future, is the key. While men are building new and beautiful skyscrapers, energy should be channeled into consciousness into this world. They are blind — make them see. Various civilizations that were highly technical, fell. When there is technology without the awareness of God, it cannot work. God is before technology and channeling the power properly will benefit and evolve mankind. It is time. The time is now for these events to happen. They only happen with individual people. That is the task at hand.

♫ Do, do, do, do♫ This message totally blew me away. Me? Was he sure? What could this possibly mean? Well, I tucked that little piece of paper safely away, stumbled upon it occasionally, but never understood its meaning.

After attending the DMA course in 1986, my instructor, David, urged me to teach the course. Well, I felt unqualified to teach as I never attended college (my old-paradigm programming) but he told me that I had the 'gift' (although I have never limited myself or my aspirations because of my lack of advanced schooling — I actually disliked school and was eager to get on living my life). I considered his appraisal of me (since it was nice... [I'm easy, huh?]), took the instructor's course, and became a certified DMA instructor. David told me that he, too, had received visions of me — that something was going to happen to me later in my life.... I asked if it had to do with singing, as I was a singer in a band at the time, but he said "No, that wasn't it, it had something to do with being on stage communicating with others. However, my singing career was part of my 'training....' Hmmm.... ♫ Do, do, do, do.♫

  Years ago I read an article on numerology disclosing the fact that I had a "Special Mission" for the world in my lifetime as indicated by my birth date which totals 33. Hmmm.... ♫ Do, do, do, do.♫ (Add your birth date in the following manner (12-7-1949) 1+2+7+1+9+4 +9=33! The remaining 2 digits are typically added, arriving at a single digit (3+3=6), except in cases where the total is 22, 33, or 44, as each of those numbers has a special significance.) Guess what? My husband is a 33, too! 6-29-1942.... ♫ Do, do, do, do.♫ Coincidence...? Serendipity...? No, Law of Attraction.

  In the summer of 1996, I decided that there must be *something* to these continual messages, so with toes curled and tongue in cheek, I set forth my intention to fulfill my Mission. Initially, I was a bit hesitant — I had no idea what I had 'signed up' for. Maybe I would *not* want to do it. What would the repercussions be to my life, my family, my current dreams, and goals? (Scary.) However, the unseen forces of the universe began their orchestration and soon I met with a very talented interior designer whose business card I had saved for more than six years. I had always wanted Marsha's assistance when Ken and I built our next home and we were then in the process of designing one. While discussing the design, our conversation ventured into another area — our searches for Truth in life. Suddenly she stared at me with a distant look in her eye and said that she didn't believe that she was at my house for this design consultation. Hmmm.... Okay.... (♫ Do, do, do, do♫) When I asked what she thought the reason might be, she was uncertain. However, she knew instinctively that it was for another reason. She then listened within and felt inspired to loan me a seminar tape by Esther and Jerry Hicks that had provided much insight along her life's journey....

The message on the tape emphasized the importance of living a joyful life, which led me to ponder what brings me joy — I felt I could always use more of that! An idea then popped into my mind, "How about a boat!" I love to water ski and imagined how much fun it would be to teach Zach. So, Ken and I ordered a wonderful boat and while searching for the financial papers necessary to secure a loan, I 'coincidentally' stumbled upon the workbooks from the DMA course I had taken eleven years before. (Angel was at it again....) Leafing through the pages, I discovered one that disclosed what I had wanted in my life at that time. Guess what? Almost every item I had written down had manifested! (Including specific positive characteristics for a husband....) I then experienced an incredible sequence of epiphanies — "Oh my God's" — when I suddenly recognized that the information in the DMA course was very similar to the information on the tape Marsha had given me! My heart began to beat even harder when I recalled that almost every person who had taken the DMA course had experienced some kind of transformation in life as a result of it. "Oh my God!" Those thoughts triggered further thoughts about the many other books I had read over the years that conveyed the exact same information, but its profound nature was never apparent to me until that precise moment! "Oh my God," "Oh my God," "Oh my God" (and yours, too!). I then experienced a physical sensation — a sign from Angel — a certainty that my Mission was to consolidate and translate this information to 'twenty-first century lingo.' I was to write a comprehensive book detailing, what I have coined, the Four-Step Formula. However, when I came off of 'Cloud Nine' and the reality of this task became clear to me, I met with my personal dragons: my doubts and fears. I then looked up and implored "Hello. Excuse me, I think a mistake has been made here. I'm actually not a writer, and I'm sure there are many *qualified* people out there who *are* writers who can do a far better job than I ever could." Well, no mistake had been made — I was to write it. Needing moral support, I called a trusted friend that I had met through a series of extraordinary circumstances. After having those experiences, I knew that Don was to be more to me than simply a telecommunications client! And indeed he was. (I now recognize him as one of my earthly "Angels," sent to guide me to the completion of this Mission.) I shared my revelation and doubts with him and on the following day he sent me a fax congratulating me on the success of this book as well as the many lives it was positively impacting! Well, then I had no choice but to write it! And from that day forward, for over four and one-half years, not a day has gone by that I have not worked on it (to the degree that my husband wondered if I was ever going to be a wife and mother again…).

I hope that you have enjoyed my labor of love and that you read and reread it again and again until you have mastered the techniques and they become second-nature to you. I hope this book has inspired you to seek joy, inner peace, and prosperity every day of your life, for that is my intention. I offer you this message with complete, pure, and unconditional love.

Your fellow sacred traveler on her own sacred journey,

Lauren

P.S. I feel this information will have a maximum effectiveness if you can work through it with a friend or group of friends. That way the busy-ness of life won't get ahead of you and you can stay on track. Arrange a meeting every week to review a specific topic in the book. Go over your progress; tackle issues that arise utilizing the Four-Step Formula, and support one another in your quests for growth and a better life. The transition from the old paradigm into the new entails a complete reorientation in thinking — from the programming of your past reactive life, to reprogramming your mind to respond in a proactive manner. It is an ongoing process that will take time to integrate into your life, so going through this transition with others can really enhance your progress! Enjoy it and have fun! (Key word — *fun*). You'll be glad you did! ☺

Climb Ev'ry Mountain

Climb ev'ry mountain,
Search high and low,
Follow every by-way,
Every path you know.

Climb ev'ry mountain,
Ford every stream,
Follow every rainbow
Till you find your dream

A dream that will need all the love you can give
Every day of your life for as long as you live.

Climb ev'ry mountain,
Ford every stream
Follow ev'ry rainbow
Till you find your dream[39]

Lyrics of "Climb Ev'ry Mountain"
by Richard Rogers and Oscar Hammerstein II

My Intention

I am visualizing your awakening to Who You Really Are.
You are experiencing joy, prosperity, and your
incredible authentic power. You are filled with an
all-encompassing love for others and our world.
You have a sense of clarity, fulfillment, and inner peace.
As I focus on these thoughts and
believe them with every fiber of my being,
I feel so excited for I know they will manifest!
I expect my vision to manifest because I know my power.
You are now a part of it and I honor you, for you are
helping not only yourself, but also our world!

November 21, 1996

I Can See Clearly Now

I can see clearly now the rain has gone
I can see all obstacles in my way
Gone are the dark clouds that had me blind
It's gonna be a bright sun shiny day
I think I can make it now the pain is gone
All of the bad feelings have disappeared
Here is the rainbow I've been praying for
It's gonna be a bright sun shiny day
Look all around, there's nothing but blue sky
Look straight ahead there's nothing but blue sky
It's gonna be a bright bright sun shiny day![40]

Words and Music by Johnny Nash

IN A NUTSHELL — YOUR TASKS FOR TODAY:

❧ My Mission is: _____

_____

_____

● ❧ This is Who I Choose To Be:

_____

_____

_____

❧ Have I "gone to work" today?

❧ Have I ordered what I want in each segment of my day?

❧ Have I been aware and sensitive to the things in life that I enjoy and been appreciative of them?

❧ The three things I appreciated today are:

_____

_____

_____

❧ Am I connected to Angel and the "Chorus of Joy?"

❧ Have I shared joy with others?

● ❧ Have I sprinkled "Magic Angel Dust" on others in need?

❧ The wrong-way signs I experienced today are:

_____

_____

_____

_____

❧ Did I make an appointment to discuss my new perspectives with those closest to me?

❧ Have I expressed to those closest to me what I believe to be their positive qualities and things about them that I appreciate?

❧ The three stations I have chosen to tune in to when I am experiencing ill feelings are:

_____

_____

_____

● ❧ Am I having pleasant thoughts?

❧ Am I being loving, compassionate, appreciative, and offering praise?

❧ Am I laughing?

❧ Am I experiencing joy?

❧ Am I enjoying freedom?

❧ Am I growing as a person?

❧ Am I placing my orders with Angel in the 'Yes' mode?

∾ I experienced the following Angacles today:

_____
_____
_____
_____

∾ Things I like having in my life:

_____
_____
_____
_____
_____

∾ Things I have accomplished in my life:

_____
_____
_____
_____
_____
_____
_____
_____
_____

∾ Things I choose to have in my life:

_____
_____
_____
_____
_____
_____
_____
_____

∾ The way I choose to feel:

_____
_____
_____
_____
_____
_____
_____
_____

Part X
The Appendices

PART X

The Appendices

Part X

The Appendices

BOOKS, PERMISSIONS, NOTES, SONGS, AND INDEX

$\mathcal{B}ooks$

I am a part of all I have read.

— JOHN KIERAN

One
by Richard Bach
© 1988 ISBN: 0-440-20562-x
Dell Publishing/Division of Bantam
Doubleday Dell Publishing Group
1540 Broadway
New York, NY 10036
to reprint anything address William
Morrow and Co. New York

*Conversations with God: An Uncommon
Dialogue Book 1*
by Neale Donald Walsch.
©1995 ISBN: 0-399-14278-9
G.P. Putnam's Sons
200 Madison Avenue
New York, NY 10016
@ Re-Creation Postal Drawer 3475
Central Point, OR 97502

*Conversations with God: An Uncommon
Dialogue Book 2*
by Neale Donald Walsch
©1997 ISBN: 1-57174-056-2
Hampton Roads Publishing Company, Inc.
134 Burgess Lane
Charlottesville, VA 22902

*Conversations with God: An Uncommon
Dialogue Book 3*
by Neale Donald Walsch.
©1998 ISBN: 1-57174-103-8
Hampton Roads Publishing Company, Inc.
134 Burgess Lane
Charlottesville, VA 22902

The Healing of America.
by Marianne Williamson
©1997 ISBN: 0-06-016374-7
Simon & Schuster Publishing
Rockefeller Center 1230 Avenue of the
Americas, New York, NY 10020

A Return to Love
by Marianne Williamson
©1992 ISBN: 0-06-016374-7
HarperCollins Publishers
10 E. 53rd Street
New York, NY 10022

*A Fourth Course of Chicken Soup for the
Soul* ™
by Jack Canfield, Mark Victor Hansen,
Hanoch McCarty and Melanee McCarty
©1997 ISBN: 1-55874-467-3
Health Communications Inc.
3201 SW 15th Street
Deerfield Beach, FL 33442-8190

HAARP: Holes in Heaven Project
by Paula Randol Smith
© 1998 Randol-Smith Productions
P.O. Box 91655
Pasadena, CA 91101-1655

The Messengers
by Julia Ingram and G.W. Hardin
©1996 ISBN: 0-671-01686-5
Pocket Books a division of Simon and
Schuster 1230 Avenue of the Americas
New York, NY 10020

Manifest Your Destiny
by Wayne W. Dyer
© 1997 ISBN: 0-06-017528-1
Harper Collins Publishers, Inc.
10 East 53rd Street New York, NY 10022

Anatomy of an Illness
by Norman Cousins
©1979 ISBN: 0-553-01293-2
A Bantam Book/Published by arrangement
with W.W. Norton & Co., Inc. 500 5th
Avenue, New York, NY 10036

Anatomy of the Spirit
by Carolyn Myss, Ph. D.
©1996 ISBN: 0-517-70391-2
Crown Publishers, Inc.
201 E. 50th
New York NY 10022

As A Man Thinketh
by James Allen
ISBN: 0-399-12828-8
The Family Inspirational Library
Putnam Publishing 200 Madison Avenue
New York, NY 10022
Publishers Grosset & Dunlap

Paradigms: The Business of Discovering the Future
by Joel Arthur Barker
©1992 ISBN: 0-88730-647-0
Harper Business/A Division of
Harper Collins Publishers
10 E. 53rd Street New York, NY 10022

New Beginnings I: A Handbook for Joyous Survival ©1988
New Beginnings II: A Personal Handbook to Enhance Your Life, Liberty, and Pursuit of Happiness. ©1991
Sara: and the Forgiveness of Friends of a Feather ©1995 ISBN: 09-621219-4-0
by Jerry and Esther Hicks
Abraham-Hicks Publications & Seminars
www.abraham-hicks.com
Jerry and Esther Hicks
PO Box 690070
San Antonio, TX 78269
830-755-2299

Awakening to Zero Point: The Collective Initiation
by Gregg Braden
©1997 ISBN: 1-889071-09-9
Radio Bookstore Press
P.O. Box 3010
Bellevue, WA 98009-3010

Living in the Light
by Shakti Gawain
© 1986 ISBN: 0-931432-14-6
New World Library
58 Paul Drive, San Rafael, CA 94903

The Path of Least Resistance
by Robert Fritz
©1984 ISBN: 0-930641-00-0
Ballantine Books c/o Random House
201 E. 50th
New York, NY 10022

Life 101: The Quote Book
by Peter Mc Williams
© 1996
Prelude Press
8159 Santa Monica Blvd. #201
Los Angeles, CA 90046

The Writings of Florence Scovel Shinn
by Florence Scovel Shinn
©1988 ISBN: 0-87516-6105
DeVorss and Co. Publications
P.O. Box 550 Marina Del Rey,
CA 90294

A Course in Miracles®
c/o The Foundation for Inner Peace
©1996 ISBN: 0-670-86975-9
Penguin Books USA Inc. 375 Hudson
Street, New York, NY 10014

The Path
by Laurie Beth Jones
© 1996 ISBN: 0-4868-6227-0
Hyperion 114 Fifth Avenue
New York, NY 10011

Jesus CEO
by Laurie Beth Jones
©1995 ISBN: 0-7868-6062-6
Hyperion 114 Fifth Avenue
New York, NY 10011

First Thunder
by MSI
©1996 - ISBN: 0-931783-07-0
The Society for Ascension
272 Biodome Drive
Waynesville, NC 28786 828-926-7853

Psychic Powers: Mysteries of the Unknown
series by Time-Life Books
©1987 ISBN: 0-8094-6308-3
P.O. Box C-32068
Richmond, VA. 23261

Spirit Guides & Angel Guardians
by Richard Webster
©1998 ISBN: 1-56718-795-1
Published by Llewellyn Worldwide, Ltd.
P.O. Box 64383, Dept. K795-1
St. Paul, MN 55164-0383

Getting in Touch with Your Inner Bitch
by Elizabeth Hiltz
©1994 ISBN: 0-9629162-0-X
Published by Hysteria
P.O. Box 8581
Bridgeport, CN 06605

Gift From the Sea
by Anne Morrow Lindbergh
©1983 ISBN: 0-679-73241-1
Published by Vintage Books/Random House Inc. 201 E. 50th Street
New York, NY 10022

Emissary of Light
by James Twyman
©1996 ISBN: 0-446-52300-3
Warner Books, Inc.
1271 Avenue of the Americas
New York, NY 10022

The Coming of the Cosmic Christ: The Healing of Mother Earth and the Birth of a Global Renaissance
by Matthew Fox
© 1988 ISBN: 0- 06-062915-0
HarperCollins® Publishers
10 E. 53rd Street
New York, NY 10022

The Seat of the Soul
by Gary Zukav
©1990 ISBN: 0-671-25383-2
Fireside Books/Simon and Schuster
Rockefeller Center
1230 Avenue of the Americas
New York, NY 10020

Soul Stories
by Gary Zukav
©2000 ISBN: 0-7432-0407-7
Fireside Books/Simon and Schuster
Rockefeller Center
1230 Avenue of the Americas
New York, NY 10020

Strangters Among Us
by Ruth Montgomery
©1979 ISBN: 0-449-20801-X
A Fawcett Crest Book
Published by Ballantine Books
Random House
201 E. 50th New York, NY 10022

Walking Between the Worlds: The Science of Compassion
by Gregg Braden
©1997 ISBN: 1-889071-05-6
Radio Bookstore Press
P.O. Box 3010
Bellevue , WA 98009-3010

The Isaiah Effect: Decoding the Lost Science of Prayer and Prophecy
by Gregg Braden
©2000 ISBN: 0-609-60534-8
Harmony Books 201 E. 50th Street
New York, NY 10022

Love Without End: Jesus Speaks
by Glenda Green
© 1999 by Glenda Green
ISBN: 0-9666623-1-8
Heartwings Publishing
P.O. Box 14251
Fort Worth, TX 76117

Present Moment, Wonderful Moment: Mindful Verses for Daily Living
by Thich Nhat Hanh ©1990
ISBN: 0-93807721-X
Parallax Press
P.O. Box 7355
Berkeley, CA 94707

Kryon: Partnering with God Book VI (Practical Information for the New Millennium)
by Lee Carroll
©1997 ISBN: 1-888053-10-0
The Kryon Writings
1155 Camino DelMar
Del Mar, CA 92014

Many Lives, Many Masters
by Brian L. Weiss, M.D.
©1988 ISBN: 0-671-63786-0
A Fireside Book
Published by Simon & Schuster, Inc.
1230 Avenue of the Americas
New York, NY 10020

Only Love is Real
by Brian L. Weiss, M.D.
©1996 ISBN: 0-446-67265-3
Published by Warner Books, Inc.
1271 Avenue of the Americas
New York, NY 10020

Creative Visualization
by Shakti Gawain
© 1978 ISBN: 0-553-24147-8
Whatever Publishing
P.O. Box 137 Mill Valley, CA 94941

The Indigo Children
by Lee Carroll and Jan Tober
© 1999 by Lee Carroll and Jan Tober
Published by Hay House, Inc.
P.O. Box 5100, Carlsbad, CA 92018-5100

Timeless Healing: The Power and Biology of
Belief by Herbert Benson M.D.
©1996 ISBN: 0-684-81441-2
Fireside Books Rockefeller Center
1230 Avenue of the Americas
New York, NY 10020

The Nature of Personal Reality
by Jane Roberts
© 1994 ISBN: 1-878424-06-8
Amber Allen Publishing/New World
Library P.O. Box 6657
San Rafael, CA 94903

The Celestine Prophecy: An Experiential
Guide
by James Redfield and Carol Adrienne
© 1995 James Redfield
ISBN: 0-446-67122-3
Warner Books, Inc..
1271 Avenue of the Americas
New York, NY 10020

The Road Less Traveled
by Morgan Scott Peck
© 1978 ISBN: 0-671-24086-2
A Touchstone book/Simon and Schuster
1230 Avenue of the Americas,
New York, NY 10020

The Ancient Secret of the Flower of Life
by Drunvalo Melchizedek
© 1998 ISBN: 1-891824-17-1
Light Technology Publishing
P.O. Box 3540
Flagstaff, AZ 86003

The Secret of the Beloved Disciple
by James Twyman
© 2000 ISBN: 1-899171-08-8
Findhorn Press
P.O. Box 13939
Tallahassee, FL 32317-3939
www.findhornpress.com

The Secret of Shambhala
by James Redfield
© 1999 ISBN: 0-446-52308-9
Warner Books, Inc.
1271 Avenue of the Americas
New York, NY 10020

The HeartMath® Solution: The Institute of
HeartMath's Revolutionary Program for
Engaging the Power of the Heart's Intelligence
by Doc Childre and Howard Martin
© 1999 ISBN: 0-06-251065-1
Published by HarperSanFrancisco™
A Division of HarperCollins® Publishers
10 E. 53rd Street New York, NY 10022

The Children of the Law of One and The
Lost Teachings of Atlantis
by Jon Peniel
© 1997 ISBN: 0-9660015-0-8
Published by Network
1007 N. Federal Highway Suite 211
Fort Lauderdale, FL 33304
www.atlantis.to

The Seven Spiritual Laws of Success
by Deepak Chopra
© 1994 ISBN: 1-878424-11-4
Amber Allen Publishing/New World
Library
P.O. Box 6657
San Rafael, CA 94903

The Four Agreements
by Don Miguel Ruiz M.D.
© 1997 ISBN: 1-878424-31-9
Amber Allen Publishing
P.O. Box 6657
San Rafael, CA 94903

Right Use of Will: Healing and Evolving the
Emotional Body
Received by Ceanne DeRohan
© 1984, 1986
Four Winds Publications
535 Cordova Road Suite 112
Santa Fe, NM 87501

Bringers of the Dawn
by Barbara Marciniak
© 1992ISBN: 0-9396808-98-X
Bear and Company, Inc.
Santa Fe, NM 87504-2860

The Journey Home
by Lee Carroll
©1997 ISBN: 1-56170-399-0
Hay House, Inc.
P.O. Box 5100
Carlsbad, CA 92018-5100

The World To Come
by Ruth Montgomery
©1999 ISBN: 0-609-60479-1
Harmony Books/Random House
201 E. 50th NY, New York, NY 10022

$\mathcal{P}ermissions$

In complete honor, gratitude, and respect, I wish to acknowledge all of the incredible writers I have quoted. The following authors and publishers have graciously granted permission to reprint passages from their copyrighted works:

Excerpted from CREATIVE VISUALIZATION by Shakti Gawain ©1978. Reprinted with permission of New World Library, Novato, CA. www.nwlib.com

Reprinted with the permission of Simon & Schuster, Inc. from THE HEALING OF AMERICA by Marianne Williamson. Copyright ©1997 by Marianne Williamson.

From ANATOMY OF THE SPIRIT by Carolyn Myss. Reprinted by permission of Harmony Books, a division of Random House, Inc.©1996

From GIFT FROM THE SEA by Anne Morrow Lindbergh. Reprinted by permission if Pantheon Books, a division of Random House, Inc.©1983

From CONVERSATIONS WITH GOD (book 1) by Neale Donald Walsch. Copyright ©1997 by Neale Donald Walsch. Used by permission of Putnam Berkley, a division of Penguin Putnam Inc.

Portions from A COURSE IN MIRACLES® copyright ©1975, ©1999, reprinted by permission of the Foundation for A Course in Miracles—1275 Tennanah Lake Road - Roscoe, NY 12776-5905

Excerpts adapted with the permission of Pocket Books, a Division of Simon & Schuster, Inc. from THE MESSENGERS; A *True Story of Angelic Presences and the Return to the Age of Miracles* by Julia Ingram and G.W. Hardin. Copyright ©1996 by Skywin, Inc.

Excerpts adapted from GETTING IN TOUCH WITH YOUR INNER BITCH by Elizabeth Hilts. Copyright ©1994 with the permission of Hysteria Publications, Sourcebooks, Inc.

Excerpts adapted from FIRST THUNDER by MSI by The Society for Ascension 272 Biodome Drive Waynesville, N.C. 28786 ©1996

Excerpts adapted from THE WRITINGS OF FLORENCE SCOVEL SHINN by Florence Scovel Shinn with the permission of De Vorss & Company 1046 Princeton Drive., P.O. Box 550, Marina del Rey, CA.90294-0550. Copyright ©1988

From MYSTERIES OF THE UNKNOWN: PSYCHIC POWERS By the editors of Time-Life Books © 1987 Time-Life Books

From EMISSARY OF LIGHT by James Twyman. Copyright ©1996 by James F. Twyman. By permission of Warner Books, Inc.

From THE CELESTINE PROPHECY: AN EXPERIENTIAL GUIDE by James Redfield. Copyright ©1995 by James Redfield. By permission of Warner Books, Inc.

$\mathcal{N}otes$

$\mathcal{A}bbreviations$

Because of the repetition of the sources I have referenced, I have adopted the following abbreviations to simplify this bibliography:

CWG 1, 2, or 3 — *Conversations With God: An Uncommon Dialogue books 1, 2, or 3* by Neale Donald Walsch
NPR — *The Nature of Personal Reality* by Jane Roberts
NB I — *New Beginnings I: A Handbook for Joyous Survival* by Esther and Jerry Hicks
NB II — *New Beginnings II: A Personal Handbook to Enhance Your Life, Liberty and Pursuit of Happiness.* by Esther and Jerry Hicks
Sara — *Sara: and the Forgiveness of Friends of a Feather* by Jerry and Esther Hicks
Hicks Seminar Quote — Quotations garnered from seminar cassette tapes
Celestine — *The Celestine Prophecy: An Experiential Guide*, by James Redfield and Carol Adrienne
The Writings of Florence Scovel Shinn:
Game — *The Game of Life* by Florence Scovel Shinn
Word is Wand — *Your Word is Your Wand* by Florence Scovel Shinn
Secret Door — *Secret Door of Success* by Florence Scovel Shinn
Timeless Healing — *Timeless Healing : The Power and Biology of Belief* by Herbert Benson M.D.
One — *One* by Richard Bach
Anatomy of Illness — *Anatomy of an Illness* by Norman Cousins
Gift From Sea — *A Gift From the Sea* by Ane Morrow Lindbergh
Path — *The Path: Creating Your Mission Statement for Work and for Life* by Laurie Beth Jones
Manifest Destiny — *Manifest Your Destiny* by Dr. Wayne Dyer
Anatomy of Spirit — *Anatomy of a Spirit* by Dr. Carolyn Myss
Miracles — *A Course in Miracles®* c/o The Foundation for Inner Peace

---

1. ♩ **DO YOU KNOW WHERE YOU'RE GOING TO?** Theme from MAHOGANY. Words by Gerry Goffin. Music by Michael Masser ©1973 SCREEN GEMS - EMI MUSIC INC and JOBETE MUSIC CO., INC .All Rights for JOBETE MUSIC CO., INC. Controlled and Administered by EMI APRIL MUSIC, INC. All Rights Reserved. International Copyright Secured. Used by Permission.
2. ♩ **THEME FROM THE VALLEY OF THE DOLLS** by Andre Previn and Dory

Previn ©1967 (Renewed) WB Music Corp. (ASCAP) All Rights Reserved. Used by Permission. WARNER BROS. PUBLICATIONS U.S. INC., Miami, Fl. 33014
3. ♩ **ALFIE** Theme from the Paramount Picture ALFIE. Words by Hal David. Music by Burt Bacharach. Copyright ©1966 (Renewed 1994)by Famous Music Corporation International Copyright Secured. All Rights Reserved

Part I

The Prelude

1. *Path* - pg 24 - in order to truly find Path
2. **CWG 2** - pg 100 - are you hurting or healing
3. *Only Love is Real* by Brian L. Weiss, M.D. page 144
4. *Love Without End: Jesus Speaks* by Glenda Green - pg 56 - the heart knows truth as free
5. ♪ **THE ROSE**, by Amanda McBroom © 1979 Warner-Tamerlane Publishing Corp. And Third Story Music Inc. All rights administered by Warner-Tamerlane Publishing Corp. All Rights Reserved. Used by Permission. WARNER BROS. PUBLICATIONS U.S. INC., Miami, Fl. 33014
6. ♪ **COME IN FROM THE RAIN** Words and Music by Carole Bayer Sager and Melissa Manchester. Copyright © 1975,1976 by Alley Music Corp., Trio Music, Company Inc., and Rumanian Pickleworks Music Company. All rights for Rumanian Pickleworks Music Company Controlled and Administered by Screen Gems-EMI Music Inc. International Copyright Secured. All Rights Reserved. Used by Permission.
7. *The Healing of America* by Marianne Williamson - pg 38 - "...it (this yearning) is penetrating the deepest levels of our psyche... and no amount of force can contain it ..." Paraphrased
8. ♪ **FLASHDANCE - WHAT A FEELING** from the Paramount Picture FLASHDANCE Lyrics by Keith Forsey and Irene Cara. Music by Giorgio Moroder Copyright 1983 © by Chappelle & Co., Budde Music, Inc. and Famous Music Corporation. All Rights Administered by Chappelle & Co. International Copyright Secured. All Rights Reserved.

Part II

The Puzzle

1. *As a Man Thinketh* by James Allen - pg 16 - man revealed by circumstances
2. *The Essene Gospel of Peace* by Szekely - Book 4 page 30
3. **CWG 1** - pg 188 - nothing occurs
4. *The Path of Least Resistance* by Robert Fritz- pg X- indeed connection
5. **Game** - pg 36 - man sees first his failure
6. **Secret Door** - pg 190 - you attract the things you give thought to
7. *Each Day a New Beginning* - pg 6–19 - one receives
8. **CWG 1** - pg 179 - a thought or word expressed
9. **Hicks Seminar Quote** - you create your life
10. **NPR** - pg 28 - regardless of the nature
11. **Miracles** - pg 17 - because of likeness to Creator
12. **CWG 1** - pg 168 - the question is not
13. *Hicks Seminar Quote* - you're responsible for your own thoughts
14. **Game** - pg 36 - Jesus said and ye shall know the truth
15. **Strangers** - pg 67 - Jesus claimed no miracles
16. **CWG 2** - pg 67 - embrace the process
17. **Celestine** - pg 29 - 90,000 thoughts
18. **NPR** - pg 45 - you are locked
19. **CWG 1** - pg 8 - go ahead and act
20. "The Power of Prayer" - Rice University
21. *Timeless Healing* - pg 32- Dr. Stewart Wolf - antinausea case study
22. "Good Morning America" Nov '97 - Mind and Machinery

23. *A Fourth Course of Chicken Soup for the Soul* - pgs 231–235 - "To Save a Life"
24. *Timeless Healing* - pg 40–41- nocebo effect on Maori aborigines - paraphrased
25. *CWG 3* - pg 61 and 71 - you are at the cause - at first you may not realize this
26. *The Ancient Secret of the Flower of Life* by Drunvalo Melchizedek - paraphrased from pgs 106 and 107
27. *Paradigms—The Business of Discovering the Future* - pg 32 - a set of rules or regulations
28. *Paradigms—The Business of Discovering the Future* - pg 125 - paradigms can be invisible
29. *Paradigms—The Business of Discovering the Future* - pg 37 - a paradigm shift...Paraphrased from pg 39- but when the rules change so can the world.
30. *Paradigms—The Business of Discovering the Future* - pg 149 paraphrased - you can resist the new paradigm
31. *Paradigms—The Business of Discovering the Future* - pg 83 - the message about paradigms... and where we are going....
32. *Paradigms—The Business of Discovering the Future* - you cannot know who will bring future, you can only listen. Pg 70
33. ♪ THROUGH HEAVEN'S EYES From THE PRINCE OF EGYPT. Words and Music by Steven Schwartz. Copyright © 1998 SKG Songs (ASCAP) Worldwide Rights for SKG Songs Administered by Cherry Lane Music Publishing Company, Inc. International Copyright Secured. All Rights Reserved.
34. *As a Man Thinketh* by James Allen - pg 64 - mind is the master power
35. *CWG 1* - pg 12 - every prayer
36. *NPR* - pg 71- your beliefs form reality
37. *As a Man Thinketh* by James Allen - preface - you will become as small
38. *As a Man Thinketh* by James Allen - pg 61 - dreams are seedlings
39. *Game* - pg 21 - invisible forces
40. *Word is Wand* - pg 163 - I will give to thee that thou seest
41. *Hicks Seminar Quote* - there is no exception to disprove the Formula
42. *NPR* - pg 16 - you form the fabric of experience thru beliefs and expectations
43. *Love Without End: Jesus Speaks* by Glenda Green - pg 190 - the law of cause
44. *CWG 1* - pg 189 - thoughts subtle energy
45. *CWG 3* - pg 115 - every time you have a thought
46. *Word is Wand* - pg 117 - thoughts are a tremendous vibratory force.
47. *Timeless Healing* - pg 30- we should not ignore compelling brain research
48. *Kryon Book 6 - Partnering With God* - pg 373 - Schumann Resonance taken from Handbook of Atmospheric Electrodynamics Volume 1, Chptr 11, Hans Volland ©1995 Published by CRC Press
49. *Hicks Seminar Quote* - as vibration of Earth increases, speed of energy increases.
50. Dr. Beverly Rubik - "Holes In Heaven" documentary (Experiments are being conducted utilizing technology developed by Scientist Nikola Tesla in the early 1900's, that deals with piercing the electro magnetic protective membrane of the Earth creating the potential for manipulation of weather patterns as well as electromagnetic warfare. Our government is clearly lacking adequate scientific knowledge to understand the mechanics of our Earth and the fragile interdependent systems that exist upon her.) We must guard against taking action without facts.
51. *Anatomy of Spirit* - pg 33 - The Human Energy Field
52. *Path* - pg 72 - physicists and subatomic articles
53. *The Purpose of Your Life* by Carol Adrienne - from the preface: a summation of Chapter Five - The Magnetic Force Field of Your Life Purpose
54. *1st Thunder* by MSI - pg 63–64 - see my flower
55. *Timeless Healing* - pg 202 - nobel laureate Leon Lederman
56. Time Life book series *"Mysteries of the Unknown" Psychic Powers* - pg 73 - one of the popular
57. *Creative Visualization* by Shakti Gawain - paraphrased from pgs 5–7 - Universe composed of energy
58. *CWG 2* - pgs 82–88 - The Matrix
59. *NPR* - pg 131 & 103- living cells have structure
60. *Love Without End: Jesus Speaks* by Glenda Green - pg 62 - there is a particle substance
61. *Love Without End: Jesus Speaks* by Glenda Green- pg 108 - adamantine particles are the building
62. *Love Without End: Jesus Speaks* by Glenda Green - pg 111 - all physical existence is comprised
63. *Love Without End: Jesus Speaks* by Glenda Green - pg 108 - the idea of energy as force
64. *Love Without End: Jesus Speaks* by Glenda Green - pg 158 - the heart is the true center of power
65. *Love Without End: Jesus Speaks* by

Glenda Green - pg 56- the heart is the bringer of miracles

66. *Love Without End: Jesus Speaks* by Glenda Green - pg 155 - the heart is your connecting link

67. *Love Without End: Jesus Speaks* by Glenda Green - pg 156 - the heart is a point within your existence

68. *Love Without End: Jesus Speaks* by Glenda Green - pg 110 - you may remember the children's

69. *Love Without End: Jesus Speaks* by Glenda Green - pg 158 - the heart is a magnetic vortex

70. *Love Without End: Jesus Speaks* by Glenda Green - pg 110 - this is your power of influence

71. *Love Without End: Jesus Speaks* by Glenda Green - pg 222 - the love, faith, and consciousness

72. *Love Without End: Jesus Speaks* by Glenda Green - pg 110 - all that you have to do is be the love

73. *Messages from the Masters* by Brian Weiss M.D. - pg 135- love is the answer

74. *"The Cosmic Lattice."* Lee Carroll from transcript of seminar given in 11-97 New Hampshire

75. *The Children of the Law of One and The Lost Teachings of Atlantis* by Jon Peniel - pg 12 - placed on top and towering above

76. *The Children of the Law of One and The Lost Teachings of Atlantis* by Jon Peniel - pg 84 - tuned to the earth's magnetic field

77. *The Ancient Secret of the Flower of Life* by Drunvalo Melchizedek - pg 118- the largest known pyramid

78. *The Children of the Law of One and The Lost Teachings of Atlantis* by Jon Peniel - pg 275 - All is vibration

79. *The Children of the Law of One and The Lost Teachings of Atlantis* by Jon Peniel - pg 58 - what many consider the mysteries

80. *CWG 1* - pg 20 - the voice within

81. *CWG 1* - pg 94 - come to me along path of heart

82. *CWG 1* - pg 44 - if you do not go within, you go without

83. *CWG 1* - pg 180 - if now there is something you want to experience

84. *CWG 1* - pg 11 - your saying you want

85. *NPR* - page 63 - quite deliberately you use your conscious mind

86. *Game* - pg 28 - in order to demonstrate

87. *Secret Door* - Jesus Matthew 21:22- pg 200 - all things ask in prayer - believe

88. *CWG 1* - pg 12 - when it is said a prayer

89. *Miracles* - pg 19 - miracles cannot occur with doubt

90. *Game* - pg 13 - if one asks for success

91.♪ **WHEN YOU BELIEVE** From THE PRINCE OF EGYPT. Words and Music by Steven Schwartz. Copyright © 1997 SKG Songs (ASCAP) Worldwide Rights for SKG Songs Administered by Cherry Lane Music Publishing Company, Inc. International Copyright Secured. All Rights Reserved.

92. *NPR* - pg 25 - the conscious mind sets goals

93. *Celestine* - pg 7 - coincidences

94. *Path* - pg 213 - Jonas Salk

95. *Strangers* - pg 166 - paraphrased-Findhorn, Scotland

96. *Word is Wand* - pg 141 - angel of destiny

97. *Celestine* - pg 19 - how did you get job?

98. *Celestine* - pg 20 - how did you meet person

99. *CWG 1* - pg 62- if there was such a thing as sin

100. *CWG 1* - pg 50 - the world is in the condition its in because of you

101. *CWG 1* - Pg 62 - for the most part your judgements

102. *Hicks Seminar Quote* - live out the dramas of others to which we acquiesced

103. *NB I* - pg 105 - our minds are full of thoughts

104. *Hicks Seminar Quote* - use your life to determine your truth

105. *NB I* - pg 28 - the power of influence

106. *The Healing of America* by Marianne Williamson - pg 36 - what catholic church did to Europe

107. *CWG 1* - pg 191 - some people don't want to be awakened

108. *One* - pg 114 - no one can solve problems

109. *NB II* - pgs 30-31 - some people think they have answers to all questions

110. *Hicks Seminar Quote* - when someone asks a question, answer is meaningful

111. *CWG 2* - pg 19 - life is an on-going

112. *CWG 1* - pg 196 - conceive, create, experience

113. *CWG 2* - pg 98 - it is only thru the exercise of the greatest freedom

114. *NB II* - book cover - joy, freedom, and growth

115. *CWG 1* - pg 65 - desire is beginning

116. *Right Use of Will* by Ceanne DeRohan - pg 9 - Desire is the magnetic energy

117. *CWG 2* - pg 76 - all thru your life,

guilty, love

118. **Hicks Seminar Quote** - spiritual versus material

119. **CWG 2** - pg 79 - the pleasure you give yourself

120. **CWG 1** - pg 130 - when life is lived damage control

121. **Hicks Seminar Quote** - focus on joy as first priority

122. **CWG 2** - pg 79 - don't force evolution

123. ♪ **ON THE WINGS OF LOVE** by Jeffery Osborne and Peter Schless ©1982 Almo Music Corp., March 9 Music, and Lincoln Pond Music All Rights Reserved. Used by Permission. WARNER BROS. PUBLICATIONS U.S. INC., Miami, Fl. 33014

124. **CWG 2** - pg 14 - soul speaks in feelings

125. **NPR** - pg 212 - going along with feelings

126. **CWG 2** - pg 80 - feeling good is your way of telling

127. **Miracles** - pg 26 - discomfort aroused

128. **NPR** - pg 134 - do not say negative feelings are wrong

129. **Getting In Touch With Your Inner Bitch** by Elizabeth Hilts - pg 21

130. **Right Use of Will** by Ceanne DeRohan - pg 53 - violence is the last resort of Will

131. **NPR** - pg 410 - the expression of normal aggression

132. **NPR** - pg 410 - preventing violence

133. **NPR** - pg 203 - a frown is a natural

134. **NPR** - pg 225 - when you allow your emotions

135. **Right Use of Will** by Ceanne DeRohan - pg 45 - Feelings are a Divine part

136. **CWG 1** - pg 8 - listen to your feelings

137. **CWG 2** - pg 15 - feelings are truth

138. **NPR** - pg 144 - if you are filled with rage

139. **CWG 1** - pg 134 - things others say

140. **CWG 1** - pg 128 - and so there are things when you react in pain.

141. **CWG 2** - pg 16 - if you share feelings share them with love, sensitivity

142. **NPR** - pg 344 - many who commit crimes

143. **NPR** - pg 344 - no feeling brings dead end

144. ♪ **WHAT ARE YOU DOING FOR THE REST OF YOUR LIFE?** Lyrics by Alan and Marilyn Bergman, Music by Michel LeGrand ©1969 (Renewed) EMI U Catalog Inc. All Rights Reserved. Used by Permission. WARNER BROS. PUBLICATIONS U.S. INC., Miami, Fl. 33014

145. **NPR** - pg 229 - when you do not embrace this conscious knowledge

146. **CWG 1** - pg 156 - for most of your life you've lived at effect

147. **CWG 1** - pg 119 - so what is your intention now?

148. **CWG 1** - pg 40 - hell is the experience

149. **CWG 1** - pg 76 - do you want life to take off?

150. **Creative Visualization** by Shakti Gawain - pg 59 - paraphrased - at our core perfect spiritual beings

151. **Hicks Seminar Quote** - you are a creator - nothing worse than not allowing energy to flow - squandering life

152. **Game** - pg 89 - may each be freed

Part III

𝒯he 𝒫resent

1. **The Healing of America** by Marianne Williamson - pg 27 - paraphrased - pretend to be happy

2. **The Path of Least Resistance** - by Robert Fritz - pg 45 - if only I had a guaranteed wage

3. **Creative Visualization** by Shakti Gawain - pg 45 - there isn't enough to go around

4. **Creative Visualization** by Shakti Gawain - pg 90 - selfish to have abundance

5. **Path of Least Resistance** - by Robert Fritz - pg 37 - I am not good enough

6. ♪ **THE WINDOWS OF THE WORLD** Lyric by Hal David. Music by Burt Bacharach. Copyright ©1967 (Renewed) Casa David and New Hidden Valley Music. International Copyright Secured. All Rights Reserved.
7. **CWG 1** - pg 191- the world is in the condition it is - sleepwalkers
8. **NPR** - pg 71 - when man feels no connection
9. *Many Lives, Many Masters* by Brian L. Weiss - pg 10 - years of disciplined study
10. *Many Lives, Many Masters* by Brian L. Weiss - pg 127 - 128 - I had been reluctant
11. *Celestine* - pg 24 - the more we mapped and named physical phenomena
12. **CWG 2** - pg 80 - no kind of evolution
13. **CWG 1** - pg 195 - you don't want to know the truth
14. *Many Lives, Many Masters* by Brian L. Weiss- pg 10 - we as a society have much
15. *Love Without End: Jesus Speaks* by Glenda Green - pg 54 - when the mind is reinforced - paraphrased
16. *Love Without End: Jesus Speaks* by Glenda Green - pg 80 - most conditions need relaxing
17. *Manifest Destiny* - pg 20 - most of us in the west
18. **NPR** - pg 171 - the integration of intellect and intuition
19. *Love Without End: Jesus Speaks* by Glenda Green - pg 166 - it is imperative that man acknowledge
20. *One* - Pgs 227 – 228 - evolution made civilization
21. **CWG 3** - pg 276 - your present technology
22. *Love Without End: Jesus Speaks* by Glenda Green - pg140 - humankind is standing precariously
23. **CWG 1** - pg 168 - it's important now
24. **CWG 3** - pg 90 - be open
25. *Love Without End: Jesus Speaks* by Glenda Green - pg 98 - the structure of scientific theory
26. *Love Without End: Jesus Speaks* by Glenda Green - pg 169 - regard the present moment
27. ♪ **JUST A LITTLE BIT OF LOVE** by Maria Christiansen, Arnie Roman, Arthur Jacobsen ©1997 Sweet Woo Music (SESAC), Mir Music (SESAC), Romanesque Music (ASCAP), Arthur Jacobsen Music (ASCAP), & W 'N"R Music (ASCAP) All rights o/b/o Sweet Woo Music (SESAC) & Mir Music (SESAC) administered by W.B.M. Music (SESAC). All rights o/b/o Romanesque Music (ASCAP), administered by WB Music Corp. (ASCAP) All Rights Reserved. Used by Permission. WARNER BROS. PUBLICATIONS U.S. INC., Miami, Fl. 33014
28. **CWG 2** - pg 189 - no one in enlightened societies
29. **CWG 1** - pg 170 - if you think your life is about doingness
30. *One* - pg 92 - soon as you learned to see; pictures
31. *Love Without End: Jesus Speaks* by Glenda Green - pg 70 - greed is the root of all evil.
32. **CWG 2** - pg 221 - system of rank obscenity
33. *The Healing of America* by Marianne Williamson - pg 25 - greed considered legitimate
34. **CWG 2** - pg 169 - what kind of glory
35. *Gift From Sea* - pg 125 - because we cannot deal with the complexity of the present
36. *Many Lives, Many Masters* by Brian L. Weiss- pg 210- lip service without behavior
37. **CWG 1** - pg 185 - go ahead and do what you love
38. *Hicks Seminar Quote* - the standard of success
39. ♪ **CALL ME,** by Tony Hatch ©1965 (Renewed) Universal-Duchess Music Corp. All Rights Reserved. Used by Permission. WARNER BROS. PUBLICATIONS U.S. INC., Miami, Fl. 33014
40. **CWG 1** - pg 186 - your life work is a statement
41. *Love Without End: Jesus Speaks* by Glenda Green - pg 191 - many people are in a state of burnout
42. *Gift From Sea* - pg 42 - now instead of planting solitude
43. *Gift From Sea* - pg 49 - as far as the search for solitude
44. *Gift From Sea* - pgs 28–29 - to be human

Part IV

$\mathcal{T}he\ \mathcal{P}ast$

1. CWG 1 - pg 122- you can choose to be a person
2. Hicks Seminar Quote - 2/3 of thoughts blame 1/3 guilt...
3. Celestine - pg 29- subtle core beliefs
4. CWG 1 - pg 61 - your beliefs form the structure
5. NPR - pg 34 - if you find great exuberance
6. Love Without End: Jesus Speaks by Glenda Green - pg 189 - there is no place where you are
7. NPR - pg 198 - you will not understand emotions unless you understand beliefs
8. NPR - pg 72 - your daily experience will justify
9. CWG 3 - pg 89 - stick to beliefs
10. CWG 1 - pg 27 - you cannot experience yourself
11. CWG 3 - pg 87 - what you have done is unimportant
12. Manifest Destiny - pg 83 - a person who has experienced traumatic
13. Word is Wand - pg 163 - this is the reason so many people
14. NPR - pg 298 - to rid yourself of annoying restrictions
15. CWG 3 - pg 146 - glorify what you are today
16. CWG 1 - pg 119 - no need to recriminate yourself
17. Game - pg 32 - subconscious mind
18. NPR - pg 58 - from the earliest stages
19. CWG 2 - pg 126 - you've seen what has resulted on planet
20. NPR - pg 72 - some of your beliefs
21. Messengers - pg 38 - people cannot be judged by their covers - paraphrased
22. CWG 2 - pg 208 - it is not for you to judge
23. CWG 1 - pg 15 - all human actions
24. CWG 1 - pg 19 - fear is the energy which contracts
25. Love Without End: Jesus Speaks by Glenda Green - pg 101 - in the beginning
26. Love Without End: Jesus Speaks by Glenda Green - pg 100 - the most import
27. Love Without End: Jesus Speaks by Glenda Green - pg 79 - once a man's sense
28. Love Without End: Jesus Speaks by Glenda Green - pg 168 - love is the power

29. Celestine - pgs 143–149 - four personality types - paraphrased
30. The Children of the Law of One and The Lost Teachings of Atlantis by Jon Peniel - pg 127 - our consciousness is the
31. CWG 1 - pg 33 - each circumstance a gift
32. CWG 1 - pg 127- when you lose sight
33. CWG 2 - pg 16 - you cannot take responsibility for truth
34. CWG 2 - pg 170 - when in doubt always err on side of compassion
35. Celestine - pg 155 - overwhelmed, stuck, powerless
36. Messengers - pg 356 - we don't have the right to judge others - paraphrased
37. Celestine - pg 96 - describe conflict - respond - feeling
38. Celestine - pg 97 - past reaction to conflict - being righteous
39. Celestine - pg 97 - letting fears run your life
40. Celestine - pg 98 - disarm conflict - be willing to look at situation from other point of view
41. ♩ YOU NEEDED ME Words and Music by Randy Goodrum Copyright ©1975,1978 by Chappelle & Co. and Ironside Music. All Rights Administered by Chappelle & Co. International Copyright Secured. All Rights Reserved.
42. CWG 1 - pg 174 - the soul leads you to right and perfect opportunity
43. NPR - pg 99 - if only positive beliefs were materialized
44. Hicks Seminar Quote - there is nothing to regret
45. NPR - pg 343 - you learn thru your creations
46. Love Without End: Jesus Speaks by Glenda Green - pg 169 - instead of look
47. Right Use of Will by Ceanne DeRohan - pg 193 - past experiences are a source of
48. Present Moment, Wonderful Moment - by Thich Nhat Hanh - peace is everywhere
49. CWG 1 - pg 121 - relationships challenging
50. Manifest Destiny - pg 79 - persistent feelings of guilt
51. Celestine - pgs 164–172 - dad, mom, and their influence

Part V

The Pathway

1. **CWG 1** - pg 78 - begin at once to imagine life the way you want it.
2. **NPR** - pg 31 - if you dwell on limitations
3. **Gift From Sea** - pg 128 - when we start at the center of ourselves
4. **CWG 1** - pg 77 - now having seen the differences
5. **CWG 1** - pg 78 - when you have a thought not in alignment
6. **CWG 2** - pg 11 - when you make up your mind
7. **NB II** - pg 12 - when you're writing
8. **Amway brochure**: The Team Approach to Business - The Plan - 1996 DST Publishing - pg 6 - quoting a Yale economic study 1973
9. ♭ **HERO** Words and Music by Mariah Carey Walter Afanasieff. Copyright ©1993 Sony/ATV Songs LLC, Rye Songs, WB Music Corp. and Wallyworld Music. All Rights on behalf of Sony/ATV Songs LLC and Rye Songs Administered by Sony/ATV Music Publishing, 8 Music Square West, Nashville, TN 37203. All Rights on behalf of Wallyworld Music Administered by WB Music Corp. International Copyright Secured. All Rights Reserved.
10. **NPR** - pg 62 - it is vital that you realize that your real work
11. **Jesus CEO** - by Laurie Beth Jones - pg 5 - The Bible - Isaiah 55:11
12. **Hicks Seminar Quote** - action-oriented
13. **CWG 1** - pg 93 - Use the great command "I am"
14. **Hicks Seminar Quote** - powerful wanting
15. **Game** - pg 30 - one ships come in
16. **Game** - pg 13 - man must prepare
17. **Manifest Destiny** - pgs 60–61 - this not prescription for idleness
18. **Manifest Destiny** - pgs 62–63 - when we speak to others
19. **Hicks Seminar Quote** - when you no longer split your thoughts
20. **The Children of the Law of One and The Lost Teachings of Atlantis** by Jon Peniel - pg 247 - make it real in your mind
21. **The Children of the Law of One and The Lost Teachings of Atlantis** by Jon

Peniel - pg 261- build strength of will slowly
22. **Hicks Seminar Quote** - never face reality.
23. **As a Man Thinketh** by James Allen - pg 61 - dream lofty dreams
24. **Strangers** - pg 151- I begin each day
25. **NB I** - pg 30 - This will leave you refreshed, exuberant, open fully to life.
26. **CWG 1** - pg 44 - begin by being still
27. **CWG 1** - pg 113 - this is a day to day
28. **NPR** - pg 295 - the present is the point of power
29. ♭ **REACH OUT, I'LL BE THERE** - Words and Music by Brian Holland, Lamont Dozier, and Edward Holland. ©1966 (Renewed 1994) JOBETE MUSIC CO. INC. All Rights Controlled and Administered by EMI BLACKWOOD MUSIC INC. on behalf of STONE AGATE MUSIC (A Division of JOBETE MUSIC CO. INC.) All Rights Reserved. International Copyright Secured. Used by Permission.
30. **The Healing of America** by Marianne Williamson - pg 41 - within each one of us is divinity
31. **Life 101** quote from **Seat of the Soul** by Gary Zukav
32. **Path** - pgs 11–12 - Mission extends beyond limited role
33. **Path** - pg 11 - Mission should interrelate - paraphrased
34. **Celestine** - pgs 48–49 - If you were wealthy
35. **1999 Writers Market** paraphrased from "Jack Canfield: Taking Chicken Soup to the Top" article by Dee Porter - pgs 59–61
36. **Path** - pg 65 - Jesus Mission statement
37. **CWG 1** - pg 49 - the world exists
38. **CWG 1** - pg 32 - do not condemn
39. **CWG 2** - pg 175 - be a light unto the world
40. **NPR** - pg 26 - you are not here to cry
41. **CWG 1** - pg 108 - the act of resisting
42. **NPR** - pg 409 - there is no justification for hatred
43. **CWG 3** - pg 125- look to see who is truly serving the world
44. **Hicks Seminar Quote** - we can never

cry enough tears
45. *Love Without End: Jesus Speaks* by Glenda Green - pg 85 - this does not mean that we turn
46. **CWG 1** - pg 32 - there are no victims
47. **CWG 1** - pg 33 - this does not mean ignore a call for help
48. **NPR** - pg 188 - the most rejuvenating idea
49. **NPR** - pg 31 - he who hates an evil creates one
50. *The Healing of America* by Marianne Williamson - pg 24 - those who lead us into cynicism
51. **CWG 1** - pg 38 - judge not
52. *The Healing of America* by Marianne Williamson - pg 28 - they rose to the occasion by defining it
53. **CWG 3** - pg 150 - enlightenment begins with acceptance
54. **CWG 1** - pg 55 - a society living in fear
55. **NPR** - pg 336 - most criminals feel forced into aggressive action as preventive measure
56. *Game* - pg 28 - bless your enemy
57. *Love Without End: Jesus Speaks* by Glenda Green - pg 81 - by recognizing our enemies potential
58. *Gift From Sea* - pgs 28–29 - hub of wheel - paraphrased
59. **NPR** - pg 32- hatred of war
60. *The Healing of America* by Marianne Williamson - pg 29 - our only true enemy

61. *Emissary of Light-* by James Twyman - pgs 200–203 - head Emissary message
62. *One* - pg 143 - tiny change today
63. *Game* - pg 25 - love and goodwill destroy enemies arrows
64. *One* - pg 114 - character comes from
65. *One* - pg 150 - by your choice you dwell you now
66. *Path* - pg 65 - a good mission statement is inspiring
67. *Word is Wand* - pg 165 - I now see clearly
68. ♮ **HIGHER LOVE** by Steve Winwood and Will Jennings ©1986 F.S. Music Ltd. (PRS)/Willin' David Music/Blue Sky Rider Songs (BMI) All Rights o/b/o F.S. Music Ltd. administered by Warner-Tamerlane Publishing Corp. All Rights Reserved. Used by Permission. WARNER BROS. PUBLICATIONS U.S. INC., Miami, Fl. 33014
69. **NPR** - pg 365 - you cannot act positively if you cannot act.
70. *One* - pg 119 - any powerful idea
71. *Messengers* - pgs 129–130 - you can make a difference - paraphrased
72. ♮ **WHERE DO I BEGIN (Love Theme)** from the Paramount Picture LOVE STORY. Words by Carl Sigman. Music by Francis Lai. Copyright ©1970,1971 (Renewed 1998, 1999) by Famous Music Corporation. International Copyright Secured. All Rights Reserved.

Part VI

The Procedures

1. **NB II** - pgs 155–156 - in your joy you offer joy
2. **CWG 2** - pg 87 - you see beauty
3. *Hicks Seminar Quote* - choose a frequency that matches your desire
4. *Hicks Seminar Quote* - only people who correspond with your frequency
5. *Hicks Seminar Quote* - appreciation begets appreciation
6. *Path* - pg 29 - do you realize transplanted heart?
7. *Hicks Seminar Quote* - every time you

praise something
8. *Game* - pg 33 - look with wonder
9. **NPR** - pg 360 - many habitual beliefs
10. *Miracles* - pg 22- tolerance for pain
11. *Game* - pg 54 - suffering is not necessary
12. *Love Without End: Jesus Speaks* by Glenda Green - pg 175 - kindness is the heart of living
13. *Game* - pg 17 - in certain instances man cannot demonstrate
14. **CWG 1** - pg 122 - Most people enter

15. **CWG 1** - pg 108 - I suggest that it is your judgements
16. **NB II** - pg 159 - anything you fail to focus on will go away
17. **Celestine** - pg 208 - romantic love retards our evolution
18. **Gift From Sea** - pgs 105–106 - the dancers who are perfectly in time
19. **Gift From Sea** - pgs 95–96 - women must come of age by herself
20. **CWG 1** - pg 123 - the purpose of relationships
21. **One** - pgs 284–285 - what is there about you that your mate ought to love?
22. **The Road Less Traveled** by M. Scott Peck - pg 167 - mountain base camp analogy - paraphrased into relationships

Part VII

The Predicaments

1. **CWG 2** - pg 17 - negativity always arises
2. **Game** - pg 10 - man can change his conditions
3. **Secret Door** - pg 202 - never voice lack or limitation
4. **Word is Wand** - pg 95 - mans word is his magic wand.
5. **The Coming of the Cosmic Christ** - pg 41 - Alice Miller - cited from **"For Your Own Good"** page xi - depression result of separation - New York Farrar, Strauss, Giroux 1984. Page 65 "soul murder"
6. **Anatomy of Illness** - pg 92 - pain-killing drugs conceal the pain
7. **Hicks Seminar Quote** - life is nothing without desire
8. **Word is Wand** - pg 165 - unless man has promised land
9. **CWG 1** - pgs 92- 93 - you get your life to take off
10. **Game** - pg 42 - mans abundance
11. **CWG 1** - pg 118 - you always get what you create
12. **Celestine** - pg 34 - preoccupations
13. **NPR** - pg 291 - concentration upon unhealthy situation
14. **Celestine** - pg 45 - preoccupations-goals
15. ♮ **A TIME FOR US (Love Theme)** From the Paramount Picture ROMEO AND JULIET. Words by Larry Kusik and Eddie Snyder. Music by Nino Rota Copyright © 1968 (Renewed 1996) by Famous Music Corporation. International Copyright Secured. All Rights Reserved
16. **Path of Least Resistance** by Robert Fritz - pg 36 - you activate the seeds of creation
17. **Life 101 Quote Book** - pg 39 - W. H. Murray - "The Scottish Himalayan Expedition"
18. **Hicks Seminar Quote** - stand in your fresh new moment of now
19. **CWG 1** - pg 118 - you are telling me you haven't gotten what you want
20. **NB II** - pg 201 - whatever you are thinking about is planning an event
21. **NPR** - pg 104 - strong contradictory beliefs
22. **Hicks Seminar Quote** - turn the tea off too early
23. **One** - pg 118 - we can have excuses
24. **Hicks Seminar Quote** - no, no, no, stop that
25. **The Path of Least Resistance** by Robert Fritz - pg 27 - study on 3-4 year olds
26. **Strangers** - pg 150 - awareness is bred out of us
27. **Hicks Seminar Quote** - child of mine
28. **Love Without End: Jesus Speaks** by Glenda Green - pg 131 - when you believe that spirit is
29. **Secret Door** - pg 205 - every day examine your consciousness
30. **Love Without End: Jesus Speaks** by Glenda Green - pg 70 - greed is the root of all evil
31. **Love Without End: Jesus Speaks** by Glenda Green - pg 94 - a man who believes in scarcity
32. **Hicks Seminar Quote** - feel your abundance little by little
33. **Path** - pg 75 - I often visualize
34. ♮ **YOU'VE GOT A FRIEND** Words

and Music by Carole King ©1971 (Renewed 1999) COL-GEMS-EMI MUSIC INC. All Rights Reserved. International Copyright Secured. Used by Permission.

35. *Celestine* - pg 184 - signs from ego
36. *Celestine* - pg 184 - signs from angel
37. *CWG 3* - pg 114 - pay attention
38. *CWG 1* - pg 4 - challenge is one of discernment
39. *Celestine* - pg 196 - formulate the questions you have - paraphrased
40. *CWG 1* - pg 210 - if you have questions
41. *Miracles* - pg 22 - whenever you are afraid
42. *Game* - pg 49 - there is no peace or happiness
43. *CWG 3* - pg 26 - fear is a natural emotion
44. *CWG 1* - pg 54 - that which you fear strongly
45. *Celestine* - pg 187 - letting go of fears
46. *Emissary of Light* by James Twyman - pg 177 - letting go of fears
48. *Celestine* - pg 186 - as soon as fear image presents itself
49. *One* - pg 119 - we generate own environment
50. *Secret Door* - pg 197 - no man gives to himself
51. *Secret Door* - pg 198 - let us free

ourselves from the tyrants
52. *Game* - pg 24 - mans work is good will
53. *CWG 1* - pg 55 - the Universe is a big xerox machine
54. *NPR* - pg 21 - your environment made visible
55. *CWG 1* - pg 119 - no need to recriminate
56. *Strangers* - pg 60 - if people wish to defy this cosmic law
57. *Sara* - pg 107 - perfect circumstances
58. *Sara* - pg 89 and 101- feel trapped
59. *Sara* - pgs 105&107 - look for things to appreciate
60. *Hicks Seminar Quote* - do your part in adding to worlds joy
61. *Hicks Seminar Quote* - Appreciation vs. Observation
62. *Strangers* - pg 212 - we are the creators of our fate
63. *NB II* - pg 84 - Who is the creator of your life? YOU.
64. **Hicks Seminar Quote** - no one can threaten you
65. *Emissary of Light* by James Twyman - pg 135 - fear is the only thing standing
66. ♪ **NEW WORLD COMING** - Words and Music by Barry Mann and Cynthia Weil ©1970(Renewed 1998) SCREEN GEMS-EMI MUSIC .All Rights Reserved. International Copyright Secured. Used by Permission.

Part VIII

The Physical Body

1. *NPR* - pg 87- a good physician is a changer of beliefs
2. *The Seven Spiritual Laws of Success* by Dr. Deepak Chopra - pg 71 - cells perform 6 trillion functions
3. *The Coming of the Cosmic Christ* by Matthew Fox - pgs 113–121 - Quoting Guy Murchie - "The 7 Mysteries of Life" Boston: Houghton-Mifflin Co. 1978
4. *Timeless Healing* - pgs 63–39 - our brains are wired
5. *Timeless Healing* - pg 39 - Belief can work against us

6. *Timeless Healing* - pg 39 - Because medicine separated & compartmentalized
7. *Anatomy of Illness* - pg. 57 - bleeding ulcers - paraphrased
8. *Timeless Healing* - pg 30 - Dr. McCallie reviewed case histories
9. *Timeless Healing* - pg 31 - Dr. Allen Roberts - ulcers
10. *Timeless Healing* - pg 44 - 2000 men beta-blocking
11. *Timeless Healing* - pg 45 - British Lancet - some didn't take medications - bad results

12. *Anatomy of Illness* - Pg 51 - placebos curing cancer

13. *Anatomy of Illness* - Pg 46 - Dr. Thomas C. Chalmers - Mount Sinai Medical Center in New York - ascorbic acid - paraphrased

14. *Timeless Healing* - pg 45 - as medical researchers we expect some exceptions

15. *Timeless Healing* - pg 31 - physicians could no longer dismiss

16. *Timeless Healing* - pg 121 - turning point in medicine

17. *Timeless Healing* - pg 95 - stodgy dichotomy system

18. *NB II* - pg 185 - doctors plummeting you into despair

19. *Timeless Healing* - pg 18 - overnight patients diagnosed with illnesses

20. *Anatomy of Illness* - pg 95 - making psychological cripples - paraphrased

21. *Right Use of Will* by Ceanne DeRohan - pg 33 - remedial medicine

22. *Timeless Healing* - pg 119 - body grandest problem-solver

23. *Right Use of Will* by Ceanne DeRohan - pg 2 - suppression of symptoms

24. *Anatomy of Illness* - pg 111 - Hippocrates avoid treatment - paraphrased

25. *Anatomy of Illness* - pg 62- robust belief

26. *Hicks Seminar Quote* - genes aren't inherited, thoughts are

27 *NPR* - pg 98 - man believing heart trouble

28. *Right Use of Will* by Ceanne DeRohan - pg 34 - body does not get sick

29. *NPR* - pg 313 - the most educated western doctors

30. *CWG 3* - pg 278 - by developing medicines

31. *NPR* - pg 333 - healings occur despite conditions

32. ♮ WE'RE ALL ALONE - Words and Music by Boz Scaggs. Copyright ©1976 by BMG Songs, Inc. International Copyright Secured. All Rights Reserved.

33. *Anatomy of Spirit* - pg xiii - biography becomes your biology

34. *NB II* - pgs 168–169 - illness state of mind

35. *NPR* - pg 29 - even false beliefs

36. *Game* - pg 46 - doubts and fears poison the mind

37. *Hicks Seminar Quote* - medicine is not about the human body

38. *NPR* - pg 334 - illness represents unfaced problems

39. *Anatomy of Spirit* - pg 34 - practitioners of energy medicine

40. *Anatomy of Spirit* - pg 40 - every thought has traveled through biological system

41. *NPR* - pg 33 - if you are sick-reason

42. *Right Use of Will* by Ceanne DeRohan - pg 34 - only seeking and healing the cause

43. *Jesus CEO* by Laurie Beth Jones - pg 48 - Dr. Bernie Siegel question

44. *Right Use of Will* by Ceanne DeRohan - pg 2 - illness is not sabotage

45. *CWG 1* - pg 36 - only when you can say "I did this"

46. *CWG 1* - pg 189 - all mental lepers

47. *Anatomy of Spirit* - pg 20 - if we look deep enough in to lives of people with illness

48. *CWG 1* - pg 188 - worry-hate-fear

49. *Manifest Destiny* - pg 84 - hanging onto earlier traumas

50. *Messengers* - pg 200&210 paraphrased - in order to heal

51. *Word is Wand* - pg 149 - when man is harmonious he is healthy

52. *NPR* - pg 216 - do not run from physical symptom

53. *Anatomy of Spirit* - pg 24 - emotional, physical, stress

54. *Anatomy of Illness* - pg 34 - Hans Selye study on the *Stress of Life*

55. *Timeless Healing* - pgs 128 - 300–400% increase of blood flow - flight or flee

56. *First Thunder* by MSI - pg 86 - anger shuts down the brain

57. *The HeartMath® Solution* by Doc Childre and Howard Martin - pgs 15-19- stress is the enemy

58. *Anatomy of Illness* - pg 39 - laughter replaced pain killers - paraphrased

59. *Anatomy of Illness* - from the forward written by René DuBos - emotional states

60. *Anatomy of Spirit* - pg 20 - HIV negative

61. *NPR* - pgs 216–217 - from *Dialogues*

62. ♮ GEORGY GIRL From GEORGY GIRL. Words by Jim Dale. Music by Tom Springfield. Copyright ©1966 by Chappelle Music Ltd. Copyright Renewed. All Rights Administered by Chappelle & Co. International Copyright Secured. All Rights Reserved.

63. *NPR* - pg 368 - you can cure yourself point of power present moment

64. *NPR* - pg 25 - conscious beliefs direct functioning of body

65. *CWG 1* - pg 118 - you cannot be ill

66. *CWG 1* - pg 188 - health will improve

67. *Hicks Seminar Quote* - not a shred of evidence

68. *Timeless Healing* - pg 38 - every

instance of remembered wellness

69. *Celestine* - pg 31 - everyday growing body of evidence

70. *Anatomy of Spirit* - pg 11 - conventional medical world

71. *Ageless Body, Timeless Mind* by Dr. Deepak Chopra - pg 4 - perception is a learned phenomenon.

72. *NPR* - pg 66 - your emotions and actions

73. *Anatomy of Spirit* - pg 47 - energy medicine

74. *Timeless Healing* - pg 30 - our brains cannot distinguish external

75. *Timeless Healing* - pg 92 - all of us have distinct neurosignatures

76. *Timeless Healing* - pg 39 - every specialty and subspecialty of medicine

77. Mary Baker Eddy - pg 5 - *"Gods Law of Adjustment"* Christian Science Publishing Society 1 Norway Street, Boston Mass. 1971. By Adam Hickey.

78. *NPR* - pg 66 - if you are ill

79. *Timeless Healing* - pg 45 - our bodies are nourished or starved

80. *Hicks Seminar Quote* - more things right than wrong in body

81. *Game* - pg 50 - man should watch himself hourly

82. *Hicks Seminar Quote* - go to sleep 6-8 hours - nonresistance

83. *Hicks Seminar Quote* - within a few days you will feel better

84. *NPR* - pg 66 - if you divert your thoughts

85. *Strangers* - pg 170 - think healthy, be healthy

86. *NPR* - pg 341 - healing involves great thrusts of energy

87. *Hicks Seminar Quote* - even the most

dreaded disease will vanish

88. *Bottom Line/Personal* - (volume 18 #15) Dr. Isadore Rosenfeld - New York Hospital-Cornell Medical Center - growing evidence of emotions influence

89. *A Return to Love* by Marianne Williamson - pg 258 - I have heard people

90. *Seminar Quote* - illness creates desire for health

91. *First Thunder* by MSI - pg 185 - the body's waking state is a creation of the mind

92. *Making Friends of Enemies* by Jim Forest - New York *Crossroad* 1988 quoted from a Christian Science leaflet

93. *Many Lives, Many Masters* by Brian L. Weiss- page 212 - we are the ones who still

94. *The Isaiah Effect* by Gregg Braden - pgs 89-91 - videotape of healing cancer

95. *First Thunder* by MSI - pg 215 - these are the dark ages

96. *NPR* - pg 320 - you are what you think

97. *NPR* - pg 29 - to change your experience

98. *NPR* - pg 102- you live in the body of your beliefs

99. *Love Without End: Jesus Speaks* by Glenda Green - pg 194 - find out for what you are hungry

100. *NPR* - pg 323 - you are overweight

101. *NPR* - pg 327 - diets momentarily

102. *NPR* - pg 326 - the reason some weight loss groups succeed

103. *Creative Visualization* by Shakti Gawain - pg 59 - the body is continuously changing, replenishing

104. *Timeless Healing* - pg 88 - we come into the world with factory-installed

105. *NPR* - pg 190 - body sculpture

Part IX

The Postscript

1. *One* - pg 118–119 - given block of marble

2. *CWG 1* - pg 65 - is to be an experience of constant joy

3. *CWG 1* - page 47 - allow each soul

4. *Hicks Seminar Quote* - your joy, freedom and growth

5. *CWG 1* - pg 84 - the soul cannot choose

if it has nothing to choose from

6. **NPR** - pg 232 - good and evil birth of choices

7. **NPR** - pg 243 - all seeming opposites

8. *Hicks Seminar Quote* - would you like to have all the answers - paraphrased

9. *Hicks Seminar Quote* - there is a Life Stream

10. *Game* - pg 89 - all power is given man through right thinking

11. *Love Without End: Jesus Speaks* by Glenda Green - pg 88 - the soul is crying for an experience

12. *Love Without End: Jesus Speaks* by Glenda Green - pg 147 - the right of choice is your freedom

13. *NB II* - pg 13- paraphrased - what you have lived before this day

14. *Creative Visualization* - by Shakti Gawain - pg 1 - every moment is infinitely

15. **CWG 2** - pg 81 - grant yourself permission

16. *Hicks Seminar Quote* - affirmations

17. *Creative Visualization* - by Shakti Gawain - affirmations pages 22–23

18. **CWG 1** - pg 86 - I am goodness and mercy

19. *NB II* - pg 203 - The Recipe For Eternal Joy

20. *Creative Visualization* - by Shakti Gawain - pg 10 - this or something better

21. ♪ **A LOT OF LIVIN' TO DO** - from BYE BYE BIRDIE. Words by Lee Adams. Music by Charles Strouse. © 1960 LEE ADAMS AND CHARLES STROUSE. All Rights Throughout the World Controlled by EDWIN H. MORRIS & CO., A Division of MPL Communications, Inc. International Copyright Secured. All Rights Reserved.

22. **CWG 3** - pg 293 - raise consciousness

23. *Love Without End: Jesus Speaks* by Glenda Green - pg 169 - follow life, serve the living

24. **CWG 1**- pg 144 - ideas will separate

you from the many

25. **CWG 1** - pg 76 - why then do it?

26. **CWG 1** - pg 144 - chosen you to be the messenger

27. **CWG 2** - pg 114 - advanced technology

28. **CWG 2** - pg 171 - the largest question

29. **CWG 3** - pg 293 - you will not change what you are doing until you

30. **CWG 3** - pg 366 - you came to the room to heal

31. **CWG 3** - pg 294 - you will wake up

32. **CWG 3** - pg 273 - your grandest ideas

33. **CWG 3** - pgs. 68–69 - behold the darkness, yet curse it not

34. **CWG 3**- pg 68 - be a bringer of light

35. **CWG 3** - pg 269 - shine on then O Illuminati

36. **CWG 3** - pg 68–69 - the world waits for you, heal it

37. *Indigo Children* by Lee Carroll and Jan Tober - pgs 219–222 - the time of the great awakening is come

38. ♪ **CABARET** from the Musical CABARET. Words by Fred Ebb. Music by John Kander. Copyright ©1966,1967 by Alley Music Corp. and Trio Music Company, Inc. Copyright Renewed. International Copyright Secured. All Rights Reserved. Used by Permission.

39. ♪ **"CLIMB EV'RY MOUNTAIN"** - Lyrics by Richard Rogers and Oscar Hammerstein II Copyright ©1959 by Richard Rogers and Oscar Hammerstein II Copyright renewed. WILLIAMSON MUSIC owner of publication and allied rights throughout the world. International Copyright Secured. All rights reserved. Reprinted by Permission.

40.♪ **I CAN SEE CLEARLY NOW,** by Johnny Nash ©1972 (Renewed)Dovan Music All Rights Reserved. Used by Permission. WARNER BROS. PUBLICATIONS U.S. INC., Miami, FL. 33014

Song List

PART I

The Prelude

PART II

The Puzzle

PART III

The Present

Index